365

THE BEST WISCONSIN SPORTS STORIES DAY BY DAY

365

THE BEST WISCONSIN SPORTS STORIES DAY BY DAY

DALE HOFMANN

CLIFF CHRISTL

Copyright© 2010 Dale Hofmann & Cliff Christl

All rights reserved. Except for use in a review, no part of this publication may be reproduced or transmitted in any form or by any means, electronic or mechanic, now known or hereafter invented, including xerography, photocopying, recording, and in any information storage and retrieval system, without written permission from the publisher, KCI Sports Publishing, 3340 Whiting Avenue, Suite 5, Stevens Point, Wisconsin 54481, Dale Hofmann and Cliff Christl.

Printed in the United States of America by Worzalla Publishing, Stevens Point, WI.

Cataloging-in-Publication Data is available from the Library of Congress.

First KCI Sports Publishing edition: 2010
ISBN-13: 978-09843882-8-8
ISBN-10: 09843882-8-1

Book Layout and Design: Nicky Brillowski

This book is available in quantity at special discounts for your group or organization. For further information, contact:

KCI Sports Publishing
3340 Whiting Avenue
Suite 5
Stevens Point, WI 54481
(217) 766-3390
Fax: (715) 344-2668

Photos courtesy of:
Green Bay Packers Hall of Fame, Inc.
Pete Ehrmann
Courtesy of the NIT — Archives & Special Collections Center, Seton Hall University
Purdue University
Manitowoc County Historical Society
University of Wisconsin-Milwaukee Athletics
Stanford University Athletics
Joyce Ziske Malison
Colorado State University Athletics
Louisiana State University
Blue Mound Golf & Country Club
Diane Kleinsteiber
UW-Whitewater Sports Information, Gregg Theune & Tom Fick
Kenosha County Historical Society
Russ Lake
Bud Lea and Tim Urban
The Oshkosh Northwestern
Valerie Strauss
University of Wisconsin Athletics
Eau Claire Leader-Telegram
Milwaukee Bucks
Milwaukee Journal-Sentinel
Pettit National Ice Center
Milwaukee Brewers
Wisconsin State Journal
AP Images

CONTENTS

Contents v
Dedication xii
Acknowledgement xiii
Foreword xiv
Introduction 17

January
1 (1994) – Badgers win their first Rose Bowl 20
2 (1966) – Neither sleet nor snow can stop Packers in title game 21
3 (2006) – Novak's 41 leads Marquette in Big East debut 22
4 (2004) – Al Harris' overtime pick silences Seahawks 23
5 (1976) – Badgers stage their biggest comeback 24
6 (1996) – Packers prove themselves in San Francisco 25
7 (1984) – UW hockey team stuns Olympians 26
8 (1999) – Holmgren leaves Packers for Seattle 27
9 (1972) – Bucks end Lakers' record 33-game streak 28
10 (1981) – Rivers' 35-footer sinks Notre Dame 29
11 (2004) – Fourth-and-26 dooms Packers 30
12 (1997) – Packers beat Carolina for Super Bowl berth 31
13 (1998) – Disgruntled Okey quits Badgers 32
14 (1968) – Preeminent Packers win Super Bowl II 33
15 (1967) – Packers conquer new world in Super Bowl I 34
16 (1993) – Pieper breaks state scoring record (again) 35
17 (1998) – Kohl Center opens for business 36
18 (1992) – Packers hire two African-American coordinators 37
19 (1975) – Abdul-Jabbar dominates Walton in first meeting 38
20 (2008) – One step from Super Bowl, Packers bow to Giants 39
21 (1970) – Packers get No. 2 pick from hated Bears 40
22 (1968) – Milwaukee lands the Bucks 41
23 (1932) – Millpond site of U.S. Speedskating championships 42
24 (1950) – Packers' Rockwood Lodge destroyed by fire 43
25 (1998) – Packers upset in Super Bowl XXXII 44
26 (1997) – Packers' wait ends with Super Bowl XXXI 45
27 (1997) – Thousands welcome Super Bowl champions 46
28 (1959) – Packers hire Lombardi 47
29 (1963) – Four Packers in first Hall of Fame class 48
30 (2003) – Michael Jordan plays his last game in Milwaukee 49
31 (1924) – The Original Celtics win in Beloit 50

v

February

1 (1950) - Lambeau resigns as Packers coach 51
2 (1950) - River Falls' scoring machine gives back points 52
3 (1968) - Marquette victory is a day at the beach 53
4 (1980) - Bucks acquire Lanier from Pistons 54
5 (1974) - McGuire takes a stand, gets a one-finger salute 55
6 (1969) - Lombardi leaves Packers for Washington 56
7 (1972) - Green Bay goalie saves U.S. hockey team 57
8 (1978) - Brewers buy back Gorman Thomas 58
9 (1950) - Auerbach escorted from game in Sheboygan 59
10 (1913) - Fond du Lac claims national championship 60
11 (1992) - Packers trade for Brett Favre 61
12 (2002) - FitzRandolph wins Olympic gold 62
13 (1977) - NBA All-Stars come to Milwaukee 63
14 (1990) - Alvarez recruits for the Rose Bowl 64
15 (2009) - Cambridge's Kenseth wins Daytona 500 65
16 (2004) - Jolene Anderson sets state scoring record 66
17 (2002) - Weary Witte takes home the gold 67
18 (1994) - Jansen sheds burdens by winning gold 68
19 (1994) - Blair wins record fourth gold medal 69
20 (2003) - Bucks trade Ray Allen to Seattle 70
21 (1959) - Conley defies Braves, stays with Celtics 71
22 (1980) - The Miracle on Ice 72
23 (1980) - Incomparable Heiden wins fifth gold 73
24 (1970) - McGuire spurns NCAA tournament 74
25 (1918) - Jack Dempsey stops Bill Brennan in Milwaukee 75
26 (1911) - Kenosha's Conley loses bantamweight crown 76
27 (2002) - Bo Ryan leads Wisconsin to Big Ten title 77
28 (1960) - Green Bay Bobcats golden in "First Miracle on Ice" 78

March

1 (1985) - Herb Kohl buys Bucks 79
2 (1959) - Badgers battered by homegrown foes 80
3 (1962) - Erickson's Badgers stun Ohio State 81
4 (2008) - Packers announce Favre's retirement 82
5 (2003) - Badgers end 56-year Big Ten drought 83
6 (1993) - Pius girls win 12th straight state title 84
7 (1980) - Dominican wins 71st straight game – maybe 85
8 (2003) - Marquette snaps Cincinnati's reign en route to Final Four 86
9 (1975) - Mickey Crowe scores record 45 in title game 87
10 (1951) - Beloit College falls short in NIT 88
11 (1942) - Oshkosh All-Stars win world tournament 89
12 (1914) - Low blow spices Wolgast-Ritchie title bout 90
13 (1969) - Marquette gets its revenge on Kentucky 91
14 (1953) - Milwaukee lands the Braves 92

15 (1969) – Mount sinks shot and Marquette 93
16 (1946) – Tiny Reedsville wears state crown 94
17 (1973) – Badgers capture first NCAA hockey title 95
18 (2006) – Oshkosh West coach wins one for dad 96
19 (1969) – Bucks win coin flip for Alcindor 97
20 (1959) – Milwaukee Lincoln roars back 98
21 (1964) – Little Dodgeville scores big triumph 99
22 (1969) – Weaver's desperation shot saves Beloit 100
23 (2000) – Badgers beat LSU on road to Final Four 101
24 (2005) – UWM's Cinderella story ends 102
25 (1974) – McGuire's technicals cost Marquette 103
26 (2008) – Bradley Center is home to McDonald's All-Stars 104
27 (1982) – Earl Anthony unstoppable in Miller Open 105
28 (1977) – Marquette wins it all in McGuire's final game 106
29 (1941) – Badgers claim NCAA basketball title 107
30 (1985) – UW-Green Bay hires Dick Bennett 108
31 (1970) – Major League Baseball returns to Milwaukee 109

April

1 (1916) – Minor league Brewers obtain Jim Thorpe 110
2 (1924) – Roundy Coughlin joins the State Journal 111
3 (1968) – Costello, not McGuire, gets Bucks' job 112
4 (1962) – Kicking legend O'Dea dies at 90 113
5 (1937) – James Braddock arrives in Wisconsin woods 114
6 (2001) – Brewers win Miller Park opener 115
7 (1970) – Brewers open at County Stadium 116
8 (1993) – Packers sign Reggie White 117
9 (1960) – UW boxer Mohr suffers fatal brain injury 118
10 (1980) – Lezcano slam wins Brewers' opener 119
11 (1964) – Marquette hires Al McGuire 120
12 (1977) – Palmer outduels Travers in Brewers' opener 121
13 (1982) – Anderson withdraws as UW basketball coach 122
14 (1953) – Braves win first home opener 123
15 (1987) – Nieves' no-hitter keeps streak alive 124
16 (1996) – Bulls win record 70th in Milwaukee 125
17 (1963) – Hornung suspended for gambling 126
18 (1971) – Bucks beat Lakers in Western Conference final 127
19 (1987) – Deer, Sveum homers lift Brewers on Easter Sunday 128
20 (1987) – Brewers' 13th straight victory ties record 129
21 (1970) – Bucks trade for "The Big O" 130
22 (1948) – Teenage boxer dies following Milwaukee bout 131
23 (1989) – Packers draft Tony Mandarich 132
24 (1959) – Lombardi jettisons Billy Howton 133
25 (1992) – Heard's relay team breaks world record 134
26 (1968) – Bob Knight changes mind, spurns Badgers 135

vii

27 (1991) – Barkley, Bucks fans mix it up 136
28 (1959) – Madison meets Cassius Clay 137
29 (1950) – Oshkosh's Hoeft pitches the most perfect game 138
30 (1971) – Bucks sweep Bullets for NBA title 139

May

1 (1991) – Brewers beat White Sox in 19 innings 140
2 (1983) – Auerbach rips Nelson for ripping Ainge 141
3 (1917) – Brewers' white manager kills black waiter 142
4 (1964) – Braves beat Mets; brawl is a draw 143
5 (1964) – Lombardi trades all-pro center Jim Ringo 144
6 (1968) – Bucks take Hetzel, Embry in expansion draft 145
7 (1988) – Antigo's Lukas gets first Kentucky Derby victory 146
8 (1984) – Brewers, White Sox play 25 innings 147
9 (1950) – Graziano scores TKO in new Milwaukee Arena 148
10 (1974) – Kareem's hook beats Celtics in double overtime 149
11 (1937) – Kenosha welcomes Joe Louis 150
12 (1974) – Bucks lose NBA title game to Boston 151
13 (1984) – Terry Porter cut from Olympic squad 152
14 (1878) – Milwaukee hosts first major league game 153
15 (1968) – Milwaukee welcomes the White Sox 154
16 (1992) – Melges steers U.S. to America's Cup 155
17 (1943) – Wisconsin women pioneer pro baseball league 156
18 (1986) – Bird-led Celtics sweep Bucks out of playoffs 158
19 (1977) – Brewers demote "The Sundown Kid" 159
20 (1888) – Borchert Field opens in Milwaukee 160
21 (1971) – "Trader" Lane lays into umpire Hank Soar 161
22 (1987) – James Lofton acquitted 162
23 (1987) – Mossy Cade convicted 163
24 (2005) – Bucks win the lottery 164
25 (1991) – Bob Johnson leads Penguins to Stanley Cup 165
26 (1959) – Haddix loses his masterpiece 166
27 (1987) – Don Nelson resigns from Bucks 167
28 (1980) – Packers' No. 1 pick flees to Canada 168
29 (1947) – Sheboygan Redskins coach fined for assault and battery 169
30 (1935) – Wisconsin's Weatherly dies in Indianapolis 500 crash 170
31 (1947) – UW's Gehrmann wins first conference mile 171

June

1 (1990) – Suzy Favor wins record eighth NCAA title 172
2 (1982) – Brewers fire Rodgers, name Kuenn manager 173
3 (1985) – Brewers make Surhoff first choice in draft 174
4 (1908) – Middleweight king Ketchel wins Milwaukee brawl 175
5 (1965) – Larry Franklin sets enduring broad jump record 176
6 (1948) – Rex Mays hits a wall, saves a life 177

7 (1935) – Jesse Owens dominates Marquette track meet 178
8 (1961) – Record home run barrage can't save Braves 179
9 (1945) – Wiesner shares NCAA high jump title in Milwaukee 180
10 (1950) – Badgers qualify for their only College World Series 181
11 (1932) – MU's Metcalfe credited with four world records 182
12 (1954) – Braves' retread Jim Wilson pitches no-hitter 183
13 (1957) – Braves take NL lead after brawling with Dodgers 184
14 (1952) – Aaron signs with Eau Claire Bears 185
15 (1957) – Schoendienst trade boosts Braves' pennant hopes 186
16 (1975) – Bucks trade Abdul-Jabbar to Lakers 187
17 (1939) – UW miler Fenske shocks Princeton crowd 188
18 (1978) – Andy North wins his first U.S. Open 189
19 (1966) – Whitworth crushes field for Milwaukee title 190
20 (2006) – Dwyane Wade leads Miami Heat to NBA title 191
21 (1941) – Showman Bill Veeck buys Brewers 192
22 (1974) – Neenah's Whitlinger rules college tennis 193
23 (2010) – DeMerit's perseverance pays at World Cup 194
24 (1998) – Bucks trade rights to Nowitzke 195
25 (1979) – Bucks con Pistons, draft Moncrief 196
26 (1960) – Waterford's Ziske wins women's Western Open 197
27 (1936) – Future gold medalist wins decathlon at Marquette 198
28 (1964) – Pancho Gonzales loses temper, doubles final 199
29 (2005) – Marquette settles again on Golden Eagles 200
30 (1934) – Bonthron edges Cunningham at wire in classic 1,500 201

July
1 (1986) – Bucks get Sikma from Seattle 202
2 (1963) – Marichal beats Spahn in epic pitchers' duel 203
3 (1971) – Matzdorf sets world high jump record 204
4 (1916) – No winner in five-hour wrestling marathon 205
5 (1970) – Ex-infielder Lockwood wins his first game 206
6 (1998) – Se Ri Pak wins U.S. Women's Open at Kohler 207
7 (2008) – Brewers trade for Sabathia 208
8 (1998) – Packers' shareholders flock to Lambeau 209
9 (2002) – Milwaukee boos, blushes over All-Star tie 210
10 (1991) – Bucks sign Moses Malone 211
11 (1965) – Richeys sweep Western Open 212
12 (1955) – Musial's blast wins Milwaukee All-Star Game 213
13 (1934) – Soap opera continues: UW names Meanwell 214
14 (1968) – Stockton wins first Greater Milwaukee Open 215
15 (1975) – NL All-Star streak stays alive in Milwaukee 216
16 (1900) – Milwaukee's Kraenzlein wins fourth gold medal 217
17 (1956) – Adcock loses cool, chases Gomez into dugout 218
18 (1974) – Jim Carter defies NFL players' strike 219
19 (1956) – Wisconsin cancels LSU games over race law 220

20 (1976) – Aaron hits No. 755 221
21 (2008) – Bill Hall ignites Brewers' sweep 222
22 (1995) – Managers Garner, Bevington mix it up 223
23 (1967) – Ashe wins U.S. Clay Court title in Fox Point 224
24 (1967) – Overflow crowd sees baseball return to Milwaukee 225
25 (1976) – Montgomery topples barrier in 100-free 226
26 (1957) – Packers trade quarterback Tobin Rote to Lions 227
27 (1996) – Harrison wins Olympic triple jump 228
28 (2005) – Alvarez steps down as coach 229
29 (1979) – Brewers sweep wild weekend set with Yankees 230
30 (1869) – Famous Cincinnati Red Stockings maul Milwaukee 231
31 (1954) – Adcock cracks four home runs 232

August
1 (1982) – Hickman dies after State Fair crash 233
2 (1964) – Legendary Mickey Wright wins at North Shore 234
3 (1936) – Metcalfe nipped by Owens in Berlin Olympics 235
4 (1940) – Guldahl sets pace in Milwaukee golf tournament 236
5 (2000) – Morel wins WBA flyweight title in Madison 237
6 (2008) – Packers trade Favre to New York Jets 238
7 (1915) – Mucks wins first national shot and discus titles 239
8 (1992) – Esther Jones races to gold at Barcelona 240
9 (1957) – "Hurricane" Hazle delivers big for Braves 241
10 (1980) – Rutherford wins Bettenhausen Classic 242
11 (1961) – Spahn joins elite company with 300th win 243
12 (1999) – Brewers fire Garner; Bando reassigned 244
13 (1933) – Sarazen rules in PGA tourney at Blue Mound 245
14 (1982) – Lee Kemp wins third world wrestling title 246
15 (2004) – Singh prevails in PGA playoff at Whistling Straits 247
16 (1941) – Zale-Pryor draws 135,000 to Milwaukee lakefront 248
17 (1961) – Sachs wins stock car race at State Fair Park 249
18 (1960) – Burdette's no-hitter stifles Phillies 250
19 (1922) – Weissmuller swims to victory in Milwaukee River 251
20 (1933) – Milwaukee's Ike Ruehl upsets Don Budge 252
21 (2004) – Controversy erupts over Hamm's gold medal 253
22 (2004) – State rowers win Olympic gold 254
23 (1946) – Hirsch stars for College All-Stars 255
24 (1929) – Armour wins Western at Ozaukee Country Club 256
25 (1987) – Molitor extends hit streak to 39 257
26 (2007) – Long wait ends for Edgerton's Stricker 258
27 (1996) – Tiger Woods turns pro in Milwaukee 259
28 (1935) – Negro League legends appear in Milwaukee 260
29 (1940) – Packers beat College All-Stars before 84,567 261
30 (1980) – Ezra Johnson hot dogs it 262
31 (1972) – Ben Peterson captures Olympic gold 263

September

1 (1904) - Milwaukee AC shines in the Olympics 264
2 (1979) - Knee injury shelves Packers' Ivery 265
3 (1989) - Greg Norman rallies to win GMO 266
4 (1944) - Scandal aside, Parker wins U.S. Open tennis 267
5 (1906) - Cochems pioneers the forward pass 268
6 (1877) - Future Hall of Fame pitcher not enough for Janesville 269
7 (1980) - Marcol's fluke TD beats Bears in overtime 270
8 (1904) - Dan Patch showcased at Wisconsin State Fair 271
9 (1992) - Yount gets 3,000th hit at County Stadium 272
10 (1955) - Racing opens at Road America 273
11 (1903) - Milwaukee site of AAU track meet for first time 274
12 (1981) - Badgers shock top-ranked Michigan 275
13 (1961) - Jay gets revenge on Braves 276
14 (1919) - Packers romp in their first game 277
15 (1985) - Thorpe holds off Nicklaus to win GMO 278
16 (1960) - Spahn throws his first no-hitter 279
17 (1935) - Baraboo's Koenecke killed in mid-air brawl 280
18 (1998) - McGwire hits 64th home run at County Stadium 281
19 (1978) - Brewers' Caldwell wins 20th game 282
20 (1992) - Favre ignites comeback in Lambeau debut 283
21 (1958) - Braves repeat as National League champs 284
22 (1935) - Hutson's first catch burns Bears 285
23 (1957) - Braves win first pennant on Aaron's homer 286
24 (2000) - Freedom's Lowney scores huge wrestling upset 287
25 (2002) - Brewers' shake-up starts at the top ...:..........................288
26 (1934) - Green Bay boxer goes 10 with Joe Louis 289
27 (1959) - Lombardi wins first game with Packers 290
28 (2008) - Brewers back in playoffs after 26 years 291
29 (1957) - Packers dedicate stadium with victory over Bears 292
30 (1978) - "The Bud Song" comes to Camp Randall 293

October

1 (1988) - Bradley Center opens with NHL exhibition 294
2 (2001) - Wisconsin gets probation for "Shoegate" 295
3 (1982) - Brewers recover to win AL East on final day 296
4 (1957) - Yankees arrive in "Bushville" 297
5 (1912) - Bragg wins grim Grand Prix in Wauwatosa 298
6 (1957) - Nippy Jones shoeshine call kick-starts Braves 299
7 (1962) - Packers win classic defensive struggle 300
8 (1982) - Brewers stay alive in ALCS 301
9 (1958) - Braves blow Game 7 of World Series 302
10 (1957) - Burdette pitches Braves to World Series victory 303
11 (1969) - Badgers celebrate after shocking Iowa 304
12 (1952) - Packers collapse against defending champs 305

13 (1982) – Without Fingers, Brewers' bullpen falters 306
14 (1996) – Jacke's overtime field goal beats 49ers 307
15 (1934) – Deserting Deans cause near riot 308
16 (1982) – Brewers' rally squares World Series 309
17 (1983) – Packers win shootout with Redskins 310
18 (1977) – Abdul-Jabbar decks Kent Benson 311
19 (1906) – World champion White Sox play in Kenosha 312
20 (1901) – Hall of Fame pitchers battle for local pride 313
21 (1964) – Braves announce move to Atlanta 314
22 (1974) – Desperate Devine trades five picks for Hadl 315
23 (1935) – Oshkosh's Revolta wins PGA tournament 316
24 (1936) – MU football team rolls toward Cotton Bowl bid 317
25 (1987) – Bucks beat Soviets in first-ever event 318
26 (1957) – Braves' Fred Haney cleans house 319
27 (1923) – MU's Dunn beats Boston College with one arm 320
28 (1928) – Babe Ruth wows Milwaukee crowd 321
29 (1949) – Ancient M&M rivalry draws national attention 322
30 (1978) – Starr, reporters clash over Duane Thomas 323
31 (1942) – Badgers upset No. 1 Ohio State 324

November

1 (2009) – Favre gets revenge in Lambeau return 325
2 (1974) – Aaron comes back to Milwaukee 326
3 (1917) – Camp Randall Stadium dedicated 327
4 (2003) – Marquette joins Big East Conference 328
5 (1989) – Packers beat Bears in instant replay game 329
6 (1997) – Brewers move to National League 330
7 (1925) – Badgers beat Iowa in a blizzard 331
8 (1924) – "Four Horsemen" trample Badgers 332
9 (2003) – Kenseth wins NASCAR title 333
10 (1962) – Wisconsin routs No. 1 Northwestern 334
11 (1944) – UW's Shafer fatally injured in game 335
12 (1967) – Travis Williams' returns crush Cleveland 336
13 (1999) – Dayne breaks NCAA rushing record 337
14 (1940) – Packers first NFL team to fly 338
15 (1992) – Star-crossed Kulwicki wins Winston Cup 339
16 (1985) – Badgers, McClain shock Buckeyes again 340
17 (1913) – Jess Willard disappoints Milwaukee fight fans 341
18 (2005) – Clay's record day rallies Racine Park 342
19 (1977) – Brewers carry out "Saturday Night Massacre" 343
20 (1989) – Yount wins second MVP award 344
21 (1959) – Hackbart drives Badgers to Big Ten title 345
22 (1962) – Lombardi takes worst licking in Detroit 346
23 (1986) – Charles Martin body-slams Bears' McMahon 347
24 (2002) – Sapp's block enrages Mike Sherman 348

25 (1950) – Packers sign Bob Mann, their first black player 349
26 (1968) – Black players boycott UW football banquet 350
27 (1991) – Packers name Wolf general manager 351
28 (1951) – Class of 14 inaugurates Wisconsin Hall of Fame 352
29 (1931) – Packers capture third straight NFL title 353
30 (1954) – Ameche named Heisman winner 354

December

1 (1985) – Packers bury Bucs in blizzard 355
2 (1957) – Packers land Taylor, Nitschke in windfall draft 356
3 (1968) – Badgers jolt No. 4 Kansas 357
4 (1993) – Badgers beat Michigan State in Japan 358
5 (1957) – Braves get Rush in five-player trade 359
6 (1976) – Brewers get Cooper for Scott on busy day 360
7 (1992) – Brewers lose Molitor to free agency 361
8 (1929) – Packers capture their first championship 362
9 (1939) – NFL draft held in Milwaukee hotel 363
10 (1939) – Packers pacify fans by winning fifth title 364
11 (1999) – Dayne walks away with Heisman Trophy 365
12 (1980) – Brewers get Fingers, Simmons, Vuckovich 366
13 (1936) – Packers win NFL title with aerial barrage 367
14 (1930) – Portsmouth tie good enough for Packers 368
15 (2007) – UW-Whitewater dethrones Mount Union 369
16 (1967) – Maravich, Cowens just part of "Classic" show 370
17 (1944) – Packers outlast Giants, Herber for NFL title 371
18 (1994) – Packers win their last game in Milwaukee 372
19 (1983) – Packers fire Bart Starr 373
20 (2003) – Wisconsin edges Marquette in local starfest 374
21 (1963) – Princeton's Bradley bedevils Badgers 375
22 (2003) – Favre stars despite father's death 376
23 (1967) – Lombardi Packers score rare upset on home turf 377
24 (1974) – Packers bow to demand, name Starr coach 378
25 (1912) – Typhoid fever claims "Keckie" Moll 379
26 (1965) – Disputed kick dooms Matte-led Colts 380
27 (1997) – Favre wins third MVP award 381
28 (2002) – UW rallies past Colorado in Alamo Bowl 382
29 (1925) – NFL gives Milwaukee Badgers the boot 383
30 (1962) – Packers survive elements, Giants to win NFL title 384
31 (1967) – Packers chill Cowboys in Ice Bowl 385

BIBLIOGRAPHY 386

DEDICATION

To Sandy, my wife, my friend and my proof reader,
and to all of the people I've covered who have told the truth.
Dale Hofmann

To my family:
Wife and best friend Shirley Christl
Daughter Kelly Christl
Daughter Cassie Schmitt, her husband Cory
and grandsons Isaac Schmitt and Beckett Schmitt;
Brother Jeff Sapiro and nephew Daniel;
sister Nancy Sapiro, her husband Lincoln Miller,
and nieces and nephews Ana, Aidan and Kathryn;
The Fabrys (stepsons, spouses and grandkids):
Keith, Ann, Jim and Zach;
Ryan, Tracy, Olivia and Sophia;
and Brandon
Cliff Christl

ACKNOWLEDGEMENT

To the old warhorses of our profession who wrote about sports for newspapers across the state during the many decades before we got into the business. We relied heavily on their prose and reporting, their details and perspective, their yarns and anecdotes. Although most of those craftsmen are no longer with us, almost all of their stories have been preserved on microfilm and we're thankful for that.

Dale Hofmann & Cliff Christl

FOREWORD *by David Maraniss*

This book speaks to me, day in and day out, like few books ever have. I grew up on Regent Street in Madison only one short block from Camp Randall Stadium and the adjacent Field House, where many of the events recalled here took place. The memories unspool with the annotated sporting calendar. March 3 (1962) – I was one of those delirious kids who stormed the court after Johnny Erickson's no-name team pulled off the biggest upset in UW basketball history, taking down the mighty Ohio State Buckeyes of Lucas and Havlicek. March 21 (1964) – I was stomping my feet in the dizzying heights of the upper deck bleachers rooting for Milwaukee North (my sentiments were always with the black teams from Milwaukee) when they were shocked by little Dodgeville in the high school tournament finals. April 9 (1960) – I was in the audience when beloved UW boxer Charlie Mohr, who lived only a few blocks from us and was great to neighborhood kids, suffered a fatal blow in the ring.

I spent my boyhood parking cars on our front lawn on Badger football Saturdays then finding a way to sneak into the games. I missed the Four Horsemen, but was in the stands, part of the crowd practicing our sixties era's favorite cheer – Ooooooh, Shit! – on the afternoon of October 11 (1969) when Johnny Coatta's ragtag squad shockingly snapped a miserable losing streak by beating Iowa. Later that night I saw Crazylegs live up to his name by performing an impromptu rooftop jig. On Sundays my Dad and I would watch the glory years Packers on the television in our living room. He would sit in the big winged chair. I would plop down on the heating grate near the coat closet. I can still hear him screaming with delight on November 12 (1967), as Travis Williams roadrunnered those kickoffs and the Pack trounced the Browns. During summer nights, we would convene on the side porch, my Dad down to boxer shorts and t-shirt, and listen to the Braves radio broadcasts of Earl Gillespie and Blaine Walsh from County Stadium. I can still see in my mind's eye the two of us listening, transfixed, on July 2 (1963), as Marichal and Spahn both went the distance in a thirteen-inning masterpiece duel.

One day or another, our state heroes are all here: Vince Lombardi and Bart Starr, Hank Aaron and Nippy Jones, Brett Favre and Reggie White, Robin Yount and Paul Molitor, Al McGuire and Bo Ryan, Alan Ameche and Ron Dayne, Kareem and the Big O. There are also guest appearances from immortals like Thorpe and Owens and Dempsey and Louis. But the beauty of sports, and life itself, is that the best stories do not need to involve the most famous people or life-altering events. How about July 17 (1956) when Joe Adcock lost his cool and chased Gomez into the dugout? Has to be a great story. And my professorial brother's favorite in Packer lore, August 30 (1980), when Ezra Johnson chomped into a hot dog on the sidelines. And what more could be fairer than the opening line to April 2 (1926) when a Madison sportswriter named Joseph Leo (Roundy) Coughlin "launched his assault on the English language." Cliff and Dale have the right touch on all of these stories, from January 1 (1994) the first UW Rose Bowl win, to December 31 (1967), which brings the year to an appropriate close with the most glorious moment in the communal history of Cheeseheads, the Ice Bowl.

INTRODUCTION

Oftentimes when we'd tell people about our project over the course of researching and writing this book, it would lead to a guessing game. The typical response would often go something like this: "You mean like The Ice Bowl? Like when the Milwaukee Bucks won the NBA championship? Like when Robin Yount got his 3,000th hit?" Then almost invariably, we'd get these quizzical looks and even if people didn't ask, we knew exactly what they were thinking: "How are you going to fill all 365 days?"

No problem.

Thanks to the rich history of our professional and collegiate sports teams in Wisconsin and the countless outstanding athletes who performed here or grew up here, the bigger problem was determining which story to select out of two, three, four and sometimes even more possibilities.

Our purpose was to choose the best ever Wisconsin sports story for each of the 365 days of the year - sorry no leap year story - in much the same way that newspaper editors pick the biggest and best story to play up in their sports sections each day. While there were many dates where the choices were as obvious as the ones that had been rattled off to us in conversation, there were many more where it wasn't so easy.

Take July 25, for example.

On that date alone, Jim Montgomery, a native of Madison, became the first swimmer in history to eclipse the 50-second mark in the 100-meter freestyle at the Olympic Games in Montreal; Yount became the first player who spent his entire major league career playing in Milwaukee to be inducted into the Baseball Hall of Fame; Paul Molitor also was inducted on that date; Laurie Merten, a native of Waukesha who moved to Phoenix as a youngster, won the U.S. Women's Open golf tournament; 14 Packers were arrested outside Lambeau Field prior to a practice game during the 1974 NFL strike; and Milwaukee Braves teammates Johnny Logan and Vern Bickford got into a fight that started in a restaurant on W. 42nd St. and spilled onto the sidewalk following a game in New York.

After carefully weighing our options, we selected the Montgomery story based on our conclusion that it was Bannister-like. Montgomery isn't as magical a name in Wisconsin as Yount or Molitor, and swimming doesn't have anywhere near the fan following here that baseball does, but Montgomery's world record time was comparable in his sport to England's Roger Bannister breaking the four-minute mile mark in track and field. Besides, we've devoted other stories to Yount and Molitor, which, to be honest, was sometimes a consideration in our selections.

Or how about the coincidences of February 2?

Three of the biggest Packer stories in the 90-year history of the franchise took place on that date. Curly Lambeau turned in his resignation to become head coach of the Chicago Cardinals; Vince Lombardi stepped aside as head coach and turned the job over to his defensive assistant Phil Bengtson; and Ron Wolf announced his retirement as the team's general manager. Lambeau, Lombardi and Wolf were the architects of the three most successful eras in the team's history.

Our choice was the Lambeau story because he was the Packers at that point and also because of the infighting and bitterness that led to his departure.

Sometimes, our choices were both obvious and difficult.

Think that's an oxymoron? For our July 9 story, we wrote about the 2002 All-Star Game that was

INTRODUCTION 17

played in Milwaukee and called after 11 innings by Commissioner Bud Selig with the score tied, 7-7. Sport stories don't get much bigger than that in Wisconsin. But that also was the date on which Selig, a Milwaukee native, was elected commissioner of baseball; Lee Elder beat Lee Trevino on the eighth hole of a sudden death playoff to win the GMO; and Pittsburgh's Randall Simon took a whack at one of the sausage racers at Miller Park.

To be sure that we didn't miss stories, we spent countless hours grinding through microfilm and paging through sports record books. And our search took us back close to 150 years before newspapers in Wisconsin even had sports pages.

Once the research was done, it was then that we asked ourselves: "Which sports story would deserve the biggest headline if we were putting out a statewide paper for that day?" The one caveat was that newspapers make their choices based on the moment. We were able to make ours through the lens of history.

For example, on April 28, 1961, future Hall of Famer Warren Spahn pitched the second no-hitter of his career at County Stadium as the Braves beat the San Francisco Giants, 1-0. On the same date, two years earlier, a relatively unknown amateur boxer named Cassius Clay won his debut in the Pan-American Trials before a sparse crowd of 3,139 at the University of Wisconsin Fieldhouse in Madison.

Spahn's feat was splashed across headlines throughout the state the next day. Clay's victory was barely covered outside of Madison. But we chose the Clay story. It was the only time that the man who became Muhammad Ali and maybe the most famous athlete in the history of the world fought in Wisconsin. The Clay story also had added appeal because it was so rich in detail. One of the more notable tidbits was that those who watched Clay from ringside paid only $1.50 for their seats. Plus, we wrote about Spahn's first no-hitter for our story on September 16.

Something we wrestled with perhaps more than anything else was how to treat stories involving athletes with state ties who made headlines while playing for teams that few in Wisconsin had any personal interest in. The issue, as we saw it, was whether a big national story was automatically a big state story.

Madison native Mark Johnson scoring two goals in the "Miracle on Ice" was both. The same was true when Sheboygan's Pat Matzdorf set a world record in the high jump.

Part of our thinking was that any time an athlete from Wisconsin did something special while representing his or her country in international competition, it was big news back home.

But how big a story was it in Wisconsin when Kenosha native Alan Ameche scored the winning touchdown in the so-called "Greatest Game Ever Played," when the Baltimore Colts beat the New York Giants in the 1958 NFL championship? Or when Craig Counsell, who grew up in Whitefish Bay, scored the winning run for the Florida Marlins in the bottom of the 11th inning of the seventh game of the 1997 World Series? Or when Green Bay's Jerry Tagge led No. 1 Nebraska to a 35-31 win over No. 2 Oklahoma in what was billed as college football's "Game of the Century?"

In the end, we decided to go with other stories that had more of a Wisconsin flavor. On the flip side, we had no such qualms about picking stories involving homegrown athletes winning or setting records in individual sports on a national or international stage. Here, again, we decided that most sports fans in the state felt a sense of pride or ownership when, for example, Andy North of Monona won the U.S. Open or when Matt Kenseth of Cambridge won the Daytona 500.

We also struggled with several choices that boiled down to picking between an unforgettable game and a major news development with a sports angle.

A good example was September 12, the date on which Wisconsin snapped a 14-game losing streak to Michigan in one of the most improbable upsets in the Badgers' long football history; and also the date on which Brown County voters approved a sales tax to rebuild Lambeau Field. Another example was October 6. That was the date of the famous Nippy Jones' shoeshine incident, the turning point when the Braves won the 1957 World Series. It also was close to 5 a.m. on that morning in 1995 when George Petak changed his vote and the Wisconsin Senate passed a financing bill that cleared the way for the Brewers to build Miller Park.

One could argue that the Lambeau referendum and Petak's change of heart were so consequential that they should have transcended any sporting event. After all, if those votes hadn't turned out the way they did, the Packers and Brewers might be heading out of town or even be long gone by now. Nevertheless, we chose to write about the two games. After all, they'd be the headline in the sports section and the two votes would be the big news on Page One.

That doesn't mean we ignored all stories that took place in boardrooms and courtrooms and anywhere else far removed from the field of play. For example, the court decision that cleared the way for the Seattle Pilots to move to Milwaukee and become the Brewers was the story we chose for March 31.

And that leads to another point. The Brewers' press guide and baseball's official encyclopedia both recognize April 1 as the day Milwaukee regained a major league team. But the court decision was actually announced in Seattle at 10:20 p.m. (Milwaukee time) on March 31 and the next morning's papers had the full story. It wasn't until April 2 that the bankruptcy referee officially signed the order, which meant that April 1 was actually a quiet news day.

We made every effort to pick and verify the dates on which events or trades or coaching changes or whatever actually occurred and were first reported, not simply when they were confirmed at press conferences. For example, the Packers list Feb. 4, 1959, as the date Lombardi was named their coach and general manager. But the announcement was actually made a week earlier. January 28 was the date of the news splash and that was the date we assigned to the story.

The one time we maybe fudged a little was over the Reggie White signing. The news actually broke on April 6, the same date that Miller Park opened eight years later. But we decided to write about White coming to Green Bay for our April 8 story. That was the date he officially signed his contract, according to a Packers spokesman. Moreover, the NFL office lists April 9 as the official date of the transaction.

Perhaps some also would accuse us of breaking our own rules with regard to Lombardi's departure from Green Bay to become head coach of the Washington Redskins. But that was a story that dragged out for five days and, again, didn't become official until Feb. 6.

If we stretched our self-imposed guidelines in a case or two, we apologize. First and foremost, our objective was to be as historically accurate as possible. But we also wanted this to be a fun book about the most memorable stories in the history of Wisconsin sports; stories that we hope will both rekindle fond memories and serve as brief history lessons in an entertaining way.

We offer 365 of them here and wish we could have told more.

BADGERS WIN THEIR FIRST ROSE BOWL

JANUARY 1, 1994

After 31 years of waiting to get back to Pasadena, Wisconsin was finding the last two minutes to be the hardest.

Brent Moss had just been stopped on a third-and-one play, which was a major upset all by itself, and UCLA had the ball with 1 minute 43 seconds on the clock. The Bruins were trailing by five points with no timeouts, but they were also facing a defense that had given up 453 yards.

It would give up 47 more before an overwhelmingly red-clad crowd of 101,327 held its collective breath as UCLA quarterback Wayne Cook barked out signals on the Wisconsin 18-yard line. Now there were 15 seconds left in the game.

Cook wanted desperately to pass to somebody, but the Badger defenders were up to the task this time. They covered everybody, forcing him to scramble way too long for way too little. He picked up three yards on the play, and as he screamed at his teammates to line up so that he could spike the ball, time ran out.

Suddenly the field was flooded with Wisconsinites. The Badgers had beaten the Bruins, 21-16, and they had their first Rose Bowl championship ever.

Coach Barry Alvarez, who had hauled the program up from the Big Ten catacombs in just four years, labeled the victory the "hugest" of his career. That might not have been a word, but it was a sentiment easy to identify with. The Badgers hadn't been to the Rose Bowl since Athletic Director Pat Richter set the game's receiving record in a 42-37 loss to Southern Cal in 1963. They hadn't won in three tries, and they certainly weren't expected to win this one. The speedy Bruins were favored to run right past the plodding Badgers, but the Badgers plodded better than anyone could have imagined.

Moss gained 158 yards on 36 carries and scored twice to win the game's Most Valuable Player award. Terrell Fletcher added 64 yards on seven carries, and then there was Darrell Bevell.

Wisconsin's slow-footed quarterback contributed the run of the day, a 21-yard scramble that reminded people of the tortoise-like O.J. Simpson car chase staged on a freeway not far away. Bevell had never carried the ball for more than nine yards at a time during the season, but when he moseyed over the UCLA goal line and the Badgers added the extra point, they had a 21-10 lead and 10:52 to protect it.

The Rose Bowl in Pasadena, California

The Bruins were discouraged, but they weren't done. Lord knows they had plenty of reason to be discouraged. While they outgained Wisconsin by more than 150 yards, they also set a Rose Bowl record by losing five fumbles. What's more, they'd been intercepted once and penalized 95 yards.

But they stopped shooting themselves in the foot long enough to put together a 90-yard drive capped by Cook's five-yard touchdown pass. Then they went for the two-point conversion, but Cook's pass fell incomplete, making it a five-point game with 3:38 remaining. When Moss was stopped on the Badgers' final possession, UCLA got a final scoring chance, only to run out of time.

The Bruins had gone into the game with the nation's best turnover ratio, and to lose that battle by a 6-1 margin had to put a significant dent in their morale. On the other hand, they seemed to get some bounce from a third quarter brawl that started with too much pre-game trash talking and ended with two players from each side getting ejected from the game. The Badgers lost receiver Lee DeRamus and fullback Mike Montgomery, and the Bruins lost two safeties.

If the fight was a draw, the outcome of the game was a joy to Wisconsinites everywhere. Nobody was happier than Richter, even though the Bruins' J.J. Stokes had obliterated his Rose Bowl record of 11 receptions. Stokes had 14 catches for 176 yards, but only one of them carried more than 25 yards and just four were in Badger territory.

"I'm happy for him, especially because we won," Richter said. "That's the important thing."

After all that time, it was the only thing.

NEITHER SLEET NOR SNOW CAN STOP PACKERS IN TITLE GAME

JANUARY 2, 1966

Jim Taylor had a groin injury. Paul Hornung hurt everywhere. Both had turned 30 during the season, and their replacements had already been signed for a combined total of more than a million dollars.

The track was sloppy, the weather was impossible, and the defending NFL champion Cleveland Browns were bringing incomparable Jim Brown to town to make them look bad. It was not a pretty picture for the Packers' once-feared backfield tandem.

Until the game was over, and they'd turned it into a masterpiece, bringing the title back to Green Bay with a 23-12 victory.

As usual, Taylor had led the Packers in rushing that season but with only 734 yards, marking the first time in seven years that he'd failed to gain 1,000. Hornung had run for only 299 yards while battling an assortment of injuries. It was only a matter of time before Jim Grabowski and Donny Anderson would claim their spots. But the time hadn't come yet.

Quarterback Bart Starr had suffered a bad case of bruised ribs the week before the Browns game, and he didn't know until Thursday whether he'd be able to play. Then four inches of snow, sleet and rain fell on an already soaked Lambeau Field, and everyone knew the issue would be decided on the ground.

The conditions should have favored Cleveland, which owned the league's top-ranked rushing attack while the Packers' ground game was rated 10th among 14 teams. Brown, the NFL eight-time rushing champion, figured to get all he wanted in the slop, but linebacker Ray Nitschke, defensive end Willie Davis and the rest of the Green Bay defense had other plans for the reigning MVP. Keying on him all day long, they helped hold him to 50 yards.

The Packers defense also intercepted two passes and blocked a field goal, and Nitschke nailed Cleveland's center so hard on an extra point attempt that place-kicker Lou Groza never had a chance to kick the ball.

The Green Bay Packers and Cleveland Browns went through their pre-game warm-ups in the snow and muck at Lambeau Field before the NFL Championship Game following the 1965 season.

But the day belonged to Taylor and Hornung. Starr threw only 18 passes all afternoon, completing 10 of them for 147 yards and a touchdown. The touchdown came on the Packers' first series when thousands of fans were still struggling with the elements on their way to the stadium. But the Packers quarterback would pass only five times in the second half, turning the game over to his running backs.

They didn't disappoint him. Hornung gashed the Browns for 105 yards on 18 carries, while Taylor simply wore them out. Green Bay's fullback always treated his matchups with Brown personally, and he didn't know how many more chances he'd have to face him. He made the most of this one, carrying the ball 27 times and gaining 96 yards. The performance not only salvaged his pride, it earned him the keys to a new car as the game's Most Valuable Player.

The people who expected to see at least one running back on his way out turned out to be right, but it wasn't either of the ones they'd thought. Hornung and Taylor both stayed one more season with the Packers before Hornung retired after being selected in an expansion draft and Taylor spent his final season with the New Orleans Saints. Brown, on the other hand, never played another game. He retired at age 29.

NOVAK'S 41 LEADS MARQUETTE IN BIG EAST DEBUT

JANUARY 3, 2006

Marquette had worked hard to join the Big East. It had been in three leagues in 16 years, and now the fourth may have been the most powerful in the country. The doubters questioned whether the Golden Eagles had gotten in over their heads.

Their answer was senior forward Steve Novak.

Marquette couldn't have drawn a tougher opponent for its first league game. Unbeaten Connecticut came to the Bradley Center ranked second in the nation and led by a 6-foot-9 sophomore who many thought would be a top three pick in the next NBA draft. Rudy Gay was supposed to be far and away the best big man on the floor. But on this night he wasn't even close.

Gay was held to two points in the first half while the Golden Eagles were taking a surprising six-point lead. On the other side, Novak scored 14 and was just getting warmed up. He would finish with 41 in a 94-79 romp that a crowd of 15,831 never saw coming.

Everyone knew that Novak could shoot. He had proved that from the time he was a freshman at Brown Deer High School playing in a program run by his dad Mike. By his third year, Steve had been named the Parkland Conference player of the year twice, made first-team all-state and been rated one of the top 10 juniors in the country.

The first man to offer him a scholarship following his freshman season was Marquette's Tom Crean, who was also the last man standing after a coast-to-coast recruiting battle with the likes of Illinois, Florida, Notre Dame, North Carolina and Wisconsin. Crean knew that he would need Novak for just the kind of challenge he was facing from Connecticut. What he didn't know was how willing the rangy local kid would be to use his gift.

The coaching staff and Novak's teammates were constantly on him to shoot more. But he just wasn't the aggressive type. At least, he wasn't until he tore up UConn.

Gay's first-half troubles were compounded when he was assigned the task of guarding Novak in the second half. Taking Gay further and further from the basket, Novak displayed the kind of stroke that couldn't be taught – especially to someone who stood 6-10. With 11 minutes 8 seconds to play, Gay fouled Novak on a three-pointer. Novak made all three free throws, and Gay went to the bench with his third personal foul. Gay was back in the last five minutes when the

Steve Novak fired up a shot against Connecticut.

Huskies tried to make a run, but he fouled out with 2:24 remaining, leaving the game with eight points.

The newly assertive Novak took 20 shots, 13 of them from three-point range. He went 12 for 20 overall and six for 13 on the threes, and he made all 11 of his free throws. Almost as important as his scoring were his 16 rebounds as the Golden Eagles held Connecticut to a 46-46 stalemate on the boards.

"At times in the past, I have been a little bit passive," Novak acknowledged after the game. "The difference has been the guys on the team really backing up what coach says. That gives me great confidence."

It also gave him a couple of conference records. His 41 points were the most ever in a Big East debut, and his combined total of 57 points and rebounds had never been equaled. Novak obviously belonged in the Big East. And so did Marquette.

AL HARRIS' OVERTIME PICK SILENCES SEAHAWKS

JANUARY 4, 2004

Mike Holmgren didn't leave empty-handed when he resigned as the Green Bay Packers head coach in 1999 to take over at Seattle. He grabbed Mike Reinfeldt and Ted Thompson from the front office as well as eight assistant coaches on the way out. Then two years later, he stole quarterback Matt Hasselbeck from the Packers in a lopsided trade.

So when the Seahawks showed up at Lambeau Field in the NFC wild-card round, the Packers were determined not to let it become a homecoming celebration. "Everybody really wanted to beat the old ball coach," said cornerback Al Harris, who proceeded to do just that with the biggest play of a 33-27 overtime victory.

A lot of strange things had to happen for the Packers to be in this game at all. The year had been especially hard on quarterback Brett Favre, who'd lost his father with two weeks left in the regular season. But he had responded to that with the best game of his career on a Monday night in Oakland, and he'd finished the 16-game schedule with 32 touchdown passes.

The Packers needed most of them, too, because they'd started the season 3-4, and only an early November upset in Minnesota and a four-game, season-ending winning streak kept them alive. When the heavily favored Vikings lost their last game in the last second to Arizona to put Green Bay into the playoffs, people were talking about the Packers as a team of destiny.

They seemed destined to beat the Seahawks, too, when running back Ahman Green rallied them from a 20-13 deficit to a 27-20 lead with a pair of one-yard touchdown runs in the fourth quarter. Interestingly enough, Holmgren had traded Green to the Packers for a little remembered cornerback named Fred Vinson and lived to regret it when Green became one of the league's most potent rushers. At least one Holmgren-Green Bay transaction had gone the Packers' way.

But Hasselbeck was having a career game at his former teammates' expense. He'd led the Seahawks on scoring drives of 74, 77 and 67 yards, and when running back Shaun Alexander capped the last one with a one-yard run with 51 seconds remaining in the fourth quarter, the game was tied. The Packers had a chance to win in the last second of regulation, but Ryan Longwell's 47-yard field goal attempt fell short.

It would have been much easier on Hasselbeck if Longwell's kick had been successful, because the next five minutes were among the most humbling of his career. Seattle won the overtime coin flip, and when

Cornerback Al Harris headed for the end zone and a game-winning touchdown in overtime in an NFL wild-card round playoff game at Lambeau Field.

the referee asked Hasselbeck what the Seahawks wanted to do, he proclaimed loudly, "We want the ball. We're going to score." The first was understandable. The second was dead wrong.

With 4 minutes 16 seconds gone in overtime, Seattle was facing a third-and-11 situation on its own 45-yard line. The Packers came with a full blitz, and Hasselbeck called an audible, going with a three-step drop and sending wide receiver Alex Bannister on a hitch route. His problem was that Harris had seen the call before.

"We actually practiced against that play," Harris said. "Hasselbeck had checked to that call two plays earlier, and the guy did the same thing. The guy ran a stop, and when I saw that, I thought, 'No, he can't be about to do the same play.'"

But he was, and Harris stepped in front of Bannister, intercepted the pass and ran 52 yards into the end zone to win the game. Hasselbeck was left to eat his ill-considered words, although Harris would be the last guy to feed them to him. "I never heard him say it," he said.

JANUARY 23

BADGERS STAGE THEIR BIGGEST COMEBACK

JANUARY 5, 1976

John Powless didn't know it yet, but he was on his way out. He was in his eighth season as Wisconsin's basketball coach, and only two of his previous teams had had winning records. This one would be worse than most, finishing 10-16.

So it came as no surprise to a sparse crowd of 5,735 at the University of Wisconsin Fieldhouse to find the Badgers trailing Ohio State, 47-25, with 3 minutes 38 seconds left in the first half. They'd seen it all before.

But they'd never seen anything quite like what came next. Nobody had.

Call it an early retirement present for Powless. Or just call it the biggest Wisconsin basketball comeback ever as the Badgers rallied again and again to beat the Buckeyes, 82-81, in overtime.

Dale Koehler

It was a strange game frequently dominated by the officials. Fifty-four personal fouls were called and three technical fouls assessed: one each on UW and Ohio State players, and one on Buckeyes coach Fred Taylor. The final margin was determined at the free throw line with the Badgers making 20 of 27 foul shots to the visitors' 17 of 25, but the biggest difference in the outcome was 6-foot-8 senior forward Dale Koehler.

Koehler, a product of Kewaunee High School, scored 26 points and claimed 14 rebounds, and his two free throws pulled Wisconsin even with 25 seconds remaining in regulation. But he wasn't the Badgers' only hero. Guard Tim Paterick hit three straight jump shots to wipe out a five-point deficit in overtime, and guard Brian Colbert sealed the victory by dropping in a pair of foul shots for Wisconsin's last points with 13 seconds to play.

UW really had no business being in this game after shooting just 29.7% in the first half compared to Ohio State's 58.3%. The Buckeyes had gone on a 22-2 run to open their biggest lead of the night, and they were still ahead, 49-31, at the break. But then the Badgers found the basket, cutting 10 points off the deficit in the first four minutes of the second half. They kept coming as Koehler scored eight points in the last 6:50 and finally tied the game at 72 from the free-throw line.

Ohio State had a final chance to win in regulation, but Larry Bolden's 20-footer rimmed out with 10 seconds on the clock to send the game into overtime. Two Wisconsin turnovers led to a three-point play and a layup as the Buckeyes took a 77-72 lead in the first 53 seconds of the extra period. But Koehler's basket broke the slump, and Paterick's three jumpers put Wisconsin ahead, 80-79. Then Colbert's free throws put it out of reach.

The victory improved the Badgers' record to 8-2 and gave them their first 2-0 start in the Big Ten in nine years. But the celebration was short-lived. They lost their next 14 games, and Ohio State turned out to be the only team to finish below them in the league standings. The Buckeyes ended the year 6-20 overall and 2-16 in the Big Ten. Wisconsin was 4-14 in the league, and Powless was replaced by Bill Cofield at the end of the season.

PACKERS PROVE THEMSELVES IN SAN FRANCISCO

JANUARY 6, 1996

Mike Holmgren had created a fuss the week before when he suggested that Green Bay "would win it all" after clobbering Atlanta in the NFC wild-card round. "Why not?" asked the Packers' normally diplomatic head coach.

It seemed like such a carefree question. The San Francisco 49ers were why not, of course.

It was an article of faith in those times that when the Dallas Cowboys didn't win the Super Bowl, the 49ers did. One or the other had claimed the last three NFL championships and five of the last seven. Holmgren, on the other hand, had never even played San Francisco, and he'd never beaten Dallas.

So when the Packers took their brash young club west, the oddsmakers saw no reason to expect them to disrupt the pattern. It was true that they were 12-5, including their victory over Atlanta, and they had won seven of their last eight games, but the 49ers were playing at home, and they had a bye week to prepare for the occasion. That was more than enough to make them 10-point favorites.

Which just added to everyone's surprise when Green Bay won easily, 27-17, and advanced to the NFC title game for the first time since Vince Lombardi left Wisconsin. It was still a little early to say the Packers had "arrived" as an elite team, but they had certainly phoned ahead with their intentions.

As 69,311 startled onlookers headed off to the streets of San Francisco, General Manager Ron Wolf said the victory had shown that the Packers were a real football team. He got no argument from the 49ers, who'd figured that out halfway through the second quarter after the visitors had raced to a 21-0 lead.

This was an equal opportunity thrashing. Green Bay's defense produced four turnovers, sacked quarterback Steve Young three times and knocked him down at least 10 more while forcing him to misfire on 33 of 65 passes. The offense gained 368 yards and played mistake-free football behind an almost flawless performance by Brett Favre. Favre completed 15 of his first 16 passes on the way to a 21-for-28 day that included two touchdowns against the league's top-ranked defense.

Hard-luck linebacker Wayne Simmons let the 49ers know where the afternoon was headed on their first snap from scrimmage. That's when Young completed a swing pass to fullback Adam Walker, who held the ball just long enough for Simmons to put his helmet on it. Cornerback Craig Newsome scooped up the fumble and took it 31 yards for a touchdown. Simmons, a third-year man plagued by knee problems in his first two seasons, led the Packers' defensive effort with 12 tackles, a sack and two passes defended, in addition to causing Walker's crucial bobble.

No question who led the Packers' offensive effort. Favre directed them to scoring drives on two of their first three possessions, and it would have been all three if Chris Jacke hadn't missed a 44-yard field goal on the first one. Taking turns with his tight ends, Favre hit Keith Jackson with a three-yard touchdown pass and Mark Chmura with a 13-yard strike that put the Packers ahead by three touchdowns.

Forced to abandon their running game, the 49ers never got closer than 11 points until they scored a consolation touchdown with 50 seconds on the clock. Their only intimidating play of the day may have come when center Bart Oates got so frustrated that he snatched the helmet of defensive lineman Darius Holland and flung it downfield.

San Francisco coach George Seifert gave the Packers all the credit in the world. "They certainly have our respect," he said. "Everybody saw what took place out there."

Everybody saw what happened the following Sunday, too, when the Packers lost at Dallas, 38-27, and failed to get to their first Super Bowl in 28 years. But they won the next one, proving that Holmgren was right after all. His timing was just a little off.

UW HOCKEY TEAM STUNS OLYMPIANS

JANUARY 7, 1984

When Jeff Sauer is right he's right. And when he's wrong ... well he can be pretty happy about that, too, sometimes.

It was Thursday, and the coach was wondering what an upcoming weekend series with the United States Olympic hockey team would do to his struggling University of Wisconsin team's morale. "It's probably not a good idea to be playing them twice," he said dryly.

He couldn't have gotten that more backward.

Playing the Olympians once did look like a mistake as the Badgers lost a ragged 4-1 decision on Friday night. But meeting them a second time on Saturday produced a shock. Three third-period scores and an unconscious performance by sophomore goaltender Gary Baxter gave Wisconsin a 4-2 victory that a giddy Sauer put on a par with winning the national championship the year before.

"It had to be," he said, "especially with the type of talent on the other team. Do you think this will make headlines in Moscow?"

It certainly created a fuss in Madison where the best local fans had been hoping for was a mercy killing and a chance to see former Badgers Marc Behrend, Tim Thomas and Chris Chelios perform with the visitors.

The touring Olympic team came to town with a 32-14-8 record that included three victories and a tie in seven games against National Hockey League clubs. Eleven college teams had gotten a crack at this collection of all-Americans and top NHL draft choices, and they'd fallen by a combined margin of 87-20. No college team had beaten an Olympic team since 1976, and these Badgers looked like a poor bet to change that pattern.

They were sitting in fourth place in the Western Collegiate Hockey Association standings and were holding a 14-9 overall record. Though they'd won their last four games they'd beaten only two winning teams all year.

The Olympians got some inspired goaltending from Behrend in the Friday night game, but they still looked lifeless to coach Lou Vairo, who called it their worst performance of the year. On a scale of one to 10, he gave it a one.

If that was designed to light a fire under his team, it didn't work. Vairo decided to give Behrend a rest on Saturday and replace him with Bob Mason, a former Green Bay Bobcat and future Milwaukee Admiral, but it really didn't matter. Anyone Vairo put in the nets would have been the second-best goalie that night. The best was Baxter by a wide margin.

A native of Don Mills, Ontario, Baxter was a sophomore who would turn out to have a limited future with the Badgers. He lettered for four years, but he played in only 38 games. He had sat out the Friday night game, and it wasn't until Saturday morning that Sauer decided to start him. It was Sauer's best decision of the weekend.

Baxter made 39 saves, including 20 in the second period when the Olympians all but punched themselves out. He snuffed six breakaways including one by teenage sensation Pat LaFontaine that brought a Dane County Coliseum sellout to its feet.

The Olympians took a 2-1 lead in the first 1 minute 31 seconds of the final period, but they were showing the effects of their 54-game road trip while the Badgers were just getting started. Two third-period goals 18 seconds apart by Gary Suter and Dave Maley gave Wisconsin its first lead. When Marty Wiitala added an insurance goal while Wisconsin was skating two players short, Sauer let his whole bench flood the ice to congratulate the Superior native.

"It was probably good for both teams," the coach said later. "It's a tremendous feat for us, but in the long run, it might help them more."

He was wrong about that, too. The U.S. finished out of the medal round at the Sarajevo Olympics with a 1-2-2 record.

HOLMGREN LEAVES PACKERS FOR SEATTLE

JANUARY 8, 1999

Mike Holmgren

His title would be almost as long as his resume. When the Seattle Seahawks hired away the only coach to win a Super Bowl in Green Bay other than the legendary Vince Lombardi, they named him "executive vice president of football operations/general manager/head coach."

They could have tossed in ticket director and marketing manager, because Mike Holmgren probably would be in charge of that stuff, too, but enough was enough. The man who came to be nicknamed "The Emperor" was leaving Green Bay for power, and he was getting enough of it to light the entire state of Washington. The money wasn't bad either.

Seahawks owner Paul Allen, the third-richest man in America, was worth $22 billion, so he could hardly be expected to miss the $32 million he'd promised to pay Holmgren over the next eight years. The contract made Holmgren the best-paid coach in the NFL and put him out of Green Bay's fiscal reach.

Even if the Packers could have matched the money, they couldn't have duplicated the position. They already had a reasonably competent general manager, a fellow named Ron Wolf, which was why Holmgren was leaving. He'd made no secret of his desire to run his own show, and his relationship with Wolf had gotten scratchy enough that Wolf had given him a 21-day window to find a team that would allow him total control. When Allen opened his checkbook, Holmgren dived out the window.

Only five days elapsed between the Packers' year-ending playoff loss to San Francisco and the Seattle press conference announcing Holmgren's hiring, prompting cynics to suggest that a deal was in place before the season was even over. Holmgren and his agent, Bob LaMonte, both denied that strenuously, not that it mattered to anyone but the Baltimore Ravens and the Philadelphia Eagles. They were interested in Holmgren, too, and he canceled visits to both of them as soon as he signed with the Seahawks.

Holmgren's departure was a huge loss for the Packers in several ways. His .670 winning percentage was topped only by Lombardi's .758 among Green Bay coaches, and he was the only coach since Lombardi to even compile a winning record. He'd taken the Packers to two Super Bowls, winning the first one. He'd also led them to the playoffs six times in seven years and formed a management team with Wolf that was irreplaceable. And on the way out the door he scooped up Mike Reinfeldt, who was in line to become the Packers' next president, and Ted Thompson, who would later become their general manager.

In return for all of that, the Packers got a second-round draft choice because Holmgren's contract had a year to run, and the problem of finding a new head coach. The draft choice was the 47th pick overall. The coach was Ray Rhodes.

Rhodes had just been fired by the same Philadelphia Eagles who were trying to hire Holmgren, and the Eagles wound up dealing the Packers another blow by hiring their fine young quarterback coach, Andy Reid, to become their new head coach. The dominoes never stop falling in the NFL.

When Holmgren left Green Bay, Wolf declared that he had neither a list nor a time frame for finding a new coach, which was a little disingenuous if technically correct. Holmgren was gone only three days before Wolf announced that Rhodes had the job. Jacksonville Jaguars defensive coordinator Dick Jauron's name had been mentioned prominently, but it was pretty clear that Wolf had one man in mind the whole time.

It was a peculiar selection. Rhodes had served well as Holmgren's defensive coordinator in 1992 and '93 before becoming the Eagles' head coach, but he had been fired in Philly for a 3-13 season. Wolf ignored the numbers. He wanted someone to make the Packers a tough team.

What he got instead was a tough season. The Packers paid Rhodes about an eighth of what Holmgren was making at Seattle and half of what Holmgren had made the previous year at Green Bay, and got what they paid for. He lasted one year, leading the Packers to one of the uglier 8-8 seasons in their history.

Holmgren, meanwhile, rescued the Seahawks from a run of 10 non-playoff seasons, but he was later stripped of most of his front office duties. Functioning again primarily as a head coach, he took Seattle to a Super Bowl. Sometimes, you have to be careful what you wish for.

BUCKS END LAKERS' RECORD 33-GAME STREAK

JANUARY 9, 1972

Half of the starters would make the Basketball Hall of Fame. Four of the NBA's top eight all-time scorers were on the floor, and pro basketball's longest winning streak ever was on the line.

A national television audience, a coast-to-coast media contingent and 10,746 paying customers were all witnesses when the defending champion Milwaukee Bucks faced the visiting Los Angeles Lakers on a Sunday afternoon at the Milwaukee Arena. NBA regular-season games just didn't get any bigger than this.

The Lakers had won 33 in a row by a staggering average margin of 16 points a game. They were 39-3, and they hadn't lost since Oct. 31. Their center was Wilt Chamberlain. Their guards were Jerry West and Gail Goodrich. All of them were future Hall of Famers, and their sixth man was Pat Riley, who was a lock to make it one day as a coach.

The Bucks' credentials were every bit as solid. They were 35-8, and they had arguably the most talented center in the league in Kareem Abdul-Jabbar and, at that point, maybe the best guard to ever play the game in Oscar Robertson. Bobby Dandridge was no slouch either. He was widely regarded as one of the premier NBA forwards of the 1970s.

The Lakers' streak had obliterated the old record set by Milwaukee at 20 the previous year. The two teams had already met once in Los Angeles with the Lakers winning, 112-105. The game was No. 11 in the streak, and the Bucks were determined that No. 34 wouldn't happen on their home court.

This had all the makings of a classic battle except for one thing. It wasn't even close. The Lakers took a 24-17 lead in the first quarter, but it was all Bucks after that as they won going away, 120-104.

Abdul-Jabbar let everyone know just how intense things were going to be when LA's Happy Hairston fouled him on the way to the basket in the second quarter. A decidedly unhappy Abdul-Jabbar turned and smacked the Lakers' forward in the face. It cost him a punching foul, but it ignited the Bucks. They outscored the visitors, 34-21, in the period to take a 51-45 halftime lead they never came close to losing.

Abdul-Jabbar turned his personal duel with Chamberlain into a rout, scoring 39 points and pulling down 20 rebounds. The Lakers' big man finished with 15 points and 12 boards, and he was called for his fourth foul in the second minute of the second half, which was unheard of. Chamberlain had never fouled out of an NBA game in his life, and he seemed determined to keep that record intact as he gave his rival all the room he needed to operate in the post.

Abdul-Jabbar took maximum advantage during an 18-2 Bucks run that put them up, 112-94, and removed all doubt about the outcome. Not only was Chamberlain neutralized, but the Lakers' lethal fast break was stymied by coach Larry Costello's game plan. Costello dropped both of his guards back and left a forward at the free-throw line after every Bucks' shot. Incredibly, Milwaukee still out-rebounded Los Angeles, 58-46.

One big reason for that was the anonymous John Block, who came off the bench to score 17 points mostly on the offensive boards. Block, a 6-foot-9½ forward, also had 10 rebounds, and back-up guard Lucius Allen contributed 18 points as the Bucks' bench dominated.

Allen was a big factor in limiting Goodrich to five-of-20 shooting. West wasn't much better. He went five for 16, thanks mostly to the defensive effort of Robertson, who had 17 points and nine assists.

When it was over, Robertson, Abdul-Jabbar and Block all got standing ovations, and Lakers coach Bill Sharman paid the Bucks a huge compliment. "If it had to end," he said of the streak, "I'm happy it was ended by a great team."

The Lakers would prove to be a greater one, winning a league-record 69 games and their first championship since they had resided in Minneapolis. They beat Milwaukee, four games to two, in the Western Conference finals. But for one Sunday at least, the Bucks were clearly the class of the NBA.

NBA'S LONGEST WINNING STREAKS

No.	Team	Start	Finish
33	Los Angeles Lakers	Nov. 5, 1971	Jan. 7, 1972
22	Houston	Jan. 29, 2008	March 18, 2008
20	Milwaukee	Feb. 6, 1971	March 8, 1971
19	Los Angeles Lakers	Feb. 4, 2000	March 13, 2000
18	Boston	Feb. 24, 1982	March 26, 1982
18	Chicago	Dec. 29, 1995	Feb. 2, 1996
18	New York	Oct. 24, 1969	Nov. 28, 1969

Source: nba.com

RIVERS' 35-FOOTER SINKS NOTRE DAME

JANUARY 10, 1981

Dean Marquardt was feeling left out. Glenn "Doc" Rivers had considered transferring from Marquette. Both were unhappy when fifth-ranked Notre Dame came to the Milwaukee Arena on a Saturday afternoon.

Two hours and one 35-foot desperation heave later, only Notre Dame fans were unhappy.

The Irish arrived with an 8-1 record, an eight-game winning streak and four future NBA players in their lineup. Marquette wasn't quite Marquette. The Warriors had lost three of their last four NCAA tournament games after winning the national championship in 1977, and they were headed for the NIT in March.

Rivers, their blue-chip freshman from Maywood, Ill., was only a sometime starter who'd recently told a Chicago newspaper reporter that he'd given some thought to leaving Marquette. Marquardt, a junior center from Milwaukee Washington High School, had met with assistant coach Rick Majerus the night before the game to ask where he fit in. He hadn't been able to crack the starting lineup.

It was hard to imagine two less likely heroes in an upset against an archrival. But that's how it worked for the Warriors as Rivers' last-second shot shocked Notre Dame, 54-52.

In a way, the game was won before it began when coach Hank Raymonds decided on his starting lineup. Raymonds had been going with three guards and two forwards much of the time, which left Marquardt out. When Marquette did start a center, Marquardt still sat, and Rivers was benched in favor of senior Artie Green.

But Notre Dame rotated three big postmen and had a quick 6-foot-9 future pro named Orlando Woolridge at one forward, and Raymonds needed the 6-9 Marquardt's size. He also needed Rivers' athleticism, so he started him ahead of Green.

For most of the game, the first move looked much better than the second. Marquardt battled the committee of Irish big men to a draw, making all six of his field goal attempts and blocking three shots in a 15-point performance that was the best of his career. Rivers, on the other hand, had taken seven shots and missed five of them.

With 3 minutes 29 seconds to play, the game was tied at 52, and Notre Dame coach Digger Phelps decided inexplicably to go into a four-corner offense and play for the last shot. He never got it. With four seconds left, Rivers and guard Michael Wilson trapped Irish guard Tracy Jackson in a corner, and Rivers tied up Jackson and created a jump ball. The tip went to Woolridge, but the ball went off his hands out of bounds giving the Warriors possession with one second to go.

That was all Rivers needed to win the game on a busted play. When Wilson took the ball in, he was supposed to go inside, but the Irish clogged the middle. That's when Wilson spotted Rivers crossing half-court and got him the ball. Rivers turned and fired from 35 feet. The ball banged off the backboard and through the net.

Glenn "Doc" Rivers

"When I let go, I didn't know where the ball was going," Rivers said afterward. "I just aimed for the backboard. But when I saw where it was going to hit on the board I jumped up and down before it even went in."

The fans did some jumping, too, flooding the floor and carrying the players off. And Raymonds, who had been Al McGuire's assistant in two NCAA Final Fours, called the victory the "most satisfying" in his 20 years at Marquette. Rivers and Marquardt were pretty satisfied, too. They both finished their college days with the Warriors.

Michael Wilson of Marquette stood on the rim of the basket at the Milwaukee Arena to celebrate his team's victory over Notre Dame.

JANUARY 29

FOURTH-AND-26 DOOMS PACKERS

JANUARY 11, 2004

Five syllables that live in infamy, synonyms for disappointment and disbelief. Down and distance. Say the words "Fourth-and-26" to Green Bay Packer fans anywhere, and they're taken back to a sunny, 15-degree day in Philadelphia where everything looked so bright.

They're at a divisional playoff, two games from the Super Bowl in what was shaping up as a season of "destiny." The Packers had started the year 3-3 and still made it into the playoffs, thanks to a stunning, last-second loss by Minnesota. Then they'd eliminated Mike Holmgren's Seattle Seahawks with a walk-off interception in overtime. Who could stop them now?

Well, the Packers could, that's who.

They had spent the afternoon at Lincoln Financial Field enduring a dizzying series of questionable judgments, blown blocks and missed opportunities, and still they led the Philadelphia Eagles, 17-14, with 1 minute 12 seconds to play. Donovan McNabb had just been sacked for an astounding eighth time, and as he took his team to the line of scrimmage on his own 26-yard line, Green Bay was in its "quarters" defense with two cornerbacks and two safeties each responsible for a quarter of the field. A linebacker and two nickel backs were underneath, and McNabb was facing fourth down needing 26 yards to keep Philadelphia in the game. Incredibly, he got 28.

Freddie Mitchell, a garrulous and largely anonymous backup receiver, found a seam that absolutely should not have been there and caught McNabb's pass in front of safety Darren Sharper for a first down at the Packers' 46. Barely a minute later, Fred Akers was kicking a 37-yard field goal to send the game into overtime.

Suddenly, destiny was wearing a different jersey. The Eagles won the coin flip and got the ball first in overtime, but they had to punt, putting the game in the capable hands of Brett Favre. Favre had been having a good day, although McNabb was having a better one. The Packers' quarterback had completed 14 of 27 passes for 180 yards and two touchdowns to wide receiver Robert Ferguson. He hadn't had a single pass intercepted. Not until that moment when he overthrew Javon Walker.

Walker was running deep down the right sideline, and the Eagles had made the correct defensive call, sending more pass rushers than the Packers could block. With hands in his face, Favre let it fly anyway, and Philadelphia safety Brian Dawkins was waiting for the ball. He ran it back 35 yards.

With 10:12 on the overtime clock, Akers was at it again. His 31-yard field goal gave the Eagles a 20-17 victory and Packer boosters a grievance that might just endure forever.

So many things had to go badly for Green Bay to suffer this indignity. They were playing their best football of the season, and they were facing a Philadelphia team that was missing four starters, including its leading ground-gainer. They had taken a 14-0 lead in the first quarter, and their running game appeared to be unstoppable as Ahman Green gained 156 yards on 25 carries.

The injury-riddled Eagles, on the other hand, were all McNabb, who passed for 248 yards and ran for 107 more. He wouldn't have been enough if the Packers could have gotten out of their own way.

They'd allowed Philadelphia back into the game by sitting on their lead, and still, they could have gone into halftime ahead, 21-7, if they'd been able to profit from a first-and-goal situation inside the Eagles' four late in the second quarter. Instead, they'd missed a key block on fourth-and-one and fallen six inches short of a touchdown.

Another fourth-and-one opportunity backfired in the fourth quarter. The Packers were on the Philadelphia 41 with 2:30 to play, and the Eagles were out of timeouts. One first down would have allowed them to run out the clock, but coach Mike Sherman elected to punt rather than go for it. The ball sailed into the end zone, bringing the ball out to the 20 and setting the stage for McNabb's dramatic completion to Mitchell.

There would be no Super Bowl. There would only be fourth-and-26.

PACKERS BEAT CAROLINA FOR SUPER BOWL BERTH

JANUARY 12, 1997

The sun was shining, the grass was green, and the wind chill at Lambeau Field was minus 17 degrees. Even the opponent was practically handpicked. What could possibly go wrong?

Well, there were the two turnovers for openers. Linebacker Sam Mills had picked off Brett Favre's slant pass on the Green Bay Packers' second possession of the game, and Favre had dropped the ball after being sacked in the second quarter. One led to a touchdown, the other to a field goal, and suddenly, Carolina's upstart Panthers had a 10-7 lead with 8 minutes 40 seconds to play in the second quarter and 60,216 fans were shivering from more than the three-degree temperature.

Turned out they didn't have a thing to worry about.

The Panthers would score only one more time on John Kasay's third-quarter field goal, and the Packers were on their way to the Super Bowl for the first time since the 1967 season. As his team put the finishing touches on a 30-13 rout in the NFC Championship Game, General Manager Ron Wolf pumped both arms in the air. The franchise revival that he'd started five years earlier was almost complete. All that remained was a 35-21 victory over New England in Super Bowl XXXI.

Nothing is certain in pro football, but the outcome of this match was as close to a foregone conclusion as it comes. The Packers players just knew if they could get this game at home they couldn't be stopped, and they were right. The team had never lost a playoff game at Lambeau Field at that point, and the conditions were perfect for facing an opponent from Dixie. Especially this opponent.

Carolina wasn't even supposed to be there. The Panthers had upset Dallas the week before, depriving Green Bay of a rematch of a 21-6 loss in November, but nobody was complaining too loudly about that. The Panthers had compiled a 12-4 season record with a respectable 10th-ranked defense, but their offense, led by the no better than adequate Kerry Collins, was a highly suspect 23rd.

The Packers, on the other hand, had the NFL's fifth-ranked offense directed by Favre, who had just won his second straight Most Valuable Player award. And their defense featuring Hall of Fame-bound Reggie White was No. 1. They were in the playoffs for the fourth year in a row, two years more than the expansion Panthers had even been in the league.

Green Bay had beaten the San Francisco 49ers, 35-14, the weekend before in a divisional playoff monsoon at Lambeau Field. The all-day rain had torn

Running back Dorsey Levens of the Packers ran past a Carolina defender on his way to gaining 205 total yards in the NFC Championship Game at Lambeau Field.

up the surface so badly that a whole new field had to be trucked in from a Maryland sod farm. The old field was sold a square at a time to the Packers' playoff-crazed customers.

Rain was not an issue in the week that followed. Snow was. The Packers sent out a community newsletter asking for people to help shovel the stands. Dozens responded. Then the temperature plunged. By Sunday, both the stadium and the fans were ready for a showdown, even if the Panthers weren't.

When cornerback Tyrone Williams intercepted a Collins pass in the last minute of the first half to set up a Chris Jacke field goal, the Packers held a 17-10 lead that they never came close to losing. Carolina couldn't make it past Green Bay's 35-yard line after Kasay's third-quarter kick.

Favre had a good day, passing for 292 yards and two touchdowns, but it was the Packers' running backs who dominated the afternoon. Edgar Bennett rushed for 99 yards, and Dorsey Levens got 88 on the ground and 117 more receiving. Green Bay's defense, meanwhile, lived up to its ranking by holding the Panthers to 251 yards and producing three turnovers.

Years later, Wolf called the victory the highlight of his 41-year career in the NFL. For the Panthers, it was the beginning of the end. They went 7-9 the next season and 4-12 in the one after that. Green Bay would get back to the Super Bowl in 1998, but Lambeau Field was never happier than it was on that frigid day when the Packers returned to glory.

DISGRUNTLED OKEY QUITS BADGERS

JANUARY 13, 1998

There wasn't much to say when Sam Okey walked into Wisconsin basketball coach Dick Bennett's office at 11 o'clock on a Tuesday morning. Okey told the coach that he'd decided to quit the team, and the coach told Okey he thought it was a good idea. It was about all they'd agreed on for the last two-and-a-half years.

Their most recent dispute had come earlier in the week when Okey missed a mandatory weightlifting session, and Bennett demoted him to the second team. It may have been the straw that broke the camel's back, but a ton of hay had piled up before that as the two clashed over Okey's work habits, his off-the-court conduct and his approach to the game.

And so when the gifted 6-foot-7 junior left the program halfway through the season, it came more as a relief than a surprise for everyone involved. Not that anyone would have expected it when Okey left little Cassville High School to become one of the Badgers' most celebrated recruits.

A two-time Wisconsin player of the year who led his team to four state tournaments and two Division 4 championships, Okey was a "can't-miss" prospect in more ways than one. He'd made an incredible 80% of his two-point shots as a senior. He finished his high school career as the fourth-leading scorer in state history, and there were those who said he was the best prep player Wisconsin had ever produced.

North Carolina wanted him, and so did Iowa. When he made a verbal commitment to the Badgers, it was a major coup for coach Stan Van Gundy. But Van Gundy never got to celebrate the accomplishment. He was replaced by Bennett the next year. On the surface, Okey seemed perfectly suited for Bennett's style and he was far more talented than almost all of the players Bennett had at his previous job at the University of Wisconsin-Green Bay.

And their first year together, they got along well enough for Okey to be named Big Ten freshman of the year while averaging 13.2 points a game and becoming the first player in conference history to lead his team in scoring, rebounding, blocked shots and assists. It was all downhill after that.

Okey's scoring average dipped to 11.2 his sophomore season, and it was at 9.8 his junior year when he left the team. Part of the falloff was due to a fundamental disagreement between coach and player. Okey wanted to develop his perimeter game for the NBA. Bennett wanted him inside.

But their biggest differences developed off the

Sam Okey

court. Okey had two run-ins with police involving underage drinking incidents, and Bennett suspended him for two weeks after allegations of marijuana use. Citizenship was always a big item with the coach.

It didn't help either that Okey dislocated his knee playing in the Badger State Games the summer before his junior year, and Bennett wasn't inclined to hold open a spot for him while he recuperated.

The next fall, following his departure from Wisconsin, Okey resurfaced at Iowa, which had recruited him heavily out of high school. But he was arrested for drunken driving in Iowa City before he'd even played a game. He wound up playing seven of them for the Hawkeyes, averaging 16 minutes, 6.6 points and 3.1 rebounds before missing the second half of the season with a broken hand.

And so ended Okey's NBA dreams. He played six months in Turkey and hated it before coming back to Iowa City and working at a moving company. His career ended with La Crosse in the Continental Basketball Association where coach Bill Klucas praised his talent but not his attitude. Said Klucas, "At some point, Sam's got to take a stand in life."

PREEMINENT PACKERS WIN SUPER BOWL II

JANUARY 14, 1968

When it was over, which was roughly at halftime, only a couple of questions remained. When would the upstart American Football League ever catch up with the NFL, and what was Bart Starr supposed to do with *two* sports cars?

Nobody really gave the AFL Oakland Raiders much of a chance against the Green Bay Packers in the second annual clash of pro football champions. These were the same Packers after all who had won five of the last seven NFL titles and who had dismantled the proud Kansas City Chiefs, 35-10, the year before.

They had nine Pro Bowl players, a decade of big-game experience, the No. 1 coach in either league, and a veteran quarterback who was the reigning Super Bowl Most Valuable Player. Maybe the Raiders had an edge at place-kicker with 39-year old George Blanda, but Green Bay's Don Chandler was about to dispute that.

So when 75,546 spectators gathered at Miami's Orange Bowl and millions more took up positions around their television sets to watch Super Bowl II, or what officially was still being called The World Championship Game, the overwhelming majority of them were expecting business as usual by the Packers. Which is exactly what they got.

Green Bay scored the first three times it had the ball, twice on Chandler field goals and once on a 62-yard pass from quarterback Bart Starr to wide receiver Boyd Dowler. The Packers allowed the Raiders to enter the argument just once, and that was when young quarterback Daryle Lamonica led them on a 78-yard, second-quarter drive that closed the difference to 13-7.

But the challengers tripped over their own feet in the closing seconds of the second quarter when Rodger Bird fumbled a high, left-footed punt by Donny Anderson and Dick Capp recovered at midfield. That led to Chandler's third field goal from 43 yards out and put the Packers ahead, 16-7, at halftime. Most observers saw that as the play of the game, because Oakland was never heard from again.

The Raiders ran just six plays in the third quarter when Green Bay added a touchdown and a final Chandler field goal. Counting the extra points, the Packers' kicker had outscored Oakland, 14-7, all by himself at that juncture. Cornerback Herb Adderley wrapped up the afternoon by returning a 60-yard interception for a touchdown and leaving the crowd far more impressed than the Packers' own coach.

"The way we played was typical of this team in the last year-and-a-half," yawned Vince Lombardi. "We took a 13-0 lead and went on vacation."

For Starr, at least, it was a working vacation. He completed 13 of 24 passes for 202 yards and a touchdown, but he was also sacked four times, and he finished the game with an injured thumb. The thumb didn't hurt badly enough the next day, though, to prevent him from taking the keys of a new sports car from *Sport* magazine, which annually awarded a vehicle to the Super Bowl MVP.

Starr had won the honor the year before, as well, and fortunately the payoff for the players on the winning team could cover the cost of a two-car garage. The Packers earned $15,000 apiece while the Raiders got $7,500 in the most lucrative football game ever played. It grossed more than $3 million, including $2.5 million from CBS for the television rights.

Defensive end Ben Davidson may have summed up the general tone of Super Bowl II better than anyone when he asked the reporters in the Raiders' locker room, "Don't you guys get a little tired of writing about all those Packer victories? Just once, wouldn't you like to write about a defeat? Sort of as a change of pace?"

The pace would change the following year after Lombardi resigned as coach, but for the time being, another championship was business as usual in Green Bay.

LOMBARDI'S THREE STRAIGHT TITLES
1965-'67
(Post-Season Scores)

DATE	GAME	SCORE
12-26-65	Western Conference Playoff	Packers 13, Balt Colts 10 (ot)
01-02-66	NFL Championship	Packers 23, Cleveland 12
01-01-67	NFL Championship	Packers 34, Dallas 27
01-15-67	Super Bowl I	Packers 35, Kansas City 10
12-23-67	Western Conference Playoff	Packers 28, L.A. Rams 7
12-31-67	NFL Championship	Packers 21, Dallas 17
01-14-68	Super Bowl II	Packers 33, Oakland 14

Source: Green Bay Packers Media Guide

PACKERS CONQUER NEW WORLD IN SUPER BOWL I

JANUARY 15, 1967

It was late in the fourth quarter when "The Hammer" officially became the nail. Fred Williamson had given himself the nickname, and running back Donny Anderson had given him cause to regret it when he hit the Kansas City cornerback so hard Williamson had to leave the game on a stretcher.

The rest of the Chiefs exited the Los Angeles Memorial Coliseum under their own power, but only after suffering major damage to their reputations and the fledgling pride of the American Football League. The Green Bay Packers struggled to a 14-10 halftime lead, but then simply skated away from the two-touchdown underdogs in the first of many Super Bowls that proved to be five parts hype to one-part performance. The final score was 35-10.

Williamson did his best to contribute to the former earlier in the week when he promised to "lower the hammer" on wide receiver Boyd Dowler. Williamson never got the chance, because the Packers' rangy wide-out left the game after injuring his shoulder on the third play. But Dowler had an adequate replacement.

Max McGee, in the twilight of an outstanding 12-year career, had caught only four passes during the regular season, but he pulled in seven more for 138 yards and two touchdowns against Williamson and his friends. McGee would play one more year, but he will be best remembered for embarrassing Kansas City's secondary and creating his own urban legend.

McGee claimed to have spent all night before the game sampling Southern California's nightlife. Dave Hanner, the Packers' defensive line coach who was in charge of bed checks, said he looked in on him three times that night and McGee never left the hotel. Dowler, on the other hand, talked briefly with McGee in the locker room before the game and said there was no doubt his fellow receiver hadn't slept much.

Whatever, it was the Chiefs who were looking a little hung over after their valiant first half. Quarterback Len Dawson and his moving pocket seemed to befuddle the Packers as he completed 11 of 15 passes for 152 yards before the break. But he went five for 12 after that for only 59 yards, and when safety Willie Wood intercepted him early in the third period and ran 50 yards to the KC 5, Chiefs coach Hank Stram admitted that everything changed. Halfback Elijah Pitts scored on the next play to give Green Bay a 21-10 lead, and the Kansas City game plan flew south.

While Dawson was getting sacked six times for 61 yards, Bart Starr was winning a car. The Packers' quarterback faced 13 third-down situations and converted 11 of them on the way to a 16-for-23, 250-yard day and the game's Most Valuable Player honor. The latter came with the keys to a 1967 Corvette compliments of *Sport* magazine.

But it was the Green Bay defense that was in the driver's seat for most of the afternoon. It limited the Chiefs' rushing game to 72 yards, 24 of which came from Dawson running around trying to stay alive. The Packers' offense, meanwhile, provided scoring drives of 80, 73, 5, 56 and 80 yards.

And yet nobody seemed overly impressed by the Packers' triumph. Least of all, the Chiefs. Cornerback Willie Mitchell, who suffered third-degree burns on McGee's first touchdown, sniffed, "They got the breaks," and Dawson said he wasn't convinced Green Bay had the better team. Stram was, but he apologized to the AFL for his club's performance, and expressed doubt that one game was a fair measure of the leagues' relative strengths.

Even the Packers weren't all that carried away by the Packers. Vince Lombardi said it wasn't one of their better games, and the locker room celebration was downright tame compared to the one the week before when Green Bay beat Dallas, 34-27, to win the NFC championship. After all, people were just starting to get the hang of this Super Bowl thing.

The Coliseum held 93,000 seats at the time, and almost 30,000 of them were empty for a game played in sunshine with temperatures in the upper 70s. CBS and NBC both carried the action live, although the telecasts were blacked out within a 75-mile radius of Los Angeles. This with a ticket price of $12, or less than what a Super Bowl program costs today.

Halftime ceremonies consisted of two college marching bands, a drill team, 10,000 helium balloons, 4,000 pigeons and four men sailing through the air with compressed air packs on their backs. There were no reports of wardrobe malfunctions.

Only "The Hammer" embarrassed himself.

PIEPER BREAKS STATE SCORING RECORD (AGAIN)

JANUARY 16, 1993

The crowd started forming two hours before the junior varsity game. Almost 500 people lined up to get seats to Anthony Pieper's record run, or roughly 150 fewer than the entire population of Wausaukee, Wis.

Scoring points had always been easy for the 6-foot-3 senior guard. Finding a spot on one of the six rows of bleachers that lined either side of the 35-year-old Wausaukee High School gym to watch him break the state career record was tougher.

Pieper needed 11 points to top the mark of 2,747 set by Mickey Crowe of JFK Prep of St. Nazianz between 1971 and '75. Or so everyone thought at the time. The truth was that Pieper had already claimed the record eight days earlier in a game at Lena, but nobody had celebrated the accomplishment because nobody had known about it.

An extensive *Milwaukee Journal* review of Crowe's numbers would show six months later that he had been credited for at least 23 points more than he'd actually scored. Nobody had ever kept official high school statistics in Wisconsin, and so there were no official records. And since JFK Prep no longer existed, it made Crowe's figures all the more suspect.

But that was all about arithmetic. This was about basketball and the pride of an entire community.

The little tourist and logging town 60 miles north of Green Bay had been keeping a close eye on Gene Pieper's boy, Andy, ever since his freshman year. Gene was the high school coach, and Andy was the name the townspeople had given his son, although he actually preferred Anthony. Either way, he was making a name for himself and for Wausaukee where he'd become a teenage celebrity.

A natural born gym rat, Anthony grew up less than 100 feet from the high school court. Of course, he had a key. His dad was a coach, his mom Sue was a coach, and his brother Phil had set the school scoring record in 1986.

Anthony became really serious about the game when he got to high school. After he'd scored 1,296 points as a freshman and sophomore, he was in line to get a major college scholarship. With that in mind, he took 20,000 jump shots in a one-month span in the summer of his junior year. His mother sat in the gym and counted every one of them.

All that practice wasn't wasted. Thirty-point nights were normal. Pieper had 66 of them over four years. In fact, he scored fewer than 30 only four times in his last two seasons. He topped 50 ten times, with his most productive game coming in a WIAA regional final against Gillett when he scored 59.

But his biggest game, the one everyone would talk about for years, came against Suring when they sold out the gym in Wausaukee to watch him break Crowe's record. Pieper started the show with a layup, and then he drove the lane and did a 180 in the air on the way to another layup. He was fouled on the play and made the free throw. Another layup and a three-pointer gave him 10 points for the first quarter and a share of the record.

He opened the second period trying to get in position for a dunk, but it didn't work. Instead with 55 seconds gone in the quarter, he dribbled up the right side of the court, pulled up 22 feet from the hoop and swished the three-pointer that made history. Pieper said it felt good when he let it go. It felt pretty good to the overflow crowd, too, as it stood and cheered. Play was stopped, and the referee gave Pieper the game ball. He handed it to his mom, who was sitting behind the bench somewhere in the vicinity of where she'd counted those 20,000 jump shots.

Pieper scored 33 points that day, and Wausaukee won the game, 74-38. He would finish his career with 3,391 points and lead his school to the state Division 4 championship. After the season, he was named the winner of the state's Mr. Basketball award, and then it was on to Marquette University.

The old high school gym was replaced the following season, but the memory of Anthony Pieper's big day will linger in Wausaukee forever.

WISCONSIN'S ALL-TIME SCORING LEADERS
(Boys High School Basketball)

Rank	Name	School	Class	Points
1	Anthony Pieper	Wausaukee	1993	3,391
2	Mickey Crowe	JFK Prep (St. Nazianz)	1975	2,724
3	Mike Koehler	Elkhart Lake-Glenbeulah	1993	2,685
4	Sam Okey	Cassville	1995	2,539
5	Craig Smith	University School	1992	2,462

Source: 2009-10 Wisconsin Men's Basketball Yearbook

KOHL CENTER OPENS FOR BUSINESS

JANUARY 17, 1998

The Kohl Center

No doubt the new place was big enough. And posh enough. And red enough. The only question was whether it was loud enough.

Herb Kohl, Wisconsin's senior senator and $25 million man, resolved that issue when he cut the ceremonial ribbon officially opening the Kohl Center as the new home of Badger basketball and hockey. He asked for a cheer, and 16,697 voices produced a howl that bounced off Bascom Hill.

And then coach Dick Bennett's University of Wisconsin basketball team proceeded to render Northwestern both deaf and dumb. The Badgers held the Wildcats to 33 points while scoring 56 of their own in a turn-back-the-clock performance that might not have looked out of place at the venue they'd left. Wisconsin had opened the UW Fieldhouse in 1930 by beating Carroll College, 17-14, and Bennett's defense was only slightly more generous than that.

The coach pronounced the Kohl Center a "defensive arena," which may have been the faintest praise it received all night. With its 17,142 bright red seats, wide concourses, private suites, spacious new locker rooms and modern, plentiful bathrooms, the Kohl Center drew lavish compliments. Well, except for one of the bathrooms. A valve in the men's room in section 219 sprung a leak and christened the concourse outside before a plumber could be rushed to the scene.

Still, the Kohl Center looked every bit like a $76.4 million bargain compared to the Fieldhouse where the Badgers had played for 68 years. That had only two bathrooms and 11,500 seats, along with the look of a boiler room. The Fieldhouse cost $650,000 to build and another $718,000 to renovate in 1976, and Kohl decided it was clearly past its prime.

So he put up $25 million to replace it, marking the largest private donation in the university's history. Former all-Big Ten basketball player Ab Nicholas and his wife Nancy Johnson Nicholas then kicked in another $10 million, and they were rewarded by having their name put on a private gymnasium adjoining the facility called the Nicholas-Johnson Pavilion.

Kohl called the building's dedication one of the highlights of his life, and his enthusiasm has been shared by tens of thousands of people who have filled the building for every men's basketball game since. The noise has never settled down.

PACKERS HIRE TWO AFRICAN-AMERICAN COORDINATORS

JANUARY 18, 1992

When it came to race relations in the National Football League or anywhere else for that matter, moving from northern California to northern Wisconsin wasn't normally viewed as progress. But all of that changed when Mike Holmgren took over the Green Bay Packers and lured Sherman Lewis and Ray Rhodes from the San Francisco 49ers' staff.

Lewis was named offensive coordinator, and Rhodes was named defensive coordinator, and both of them happened to be black. By becoming the first NFL team ever to have two African-American coordinators, the Packers went a long way toward ending a stereotype and winning a Super Bowl.

From the time the Vince Lombardi heydays ended in 1968, there was a growing feeling in the league that Green Bay was not somewhere black players wanted to play. A 1987 story in *Sports Illustrated* magazine went so far as to suggest the Packers should move to Milwaukee to solve that problem. "There is little argument that a lot of players don't want to spend their salad days in a one-horse town," wrote SI's Frank Deford. "This is especially true of black players, who bemoan the lack of a normal social life."

Deford leveled that criticism in 1987, and Holmgren answered it belatedly in 1992 by recruiting Lewis and Rhodes. A year later, Reggie White put it to bed when he signed with the Packers as a free agent.

The problem of racial equality among NFL teams hasn't gone away, but there's been progress since Lewis and Rhodes came to Green Bay. At the time, Minnesota's Tony Dungy was the only black coordinator in the league, and he was one of just four who had ever held that title or a similar one with similar responsibilities. The others were Jimmy Raye in Tampa Bay and New England, Ray Sherman in Atlanta, and Billie Matthews in Indianapolis.

There could be no question that Lewis and Rhodes had earned their shot. The 49-year-old Lewis had spent the last nine seasons coaching running backs and wide receivers, and the 41-year-old Rhodes had coached defensive backs for the last 11 years while San Francisco was becoming pro football's most successful franchise. Lewis had held out some hope that the 49ers would offer him the offensive coordinator job that was vacated when Holmgren went to Green Bay, but it went to Mike Shanahan instead, and Lewis rejoined his old colleague.

Rhodes spent two seasons running the Packers' defense and elevating it from 23rd to second in the league before he returned to San Francisco as defensive coordinator and then went on to become head coach at Philadelphia for four years. Lewis stayed for eight years, and in that time the Packers made the playoffs six times, won three division titles and went to two Super Bowls, winning one of them.

Eleven NFL head coaching jobs had come open when the Packers beat New England in Super Bowl XXXI, and Lewis had reason to believe he'd get at least one of them. But he didn't, and Dungy, who had become the head coach at Tampa Bay, was disgusted. "If Sherman Lewis were white, do you think he would have gotten a job this year?" he asked in a *New York Daily News* story.

Meanwhile, Rhodes struggled in Philadelphia. He was named NFL coach of the year in his first season with the Eagles, but things went steadily downhill after that. He was fired after posting a 3-13 record in 1998, but he wasn't on the street for long. The Packers made him their first black head coach in 1999.

When Lewis agreed to stay on as the Packers' offensive coordinator after Holmgren left to go to Seattle that put Lewis and Rhodes together again, and for the first time Lewis was allowed to call plays. But the Packers finished a disappointing 8-8 in 1999, and Rhodes was gone after one season. He went on to serve as defensive coordinator with Washington and Denver before combining with Holmgren again for five years in Seattle. In 2008 Rhodes took a job as assistant defensive backs coach with the Houston Texans.

Lewis spent two years as offensive coordinator in Minnesota and two more in the same job in Detroit. He retired from football after the 2004 season, never having landed a job as an NFL head coach. However, four weeks into the 2009 season, he was summoned out of retirement by the Washington Redskins to serve as a consultant and to try and revive their struggling offense.

ABDUL-JABBAR DOMINATES WALTON IN FIRST MEETING

JANUARY 19, 1975

The two best centers in the storied history of UCLA basketball were meeting for the first time as pros, and Kareem Abdul-Jabbar had a point to make. So he made 50 of them.

The Milwaukee Bucks star also pulled down 15 rebounds, handed out 11 assists and blocked three shots on a Sunday afternoon at the Milwaukee Arena when he simply owned Bill Walton of the Portland Trail Blazers

The result didn't surprise anyone. Abdul-Jabbar had been in the league for six years, while Walton was only a rookie. And Walton had missed almost two months of the season with a bone spur on his ankle. But the gap between the two was startling.

Abdul-Jabbar had Walton in foul trouble all afternoon. The Blazers' No. 1 draft choice played just 21 minutes, and in that time, he took only five shots. He made two of them while going three for four from the free-throw line and getting six rebounds. He did demonstrate his remarkable passing ability with seven assists, which was pretty typical of his game.

"He had shots he didn't take," said Bucks coach Larry Costello. "He doesn't look for them that much. Maybe he's not that good a shooter."

Costello was being kinder than the fans. A capacity crowd was on hand to witness the confrontation, and the people took every opportunity to boo Walton. The Portland center was never much for public relations, and it didn't help that he'd come to town knee deep in controversy.

A report in *The New York Times* had said that he was trying to void his $2 million contract with the Blazers so that he could play somewhere else. He was quoted as saying it was too frigid in Portland, that his feet got cold at practice. That didn't play well in Milwaukee where Oregon's weather seemed tropical by comparison.

Walton didn't deny the report. He didn't confirm it either. He simply refused to talk about it, which was his standard approach to the media. He did acknowledge that he was a friend of Black Panther Party attorney Charles Garry, but he didn't say whether Garry had replaced UCLA booster Sam Gilbert as his representative. Gilbert had arranged Walton's lucrative deal with the Trail Blazers, and he said Walton was doing everything he could to get out of the deal.

None of which had anything to do with what occurred on the court. That was all dictated by Abdul-Jabbar. His 50 points left him five short of his career high, but that was probably because he was looking so much for open teammates. The Bucks did have a game to win, and they did it with relative ease, 122-108.

Abdul-Jabbar took 30 shots and made 18 of them. He also made 14 of 16 free throws and totally neutralized Walton on defense. Asked about his fellow Bruin following the game, he said, "I really haven't seen him play that much. If I commented, it would be on how he's not playing. I'm not criticizing him. He's not contributing to his team for whatever reason he has. That's a statement in itself."

Two years later, Walton made a major contribution to the Trail Blazers when they won an NBA title. He also played a key reserve role for the 1986 champion Boston Celtics. By the end of their careers, the gap between the former UCLA stars had narrowed enough for both of them to qualify for the Basketball Hall of Fame.

But Abdul-Jabbar would play 20 years and win six titles to Walton's two. He took a big lead on the big redhead that day in Milwaukee, and Walton never really caught up.

ONE STEP FROM SUPER BOWL, PACKERS BOW TO GIANTS

JANUARY 20, 2008

Donald Driver never had a chance. The pass was underthrown, and when New York Giants cornerback Corey Webster stepped in front of him and took it nine yards in the wrong direction, all of those things that had been falling into place for the Green Bay Packers fell apart.

The dream season was gone, the Super Bowl was gone, and soon the quarterback would be gone, too. Brett Favre's second errant pass of the NFC Championship Game was also the last one he would ever throw for the Packers.

He simply didn't get enough on the ball as Driver ran a deep sideline route and Webster did his job. The play ended up on Green Bay's 34-yard line, and three downs later Lawrence Tynes kicked a 47-yard field goal that left the Packers with a 23-20 defeat and a lot of explaining to do.

They'd entered the game as 7½-point favorites with so much going for them. Not only were they at home where the Packers were 5-0 all-time in NFL or NFC championship games, but the Giants had knocked off their nemesis in Dallas the week before. New York needed to win three road games in a row to get to the Super Bowl, something only two teams in NFL history had ever done. And the weather was atrocious, which was always supposed to be in Green Bay's favor. With a one-degree air temperature and a minus 23-degree wind chill, it was the second coldest game in Lambeau Field history. Only the 1967 Ice Bowl had been chillier.

Fortune hadn't just smiled on the Packers during their completely unpredictable 13-3 regular season, it had almost laughed out loud. But the grin got a little lopsided when their pass defense collapsed and they got dominated on both lines of scrimmage by the Giants. The truth was Green Bay was only in this game because Tynes had missed two field goals in the final seven minutes of regulation. The Giants' kicker hadn't made a game-winner all season, and he'd kept that record intact by blowing a 36-yarder with four seconds left in the fourth quarter.

New York's dominance was reflected in a 17-minute advantage in time of possession and a resounding 134-28-yard edge on the ground. The Packers had managed only one play of more than 20 yards all day, and that resulted in a 90-yard touchdown pass to Driver. Their other scores were set up by Tramon Williams' 49-yard kickoff return and tackle Mark Tauscher's fumble recovery after Favre's first interception. The Giants, on the other hand, rolled up 380 yards of offense. Eli Manning passed for 254 of those yards, hitting Plaxico Burress 11 times as his favorite receiver turned Packers cornerback Al Harris into a statue.

Fortune's final gesture was to allow the Packers to win the overtime coin flip, but that just deepened their disappointment. They returned the kickoff to their 26-yard line, and after a frustrated Ryan Grant gained two yards on first down, they faced a second-and-eight situation.

That's when Webster intercepted Favre and evoked memories of the fourth-and-26 debacle in Philadelphia four years earlier. That had been the last time the Packers had seemed to be on the verge of reaching the Super Bowl, and it had ended the same way with Favre throwing an interception, and the opponents winning the game with a field goal.

This pass wasn't as bad as that one, but the feeling afterward was the same.

"All the plans and the hopes we had are out the window," said General Manager Ted Thompson. "It's a shame. I certainly don't think we played our best, and the Giants played very well."

The loss was the sixth in the Packers' last nine playoff games and the worst upset they'd suffered since they'd gone into Super Bowl XXXII as 11½-point favorites against Denver. That may have been a lesson too easily forgotten.

"I'm not going to say I thought we had this one," said Favre, "but I felt like everything had fallen into place. All that was left was to play the game."

There is always that.

PACKERS GET NO. 2 PICK FROM HATED BEARS

JANUARY 21, 1970

No one could remember the Green Bay Packers ever making a major trade with the Chicago Bears. They were always cautious about helping their bitter rivals. They had nothing to worry about this time.

In what looked like a very big deal at the time, they sent veteran linebacker Lee Roy Caffey, popular running back Elijah Pitts and promising center Bob Hyland to the Bears for the second choice in the NFL draft.

The Bears were coming off a 1-13 season, and they were looking for immediate help. The Packers had gone 8-6, but needed some young blood two seasons into the post-Lombardi era. Besides, they knew just the man they wanted with that No. 2 pick. Mike McCoy, a 6-foot-5, 284-pound defensive lineman from Notre Dame, was widely considered to be the best available talent in the country next to quarterback Terry Bradshaw, and he was perfect for the Packers who were losing defensive starters Willie Davis and Henry Jordan to retirement.

Or so it appeared. But McCoy turned out to be nothing more than a solid starter. And the three departing Packers barely made a dent in the Bears' problems. In other words, this was a much ballyhooed deal that favored the Packers, but neither side benefited to the extent that they expected.

In Caffey, Hyland and Pitts, Chicago got a player who'd asked to be traded, a player who complained that he was being used wrong and a player who was barely being used at all. Caffey started on Green Bay's three straight NFL championship teams but he requested a trade for personal reasons and wound up staying just one season with the Bears. Hyland, a promising 24-year-old who was unhappy with his playing time, also lasted just a year in Chicago before being shipped to the New York Giants. And Pitts, who had been on five Packer title teams but carried the ball only 35 times during the 1969 season, was cut in training camp.

The Packers had a better draft in 1970 after having a terrible one in 1969 when they squandered their first-round choice on Rich Moore, a defensive tackle from Villanova who proved to be a colossal bust. They chose five future starters in McCoy, tight end Rich McGeorge, linebacker Jim Carter, and defensive backs Al Matthews and Ken Ellis. But it could be argued that, dollar for dollar, McCoy was the most disappointing of the group.

He was a capable starter for seven seasons in Green Bay, but he never made it to a Pro Bowl. In fact, he was so unspectacular that at one point the Packers tried to make an offensive lineman out of him. The scouts were crazy about his size and speed, but the coaches discovered that he tended to play too high, and after undergoing knee surgery in 1973, he was extremely careful about being cut.

But in a way he did hold his value. The Packers dealt McCoy to Oakland in 1977 and got a first-round choice for him, giving them two in the 1978 draft. They used them on wide receiver James Lofton and linebacker John Anderson, two players who would make the franchise's Hall of Fame.

And ironically, they eventually got back two of the players they'd sent to the Bears. Pitts returned for six games in 1971, and Hyland rejoined them for the 1976 season.

MILWAUKEE LANDS THE BUCKS

JANUARY 22, 1968

Wes Pavalon knew just what he wanted when he and Marv Fishman put together their syndicate to bring a National Basketball Association franchise to Milwaukee. He wanted a new arena, a statewide schedule and a hockey team.

He got none of the above. But the city got its pro basketball team, soon to be named the Bucks.

Pavalon, a 34-year-old self-made millionaire, and Fishman, a 42-year-old real estate developer, had an important advantage when they met with the 12 NBA owners on a Sunday afternoon in New York. If they were granted a franchise, basketball would be the only game in town.

The city had lost its Major League Baseball team in 1965 and its NBA team 10 years before that, leaving only the Packers. And, at the time, they played four of their seven home games in Green Bay. And so for $2 million - less than the average NBA player makes today - pro basketball returned to Milwaukee.

Phoenix, which was similarly bereft of professional sports, was admitted at the same time as the NBA took another step in its ambitious expansion plans. Pavalon had ambitions of his own.

As the team's new president, he made it immediately clear that he considered the Milwaukee Arena to be temporary quarters. "We are very anxious to have a sports arena built," he told *The Milwaukee Journal.* "The dates at the Arena are totally inadequate. Something must be done to hasten the construction of a new building. We are also interested in a team in the National Hockey League, and for that, a new building seating at least 15,000 persons is necessary."

Pavalon was long gone when the Bucks finally got a new home in the Bradley Center 20 years later, and an NHL franchise never did make it to Milwaukee. He also announced plans to schedule at least 10 or 12 home games in places like Madison, Green Bay and Kenosha. Current Bucks owner Herb Kohl, who had tried to acquire an NBA franchise earlier but dropped out when he couldn't get the terms he wanted, had reserved a number of dates in Madison that he was happy to turn over to Pavalon's group.

But Madison got only four games in the Bucks' first year and Green Bay got two. That was cut to two Madison games the following season, although two playoff games also were played there out of necessity.

The new franchise faced an uphill battle. It was placed in the NBA's tough Eastern Division with the likes of the Boston Celtics, Philadelphia 76ers and the New York Knicks, while Phoenix went to the West where there were already three expansion franchises. What's more, the expansion draft where the team was to get its talent allowed each of the existing clubs to protect seven players, and the Bucks' first pick in the college draft was only seventh overall.

But the management was optimistic, and the fans were enthusiastic. A statewide contest to name the team drew more than 14,000 entries, 45 of which suggested "Bucks." R.D. Trebilcox of Whitefish Bay won a new car for his submission when he pointed out that bucks are "spirited, good jumpers, fast and agile."

The 1968-'69 team lived up to that description enough to win 27 games despite blowing its first draft choice on a 6-foot-9 forward named Charlie Paulk, who averaged three points in his only season with the Bucks. But Pavalon admitted he was already thinking about the 1969 draft when his group brought the team to town. A 7-2 center from UCLA named Lew Alcindor would become available then.

When Milwaukee won a coin toss with Phoenix for Alcindor's rights, everything changed. The Bucks new owners didn't get their arena, but they did get a championship.

JANUARY 41

MILLPOND SITE OF U.S. SPEEDSKATING CHAMPIONSHIPS

JANUARY 23, 1932

Normally a non-contact sport, speedskating can have hazards of its own: Fist-fighting for instance, not to mention collisions at the finish line and falling through the ice.

The first two actually happened when the United States Outdoor Championships came to Oconomowoc for the second straight year in 1932, and the third could have if the meet hadn't been moved twice.

More than 250 competitors, including the nation's top 40 women, got too warm a welcome when they came to southern Wisconsin vying for individual national titles and, in some cases, a trip to the Winter Olympics. The meet also served as the Olympic Trials for women, although speedskating didn't become an official Olympic sport for them until 1960. Still, it was a demonstration sport in 1932, and so the leading finishers earned a trip to Lake Placid.

The meet was originally scheduled for Fowler Lake, but unusual warm January weather had created thin ice and forced a postponement. When things still hadn't improved after a week, the operation was moved to Lac La Belle where the ice was seven inches thick in most places. But there was a danger of holes out there, and officials couldn't risk having the cream of American speedskating disappearing into the deep. So there was another change of venue, this time to the millpond in Monterey, three miles north of Oconomowoc.

An estimated 3,000 fans gathered for the opening day of competition, and they were entertained by bands from the local American Legion post and St. John's Military Academy. Temporary bleachers were erected, and hot coffee and sandwiches were available to participants and fans. It was a festive occasion except for a clash between Wisconsin State Skating Association President Bill Kritter and Harry Berz, chairman of the Western Illinois Skating Association's registration committee, over the eligibility of Chicago skater Marie Becker.

Only amateurs were allowed to compete at that time, and Berz claimed that Becker was ineligible because she'd been charged with being a pro. Kritter said nobody had told him that, and Becker was good to go. Heated words were followed by fisticuffs. Becker did skate, but didn't place.

The women's competition consisted of 500-, 1,000- and 1,500-meter races, with the top six overall finishers going to the Games in Lake Placid. When the mercury finally plunged by Saturday, Jan. 23, the ice got very fast, and records began falling like snow. Dorothy Franey of St. Paul, Minn., shattered the world mark in the 500 with a time of 54.6 seconds, and Helen Bina of Chicago did the same with a time of 2 minutes 4.8 seconds in the 1,000. The men's competition, on the other hand, produced no records.

When skating resumed on Sunday, the crowds doubled, and the fans were treated to some more extracurricular activity. Only the 1,500 was on tap for the women on the final day, and when Kit Klein of Buffalo, N.Y., won it, she and Bina were left tied at the top of the standings. So a special match race at 1,000 meters was held to break the tie.

Klein took the lead and held it most of the way, but Bina closed the gap on the final straightaway. With 20 meters to go, Klein still had a half-length lead, and that's when things got interesting. Klein swerved slightly from her inside track, and her arm caught the onrushing Bina. Both skaters went down, and they skidded across the finish line. Klein got there first, but the judges ruled that she'd fouled her opponent, and Bina was declared the winner. Some observers believed Bina had grabbed Klein's arm to avoid falling, but the ruling stood.

And so Bina was crowned the women's national champion, while Jimmy Webster of St. Paul won the men's title. Two weeks later, American women, including Klein, took firsts in two of three events at Lake Placid.

Oconomowoc played host to the outdoor championships again in 1933 and '35; and La Crosse served as host from 1939-'42, where the races were held on a lagoon rink in Pettibone Park. Following World War II, the outdoor championships found a regular home at Como Park in St. Paul. It wasn't until 1966 that the first permanent 400-meter track with artificial ice was built in the United States at State Fair Park. The ice was much more reliable after that.

PACKERS' ROCKWOOD LODGE DESTROYED BY FIRE

JANUARY 24, 1950

Twelve-year-old Danny Flagstead spotted the smoke at around 2 o'clock in the afternoon and ran outside in his bare feet, along with his mother and his nine-year-old sister. His father, caretaker Melvin Flagstead, cut his hand while jumping out of a second-story window. There were no other injuries, just accusations.

The joke going around town was that Curly Lambeau himself had torched Rockwood Lodge, the controversial Green Bay Packers' training quarters he'd purchased four years earlier. Of course, the fire was no joke to the Flagstead family, which lived there and took care of the place, and, thankfully, survived it.

But the organization had long since lost its sense of humor where Rockwood Lodge was concerned, and the fire that leveled it in a matter of hours proved to be a financial blessing for the Packers. Faulty attic wiring was blamed, which was oddly appropriate since the entire franchise was short-circuiting at the time.

The Norbertine Fathers had built the place in 1937 as a social center on 3,000 feet of Green Bay shoreline – the bay is a sub-basin of Lake Michigan – just outside of Dyckesville, and they'd done a spectacular job of it. All limestone and oak and big windows, it resembled a centuries-old European chateau, except that it had tennis courts, a baseball diamond and an outdoor theater. Weddings and banquets and sales meetings were held there until World War II gas rationing came along, and it lost its usefulness.

So the Fathers sold it to a couple of private citizens, who in turn sold it to the Packers in 1946 when Lambeau decided it was time for the team to have its own permanent training quarters. The price was $32,000, which was either a bargain or a boondoggle, depending on how people felt about Lambeau. And there were lots of feelings about Lambeau by 1950.

The team was losing both games and money, having gone without a championship for five years, and the franchise's co-founder, coach and general manager had become a lightning rod. His critics didn't like what was happening on the field or on the balance sheet or even in Lambeau's personal life. He'd married a stranger from California, and then he'd divorced her and married another one from the same state and hired her to decorate the facility that his detractors thought he never should have bought in the first place.

But Lambeau believed there were major advantages to Rockwood, where the Packers could house and feed their players not only during training camp, but also during the season. Most NFL franchises would eventually agree with him and build their own places.

Rockwood Lodge

In a sense, Lambeau was a pioneer of the practice scene, but the Packers were the only franchise at the time to test the concept, and it came with problems.

What it didn't come with was a football field. The team had to build one of those over the solid limestone on which the lodge sat, and it proved to be inadequate. After one three-hour practice session, the players were working out again at City Stadium, the groundskeeper having to admit the new field was "pretty rocky."

So was Lambeau's relationship with the fans who had gotten used to having the players in their midst in downtown Green Bay rather than 15 miles away. And with the accountants who thought Rockwood was much too expensive at a time when the organization had to hold a special Thanksgiving Day intra-squad game just to pay the bills.

There was talk of selling the place, but there were no readily available buyers. More important, there was talk of getting rid of Lambeau. He was offered a two-year contract extension, but there were plenty of people on the Packers board of directors who were still unhappy with him. Rockwood Lodge was one of the major sources of their discontent.

The source was removed on a rainy, sleety, windy day in January when flames shot 500 feet into the air leaving only two crumbling walls and a chimney where Rockwood Lodge once stood. Four men from the Duquaine Lumber Co. in nearby New Franken arrived with a pumping unit and 600 feet of hose, but there was no point. They never even used them.

The building was fully insured, and the Packers collected $75,000, which went a long way toward keeping them afloat. Eight days after the blaze, Lambeau resigned.

The site of Rockwood Lodge is now a county park and campground. It was formally dedicated as Bay Shore Park on May 26, 1974, some 24 years after the building burned to the ground.

PACKERS UPSET IN SUPER BOWL XXXII

JANUARY 25, 1998

Say this for Ron Wolf. What he lacked in diplomacy, he could always make up for in color.

After the Green Bay Packers trudged off the field at Qualcomm Stadium in San Diego following their second Super Bowl run in two seasons, Wolf snorted to the *Milwaukee Journal Sentinel*, "We're a one-year wonder. Just a fart in the wind. Now this will stop all this idiotic talk about a dynasty."

The general manager had a point. As dynasties go, the Packers' was definitely among the briefer ones. It lasted just one day short of a year, and it ended in a 31-24 loss to the 11½-point underdog Denver Broncos.

The Packers were coming off their second straight 13-3 season, having won their last seven games and 12 of their last 13 including playoffs. The Broncos were 12-4 and a wild-card team, and wild-card teams never won Super Bowls. At that point, the 1980 Oakland Raiders had been the single exception.

Green Bay had Brett Favre, Reggie White and most of the other major ingredients left from the team that had beaten New England in the championship game the previous year. Denver had John Elway, Terrell Davis and a quick blitzing defense with an attitude. Coach Mike Shanahan had ordered his players to keep a low profile in the two weeks leading up to the game, and linebacker Bill Romanowski said afterward that he was so tired of saying how good the Packers were, he "could puke." Romanowksi was pretty colorful himself.

The Packers had it all going for them early in the game when they not only took a 7-0 lead on Favre's 22-yard pass to Antonio Freeman, but they delivered a shot to Davis' head that had him nursing a migraine from the sidelines for the entire second quarter.

Davis was still feeling good, though, when he tied the score with 5 minutes 39 seconds to play in the first period with a one-yard run. And then Elway's one-yard scramble put the Broncos up, 14-7, five seconds into the second quarter after a Favre interception. Favre also fumbled the ball midway through the quarter, and the Broncos took advantage of that, too, getting a 51-yard field goal to take a 17-7 lead.

It was that kind of day for the Packers' quarterback. Favre completed 25 of 42 passes for 256 yards and three touchdowns, but his two first-half turnovers were crucial, and he wasn't his usual heroic self at the end. When the Packers needed him to make a game-saving play on their last possession, he threw three incomplete passes instead.

Still, he looked pretty familiar on the closing drive of the first half. It covered 95 yards in 17 plays and ended with a six-yard touchdown pass to tight end Mark Chmura as the Packers closed their deficit to 17-14 at halftime.

Davis was back to open the third quarter, although he might have wished he'd sat out a little longer when his fumble set up a game-tying, 27-yard field goal by Ryan Longwell. Davis wouldn't make any more mistakes.

Green Bay just never could get a handle on him as he rushed to the game's Most Valuable Player award with 157 yards on 30 carries. That was particularly frustrating for defensive coordinator Fritz Shurmur, who admitted that the Packers' whole plan was predicated on stopping the run.

The Broncos' whole plan was predicated on harassing Favre half to death. They blitzed on almost every play, and while they sacked him only once they hurried him all day long.

Elway, on the other hand, had a competent day with his arm and a memorable one with his feet. He provided the signature play of the afternoon late in the third quarter when he kept a Denver drive alive by scrambling up the middle for eight yards and diving into a pile of three Packers inside the Green Bay five-yard line. Davis' one-yard run climaxed the march and gave the Broncos a 24-17 lead.

Safety Eugene Robinson's interception led to a 13-yard touchdown pass from Favre to Freeman that tied the game again at 24, but the Broncos got the last word. They started the game-winning drive at midfield after a punt and needed just four plays and a key facemask penalty to make it to the one against a plainly fatigued Packers defense. Davis was strangely alone as he stepped into the end zone with 1:45 left in the game.

It was learned later that coach Mike Holmgren had told his players to let Davis score, so that the Broncos couldn't run out the clock and win with a short field goal. The strategy failed when the Packers couldn't connect on their last three passes. One-year wonders indeed. Denver left them wondering what had happened to them.

PACKERS' WAIT ENDS WITH SUPER BOWL XXXI

JANUARY 26, 1997

They started the scoring with a reject and ended it with a castoff. The Green Bay Packers experienced plenty of nervous moments in between, but nothing that could deny them their first Super Bowl championship in 29 years.

On the second play from scrimmage, wide receiver Andre Rison spun New England Patriots cornerback Otis Smith like a centrifuge and loped into the open to catch a 54-yard pass from Brett Favre. A four-time Pro Bowl selection whose antics had worn out his welcome at Atlanta, Cleveland and Jacksonville, Rison put the Packers up by a touchdown less than four minutes into Super Bowl XXXI with his catch.

Five touchdowns and two field goals later, Desmond Howard caught a New England kickoff on his one-yard line and burst straight up the middle of the field. The former Heisman Trophy winner, who'd been cut by Jacksonville and Washington before the Packers signed him in July, was barely grazed while racing a Super Bowl record 99 yards to the clinching score in Green Bay's 35-21 victory.

Defensive end Reggie White, who was General Manager Ron Wolf's biggest free-agent acquisition, sacked quarterback Drew Bledsoe twice on the Pats' next possession, and the game was over. So was the wait.

Not since January, 1968 when Vince Lombardi led the Packers past Oakland in Super Bowl II had they won a National Football League championship. They'd been a permanent afterthought from then until Wolf and coach Mike Holmgren had taken over the operation in 1992. Now they had people talking dynasty.

This was a young team coming off a 13-3 regular season, whose offense was led by MVP quarterback Brett Favre and whose defense was anchored by White, a lock for the Pro Football Hall of Fame. The machine's other moving parts weren't bad either as they showed while neutralizing New England.

Not that it was easy. It just started out looking that way. Following Rison's touchdown, cornerback Doug Evans intercepted a Bledsoe pass to set up Chris Jacke's 37-yard field goal, stretching the Packers' advantage to 10-0 and prompting a crowd of 72,301 to wonder whether they might be leaving the New Orleans Superdome early. But then Bledsoe needed just over four minutes to throw two touchdown passes and put the Pats up, 14-10.

It would be the last time they'd hold the lead. Favre opened the second quarter by collaborating with wide receiver Antonio Freeman on a record-setting 81-yard

Mike Holmgren, Ron Wolf and Bob Harlan stand with the Lombardi Trophy at the victory party following Super Bowl XXXI.

touchdown pass, and then Jacke kicked a 31-yard field goal to cap a drive that began after Howard returned a punt 34 yards. With his team ahead, 20-14, Favre turned into an acrobat. With about 90% of his body out of bounds, he dived over the goal line from two yards out and reached the ball back into the end zone. When the play was ruled a touchdown, the Patriots were incensed.

They were also behind, 27-14, at halftime and might have been left for dead if Curtis Martin hadn't scored on an 18-yard run with 3 minutes 27 seconds remaining in the third quarter to return the customers to the edge of their seats. That's when Howard's 99-yard sprint sat them right back again. When Favre found tight end Mark Chmura in the end zone for a two-point conversion, the Pats were flattened.

Howard would finish his day with a Super Bowl record 244 yards in kick returns and a 1997 Ford Taurus after being named the game's Most Valuable Player. When he got the keys, his trademark grin could have filled a bayou.

Favre would finish with 14 pass completions in 27 attempts for 246 yards and two touchdowns. He was sacked five times, but down never meant out for the 27-year-old quarterback who'd promised before the season that he would one day lead the Packers to the Super Bowl.

But it was Wolf who gained the greatest vindication after ripping up the roster of a 4-12 team five years earlier and taking some major gambles in the process of acquiring the likes of Favre, White, Howard, Rison and, of course, Holmgren. Jacke and safety LeRoy Butler were the only players left from the squad that Wolf had inherited.

JANUARY 45

THOUSANDS WELCOME SUPER BOWL CHAMPIONS

JANUARY 27, 1997

You can question their judgment and maybe even their sanity, but you can never question the patience of Green Bay Packers fans. They waited 29 years for a Super Bowl, so what was several more hours standing around in sub-freezing temperatures waiting to celebrate it all?

Naturally, it was snowing as well as brutally cold when an estimated 100,000 people lined a parade route from downtown Green Bay to Lambeau Field where another 60,000 officially welcomed the Packers back from their triumph in Super Bowl XXXI. If this wasn't the largest homecoming celebration any pro team has ever enjoyed, it was easily the bravest.

"It's been an extreme honor to play in front of you guys," said a shivering Reggie White when the buses carrying the world champions finally arrived at their destination two-and-a-half hours late. Some of the people he was talking to had been tailgating since breakfast, and some of the people he'd passed on the route had been staking out their spots since well before lunch.

The smiles were frozen on their faces by the time the players in the procession got to them, but they didn't seem to mind because the Packers literally shared their pain. The marketing department that organized the parade had had the windows removed from the buses, so that the players could reach out and touch someone. Most of them did, and all the handshaking and high-fiving turned a 45-minute ride into three hours. "It was a lonnnnng ride," said safety Eugene Robinson.

And a fun one at first, but a few of the honorees were too chilled to be thrilled by the end. Among them was coach Mike Holmgren, who had arrived at the airport wearing just a suit and had found relief only by borrowing a jacket from a sheriff's deputy. It was fitting that Holmgren looked like a motorcycle cop when he strode to the podium to make a few brief remarks, because there was a new machine waiting for him at Lambeau Field, compliments of Harley-Davidson.

The real police had a full but fairly tame day keeping track of all the well-wishers. They encountered their biggest problem outside the stadium where they had to clear a couple thousand people off the street to let the buses in. "Unbelievable," said Green Bay police captain Glenn Mercier. "I never saw anything like this in my life."

As a 28-year-veteran of the force, Mercier had seen a lot, but his department was happy to announce that only one arrest was made all day and that for disorderly conduct. The fans were too happy to be troublesome.

At least, most of the fans were. The exceptions were the ones deployed south of the stadium on Oneida Street when the parade stopped short in the interest of time and left them very much out in the cold. When news of the detour reached them, many of them raced for their cars to get a glimpse of the proceedings, but many more simply left for home.

The people who'd been waiting at Lambeau Field were rewarded by speeches from Holmgren, General Manager Ron Wolf, President Bob Harlan and several players. They didn't hear anything from Brett Favre, however. The quarterback had gone ahead to Hawaii for the Pro Bowl.

Meanwhile back in Massachusetts, the losing New England Patriots were getting a welcome of their own at their stadium. Four hundred people came.

PACKERS' CHAMPIONSHIP HOMECOMINGS

Dec. 9, 1929 - An estimated 20,000 fans greeted the Packers at Green Bay's Chicago & North Western depot, the day after they won their first title by beating the Bears in Chicago.

Dec. 15, 1930 - About 3,000 fans greeted the team at the North Western depot following a title-clinching victory in Portsmouth, Ohio.

Dec. 1, 1931 - Nearly 2,500 fans greeted the team at Green Bay's Milwaukee Road two days after the Packers had clinched their third straight championship with a victory in Brooklyn.

Dec. 14, 1936 - An estimated 10,000 fans were at the Milwaukee Road depot when the Packers arrived home the day after beating the Boston Redskins in the championship game in New York.

Dec. 11, 1939 - Several thousand fans greeted the team at the Milwaukee Road depot a day after the Packers had beaten the New York Giants in the title game at Milwaukee.

Dec. 18, 1944 - A crowd of about 1,500 welcomed the team at the Milwaukee Road station after it had completed a 24-hour train ride from New York, where it had won the NFL championship the day before.

Dec. 30, 1962 - A crowd estimated at anywhere from 8,000 to 14,000 greeted the Packers at Austin Straubel Field when they arrived at 11 p.m., hours after winning the NFL title in New York.

Jan. 16, 1967 - Only about 1,000 fans welcomed the team when it arrived at Austin Straubel Field on Monday afternoon, a day after winning Super Bowl I. The team had been scheduled to arrive the night before, but didn't get out of Los Angeles due to fog.

Jan. 14, 1968 - About 4,000 fans jammed Austin Straubel to welcome the team home from Miami after its Super Bowl triumph over Oakland.

(Note: The Packers played in Green Bay when they won championships in 1961, '65 and '67.)

Source: Green Bay Press-Gazette

PACKERS HIRE LOMBARDI

JANUARY 28, 1959

Vince Lombardi

Coaching football wasn't Vince Lombardi's first career choice before he took a job as an assistant at St. Cecilia High School in Englewood, New Jersey. He'd spent four good years playing at Fordham University as part of "The Seven Blocks of Granite" line, but he found himself lost in the real world following his graduation in 1937. He spent two aimless years looking for his niche in life and playing some semi-pro football.

He even tried law school, but lasted only a semester. So when he was offered a teaching and coaching job in 1939, he jumped at it. Three years later, he was named head football coach and forged a powerhouse, at one point going 32 straight games without a loss. That was enough to make Lombardi decide his future was in football. Now 20 years after accepting his first coaching job, he was celebrating that decision after being named head coach and general manager of the Green Bay Packers.

By the end of the next season, the Packers would be celebrating, too, and it had been a long time since they'd done much of that. Fourteen years had passed since their last championship and 11 since their last winning season. First-year head coach Scooter McLean had resigned on Dec. 17 after stumbling to a 1-10-1 record, the worst in franchise history, and the organization knew it had to do something drastic.

Hiring Lombardi certainly qualified.

Although he'd been running the New York Giants' offense as Jim Lee Howell's backfield assistant for the past five years, he'd never held a head coaching position except in high school. But the Packers executive committee not only gave the 45-year-old New Yorker an eyebrow-raising five-year contract, they made him both head coach and general manager. Cleveland's Paul Brown was the only other man in the league holding both titles, although George Halas of the Chicago Bears was both owner and coach.

Assistant coaches were a pretty anonymous bunch at that time, and bigger names than Lombardi's had surfaced during the Packers' six-week search. The biggest was Iowa's Forrest Evashevski, who reportedly had toured Green Bay with Packers President Dominic Olejniczak three days earlier and subsequently turned down the job. Former Philadelphia Eagles coach Jim Trimble was also prominently mentioned as a candidate.

It may have been that the Packers settled for Lombardi after Evashevski rejected their offer, but it was only a matter of time before someone was going to hire him. Commissioner Bert Bell said that two or three other NFL teams had wanted to hire Lombardi over the past four years, and it was rumored that he'd turned down the top job at Army. But Lombardi couldn't pass on a Packers' offer that featured the two elements that all coaches covet – power and security.

Lombardi was promised "a free hand" in running the team, and a multi-year contract looked pretty good to a man with a wife and two kids. He could even afford to give up his off-season banking job in New York.

The Packers announced that Lombardi had accepted the job at a 3 p.m. press conference on Wednesday, Jan. 28. He arrived in Green Bay five days later and was introduced at another press conference at the Northland Hotel on Feb. 3, the day he was scheduled to officially sign his contract.

"My word will be final," Lombardi said from New York the day he was actually hired. "I've never been connected with a losing team and I hope to instill a winning spirit in the Packers in a lot less than five years."

The Packers were counting on it, and some of the league's heaviest hitters seemed to think they had good reason for optimism. Cleveland's Brown, as well as Halas, praised the Packers' selection. They had watched Lombardi take control of the Giants' offense and make it one of the most fundamentally sound in the NFL. The Giants' defense was run pretty well, too, by a young assistant named Tom Landry.

Both would enjoy remarkable head coaching success. Lombardi's was immediate. He led the Packers to a 7-5 record in his first season, which was good enough to earn him NFL Coach of the Year honors from both the Associated Press and United Press International. He did it with experience, skill and most of all with a hard-nosed approach to defense and discipline.

Once an aspiring attorney, Lombardi proved in Green Bay that he could both coach and lay down the law.

FOUR PACKERS IN FIRST HALL OF FAME CLASS

JANUARY 29, 1963

Their skills were all remarkable, but their reputations couldn't have been much different. A founder, a flier, an umpire and a flake.

The Pro Football Hall of Fame took on a decided green and gold tinge when it announced its 17-member charter class for enshrinement in Canton, Ohio. Included were Curly Lambeau, Don Hutson, Cal Hubbard and Johnny "Blood" McNally, all of them Green Bay Packers for the best years of their careers.

Without Lambeau there would have been no Packers. A player for 11 years and a coach for almost 30, he established the franchise, pioneered the forward pass at the pro level, was credited with 209 regular-season victories and won six National Football League championships. Later, the Packers would let him know how much they appreciated him by naming their stadium after him.

Hutson was the best player Lambeau ever coached and the best receiver the game had ever known. He combined size, soft hands and ridiculous speed to do things no one had even thought of doing before at his position. And that was just part of his game. He also place-kicked and played safety on defense. He led the league in receptions for the eighth time in his 11th and final season, and he owned 19 NFL records when he retired at the age of 32 following the 1945 season.

Hubbard is still one of a kind. At 6-foot-3 and 255 pounds, he was a giant of a man when he joined the Packers in 1929 as an offensive and defensive tackle. He was considered the greatest lineman of his era, and he was still playing football when he started a second Hall of Fame career in another sport. He began umpiring in the minor leagues in 1927, and eight years later he was hired by the American League. A hunting accident left shotgun pellets in his left eye and forced him off the field, but he spent 16 more years serving as the AL's supervisor of umpires. In 1976 he became the only man ever to be elected to both the pro football and baseball halls of fame.

And then there was Blood, who combined his physical gifts with the kind of color that made Max McGee and Paul Hornung look like Eagle Scouts. Blood held all of the important NFL receiving records until Hutson broke them, and he was an outstanding runner and passer and a fierce tackler as well.

The son of a prominent New Richmond, Wis., family, he was born with talent, money and an insatiable thirst for adventure. He also had a different name until he was 20 years old. He was baptized John Victor McNally, and he was smart enough to graduate from high school at the age of 14. He began his collegiate career at St. John's of Minnesota after trying to join the Navy at 15 but getting turned down.

In 1924 he and a teammate decided to sign up with a local pro team in Minneapolis called the East 26th Street Liberties, but in order to maintain their amateur standing, they needed to play under false names. They pulled their aliases off a movie marquee. *Blood and Sand* starring Rudolph Valentino was playing at the time, and young McNally became "Blood" while his friend became "Sand." A year later, McNally began his NFL career with the Milwaukee Badgers. He joined the Packers in 1929 and was their top playmaker as they won three straight NFL championships.

The name Blood fit McNally's reckless streak, which surfaced frequently off the field. His most entertaining exploits tended to involve transportation. He stole a cab once when he was on a date, and he couldn't find the driver. The police caught him, but no charges were pressed as long as he paid the 35-cent fare. He also got into an altercation with Packers teammate Lavvie Dilweg, who chased him through several cars on a speeding train. Dilweg might have caught him, too, if Blood hadn't rushed outside and climbed up on top of the car and clambered from roof to roof before lowering himself into the locomotive.

Legend has it that when Blood signed with the Packers, Lambeau offered him $100 a game but promised to make it $110 if Blood didn't drink from Wednesday through Sunday. Blood took the lower offer and allegedly imbibed heavily, Prohibition or not, during his seven-year stay in Green Bay.

Blood settled down some after retiring from the game, returning to St. John's in the late fifties to coach and teach economics. But his reputation was indelible. The inscription in his niche at the Hall of Fame begins, "Famed vagabond, halfback and totally unpredictable funster."

MICHAEL JORDAN PLAYS HIS LAST GAME IN MILWAUKEE

JANUARY 30, 2003

It happened all the time when Michael Jordan played at the Bradley Center and it was happening again. A bald-headed guard was taking over the game in the fourth quarter.

He would score 31 points, including 12 in the final period and 10 in the last four minutes to rally his team to victory. And once again he did it before a sellout crowd. The only difference was that this time the bald-headed guard was Sam Cassell, and he was playing for the Milwaukee Bucks.

Cassell did all he could to spoil the great Michael Jordan's 32nd and final appearance in Milwaukee, and his efforts were rewarded by a 97-90 triumph. But it was still "His Airness" who got the lion's share of attention from the 18,717 people who'd paid to say good-bye.

There were no pre-game gifts for the oft-retired Jordan, but a 40-second standing ovation greeted him when he was introduced, and it would have lasted longer if the management hadn't dimmed the house lights to introduce the Bucks. He was cheered wildly again when he re-entered the game for the last time with 9 minutes 34 seconds to play. No question he deserved it.

While Jordan usually left the local fans disappointed, he almost always gave them a show. He'd averaged 33 points a game in 21 previous appearances at the Bradley Center and 33.4 in 10 more at the Milwaukee Arena. On one April night in 1987, he'd scored 50 points and pulled down nine rebounds.

The Chicago Bulls had won 19 of their 30 games in Milwaukee with Jordan in the lineup. But now he was back for a second time with the Washington Wizards. The Bucks had won the first match the previous year, and they were determined to send him home disappointed in his finale.

Ray Allen drew the defensive assignment on Jordan, and at times it was hard to tell which of the two guards was 40 years old. Jordan scored 24 points in 38 minutes against Allen. But then in the final minute, Bucks coach George Karl switched the mountainous 6-foot-8 Anthony Mason onto Jordan. In his prime, Jordan would have been much too quick for Mason, but the years showed as he missed his last three shots.

As usual, the crowd was bipartisan. While most of the people rooted for the home team, they cheered for Jordan throughout the game. At one point during a timeout, a young fan came out of the stands and asked him for an autograph.

Jordan made 11 of 24 shots, added four rebounds and four assists, and when the game was over he called Milwaukee "the next-best thing to Chicago." Allen went six for 17 for 16 points and acknowledged later that Jordan had had the best of their match-up. As he put it, "He's older and slower, but he's still Michael Jordan."

And Cassell was Cassell. "It was a win for us," he said. "That's all I care about."

MICHAEL JORDAN GAME-BY-GAME IN MILWAUKEE

Chicago Bulls
(at the Milwaukee Arena)

Date	Points
Oct. 27, 1984	21
Nov. 21, 1984	35
Feb. 17, 1985	26
April 1, 1986	28
Dec. 12, 1986	41
Feb. 5, 1987	36
April 13, 1987	50
Nov. 25, 1987	33
Feb. 12, 1988	27
April 6, 1988	37

(at the Bradley Center)

Date	Points
Dec. 17, 1988	36
Feb. 19, 1989	23
March 29, 1989	32
Jan. 6, 1990	35
Feb. 18, 1990	39
March 6, 1990	35
Dec. 11, 1990	31
March 13, 1991	39
Nov. 2, 1991	46
Jan. 3, 1992	44
Feb. 28, 1992	24
Nov. 13, 1992	34
April 6, 1993	30
April 23, 1995	33
Dec. 9, 1995	45
April 16, 1996	22
Dec. 3, 1996	40
Jan. 10, 1997	33
Jan. 16, 1998	27
March 29, 1998	30

Washington Wizards

Date	Points
Jan. 11, 2002	22
Jan. 30, 2003	24

Source: michaeljordansworld.com

THE ORIGINAL CELTICS WIN IN BELOIT

JANUARY 31, 1924

Americans were living large in the early twenties, looking for new ways to be entertained, and pro basketball was just starting to get noticed.

It was mostly an Eastern game in the beginning, with teams playing home games to packed houses of as many as 4,000 fans. But leagues tended to come and go, and promoters soon realized that they'd have to take their show on the road to pay the bills. One such promoter was James Furey.

Furey gathered a talented group of New Yorkers and embarked on a 141-game national schedule that took him as far west as Wisconsin. He called his team the Original Celtics of New York, and his lineup featured 5-foot-11 Nat Holman, 5-10 Johnny Beckman, 5-11 Dutch Dehnert and giant 6-5 center Joe Lapchick. All four eventually made the Basketball Hall of Fame as individuals. But the Celtics were so dominant and so influential in promoting the game that they were inducted first as a team in the Hall's charter class in 1959.

Barnstorming wasn't an easy life. Teams would take the court six nights a week, sometimes playing doubleheaders on Saturdays, and although salaries could soar as high as $10,000 they weren't necessarily paid on time. The pros almost always won, but they rarely won by much. Running up the score was a bad idea if a team wanted to get invited back to a town.

But that was not a consideration when the Original Celtics journeyed to the Badger State to face the Beloit Fairies, among others. The Fairies were an industrial team sponsored by Fairbanks-Morse & Company, an employer with a love for sports. Fairbanks-Morse also had a baseball team that beat the Chicago White Sox in an exhibition game and a football team that handed the Green Bay Packers their only loss in 1919.

And the basketball Fairies were almost good enough to upset the Original Celtics. The New Yorkers came to town with an 82-4 record and a taste for big crowds, having drawn as many as 24,000 for two games in Detroit and 23,000 for two more in Cleveland. There wasn't room for nearly that many in the Beloit gym, but extra seats were added for the game, and it sold out.

Amateur rules were in force, although the five-foul maximum was waived, so that the visitors' regulars could go the distance. Beloit played nine men, while the Celtics used only five.

The home-court advantage helped the Fairies take a 12-8 lead at halftime. But then the Celtics' famous fast break kicked in with four players running down the floor with the two forwards, Beckman and Holman, usually taking the shots. The Celtics also had great success when they placed guard Chris Leonard in front of the basket, and then crisscrossed in front of him, with one of them getting the ball back for an open shot.

The tactic seemed to confuse the Fairies, who lost the lead and eventually the game by a 24-16 score. Leonard led all scorers with nine points. And the packed house couldn't have seen a better show.

Little did the fans know that The Original Celtics would be one of only six teams inducted into the Basketball Hall of Fame in its first 50 years.

LAMBEAU RESIGNS AS PACKERS COACH

FEBRUARY 1, 1950

He left Wisconsin for Chicago on Tuesday afternoon and mailed in his resignation on Wednesday morning. Earl Louis "Curly" Lambeau, co-founder, player, coach, general manager, vice president of the executive committee, you name it, was no longer a Green Bay Packer.

"Not entirely unexpected" is how team President Emil Fischer described Lambeau's decision to bolt the franchise he'd created, and that was true enough. A struggle at the top of the Packers organization had been reported for months.

Leaving a two-year contract extension unsigned, Lambeau became coach and vice president of the Chicago Cardinals for the princely sum of $25,000 a year, which was also what he was believed to be making with the Packers. "This difference of opinion, honest though it be, has brought about a dangerous disunity of purpose within the corporation, one which in my opinion threatens the existence of the club," he wrote in his resignation letter.

It didn't help, of course, that the Packers were coming off a 2-10 season after having gone 3-9 the year before that, but their fade on the field might have had less to do with those differences than their sagging bottom line. They'd been forced to hold an intra-squad game on Thanksgiving Day to raise enough money to survive the 1949 season, and a stock sale was planned to keep the franchise afloat.

Lambeau's prowess as a coach was never as much an issue as his ambitions as an executive. After all, he was credited with 209 regular-season wins and six championships in the 29 years that the Packers had been part of the National Football League, and he had suffered only one losing year before 1948. It could even be argued that the 2-10 record was somebody else's fault, because he had relinquished the bench duties to his three assistants following a 17-0 loss to the Chicago Bears in the opener.

No, what may have created the greatest ruckus in the boardroom, was Lambeau's plan to turn the Packers into a for-profit corporation. He had four friends in mind to buy up $200,000 worth of stock and hand him complete control of the Packers' operation, according to the book, *The Packer Legend: An Inside Look*, by former executive committee member John Torinus. But the board of directors had other ideas, although they had voted to give Lambeau a two-year contract extension in a dramatic Nov. 30, 1949, meeting. He never signed on the dotted line.

The notion of a Lambeau-less Packer franchise would have been unthinkable just a few years before. Lambeau had grown up in Green Bay and starred as a halfback at East High School before playing fullback for a year under Knute Rockne at Notre Dame. He went to work at the Indian Packing Company as a shipping clerk, and in 1919 he convinced management to put up $500 to buy jerseys for a fledgling football team. Two years later, the Packers joined what became the NFL. Lambeau was a 5-foot-10, 187-pound player-coach through the 1928 season, and in 1929, he coached the team to the first of three straight championships.

Lambeau did as he pleased with the Packers until the mid-1940s when friction surfaced within the board of directors. One source of it was the purchase of a lodge on the shores of Green Bay that Lambeau converted into a training center. Rockwood Lodge cost $32,000 to buy and $8,000 to renovate, and his critics believed it was too expensive under the Packers' current fiscal circumstances.

There was also an uproar over the firing of the team's co-founder and publicity director, George Whitney Calhoun, and his replacement by former *Chicago Tribune* sportswriter George Strickler, as well as differences over playing part of the Packers' schedule in Milwaukee.

It all added up to Lambeau leaving for Chicago where he was given total control over the team's football operation. He would coach two losing seasons with the Cardinals before resigning and bitterly charging the team's upper management with interference. He took over as coach of the Washington Redskins in 1952 and lasted two more seasons, compiling a 10-13-1 record. After being fired by the Redskins, he coached the College All-Stars for three years before retiring completely and splitting his time between Door County and California.

He died of a heart attack on June 1, 1965, at the age of 67 while cutting the lawn at the home of friends in Sturgeon Bay. Three months later, the Packers rededicated their stadium. They called it Lambeau Field.

RIVER FALLS' SCORING MACHINE GIVES BACK POINTS

FEBRUARY 2, 1950

Before the legendary exploits of small-school superhero Bevo Francis captured headlines across the country in the early 1950s, there was Nate DeLong.

DeLong's scoring records at River Falls State Teachers College didn't survive Francis' onslaught at the national level, but they remain unsurpassed in the Wisconsin Intercollegiate Athletic Conference.

Francis gained his fame at tiny Rio Grande College in southeastern Ohio, where he once scored 113 points in a game against Hillsdale College of Michigan. In fact, Francis' 113-point effort still stands as the all-time single-game scoring record in college basketball. When the 6-foot-9 Francis left Rio Grande in 1954, he owned five of the seven highest single-game scoring totals in collegiate history and he still owns three of the top five. Francis was such a national sensation that in 2000, he was featured by ESPN Classic in one of its *SportsCentury* segments.

DeLong was Wisconsin's version of Francis.

DeLong scored so many points in four seasons at what is now UW-River Falls that he could afford to give more than 300 of them back. And that's exactly what he did.

The one-time Chippewa Falls High School star had totaled 310 points as a first semester freshman in 1943, but then the Wisconsin State Teachers College Conference suspended play because of World War II, and DeLong went off to join the Navy. He returned to school in 1946 and scored 2,281 more points, giving him 2,591 with another six weeks to play in his senior season. That also made him the top scorer in college history, but it created a problem.

The conference had wiped out DeLong's 1943 semester so that he'd have four full years of eligibility when he came back from the service. But record-keepers and newspapers still counted his points from that time. At least they did until DeLong voluntarily relinquished the 310 points he'd scored six years earlier, figuring a record achieved in four-and-a-half seasons would be tainted if everybody else had only four years.

Though magnanimous, the sacrifice wasn't especially costly because DeLong's reduced total still left him with the collegiate scoring record. "It's certainly the first time I've ever heard of an athlete voluntarily giving up something to which he's entitled," said River Falls coach George Schlagenhauf in making the announcement.

It was a rare gesture, but then DeLong was a rare talent. Opposing coaches and players liked to say that he'd never really be a good player because he was so clumsy and slow. And it was true that at 6-6 and 215 pounds DeLong wasn't quick and he was certainly no gazelle. But he stood a head taller than most of his opponents back then, and he put the ball in the basket more than anyone else before him whether they came from big colleges or small ones. Statisticians didn't make a distinction in those days.

DeLong finished up at River Falls with 2,592 points, an average of 25.4 per game which made him America's all-time leading college scorer at the time. The total remains a WIAC record, and he still holds the WIAC marks for single-season and single-game scoring as well.

He set the single-game record of 72 in a non-conference matchup against Winona (Minn.) State Teachers College. Before the start of the 2008-'09 season that 72-point performance was still tied for 12th all-time in the NCAA Men's Basketball Record Book and was the oldest of the top 25 totals listed.

DeLong also held the single-game scoring record in the National Association of Intercollegiate Athletics tournament in Kansas City for 25 years. As a freshman, DeLong scored 56 against what is now Marshall University, and the record stood until Travis Grant of Kentucky State broke it in 1972.

DeLong's critics had their day when he moved on to the pros. He averaged 10.2 points per game in one season for Sheboygan of the National Professional Basketball League, an organization formed from teams that either split from the National Basketball Association or were dropped by it, and then he signed with the NBA's Milwaukee Hawks and played in only 17 games during the 1951-'52 season.

But, to this day, not even the highest scorers at Wisconsin's four Division I basketball programs have eclipsed his all-time, single-season and single-game scoring totals.

MARQUETTE VICTORY IS A DAY AT THE BEACH

FEBRUARY 3, 1968

The question was who threw the first elbow, and the referee didn't waste any time waiting for the answer. With a minute gone in a scoreless game, he ejected both teams' centers.

This was quick work even for a Marquette-DePaul game. The dispute would last much longer. It started grimly in a gym in Chicago and it ended comically on a beach in Milwaukee. In the two days in between, the future of the fierce, 50-year-old rivalry between neighboring Catholic schools was up for grabs.

Marquette's Al McGuire had an undersized pivot man named Pat Smith, who couldn't shoot and was visually impaired to boot. But there were two things he could definitely do. He could rebound, and he could take care of himself. So it came as no surprise when the 6-foot-3 New Yorker missed a shot from close range in the opening seconds against DePaul and waded into the fray looking for a put-back.

On the way, he encountered Bob Zoretich, De Paul's 6-7 pivot man. The two exchanged elbows, and suddenly the court was awash in martial arts. DePaul's Ken Warzynski and Marquette's George Thompson lost some blood in the fracas, but more importantly Blue Demons coach Ray Meyer lost his temper after the officials tossed Smith and Zoretich.

When the melee was over Marquette bolted to a 28-12 lead. DePaul went without a field goal for more than nine minutes as the Warriors won the game, 58-53, and succeeded at the Blue Demons' Alumni Hall for only the second time in their last 11 tries. When the players walked off the court, Smith stopped at the DePaul bench where he appeared to be apologizing. Appearances can be deceiving. According to Zoretich, what Smith really said was, "If you want to finish it, see me after the game."

Meyer also was still seething after watching Joe Thomas score 13 points and claim 10 rebounds filling in for Smith, while DePaul's Tom Hunter was held to seven points and seven rebounds while replacing Zoretich.

"Of course, they could stand the loss better," fumed Meyer. "You don't lose your leading scorer and rebounder while they lose some stumblebum without getting hurt. Smith couldn't throw the ball in the ocean if he was standing on the beach."

McGuire took exception to Meyer's remarks but not to his assessment of Smith's shooting skills. He saved that for later. He just didn't like the "stumblebum" reference.

"Pat can't see," McGuire said. "The guy who passes the ball to him in a game comes out right away. But he can rebound. I think Ray must have forgotten that Pat is a junior. He's too smart a coach to say that about a kid, especially when he has to play him again."

The next day there was some question whether he'd have to play him again at all. A report had gotten back to Meyer that McGuire had prearranged the Smith-Zoretich encounter. The report turned out to be false, but Meyer had been quoted in a wire service story saying, "I'm so burned up I would like to discontinue the series."

The misunderstanding was cleared up, and on the Monday after the game Meyer said he had been misquoted and as far as he was concerned, the issue was settled. But it wasn't as far as McGuire was concerned. This was too good a public relations opportunity for him to pass up. And so he decided to prove that Smith could, too, throw the ball in the ocean.

Of course, Marquette was a landlocked campus, and no ocean was available. Lake Michigan would have to do. First McGuire summoned his center, and then he called a photographer and posed Smith, right arm cocked, taking dead aim at the water with a beach ball. The picture appeared in *The Milwaukee Journal* on Tuesday, Feb. 6.

For the record, the ball did land in the drink, although it was dropped in rather than thrown in. Even if Smith couldn't shoot, he could always dunk.

After DePaul coach Ray Meyer said center Pat Smith of Marquette "couldn't throw the ball in the ocean if he was standing on the beach," coach Al McGuire of the Warriors seized the opportunity to stage a publicity stunt. McGuire took Smith to the shores of Lake Michigan and had him drop the ball in the water to prove Meyer wrong.

BUCKS ACQUIRE LANIER FROM PISTONS

FEBRUARY 4, 1980

The trade rumors began before Christmas. The Milwaukee Bucks needed a center, and Bob Lanier wanted a ring. They seemed to be made for each other.

According to a report in *The Milwaukee Journal*, the deal was virtually completed six weeks earlier, but when the Detroit Pistons' big-man fractured the little finger on his shooting hand, it was put on hold. When Lanier's recovery was complete, the Bucks announced on a Monday night that they'd sent center Kent Benson and their No. 1 draft choice to Detroit for the Pistons' all-time leading scorer.

It was one of the two or three most important trades in the history of the franchise, and it came with some risks. While Lanier was a seven-time All-Star, Benson had been the No. 1 choice in the draft three years earlier, and he was only 25 years old. Lanier was 31 with famously bad knees, and he was making close to $400,000 a year or about $250,000 more than Benson.

The Bucks had to do something, though. Their 29-27 record had put them 4½ games behind first-place Kansas City in the Midwest Division, and they'd been without an inside scoring threat since the departure of Kareem Abdul-Jabbar in 1975. They'd also qualified for the playoffs only twice in the four seasons since.

Lanier had been a dominant presence for 10 years with Detroit, but he wasn't happy. The Pistons were rebuilding, and he wanted a chance at a championship ring. "I'm in a dilemma," he had said in December. "My head is all screwed up. I'd like to get on a team that has some semblance of going somewhere."

The Bucks were that team. They were young and unquestionably talented. Seven retired jerseys hang in the rafters at the Bradley Center today, and four of them were worn by players who were on Lanier's first team with the Bucks. In addition to Lanier himself, they include Brian Winters, Sidney Moncrief and Junior Bridgeman, and a strong case could be made for a fifth. The team's leading scorer that season was Marques Johnson, who is in their top five in every important career offensive category.

Two days after the Bucks announced the deal, it began to pay off when Winters hit a jump shot from the top of the key in the last two seconds of a 111-109 victory over Cleveland. With the Cavaliers' defense sagging on Lanier, Winters had more than enough room to get off the shot. "He's like a magnet," said the Bucks' guard.

Lanier played 24 minutes in that first game, scoring 14 points, grabbing six rebounds and blocking two shots. "He looked rusty, but he also looked awful good to me," said coach Don Nelson.

The Cleveland victory started the Bucks on a six-game winning streak. They would lose only six more times during the rest of the regular season and sell out the Arena for every home game. They won the division championship, and they won it again in each of the four seasons that Lanier played after that. And they made it to the conference finals in Lanier's last two seasons only to be turned back by Philadelphia and Boston.

As for the Pistons, they won only two of their final 28 games. Benson played six more years with them, but his scoring average slipped every year from 15.7 to 6.5. In his final three seasons, Benson was a sometime starter and the Pistons made the playoffs each time, but they won only one first-round series. They got even less out of the No. 1 pick. The Pistons used it to take Larry Drew, who played one year with them and then nine more years with three different franchises.

Lanier got much closer to a title with the Bucks than he would have with the Pistons, but he never got his ring. He was inducted into the Basketball Hall of Fame, however, in 1992.

Bob Lanier

McGUIRE TAKES A STAND, GETS A ONE-FINGER SALUTE

FEBRUARY 5, 1974

Fifty-seven years of rivalry was all wrapped up in a single picture. It ran over two columns in *The Milwaukee Journal*, and naturally it featured Al McGuire.

There was Marquette's flamboyant basketball coach standing, of all places, on top of the scorer's table at the Milwaukee Arena. He was facing the crowd with his fist raised in the air.

And there was an enraged Wisconsin fan with his hand also raised in the air, but with only one finger showing. You can guess which one.

In the foreground was Wisconsin coach John Powless walking off the court like a prisoner on his way to the gallows. It was easy to understand the emotions of all three men.

The fellow with the finger was Glenn Hughes, father of 6-foot-11 Badger twins Kim and Kerry Hughes, and he was having a bad night. Kim had taken two free throws with 17 seconds to play in an incredibly tense game. He missed them both, and 16 seconds later Marquette star Maurice Lucas fumbled a pass from teammate Dave Delsman, turned to the basket and heaved up a 20-foot wish.

The ball went straight through the hoop, a sellout crowd of 10,938 went nuts, and McGuire hopped up on the scorer's table to celebrate. McGuire admitted later that the Warriors had no right to expect to win after missing 40 of 64 shots and going down by nine points with nine minutes to play. But win they did by a final score of 59-58.

Powless, who had not beaten Marquette since his first year at Wisconsin in 1968, got exactly what he wanted on the final play, shutting off the Warriors inside and forcing them to take a bad shot. It just wasn't bad enough.

Making it even more painful for the Badgers was another shot taken by 6-8 forward Dale Koehler at the end of the first half from a little further away. Koehler's attempt, like Lucas', also came at the buzzer, and like Lucas', it went in. But the official said it came too late and waved it off, sending the Badgers into the locker room up by two points and arguing vehemently that they should be up by four.

It didn't appear to make much difference when Wisconsin breezed to a 43-34 lead with nine minutes

Al McGuire exulted in victory by hopping on to the scorer's table at the Milwaukee Arena after Marquette had beaten Wisconsin in a tight, fierce battle. Glenn Hughes, father of Wisconsin twins Kim and Kerry Hughes, responded by giving McGuire a one-finger salute. However, Glenn Hughes' middle finger was blocked out by one of the Milwaukee newspapers.

to play. The Badgers were outshooting the Warriors and ruling the backboards, and Koehler was upstaging Lucas. He would finish the game with 19 points and 12 rebounds, while Lucas made only six of 14 shots on the way to 17 points.

But Koehler got into foul trouble, picking up his fourth with 13:35 left, and Marquette stepped up its full-court pressure. With 3:26 on the clock, Wisconsin's lead was down to 52-51, and it was a 58-57 advantage when Hughes missed his free throws and set up Lucas' game-winner.

"We played too good defense on that last shot," Powless told the *Wisconsin State Journal* later. "It's like there isn't any justice."

Not for the Badgers anyway. They finished the season 16-8, while Marquette played for the national championship in March and lost to North Carolina State in another game marked by McGuire's antics. He didn't get up on the scorer's table. He got two technical fouls instead.

LOMBARDI LEAVES PACKERS FOR WASHINGTON

FEBRUARY 6, 1969

Breaking up is hard to do.

Harder probably than Vince Lombardi thought when he surprised the Green Bay Packers by submitting a letter of resignation on Feb. 3, and certainly harder than the Washington Redskins expected when they planned a press conference that day to announce that the Packers' general manager had become their new head coach, executive vice president and part-owner, only to have to twice postpone it.

At least as early as November 1968, when the Packers played at D.C. Stadium, Lombardi and Redskins owner Edward Bennett Williams engaged in secret talks to pave the way for Lombardi to get part ownership in the Redskins and to return to coaching.

On Feb 1, the *Washington Post* finally broke the story and said Lombardi would ask the Packers to release him from his five-year contract as general manager. Two days later, Lombardi submitted his resignation.

Meanwhile, in Washington, D.C., Williams scheduled a press conference for noon that same day to make the announcement, but he had to postpone it when the Packers executive committee declined to rubber stamp the move. He postponed it twice, in fact, and then finally met with the Washington media at 4:30 in the afternoon to tell them he had nothing to tell them. It took him three minutes to apologize for the inconvenience.

It would be Wednesday evening, Feb. 6, before Packers President Dominic Olejniczak would announce that the franchise's board of directors, on the recommendation of the seven-man executive committee, had freed Lombardi from his contact. And it would be another day before the Redskins finally were able to hold their press conference and introduce Lombardi as their new coach.

The Packers were in no hurry to part with such an important asset. After the board finally agreed to allow Lombardi out of his contract following a two-hour meeting, Olejniczak said the Packers would have turned down an offer of "15 good players" or "$1 million" to keep him. Olejniczak no doubt was serious, and he also was clearly annoyed.

The Redskins had never asked the organization directly for permission to talk with Lombardi, and Lombardi hadn't informed anyone connected with the Packers either. As late as Monday, the day Lombardi submitted his resignation, Olejniczak said the Redskins still had not asked the Packers for permission for anything. Not only was Lombardi bound to the Packers for five more years, but he had reportedly agreed to a clause that he wouldn't coach anywhere else until at least 1974.

It also would eventually come to light that Lombardi did the Packers no favors when he quietly sat in his office at Lambeau Field on draft day, Jan. 28, a week before resigning and probably after he had agreed to take the Redskins' job. He allowed Head Coach Phil Bengtson to tab defensive tackle Rich Moore, who turned out to be a colossal bust, with the team's No. 1 pick.

Privately, the Packers' hierarchy was steaming over how the whole situation was handled. But Olejniczak and others finally had to admit there was no point in trying to tie down a man who was determined to move on. Especially this man, who had taken them on the 10-year ride of their lives, winning five NFL championships and the first two Super Bowls during his last seven as coach.

So in the end, there were no harsh comments. Just harsh times. Green Bay would make it to the playoffs only twice in the next 24 years.

As much as the Packers knew they would miss Lombardi, they couldn't give him the one thing he wanted, which was a piece of the action. The Redskins offered him complete control of their football operation and a reported annual salary of $110,000 a year for five years, but that wasn't the important part. They also offered him a percentage of the team.

The Packers could have matched the money, but they couldn't match the ownership stake, because they were public property. Control was a problem, too. Lombardi had relinquished his coaching job in Green Bay to Bengtson one year earlier, and while the team had finished a disappointing 6-7-1, there was no going back on that now.

Lombardi would coach one year in Washington, breaking the Skins' string of 13 losing seasons with a 7-5-2 record. And then he died of cancer on Sept. 3, 1970. He was 57.

GREEN BAY GOALIE SAVES U.S. HOCKEY TEAM

FEBRUARY 7, 1972

The players would have had to leave their skates at home for things to look any worse for the United States Olympic hockey team after one match in Sapporo, Japan. The Americans had to win an elimination game against Switzerland to qualify for the Group A pool; they'd just been blown out, 5-1, by Sweden; and their next two games were against second-ranked Czechoslovakia and the top-ranked Soviet Union.

What's more, their best goalie hadn't even been on the roster three weeks earlier. The Green Bay Bobcats had lent Mike Curran to the Olympians reluctantly on Jan. 19, and only then because there was nobody else who could do the job.

Bobcats President Jim Van Essen was happy for Curran, but steamed at the U.S. Olympic Ice Hockey Committee when it came looking for his star. "Last September they told us that there was no way that they would consider Mike, and we built our team accordingly," he said. "Now they feel their goaltenders are not consistent enough and they come and get Mike."

It didn't seem to matter who the Americans had in the nets anyway. They were a struggling team of amateurs in a tournament dominated by pros. It was an open secret that the Soviets and the Czechs paid their players, which was why Canada was boycotting the competition for the first time ever. The Americans, meanwhile, hadn't won a medal since capturing the gold in a colossal upset of the Soviets in 1960.

They'd finished sixth in 1968, forcing the elimination game with Switzerland. Sixteen hours after beating the Swiss, they'd been obliterated by Sweden, and now they faced the very real prospect of going 0-3 after the Czechs and the Russians were done with them.

Despite the five-goal Swedish onslaught, Curran was their best hope of staying alive in the competition. The 27-year-old International Falls, Minn., native had accumulated a fair amount of international experience as well as a full supply of bad luck over the past two years. After leading the University of North Dakota to the NCAA finals for two years in a row, he'd earned a spot on the U.S. team in 1969-'70, but missed the World Tournament because of a bleeding ulcer. He played with the national team the next year, too, but a knee injury sidelined him during the World Games in Europe.

He was in good health for the Czechoslovakia game, though, as he turned in one of the most brilliant individual performances in Olympic history. The Czechs took 52 shots, and Curran stopped 51 of them. The only exception came early in the first period when the U.S. was shorthanded. The Americans got that goal back before the period was over, and when they scored three more in the second the frustrated Czechs were done.

An insurance goal in the third period made the score 5-1 and left Curran ecstatic. "I can't think of any win that's made me happier," he said.

Two days later, the Soviets brought the U.S. team back to earth. They scored two goals in 26 seconds while handing the Americans a 7-2 loss that left Curran so frustrated he broke a stick over one of the Russian players' backs, surprisingly, without drawing a penalty. Still, the U.S. medal hopes weren't dead.

Curran stopped 35 of 36 shots in a 4-1 victory over Finland that evened the Americans' record at 2-2, and when they beat Poland, 6-1, they finished the tournament with a 3-2 record and a tie with Czechoslovakia. Since they'd beaten the Czechs head-to-head, they earned the silver. The Soviets got the gold, but Curran didn't seem to mind.

When he got home to Green Bay, he said, "It's the first time I've ever been satisfied finishing second."

There was more satisfaction to come. While he was in Japan, he was drafted by the Minnesota Fighting Saints of the upstart World Hockey Association, which took on the established National Hockey League from 1972 to '79. Curran played five seasons for Minnesota before retiring. In 1998 he was inducted into the United States Hockey Hall of Fame.

BREWERS BUY BACK GORMAN THOMAS

FEBRUARY 8, 1978

Gorman Thomas always understood his own popularity. "The fans come out to see me strike out, hit a home run or run into a fence," he said once. "I try to accommodate them at least one way every game."

That may have been how the fans felt, but at the start the Milwaukee Brewers management wasn't willing to settle for two out of three. And so the rough-edged outfielder spent most of the first nine years of his career in their farm system.

The Brewers loved the home runs and hated the strikeouts. In two years with Class A Danville and Class AA San Antonio, Thomas was the league leader in both before he made his debut with the Brewers in 1973 and failed to improve on the pattern. He spent most of the 1974 season with Class AAA Sacramento where he hit 51 home runs, which was very good, and struck out 175 times, which was very bad.

And so it went. The Brewers kept him in Milwaukee for the next two seasons, but when he batted .188 and hit only 18 home runs they'd had enough. They cut him in spring training and sent him to Class AAA Spokane. "We don't have room for Gorman," said Jim Baumer, the Brewers' director of baseball operations. "There are other guys who deserve it more. It's a lack of contact. He's had that problem all his life."

Since the Brewers had used up all their options on Thomas and couldn't recall him again from the minors, he appeared to be somebody else's problem from that point on. True to form, he hit 36 home runs and whiffed 115 times with Spokane. On Oct. 25, 1977, Baumer designated Thomas the player to be named later in a deal with Texas that had brought journeyman outfielder Ed Kirkpatrick to Milwaukee in late August.

That almost certainly sealed the end of Thomas' association with the Brewers. But had they really given up on the free-swinging slugger?

Less than four months later, they bought him back from Texas for an undisclosed amount of cash in a deal that looked a little slippery. The rules said the Brewers couldn't call Thomas up from the minors again without exposing him to waivers, but there was nothing illegal about trading him to another big league club and then buying him back. The suspicion was that they had a gentleman's agreement with the Rangers to do just that.

The sale was approved by Commissioner Bowie Kuhn and American League President Lee MacPhail, although MacPhail's office did say any prior agreement between Texas and Milwaukee would have been wrong. But the league chose to believe the two clubs when they said it was simply a matter of the Brewers wanting Thomas and the Rangers being unable to sign him.

The fact that Harry Dalton had replaced Baumer in November may have helped the Brewers' credibility in this case. "I've always liked Thomas," said Dalton. "I don't know anything about any arrangements when he went to Texas."

If that was true, ignorance was bliss. What appeared to be a minor transaction turned out to be one of the best moves of Dalton's 14 years as general manager. Thomas won the Brewers' starting center-field job in the spring of 1978 and held it for the next five seasons, becoming one of their most beloved players along the way. When he wasn't crashing into the fences at County Stadium, he was hitting balls over them. He led the American League in home runs in 1979 with 45, and tied for the title with 39 in 1982 when the Brewers won their only pennant.

The following year he ran into shoulder problems, and the Brewers sent him to Cleveland in one of the least popular trades the franchise would ever make. Thomas struggled badly with the Indians, who then dealt him to Seattle where he bounced back with 32 home runs in 1985. When he returned to County Stadium as a Mariner early in the 1986 season, the crowd cheered his every move.

Thomas appreciated the sentiment. He also understood it. "Success changes some people's personality," he said. "I didn't change."

He was certainly right about that. When Thomas retired after the 1986 season, following a final two-and-a-half month stint with the Brewers, he had 268 home runs. And 1,339 strikeouts.

Gorman Thomas

58 365 BEST WISCONSIN SPORTS STORIES

AUERBACH ESCORTED FROM GAME IN SHEBOYGAN

FEBRUARY 9, 1950

"Irascible" was the word frequently used to describe Red Auerbach. "Under arrest" were two others that almost applied when the future Boston Celtics legend visited Sheboygan as a 32-year-old head coach.

Auerbach didn't like Sheboygan. He particularly didn't like the Sheboygan Municipal Auditorium where he brought his Tri-Cities Blackhawks team to play during the National Basketball Association's first season. He thought the facility was less than major league.

The citizens of Sheboygan naturally disagreed. They were proud of the eight-year-old building that their Redskins shared with the National Guard. It had been built as a Works Progress Administration project for $200,000, and it seated 3,400 people in relative comfort. It still stands today overlooking Lake Michigan.

Sheboyganites were also proud of their team. The Redskins had been a power in the old National Basketball League for 11 years before six of the NBL franchises were absorbed by the Basketball Association of America to create the newly named NBA.

So there wasn't much love lost between the crowd and the visiting coach when Auerbach walked into the Auditorium. There was even less after he'd been there awhile. As the *Sheboygan Press* described it: "Auerbach's unsportsmanlike conduct was further demonstrated when he commenced swearing before the scores of school children seated on the stage and continued a constant flow of vile language throughout the game."

Part of Auerbach's problem was the stage. There were no benches on the floor, so he was forced to jump down from it to talk to his team during timeouts. Another part were the 90 fouls called during the course of the game.

Those were just the personal fouls. It was a technical foul that earned the excitable redhead an early exit.

The *Press* story said he'd been arguing all night with the fans, the officials and even the scorer's table. In fact, it said, "He had very nearly become engaged in fisticuffs with a couple of spectators." And so it came as no great surprise when referee Bud Lowell blew his whistle and made the sign of a "T" when Auerbach disputed another call a little too loudly.

Incensed, Auerbach raced out onto the floor to protest and the cops had to escort him off in order for the game to proceed without him. Lowell may actually have done Auerbach a favor. At least he didn't have to watch the Blackhawks getting manhandled, 104-82, by the home team.

It was kind of the Redskins' last hurrah. They finished the season fourth in the six-team Western Division with a 22-40 record, and a year later Sheboygan and five other cities dropped out of the NBA. The Blackhawks, meanwhile, would play one more year in the Davenport-Moline area and then move to Milwaukee where they became the Milwaukee Hawks.

As for Auerbach, he landed in Boston where he led the Celtics to eight straight championships and nine overall as coach. He was voted into the Basketball Hall of Fame in 1969. Sheboygan didn't have a vote.

FRANCHISES IN NBA'S FIRST SEASON (1949-'50)

Eastern Division
Baltimore Bullets
Boston Celtics
New York Knickerbockers
Philadelphia Warriors
Syracuse Nationals
Washington Capitols

Central Division
Chicago Stags
Fort Wayne Pistons
Minneapolis Lakers
Rochester Royals
St. Louis Bombers

Western Division
Anderson Packers
Denver Nuggets
Indianapolis Olympians
Sheboygan Redskins
Tri-Cities Blackhawks
Waterloo Hawks

Source: The Official NBA Basketball Encyclopedia

FOND DU LAC CLAIMS NATIONAL CHAMPIONSHIP

FEBRUARY 10, 1913

It didn't get much better than the old Fond du Lac Armory on East Second Street. According to the book *Cages to Jumpshots,* it was one of the few gymnasiums in the country that had glass backboards and a "cage," which was a three-foot high wooden fence plastered with advertising posters surrounding the court. In those days that made it a place fit for kings, which was exactly what the city's famed basketball team planned to become once again.

The lads from the Fond du Lac National Guard Company E Athletic Association had claimed the basketball championship of the United States at the turn of the century by beating a Yale squad that had traveled all the way from New Haven, Conn. Now, 13 years later, it was facing the touring New York Nationals with hopes of recapturing the crown.

And so it did. And as befits a National Guard company, it was war, albeit in sneakers.

Fond du Lac was called for 15 fouls, the Nationals for 16, and referee Roy Rogers, athletic director at the Presbyterian Club of Oshkosh, ejected a player from each team for fighting. There were some particularly anxious moments in the first half when the Nationals were so distressed at a call that they refused to play on. Rogers gave them three minutes to resume action.

When the timer's final whistle sounded, Company E had won the second game of the proposed three-game series, 28-25, and an overflow crowd of approximately 1,500 went wild, standing and clapping and tooting tin horns. Peter Lapine led Fond du Lac with 15 points. George Fogarty, one of the early stars of basketball and a player that the Fond du Lac team imported from New York, was one of the players ejected, and he was held to four points.

There was no national sanctioning organization in those days and very few burdensome rules. If two teams decided they were playing for the national championship, it was up to others to disprove it. There was certainly no disputing that Fond du Lac was a hotbed of hoops.

The local high school won the 1905 Lawrence Invitational, the first high school basketball tournament ever held in the United States and forerunner to the Wisconsin state tournament, and it was victorious again in 1916 in what is recognized as the first official Wisconsin Interscholastic Athletic Association state tournament. And of course, there was Company E's historic conquest of Yale, starting with a game on Dec. 30, 1899, and ending with one on Jan. 3, 1900.

Carl Brugger, Company E's team manager, incurred $1,000 in expenses bringing the proclaimed national champions west to Wisconsin. It was generally recognized as the longest trip ever taken by a college team at that time, and it wasn't an easy journey. The train was delayed twice by accidents on the tracks, and when the Yale players arrived in Fond du Lac they had to be rushed from the railroad depot to the Armory by horse-drawn carriage.

The series wasn't even close. Company E coasted to a 27-18 victory in the opener, and then romped, 27-6, in the second game to clinch the title. Yale got its best effort in the meaningless finale, but still lost, 21-13.

When Company E claimed the national title again in 1913, it did so after sweeping two games from the Nationals. It won the first game on Feb. 8, 43-23. The third game wasn't necessary, but the Nationals returned to Fond du Lac for another game on March 16. Company E, proving the earlier series was no fluke, won again, 40-35, to finish its season with a 35-3 record.

Company E would sweep Oswego, N.Y., in three games in 1914, finish the season unbeaten and claim its third national title. But then in 1915 the soldiers were routed by Troy, N.Y., losing the third game, 49-15. Newspaper accounts claimed the Company E players weren't as fit as those from Troy.

Sometimes champions just get complacent.

PACKERS TRADE FOR BRETT FAVRE

FEBRUARY 11, 1992

Bob Harlan's favorite Ron Wolf story takes place in the press box in Atlanta. It's the new general manager's first weekend on the job, and he sits next to the Packers' president about an hour before kickoff and tells him he's going down on the field to watch the Falcons' third-string quarterback throw the ball. Harlan looks at his flip chart trying to figure out who the Falcons' third-string quarterback is.

After about 45 minutes Wolf comes back and says to Harlan, "We're going to make a trade for Brett Favre." Ten weeks later, Favre is property of the Green Bay Packers. It's a busy 10 weeks.

Although Wolf told the *Green Bay Press-Gazette* years later that he never made it to the field, he recalled talking to Ken Herock, Atlanta's director of player personnel, at least every other day during that time, hammering out a deal for this hell-raising, 22-year-old from Southern Mississippi. Wolf tried to get him for a second-round draft choice, but Herock liked Favre as much as Wolf did, and he held out for a No. 1. Herock preferred not to trade Favre at all, but Falcons coach Jerry Glanville wanted him gone.

Wolf and Herock finally settled on the Packers' second choice in the first round of the 1992 draft, the 17th pick overall acquired the year before from Philadelphia. Wolf announced the trade, and thousands of Packers fans thought he'd lost his mind.

Wolf being Wolf didn't care what thousands of Packers fans thought. He said his success would one day depend on Brett Favre. He was a smart man. It was a great trade.

It might never have happened if Wolf and Herock hadn't become friends when they'd worked together for the Oakland Raiders. Or if Glanville hadn't wanted to claim Browning Nagle with the Falcons' pick in the second round of the 1991 draft. Herock said he overruled his coach and took Favre, and a resentful Glanville never gave Favre a chance.

Playing behind former Pro Bowler Chris Miller and the forgettable Billy Joe Tolliver, Favre threw only four passes for Atlanta as a rookie, got two of them intercepted and didn't complete any of them. While he couldn't find a receiver, he was able to locate the nightspots in Atlanta, which also failed to endear him to Glanville. The coach fined him $1,500 for missing the team picture and relegated him to the scout team.

But Wolf cheerfully ignored all of the above and the fact that he was giving up a No. 1 draft choice for a player who had gone in the second round the year before. He reasoned that the Atlanta system was all wrong for Favre, a drop-back passer who was being told to roll out in Glanville's run-and-shoot offense. Wolf also figured that he was going to need to draft a quarterback if he didn't get Favre. After all, since 1971, Bart Starr's last season with the Packers, they had used 27 different quarterbacks, including 17 different starters. Over those 22 seasons, only Lynn Dickey in 1983 and '84, and Don Majkowski in 1989 had finished in the top 10 in the NFL in passing.

So the deal got done, and a reluctant Herock told Wolf, "You got a hell of a quarterback." He didn't know the half of it.

The Packers finished the 1992 season with a 9-7 record behind Favre, who proceeded to tear up their record book over the next 16 years. The Falcons went 6-10 and hit the skids for more than a decade.

Brett Favre

FITZRANDOLPH WINS OLYMPIC GOLD

FEBRUARY 12, 2002

Eric Heiden had tears in his eyes when Casey FitzRandolph skated over to him - two American speedskating heroes, the greatest and the latest, celebrating a triumph 22 years in the making.

Verona's FitzRandolph had just won a gold medal in the Salt Lake City Olympics, and nobody knew that feeling better than Heiden, who had won five of them in the 1980 Games in Lake Placid, N.Y. FitzRandolph earned his in the 500 meters by the slimmest of margins - .03 seconds or about the length of a blade - over Japan's Hirroyasu Shimizu. The last American man to win that event? Heiden of course.

The Madison native had swept all of the men's events at Lake Placid, and if he hadn't, FitzRandolph's time might never have come. FitzRandolph was five years old and a peewee hockey player when he watched Heiden dominate the ice, and he decided on the spot that he wanted to be a speedskater. Before long, he was one of America's best.

FitzRandolph won two World Cup races at 1,000 meters in 1997, and he looked like a good bet to medal in 1998 in Nagano, Japan. But the sport underwent a major technical change in the mid-nineties with the introduction of "clap skates," an innovation that set FitzRandolph and a number of other world class racers back until they adapted to the newer, faster equipment.

After a deflating sixth-place finish in the 500 at Nagano, FitzRandolph moved to Calgary to train with the Canadian team and hit his stride again on the World Cup circuit. When Salt Lake City rolled around, he was ready.

And so was another Wisconsin athlete, Kip Carpenter of Brookfield, who skated with FitzRandolph in his final 500 pair and shocked everyone by winning the bronze. Carpenter, who was ranked only 17th at the distance in the World Cup standings, actually beat FitzRandolph that day, finishing in 34.79 seconds to his teammate's 34.81. But the standings in the 500 are determined by total time in two heats, and FitzRandolph had set an Olympic record at 34.42 in his first heat the day before.

Casey FitzRandolph

Heiden was in Salt Lake serving as the U.S. speedskating team doctor when FitzRandolph crossed the finish line and then joined him to share his big moment. They had spoken often about how the one had inspired the other. And so it was a big day for three American skaters when FitzRandolph and Carpenter mounted the podium. And a huge one for Wisconsin.

NBA ALL-STARS COME TO MILWAUKEE

FEBRUARY 13, 1977

All of pro basketball's best gathered on the same floor for the first time in 10 years to put on a show with a strong local flavor and a sour aftertaste.

The first NBA All-Star Game played after the demise of the renegade American Basketball Association included no Milwaukee Bucks, but two of the game's brightest stars had been drafted by the franchise. One of them left the Bucks at his own request, and the other one never joined them.

Kareem Abdul-Jabbar made thousands of friends among a sellout crowd of 10,938 at the Milwaukee Arena before the All-Star tip-off by wearing Bucks warm-ups, while Julius Erving heard boos when he was named the game's Most Valuable Player. It was that kind of day.

Defense and teamwork, normally orphans in these affairs, played key roles in the West's 125-124 victory over the East. The West had an unheard of 42 assists, and the game ended when Paul Westphal stole the ball from Pete Maravich with seven seconds to play. Naturally, Maravich said he was fouled, but nobody was listening.

Erving's MVP selection, on the other hand, got plenty of attention. He scored 30 points to tie Bob McAdoo for game honors, and his 12 rebounds topped everyone. In one whirlwind stretch of the fourth quarter, Erving scored 11 of the East's 15 points. Still, he was on the losing team, and that didn't sit well with the customers or even some of the players.

The fans booed when NBA Commissioner Larry O'Brien presented the award, but it was hard to tell whether they were booing Erving or the media that had voted him in. Neither was really at fault, because TV had dictated that the ballots be cast with four minutes to play and the outcome very much in doubt.

"It's one of the most foolish things I've ever seen," said veteran Golden State forward Rick Barry. "They take the vote before they know what's going to happen. The guy they voted for made a big mistake at the end of the game. How can that guy be the Most Valuable Player?

"Julius played for one stretch, and it helped them to get where they were. Fine. But it had no relation to the outcome. How can they do that? They should have two awards. One for the Most Valuable Player and one for the outstanding player. The outstanding player is not always the most valuable."

Erving didn't seem concerned about being named either. "I just try to go out and play as hard as I can," he said. "I'm not looking for any particular award or reward. There was no time to think about being offended or anything like that when I was named and they booed me."

Westphal appeared to be the people's choice. The Phoenix guard finished with 20 points, scored what proved to be the winning basket on an uncontested dunk and had the key steal against Maravich. And the crowd was chanting his name while O'Brien tried to talk.

Westphal himself had no complaints about the process. "Dr. J had a fantastic game," he said. "And so did four or five guys on our team. I wasn't bothered by that at all."

The fans' second choice might have been Abdul-Jabbar, who led the West with 21 points and got a standing ovation in pre-game introductions after warming up in Milwaukee colors. It was a grand gesture, and it would have been even grander if he'd done it on purpose. But he'd left his own stuff in Los Angeles and had to borrow a jacket from the Bucks' trainer.

Abdul-Jabbar was relieved to see he'd been forgiven for demanding a trade out of Milwaukee a little more than two years earlier. As for Erving, who had been drafted by the Bucks in 1972 even though he had left the University of Massachusetts a year early to play for the ABA's Virginia Squires and had spurned them before the 1976-'77 season when he joined the Philadelphia 76ers... well, he was philosophical. He pointed out that he hadn't come to enter a popularity contest, so he didn't see how he could lose one. He did lose the game, though, and it was a memorable one.

ALVAREZ RECRUITS FOR THE ROSE BOWL

FEBRUARY 14, 1990

Within 24 hours of being introduced as the new University of Wisconsin football coach, Barry Alvarez hit the road trying to change minds and perceptions. One of the stops on his whirlwind tour of the state was Racine, where he went to the home of running back Brent Moss, who was leaning toward Michigan State. He also visited with Moss' high school teammate at Racine Park, receiver J.C. Dawkins, who was leaning toward Purdue. Another stop was Marinette where Jeff Messenger, an option quarterback, was thinking of playing football at Iowa or Michigan State or baseball at Arkansas.

Moss changed his mind and committed to Wisconsin before Alvarez walked out the door. Dawkins and Messenger hopped on board, too.

Alvarez was providing the two things his new football program at Wisconsin most urgently needed, some master salesmanship and a little elbow grease to recover from the train wreck that his predecessor, Don Morton, had left him. The Badgers had won exactly six games in three seasons under Morton, and for a very good reason. They didn't have very many good players.

Six weeks after taking the job, Alvarez demonstrated that that was about to change when he revealed his first recruiting class on national signing day. Included in the group of 23 players were Moss, Dawkins, Messenger and eight others who would start for the Badgers' Rose Bowl champions four years later.

Alvarez promised to build a fence around Wisconsin that would keep the top local football prospects at home, but two of the best hopped the fence in that first year. Jim Flanigan of Southern Door High School picked Notre Dame, and Milwaukee Marquette's Greg McThomas chose Michigan. Both were linebackers, and both were Parade All-Americans.

Flanigan went on to become an outstanding player with the Irish and then put together a solid 10-year pro career. McThomas, who at different times during the process had given verbal commitments to Wisconsin and Notre Dame, was just a backup after he settled on Michigan.

Alvarez had no illusions that he could compete for national recruits of that caliber when he started out, but he knew that he needed to get enough quality homegrown players to at least lay a foundation for future success. Moss, a 5-foot-9, 190-pound running back who had rushed for 2,223 yards and scored 31 touchdowns the previous fall, was a good place to start. Four years later, he turned out to be the Big Ten offensive player of the year and the Most Valuable Player in the Rose Bowl.

The Badgers turned Messenger into a cornerback, and he led them in interceptions and was a first-team all-Big Ten choice during the turnaround 1993 season. Dawkins caught 32 passes in that Rose Bowl season. Among other in-state recruits, offensive lineman Mike Verstegen of Kimberly was honorable mention all-Big Ten, and Mike Thompson of Portage started on the defensive line.

Alvarez had one advantage when he signed on at Wisconsin. He'd learned the Chicago area well in his time as an assistant coach at Notre Dame. Morton had been shut out there in his last year, but Alvarez was determined to reestablish a Wisconsin pipeline to Illinois. He signed five Illinois players, although his best out-of-state recruits came from further away. Joe Rudolph, another future all-conference offensive lineman, was from Pennsylvania, while tight end Michael Roan came from Iowa and linebacker Yusef Burgess from New York.

National recruiting "experts" were hardly blown away by the 43-year-old Alvarez's first effort. "It's not outstanding," said *SuperPrep* magazine's Allen Wallace, who ranked the class near the bottom of the Big Ten. "You're not going to find kids on their list who have been recruited by schools all over the country. It's impossible to expect them to put together a great class."

Alvarez wasn't fazed. "All the evaluations by analysts go out the door when they show up," he said.

Four years later, his first recruits showed up in a big way.

CAMBRIDGE'S KENSETH WINS DAYTONA 500

FEBRUARY 15, 2009

After 36 straight disappointments, Matt Kenseth was starting to wonder. He'd never run that many NASCAR Sprint Cup Races in a row before without finishing first in at least one of them.

But he'd gone winless in 2007 for the first time in seven years, and here he was starting a backup car four spots from the rear in auto racing's answer to the Super Bowl. What could happen to him next, a rainout?

Well, not quite, but close enough.

The 35-year-old Kenseth had experienced plenty of weather growing up in Cambridge, Wis., but he'd never appreciated precipitation more than he did on a grey Sunday along the eastern coast of Florida when a driving rain helped him win his first Daytona 500. Or as some people would call this particular edition, the Daytona 380.

That's how many miles Kenseth drove before the rest of the rain-shortened race was called off with him at the front of the pack. Mother Nature's timing couldn't have been better. If the wet stuff had started even a minute earlier, Kenseth would have finished second. Instead, he posted his biggest victory during one of the lowest periods of his career.

"Yesterday I was sitting in the motor home telling (wife) Katie that I was really getting fed up with not winning, with not being a contender," he said after the race. "It was actually starting to weigh on me more than I thought. When you don't win for awhile, you kind of wonder if you're ever going to win again."

Kenseth didn't have time for that kind of reflection when he started the 146th lap of the race running second to Elliott Sadler. Sadler strayed wide, and Kenseth dived inside of him to take the lead with Kevin Harvick right on his tail. Moments later, Aric Almirola spun on the backstretch and the yellow flag came out, directing the drivers to hold their positions. That's when Kenseth saw the first raindrops on his windshield.

The field ran six stately laps behind the pace car while NASCAR officials pored over the weather reports. The radar was adamant. It would be raining for hours. The race was over.

And so was Kenseth's personal dry spell. The following week he went to Fontana, Calif., for the Auto Club 500 and won there, too. There were four short rain delays in Fontana, but nothing to prevent him from becoming only the fourth driver in NASCAR history to capture the first two points races of the season. This was more like it.

When Kenseth began racing on the short tracks around Wisconsin at the age of 16, he never dreamed he would rule Daytona some day. But he won championships in Madison, Slinger and Kaukauna and later graduated to NASCAR's Busch Series where he finished second one year and third the next before getting a ride in the big time.

NASCAR's premier series was called the Winston Cup then, and Kenseth made himself right at home by getting selected as its Rookie of the Year in 2000. Three years later, he became the first Wisconsin racer since Alan Kulwicki to win the driver's title. But he caused a fuss because he won only one race.

NASCAR responded by creating a season-ending playoff format among the points leaders called the "Chase for the Cup." Critics dubbed it "The Kenseth Rule." Kenseth didn't care what they called it as long as he got to participate. He and Jimmie Johnson were the only drivers who qualified for all five of the first Chases, but he wasn't happy when he finished 11th in the standings in 2008.

Something had to change, and in Kenseth's case, it was his crew chief. Drew Blickensderfer was hired to take over in the pits, and the revised team got off to a rocky start at Daytona when Kenseth's No. 17 Ford was damaged in a qualifying crash. That forced him to start 39th in the 43-car field in his backup machine.

It didn't matter where he started, though, because he had the $1,536,388 winner's check when he finished. The victory was the 17th of his career and easily the most satisfying, regardless of how many laps he had to run to get it.

Kenseth said the circumstances didn't make him think any less of the victory. He was no longer a worried man. "Winning," he said, "cures a lot of things."

JOLENE ANDERSON SETS STATE SCORING RECORD

FEBRUARY 16, 2004

Before the 34 points, the 14 rebounds and the five assists, there was a short musical interlude. Jolene Anderson couldn't even think about setting a state scoring record until after she'd sung the national anthem on a frigid Monday night in Port Wing.

The most productive player in Wisconsin girls' basketball history was also the busiest. In addition to her vocal and athletic duties, the South Shore High School star also played in the band. Just not on game nights. Even she had her limits.

But she didn't have many when South Shore romped to an 81-45 Indianhead Conference victory over Drummond. With 27.2 seconds left in the first half, Anderson's six-foot, put-back shot broke the Wisconsin girls' all-time scoring record of 2,601 points set by Niagara's Anna DeForge. Anderson finished the night with 2,622 points and the second leg of the state's individual triple crown.

She'd already set the single-game record of 58 points a month earlier in a game against Bayfield, and she was on her way to the single-season mark of 957. Not what you'd normally expect from a player at a high school with 95 students.

But as Anderson explained once to the *Milwaukee Journal Sentinel*, there are advantages to growing up in a very small town. "There is really nothing to do besides sports," she said.

Well, there's music, too. In addition to playing trumpet and saxophone in the band, Anderson sang the *Star Spangled Banner* before every home game. She also was an all-state honorable mention volleyball player for three years, and she qualified for the state high school track meet in the long jump and the shot put.

But basketball was clearly her best sport. She would score 259 points after the Drummond game to give her a total of 2,881. In the process, she led her team to a 24-2 record and the state championship game. South Shore lost the title game to Racine Prairie, but not before she broke the tournament record with 46 points in the semifinals.

Jim and Julie Anderson suspected they had a special athlete on their hands when they found Jolene spending most of her spare time shooting hoops in the hayloft of their barn at the tender age of seven. The barn was two miles outside of Port Wing, which is quite a few more miles than that from anywhere you've ever heard of except Lake Superior.

It didn't matter whether the winter wind was blowing through the cracks in the barn or the summer sun was baking it, Jolene was there. Both of her parents had played basketball, but Julie was the better of the two, and her daughter rewarded her support by breaking her high school scoring records.

Naturally, as Anderson's numbers grew, so did the number of doubters After all, it was just girls' basketball, and the competition was decidedly small time.

On the other hand, in a school district that covered 300 square miles, the available practice partners were few and far between, so Anderson had the advantage of playing against boys much of the time. "She plays basketball like a basketball player, boy or girl," said her coach, Don Moore.

People understood what he meant when Anderson began competing in Amateur Athletic Union tournaments in the summer after her freshman year and starring in national tournaments from Fort Worth, Tex., to Detroit.

She was named Miss Basketball by the Wisconsin Basketball Coaches Association following her senior year, and then she proceeded to erase all of the remaining doubts about her national credentials at the University of Wisconsin. She led the Big Ten in scoring twice and became the school's all-time leading scorer – men or women – with 2,312 points over her four years with the Badgers.

The Connecticut Sun of the Women's National Basketball Association drafted her in the second round in 2008, and she averaged four points a game as a rookie. She was not quite as versatile, however, as she was in high school. She didn't sing the national anthem in the pros.

WEARY WITTE TAKES HOME THE GOLD

FEBRUARY 17, 2002

"Sick and tired" would be the best way to describe Chris Witte when she arrived at the Salt Lake City Olympics.

The West Allis speedskating star had lost her stamina, her technique and every World Cup race she'd skated during the 2001-'02 season. A double-medal winner at the Nagano Olympics in 1998, she hadn't posted so much as a third-place finish in a World Cup event, and that hadn't happened to her in seven years on the circuit.

Something was wrong. If she practiced hard one day, she'd have to spend the next day resting, a routine hardly calculated to get a world class athlete ready for her sport's biggest stage. And then a month before the Games, the doctors came up with an explanation. She had mononucleosis, a strength-sapping viral infection that left her drained and most experts convinced she had no chance at Salt Lake.

Witte was determined to prove those experts wrong as she joined Catriona Le May Doan at the starting line in the 15th of 18 pairs in the 1,000-meter race. Le May Doan, considered to be the fastest women's sprinter in the world, had already won the 500 gold, but Witte had a game plan. She figured if she could go out fast enough in the first 200 meters, she'd have a chance to chase the Canadian down on the last straightaway.

And so she skated the fastest opener of her career, covering the 200 meters in 17.88 seconds, and then finding the strength to not only edge out Le May Doan but to set a world record at 1 minute 13.83 seconds. All that left was the waiting.

The record Witte had broken belonged to Germany's Sabine Voelker, and Voelker was skating in the 17th pair. Witte said she felt like her head was going to explode as she watched Voelker cover the first 600 meters .09 seconds faster than she had. But the German faded, coming home in 1:13.96 and settling for silver while another American, Jennifer Rodriguez, who had lived and trained in Milwaukee in the 1990s, claimed the bronze.

Gerard Kemkers, Witte's former coach who was now employed by the Dutch team, said he believed in Witte all along.

"She is something special at the Olympics," he said. "She might skate the whole year, 10th, 10th, 10th, but when the Olympics come, she will step up. You put your money on that."

Chris Witte

Witte was 26 at the time and had won silver and bronze medals at Nagano. She won the silver in the 1,000 meters and the bronze in the 1,500. She also had competed in cycling in the 2000 Summer Games at Sydney, Australia.

Now there was a different way to describe Chris Witte: "Gold medalist."

JANSEN SHEDS BURDENS BY WINNING GOLD

FEBRUARY 18, 1994

Dan Jansen turned speaker after he retired from speedskating.

He apologized to a city, and then he thrilled a country. Dan Jansen had struck gold at last.

In his final Olympic race, one that he had no business winning, West Allis' world champion shattered a record and brought a dramatic end to six years of pain and frustration. The distance was 1,000 meters, the place was Hamar, Norway, and the story was irresistible.

It began at the Calgary Games in 1988 when the 22-year-old World Cup star was expected to medal twice and fell twice instead. Just hours before the 500-meter final, he learned that his sister Jane had died of leukemia at the age of 27, and 100 meters into the race, he went sprawling. Four days later, he was skating ahead of everyone in the 1,000 and he fell again with one lap to go.

When he finished fourth in the 500 and a disastrous 26th in the 1,000 at the 1992 Games in Albertville, France, questions were inevitably raised about his head and his heart. And when he slipped in the final turn of the 500 at the Lillehammer Games and came home eighth, his best chance for the biggest prize in his sport appeared to vanish in a spray of ice.

An icon among speedskating fans throughout the world, the runaway favorite in the 500 and the only man ever to skate one under 36 seconds, Dan Jansen had failed in the Olympics again. "Sorry, Milwaukee," he said after the race, and he meant it.

This was on Monday. The 1,000 was Thursday, and Jansen was given little chance to win it, or even to finish among the top three. He'd posted respectable times at the distance during the World Cup season, but no fewer than seven skaters had posted better ones. Two of them raced in the first pair.

Igor Zhelezovsky of Belarus had dominated the 1,000 all year the way Jansen had dominated the 500. He was everyone's choice to win the gold, particularly with Russia's Sergei Klevchenya in the same pair to push him. And push him he did. Both skaters broke the Olympic record with Zhelezovsky edging the Russian by thirteen-hundredths of a second. Two pairs later, it was Jansen's turn.

A blazing first 600 meters left him one-tenth of a second ahead of Zhelezovsky's pace, but could he keep it up? And then Jansen slipped coming out of the seventh turn, and the crowd held its breath. But the 1,000 is a more forgiving race than the 500, and Jansen was able to brush the ice with his hand and dig in. He crossed the finish line in 1 minute 12.43 seconds, breaking the world record by eleven-hundredths of a second.

Three skaters who had better personal bests in the 1,000 than Jansen had yet to skate, but none of them came close to that time. When the last pair cleared the ice, Jansen mounted the podium, looked to the sky and gave a little salute. The salute was for his sister Jane.

But there was another Jane about to experience an Olympic moment. As the national anthem played, Jansen's wife Robin made her way down the stands carrying their nine-month-old daughter in her arms. Little Jane, who had been named after the aunt she'd never known, was delivered to her dad, who made one last Olympic lap.

With his daughter in his right arm and a bouquet of flowers in his left he skated around the rink, a spotlight following him the whole way. The light caught the gold draped around Dan Jansen's neck.

BLAIR WINS RECORD FOURTH GOLD MEDAL

FEBRUARY 19, 1994

For Bonnie Blair "Olympic glory" was an oxymoron. The world's greatest women's speedskater participated in the world's grandest competition for only two reasons. She loved her sport, and she loved to win.

But when the 29-year-old pride of Champaign, Ill., who was now living in Pewaukee, crossed the finish line in the 500-meter race at Hamar, Norway, glory caught up to her whether she wanted it or not. Winning the race by a breathtaking .36-second margin over Canadian runner-up Susan Auch made Blair only the fourth American woman ever to win four Olympic gold medals. She was also the first ever to win the same event for three Olympics in a row.

What's more, she was just getting started.

Four days later, Blair won the 1,000-meter race by an even more preposterous 1.38 seconds over silver medalist Anke Baier. That was her last Olympic race, and it left her all alone in two major Olympic categories. No other American woman had ever won five golds before, and no American athlete of either gender had won six medals overall in the Winter Games. She'd also captured a bronze in the 1,000 at the 1988 Games in Calgary.

As big a part of Olympic history as Blair was, Olympic history wasn't even a small part of Blair. Throughout the Lillehammer Games, she would talk only about her last race or her next one, never about the entire body of her work. Finally, when the Games were over and she was asked what all of her accomplishments said about her, Blair pronounced herself "stumped."

She may have been the only one who didn't know how good she was. She won the Sullivan Award in 1992 as the world's top amateur athlete, and *Sports Illustrated* made her its "Sportswoman of the Year" two years later. She'd also shaken the hands of three presidents and been named grand marshal of the Indianapolis 500 auto race.

But Blair's greatest admirers were the people who'd been around her the longest. The "Blair Bunch," a group of 60 close friends and relatives dressed in white sweatshirts and gold hats, gained fame of their own as they cheered her every move in Hamar. The group was headed by her mother Eleanor, and it was made up mostly of people from Champaign. Wisconsin didn't adopt her until 1992 when she moved to the Milwaukee area to train at the Pettit Center.

Bonnie Blair

Blair was the quintessential grassroots athlete. She was the youngest of six kids, and her father missed her birth because he was watching the other five compete in a speedskating meet. She was able to compete in her first Olympics in Sarajevo in 1984 only because the Champaign Policemen's Benevolent Association collected $7,000 to pay for her training expenses in Europe. She placed eighth in the 500 meters, the only Olympic race she'd ever skated and failed to medal in.

And then she won gold in the 500 and bronze in the 1,000 at Calgary in 1988 before going on to double gold in Albertville, France, in 1992. It all set the stage for her 500 triumph in Norway. Skating in the third pair, she set a track record on her way to the historic gold and then celebrated the way Bonnie Blair would be expected to celebrate.

She climbed into the stands to be with her mom.

FEBRUARY 69

BUCKS TRADE RAY ALLEN TO SEATTLE

FEBRUARY 20, 2003

Ray Allen

The Milwaukee Bucks were in Seattle for a Friday game, and the rumors started flying on Thursday morning. By the time the team got to KeyArena for a light practice that afternoon, the place was packed with media.

Ray Allen's jaw dropped when he first heard of a possible deal from a reporter while he was making his way to the weight room. A couple of hours later, he learned he was now a Seattle SuperSonic.

Allen's disbelief was echoed in Milwaukee when word got back that the Bucks had swung their biggest trade in years, and one that had all the makings of also being one of their worst ever.

They'd given up their leading scorer, a three-time all-star and potentially the best three-point shooter in the history of the NBA along with backup guards Kevin Ollie and Ronald Murray and what turned out to be a first-round draft choice for point guard Gary Payton and swingman Desmond Mason.

Payton, a nine-time All-Star, was 34 years old and a free agent who refused to give the Bucks any assurances that he would re-sign in Milwaukee after the season was over. Mason was 25, two years younger than Allen, and his major claim to fame was finishing second in the NBA slam-dunk contest.

Critics of the trade envisioned the Bucks giving up perhaps the best pure shooter in the game and maybe even a future Hall of Famer, plus a No. 1 choice, for a sixth man with a 14.1 scoring average and the use of Payton for 28 games before he left to join another team. And that's exactly what happened.

Payton averaged 19.6 points per game for Milwaukee for the rest of the season and then left the following year for the Los Angeles Lakers with no compensation to the Bucks. An enormous fan favorite in Seattle and the career franchise leader in scoring and assists, he'd made it clear that he wanted to test the free-agent market after the Sonics had refused to sign him to a multi-year contract extension.

Mason started 25 games and averaged 14.8 points for the Bucks over the remainder of the 2002-'03 season, but he was traded in 2005 along with another first-round draft choice and cash for Jamaal Magloire.

Making the Allen-Payton trade even more puzzling was the fact that the Bucks already had a starting point guard in Sam Cassell, who like Payton, saw himself as a scorer. What's more, they had virtually no one to play inside. It seemed likely that if they were to deal Allen at all it would be for a big man.

But Allen, who had become almost as popular in Milwaukee after six-and-a-half years as Payton was in Seattle, was frequently at odds with coach George Karl. Karl had coached Payton in Seattle, and he thought he brought the kind of defensive toughness the Bucks would need to succeed in the playoffs. General Manager Ernie Grunfeld agreed, insisting that Payton and Cassell would get along just fine in the Bucks' backcourt.

It was never totally clear who instigated the trade. Was it Karl, was it Grunfeld or was it owner Herb Kohl? The Bucks had a $57 million payroll at the time, and it was reported that Kohl had ordered Grunfeld to cut costs because the franchise was on the threshold of having to pay the league luxury tax. Allen's $12 million-plus salary was wiped off the books by the deal.

The team was also for sale at the time, and a lower payroll would make it a more attractive commodity. There were widespread reports that Michael Jordan was interested in buying the franchise and moving it to Las Vegas. Kohl would later take the team off the market.

Neither Payton nor Allen played in the Friday night game in Seattle, which the Bucks lost, 88-58. They lost 12 of their next 19 while Payton was getting assimilated, but then they took an 8-1 streak into a first-round playoff series with New Jersey.

Payton averaged 18.5 points in the series, which the Bucks lost in six games. And then he was gone before the 2003-'04 season opener.

So was Karl. So was Grunfeld. And in two more years, so was Mason. Five years later, Allen averaged 17.4 points per game as his latest team, the Boston Celtics, won the NBA championship.

CONLEY DEFIES BRAVES, STAYS WITH CELTICS

FEBRUARY 21, 1959

Before Michael Jordan couldn't hit the breaking ball or Bo Jackson couldn't stay healthy, there was Gene Conley.

Only special athletes can even consider playing two big-league sports at the same time, and the 6-foot-8, 225-pound Conley was special. He pitched in two All-Star games for the Milwaukee Braves and played on three National Basketball Association championship teams with the Boston Celtics. But even in the fifties, the two schedules overlapped.

And that was the Braves' problem with their veteran right-hander when they opened spring training on a Saturday at Bradenton, Fla., while the Celtics were getting ready to face Minneapolis in the NBA Finals. Manager Fred Haney expected Conley to be throwing strikes, but Conley wasn't through pulling down rebounds.

When Conley failed to report, Haney threatened to suspend him. Conley didn't care. "I couldn't work out if I was there, because I don't have a contract," he said. "They want me to take a 25% cut, and I'm dissatisfied. Nobody from the Braves has been in touch with me for a month, and I'm not reporting for training until I sign."

Baseball's rules were on Conley's side. The Braves couldn't suspend him until the season started, but all that did was frustrate them, because they knew their pitcher had a lot of work to do. He'd been their fourth starter when they won the pennant in 1957, but he was a sore-armed 0-6 in '58.

A clause in the standard contract prohibited Conley from playing pro basketball, but the Braves said they had waived it with the understanding that he'd come to spring training on time. Conley had played the 1952-'53 season with the Celtics, and then he'd interrupted his basketball career for five years at Milwaukee's request before going back to them in 1958.

An angry Birdie Tebbetts, the Braves' executive vice president, pointed out that the team had paid Conley the princely average of $22,500 over the last five years including World Series money. That only annoyed Conley, who said it was nobody's business what he made.

Despite his struggles on the mound in 1958, Conley was well worth fighting over. He'd been the minor league player of the year in 1953 before he'd caught on with the Braves for good the following season. A 14-game winner in 1954, he finished third in the Rookie of the Year balloting behind Wally Moon and Ernie Banks, but ahead of teammate Henry Aaron. Conley also pitched in the 1954 and '55 All-Star games.

While not a prolific basketball scorer, he was a good defender and rebounder who enjoyed a six-year NBA career even though he'd taken five seasons off in his prime. When he started having arm problems, it was suggested that he might want to give up baseball, but his response to that was, "Are you kidding? I'd never quit baseball."

The Celtics were glad he felt the same way about basketball when he helped them to a four-game sweep of the Lakers in the 1959 title series, scoring 10 points in the final game. But 10 days earlier, on March 31, the Braves shipped Conley to Philadelphia in a six-player trade that brought them veteran catcher Stan Lopata.

The deal was engineered by Phillies General Manager John Quinn, who had left the Braves' front office just two months earlier. Quinn believed Conley's arm was just fine, and Conley rewarded his confidence by posting a 12-7 record and a 3.00 earned run average in the 1959 season. Conley pitched one more season with Philadelphia and three more with the Boston Red Sox before retiring with a lifetime record of 91-96.

His hoops career lasted one year longer. In all, he played four seasons with Boston and two more with the New York Knicks before leaving the game in 1964 with a 5.9-point average. It was time. He hadn't had an off-season in five years.

Gene Conley

THE MIRACLE ON ICE

FEBRUARY 22, 1980

All Mark Johnson wanted was to make the United States Olympic team. The 22-year-old phenom from Madison, Wis., was widely regarded as the best college hockey player in America, and he'd grown up with the game, starring at Madison Memorial High School before joining his dad at the University of Wisconsin. But that was the problem.

Badgers coach Bob Johnson had had a long running feud with Herb Brooks when Brooks was coaching at the University of Minnesota, and now Brooks was coaching the U.S. Olympians. Would Johnson's bitter rivalry with Brooks cost his son a chance to skate at the Winter Games?

The answer was an emphatic no. Brooks told Mark Johnson in Oslo, Norway, during the team's pre-Olympic tour that he not only wanted him as a player, he wanted him as a leader. Johnson was relieved that his family ties didn't get him cut. "Hey," he said, "stranger things have happened in hockey." He certainly had that right.

The strangest of all happened at Lake Placid, N.Y., when the U.S. team stunned the sporting world by beating the Soviet Union, 4-3, in the Olympic semifinals. It couldn't have happened without Johnson's two goals, and by all logic, it shouldn't have happened at all.

The Soviets were tough, talented and most of all experienced in the international game. They had seven players back from the team that won the gold medal in 1976, and they'd won the last four golds dating back to 1960.

The Americans, on the other hand, were a collection of unpaid collegians and NHL hopefuls. The average age on the 20-man team was 22, and the oldest player was Mike Eruzione, 25, who was ignored by the pros after a four-year career at Boston University. Everyone knew they were totally outclassed when the Soviets beat them, 10-3, in an exhibition game at Madison Square Garden a week before the Olympics.

Some believed Brooks' incredibly demanding conditioning drills and sometimes acid tongue were designed to unite the team – against him. He told his players that they weren't talented enough to win on talent alone, that they had to outwork their opponents.

But Brooks' conditioning paid off as the Americans consistently outlasted their opponents, outscoring them, 61-27, in the second and third periods in their seven games at Lake Placid. They beat Sweden, Czechoslovakia, Norway, Romania and West Germany to take a 5-0 record into the semifinals against the Soviet Union, which was also 5-0. The difference was the Soviets had been seeded first; the Americans, seventh.

This was the height of the Cold War, and American flags were everywhere in the crowd when the two teams faced off at center ice. The fans were quickly disappointed when the Soviets scored the game's first goal.

Then Buzz Schneider, a holdover from the 1976 Olympic team and a former Milwaukee Admiral, tied the game. Schneider was one of three U.S. players with Wisconsin ties. Bobby Suter, a onetime Madison East High School star and Johnson's teammate at Wisconsin, was also on the roster.

The Soviet Union went ahead again, 2-1, only to have Johnson tie the game once more with his first goal with one second remaining in the first period. But the Soviets were relentless. They would take 38 shots during the game, and when they reclaimed the lead at 3-2 going into the third period, no one would have been surprised if the U.S. had folded.

Instead, Johnson scored again on a power play 8 minutes 39 seconds into the period, setting the stage for the most famous goal in Olympic history. It was scored by the captain, Eruzione, two minutes later.

Fans lined the route as the team bus crept from the arena to the post-game press conference. They were banging on the bus when one of the players began singing *God Bless America*, and the others joined in. Everyone seemed to forget that the players still had work to do. Awaiting them was a tough team from Finland and the gold medal game two days later. Lose it, and the U.S. would finish fourth and fail to get even a bronze.

Typically, the Americans fell behind, 2-1. But then they scored three goals in the final period to win, 4-2. Johnson assisted on the go-ahead goal and scored the last one, giving him five goals and six assists in seven games. And yet he insisted that the Soviets were still the best in the world. "It just happened on one night that we beat them," he said. "I don't know if it will ever happen again."

Once was enough.

Mark Johnson

72   365 BEST WISCONSIN SPORTS STORIES

INCOMPARABLE HEIDEN WINS FIFTH GOLD

FEBRUARY 23, 1980

Eric Heiden

Before Madison native Eric Heiden could make Olympic history, he wanted to witness it. The greatest speedskater the world had ever known was facing the biggest event of his life on Saturday morning in Lake Placid, N.Y. It would be a grueling test against an international field of champions, and, by all logic, Heiden should have spent his Friday in a peaceful setting that wouldn't drain his emotions.

But the United States hockey team was scheduled to take on the heavily favored Soviet Union, starting in the late afternoon, and there was no way Heiden wanted to miss that. So he spent his time cheering a "Miracle on Ice." Close to 12 hours later, he created another one.

As shocking as the American hockey upset was, it was no less likely than what Heiden did when he skated away with his fifth gold medal of the Games, winning the 10,000-meter race and bettering the world record by more than six seconds.

American swimmer Mark Spitz had won seven golds in Munich in 1972, but three of those were in relay races. No Olympian had ever won five by himself, and none would again until another American swimmer, Michael Phelps, dominated his sport in Beijing 28 years later, winning five individual golds and three more in relays for a total of eight. Heiden's five individual golds were more than the whole American team had won in any Winter Games since 1932.

Speedskating is a sport of specialists. There are sprinters, and there are all-arounders, and normally they cross paths only in the 1,500-meter race. But there was nothing normal about Heiden's performance at Lake Placid.

Eight days before his climactic triumph at 10,000 meters he had edged out Russian world record-holder Yevgeny Kulikov by milliseconds at 500 meters, breaking the Olympic record in the process. And then over the next week, he'd blazed through the 5,000, the 1,000 and the 1,500, all in Olympic record time.

That left just the 10,000, skating's toughest race. If Heiden could add that to his gold medal collection, it would be the equivalent of the 100-yard dash champion winning the Olympic marathon. Heiden had his doubts going into the final race. He wasn't sure he had the experience to win it.

Standing between him and his fifth gold was the Soviet Union's Viktor Loshkin, the world record-holder at 10,000 meters. As luck would have it, Heiden and Loshkin skated in the same pair. When they were done, they were barely in the same time zone.

Heiden crossed the finish line in 14 minutes 28.13 seconds, beating Loshkin by almost eight seconds and the world record by more than six. Suddenly he was sharing the spotlight with the U.S. hockey team.

Unlike the hockey players, though, he wasn't comfortable there. He called the hype surrounding his accomplishment "The Great Whoopee" and while he was polite to the press, it was clear he could live quite happily without his new-found notoriety. About the only trapping of fame he truly enjoyed was turning over his gold, skintight racing suit to the Smithsonian.

"We have no idea how to train to beat him," said Norwegian coach Sten Stenson. "We just hope he retires."

Stenson got his wish when Heiden hung up his skates after the 1980 season at the age of 21 to become a pre-med student at Stanford. He said he'd wanted to be a doctor ever since he was a little kid, and now was the time.

"You can only use that athletic talent when you're young," Heiden said.

Nobody on ice ever used it better.

McGuire Spurns NCAA Tournament

FEBRUARY 24, 1970

"Power politics," fumed Al McGuire. "Jealousy." And he was just getting warmed up.

The field had been announced for the 25-team NCAA basketball tournament, and Marquette's always excitable coach was beside himself. Of course, his Warriors were in. With a 19-3 record and a top-ten ranking in both wire-service polls they could hardly be left out. But the problem wasn't whether they'd be invited. It was where.

"I feel a power complex within the NCAA has buckled under and tried to treat us like little brothers," McGuire raged, and that was before he questioned the ethics of the Mideast selection committee. "They worry more about giving a T-shirt to a ballplayer than their own ethics," he said.

"Hogwash," fired back Kentucky coach Adolph Rupp, one of the five committee members. "He's apt to say anything."

No doubt, that was always true, but this was something special even for McGuire. The committee had moved his team out of its home Mideast Regional in Dayton, Ohio, and plunked it into the Midwest and Fort Worth, Texas, and he wasn't about to tolerate the slight. So he didn't.

After more than five hours of meetings with his Athletic Director Sam Sauceda, his players and members of his athletic board, McGuire announced that the Warriors wouldn't be going to the NCAA tournament at all. They would be accepting a bid from the National Invitation Tournament instead.

The decision shocked the college basketball establishment, and it would later become illegal, but the maverick Warriors considered it a matter of principle. As Marquette star Dean Meminger put it, "You must stand up to the establishment."

You must also do the math, and that was a little tenuous. Only two at-large teams could be sent to the Mideast, and the committee picked Notre Dame and Jacksonville ahead of Marquette. Jacksonville was 20-1 and Notre Dame was 20-5. McGuire reasoned that his team played a better schedule than Jacksonville and had a better record than Notre Dame.

Of course, Notre Dame played a better schedule than Marquette, and Jacksonville had a better record, and the Irish had beaten the Warriors in double overtime that year in South Bend. But McGuire theorized that the real issue might have been something between him and the committee members.

It was not out of the question. The Warriors had beaten Rupp's Kentucky team, 81-74, in the regional tournament the previous year in Madison, and the two coaches weren't exactly golfing buddies.

But none of that mattered now. Kentucky was going to the NCAA regional in Dayton, and Marquette was off to the NIT in New York where, incidentally, McGuire liked to recruit. As it turned out, the Warriors had a much better trip.

With four starters back from the previous year's 24-5 team, they dismissed Massachusetts, 62-55, and mauled Utah, 83-63, in the first two rounds before eliminating Louisiana State and Pete Maravich, 101-79, in the semifinal. That set up a championship match with St. John's, which was coached by McGuire's friend Lou Carnesecca and led by 6-foot-11, 235-pound center Billy Paultz.

Paultz got 15 points and 17 rebounds, but the Redmen shot only 34%, and after Marquette won the game and the championship, 65-53, Carnesecca called the Warriors the best defensive team he'd ever played against. While Meminger was named the tournament's Most Valuable Player, Marquette's leading scorer against St. John's was Grafton product Jeff Sewell, who had 22 points.

Kentucky, meanwhile, got a first-round bye in Dayton and then drilled Notre Dame, 112-82, in a second-round matchup that might have featured Marquette if the Warriors had gotten their way. But then Rupp's top-ranked Wildcats fell, 106-100, to, of all teams, Jacksonville. The following week, 7-2 center Artis Gilmore would carry Jacksonville to the national championship game where it lost to UCLA.

There was no telling whether Marquette would have gotten that far, but the Warriors seemed content with their NIT championship. Said McGuire: "Frankly, I don't care what other people think about us being here."

JACK DEMPSEY STOPS BILL BRENNAN IN MILWAUKEE

FEBRUARY 25, 1918

It was a long way from the West Coast to the boxing rings of Wisconsin in the early 20th century, and Jack Dempsey made the trip just twice.

The first time he destroyed a lanky pretender named Homer Smith in less than one round at Racine's Lakeside Auditorium. Then a month later, he traveled to the Elite Roller Rink in Milwaukee where he took a long step on the road to the world heavyweight championship.

The rink on National Avenue held only 4,200 people, but it served as the site of some of Wisconsin's most storied pro fights. Dempsey's crushing sixth-round TKO of Bill Brennan was easily one of those.

Not many people in the Midwest had heard much about Dempsey before he took on the Irish contender, mainly because most of his fights had been fought in Colorado, Utah, Nevada and California. But he was running out of meal money, and he needed fights wherever he could find them. Brennan, the second-ranked heavyweight contender at the time, had met and befriended Dempsey in a New York gym a couple of years earlier, and he did him a favor by giving him the fight.

Brennan considered the bout to be no more than a tune-up for a match with Fred Fulton, who was considered the No. 1 challenger to heavyweight champion Jess Willard. In fact, according to one Dempsey biography, Brennan went to Dempsey's dressing room before the fight and apologized in advance for what he was about to do to him.

No apology was necessary. Different accounts of the fight had Dempsey putting the Irishman on the deck anywhere from four to six times before he stopped him in the sixth round. Brennan had gone down either three or four times in the second before being saved by the bell as Dempsey's corner pleaded with the referee to stop the fight. One story had Brennan's manager instructing his fighter to "keep away from his right," and then adding as an afterthought, "Keep away from his left, too."

Brennan could do neither in the sixth when Dempsey nailed him with a right cross that sent him spinning to the canvas, cracking his left ankle on the way down. Brennan dragged himself to his feet at the count of nine, but the referee stopped the fight seconds later.

Bill Brennan   Jack Dempsey

The victory made Dempsey enough meal money that he was able to wrap $150 in newspaper and send it to his mother. More important, it put him, instead of Brennan, in the ring with Fulton five months later in Harrison, N.J. Dempsey finished Fulton in the first round, and on the Fourth of July in 1919, he knocked out Willard in three rounds in Toledo, Ohio, to win the championship.

Dempsey, known as "The Manassa Mauler," would keep that belt for seven years and also knock out Brennan again in 12 rounds in a championship fight in 1920. In 1950 in an Associated Press poll, Dempsey was voted the greatest fighter of the half-century. Brennan's story didn't end nearly as happily. On June 15, 1924, he was gunned down by gangsters in a New York speakeasy.

Ten years later, on April 14, 1934, the Elite Roller Rink burned to the ground.

KENOSHA'S CONLEY LOSES BANTAMWEIGHT CROWN

FEBRUARY 26, 1911

Frank Conley was so tough that the kids in his grade school made him an honorary Irishman. One of Wisconsin's greatest boxers, Conley came to Kenosha as a little boy from Platania, Italy. He was born Francesco Conte, but his Irish friends at St. Mark's parochial school changed that to Frank Conley after he beat up a bully who outweighed him by 40 pounds. That's the story anyway, and nobody wanted to argue the point.

Whatever they called him, Conley's name was synonymous with fearlessness and grit. A natural bantamweight, he usually faced opponents bigger than he was because of a shortage of fighters in his weight class. But he was having the opposite problem when he took on Chicago's Johnny Coulon for the world bantamweight championship in New Orleans. He had to starve himself for eight days to make the 116-pound limit.

If Conley had won, it would have been worth the effort. He came into the scheduled 20-round bout with a small piece of the title, having knocked out Monte Attell in the 42nd round in Los Angeles when the crown was vacant in 1910. That got him recognized as the champion in California, but Coulon was king everywhere else.

Conley wanted to schedule the fight for 45 rounds. He didn't think anything less than that was a true test of a boxer's ability. Coulon compromised and agreed to 20. He clearly outpointed the challenger, winning all but two rounds, but Conley's backers went away convinced that their man would have won if the fight had gone 25 more. The champ seemed to think 20 had been hard enough.

"I consider Conley the best boy I ever met," said Coulon, a Hall of Fame fighter who held the title for four years. "I hit that chicken a million times..., but I didn't hurt him. I expected and got the toughest battle of my career."

Conley's head-down, bulldoggish style was not conducive to defense, and it didn't always conform to the rules. In a 1997 article for *The Ring* magazine, veteran boxing writer Pete Ehrmann quoted Coulon saying, "Conley tried butting me. I had a tooth longer than the others and as sharp as a tiger's fang. I must have made 20 holes in Conley's head before he quit butting."

Conley's head healed up in time for a rematch in Vernon, Calif., a year later, and Coulon beat him again in 20 rounds. But Coulon couldn't knock him out. Official records had Conley being knocked out only four times in 81 pro bouts, but he disputed both numbers. He said he'd had more than 500 fights, had been stopped just once and never been counted out.

Recordkeeping was sketchy in those days. The truth may have landed somewhere in between, but there was no doubt that Conley was one of the four or five best fighters ever to grow up in Wisconsin. He was one of just three to earn a claim to any portion of a world title. The other two were Milwaukee's Myron "Pinkey" Mitchell, who was proclaimed junior welterweight champion in 1922 through a poll taken by *The Boxing Blade*, and Eureka's Eddie McGoorty, who was recognized as the middleweight king in Australia in 1914.

According to an account by Ehrmann, future lightweight champion Johnny Dundee was credited with one of the four TKOs suffered by Conley. The bout went 19 rounds, and one of the spectators was a heavyweight contender named "Fireman" Jim Flynn. Flynn had taken a lot of punishment himself in his time, but he said of Conley, "That little fellow took a beating that would have sent a heavyweight to the hospital. He's the gamest kid in the world."

Conley retired with an official record of 37 victories, 11 losses, 10 draws and 23 no-decisions. He spent the rest of his life working in a mattress factory. It was a strange job for a battler who never looked for a soft place to land.

BO RYAN LEADS WISCONSIN TO BIG TEN TITLE

FEBRUARY 27, 2002

The question was whether Bo Ryan could compete in the Big Ten after winning four NCAA Division III championships at UW-Platteville. The answer he gave on the day he was hired at the University of Wisconsin was "wait and see."

The wait couldn't have been much shorter.

Eleven months after Ryan became the Badgers' coach, they mauled Michigan, 74-54, to clinch their first share of a Big Ten championship in 55 years. Leading a group that had lost four starters from an NCAA tournament team the year before, Ryan had no trouble adapting his trademark swing offense and cantankerous defense to the big time.

Wisconsin got 23 points from Kirk Penney, a sharp-shooting junior guard from New Zealand, and 21 from freshman Devin Harris of Wauwatosa against the Wolverines. The Badgers made 13 of 19 three-pointers, held Michigan scoreless for almost seven minutes of the first half and plainly delighted a sellout crowd of 17,142 at the Kohl Center.

It was the last thing anyone expected from an injury-plagued squad that had started the season with only eight scholarship players and had been picked to finish ninth in the Big Ten. The Badgers obliged the prognosticators by dropping two of their first three league games, but then they went to East Lansing and ended Michigan State's 53-game home winning streak. When they won their last six conference starts and earned the No. 1 seed in the Big Ten tournament, the 53-year-old Ryan had routed the doubters.

There was certainly no shortage of them in Madison when Athletic Director Pat Richter gave Ryan the job. Utah's Rick Majerus, a Milwaukee native and former Marquette coach, had been Wisconsin's first choice, but Majerus politely declined.

Richter had interviewed Ryan eight years earlier and taken Stu Jackson instead, but he atoned for his mistake this time by spiriting Ryan away from UW-Milwaukee. The only question Ryan's legion of state fans had then was "What took so long?"

After serving eight seasons as an assistant at Wisconsin under Bill Cofield and Steve Yoder, Ryan had taken over the program at Platteville, gone 9-17 his first year and proceeded to become a Division III legend. He won 353 games there and lost only 76 for a ridiculous .822 winning percentage, and he was named the division's national Coach of the Year four times. No coach on any level won more games than Ryan did in the 1990s.

Then he moved on to UW-Milwaukee and made the Panthers respectable immediately. An 8-19 team when he got there, they went 15-14 and 15-13 before he left to replace the fired Brad Soderberg, who had taken over for Dick Bennett four games into the 2000-'01 season.

Bennett took the Badgers to the Final Four in 2000, but not even he could win a Big Ten championship with them. Ryan won two in his first two tries. Wisconsin shared the throne with Indiana, Ohio State and Illinois in his first year and won it outright in his second. To no one's surprise, he was named Big Ten Coach of the Year both times.

The Badgers had signed him to a five-year contract for a reported $2 million, and he never made them sorry. In his second season, the team was 12-4 in the Big Ten and went three games deep into the NCAA tournament before losing to No. 1-ranked Kentucky. After that, Wisconsin was simply expected to succeed in the Big Ten.

But it was all new in 2002 when the Badgers ended a title drought that had begun in 1947. Ironically, that was the year Bo Ryan was born.

Bo Ryan

GREEN BAY BOBCATS GOLDEN IN "FIRST MIRACLE ON ICE"

FEBRUARY 28, 1960

Before the 1980 "Miracle on Ice," there was another United States Olympic hockey team that scored an improbable victory, although with much less fanfare. And just as the 1980 U.S. gold medal team had a distinct Wisconsin flavor, so did the 1960 team that won the U.S.'s first gold medal in hockey.

There were plenty of heroes on that 1960 team that knocked off the world's best at Squaw Valley Calif., and John Mayasich and Paul Johnson, both on loan from the Green Bay Bobcats, were certainly among them.

In the gold medal game against Czechoslovakia, played at 8 a.m. on the final Sunday of the Olympics, Mayasich set up the go-ahead goal in the third period to give the U.S. a 5-4 lead and assisted on another goal later in the period by Roger Christian. Trailing, 4-3, after two periods, the U.S. rallied for six goals, including a hat trick by Christian, to win in a 9-4 rout. Johnson also pitched in with an assist on the first U.S. goal of the game

Johnson, a native of West St. Paul, Minn., regarded as one of most explosive scorers in American hockey, left the Bobcats to join the U.S. Olympic team in early January. At the time, he was the leading scorer in the Central Hockey League, a semipro circuit loaded with talent back when the National Hockey League consisted of only six franchises. Mayasich, player-coach of the Bobcats, didn't join the Olympic team until more than a month later, just two days before the Winter Games were to begin.

After leading Eveleth High School to four consecutive unbeaten seasons from 1948-'51, Mayasich entered the University of Minnesota, where he became the school's all-time leading scorer. Mayasich was such an exceptional talent that he was sometimes compared to Jean Beliveau, the legendary Montreal Canadiens center, but Americans were shunned by the NHL in the 1950s and Mayasich settled for joining the newly formed Bobcats in 1958.

Two years earlier, he was a center and the leading scorer for the U.S. Olympic team that won a silver medal at Cortina d'Ampezzo, Italy. At the time, it was the Canadians, not the Russians, who had dominated Olympic hockey, winning six of the first seven gold medals in the sport. Thus, when the U.S. knocked off Canada, 4-1, in the second game of the round-robin finals with Mayasich scoring three goals, it was the most significant victory in the history of American hockey.

But four years later, the U.S. team topped it, not once, not twice, but three times. This time, U.S. hockey officials believed they had their best team ever, but their enthusiasm wasn't shared very widely outside their own borders.

Mayasich, now playing as a defenseman, wasted no time in changing world opinion as he scored three goals and assisted on another in a 7-5 victory over the Czechs in a Group C preliminary round game. Then he got two more in a 12-1 romp over Australia to put the U.S. into the six-team finals. When Johnson got into the act by scoring a goal in a 6-3 coast past Sweden, Uncle Sam had everyone's attention. Mayasich scored two more goals in a 9-1 victory over Germany. But the hard part was still to come.

Canada was unbeaten and had outscored its first four opponents, 40-3, when it faced off against the Americans on a Thursday night before a standing room only crowd of 8,500. But it lost its air of invincibility when Johnson intercepted a pass at his own blue line and scored the game-winning goal late in the second period to produce a monumental 2-1 upset. The Soviet Union was next.

The Americans had never beaten the Russians in hockey, but they remedied that situation with a 3-2 triumph on Saturday as Bill Christian scored the tying and winning goals. That left the U.S. with a 4-0 record while Canada was 3-1 and the Soviets 2-1-1. All the U.S. had to do was tie Czechoslovakia in a rematch to wrap up the gold.

The Bobcat recruits not only shared in making hockey history against the Czechs, but they also were witnesses to a small thaw in the Cold War. When the Czechs were leading, 4-3, after the second period, Soviet captain Nikolai Sologubov appeared in the U.S. locker room with an oxygen bottle. He told the Americans that they should try the stuff to combat Squaw Valley's 6,200-foot altitude. They appreciated the gesture, used the oxygen and buried the Czechs the rest of the way.

And all the Bobcat fans in Green Bay breathed easier, as well.

HERB KOHL BUYS BUCKS

MARCH 1, 1985

The Milwaukee Bucks were winning games but losing money. Playing in the National Basketball Association's smallest arena and in one of its smallest markets, they'd spilled red ink on their last two seasons. Jim Fitzgerald, their principal owner, had hoped a new cable television enterprise would provide new income, but when it failed, he wanted out.

Herb Kohl didn't need a basketball team. But he knew Milwaukee did, and he didn't want to see this one leave town. So he bought Fitzgerald's Bucks, along with all of their fiscal challenges. Within days, a new arena dropped into his lap.

Sometimes it's the road to success that's paved with good intentions.

Kohl bought the team for $18 million, a reasonable price in those times for a city Milwaukee's size. But he had no idea what a bargain he was getting. On the day the sale was announced he said he believed action would be taken quickly on a new arena. He just didn't know how quickly.

Four days later, Jane and Lloyd Pettit announced at a news conference that they planned to build a new arena for the community that would be used as a new home for the Bucks.

Civic leaders had been talking for years about upgrading the team's venue. Maybe an overhaul of the 11,052-seat Milwaukee Arena. Or maybe a new place across the street. Or one next to County Stadium. But Milwaukee moves slowly in these matters, and on Feb. 5, when Fitzgerald announced that the team was for sale, important people began to fear that it would be leaving town.

It could have, too. Fitzgerald got three local bids, but none of them was as good as two others that came from out of state. A group from Minneapolis made an offer, and another one from Orange County, Calif., did the same. Fitzgerald said their numbers were 10% to 20% better than the local propositions, but he had been running the Bucks in Milwaukee since 1976, and he didn't want to see them leave either.

When Kohl entered the picture, Fitzgerald stopped talking to anyone else. Negotiations continued around the clock for eight days, and the deal was sealed at 4 o'clock on a Friday morning.

Kohl, an heir to his family's thriving grocery and department store business, was no stranger to this type of thing. He'd made a run at an expansion franchise for Milwaukee in 1967, but then stepped back when the Bucks' original owners got the team for

Herb Kohl

$2 million. He was also part of the group that brought the Milwaukee Brewers from Seattle.

A private man who led a very public life, he'd served as the chairman of the state Democratic Party from 1975 to '77, and he would soon become a United States senator. But he was never more popular than he was on the day when he stepped forward to keep the Bucks in Wisconsin.

And then the Pettits topped him. Already among Wisconsin's leading philanthropists, they would invest $90 million in the new Bradley Center that would house the Milwaukee Admirals hockey team and the Marquette University basketball team in addition to the Bucks. It wasn't easy to give away the money either as the politicians bickered for months over where the place would be built.

When the wrangling finally stopped, the franchise's new owner had a building that would fill the Bucks' needs for the foreseeable future, and the old owner went on to buy another team in San Francisco. He got it for an unusually good price, but nothing like the bargain that Kohl got for keeping the Milwaukee Bucks at home.

BADGERS BATTERED BY HOMEGROWN FOES

MARCH 2, 1959

The problem was obviously twofold as the University of Wisconsin basketball team went six years without a winning season: Mediocre talent and a severe trade imbalance. Wisconsin was exporting its best high school players and not importing anyone else's.

Never was the dilemma more glaring than it was when the last-place Badgers traveled to first-place Michigan State with two games remaining in the Big Ten season. An upset would have required an act of God or at least a ruling by the Interstate Commerce Commission. The Spartans were 17-3, and four of their top six players were Wisconsin high school graduates.

Their leading scorer was Bob Anderegg of Monroe, while their starting guards were Lance Olson of Green Bay West and Tom Rand of Green Bay East. Their sixth man was Dave Fahs, Anderegg's former Monroe teammate. Anderegg scored 18 points, while All-American center Johnny Green had 28 as Michigan State made short work of the Badgers. The Spartans threatened to pitch a shutout, scoring the first 13 points on the way to a 93-73 victory.

Losing had become ordinary for the Badgers, but this was no ordinary loss. It assured them of having the worst record in the history of the program. A week later they tumbled to Indiana, 97-71, to finish 3-19, and they did it with a lame duck coach. Bud Foster submitted his resignation on the Wednesday after the Spartan spanking, and it was accepted on the morning before the Hoosier humiliation.

In accepting Foster's letter, university President Conrad Elvehjem emphasized that there was no pressure on him to quit. Maybe that was part of the problem. Foster had compiled a 265-267 record in 25 years, and most of the losses had come in the last 10. He had led the Badgers to a national championship in 1941 and a Big Ten title and NCAA bid in 1947, but the game had clearly passed him by over the last decade.

He was married to an old, walk-up style of play, and he seemed to have lost interest in recruiting. Especially in recruiting close to home. Four years earlier, Minnesota had finished second in the Big Ten, while Wisconsin tied for sixth. Three of the Gophers' starters were Wisconsin prep products: Chuck Mencel of Eau Claire, Dave Tucker of Superior Cathedral and Buck Lindsley of West De Pere.

Foster said Big Ten regulations and his university's stringent academic requirements made it much too hard to recruit top players. He also acknowledged losing many of the best state prospects to Marquette. His defenders ripped Big Ten rivals for "raiding" Wisconsin, but Michigan State coach Forddy Anderson exploded that argument when he said he never had to leave his office to get Anderegg, Olson, Rand or Fahs. They all came to him.

It was clear that Foster's archaic style and declining record were driving Wisconsin's best elsewhere. He recognized the problem by calling it quits and getting reassigned as the head of the university's grant-in-aid program. He said the basketball program might benefit from "new blood."

It got young blood instead. The Badgers considered DePaul's Ray Meyer and former Marquette coach Tex Winter, both of whom would go on to Hall of Fame careers. They also interviewed Arizona State's Ned Wulk, a native of Marion, Wis. But they settled on Foster's assistant, 31-year-old John Erickson. He stayed nine years and had only two winning seasons in the Big Ten before taking over as general manager of the Milwaukee Bucks.

The problems took 27 more years to go away. In that time, the Badgers had five more coaches and only five winning seasons. They won no Big Ten titles, never finished better than fourth in the conference and appeared in one NCAA tournament.

In-state players continued to pour over the border or choose Marquette. While the likes of Joe Wolf, Max Walker, Bill Hanzlik, Kurt Nimphius, Jim Chones, Tony Smith, John Johnson and Fred Brown left, the Badgers' only native grown all-Big Ten player was Madison Central's Joe Franklin.

It took Dick Bennett to stem the tide when he arrived in 1995. He was more than 35 years overdue.

ERICKSON'S BADGERS STUN OHIO STATE

MARCH 3, 1962

The nation's top-ranked team was coming to Madison, and John Erickson was into reverse psychology.

"If we can make a game of it, we'll be happy," said the Wisconsin basketball coach. "Every team that plays Ohio State regards the game as a big chance, but if they can stay within 15 points, they consider it a close one."

The Badgers didn't stay within 15 points, and it wasn't a close one. They won by 19 against one of the greatest basketball dynasties in the history of the Big Ten.

That probably wasn't what Erickson had in mind, but who knows? While praising the Buckeyes, he neglected to mention that he had the best Wisconsin team anyone had seen since 1950. The Badgers would finish the season 17-7 overall and 10-4 in the Big Ten, good for second place for the first time in 12 years.

Still, there was no question that Ohio State was a forbidding opponent, even though it had little to play for after clinching the outright conference title five days before coming to the UW Fieldhouse. The Buckeyes were led by Jerry Lucas, John Havlicek and Mel Nowell, three seniors who hadn't lost in the Big Ten in 27 games over the last three years. Ohio State's only loss in its previous 54 starts was to Cincinnati in the 1961 national championship game. The current Buckeyes' average margin of victory was 21 points.

Containing one or two of their big three was a huge challenge. Shutting down all three was almost impossible, and so Erickson didn't try. Instead he packed in his defense and dared Ohio State to beat the Badgers from the perimeter. That worked for Nowell, a 6-foot-2 guard, who took 21 shots and made nine of them. But Lucas, a 6-8 center, went a sub-par eight for 18 and Havlicek, a 6-5 forward, made only three baskets.

Meanwhile, sophomore guard Don Hearden scored 29 points for Wisconsin, tying a school record with 14 field goals, as the Badgers won a shootout, 86-67. Forward Ken Seibel added 22 points, and fellow forward Tom Hughbanks scored 11 and grabbed 11 rebounds.

Lucas scored 11 points in the first half, but the Buckeyes fell behind, 37-30. The Badgers pushed their lead to 15 points midway through the second half, and the difference grew to 19 with 4 minutes 17 seconds to play. Ohio State never got it under double figures after that.

Tom Hughbanks

A crowd of 13,545 swarmed the floor after witnessing what remains one of biggest upsets in Wisconsin basketball history. "Like I told the team in practice," Erickson said. "You'll always remember playing a great team like Ohio State, but you'll remember it more if you beat them."

How rare was it for a team to beat Ohio State during that period? During the three years that Lucas, Havlicek and Nowell played together, they went 78-6.

The date March 3 also had a special charm for the Badgers. Seventeen years later to the day, they beat eventual NCAA champion Michigan State with Magic Johnson, 83-81, at the UW Fieldhouse on a 55-foot shot at the buzzer by Wes Matthews.

PACKERS ANNOUNCE FAVRE'S RETIREMENT

MARCH 4, 2008

Mike McCarthy was at his daughter's high school basketball banquet in Austin, Texas, when Brett Favre called him on his cell phone with some bad news. At least, Green Bay Packers fans thought it was bad news. What McCarthy, the Packers' head coach, and general manager Ted Thompson thought may never be clear.

Favre was calling to say he had made up his mind to retire after 17 years in the National Football League. Forty-four days had passed since the greatest player in franchise history had thrown an overtime interception against the New York Giants, leaving the Packers one game short of a Super Bowl. The Packers announced his decision with regret.

Favre had publicly mulled his retirement after each of the last three seasons, and it wasn't clear what had tipped the balance this time. Favre was unavailable for comment, and he didn't say when he would be around to talk. His only comment on the situation came in a voice mail to ESPN's Chris Mortensen. The network played the tape endlessly throughout the day, and the rambling message boiled down to three words. "I'm just tired," Favre said.

Other people close to the situation had plenty to say. James "Bus" Cook, Favre's agent and longtime friend, indicated that the Packers didn't exactly fall all over themselves to welcome their quarterback back. "I know he wants to play one more year," Cook told the *Milwaukee Journal Sentinel.* "I don't think anyone forced him to make that decision, but I don't know that anyone tried to talk him out of it."

Favre's brother Scott expressed similar sentiments in an interview with WTMJ-TV of Milwaukee, saying the Packers could have done more to let Favre know how much they needed him. He thought there had been a lack of communication.

McCarthy might have taken exception to that, since he said he had communicated with Favre at least once a week after the Giants game until Favre announced his decision. Thompson, meanwhile, responded to the contention that he hadn't tried hard enough to keep the three-time league MVP by saying, "For me to be presumptuous enough to talk a grown man into making a life-changing decision that he's already made is wrong." Only the three of them will ever know exactly what they had said to each other.

It was generally understood, though, that Favre would have liked the Packers to do more about building the team around him for a final Super Bowl drive. Specifically, he had wanted them to acquire free agent receiver Randy Moss, another Cook client, a year earlier.

Thompson's many critics charged that his agenda wasn't so much getting on-field help for Favre, as it was getting him out of the way so that three-year backup Aaron Rodgers could take over the quarterbacking job.

It was also known that Thompson and McCarthy weren't prepared to wait forever for Favre to make his decision. He had drawn it out for months in the two previous seasons, and the Green Bay brain trust wanted to know whether it was time to move on before the draft. If Favre left, the Packers would have an additional $11.4 million in salary cap room and a pressing need for a backup quarterback. If Favre stayed, Rodgers would have to wait another year for his chance.

A tearful press conference in Green Bay two days later did little to clear up how much those issues had to do with Favre's decision. Noting that Favre had enjoyed the third highest passer rating in his career while leading the Packers to a 13-3 season, McCarthy acknowledged that he had "plenty left in his tank." Thompson said he was sure Favre had based his decision on what was best for him and his family.

Favre, who shed all the tears, said "It's been a great career for me, and it's over." He added, "I don't think I've got anything left to give."

But the most prescient comment on the subject may have come from, of all places, Minnesota. Vikings safety and former Favre teammate Darren Sharper told the *Journal Sentinel,* "Come midsummer when everyone starts talking about football and he's done about four months worth of fishing and playing golf, it wouldn't surprise me to hear speculation that Brett Favre might be coming out of retirement."

Five months later, Favre was back in uniform. The uniform belonged to the New York Jets.

BADGERS END 56-YEAR BIG TEN DROUGHT

MARCH 5, 2003

It took only 59 games, 39 minutes and 59.6 seconds for coach Bo Ryan and the University of Wisconsin basketball team to prove to everyone that they were for real. Devin Harris provided the clinching argument.

Harris, a Milwaukee native and the pride of Wauwatosa East High School, stood on the free throw line with four-tenths of a second remaining in the Badgers' Big Ten finale against two-time defending champion Illinois. A Kohl Center crowd of 17,142 was on its feet as the sophomore guard took the first of two shots that could end Wisconsin's 56-year stretch without an undisputed conference title.

Naturally, he prolonged the suspense by rimming it out. But then he calmly swished the second one to seal a historic 60-59 victory, giving Ryan his second Big Ten championship in his two years in charge. Wisconsin had tied for the title with three other teams, including Illinois, the year before, but the Badgers didn't get a lot of credit for that. They needed an outright title to convince the public.

When the season began, they were picked to finish no better than fourth in the Big Ten, and when they lost their first two league games to league favorites Illinois and Michigan on the road, they became more lightly regarded than that. They'd been left out of the top 25 ratings from early December until two days before the rematch with Illinois.

High school teams had more size than this outfit. Wading pools had more depth. Only one man in the starting lineup topped 6 feet 5 inches. Eighty per cent of the minutes were played by the starters. But somehow or other, the Badgers had put together a 21-6 record at that point, playing for a man who'd spent his entire head coaching career in Division III and the mid-majors until he came to Madison.

Ryan used tenacious, all-day defense, a patented swing offense and a hellacious home-court advantage to help the Badgers beat Illinois and claim their 26th victory in their last 27 games at the Kohl Center. Of course, they had some players, too.

Harris, a sophomore on his way to a productive NBA career, led a typical balanced attack with 13 points and nine rebounds, while senior Kirk Penney earned a ride off the floor on the shoulders of the fans with 14 points in his last home game. Freshman Alando Tucker chipped in with 12 points, and sophomore Mike Wilkinson added 11. Plus, Wilkinson's seven rebounds contributed to the Badgers' 31-25 advantage on the boards over the much bigger Illini.

Devin Harris

When it was over, Illinois coach Bill Self said, "You work your butt off all year long, and it comes down to one second." Well, not exactly. The Badgers had been working for this much longer than that.

Since 1947 to be precise.

PIUS GIRLS WIN 12TH STRAIGHT STATE TITLE

MARCH 6, 1993

Jenny Heft was going through her terrible twos when Milwaukee Pius XI High School started its record streak of girls state basketball championships. Now she was in charge of keeping the string intact.

Coach Joel Claassen had decided to spread the floor to protect a six-point lead with 4 minutes 55 seconds left in the Wisconsin Independent Schools Athletic Association title game with Appleton Xavier at the Milwaukee Arena. It seemed like sound strategy as long as his point guard didn't suddenly remember that she was 14 years old.

She didn't, and the Popes finished on top one more time with a 49-36 victory.

No girls basketball team in the country had ever won nine state high school basketball championships in a row before, and now Pius had 12. The 5-foot Heft preserved the triumph with 12 points, three assists and a near-flawless floor game, while 5-10 senior Brenda Brunner dominated inside with 12 points and 16 rebounds. Old and young, big and small, the Popes were still in a class by themselves.

Pius had already won three straight championships when Claassen took over as head coach, and he extended the streak to a national prep record of nine when the Popes beat Xavier in 1990. That time they'd held Xavier to a single field goal in the second half of a 57-30 romp.

Claassen never lost a state tournament game in his first nine years in charge, and he put together a 92-game winning streak from February 1988 to December 1991. The Popes were 25-1 after they'd won the 1993 title game.

They were back at the Arena the next year trying to run their state tournament streak to a baker's dozen, but Wisconsin Lutheran spoiled the fun. Lutheran, which appropriately enough had been the last team to beat Pius in the WISAA tournament in 1981, pulled off a 63-60 upset.

If Claassen was discouraged by the loss, it didn't show. His teams won five additional titles and probably would have won more if the state private schools association hadn't disbanded in 2000. Two years later, he retired as the program's coach. "I've had a great time," he said, "but for the last few years, the pressure to win has gotten to me."

Claassen's record with the Pius girls was 419-37. Like Heft, he'd handled the pressure pretty well.

**PIUS GIRLS' 12 STRAIGHT TITLES
WISAA STATE
CHAMPIONSHIP GAMES**

YEAR	SCORE
1982	Pius 45, Racine St. Catherine's 30
1983	Pius 39, Stevens Point Pacelli 33
1984	Pius 53, Appleton Xavier 37
1985	Pius 52, La Crosse Aquinas 43
1986	Pius 64, Appleton Xavier 44
1987	Pius 62, Appleton Xavier 61
1988	Pius 67, Appleton Xavier 66
1989	Pius 73, La Crosse Aquinas 57
1990	Pius 57, Appleton Xavier 30
1991	Pius 42, Appleton Xavier 31
1992	Pius 36, Appleton Xavier 35
1993	Pius 49, Appleton Xavier 36

Source: WISAA State Tournament Records
by Rudy Talsky

DOMINICAN WINS 71ST STRAIGHT GAME – MAYBE

MARCH 7, 1980

There was no doubting the outcome. Whitefish Bay Dominican High School barely broke a sweat while running over Fox Valley Lutheran of Appleton, 62-45, in the quarterfinal round of the Wisconsin Independent Schools Athletic Association state basketball tournament.

Officially, it was the Knights' 71st straight victory, a state record. Unofficially, their streak had ended almost six weeks earlier in a 58-57 triple overtime loss to Milwaukee Thomas More. The difference was nine games and one of the messiest chapters in Wisconsin high school sports history.

The mess began half a country away in New York City where Nigel Wallace, a gifted 6-foot-4 forward who was one of seven children, lost his mother in the spring. The family was split up when the mother died, and Wallace moved to Milwaukee where Tim Rueth, a Marquette University law professor and a friend of Wallace's summer league coach, was named his guardian.

Wallace enrolled at Thomas More in October and opened the season with the basketball team, which is when matters got complicated for him, his new school and ultimately Dominican. Under WISAA rules, a student wasn't eligible to participate in a sport unless he enrolled in the first 17 days of the semester. Wallace missed that deadline, but there was an exception to the rule that stipulated if the athlete came from another city and acquired a legal guardian he could play.

Thomas More got permission from WISAA to play Wallace, but what it never got were documents from Rueth proving that he was Wallace's legal guardian. Athletic Director Joe Zolecki said the school had tried to obtain the papers, and when Rueth finally said he didn't have them, the school called WISAA Executive Director Steve Pavela five days before the state tournament was to begin in Milwaukee. Thus, Wallace was ruled ineligible, and all of Thomas More's victories were forfeited, including its overtime decision over Dominican.

Wallace had scored 32 points in that game, and Dominican coach Don Gosz figured if his defense couldn't stop him, a bureaucratic ruling shouldn't either. "As far as Dominican is concerned and our players are concerned, we lost that game," said Gosz. "They can continue the streak on, but as far as I'm concerned it's 62 games overall and 42 in conference. My only question is 'Why now? Why wasn't this all done in November?'"

It was a good question. A better one was whether Wallace would be allowed to play in the state tournament, and the answer to that didn't come until three hours before Thomas More's first game with Delafield St. John's Military Academy. A group of Thomas More parents won an injunction overturning the WISAA ruling and putting Wallace back in uniform. WISAA appealed, and the appeal was rejected shortly before tip-off.

So Wallace was eligible again, but that was the least of Gosz's concerns as he got his team ready for a semifinal game with Milwaukee Marquette. Dominican had beaten Marquette twice during the regular-season, but they had been close games. The third one was, too, only this time the Hilltoppers won, 47-45, setting up a title match with Thomas More and officially ending a Dominican winning streak that had stretched over three seasons and included two state championships.

There was still a lot of legal uncertainty and a fair amount of bad blood when Marquette and Thomas More met for the championship. WISAA was appealing the latest ruling, and there was a good chance that even if Marquette lost the game, it would win the title if the association prevailed in court. The Hilltoppers didn't have to worry about that, though, because they won, 52-47.

WISAA also ultimately won in the courtroom and Thomas More's victories were all forfeited. Dominican had its 71-game winning streak whether it wanted it or not.

MARQUETTE SNAPS CINCINNATI'S REIGN EN ROUTE TO FINAL FOUR

MARCH 8, 2003

The schedule-makers didn't do Marquette any favors when they sent Cincinnati to the Bradley Center for Senior Day. Nobody invited the Bearcats to a farewell party on purpose.

The Conference USA championship figured to be up for grabs when the two teams met on the final Saturday of the regular season, and Cincinnati always won the Conference USA championship. Always. The league was seven years old, and the Bearcats had won or shared seven league titles.

But nothing is forever, and when Tom Crean's eighth-ranked Golden Eagles sent a sellout crowd spilling onto the floor after a convincing 70-61 victory over their latest worst enemies, they ended something annoying and started something huge. They couldn't have known it at the time, but they were on their way to Marquette's first Final Four in 26 years and only their third one ever.

As usual, junior guard Dwyane Wade did the heaviest lifting against Cincinnati, scoring 26 points and adding 10 rebounds, five assists, three steals and three blocked shots. The Golden Eagles scored the last six points of the afternoon while Cincinnati was missing five shots in the final 3 minutes 39 seconds. "We could have won the game," said Bearcats coach Bob Huggins. "We just didn't make any shots."

Marquette liked to think it had some influence on that circumstance, although five days later it would know the feeling when Alabama-Birmingham spilled the Eagles out of the conference tournament in the first round. It would be the last game Marquette would lose until it collided with Kansas in the semifinal round of the Final Four on April 5 in New Orleans.

The Golden Eagles entered play in the NCAA Midwest Regional with a highly respectable third seed, and sophomore point guard Travis Diener took some of the load off of Wade's shoulders when he scored 29 points in a 72-68 first-round victory over Holy Cross at Indianapolis. It was the first time Marquette had won an NCAA tournament game since 1996, and it wouldn't have happened if Wade hadn't scored 13 of his 15 points in the second half to wrap it up.

Next up was Missouri and near-disaster. The Eagles frittered away an 11-point lead with 8:16 to play in regulation, and it took three three-point shots from freshman Steve Novak to rescue them in overtime. They set a school scoring record for a NCAA tournament game while winning, 101-92, and moving on to a Sweet Sixteen date with fourth-ranked Pittsburgh in Minneapolis.

Same pattern, same result. This time Marquette allowed all but one point of a 10-point lead to slip away in the final five minutes and needed a pair of free throws by forward Scott Merritt with 11 seconds remaining to pull out a 77-74 squeaker and earn the dubious distinction of facing Kentucky in the Elite Eight.

Dwyane Wade drove to the basket against Cincinnati.

The Wildcats were 32-3, they had a 26-game winning streak, and they were ranked No. 1 in the nation. They had also just polished off Wisconsin on the same night and in the same building where Marquette was surviving Pittsburgh. But Kentucky had no clue what to do with Wade.

When he torched them for 29 points, 11 rebounds and 11 assists, Marquette had its easiest victory of the tournament, 83-69, and a spot in the Final Four. "If this is a dream," said forward Todd Townsend, "I'm going to commit suicide when I wake up."

Marquette got murdered by Kansas instead. The Golden Eagles shot 25.6% in the first half and were never a part of the argument in a 94-61 whipping by the sixth-ranked Jayhawks in the semifinals. Wade's 19-point performance led the Golden Eagles, but it couldn't save them. It turned out to be his last game as he opted for the NBA draft.

Considering the ride he'd given Marquette after the Cincinnati sendoff, most people would say he'd done enough.

MICKEY CROWE SCORES RECORD 45 IN TITLE GAME

MARCH 9, 1975

The Wisconsin Independent Schools Athletic Association small-school championship game was slipping away when Mickey Crowe decided to take charge. The skinny senior with the floppy hair jacked up 15 shots and made 10 of them, scoring all 23 of his team's points in the fourth quarter.

When the game was over, he had broken the tournament record with 45 points. And still, it wasn't enough as JFK Prep of St. Nazianz lost the Class B title, 72-58, to Racine Lutheran. In many ways, that afternoon at the Milwaukee Arena was Mickey Crowe's last hurrah.

The 6-foot-5, 180-pound showman was the nation's highest scoring high school player as a senior. He shattered the Wisconsin record with 2,724 points in his four seasons at JFK Prep, scoring as many as 72 points in a single game. *Sports Illustrated* mentioned him in its "Faces in the Crowd" feature when he rang up 61 and 64 points in consecutive games as a sophomore. Even Heywood Hale Broun, colorful CBS sports commentator, showed up in St. Nazianz to tell the Mickey Crowe story.

If Crowe wasn't the most gifted player the state had ever seen, he was certainly among the most colorful. And maybe the most troubled.

Crowe was coached by his father Marty, and Mickey's flowing hair and floppy socks made it inevitable that the two would be compared to the famous father-son pair of Press and Pete Maravich at Louisiana State. The Crowes played up the comparison and drew big crowds wherever they went. But the cheering stopped after the loss to Racine Lutheran, and it never really started again.

Mickey and Marty took their act to little Silver Lake College in Manitowoc the following fall, but the program never took off. Then Mickey moved on to four different schools in four years, displaying more erratic behavior at every stop.

As important as basketball was to him, alcohol and marijuana seemed to become more important. He went to the University of Wisconsin-Fond du Lac extension and then to St. Norbert College and then to the University of Minnesota. Finally he landed at UW-Superior where he was so unpopular that his teammates refused to pass the ball to him.

Minnesota coach Jim Dutcher may have summed up Crowe's game best when he said, "I think basketball was a bigger part of his life than it should have been. His dreams were greater than his ability."

Crowe left Superior without a degree and went to Washington, D.C., to sell magazines over the phone. But he lost that job and became homeless and delusional. He began following Ronald Reagan in the president's appearances around Washington, becoming so conspicuous that he was questioned by FBI agents when Reagan was shot by John Hinckley in 1981.

In May 1984, Crowe was committed to the Trempealeau County Health Care Center after a court-ordered mental competency hearing. After 22 months there, he said he was through with drugs and alcohol, but he was on disability and couldn't handle a job.

Out of work and out of basketball, Mickey Crowe had only his scoring record for anyone to remember him by. That disappeared in 1993 when it was broken by Wausaukee's Anthony Pieper.

Mickey Crowe launched a shot.

BELOIT COLLEGE FALLS SHORT IN NIT

MARCH 10, 1951

Your hair was cut short, and you wore a coat and tie on the road when you played for Dolph Stanley. You ran all night, but you never took so much as a sip of water during a game. And you never, ever sat down for a timeout. And you won.

In the 12 years that the taskmaster from Taylorville, Ill., coached basketball at little Beloit College, the Buccaneers compiled a 242-58 record playing teams from 27 states and Hawaii, then a United States territory. Its victims included big schools like DePaul, Loyola of Chicago, Washington State, Florida State and Brigham Young. Its players included the likes of Johnny Orr, John Erickson and Ron Bontemps, and they played at Chicago Stadium, San Francisco's Cow Palace and, best of all, Madison Square Garden.

The big-time squad from the small Wisconsin city traveled to New York to meet Seton Hall on a Saturday night in the first round of the National Invitation Tournament. It was the 14th annual NIT, which at that time was the place to be in college basketball. Teams had been known to turn down NCAA bids to play in the NIT.

The pressing, fast-breaking Bucs hoped to match their speed against the size and power of Seton Hall in the first round. And for a half they did. But in the end, they couldn't measure up to Walter Dukes.

Dukes was a 6-foot-10 sophomore who would grow two more inches before beginning an eight-year career in the NBA. He scored 20 points as the Pirates raced away from a 36-33 lead to win, 71-57. The Buccaneers got 24 points from Bontemps, who would go on to play for the United States Olympic team a year later, but only five of those came in the second half.

Bontemps, a 6-3, 176-pound center, had played for Stanley at Taylorville High School in 1944 when the downstate powerhouse won 45 games and the Illinois state high school championship. He started his college career at the University of Illinois, but transferred to Beloit after a military stint. Veterans were the lifeblood of Stanley's program, which became so potent that it got kicked right out of the Midwest Conference.

The coach made some lasting enemies in the Midwest by running up scores such as 122-43 and 141-53, and the conference decided that his national ambitions were out of step with the rest of its members. The two biggest schools in the state avoided the Buccaneers as well. Marquette crushed them, 72-43, in Stanley's second year, but the then-Warriors wanted no part of them after that. Wisconsin wouldn't risk playing them at all.

Beloit's 85.3 scoring average led the country in 1951, and it set a Chicago Stadium scoring record by smoking DePaul, 94-60. Three days later, DePaul coach Ray Meyer said the Bucs, on a good night, might be able to knock off top-ranked Kentucky or Oklahoma A&M.

Stanley left Beloit in 1957 never having suffered a losing season. The school eliminated his athletic director's duties that year, and he moved on to become the AD at Drake. Beloit scaled back the basketball program after that, but the memory of Wisconsin's biggest small college story lingers on.

NIT program cover

OSHKOSH ALL-STARS WIN WORLD TOURNAMENT

MARCH 11, 1942

Lon Darling sold seeds for a living, and people in Oshkosh didn't need many seeds in November. What they needed was entertainment to help get them through the long Wisconsin winters.

So when *Oshkosh Daily Northwestern* sports editor Arthur Heywood suggested to Darling in 1929 that Oshkosh could use a pro basketball team to warm up some of those chilly nights, he'd come to the right man. The star salesman for the G.H. Hunkel Co. had never played basketball in his life, but he liked to stay busy. Darling formed the Oshkosh All-Stars as a semi-pro team and by 1937, he had helped create the National Basketball League.

Five years later, the All-Stars won the World Professional Basketball Tournament with a 43-41 victory over the Detroit Eagles in a game played before 11,500 people – or more than a quarter of the population of Oshkosh – at Chicago's International Ampitheater.

Basketball was a seat-of-the-pants operation when Darling got involved. Traveling teams would visit towns all over the country. They'd play local squads, have a few beers with the citizens and move on to the next stop. Players could make between $15 and $25 a game doing that, which was big money for those times.

Darling, a high school dropout with a brother who played for the Green Bay Packers, put the All-Stars together mostly from state college squads. Soon, he expanded his recruiting efforts and his first big star was Leroy "Cowboy" Edwards, a 6-foot-4 center who had dropped out of the University of Kentucky. Edwards joined the All-Stars in 1937, the first year of the NBL, and led the league in scoring.

The NBL would last 12 years before merging with a collection of franchises from larger Eastern cities called the Basketball Association of America to form what became the National Basketball Association. In the 12 years of the NBL, the All-Stars won two championships and lost in the championship series four other times.

Their best season came in 1942 when they not only won the league title for a second straight year, but also won the World Tournament. The tournament, a five-day affair featuring the best teams in the country, was in its fourth year, and it would survive six more.

On their way to the title game, the All-Stars knocked off the Davenport Rockets, the New York Rens and the Harlem Globetrotters. The victory over the Rens was particularly satisfying. Named after a Harlem casino, "The Renaissance," the Rens were one of the nation's first all-black teams and were always a formidable opponent.

The Ampitheater was overflowing when the All-Stars faced Detroit, led by future Hall of Famer Buddy Jeannette, on a Wednesday night. The Eagles had beaten them, 39-37, in the championship game the previous year, and the All-Stars may have been remembering that when they raced to a 20-10 halftime lead. But Detroit rallied to go ahead, 39-38, late in the fourth quarter.

It was the only lead the Eagles would have all night as Gene Englund, one of Darling's part-time seed salesmen, scored the clinching basket from underneath with five seconds to play. Englund finished the game with 17 points, while Edwards added five crucial points in the fourth quarter while playing on a bad knee.

More than 5,000 people gathered at the Oshkosh train station the following night to welcome the team home. But the love affair between the All-Stars and the city ended when Darling folded the franchise in 1949. Salaries had risen, and the junior high gyms where the All-Stars played were too small to provide the revenue needed to keep up.

Darling was devastated. He would have what his sister described as "a nervous breakdown," and he died two years later at age 48 after a series of heart attacks.

WORLD PROFESSIONAL BASKETBALL TOURNAMENT
(Played at Chicago, 1939-'48)

YEAR	CHAMPIONSHIP GAME
1939	New York Rens 34, Oshkosh All-Stars 25
1940	Harlem Globetrotters 31, Chicago Bruins 29
1941	Detroit Eagles 39, Oshkosh All-Stars 37
1942	Oshkosh All-Stars 43, Detroit Eagles 41
1943	Washington Bears 43, Oshkosh All-Stars 31
1944	Fort Wayne Zollner Pistons 50, Brooklyn Eagles 33
1945	Fort Wayne Zollner Pistons 78, Dayton Acmes 52
1946	Fort Wayne Zollner Pistons 73, Oshkosh All-Stars 57
1947	Indianapolis Kautskys 62, Toledo Jeeps 47
1948	Minneapolis Lakers 75, New York Rens 71

Source: apbr.org

LOW BLOW SPICES WOLGAST-RITCHIE TITLE BOUT

MARCH 12, 1914

They loved Ad Wolgast in Milwaukee. The free-swinging lightweight from Cadillac, Mich., considered it his adopted home and fought there 27 times over the course of his career. And he might have regained his championship there, too, if not for an alleged low blow.

In the days when $100 a month was a great paycheck, 7,916 people paid as much as $7.50 a ticket to watch their favorite take on reigning champion Willie Ritchie of San Francisco, Calif., at the sold-out Milwaukee Auditorium.

The receipts topped $39,000, which stood as a local record for 36 years. Many of the customers left disappointed, but all of them got their money's worth from one of the greatest and most controversial pro fights the city has ever seen.

Wolgast was a slugger with a reputation for shading the rules. He had held the lightweight title from 1910 until 1912 when he lost it to Ritchie on a foul in the 16th round of a fight in Daly City, Calif. Perhaps Wolgast could have won it back the same way in Milwaukee, but his instincts got in the way.

They called Wolgast "The Michigan Wildcat," and he was living up to his name by carrying the action to the favored Ritchie for the first six rounds. While Ritchie went almost exclusively to the head, Wolgast concentrated on the body in what was a furious and close fight to that point. But early in the seventh, Ritchie switched strategies and decked the challenger with an uppercut to the gut. The question was just where that punch landed.

As referee Harry "Silk Shirt" Stout stood counting, Eddie Brunner, who was in Wolgast's corner, ran around the ring screaming, "The punch was low. You can't count." But Stout kept counting anyway, and a wobbly Wolgast knew he could either get up or get counted out.

He made it to his feet at "six" and hung on for the rest of the round. The fight remained close for the next two rounds before Wolgast almost put the Californian down in the tenth with a left to the stomach. But there was only one knockdown in the 10 rounds, and it helped Ritchie keep his title.

Ad Wolgast

Willie Ritchie

This was when newspaper reporters functioned as judges, and while the bout was officially recorded as a no-decision, a majority of the writers gave the nod to Ritchie. Five writers called the fight a draw; four gave Ritchie a slight edge; and two favored Ritchie without qualifying the difference.

Meanwhile, four doctors examined Wolgast after the fight, and they concurred that he had been fouled. One newspaper suggested if Wolgast had stayed down in the seventh, he might have been awarded the championship on a disqualification.

Ritchie would lose the title four months later to Freddie Welsh. Wolgast would lose much more.

Never one to pay much attention to defense, he had absorbed far too many blows to the head in a career that ended in 1920. He was in and out of mental institutions several times; and in 1927, he was committed to the California state mental institution at the age of 39. He would die there 28 years later.

MARQUETTE GETS ITS REVENGE ON KENTUCKY

MARCH 13, 1969

Kentucky and Marquette weren't exactly rivals when they met in Madison in the NCAA Mideast Regional tournament. They hadn't played each other enough for that. They were more like enemies.

Kentucky had the nation's seventh-ranked team, a 22-4 record, a 92-point scoring average and a reasonable chance of giving coach Adolph Rupp an unprecedented fifth national championship. Marquette had the nation's 14th-ranked team, a 23-4 record and a major grudge after Kentucky had ripped the Warriors, 107-89, in the regionals a year earlier in Lexington, Ky.

It was the most points ever surrendered by a Marquette team, and coach Al McGuire believed Rupp had run up the score. If that was true, "The Baron" might have had his reasons. McGuire had insulted him in his hometown when he had rejected an invitation to appear on Rupp's television show before their regional match. McGuire had objected strenuously to having to play a tournament game on his opponents' court, and he wanted no part of the local scene.

But now he was on his turf. Or at least close to it. The UW Fieldhouse was 80 miles from the Marquette campus, and Marquette fans had gobbled up plenty of tickets. At the time, the NCAA tournament was a 25-team affair and Marquette, then an independent, had played a first-round game five days earlier in Carbondale, Ill., where it beat Murray State, 82-62.

In Madison, a full house of 12,275 fans was there, and the Warriors gave them what they'd come for, beating Kentucky, 81-74, and making their coach a very happy man.

Moments after the final horn sounded, McGuire threw his sport coat in the air in celebration. "I don't think I've ever wanted anything in my life more than I wanted this," he said.

He got it the way Marquette got most things, with balance, patience and defense. George Thompson led four Warriors in double figures with 22 points, while Ric Cobb had 17 points and 14 rebounds.

Marquette dominated the pace and frustrated Dan Issel, Kentucky's All-American center, who had scored 36 points against the Warriors a year earlier. He scored only 13 this time, thanks mostly to the defensive work of forward Joe Thomas.

There were some dust-ups between Marquette and Kentucky players during the game and some jostling at the free throw line, but there were no punches landed or blood drawn. When it was over, an estimated 900 Marquette students marched happily through the streets of Milwaukee.

Thompson, who had fouled out in 17 minutes in Lexington and taken it personally, captured the mood when he said, "We had a whole year to wait for this."

Marquette's George Thompson (24) and Pat Smith (11) reached for a rebound behind Kentucky star Dan Issel (44) in an NCAA tournament game at Madison.

MILWAUKEE LANDS THE BRAVES

MARCH 14, 1953

More than 40 years before the movie, Milwaukee had its own "Field of Dreams." The county built it, and the Boston Braves came.

When the three-year construction project known as County Stadium was finished for the handsome sum of $5 million early in 1953, it had 28,111 permanent seats and a minor league tenant. It would have been the pride of the American Association had the Class AAA Milwaukee Brewers ever played there. But the place was built to be expanded into a home for a major league team, and the concrete had barely dried before Milwaukee had one.

While a new ballpark was going up in Wisconsin, the Braves' fiscal fortunes were going down in Massachusetts. Club President Lou Perini claimed he'd lost more than $1 million since his team had gone to the World Series in 1948. Boston, he'd decided, just wasn't big enough for the both the Braves and the Red Sox.

This was hardly a minor decision. It had been more than 50 years since anyone had relocated a major league franchise, and now two of them were ready to pack their bags. Bill Veeck's St. Louis Browns were also looking for a new home. County Stadium made Milwaukee a popular option for both franchises, but Perini headed off Veeck, who moved to Baltimore a year later.

Two major items had to be settled to get the Braves to Milwaukee, and both involved the stadium. The rent had to be cheap and there had to be more seating. After weeks of negotiations, a special meeting of the Milwaukee County Park Commission was held on a Saturday morning to consider a five-year lease that called for $1,000 annual rent for the first two years and 5% of the receipts for the next three, and the addition of up to 12,000 temporary seats, all of which was subject to approval by the full County Board.

Enough was accomplished for a noon press conference to be held in Bradenton, Fla., where Perini announced that he would petition the National League for permission to move the Braves to Milwaukee. He would need the unanimous consent of all of the other owners in the league, but he was confident that he could get it. After a 52-year wait following a one-season fling in the American League, the *Milwaukee Sentinel* proclaimed in a big, bold headline, "BIG LEAGUE BALL HERE THIS YEAR."

Perini's colleagues justified his confidence four days later when they approved the franchise shift with little discussion. The Braves' dwindling crowds in Boston and the addition of a team in the Midwest that would save on travel expenses made it an easy call. Milwaukee took over Pittsburgh's schedule, while the Pirates played the original Boston schedule. At the same time, the minor league Brewers were moved to Toledo.

"The presence of the team here is certainly a direct result of construction of the new County Stadium, considered throughout the country perhaps as the best modern ballpark," said Mayor Frank Zeidler.

Zeidler's enthusiasm was matched by his constituency as 12,000 people lined the tracks and gathered in the train station to welcome the team to its new home when it arrived from spring training almost a month later. Another 60,000 gathered for a downtown parade and 5,000 more paid their way into a reception at the Milwaukee Arena. The city's love affair with its ball club was just getting started.

Perini had said that he needed at least one million fans a year to make a profit, and Milwaukee came through with more than twice that many. The Braves averaged more than two million fans a season in their first seven years in the city, topping out at 2,215,404 in 1957.

Fans crowded around the Milwaukee Road train station to welcome the Milwaukee Braves once they arrived in town from spring training. The automobiles were waiting to carry the arriving players in a parade. The crowd was estimated at 12,000.

MOUNT SINKS SHOT AND MARQUETTE

MARCH 15, 1969

Everyone in the stands at the University of Wisconsin Fieldhouse knew that Rick Mount would take the shot that could deny Marquette its first trip to the Final Four. It just came as news to Rick Mount.

Twenty-six seconds remained in overtime at the Mideast Regional final, and a crowd of 13,025 looked on as Purdue called timeout. Mount had already scored 24 points, and there was no purer shooter in the game. A consensus All-American with a 33.3 scoring average, the skinny 6-foot-4 junior from Lebanon, Ind., was born for this kind of thing.

His father had him shooting tennis balls through a bottomless coffee can when he was a little boy, and *Sports Illustrated* had him on its cover when he was in high school. He had led the Boilermakers to a 20-4 regular-season record and a No. 6 national ranking, and now he was in the biggest game of his life.

Marquette coach Al McGuire blamed himself for what happened next. The Boilermakers took the ball inbounds and proceeded to play keep-away while the Warriors tried to make one more defensive stand. Then Mount came off a screen, broke to the corner and let fly with his trademark arching jump shot. There were two seconds on the clock when it went through the net, giving Purdue a 75-73 victory and a ticket to Louisville, Ky., for the NCAA semifinals.

After the game, Mount explained that the plan called for the Boilermakers to station two men on the high post, kill all but seven seconds and then have one of the remaining three players take the last shot. It could have been him, but it also could have been teammates Larry Weatherford or Herm Gilliam. Whoever was open.

McGuire said it was his fault that Mount was the one who was open. When George Thompson made a layup that tied the score and sent Purdue to the sidelines for its timeout, McGuire said the notion of fouling center Jerry Johnson went racing through his mind. But he decided against it. Johnson was a bad free throw shooter, and even if he had made both shots, Marquette would have had time to come back. The Warriors after all had been coming back all day.

They had fallen behind, 14-3, in the opening minutes, and they had been down a point with two seconds left in regulation when Ric Cobb made one of two free throws to send the game into overtime. And then they had trailed by four points early in the extra period. But their defense never let Purdue get out of range as they kept the Boilermakers 18 points under their average. "I don't know how they won," McGuire said.

The Boilermakers would go on to win again, burying North Carolina, 92-65, behind Mount's 36 points in the semifinals of the Final Four. But then they lost the title game to UCLA, 92-72, when Mount took 36 shots and missed 24.

Rick Mount

TINY REEDSVILLE WEARS STATE CROWN

MARCH 16, 1946

As Reedsville High School got ready to face Racine Park in the quarterfinal round of the Wisconsin Interscholastic Athletic Association state basketball tournament, the story around town was that Park had more teachers than Reedsville had students.

The entire population of this Manitowoc County village would have fit easily into the halls of its big-school opponent. It had 476 citizens and 87 high school students. But it also had a basketball team that had been playing together forever, and that was enough to make Reedsville the smallest town ever to win a state basketball championship back in the days of a one-class tournament.

If there was ever a Wisconsin team that would have fit the script for the popular 1986 movie *Hoosiers*, this was it.

Hardly anyone in Madison took Reedsville seriously when the tournament began, least of all the WIAA officials who switched the Panthers' first game from the evening to the afternoon session in the interest of selling tickets. Reedsville was not only unranked, it was unheard of.

But first-year coach John Gable had a wealth of experience back – one four-year starter and two three-year starters – from a team that had been expected to make state the season before. Ed Shimon, a 6-foot-4 center, led the group, and all of the starters had grown up in Reedsville where they played with one another 12 months a year.

Fourth-ranked Park was the first to regret overlooking the 19-2 Panthers. The Racine team took a seemingly safe 28-19 lead late in the third quarter, but Reedsville scored the last 11 points of the game to win, 30-28, and set up a semifinal match with second-ranked Wisconsin Rapids. The Panthers scored the only points in overtime on baskets by Henry Behnke and Roman Kugle to win that one, 47-43, putting them in the championship game against sixth-ranked Eau Claire.

Eau Claire had already won two state titles and had finished second two other times, and it had a center named Warren Hoff, who had scored a tournament-record 32 points the night before. The question was whether Shimon could hold his own in the battle of the big men.

A record crowd of 13,800 showed up at the University of Wisconsin Fieldhouse to find out, and Shimon didn't disappoint anyone. With most of the stands rooting for the Panthers, he scored 24 points while helping to hold Hoff to 10, including just two in the second half. Bernard Kubale added 14 for the Panthers, who scored the game's last nine points and ran away with a 48-39 victory.

The welcome home celebration that Reedsville threw for its young heroes rivaled V-J Day at the end of World War II, according to old newspaper accounts. The community also threw a banquet for the team that attracted dignitaries from around the state.

Asked years later to explain his tiny school's unlikely triumph, Gable said, "We were lucky, we were well prepared, and we had a good group of boys." Maybe when you have all of that, the size of your student body doesn't matter.

The starters on Reedsville's state championship team kneeled in the front row of this team picture. From left to right, they were Carl Maertz, Henry Behnke, Ed Shimon, Barney Kubale and Roman Kugle.

BADGERS CAPTURE FIRST NCAA HOCKEY TITLE

MARCH 17, 1973

Ten years after hockey was revived at the University of Wisconsin, the Badgers won their first national championship. Coach Bob Johnson's team did it by beating the University of Denver, 4-2, in the title game at the Boston Garden, but the real drama took place the night before on March 16 when it rallied from four goals down to shock Cornell in the semifinals.

The Badgers had cut a 4-0 deficit to 4-2 in the second period of the semifinal, only to face near-certain doom when Cornell scored 40 seconds into the third. But eight minutes later, Gary Winchester slammed home a Wisconsin goal that would begin one of the least likely comebacks college hockey had ever seen.

The Badgers made it 5-4 at the 16-minute 49-second mark, and then sophomore forward Dean Talafous tied the game on a breakaway with five seconds left in regulation and close to a minute after Johnson had pulled his goalie. Talafous struck again on a rebound shot with 33 seconds remaining in overtime for a 6-5 victory, putting Wisconsin in the Saturday night title game for the first time in three trips to the finals.

"We could have beaten anyone Saturday night," senior Norm Cherrey told the *Wisconsin State Journal* after the tournament. "We were so high on that victory."

Denver, on the other hand, had been sitting and watching after winning its semifinal on Thursday, but it was still the favorite. The Pioneers had split two earlier one-goal games with Wisconsin and then gone on to win the Western Collegiate Hockey Association regular-season title, while the Badgers had lost three of their last four league games and finished third.

But Johnson had his team playing its best hockey at the best possible time, and after the Badgers wiped out a 2-1 deficit with 4:17 gone in the second period, Denver never scored again.

Once again, it was Talafous, a 6-foot-4 sophomore, who put Wisconsin ahead for good in the second period. Jim Johnston's goal in the first three minutes of the third wrapped up a 4-2 victory and sent 1,000 traveling Badger fans spilling out of the Garden to celebrate St. Patrick's Day and Wisconsin's first national hockey championship.

The Badgers' ascension into the ranks of college hockey's elite was a long time coming. They had dropped the sport after the 1934-'35 season, and they hadn't picked it up again until 1963. Three years later, Johnson signed on, and the program was on its way.

The coach his players called "Hawk" also led his teams to the finals in 1970 and '72, but they finished third both times. This group looked like a long shot to improve on either of those performances. It had only seven seniors, and it had faded badly in the regular-season stretch.

But those seven seniors rallied behind their coach in the tournament. A Minnesota native, Johnson had taken some grief for defecting to Wisconsin from Gopher fans who nicknamed him "Badger Bob," but he seemed to regard it as a compliment. He would coach nine All-Americans in his time in Madison while compiling a 367-175-23 record and winning two more national championships in 1977 and '81.

Three more came later under other coaches, but the Badgers' first big step was taken in Boston with Johnson in charge.

UW NCAA MEN'S HOCKEY CHAMPIONSHIPS
(Frozen Four Final Games)

Date	Score
March 17, 1973	Wisconsin 4, Denver 2
March 26, 1977	Wisconsin 6, Michigan 5 (ot)
March 28, 1981	Wisconsin 6, Minnesota 3
March 26, 1983	Wisconsin 6, Harvard 2
April 1, 1990	Wisconsin 7, Colgate 3
April 8, 2006	Wisconsin 2, Boston College 1

Source: University of Wisconsin Men's Hockey Guide

OSHKOSH WEST COACH WINS ONE FOR DAD

MARCH 18, 2006

When Lance Randall saw people lined up for three blocks at his father's wake, he knew he had two choices. He could return to college coaching, or he could finish what his dad had started.

He accomplished the second two years later at the Kohl Center when Oshkosh West upset Madison Memorial, 52-40, for the Wisconsin Interscholastic Athletic Association Division 1 state basketball championship.

Nobody had given Randall's Wildcats much of a chance to knock off Memorial's defending champions in the title game because no team from the Fox River Valley area had won a big-school state title since Sheboygan North 20 years earlier. The Madison team had beaten Milwaukee King the night before in what many thought was the "real" state championship. But as West's coach put it: "I think this team has a bigger goal and a little more motivation than some of the other teams in the tournament."

That was certainly true of Randall.

In October 2004, Lance Randall's father Steve was recovering from an angioplasty and looking forward to his 16th season as basketball coach at Oshkosh West when he told his wife that he wasn't feeling well. He decided to lie down on the couch. And he never got up. Something had gone horribly wrong with the heart procedure, and Steve Randall was dead at 53.

Lance was following in his father's coaching footsteps as a 33-year-old assistant at Saint Louis University. When he came home and saw 3,000 people attending Steve's wake, he knew there was important work left to be done in Oshkosh. He left his $56,000 a year position at Saint Louis and moved his wife and one-year-old daughter in with his mother. Then he went to work for the Experimental Aircraft Association and took over his dad's team. The coaching stipend was $4,000. The experience was priceless.

If life was a Walt Disney fairy tale, West would have won the state championship in 2005. The Wildcats were probably good enough to do it, too. They were 21-0 when they faced Wisconsin Rapids in a sectional semifinal, but they lost the game and their best shot at a state title since Steve Randall's team had fallen to Milwaukee Vincent in the 2001 final. Disney would have to wait a year.

Oshkosh West coach Lance Randall pointed the way for Andy Polka during his team's state quarterfinal game.

Lance Randall could have gone back to the college game at that juncture, but he didn't think it would be fair to his family to move it again that soon. So he got his emergency license as a special education teacher and returned to West. The Wildcats had lost two starters off the 2005 team, but they had more than enough left to win a third straight Fox Valley Association championship. This time there was no stopping them as they took a 25-0 record into the showdown with Madison Memorial.

The game featured a match-up of two big men. Memorial had 6-foot-7 junior Keaton Nankivil. West had 6-6 senior Andy Polka. When Polka won the battle, West won the war. Nankivil scored 14 points, while Polka had 21 points, 12 rebounds and five assists. He made three baskets in a row to give the Wildcats a 40-28 lead with 2 minutes 39 seconds to play, sealing the first state basketball championship in West's history.

Randall stayed one more year at Oshkosh West and his team repeated as champion. He signed on as an assistant at Loyola University for the following season, ending a three-year interruption of his collegiate career. Oshkosh would never forget his detour.

BUCKS WIN COIN FLIP FOR ALCINDOR

MARCH 19, 1969

Lew Alcindor signs with the Milwaukee Bucks as Bucks' general manger and vice president John Erickson, right, and coach Larry Costello, rear, look on.

A single five-letter word brought the Milwaukee Bucks riches, respectability, and ultimately, their only championship. The word was "heads," and it was uttered over the telephone by a man named Richard Bloch.

Three weeks before the first two rounds of the National Basketball Association college draft, the Bucks and the Phoenix Suns each had a 50% chance of landing the No. 1 choice by virtue of having the worst records in their respective conferences. Everyone knew that pick would be used on 7-foot-2 center Lew Alcindor of UCLA, but the question of which team would get to make it rode on a coin toss to be conducted on a Wednesday morning in the NBA offices.

Milwaukee had posted a 27-55 record in its first season, while Phoenix had gone 16-66. Naturally, the Suns thought the process was unfair. As veteran guard Gail Goodrich put it: "We obviously had the worst team in the league, so we should have the first choice."

Goodrich's argument didn't impress NBA Commissioner Walter Kennedy, the man who would be flipping the coin. As members of the New York media looked on as witnesses, Kennedy held a draw to decide which team would have the option of calling the toss. On the phone from Milwaukee was Bucks' board chairman Wes Pavalon. On the phone from Phoenix was Bloch, one of the Suns' owners.

Bloch won the draw and elected to make the call. Kennedy flipped a 1964 half dollar, and Bloch called "heads." The coin came up "tails," and the Bucks were on their way to the NBA throne room.

It would take them two seasons to get there, but they became instant contenders on April 2, when Alcindor signed a contract. The three-time All-American would later change his name to Kareem Abdul-Jabbar, but not until after he'd changed everything for the Bucks.

Pavalon was expecting no less. In fact, he said he might not have bid for the franchise at all if there hadn't been a good chance of the Bucks getting their big man. Alcindor had led UCLA to three straight national championships, and he'd averaged 24 points and more than 14 rebounds a game as a senior. Less than a month short of his 22nd birthday, he was the most coveted athlete on the planet. He was also on the verge of becoming one of the richest.

Drafting Alcindor was one thing. Signing him was another. The rival American Basketball Association wanted him every bit as badly as the Bucks and Suns had. The New York Nets held his ABA rights, but the Nets' rivals were willing to chip in to make him an offer that would bring instant credibility to their league.

Alcindor wasn't interested in a messy auction. His agents told the Bucks and the Nets that they could each submit one sealed bid, and he'd make his final choice from those. When the bids were opened, the Bucks' offer was easily the best. Exact terms weren't disclosed, but it was widely believed that the deal was worth more than $1 million over five years.

That was crazy money in those days, and things got crazier when it was reported that the ABA had come back with a $3.25 million proposal. The report led to a strike threat from the ABA players, who suddenly felt badly underpaid. It didn't lead to Alcindor changing his mind. He called the alleged offer "newspaper talk" and ripped the young league for its circus atmosphere.

The Bucks' ticket office was swamped with requests on the day that Alcindor signed. Pavalon was delighted. He said he'd worn a Christopher medal, an Italian good luck piece, on the day of the coin flip. He probably would have been happy to swap it for the commissioner's half dollar.

MILWAUKEE LINCOLN ROARS BACK

MARCH 20, 1959

Chuck Houston was on the junior varsity, and Lincoln High School was on nobody's radar screen when the 1958-'59 Milwaukee high school basketball season began. The Comets were dark horses at best in the City Conference, while defending champion North and last year's runner-up, Washington, were loaded.

Lincoln had never been to the state tournament, and when coach Dick Wadewitz's team lost its season opener to Lake Geneva, there was no reason to think this year would be any different. The Comets had just three 6-footers on the roster and nobody over 6-1. Houston stood a mere 5-foot-8, and that was just one of his challenges. He was also missing two fingers on his right hand, which was deformed at birth.

So he shot left-handed, and four months later, he was a hero in one of the most stirring state tournament journeys Wisconsin high school basketball has ever seen.

Houston would play a key role in all of the stops along the way, but he was at his very best on Friday night, March 20, at the University of Wisconsin Fieldhouse when the Comets rallied from 22 points back to beat fourth-ranked La Crosse Logan, 79-77, in overtime in the semifinal round.

Lincoln was trailing Logan, 51-29, midway through the third quarter, and it was still down, 58-46, when the final period began. That's when Houston came off the bench to hit two shots that triggered a 14-point run and led to a 60-60 tie. His long jumper with 16 seconds on the clock sent the game into overtime. And then he scored four more points in the extra period.

Forward Harold Lamar's basket with three seconds left provided the victory for the Comets, and 6-1 center Andy Chesser led them with 22 points. But Logan coach Rod Martin said, "The little boy with the crippled hand hurt us the most."

Houston, who was a junior, was pulled up to the varsity at the semester break, just in time to help Lincoln pull off one upset after another on the way to its first state basketball title and the first ever for a Milwaukee public school.

Just making it to Madison was a huge accomplishment for the Comets, who were 14-4 and unranked going into the sub-regionals. In their second tournament game, they disposed of Washington, 76-63, after losing to the Purgolders by nine in the conference season. Later, they upset defending state champion Madison East, 75-73, in the sectional semifinal. Houston saw little action in that game until the fourth quarter when he scored 11 points, recorded several key steals and tipped in a game-tying basket over 6-5 East star Pat Richter.

It just got tougher for the Comets when they got to the Thursday night quarterfinals in Madison and faced undefeated, top-ranked Kimberly. They fell behind, 26-14, in the first quarter, and they were down, 71-63, with six minutes to play before Houston's two baskets capped a 10-1 streak that put Lincoln ahead by a point. Guard Paul Ramseur's layup with 11 seconds to play gave Lincoln an 82-81 victory when Kimberly's Don Hearden had a buzzer-beating basket waved off by a traveling call.

Another last-second decision had saved the Comets in the Logan game when Dave Horton hit a half-court shot that would have tied the score if the referees hadn't ruled that he'd gotten it off too late.

Lincoln didn't need any help from the fates in wrapping up the championship with a 65-56 triumph over City Conference rival North. Houston contributed nine points to that one, and a long run of state tournament success was just getting started for the Comets. Lincoln would win four more state titles in the next eight seasons, and, then, in 1979, its doors were closed for so-called economic reasons by the Milwaukee School Board.

LITTLE DODGEVILLE SCORES BIG TRIUMPH

MARCH 21, 1964

If he played 10 games against Milwaukee North, John "Weenie" Wilson figured he would have lost seven. Or so he told the losing coach.

But once was enough. As 13,217 people watched in disbelief at the University of Wisconsin Fieldhouse, Wilson's Dodgeville High School team used five players and a ferocious defense to shut down one of the highest scoring offenses the state had ever seen.

Dodgeville, a school of 411 students, put a cap on a 26-0 season by taking just 38 shots and making 18 of them while North, a school of 1,200, was missing 52 of 71. The Dodgers became only the ninth state champion in the 39-year history of the Wisconsin Interscholastic Athletic Association tournament to finish undefeated, and they won going away, 59-45.

Wilson, who was also Dodgeville's baseball coach and former head football coach, wasn't even supposed to be on the bench that night. His doctor had told him to get out of the business three years earlier when he'd spent nine weeks in critical condition after suffering two heart attacks. But Wilson insisted he had pills to take care of that problem, and he certainly never felt better than he did when the Dodgers came back to win their first state basketball championship after losing to Manitowoc in the title game the year before.

North came into the game with a 24-1 record having topped 100 points five times during the season. The Milwaukee City Conference champions had scored 129 in one game, and they'd put up a tournament-record 94 while beating Waterloo in the semifinals the night before. Blanton Simmons, a 6-foot-4 guard who would soon join Al McGuire's first recruiting class at Marquette, scored 36 points in that game.

Dodgeville, on the other hand, had held its opponents under 50 points 18 times. North would be victim No. 19. In fact, Dodgeville didn't allow more than 48 points in any of its nine tournament games.

Neither team could find the basket in the first half. North made only 11 of its 42 shots before the break while Dodgeville went nine for 24. But North's Blue Devils broke on top, taking a 12-9 first-quarter lead and expanding it to 23-19 at halftime. They would have had more breathing room if they hadn't missed seven of eight free throws.

Simmons struggled mightily all night, finishing with only one basket and three points. Teammate and all-state center Esthesial Ford led North with 17 points and 11 rebounds. But his counterpart, 6-5 Dodgeville center Rick Brown, came alive in the second half and outshoned him. The Dodgers went on a 12-0 run in the third quarter and outscored North, 17-6, for the period, with Brown getting nine of his game-high 20 points.

The Dodgers, who never substituted in the game, dictated the pace the rest of the way. In fact, their starting five – forwards Pat Flynn and Carlos Evans, and guards Bruce Harrison and Bob Rock in addition to Brown – essentially went the distance in all three state tournament games.

Free throws and rebounds plagued North. The Blue Devils got only seven points from the line to Dodgeville's 23, and they lost the backboard battle, 40-39, after leading it, 30-19, at halftime. But coach Vic Anderson figured it was their 26.8 field goal percentage that did them in. "I knew if we were going to lose a game, it would be one where the boys got real cold," he said.

The victory topped a remarkable career for Wilson, who had played baseball in the St. Louis Cardinals' organization after going to training camp with the Green Bay Packers. And he was so happy he didn't know what to say, other than pay his respects to North, which he called one of the best teams ever to make it to state. Four years later, Wilson died of a heart attack while teaching a physical education class.

WEAVER'S DESPERATION SHOT SAVES BELOIT

MARCH 22, 1969

He was seven feet short of midcourt just inside the left sideline. According to the Pythagorean Theorem, it was a 55-foot shot. According to everyone at the University of Wisconsin Fieldhouse, it was a miracle.

Lamont Weaver would go on to have a fine college basketball career at Wisconsin, but nothing he did there could ever top the desperation heave he made for Beloit High School in its state championship game with Neenah. It came with two seconds left in regulation, and it not only sent the game into overtime, it gave Weaver the chance to be a hero twice on the same night.

The 6-foot-1 junior guard would sink two free throws in a second overtime to give Beloit an 80-79 victory and what was then a record sixth state basketball title in what may be the most memorable state title game ever.

It took some triangulation to determine just how far Weaver's shot traveled, and it took some luck and a mix-up in the Neenah defense for him to make it. Neenah had led throughout the first half, and it took Beloit until midway through the third quarter to catch up. The teams traded baskets after that until guard Pat Hawley's jump shot with four seconds to play put Neenah ahead, 70-68.

The Knights lost two more seconds calling timeout, and when they went to the sidelines they were one discouraged bunch. But coach Bernie Barkin told them it wasn't over yet. His plan was simple: Get the ball to Weaver, let him throw it as far as he could and hustle down the floor to try to get a tip-in. Of course, with two seconds to play there wasn't much chance for a tip-in, but Barkin was an optimist.

When the teams came back onto the court, the Neenah player who was supposed to guard the inbounds pass got caught out of position, and the player who was supposed to guard Weaver went after the passer instead.

That gave Weaver just enough time to get the ball, turn around, take two dribbles and let fly with a left-handed wish. The ball banged off the backboard and through the rim, stunning a crowd of 12,923 and creating an enduring moment in state basketball history.

"It looked good, but I didn't know," Weaver said later. "I've never made a shot like that before. I don't remember trying one."

Coach Ron Einerson's Neenah team recovered quickly from the shock and gave Beloit all it could handle through the two extra periods. A pair of Hawley free throws ended the first overtime in a 75-75 tie, and Beloit was trailing, 79-78, with 36 seconds to play in the second one when Weaver stepped to the line with a one-and-one. He swished both shots to put the Knights ahead for good. Neenah got another chance when Beloit missed a free throw with seven seconds remaining, but its last shot fell far short. Weaver finished with 25 points, while Beloit's 6-7 center Bruce Brown scored 26. Neenah forward Tom Kopitzke led all scorers with 27.

When the buzzer sounded, Beloit fans flooded the court, and carried Weaver and Barkin off the floor. Thousands more waited back in Beloit for the team to come home. When the bus arrived that night, there was a mile long line of cars waiting for it on the freeway, and a fire truck and a fleet of squad cars ready to escort it from the exit to the high school. Police estimated 3,000 cars and 15,000 people joined the parade to the parking lot.

Had Beloit lost, the disappointment would have been as crushing as the celebration was wild. The Knights had fallen to Manitowoc, 63-51, in the 1968 championship game, and they hadn't lost since. They were 25-0 going into the title game, while Neenah was a definite underdog at 21-4.

A year later, Neenah made it back to the championship game and the Rockets had their hearts broken once again. Appleton West beat them, 58-57, on a shot by Scott Hanson with four seconds to play. At least that one came from the corner, not from behind the half-court line.

BADGERS BEAT LSU ON ROAD TO FINAL FOUR

MARCH 23, 2000

People used a four-letter word to describe Dick Bennett's Wisconsin basketball team, and it wasn't "good," and it certainly wasn't "fast."

But there were the Badgers, one of only 16 teams in the country still standing as the NCAA West Regional semifinals got started in Albuquerque, N.M. Unranked and eighth-seeded, they didn't have an All-American or even an all-Big Ten player in the lineup, and no one was scoring as many as 13 points a game for them. They survived on fierce defense and numbing patience. Only this group could take "ugly" as a compliment.

They just did what they did, and they were about to do it again to fourth-seeded Louisiana State while taking a giant step to the school's first Final Four appearance in 59 years. LSU had a 28-6 record and an imposing frontcourt featuring twin towers Stromile Swift and Jabari Smith. Wisconsin had a 20-13 record and no towers. It was built more along the lines of a pole barn.

It had scored no style points and not too many of the other kind while advancing to the Sweet Sixteen at the expense of Fresno State and Arizona at Salt Lake City. The Badgers' 66-56 triumph over ninth-seeded Fresno was expected, but their 66-59 triumph over No. 1 seeded and fourth-ranked Arizona shocked everyone. As they left Utah, Fresno State coach Jerry Tarkanian sounded a warning. "They don't look physical in the team picture," he said, "but they are very physical."

"Physical" is often used as a code word for "non-athletic," but Bennett saw it as a synonym for "tough." This was Bennett's fifth Wisconsin team, and while he acknowledged that it may not have been his best, he said it was definitely his toughest. What's more, it had already gone further in the tournament than any UW team had since the 1941 national championship squad.

But none of that left LSU overly impressed. The Tigers were ranked 10th in the country, they were averaging 76.7 points a game, and they had their twin towers. At least, they did until the Badgers blew them down.

The 6-foot-11 Smith had been getting 12 points a game, and that's what he got against Wisconsin, but seven of them came in the last three minutes long after the issue had been decided. The 6-9 Swift was averaging 16.3 points, and he also scored 12. Put the two stars together and they got exactly half of the Tigers' points as Wisconsin walked away with a 61-48 victory that was never in doubt after halftime.

The Badgers double-teamed Swift and Smith whenever they got the ball in the post, and since neither of them passed particularly well and the Tigers weren't a good perimeter team, they were easy prey for Wisconsin. "You could see that confused look, that sense of frustration," said UW center Andy Kowske.

The frustration peaked when the Badgers turned LSU over 11 times while going on a 13-3 run that left them ahead, 22-14, at halftime. Point guard Mike Kelley had five steals as LSU finished the game with season lows in points, field goals and assists. Jon Bryant made three, three-point baskets on the way to a team-leading 16 points, and while the Badgers connected on only 21 of 55 shots, nobody cared. They'd earned a date with conference rival Purdue in the Elite Eight.

This was the fourth match between the Badgers and the sixth-seeded Boilermakers, and the result was similar to the last two. Bryant stayed hot, scoring 18 points, and Wisconsin hounded Purdue into a 21-for-53 shooting performance. The final score was 64-60, and the Badgers had become only the third eighth-seed in NCAA history to make the Final Four.

Their improbable ride ended suddenly in Indianapolis when they ran into the only team that had beaten them in the past two months. That team was Michigan State, and the Spartans had done it three times.

Michigan State led by the preposterous score of 19-17 at halftime and then slogged away to a 53-41 victory. The Spartans shot less than 35%, but they out-rebounded Wisconsin, 42-20. In other words, they beat the Badgers at their own game before going on to win the national title. For one weekend at least, ugly was in.

UWM'S CINDERELLA STORY ENDS

MARCH 24, 2005

Bruce Pearl   Joah Tucker

"Still not satisfied" was the rallying cry for the University of Wisconsin-Milwaukee basketball team as it entered the 2004-'05 season. The phrase was on the cover of the Panthers' media guide and in the thoughts of their fans when they faced top-ranked Illinois in the NCAA Sweet Sixteen at Rosemont, Ill.

Even if they weren't satisfied, the players on Bruce Pearl's mid-major surprise package had reason to feel pretty good about themselves after ringing up two huge upsets in the first two rounds at Cleveland, Ohio. No UWM team had ever won an NCAA Division I tournament game before, let alone knocked off a fifth and fourth seed.

But these Panthers were getting used to doing things differently. In 2002-'03, Pearl's second year as coach, they'd compiled a 24-8 record, earned their first Division I tournament bid and come within a point of upsetting Notre Dame in the first round. The following year, they'd gone 20-11, won their first regular-season conference championship and gone to the NIT.

Now they had four starters and 61% of their scoring back, and they weren't resting on their laurels. They'd finished the regular season with a 24-5 record and another Horizon League title, but they'd barely gotten past Detroit, 59-58, to earn the league's automatic bid. And then they'd become the Cinderella team of the tournament by stunning fifth-seeded Alabama, 83-73, and upending fourth-seeded Boston College, 83-75.

The victory over BC was particularly impressive because they'd come back from a 75-74 deficit in the last minute-and-a-half to win going away. That was enough to get Bruce Weber's attention. "They play a chaotic style," said the Illinois coach and a Milwaukee native. "It's different than the norm in college basketball. They try to get you to go faster than you want."

Alabama learned that when UWM caused it to turn the ball over 19 times. Two days later, Boston College committed 22 turnovers. But the question was whether the Panthers' pressing defense could rattle a veteran Illinois backcourt that was widely considered to be the best in the country. Unfortunately for Cinderella, the answer was no.

There was a reason why Illinois was a No. 1 seed while UWM was the lowest seed remaining in the tournament at No. 12. Everyone would prove to be outmanned by the Illini as they went on to win the national championship that year, but in UWM's case, the matchups were especially bad. Pearl relied on pressure, and Illinois was impervious to it. The Illini had basically three starting point guards in their lineup.

They also had a size advantage up front and approximately 15,000 supporters with a grudge. The game was played at the Allstate Arena, which was less than 150 miles away from the Illinois campus, and most of the fans had heard about Pearl's days as an assistant coach at Iowa where he'd been instrumental in getting Illinois placed on probation because of a recruiting scandal.

Pearl was drowned in boos when he stepped onto the court, but his unpopularity didn't seem to affect the Panthers as they made their first five shots to take a 12-8 lead. But then Illinois scored the next six points and never trailed again. Pearl had to abandon the press, and the Illini committed just nine turnovers all day long.

While all five Illinois starters scored in double figures, junior forward Joah Tucker carried the whole load for UWM with 32 points. Ed McCants, the Horizon League player of the year, was shut out in the first half and finished with 13 points on four-of-17 shooting. When the Illini went on a 12-2 run midway through the second half, the issue was decided. The final score was 77-63.

Two days later, Pearl had a meeting with the University of Tennessee president as well as the school's athletic director. Tennessee had noticed the Panthers, too, and it came after their coach waving a checkbook. UWM was paying him $275,000 a year. The Volunteers put together a package worth up to $1 million. Pearl left for Knoxville the following Tuesday, telling his players he would always be part of their lives.

And so, of course, would be their big-time battle with Illinois. "We had an opportunity to shock the world, and we had the weapons to do it," Tucker said. "It was a huge opportunity."

No moral victories there. As usual, the Panthers still weren't satisfied.

McGUIRE'S TECHNICALS COST MARQUETTE

MARCH 25, 1974

Al McGuire never denied that he drew technical fouls on purpose. Sometimes he did it to fire up his team and other times he did it to get the officials' attention. But he usually picked his spots.

Marquette's NCAA championship game with North Carolina State was definitely not one of those spots.

McGuire's Warriors were 13-point underdogs when they took on the Wolfpack in college basketball's biggest game at the Greensboro Coliseum less than 100 miles from the opponents' campus. They were facing a lineup that featured David Thompson, soon to be one of pro basketball's biggest stars, along with NBA-bound 7-foot-2 center Tom Burleson and 5-7 guard Monte Towe, as well as Tim Stoddard, who would become a major league pitcher.

The Warriors had four future pros themselves in Maurice Lucas, Earl Tatum, Bo Ellis and Lloyd Walton, but the last thing they could afford was to give away easy points. And they gave away a ton of them in a frantic space of 1 minute 13 seconds late in the first half, thanks to a pair of technical foul calls on McGuire. When they lost the game, 74-64, McGuire blamed himself for costing his team the championship.

Many observers believed top-ranked NC State had already earned the title in the semifinals two nights earlier when it beat UCLA with Bill Walton in double overtime to end the Bruins' seven-year reign as national champions. Third-rated Marquette, meanwhile, had beaten No. 6 Kansas, 64-51.

But the Warriors were holding their own in the final, taking a 28-27 lead on Marcus Washington's layup with 2:48 to play in the first half. That's when McGuire touched off his 73 seconds of fireworks. Washington was whistled for charging Thompson on the layup, and McGuire stormed over to the scorer's table and kicked the NCAA emblem whereupon he was promptly whistled for his first technical.

Thompson hit three free throws – two on the personal foul and one on the technical – and after the Wolfpack inbounded the ball at half-court, Burleson scored from underneath. Burleson connected again to put the Wolfpack up, 34-28, and then Ellis was called for goaltending on a basket by N.C. State's Phil Spencer, sending McGuire back onto the court and into orbit.

That was technical No. 2, and when Thompson made the free throw, the Wolfpack had a 37-28 advantage that it would never lose. North Carolina State expanded its lead to 19 in the first five minutes of the second half, and the game was all but over.

Marquette's Lloyd Walton scanned the floor in the NCAA championship game in 1974.

Asked later if there had been a method in his madness, McGuire said, "No way. Not unless I got a case of the DTs or something. It was a mistake on my part. The technicals cost us the game. I would say I lost the game."

McGuire wouldn't back down on the calls that led to the Ts, however. "I'd rather not discuss them," he said, "because I'm absolutely correct."

Thompson had a big game for North Carolina State with 21 points and seven rebounds, and Burleson added 14 points and 11 boards, but the best player on the floor that night was Lucas. He scored 21 points, cleared 13 rebounds and used his performance as a springboard into the pro game.

He would skip his senior season at Marquette, but he did leave McGuire a little going away present when he was asked if he was mad at the coach for giving North Carolina State all that momentum. "Mad at him? How can I be mad at him?" he told *The Milwaukee Journal*. "He's the coach, and he's the coach of the year. We all go uptown together or we all go down together."

BRADLEY CENTER IS HOME TO McDONALD'S ALL-STARS

MARCH 26, 2008

Defense was kind of an afterthought, but the entertainment was superb as Milwaukee played host to the best high school basketball players in America for the first time ever.

The boys' teams jacked up a combined 171 shots in the East's 107-102 victory over the West at the 31st annual McDonald's All-American Game, and 91 of them went in. Flyers upstaged marksmen by a wide margin throwing down 11 dunks, while three-point shooters succeeded only seven times in 41 tries.

Basketball purists might have some problem with that, but there didn't appear to be any major complaints from the 10,914 people who paid their way into the Bradley Center hoping to see the next Magic Johnson or Michael Jordan.

More than 850 high school players had been named to play in past games, including Johnson and Jordan, and more than 150 of those were playing at that time in either the NBA or the WNBA. Playing in the McDonald's game doesn't absolutely guarantee anyone a Division I scholarship, but it comes pretty close. Ninety-six percent of past participants had gone on to play D-I ball.

If you were a major college prospect or a hopeless hoops junkie, the Bradley Center was the place to be. Every March a panel of high school coaches, scouts and writers picks 48 seniors for the two boys' and two girls' squads from a field of more than 2,500 candidates and sends them to the temporary capital of prep basketball. This time it was Milwaukee, and although there were no Wisconsin players on any of the rosters, there was one future Milwaukee Buck. Brandon Jennings, the team's No. 1 draft pick in 2009, played for the West team and scored 12 points.

Moreover, the event couldn't have had a more local flavor if McDonald's had served brats. Directing the boys' West team were Milwaukee City Conference coaches Jim Gosz of King, Tom Diener of Vincent and Marc Mitchell of Custer. Leading the girls from the West were Tom Klawitter and Jane Dooley of Janesville Parker and Heidi Hamilton of Arrowhead.

In case you'd lost track of Hamilton, she used to be Heidi Bunek, and she used to lead Milwaukee Pius to a state championship just about annually. She went from there to play for Notre Dame, and the only reason she never appeared in the McDonald's game was that girls weren't included until 2002.

Gosz contended that at least two or three Wisconsin players were good enough to play in this game, and he did have some history on his side. Joe Wolf, Calvin Rayford, Sam Okey and Brian Butch had all played in past boys game; and Mistie Bass had played in the first girls game.

But this day was more about the future than it was about the past, and one player who seemed to have a bright one was 6-foot-6 swing man Tyreke Evans of West Chester, Pa., which just happened to be Wisconsin coach Bo Ryan's hometown. Evans scored 21 points and pulled down 10 rebounds to earn Most Valuable Player honors in the boys' game.

Wisconsin's coaching contingent fared better in the girls' game than it did in the boys' as the West ran right by the East, 80-64. But it was the local Ronald McDonald House charities that made out best of all. They got the proceeds from the game, which was reason enough to celebrate its stop in Wisconsin.

EARL ANTHONY UNSTOPPABLE IN MILLER OPEN

MARCH 27, 1982

It wasn't broke, and Earl Anthony wasn't about to fix it. The world's greatest bowler was competing in maybe the world's best bowling city, and he knew if he just kept on doing what he was doing, he'd be $23,000 richer by the end of the day.

"I just kept telling myself, 'Repeat the shot. Repeat the shot.' It's just a matter of repetition," Anthony said after claiming the winner's share of the $135,000 Miller Open bowling tournament at Milwaukee's Red Carpet Celebrity Lanes.

He repeated it 18 times in 20 frames while rolling past Jeff Mattingly and Frank Ellenburg in the last two games of the stepladder finals. His 268-232 victory against Mattingly included nine strikes and a single spare in the sixth frame, and then he struck nine more times while posting a 269-235 decision over Ellenburg, missing only in the second frame.

A standing room only crowd was there to watch the Dublin, Calif., left-hander atone for an embarrassing, 277-165, loss to Mike Durbin in the 1981 Miller final. Anthony also had finished second in Milwaukee in 1975. But this time the people got what they were expecting from the pro tour's first millionaire. The first-place check boosted his earnings to $97,980 for the season and $1,043,945 for his career.

Anthony joined the tour in 1963 after a broken ankle derailed his plans to be a pro baseball pitcher, but he wasn't ready to compete at that point. So he went home, practiced whenever he could, and worked as a mailman before returning to the sport in 1970. He was definitely ready after that, winning 41 tour events and earning six player of the year awards before leaving the tour following the 1987 season. Thereafter, he joined the Senior Tour and won seven more events before retiring because of arthritic knees.

Milwaukee and "Square Earl" as Anthony was called on the pro tour were a good fit. Suburban Greendale had been the longtime headquarters of the American Bowling Congress, and Anthony was a frequent visitor to the area during and after his career. His friends described him as "one of the guys," someone who liked to hang out, tell stories and have a couple of beers. Tragically, he died in Wisconsin at the age of 63.

Trim and athletic as he was, Anthony had suffered a heart attack in 1977, and heart problems may have contributed to his death. He was found dead at the bottom of a flight of stairs in the New Berlin home of his friend Ed Baur on Aug. 14, 2001. An autopsy indicated the cause of death was a head injury caused from the fall onto a marble floor, but it was speculated that he'd blacked out before the fall.

When Anthony died, he held the PBA record for most tournament victories. And eight years later, when the PBA celebrated its 50th anniversary, Anthony was named the greatest bowler of all time.

Earl Anthony

MILWAUKEE PBA WINTER TOUR WINNERS
Miller High Life Open

Year	Winner
1966	Bill Lillard
1967	Dave Davis
1968	Johnny Guenther
1969	Billy Hardwick
1970	George Pappas
1971	Dave Soutar
1972	Nelson Burton Jr.
1973	Don McCune
1974	Johnny Guenther
1975	Dave Davis
1976	Dave Soutar
1977	Eddie Ressler
1978	Fred Jaskie
1979	Johnny Petraglia
1980	Alvin Lou
1981	Mike Durbin
1982	Earl Anthony
1983	Mark Fahy
1984	Rickie Sajek

Lite Beer Championship

Year	Winner
1985	Wayne Webb
1986	Don Genalo
1987	Tom Milton
1988	Jeff Bellinger

Source: pba.com

MARQUETTE WINS IT ALL IN McGUIRE'S FINAL GAME

MARCH 28, 1977

They were the original bad guests. Al McGuire's Warriors had no business being in Atlanta in the first place, and now they wouldn't leave.

Marquette fans could think of three or four better McGuire teams than the one that arrived at The Omni for the NCAA semifinals. The coach himself doubted that this one would even make the tournament when it faced a season-ending, five-game road trip after losing three in a row at home in mid-February.

McGuire had announced his retirement three months earlier, and, for a time, he seemed destined to exit from a stage in Ann Arbor, Mich., where the Warriors played their last regular-season game. But then his team won four straight on the road before falling to the third-ranked Wolverines, 69-68, for their seventh loss of the season.

While nobody had ever won a national championship as a seven-game loser, the Warriors earned an at-large bid in what was then a 32-team NCAA field and beat Cincinnati in a first-round game before knocking off Kansas State and Wake Forest in the Midwest Regional at Oklahoma City.

Somehow the Warriors became reenergized down the stretch and McGuire couldn't explain the turnaround. The only thing he could think of was the players had stopped listening to the coach.

One thing was sure: They would never be listening to him again. Back in December when he was asked why as a relatively young 48-year-old man he'd decided to call it quits, he had said, "Because it's over. It's time. I've had my run."

Not quite. He had two fast laps to go in Atlanta.

None of the other teams in the Final Four had lost more than four games, and there were those who believed the real championship would be played on Saturday when 28-2 Nevada-Las Vegas faced 27-4 North Carolina. Waiting for Marquette was 28-3 North Carolina-Charlotte featuring future pros Cedric Maxwell and Chad Kinch.

The Warriors took an early 14-point lead on Charlotte, and then "The Fox" outfoxed himself by going into a delay with six minutes left in the first half. Suddenly, Marquette's momentum was gone, and so was its big lead as the 49ers closed the difference to 25-22 at halftime. The teams traded punches after that, leaving the score tied at 49 with three seconds remaining.

Following a timeout, center Jerome Whitehead scooped up a loose ball and banged it off the board and through the basket as time expired. It took a long conference at the scorer's table to determine that Whitehead had gotten the shot off on time, and the Warriors had survived, 51-49. Next up was Carolina.

The Tar Heels had their share of excitement as well in slipping past Vegas, 84-83. Now it came down to a matchup between two storied coaches, Carolina's Dean Smith and McGuire, with teams that were led by perhaps the two best guards in the country, MU's Butch Lee and Carolina's Phil Ford. Drawing the defensive assignment on Ford was Jimmy Boylan, a transfer student from Assumption College.

While Boylan helped limit Ford to six points for the night, Lee dominated the individual battle by scoring 15 in the first half alone as the Warriors took a surprising 39-27 lead. Then the Tar Heels caught fire in the next eight minutes, going on an 18-6 run to tie the game, 45-45.

That's when Smith made a fatal mistake. He pulled his offense back and went into his patented four-corner delay game for the next two-and-a-half minutes, hoping to take Marquette out of its zone defense and get some easy baskets on layups.

Instead, Smith halted his own team's momentum, just as McGuire had two nights earlier. Carolina got its layup, but it was blocked by Bo Ellis. A basket by Boylan and a flurry of free throws put Marquette ahead, 53-49, with 1 minute 45 seconds remaining, setting up the strangest play of the night.

The Warriors' Bernard Toone and the Tar Heels' Mike O'Koren were struggling for a loose ball when O'Koren inadvertently poked Toone in both eyes. Blinded, the Marquette forward swung his elbows wildly to protect the ball, and the officials charged him with a technical foul and O'Koren with a personal. Toone missed his free throw, while Carolina's Walter Davis made a pair on the technical to cut the MU lead to 53-51.

But the Warriors claimed the ensuing tip and wrapped up the victory on six straight free throws. The final score was 67-59, and the enduring final scene was McGuire sitting at the end of the bench with his head in his hands weeping.

"I don't know if this was destiny for me to win now," he said. "I don't look at it that way. I'm pleased for the guys."

College basketball was pleased for Al McGuire.

BADGERS CLAIM NCAA BASKETBALL TITLE

MARCH 29, 1941

They were singing "There Will Be a Hot Time in the Old Town Tonight" on the streets of Madison, and they weren't kidding. A fire engine met Wisconsin's new national collegiate basketball champions at the train station in the wee hours of Monday morning to take them to the Capitol, and so many fans hopped on along the way that the motor burst into flames trying to make it up King Street.

A fire engine catching on fire was no more improbable than these University of Wisconsin Badgers beating heavily-favored Washington State, 39-34, to win the school's only NCAA basketball championship. Bud Foster's Badgers were coming off a 5-15 season, and they hadn't had a winning record in five years. So when they got off to a 5-3 start, despite adding two talented sophomore starters in Johnny Kotz of Rhinelander and Fred Rehm of Milwaukee, no one was expecting anything special.

But then they went on a 14-game winning streak that included Eastern Regional victories over Dartmouth and Pittsburgh before sellout crowds of 13,000 at the 11-year-old state of the art UW Fieldhouse. There were only two regionals in those days, and just eight teams in what was only the third annual NCAA tournament.

With 6-foot-7 center Paul Lindeman leading the way, Washington State had put together a 25-5 record, and the Cougars were considered unstoppable when they got to Kansas City for the national championship. But Wisconsin was now 19-3 and had a big man of its own in Gene Englund. While the senior center carried less than 200 pounds on his 6-4½ frame, he had sharp elbows and an attitude to go along with a deft hook shot.

Foster used Englund and a forward to double-team Lindeman, limiting him to three points, all on free throws. Englund, meanwhile, scored 13 points and Kotz added 12. Kotz also was named the game's Most Valuable Player.

The Badgers held the Cougars scoreless for a nine-minute span on the way to a 21-17 halftime lead. Washington State managed a 24-24 tie four minutes into the second half, but never got ahead and Wisconsin sealed the victory by scoring five of the game's last seven points. Kotz scored a crucial basket, and reserve Ted Strain added a big free throw.

Defense was everything as the Badgers made just 16 of 67 field goal attempts but held the Cougars to 14 of 63.

John Kotz

The train from Kansas City pulled into Madison at 1:20 am. Monday, March 31, and an estimated 12,000 people were on hand to greet it. It was an impressive number considering the fact that the city's population was only 67,000 at the time. The players were all sporting the new wristwatches that the NCAA had awarded them, and Foster had the team trophy. It was a festive occasion for everyone but Englund, who missed it altogether. He'd gone straight to Kenosha, his hometown, for a date with his draft board.

UW-GREEN BAY HIRES DICK BENNETT

MARCH 30, 1985

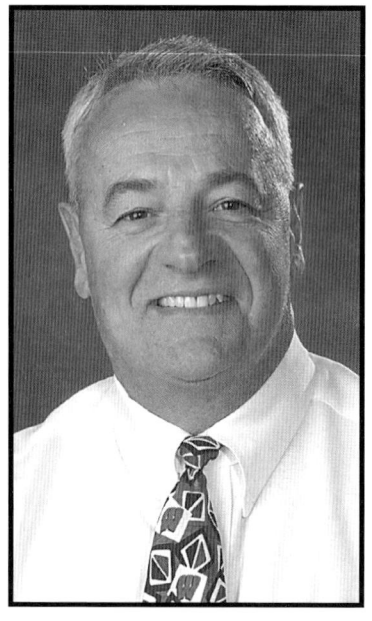

According to the legend, the Phoenix is a magnificent bird that lives for 500 years. As death nears, it builds a nest of branches and incense that's ignited by the sun, and when the flames engulf the bird, a new Phoenix rises from the ashes of the old one.

The University of Wisconsin-Green Bay adopted the Phoenix nickname when it began its basketball program in 1969-'70. Twelve years later, following a successful run at the NCAA Division II level, it moved up to Division I. And by the time it hired Dick Bennett it needed a rebirth. Sixteen years is just a small fraction of 500, but the former UW-Stevens Point coach was still stepping into some seriously deep ashes when his appointment was announced on a Saturday morning at the Phoenix Sports Center.

Green Bay had a 14-13 record in its first season of Division I competition in 1981-'82, but that was followed by two 9-19 years and one of 4-24 under Dick Lien. Bennett had begun building a reputation for rescuing distressed basketball programs in 10 years at four Wisconsin high schools and nine at Stevens Point. Now he was facing his biggest challenge.

It was easy to see why the Phoenix would want Bennett. He'd won 159 games while losing only 57 as a high school varsity coach, and then he'd gone 173-80 at Stevens Point where he'd led the Pointers to the National Association of Intercollegiate Athletics championship game and produced future pro Terry Porter.

The question was: Why would Bennett want the Phoenix rather than maybe waiting for a more promising opportunity?

It was a step up from the Division III ranks to Division I, but at a school with a short history and a seemingly bleak outlook in its new classification.

There was a modest raise, of course. Green Bay was offering a $42,000 a year rolling terms contract, although Bennett was already making $36,000 at Stevens Point and running a lucrative summer basketball camp. What's more, he'd won 101 games in the past four years and played to capacity crowds while Green Bay was struggling to reach double digits in victories and facing a sea of empty seats at Brown County Veterans Memorial Arena.

So what was the lure? The answer was the challenge.

"There is a point in time where each of us takes a long look at himself," said the 41-year-old Bennett. "I feel the need to stretch."

Bennett's particular genius was in attracting and developing players who felt the same way. He knew he couldn't recruit nationally known prospects for Green Bay, but he believed he could build a program with highly motivated, under-the-radar state kids like Porter. And like his own son. Tony Bennett became the Phoenix all-time leading scorer while playing for his father, and then he went on to play in the NBA. Two other Green Bay alums, Jeff Nordgaard of Dawson, Minn., and Logan Vander Velden of Valders, also had brief stints in the NBA after playing for Bennett.

The Phoenix were 5-23 in Bennett's first year, but they finished under .500 only once during the other nine. They also went to three NCAA tournaments in that time. They lost to Michigan State, 60-58, in their first tournament appearance and they were edged, 49-48, by Purdue in their last one, but it was the middle one that got people's attention.

No one gave them much of a chance at the West Regional in Ogden, Utah, in 1994 when they faced a 16th-ranked California team that featured two future pros in Jason Kidd and Lamond Murray. But Green Bay limited the two Cal stars to 30 points on a combined 10-for-38 shooting effort while pulling off a 61-57 upset.

Bennett had become one of the nation's worst kept coaching secrets at that point. He could have moved up to a number of major schools if the job he really wanted hadn't been 130 miles away in Madison. The University of Wisconsin had overlooked him twice before in favor of Stu Jackson and Stan Van Gundy, but Athletic Director Pat Richter didn't make that mistake again.

He hired Bennett in March 1995, and five years later, the Badgers were in the NCAA Final Four for the first time in 59 years. They'd been to three NCAA tournaments in the 97 seasons before Bennett got to Madison, and they were in three in the five he was there.

When he resigned three games into the 2000-'01 season, saying he was "just drained," he left much more than ashes behind.

MAJOR LEAGUE BASEBALL RETURNS TO MILWAUKEE

MARCH 31, 1970

The Milwaukee Braves hadn't even left town yet when Bud Selig started looking for ways to replace them. It was 1965 and the Braves had their bags all but packed for Atlanta when the local Ford dealer gathered nine other investors dedicated to bringing Major League Baseball back to a place it never should have left in the first place.

Each of the ten chipped in $150,000 to form something called the Milwaukee Brewers Baseball Club, which may have been the most stubborn lobbying group west of Washington, D.C. With heavyweights such as Cutler-Hammer's Edmund Fitzgerald and Schlitz Brewing's Robert Uihlein Jr. on board, Selig's group tried everything from applying for expansion franchises to luring an existing club to Milwaukee. None of it worked until somebody went bankrupt.

The Seattle Pilots had managed not only to finish last in the West Division, but to go $8.13 million in debt in just one year in the American League. To satisfy their creditors the owners had to sell the team, and there was no more eager buyer than Milwaukee. Dallas-Fort Worth made a run at the franchise, too, but on a fateful Tuesday night, Federal Bankruptcy Court Referee Sidney Volinn approved the sale to Selig's group for $10.8 million, or about one-tenth of what the Brewers would offer just one pitcher 38 years later.

"This is the culmination of years of frustration and disappointment," said Milwaukee County Circuit Judge Robert C. Cannon, vice president of the Brewers.

Volinn announced his decision at 10:20 (Milwaukee time) the night of March 31, in a Seattle court room packed with about 100 fans, and the Milwaukee papers splashed the news across the top of their front pages the next day. On April 1, the new Milwaukee franchise opened for business. The day after that, Volinn officially signed the papers that finalized the sale.

Milwaukee was as delighted to get the Pilots as Seattle was disgruntled about losing them. The city and the state of Washington proceeded with its lawsuit against the American League – for damages, not to keep the club – while AL President Joe Cronin sent the Brewers a telegram welcoming Milwaukee into the fold. Selig read the telegram aloud at a Wednesday press conference at the Pfister Hotel, and also announced that a "Welcome Brewers" luncheon would be held the following Monday.

Fortunately, the suit wasn't the Brewers' problem, although just about everything else was. The team was scheduled to arrive at Mitchell Field on Sunday night less than 48 hours before it was to open its season at County Stadium. All it needed in the interim were fans, uniforms, people to operate the stadium and 25 decent major league players.

The fans proved not to be a problem. More than 1,000 of them bought season tickets on the first day they went on sale. No question the price was right. The most expensive seat in the house was in the mezzanine, and it went for $5. Bleachers cost a buck.

Uniforms weren't much of an obstacle either. The team simply ripped the word "Pilots" off the front of the old jerseys and sewed "Brewers" on instead. And the stadium personnel was up and running in plenty of time. Ushers had been fitted before the team even got to town. The Brewers Baseball Club had been playing host to Chicago White Sox games for the past two seasons, so it wasn't totally unprepared.

The 25 major league players, on the other hand, were kind of elusive. The Brewers posted a well-earned 65-97 record in their first season, finishing just one game better than the Pilots had in 1969. Still, they drew 933,690 people – some 255,000 more than the Pilots the previous year – and it didn't take much to pay the rent. Their stadium deal called for them to pay the county one dollar a year and to keep all of the concession revenues up to the one-million mark in attendance.

And so on an uncharacteristically warm April Tuesday, the Brewers opened their season against the California Angels. They lost the game, 12-0, but most people thought they were worth the wait.

Bud Selig

MINOR LEAGUE BREWERS OBTAIN JIM THORPE

APRIL 1, 1916

The world's greatest athlete could run, jump throw, catch, block and tackle. He won 11 college varsity letters in every kind of sport, All-American honors in football, two Olympic gold medals in track and even an intercollegiate ballroom dancing title. But there was one thing that Jim Thorpe couldn't do.

He couldn't make winners of the Milwaukee Brewers baseball team.

Excitement reigned in Milwaukee when the two-time Olympic champion was released to the Class AAA Brewers on a Saturday night in an option deal with the New York Giants. Manager John McGraw of the Giants had done his best to teach the versatile Thorpe the one skill that consistently eluded him. He couldn't hit the breaking ball. The result was a .161 batting average over parts of three big league seasons.

But Thorpe had had better success in a previous stint on the minor league level, and when McGraw sold his contract to the Brewers he reserved the right to reclaim him if he needed him later. The Brewers thought they had a steal, although there was some skepticism in the press. Manning Vaughan wrote a story that appeared in the *Milwaukee Sentinel* three days later saying the team may have "picked a lemon."

Thorpe proved he was hardly that as he became the Brewers' best player in his one season in Milwaukee. He topped the American Association in stolen bases with 48 and hit .274 with 49 extra base hits, even though he struck out a league-high 117 times. But the team finished with a 54-110 record, the worst in the history of the franchise.

After leaving the Brewers, Thorpe went on to play three more mediocre major league seasons, finishing with a .252 career batting average before concentrating on professional football. Baseball just wasn't his game, and it was surprising that he stuck it out that long. But Thorpe wasn't easily discouraged.

He was born in 1888 on a farm in what was then called the Oklahoma Territory, and he'd seen more than his share of hard times before he was even a teenager. His father was part Irish and part Sac and Fox Indian; and his mother was French and Potawatomie and Kickapoo Indian. He lost his twin brother to pneumonia when he was eight, and his mother died when he was 12. His father died three years after that.

Thorpe's athletic career began in 1907 when he was a student at the government-run Carlisle Indian Industrial School in Pennsylvania. Four years later as a halfback on the football team he gained national prominence when he kicked four field goals and scored a touchdown in Carlisle's 18-15 upset of Harvard. The rest was history with some modern tragedy mixed in.

In 1911 and '12, Thorpe was chosen as a back on Walter Camp's All-American football team, and, between the two seasons, he went to the 1912 Olympics in Stockholm, Sweden, and won both the decathlon and the pentathlon. But he didn't get to keep the gold medals for long. It was discovered that he'd played minor league baseball for $25 a week while he was at Carlisle, which in the eyes of the inflexible Amateur Athletic Union made him a professional and cost him his Olympic titles. Seventy years later, his children got the medals back.

Thorpe's reputation was restored much sooner than his medals. In 1950 an Associated Press poll voted him the "Greatest Male Athlete" of the first half of the 20th century. He was also voted "Greatest Football Player" for his performance in college and an eight-season career in the NFL, and he finished second to Jesse Owens in the voting for "Greatest Track and Field Performer."

While Thorpe made a bigger splash in football than baseball and was inducted as a charter member of the Pro Football Hall of Fame in 1963, he never played in Green Bay. But he played twice in Milwaukee against the NFL Badgers and once in Racine against that city's NFL team.

Thorpe's prowess as an athlete made him famous, but never made him rich. He was hospitalized with lip cancer as a charity case in the early 1950s and died of a heart attack in 1953 at the age of 64.

ROUNDY COUGHLIN JOINS THE STATE JOURNAL

APRIL 2, 1924

Joseph Leo Coughlin launched his assault on the English language for the *Wisconsin State Journal* on the day he walked into the newsroom. Forty-seven years later he had brought it to its knees. In between, he became one of the most popular and colorful journalists Wisconsin has ever known, and in his spare time he helped raise more than $120,000 for needy kids and people with disabilities.

Roundy Coughlin

"Roundy" Coughlin set the ground rules for his career when he wrote in one of his early *State Journal* sports columns: "I have not had no education, and I don't intend to be smart. My English ain't the best, and I have things to learn every day. But I will keep on writing in the same manner I have always done, giving the fans the truth and in words they can understand."

He got no argument from the paper's editors, who had gone to a lot of trouble to hire him away from the rival *The Capital Times* of Madison. They did it by doubling his $35 weekly salary and giving him a bright red sports car with his name painted on the side. The *Daily Cardinal* student newspaper broke the story on April 2, 1924, six days before Coughlin's first column appeared in the *State Journal*.

Those were different times, and Coughlin was a very different character.

The son of an Irish immigrant, he dropped out of school at the age of 14 to help support his six brothers and sisters when the family grocery story went bust. He drove a butcher wagon, shined shoes, worked for the railroad and almost got himself killed climbing telephone poles before he wandered out of a pool hall and into journalism. The 40-foot fall he suffered while working on telephone wires fractured his skull, broke his neck and cost him most of his hearing, but it didn't dampen his enthusiasm for physical activity.

The one-time sandlot football player and minor league baseball teammate of Casey Stengel loved to play and talk sports. He was doing a lot of the latter while working in a Madison billiards establishment when he attracted the attention of Irwin Maier, the business manager of The *Daily Cardinal* and later the editor of *The Milwaukee Journal*.

Before long, Roundy's comments and predictions were showing up in Maier's newspaper. That morphed into a $5 a week part-time job writing a weekly column at the *Capital Times* and then a fulltime position there before the *State Journal* stole him away. The rest was history ... or something. It certainly wasn't English.

Almost five decades of scattershot "Roundy says" columns became all but required reading throughout the state. The writer bounced from sport to sport, but he was at his best with University of Wisconsin football. Once when the Badger backs had spent most of an afternoon trying futilely to run wide on their opponents, he wrote, "If they hadda put the goal posts on the sidelines we woulda won." Another time, he critiqued the UW kicking game by saying, "32,000 here at school, and they can't get a punter."

But perhaps his most famous effort came after the Badgers upset Iowa in a snowstorm: "Wisconsin 6, Iowa 0. Right there on there on there own gridiron and in there own snow. What more could be fairer?"

Coughlin's reach extended into radio and television, and his subjects weren't always sports. He interviewed Calvin Coolidge, Charles Lindbergh and Gertrude Stein, and he even drew raves from the famous American poet Amy Lowell, who told a visiting London scholar who had come to study the English language: "We have only one who speaks it in this country. His name is Roundy Coughlin, and he lives in Madison, Wisconsin."

As the nation's only English speaker, he put his popularity to good use by establishing a "Fun Fund" for kids in 1947. It raised $121,420 dollars for 43 different organizations.

Coughlin never married. His job was his life – almost literally. Aching legs forced him to retire on Jan. 2, 1971, and he spent most of his last year in bed in a nursing home before dying a little more than 11 months later at the age of 84. Doctors said he succumbed to "the general infirmities of old age."

Undoubtedly, Roundy Coughlin would have found a better way to put that.

COSTELLO, NOT McGUIRE, GETS BUCKS' JOB

APRIL 3, 1968

The Milwaukee Bucks' new coach was in a peculiar situation. He wasn't replacing anyone, but he still had a tough act to follow.

Larry Costello seemed to be just the man to lead the expansion Bucks into their first season as they introduced him and John Erickson at a press conference at the Pfister Hotel. Although Costello had no NBA head coaching experience, he was young, enthusiastic and knowledgeable. What he wasn't was Al McGuire.

That, of course, wasn't Costello's fault, but he was clearly not the team's first choice. Neither was Erickson, the University of Wisconsin coach who'd been named the franchise's first general manager. Plan A for both jobs had been McGuire.

A month earlier, the charismatic New Yorker, who had turned the Marquette University program around in four years, created a major storm when he let it be known that he was talking contract with the Bucks. The fallout made Costello's hiring an anti-climax.

Over the years McGuire would develop a reputation for controversy, and he got an early start on it when he became the subject of a public tug-of-war between Milwaukee's newest pro franchise and the Jesuit fathers. The fracas started on March 4 when McGuire met with his players and told them he would be leaving the team after the season to become the Bucks' coach and general manager if the university would let him go.

That came as an unpleasant surprise to Father Raymond McCauley, the school's executive vice president, who got the word while he was in Chicago. McCauley hustled home to hold a press conference where he made it clear that Marquette would not let McGuire leave. He pointed out that the coach had just recently signed a five-year contract, and the university intended to hold him to it.

McCauley said he'd had a couple of meetings with McGuire about the coach's interest in the Bucks, and he'd never given him permission to talk to them. He wasn't pleased either that McGuire had gone public when the Warriors had an NCAA tournament game scheduled with Bowling Green in Kent, Ohio, just five days away.

McGuire replied that the game was the reason he'd gathered his players in the first place. He knew there were rumors floating around, and he wanted to confront them rather than let the speculation become a distraction. He also said that Dean of Men Ed Kurdziel had given him permission to talk to the Bucks.

There are varying accounts of how McGuire and the Bucks got together in the first place. In McGuire's biography *You Can Call Me Al*, the late Roger Jaynes wrote that a member of the Bucks' ownership group approached *Milwaukee Journal* reporter Terry Bledsoe to find out whether McGuire would be interested in leaving Marquette. Bledsoe then asked McGuire, who told him he'd like to talk about it. McGuire tried to contact McCauley and Father John Rayner, the university president, but both were out of town, so he tried Kurdziel next. Kurdziel told McGuire he couldn't stop him from talking, but he couldn't give him permission either.

A different version came from the late Marv Fishman, one of the Bucks' primary owners, in his autobiography *Bucking the Odds*. Fishman wrote that McGuire's lawyer, Gene Smith, contacted a Bucks board member about McGuire, but the Bucks were careful not to talk directly with McGuire because that might be considered tampering. Fishman says McCauley's first reaction was to let McGuire go because he'd been difficult to work with, but McCauley came under fire from Marquette fans, and so he changed his position.

McCauley's press conference didn't appear to bother the Bucks. Team President Ray Patterson said that McGuire was still their man, although he added that the Bucks "would not want to bring about a confrontation with Marquette."

In the end, McGuire stayed put. The Warriors beat Bowling Green, 72-71, in the first round of the Mideast Regional, but then they lost to Kentucky. One day after leaving Lexington, McGuire announced that he'd be staying at Marquette.

Two weeks after that, Costello and Erickson were hired to split the duties that McGuire would have held by himself. Erickson said the job "fulfilled every dream in my life." It also ended a public relations nightmare for the Bucks.

KICKING LEGEND O'DEA DIES AT 90

APRIL 4, 1962

One day after being elected to the College Football Hall of Fame, the University of Wisconsin's greatest kicker was pronounced dead in a San Francisco hospital. This time it was official.

No question there was magic in Pat O'Dea's right foot, and the same might be said for the rest of him. Not only had he punted, drop-kicked and place-kicked a football further than Badger fans had ever seen before and maybe since, he'd also made himself disappear for the better part of two decades. When he succumbed at the age of 90 after a three-month hospital confinement, it was clear he wouldn't be coming back.

That was not the case some 45 years earlier when he'd dropped out of sight following a brilliant career with the Badgers. From about 1917 to 1934, the man they called "The Kangaroo Kicker" for his long legs was presumed to be a casualty of World War I, which was just the way he'd wanted it.

O'Dea was a most unlikely football hero, and fame had weighed heavily on him. The story goes that he'd traveled from his native Australia to Madison in 1896 to visit his brother Andy, who was coaching the UW crew at the time. The brothers attended a Badger football practice, and when a stray ball rolled over to them, O'Dea, a rugby star in Melbourne, kicked it back onto the field. His boot made such an impression that he was recruited on the spot.

A broken arm suffered in practice cost O'Dea all but one game of his freshman year, but over the next three seasons he made history while becoming the first Badger player to receive All-American mention.

The ball was rounded at the ends in those days, which made it easier to boot a long way, but O'Dea's best efforts were still the stuff of legend at a time when the field was 110 yards long, field goals were worth five points and drop kicks for field goals were the norm. He got off a 62-yard drop kick against Northwestern, a 110-yard punt against Minnesota and a rare 57-yard place kick on a free kick against Illinois.

Another 42-yard drop kick that he made on the dead run against Minnesota in 1899 was for many years considered the greatest play in the history of college football. O'Dea also starred at fullback, rowed for the crew, ran hurdles for the track team and earned his law degree in his spare time.

He coached for two years at Notre Dame and one at Missouri after graduating from Wisconsin and then moved to San Francisco to start a law practice. But while O'Dea had switched his focus to writs and torts, all anyone wanted to talk to him about were punts and field goals. Tired of the constant football conversation, he created a new identity for himself. Pat O'Dea disappeared, and in his place was a fellow named "Charles Mitchell," whom nobody knew anything about.

The prevailing theory was that O'Dea had joined up with an Australian regiment passing through San Francisco on its way to France, and he'd been killed in the war. The Australian army did have a record of a casualty named "Pat O'Day", which was close enough for the curiosity seekers.

But then in 1934 O'Dea had had enough of anonymity, and he surfaced in Westwood, Calif., using his given name. Family and old teammates had believed he was dead the whole time, and he had to produce a picture, his Wisconsin diploma, a scrapbook and an old letter to convince them that he was who he said he was.

The university brought him back to Madison as an honored guest at homecoming, and he became an avid Badger booster for the rest of his life. O'Dea turned 90 on St. Patrick's Day 1962, and several days later John F. Kennedy sent him a birthday message. "As a fellow son of Erin and a longtime admirer of your fine sports record, I wanted to wish you a belated but very sincere happy birthday," wired the president.

On April 3, O'Dea was named to the National Football Foundation's college hall of fame. When he died a day later, there was no mistaking who he was.

JAMES BRADDOCK ARRIVES IN WISCONSIN WOODS

APRIL 5, 1937

Paul Bunyan himself would have had to come riding up on Babe the Blue Ox to create a bigger fuss than James Braddock did when he arrived at Little Sissabagama Lake in far northwestern Wisconsin to begin training for his title defense against Joe Louis.

The heavyweight champion of the world needed a whole day to make the 425-mile drive from Chicago to the lakeside resort located between Spooner and Hayward, because every town along the way wanted to welcome him. The good people of Rice Lake even slung a rope across the road to stop his motorcade.

In those times, any heavyweight champ was regarded like LeBron James, Tom Brady and Alex Rodriguez all rolled into one, and the notion that Braddock would be spending five weeks in the North Woods made people downright giddy.

When Braddock, his trainer and two sparring partners pulled up at the exclusive private resort owned by former middleweight contender Karl Ogren, there were three inches of snow on the ground and a posse of press waiting for them. It was just after one o'clock in the morning, and it would be three hours before Braddock finished answering questions and posing for pictures and got to bed.

The plan was for Braddock to spend five weeks at the resort strengthening his legs and sharpening his skills for his first title defense since he'd lifted the heavyweight crown from Max Baer on June 13, 1935. His 15-round decision over Baer had been such a staggering upset that journalist Damon Runyon had labeled Braddock "The Cinderella Man."

The Louis bout was scheduled to take place in Chicago in June, and Braddock, who was 30 at the time, just wanted to shed some pounds and toughen his body for the showdown with the 22-year-old Louis before finishing his training in Chicago. Braddock planned to accomplish that by doing miles and miles of roadwork and chopping wood.

"I'm eager," he said. "That woodpile over there looks good to me for a couple of hours work tomorrow. I'm intending to make every minute count."

And he might have, too, if Mother Nature had been more cooperative. Reporters from all over the country had taken whatever hotel rooms they could find in the area to cover the training, and the first sign of trouble came when they found themselves struggling to get to the camp.

Ogren's resort was six miles off the highway that led to the nearest town, Stone Lake, and the combination of frost heaves and April precipitation had turned the access road into a swamp. The Soo Line Railroad donated three carloads of cinders to help firm up the dirt surface, but they hardly made a dent in the problem. Braddock was ankle deep in mud most of the time when he tried to do his roadwork, and his trainer was extremely wary of sprains.

The champ did give his all with the axe, though, but even that backfired when he developed blisters on his hands that caused him to miss two days of workouts and switch to the heavy bag. While Braddock's training suffered, his popularity remained intact. Towns all around vied for personal appearances, and it was a major event when he disclosed plans to go to church in Hayward. There was talk of outside sparring exhibitions, but it was too cold for that.

In the end, it was too cold and too wet for just about anything. Eleven days after his grand entrance, Braddock was in Minneapolis when he called *The Evening Telegram* in Superior and announced he'd be leaving northern Wisconsin and heading back to Chicago. He claimed he'd never planned to stay any longer than a couple of weeks anyway, but everyone knew better.

Braddock managed to lose seven pounds and chop down several pines, but he'd sparred only six rounds and gotten in just three days of roadwork in his 11 days. It obviously wasn't enough, because he didn't have any better luck with Louis than he did with a Wisconsin spring. On June 22, 1937, "The Brown Bomber" took him out in eight rounds.

James Braddock

BREWERS WIN MILLER PARK OPENER

APRIL 6, 2001

Metal detectors, bomb-sniffing dogs, 42,024 spectators, a visit from the president of the United States and a $400 million stadium might seem like an elaborate cure for a four-game losing streak, but then Milwaukee has been known to do things the hard way.

That was never more evident than it was in the Brewers' 14-year quest for a modern baseball facility. Local political leaders formed the first task force to look into a new ballpark in 1987, and the culmination of those efforts came on a 40-degree Friday night when the Brewers beat the Cincinnati Reds, 5-4, at brand new Miller Park. It was their first victory of the season after four losses

In between was a dizzying array of legislative maneuvering, political posing, deep thoughts and dire warnings that wound up costing State Senator George Petak his job and hundreds of thousands of taxpayers a nickel on every $10 they spent in five counties surrounding the stadium. And on this night, it all seemed worth it.

Manager Davey Lopes told reporters before the game that he "wasn't depressed" by his team's four-game skid, and then he went out and caught President George W. Bush's ceremonial first pitch. Lopes had to backhand the ball when it bounced six feet in front of the plate, but he called the pitch a strike when he talked about it later.

If the manager wasn't depressed, everyone else was impressed by the 1.2 million square foot playground that had been almost a decade-and-a-half in the making. "You can't believe you're in Milwaukee," said Jim Gantner. "A slight upgrade," grinned Reds Manager Bob Boone.

In an effort to beat the traffic, Bush left the park in the fourth inning, but he caused plenty of commotion while he was around, touring both clubhouses, signing balls for the players, and creating something of a security circus involving the metal detectors and the dogs.

But there weren't many complaints from the customers who were getting the first official look at the new place. The first unofficial look had come the week before when the Brewers opened the gates for an exhibition game against the Chicago White Sox. They won that one by the same 5-4 score, but people were paying much more attention to the setting than the ballgame on that night.

This one was a little higher key. This was ceremonies, speeches, backed-up freeway ramps, ticket scalpers charging $250 a copy, an American flag that covered the outfield for the national anthem and a bi-partisan feeding frenzy. Russ Feingold, Jim Sensenbrenner, Scott McCallum, Tommy Thompson, John Norquist and Condoleezza Rice were just some of the political figures who made themselves available for photo ops.

There were some important people there, too. Like Gantner, Robin Yount, Gorman Thomas, Johnny Logan, Teddy Higuera and, of course, Fuzzy Thurston. An event is not an event in Wisconsin unless a Green Bay Packer is on hand to help.

Baseball Commissioner Bud Selig, who did all of the heaviest lifting to get this project off the ground while he was the Brewers' president, admitted that it was hard for him to say in words what he was feeling, but he did it anyway and gave the fans most of the credit.

At 7:17 p.m., the Brewers' Jeff D'Amico threw the first pitch that ever counted at Miller Park to Cincinnati's Barry Larkin, and it was a called strike. Three innings later, the Reds' Michael Tucker drove a D'Amico changeup into the right-field bleachers for the first home run ever hit at the stadium. Brewers fan Tim Shields of Shorewood, Wis., bowed to peer pressure and threw the ball back onto the field.

In the sixth inning Jeromy Burnitz hit the Brewers' first home run in their new digs. It landed in the right-field corner, and nobody threw it back. In the bottom of the seventh inning, the bratwurst won the first sausage race ever at Miller Park, and no one was surprised.

Finally, in the eighth inning clean-up hitter Richie Sexson whacked a 430-foot home run off Cincinnati lefthander Dennys Reyes to win the game. The victory required 2 hours 54 minutes to accomplish, and it was followed by a ceremonial opening and closing of Miller Park's 13-acre retractable roof. That same roof had leaked all over the customers in the exhibition game a week earlier, but it held up just fine this time.

So the fans went home happy and dry, and Milwaukee had a state of the art baseball stadium. And the Brewers were no longer winless.

BREWERS OPEN AT COUNTY STADIUM

APRIL 7, 1970

Warm breezes, unruly teenagers, exploding bullpens and 50-cent beer. The Milwaukee Brewers' first game at County Stadium had a little bit of everything, but none of it saved the home team from being drilled by the California Angels.

A week after they moved into town, the players formerly known as the Seattle Pilots were hoping to make a big first impression. And maybe they did, although they failed to make any dent at all on California right-hander Andy Messersmith.

Messersmith held them to four hits in a 12-0 defeat. Still, the day was an entertainment and commercial success. Drawn by comfortable temperatures in the 50s and the novelty of a having their own big league team for the first time in five years, 37,237 fans came to County Stadium to watch the Brewers' home opener. Eleven hundred of them got in on passes, but the number still put Seattle to shame. The Pilots never drew as many as 15,000 people at any game the year before.

Messersmith's pitching and the Brewers lack of it accounted for the final score, although there may have been an element of stage fright involved as well. "I had butterflies so big they felt like damn turkeys," said outfielder Danny Walton.

Something must have been stirring in the rookie slugger's tummy when he played a fly ball into a triple in the top of the third inning and grounded out with the bases loaded in the bottom to kill Milwaukee's only threat. The Brewers loaded them with two walks and an error, which was a pretty good indication of their offense that day.

Steve Hovley, a 24-year-old right fielder, got three of their four hits, and Tommy Harper, an All-Star in waiting, got the other one. Milwaukee starter Lew Krausse and friends would need much more than that.

Krausse went three innings giving up four runs on three hits before turning the game over to the relief corps. Manager Dave Bristol employed four firemen after that, and they surrendered eight more runs and 11 more hits.

The management might not have done much worse if they'd tossed a couple of the visiting dignitaries in there. The mayor, the governor and the chairman of the county board were all in attendance, as was County Executive John Doyne, who threw a strike with the opening pitch. So was baseball Commissioner Bowie Kuhn, who drew some boos and American League President Joe Cronin, who drew nothing else. The people hadn't forgotten that Cronin had tried his best to keep the Pilots in Seattle.

Despite the disappointing action on the field, the fans managed to amuse themselves through most of the 2 hour 46 minute game, with few of them heading for the parking lots until the eighth inning. But bleacher seats costing a dollar and beer costing half that much did combine to create some problems.

There was a shortage of vendors for one thing, leading to long lines at the concession stands, but a bigger fuss was caused by customers straying onto the field during the game. Things got really out of hand in the middle of the ninth when the final tally showed 14 arrests, most of those people under the age of 20.

It took 45 minutes for 8,000 cars to clear the parking lot, but that may have been good practice for local partisans who would have to learn patience. It would be four more days before the Brewers beat the Chicago White Sox, 8-4, at Comiskey Park for their first victory, and almost a month before they would win at home. They beat Boston, 4-3, on May 6, and nobody ran onto the field.

PACKERS SIGN REGGIE WHITE

APRIL 8, 1993

You could make the argument that the Green Bay Packers' road to Super Bowl XXXI began with a detour.

Reggie White wasn't going anywhere but home after he'd visited Detroit in early March to listen to the Lions make their pitch for his services. The NFL's dominant defensive end was being recruited all over the league, and he didn't need any extra plane rides. Besides, Green Bay was about the last place top free agents could be expected to venture. Not only was the city small and frozen, but the team had had just four winning seasons in its last 20.

But the Packers just wouldn't stop calling, and White was more or less in the neighborhood. So he told his agent, Jimmy Sexton, that they might as well see what Green Bay was talking about. Less than a month later, White was a Packer, and the team had the last big asset it needed for a championship.

White had agreed to terms on April 6 and appeared at a press conference in Green Bay that day, but he didn't officially sign his contract until April 8, and the NFL didn't record the transaction until April 9.

The Packers already had the right general manager, the right coach and the right quarterback, but they also had the league's 23rd-ranked defense before White took his fateful plane ride to Wisconsin. He took it on a private jet dispatched by the Packers in the interest of showing him how serious they were.

He was met at the airport by General Manager Ron Wolf, coach Mike Holmgren, defensive coordinator Ray Rhodes and defensive line coach Greg Blache and whisked to Lambeau Field and then on to a restaurant. The restaurant was Red Lobster, and the whisking was done in a Jeep Wrangler. White had been treated like royalty during his tour, but the Packers took a simpler approach. They also took along their checkbook.

Their offer for four years and $17 million blew away the competition. A $4.5 million signing bonus plus a $4.5 million salary guaranteed him $9 million in his first season in Green Bay. Quarterbacks John Elway and Dan Marino were the only two players in the history of the game to get paid that much, and the upfront money scared off the other major suitors including Cleveland, San Francisco and Washington.

The Packers had reinforced their case when Holmgren and Rhodes flew down to Knoxville, Tenn., to meet White's family a week after his visit to Green Bay. They sealed the deal over the phone with Sexton early on a Tuesday afternoon, and Packers negotiator Mike Reinfeldt informed team President Bob Harlan. Harlan, in turn, told Wolf and Holmgren, and the celebration was on.

Reggie White

Investing that kind of money was a huge gamble for the Packers. The NFL salary cap was due to kick in the following season, and they had committed almost 15% of their payroll to one player. Harlan acknowledged that the team would have to make some major cuts, but the benefits easily outweighed the expense.

The charismatic White had an immediate positive effect in the locker room, and his decision to come to lonely little Green Bay made the Packers an instant factor in the free-agent market. He could also play a little bit.

White had made the Pro Bowl seven straight years after joining the Philadelphia Eagles in 1986 following two seasons in the United States Football League. He had 124 sacks in 121 NFL games, ranking him second all-time behind the New York Giants' Lawrence Taylor. Fourteen of those sacks had come in 1992.

Still, he was 31 years old, and there was some question whether his skills were beginning to taper off. White routed the doubters with 13 sacks, 67 unassisted tackles and another trip to the Pro Bowl in his first season in Green Bay. He would make five more Pro Bowls in Green Bay while elevating the Packers defense to No. 1 in the league by 1996. And along with Favre, he would lead them to their first championship in 29 years.

On the day White signed with the Packers, Sexton said, "We shocked the world, didn't we?" Maybe not the whole world, but they certainly shook up football.

UW BOXER MOHR SUFFERS FATAL BRAIN INJURY

APRIL 9, 1960

This was always going to be Charlie Mohr's last fight. The 22-year-old University of Wisconsin senior had had a nice four-year run in the ring, and he was capping it by defending his 165-pound title at the NCAA boxing championships.

Then it was on to graduation later that spring and a career in youth work. But those things never happened.

Mohr suffered a brain injury in his bout with Stu Bartell, a rival and a friend from San Jose State, in the 165-pound finals at the UW Fieldhouse, and underwent emergency surgery at a Madison hospital. Eight days later, Mohr was dead, and three weeks after that, so was boxing at Wisconsin.

Mohr and Bartell, a 23-year-old navy veteran, liked to talk boxing together whenever their teams faced each other. Mohr was a lefty and a boxer. Bartell was a puncher. They'd split a couple of decisions during the regular season, with Mohr winning their last bout easily on April 2.

Mohr had been named the "most outstanding boxer" at the 1959 tournament, and he had a chance of keeping that title, too, as he outpointed Bartell in the first round. But the bout shifted dramatically in the second when Bartell landed a right to the chin that put Mohr on his back. The dazed fighter got to his feet and took a standing nine-count. Bartell was all over him until referee John O'Donnell stopped the fight at 1 minute 49 seconds of the round.

As he tottered back to his corner, Mohr apologized to Wisconsin coach Vern Woodward for letting the team down. Woodward made him sit and rest for awhile before he left the ring. The coach asked the fighter if he knew what day it was. "It's Saturday," Mohr replied. "Don't worry about me." When he finally got up, he signed a few autographs on his way out of the arena.

And then while sitting in the dressing room, he collapsed. He was rushed to University Hospital where he was joined by his two sisters who lived in Madison and who had been there to see the fight. Five doctors performed surgery on Mohr's brain to combat the effects of a cerebral hemorrhage. The operation lasted past midnight, and the patient was given last rites on the operating table.

Mohr's parents were called, and they flew to Madison from their home in Merrick, N.Y. The family spent the next eight days at the hospital, along with Woodward, boxing team members, friends and people from the athletic department. But the doctors held out little hope. They said a condition existed in Mohr's head that may have made the blood vessels more susceptible than usual to injury. There was no way to know which blow had caused the bleeding in his brain.

Bartell kept his own vigil at home in Brooklyn. "We're good friends," he said. "Only a few minutes before the bout, we were talking. I don't think one of my punches landed on his head."

While Mohr's condition worsened, the UW board of regents indicated that the boxing program at the university would be given a full review.

At 8:40 a.m. on April 17, Easter Sunday, Charlie Mohr died. His father said he didn't blame boxing. He sent a letter to Bartell saying that he didn't blame him either.

On May 9, Wisconsin, which had won a record eight NCAA titles, discontinued boxing as a varsity sport.

Charlie Mohr

LEZCANO SLAM WINS BREWERS' OPENER

APRIL 10, 1980

George Bamberger

Even in Bambi's absence, the 1980 Milwaukee Brewers were still "Bambi's Bombers."

Four home runs had already proved that when Sixto Lezcano stood facing Boston reliever Dick Drago with two out in the ninth inning of the home opener. A County Stadium crowd of 53,313 had gotten its money's worth before Lezcano even stepped to the plate, but the Brewers right fielder had a special treat left for them and for his ailing boss.

George Bamberger, the club's manager for the past two seasons, was home in Florida recovering from heart surgery, and Buck Rodgers was filling in. But Bamberger was there in spirit. And he'd also been there in living color before the game began when he'd delivered a taped message of encouragement to the team on the new County Stadium scoreboard.

The Red Sox weren't exactly moved by the occasion as they took a 3-0 lead after three innings. But the Brewers had wiped that out in typical fashion with home runs by Ben Oglivie, Paul Molitor and Don Money, as well as the first of two by Lezcano, putting them on top, 5-3, going into the ninth. Back came Boston with solo shots by Carl Yastrzemski and Butch Hobson making it a 5-5 game.

A single, a sacrifice, a pop out and an intentional walk in the bottom of the inning put runners on first and second for Gorman Thomas. The Milwaukee slugger had the fans on their feet as he drew a dramatic eight-pitch walk to load the bases for Lezcano. They were up again seconds later when Lezcano drove Drago's first pitch into the bullpen for a grand slam and a 9-5 victory.

"I thought I was going to have a stroke. I couldn't believe it," Lezcano said as he recalled the moment when the ball disappeared over the wall.

He was still a couple of steps from first base when he threw his arms in the air in celebration, and he hadn't reached second yet when Bamberger got the news in Florida. General Manager Harry Dalton had called him on the phone while Lezcano was circling the bases. If he could have, Lezcano would have dialed the number himself.

"I saw him on the scoreboard," he said after the game. "His eyes were kind of watery as if he really misses us. We miss him a lot. The whole season is dedicated to him coming back."

The customers had shown some dedication of their own that day just by being there. The temperature for the first pitch was 43 degrees, and it dropped steadily throughout the afternoon. But it was still the fifth-largest crowd in franchise history and the third-largest for an opener.

The second-happiest man in the Milwaukee clubhouse may have been right-hander Reggie Cleveland, who got the victory after being booed in the pre-game introductions for his dreadful 1979 season, when he went 1-5. Cleveland said it was a special day for him, but he knew it was more special for Lezcano, who finished the afternoon with two home runs and six RBIs. Said Cleveland: "He had a good week out there today."

Just short of two months later, Bamberger returned to the dugout and the Brewers held "Welcome Back Bambi Night."

APRIL 119

MARQUETTE HIRES AL McGUIRE

APRIL 11, 1964

The search lasted three weeks, and when it was over Marquette University fans figured they'd gotten the wrong McGuire. The rumor was that Frank was coming to Milwaukee.

If the rumors had been true, the Warriors would have had a much bigger name and a lot less fun. Little did they know when they hired the 35-year-old New Yorker from Belmont Abbey College that they were about to hop on the back of his motorcycle and take the ride of their lives.

Al McGuire

The genial Frank McGuire, who'd enjoyed success at both Carolinas over the course of his career – North and South – was involved in the hiring process but only as an adviser. He'd coached Al at St. John's University, and he recommended him to the Jesuit fathers.

More than 50 candidates applied when Marquette fired Eddie Hickey and went looking for a coach, but only three were interviewed. The others were Bob Luksta, an assistant coach at DePaul, and Hank Raymonds, who would become Al's friend, "co-coach," successor and real estate agent. Raymonds had been Hickey's assistant for three years, and most people figured he had the inside track on the job. When McGuire got it instead, Raymonds wished him luck.

McGuire, in turn, asked Raymonds to stay on, and then he handed him a blank check. He had gone house-shopping while he was in town and spotted a place he liked in suburban Brookfield. He asked Raymonds to go buy it for him while he returned to North Carolina for a couple of weeks to tie up the loose ends at his old job. Raymonds did, and the McGuire family never lived anywhere else.

When Marquette hired McGuire the school knew it was getting a streetwise young coach who'd been a co-captain at St. John's, and played three-and-a-half mostly undistinguished seasons in the NBA. He won 109 of 173 games at Belmont Abbey, a school of 720 students, 90% of them men. It didn't know the half of it.

The Warriors were coming off a 5-21 season under Hickey, and McGuire understood that he had a huge job on his hands drumming up support for the program in an area of the country that he barely knew. According to one popular story, when his wife Pat asked him where Marquette was, he told her he thought it was in Minnesota.

When he got to Wisconsin, McGuire made up to 150 speeches a year, and spent hours and hours on the telephone. Former Green Bay Packers president Bob Harlan, who was MU's sports information director at the time, tells of how in his first year McGuire would call potential boosters and identify himself to their secretaries as Milwaukee Mayor Henry Maier so that he could get their bosses on the phone.

He could have had a much tougher sell as the Warriors stumbled to an 8-18 record in that first season, but they made plenty of friends by beating archrival Wisconsin twice and knocking off seventh-ranked St. John's. The 8-18 year was the only one in which a McGuire team ever finished below .500 at Marquette. The following season, the Warriors went 14-12, and then they never won fewer than 20 games until he retired in 1977 after winning a national championship.

Recruiting the playgrounds of New York and other "cracked sidewalks" venues around the country, McGuire enticed some of the nation's most gifted players to a middle-sized Catholic university in a middle-sized midwestern city where he convinced them to play patient, pattern offense and ferocious, hard-nosed defense. Most of those players were black, and McGuire's singular talent for handling delicate race relations, or as he called it "the checkerboard," helped him to achieve a 295-80 record at Marquette.

Along the way there was an NIT championship, a second place in the Final Four, national coach of the year honors in two different seasons, 26 players drafted by the NBA or the ABA, a 92% graduation rate, bumblebee uniforms, feuds with Adolph Rupp and the NCAA, induction into the Naismith Basketball Hall of Fame and a whole new lexicon of terms in which centers became "aircraft carriers," referees became "zebras," university administrators became "memos and pipes" and good times were "seashells and balloons."

There was also a colorful eight-year stint as a TV commentator after he retired from coaching, and countless motorcycle treks into the countryside in search of tin soldiers and leaded glass windows.

In 2001, McGuire died of a blood disorder at the age of 72. The funeral was at Gesu Church on the Marquette campus, and a whole city was in tears.

PALMER OUTDUELS TRAVERS IN BREWERS' OPENER

APRIL 12, 1977

Shutouts and whiteouts and presidents and kings. You get it all at Milwaukee Brewers home openers, which is why people take so much trouble to get to them.

The Brewers may not always play their best baseball in the first home game of the season, but they usually make it interesting. They lost the first one, 12-0, to California in 1970, and they postponed the fourth one for four days when 13 inches of snow fell on the city in early April. Two years later, they beat Cleveland in a special "Welcome Home Henry" celebration for home run king Henry Aaron, and a little more than three months into a new century, President George W. Bush watched them open Miller Park with a 5-4 victory over Cincinnati.

Kids have been known to skip school and their parents to take six-hour lunches on the local holiday known as Opening Day, and sometimes they've been greatly entertained and sorely disappointed on the same afternoon. One of those afternoons was a gorgeous, sunny, 83-degree Tuesday when Baltimore's Jim Palmer beat Bill Travers, 1-0.

Palmer had already won three Cy Young Awards, and he was on his way to the seventh of eight 20-game seasons when he faced Travers before what at the time was the biggest baseball crowd in County Stadium history. There were 55,120 fans on hand, breaking the record of 51,480 set at the 1975 All-Star Game. And, as it turned out, in 31 years of Brewer openers at County Stadium, this was the only one where shorts and tank tops were fitting attire. The second warmest was a 62-degree day in 1992. And in the seven home openers before this one, it had never been warmer than 46 degrees.

For fans who loved pitchers' duels and watching baseball on a picture-perfect day, it never got any better than this. Palmer gave up just two hits all day and let only one runner get as far as second base. Travers, the left-handed mainstay of the Brewers' staff through the late seventies, was almost as good. He yielded five hits, but unfortunately for him, two of them came in the ninth inning when the Orioles scored the game's only run.

By waiting until the last inning to decide the outcome, the teams guaranteed that the traffic leaving the stadium would be as tangled as it was coming in, and that wasn't easy. Interstate 94 had backed up for miles with fans anxious to start their tailgate parties, and 40 of the really impatient motorists had simply pulled off the road and parked on the side of the stadium freeway. The parking tickets were $5 apiece, a bargain under the circumstances.

Palmer made sure none of the Brewers' late-coming fans missed any offensive fireworks by allowing just one stingy single to Sixto Lezcano in the second inning and then proceeding to retire the next 18 batters.

Travers was used to that kind of treatment. The Brewers had been just as non-supportive when he'd pitched the season opener in New York and lost, 3-0, to the Yankees. But he wasn't taking it personally. "They promised me a run next time out," he said after the game.

The Orioles weren't making any promises, but they delivered the only offense Palmer would need when designated hitter Eddie Murray led off the top of the ninth with a single, went to second on Lee May's sacrifice bunt and came home on a single up the middle by, of all people, Rick Dempsey.

Murray, a future Hall of Famer, had hit into two double plays earlier in the game and maybe was overdue to start a rally, but Dempsey was an unlikely candidate to finish it. He'd gone one for 13 on the season before he rapped his game-winning hit. He followed that up with the defensive play of the day in the bottom of the ninth.

That's when Jim Wohlford got the Brewers' second hit, and Charlie Moore tried to bunt him to second. But Dempsey pounced on the bunt in front of the plate and started a double play that snuffed out any hope of a Milwaukee rally.

After providing half of the Brewers' attack, Lezcano had nothing but good things to say about Palmer. "He was just throwing strikes, making everybody swing," he said. "He just challenged us."

Which didn't surprise Orioles Manager Earl Weaver a bit. "That was just the normal Jim Palmer out there," he said. "This was a typical day."

As Brewers home openers go, it was a little better than that.

ANDERSON WITHDRAWS AS UW BASKETBALL COACH

APRIL 13, 1982

It took Ken Anderson 14 years to make his name at the University of Wisconsin-Eau Claire, and it took the chairman of the UW-Madison athletic board less than two minutes to forget it. Bad start. Worse finish.

Anderson reigned for a little less than four days as Wisconsin's basketball coach, time enough to turn a mere embarrassment into a comic skit. It was Friday afternoon, April 9, at the UW Fieldhouse when athletic board chairman David Tarr announced Anderson's selection to the assembled media. A three-time NAIA Coach of the Year who had never had a losing season, the 49-year-old Abbotsford native seemed like an ideal choice.

Tarr kicked off the press conference by saying, "Ladies and gentlemen, after the review and the recommendation of the athletic board, I'd like to introduce the new basketball coach, Ken Davis ... er Ken Anderson."

Tarr, who would later refer to Anderson as "Ken Johnson," as well, apologized by saying, "You can see how tired I am. This has been a long, exhausting process."

And it wasn't over yet. The following Tuesday afternoon, April 13, associate athletic director Otto Breitenbach announced that Anderson had changed his mind and was revoking his oral contract with Wisconsin for "personal reasons" that he declined to reveal.

Tarr's "Davis" slip was undoubtedly Freudian. Former Boston College coach Tom Davis, a native of Ridgeway, Wis., was the man the Badgers wanted most, but he'd just taken a job with Stanford before they could make him an offer. Johnson was an assistant to Bill Cofield, who'd started the whole fuss when he'd resigned under fire as UW basketball coach five weeks earlier.

Tarr, a political science professor, had become the point man in the coaching search by default because Athletic Director Elroy Hirsch was somewhere else. Hirsch's explanation of his whereabouts involved golf and a high seas junket. He said he'd injured his back at a celebrity pro-am golf tournament in Miami, and when he got back home he checked himself into a Madison hospital for undisclosed reasons. When he got out of the hospital he went on a Caribbean cruise where he entertained boosters as he did every year.

The hospital stay gave rise to rampant rumors that Hirsch was actually in alcohol rehab during the coach selection process. Hirsch denied that, but one thing was certain. He didn't meet with Anderson, which made it look as if basketball wasn't a major priority with him.

Anderson couldn't have been pleased by that, and he might have been a little miffed, too, at the wide variety of candidates Wisconsin considered before it got around to talking to him. Davis was its first choice and other prospects who came and went were Marquette's Rick Majerus, Toledo's Bob Nichols, Evansville's Dick Walters and Illinois State's Bob Donewald. Breitenbach said that Donewald had been offered the job the night before Anderson got it, but he pulled out because he decided Wisconsin's stringent academic standards would make it too hard to recruit top players.

Ken Anderson huddled with one of his UW-Eau Claire teams.

Which led to another possible explanation for Anderson's hasty departure. He had planned to recruit two promising junior college prospects from Oklahoma only to learn that he couldn't get them into school.

Money may have been another issue. Anderson was making $28,500 as an associate professor and coach at Eau Claire, but he ran a lucrative basketball camp, and leaving it would have been expensive. Anderson, however, said he'd be satisfied with what Donewald was offered – but not a penny less.

Talent, or lack of it, also might have been as big a consideration as compensation. Cofield had started freshmen Carl Golston, Cory Blackwell and Brad Sellers the previous year, and it was feared that they would leave when he went. As it turned out, Golston left that summer, while Sellers waited a year before transferring to Ohio State and Blackwell left for the pros after his junior season.

Making the job even less appealing were stubborn rumors that the Badgers were about to be punished by the NCAA for recruiting violations involving a New York prospect named Jerry "Ice" Reynolds, who was ineligible but living in Madison.

A week after Anderson stepped down, Steve Yoder was hired away from Ball State. Back in Eau Claire, Anderson wished Yoder well without shedding any additional light on his brief interlude with the Badgers. All he'd say was, "I did them a favor."

122   365 BEST WISCONSIN SPORTS STORIES

BRAVES WIN FIRST HOME OPENER

APRIL 14, 1953

Billy Bruton was one of baseball's fastest men, but he didn't need to hurry this time. He was in a home run trot.

He'd just hit a Gerry Staley knuckleball over the right-field fence, and all he had to do was circle the bases. Or so he thought. As the Milwaukee Braves' rookie rounded second and headed for third, umpire Lon Warneke waved him back. Warneke thought that the ball had either bounced over the fence or a fan had interfered with it. Now it was Charlie Grimm's turn to show some speed.

The Braves' manager raced onto the field to protest, and it was ruled that there had indeed been a mistake. So Bruton came home, and so did the Braves.

The center fielder's 10th inning home run was the only one he would hit all year, but it was enough to give Milwaukee's new National League team a 3-2 victory over the St. Louis Cardinals in its first game at County Stadium. While 34,357 ticketholders celebrated, Bruton was mobbed by his teammates at home plate.

He couldn't have had a much better day. He'd also singled in the sixth inning, saved two runs in the top of the eighth with a spectacular running catch on Stan Musial, and tripled and scored in the bottom of the inning to put his team ahead, 2-1. But St. Louis tied the game in the ninth, setting the stage for Bruton's one-out game-winner.

He'd gotten his first two hits on fastballs, which may have been why Staley tried to catch him off guard with a first-pitch knuckler. Bruton wasn't fooled. He drove the ball to right field where Enos Slaughter tried to make a leaping catch. Cards Manager Eddie Stanky said he saw Slaughter get a glove on the ball, but his elbow hit the top of the four-foot fence and it dropped over for a home run. "When I hit a ball that far, it has to be just right," said Bruton.

"Just right" might serve as a pretty good description of the whole opening day affair. The Braves got a complete game six-hitter from Warren Spahn, a tense, second straight victory and a memorable welcome from a city that had been waiting 52 years for the return of big league baseball.

Even the weather cooperated. It was windy, and it wasn't warm, but 51 degrees was pleasant enough to fill the new County Stadium and a whole lot better than the rain and cold that postponed the next day's game. Baseball Commissioner Ford Frick was there, and so was National League President Warren Giles, along with just about the entire political establishment of Wisconsin.

There watching Governor Walter Kohler throw out the first ball from his box seat were most of the state legislature, Mayor Frank Ziedler and all of the city council, and the Milwaukee County Board not to mention a number of suburban officials. It would be safe to say that no serious government business got transacted on this Tuesday afternoon.

And hardly anyone left early. With the Cardinals batting in the bottom of the ninth with two outs, some of the customers in the center-field stands began making their way to the exits, but home plate umpire Jocko Conlan told the public address announcer to ask them to sit still, because they were disturbing the hitters. The fans complied, and the Cards tied the game.

That may have contributed to a gigantic traffic jam as more than 7,000 cars left at once and mingled with the afternoon commute, but everyone got home eventually. Meanwhile, Braves President Lou Perini stopped in the clubhouse and told his players, "This is just a start, boys. We're really going to roll now." And he was right. Four years later, the Braves won the World Series.

County Stadium in 1953

NIEVES' NO-HITTER KEEPS STREAK ALIVE

APRIL 15, 1987

He couldn't throw a slider, and he couldn't keep his change-up down. Two innings into the game, Juan Nieves said he "felt like a pregnant lady." Seven innings after that, he'd given birth to the only no-hitter in Milwaukee Brewers history.

His team was riding an eight-game winning streak when Nieves took the mound against the Baltimore Orioles in Memorial Stadium, and he'd given up six runs and eight hits over $5\frac{1}{3}$ innings in his last start. A no-hitter wasn't exactly what Tom Trebelhorn had in mind for his 22-year-old left-hander. In fact, as late as the sixth inning, the manager was still considering taking him out of the game. Nieves had already thrown more than 90 pitches at that point.

He would throw a total of 128 and walk five batters before he was done. But no base runner got past first, and the Brewers' batters made Trebelhorn's decision to leave Nieves in easier by scoring two runs in the seventh inning and three more in the eighth on their way to a 7-0 victory.

Nieves got plenty of defensive support as well, mainly at the expense of Baltimore slugger Eddie Murray. Rookie left fielder Jim Paciorek robbed Murray of a base hit with a diving catch in the second inning, and Robin Yount did it to him again for the last out in the ninth. In between, Nieves regained command of his change-up and slider and kept his fastball moving while striking out seven. The Orioles were impressed.

"He wasn't overpowering," said veteran Fred Lynn, "but you have to give him credit. He pitched very well."

Catcher Bill Schroeder was more than willing to give Nieves credit, dismissing any praise for his own contribution to the gem. "The way he pitched, Bingo Long and the guy with the monkey could have called that game," Schroeder said.

When it was over, Nieves tried to pretend that he didn't know he had a no-hitter going until the final out, but no one was buying that. He would have had to be blind and deaf to miss it.

A sparse but suddenly bipartisan crowd of 11,407 was on its feet chanting "No-hitter" as he walked out onto the field for the bottom of the ninth. Ken Gerhart opened the inning by grounding out to Paul Molitor at third. Rick Burleson followed with a liner, also to Molitor, bringing up Murray, who had been trouble all night long.

In addition to his second inning near-miss, Murray had drawn a four-pitch walk to open the seventh and brought pitching coach Chuck Hartenstein to the mound for the only time in the game. Murray wasn't nearly as patient this time. The first pitch was a fastball up and in, and he spanked it to right-center field.

Yount got a good jump on the ball, but it was sinking fast. The center fielder was airborne for what seemed like forever before he extended his glove and swallowed up the ball.

Nieves threw his hands into the air just in time to catch Molitor, who leaped into his arms followed by the rest of the Brewers as they celebrated baseball history. Nieves, who had taken a far more modest goal into the game, said he just wanted to keep the Brewers' winning streak going.

You'd have to say he delivered.

BULLS WIN RECORD 70TH IN MILWAUKEE

APRIL 16, 1996

The Milwaukee Bucks looked like highly unlikely spoilers when the Chicago Bulls came to town planning to make history at their expense. The Bucks certainly hadn't spoiled their fans.

They were on their way to a fifth straight catastrophic season, and they weren't expecting a lot of loyalty from a sellout crowd of 18,633 on hand to see them play their neighbors. Traveling Chicagoans normally filled about half the seats whenever the Bulls visited the Bradley Center, and there was nothing normal about this game. The Bulls needed it to post their 70th victory of the season, a number no NBA team had ever reached before.

They came in hoping to blow the Bucks away early and get a little rest from the pressure they'd been creating for themselves all year long. They had started talking about breaking the record of 69 victories set by the 1971-'72 Los Angeles Lakers as early as December, and when they won 18 in a row from Dec. 29 through Feb. 2, there wasn't much else to talk about.

The Bucks had done their fair share to contribute to the Bulls' success, losing three games to them by an average margin of 17 points. They'd also dropped 26 of their last 31 starts.

In other words, it had been forever since pro basketball had caused any excitement at the Bradley Center, and the scalpers took full advantage of this opportunity. Lucky shoppers were getting floor-level seats for $200, but some prime locations drew as much as $700. Even after the game, souvenir hunters were paying up to $10 apiece for ticket stubs. With signs and banners backing the Bulls hanging from every corner of the arena, this had all the elements of a major humiliation.

But it didn't turn out that way. The Bulls grabbed a modest three-point lead in the first quarter, but then they took a little nap until halftime. The Bucks outscored them, 24-12, in the second period and went into intermission ahead, 49-40. Center Vin Baker was having his way in the middle where he would wind up with 28 points and 12 rebounds, while Michael Jordan finished well below his average with 22 points.

But the Bulls were still the Bulls, and the Bucks, while much better than they usually were, still weren't good enough. They were trailing, 82-80, with 4 minutes 19 seconds to play, and then they neglected to score again. The final verdict read, 86-80, and the Bulls had their record.

"Getting it over with was more of a relief," said Dennis Rodman after turning in a seven-point, 19-rebound performance. "We played like crap."

Jordan was more tactful. "That was an ugly game," he said, "but sometimes ugly is beautiful."

Then again, the Bulls might not have expected this when they began the season. The previous year, Jordan had taken an extended leave of absence to try his hand at hitting baseballs, and when he found out he couldn't do it he'd played in just 17 games. When the Bulls lost to Orlando in the 1995 Eastern Conference semifinals, the management knew it had to do something different.

They don't come much more different than Rodman, whom the Bulls acquired in an off-season trade in the hope that his defense and rebounding would compensate for his disruptive personality. Putting aside a six-game suspension for head-butting a referee, Rodman fulfilled their wishes, and the Bulls coasted to their fourth NBA championship.

They also won two more regular-season games after they left Milwaukee to finish the year with a 72-10 record. But they didn't celebrate that nearly as much as they did the championship.

In fact, after they beat the Bucks, Jordan and teammate John Salley were the only Bulls who commemorated the victory at all. They passed out cigars in the locker room, a gesture Milwaukee might have appreciated. At least the Bucks didn't get smoked.

HORNUNG SUSPENDED FOR GAMBLING

APRIL 17, 1963

Paul Hornung

Before there was Pete Rose, there was Paul Hornung. The Green Bay Packers' "Golden Boy" was severely tarnished at a press conference in New York when NFL Commissioner Pete Rozelle announced that he and Detroit Lions defensive tackle Alex Karras had been suspended indefinitely for betting on league games.

"Indefinitely" turned out to be one season, and a couple of decades later, Hornung was in the Pro Football Hall of Fame. That was a much different fate than Rose suffered when he was banned from baseball for gambling, but Hornung's story was almost as big at the time. The difference was the Packers' running back admitted what he'd done immediately, and there was no evidence that he'd ever bet on his own team. It also was a different era, and even those inside the game didn't look askance at small-time betting.

"I made a terrible mistake. I am truly sorry," Hornung said in a statement from his home in Louisville, Ky., after Rozelle had announced his findings that the NFL's three-time scoring leader had bet on college and pro games between 1959 and '61, and had helped a friend bet by giving him specific information.

Rozelle found that the friend wasn't a professional gambler, he was just a businessman who liked to bet on games. His name was Bernard M. Shapiro, and Hornung met him in San Francisco when he played in the 1956 East-West Shrine Game. Hornung began placing $100 and $200 bets through Shapiro in 1959. Once in a while, he'd risk as much as $500. Rozelle's investigation showed that Hornung generally broke even until he stopped betting in the spring of 1962, although he did make $1,500 one year.

Hornung's name was first mentioned with regard to the betting scandal in early January. He was connected to Abe Samuels, a friend who admitted to betting heavily on pro football. Suspicions also were raised when the Packers were taken off the board for a number of games during the 1962 season. Rozelle said that happened mainly because of Hornung's chancy health. He played in only nine games that year because of a knee injury.

No one was accused of shaving points or giving information to professional gamblers, but betting on football was expressly forbidden in the standard NFL player contract. And so Hornung and Karras went down. Five other Lions players were also fined the maximum of $2,000 apiece for placing $50 bets on a single game – the Packers' championship match with the New York Giants. And the Lions franchise was docked $4,000 for not telling the league that they'd been warned by Detroit police that some of their personnel was associating with "hoodlum elements."

Rozelle said that Hornung not only admitted his infractions, he helped move the investigation along by volunteering information that filled in some of the blanks. Karras' reaction was entirely different.

Although the Lions' all-pro tackle was accused of betting on his own team – a $100 bet that the Lions would win at Green Bay in 1962 – he said, "I haven't done anything I'm ashamed of. I am not guilty of anything. This is guilt by association and innuendo."

Whatever kind of guilt it was, it was expensive. Neither player was to be paid during the suspension nor did either player have the right to appeal. The money didn't bother Karras. He used the time off to further his pro wrestling career, claiming that he could make twice as much on the mat as he could on the gridiron. Hornung, who had a numer of endorsements and investments, got by, too.

There was some question about how Packers coach Vince Lombardi would handle the matter. He supported Rozelle's verdict, but he also said two months later that he had considered quitting because he felt he had failed somewhere along the way. Hornung had always been his favorite pet on the Packers.

In March 1964, the NFL reevaluated the suspensions and let both players back into the league. The 28-year-old Hornung would go on to play three more seasons for the Packers, but injuries and advancing age kept him from ever regaining the form that had earned him NFL Most Valuable Player honors in 1961.

Karras returned to the Lions and never showed even a trace of remorse. When he was asked to call the coin toss before a game in 1964, he supposedly told the referee, "I'm sorry, sir, but I'm not permitted to gamble."

BUCKS BEAT LAKERS IN WESTERN CONFERENCE FINAL

APRIL 18, 1971

Greg Smith didn't seem to mind being ignored. In fact, he may have preferred it.

Playing with Lew Alcindor, Oscar Robertson and Bobby Dandridge, the fourth-round draft choice from Western Kentucky was distinguished mainly by being the Milwaukee Bucks' fifth starter. Not a great perimeter shooter or an imposing post-up presence, he'd played 262 games for the same team and never led it in scoring. For that matter, he couldn't even remember ever leading Western Kentucky in scoring.

And so the undersized 6-foot-5 power forward had to be about the last thing on the Los Angeles Lakers' minds when they came to the Milwaukee Arena trying to stave off elimination in the best-of-seven Western Conference finals.

The Lakers' hopes rested with 34-year-old Wilt Chamberlain, who was still one of the two most dominating big men in the NBA. The other one was Alcindor. The two 7-footers had waged an epic duel in the first four games of the series, and Alcindor was winning it, albeit slightly, three games to one, because he had much better help.

LA was playing without Elgin Baylor and Jerry West, two sure Hall of Fame choices who were gone for the year with injuries. They'd also lost starting forward Keith Erickson with a stomach ailment that landed him in a Milwaukee operating room during the series.

The Bucks, on the other hand, had their own Hall of Fame shoo-ins in Alcindor and Robertson to go along with the future all-star Dandridge and perimeter wizard Jon McGlocklin. And they had Smith, who made better use of his time that day than anyone.

Plagued by foul trouble, he still managed to score 22 points in 23 minutes as the Bucks disposed of LA, 116-98, to earn their first trip to the NBA Finals.

"I concentrated so much on Alcindor that at times it was detrimental elsewhere," said Chamberlain. "I didn't switch off on their forwards enough, and it gave them too many open shots."

Smith got 14 shots and made nine of them. He also converted four of six free throws and pulled down nine rebounds.

"I felt light out there today," he said afterward. "That's when I get a lot of fouls and also a lot of rebounds. But lead the scoring? No way. That's the first time I've done that since I was in high school."

The Alcindor-Chamberlain battle ended in a virtual draw. Alcindor outscored the LA giant, 125-110 for the series, but Chamberlain finished with a 94-86 advantage in rebounds. He also blocked five of the Milwaukee center's shots in the fifth game. "There was a lot of give and take out there," said Alcindor. "Wilt was on his job. He's so strong, and yet it isn't especially exhausting to play him. You don't shove him around, because he's just about immune to it."

An Arena sellout crowd of 10,746 knew a great big man when they saw one, and this time they acknowledged seeing two.

With 2 minutes 25 seconds to play and the game out of reach, Chamberlain walked to the bench and got a standing ovation that lasted most of the way through the timeout. Less than a minute later, Alcindor left the game and got the same treatment.

Nobody stood and cheered when Smith left. He didn't appear to notice.

Lew Alcindor (33) and Oscar Robertson (1) fight for the rebound against Los Angeles Lakers Wilt Chamberlain, right.

DEER, SVEUM HOMERS LIFT BREWERS ON EASTER SUNDAY

APRIL 19, 1987

An 11-game winning streak and a ton of ground beef were on the line when Rob Deer stepped to the plate in the bottom of the ninth inning on Easter Sunday.

The Milwaukee Brewers were trailing the Texas Rangers, 4-1, with two men on and one out, and their left fielder was disgusted with himself. He'd let a short fly ball pop out of his glove in the fifth inning, helping the Rangers take a 4-0 lead. Although he'd gotten one of those runs back with a solo homer in the bottom of the inning, he still thought he'd let the fans down.

Two pitches later, Deer launched a towering apology into the left-field bleachers. His league-leading seventh home run came on an 0-1 breaking ball from right-hander Greg Harris, and it landed two rows from the top of the seats. As dramatic as Deer's game-tying blast was, it was only the second biggest hit of the day. Dale Sveum topped it.

Harris, who had come on in relief of Mitch Williams with two on and one out in the ninth, struck out B.J. Surhoff, but Jim Gantner kept the Brewers alive by drawing a walk. That left everything up to Sveum, who was batting ninth and had gone hitless in three previous at bats. He was saving the best for last.

The Brewers' shortstop worked the count full and then lined a fastball into the right-field bleachers, giving the Brewers a 6-4 victory and extending their streak to 12 games, one short of the major league record for the start of a season.

Sveum made it to the dugout after he was mobbed by his teammates at home plate, but 29,357 County Stadium customers wouldn't let him stay there. While the strains of the Monkees' *I'm a Believer* rang in their ears, the fans stood and clapped until Sveum and Deer made a curtain call. Then they had to make another one. And still another one before the fans headed for the parking lots.

Meanwhile, the cooks at George Webb Restaurants were getting ready to fire up their grills. The local hamburger chain had promised to serve free hamburgers all over town if the Brewers won 12 in a row. They would have a very busy next three days, giving away 168,194 hamburgers.

The loss was the Rangers' ninth straight, but Texas Manager Bobby Valentine had commented publicly the day before that he wasn't particularly impressed by what the Brewers were doing. Naturally, the newspaper story found its way into the Milwaukee clubhouse. "I'm not impressed either," said Brewers coach Larry Haney. "I'm awed."

So were the citizens of Milwaukee. The Brewers had thrilled them during the streak with three one-run victories and an extra-inning game, not to mention the only no-hitter in the history of the franchise. Lefthander Juan Nieves had provided that four days earlier by shutting down the Baltimore Orioles, 7-0. The Brewers would try to make it 13 straight in Chicago the next night. Nieves would be on the mound.

BREWERS' 13TH STRAIGHT VICTORY TIES RECORD

APRIL 20, 1987

More than 24,000 people were on their feet hanging on Milwaukee Brewer closer Dan Plesac's every pitch, and at least half of them were looking for a strikeout. And this was in Chicago.

The White Sox had a man on first in the bottom of the ninth inning, and the Brewers were one out from running their unbeaten string to 13 games. The 1982 Atlanta Braves were the only other major league team to start a season, 13-0, and this was about the last team anyone expected to threaten that record. Most of the experts had picked the Brewers to finish last or close to it after they had come in sixth in the seven-team American League East the year before.

But Plesac and Co. had brought their own experts, and they'd spent much of the night chanting "Here we go, Brewers!" Milwaukee fans had taken over much of Comiskey Park, and Plesac was about to make them very happy.

He'd given up an infield single to start the ninth, but then he'd struck out Ivan Calderone and retired Carlton Fisk on a fly ball. That left just Greg Walker. Walker never had a chance. Plesac fired three fastballs, and Walker swung and missed at all three. The final score was Brewers 5, White Sox 4, and the streak remained alive.

Manager Tom Trebelhorn's club won this one like it had won six of the others. By coming from behind. Juan Nieves, the no-hitter hero of five days ago, had struggled from the start as the White Sox took a 4-3 lead and then loaded the bases with two out in the fifth. That's when Trebelhorn replaced Nieves with a rookie so obscure that his name was misspelled on the scoreboard. But Chuck Crim looked like Bob Feller to Chicago catcher Ron Karkovice when he struck him out to end the rally.

Crim gave up only one hit over the next three innings before Plesac took over. Meanwhile, the Brewers' offense provided just enough with a two-run seventh inning capped by Robin Yount's most celebrated pop fly.

Jose DeLeon had retired 11 Brewers in a row when he walked Bill Schroeder to open the seventh. Ground balls by Jim Gantner and Dale Sveum moved pinch-runner B.J. Surhoff to third, and when Paul Molitor ripped a double to left, the score was tied and DeLeon was gone. White Sox closer Bobby Thigpen came on to face Yount, who fought off an inside pitch and looped it just over the right side of the infield to drive in the winning run.

Crim and Plesac did the rest as the Brewers made it 13 in a row. The streak ended the following night when the White Sox reached rookie Mark Ciardi for five runs in $2^{1}/_{3}$ innings in a 7-1 victory. But the Brewers won their next four games, tying an American League record with a 17-1 start.

And then the wheels came off. They lost 12 in a row in May, dropping out of first place and earning a lasting nickname. The 1987 Brewers would always be remembered as "Team Streak."

BREWERS' 13-GAME WINNING STREAK
(To start 1987 season)

Date	Score	Site
April 6	Brewers 5, Boston 1	County Stadium
April 8	Brewers 3, Boston 2	County Stadium
April 9	Brewers 12, Boston 11	County Stadium
April 10	Brewers 11, Texas 8	Arlington Stadium
April 11	Brewers 8, Texas 6	Arlington Stadium
April 12	Brewers 7, Texas 5 (12 inn.)	Arlington Stadium
April 13	Brewers 6, Baltimore 3	Memorial Stadium
April 14	Brewers 7, Baltimore 4	Memorial Stadium
April 15	Brewers 7, Baltimore 0	Memorial Stadium
April 17	Brewers 10, Texas 2	County Stadium
April 18	Brewers 4, Texas 3	County Stadium
April 19	Brewers 6, Texas 4	County Stadium
April 20	Brewers 5, Chicago White Sox 4	Comiskey Park

Source: Brewers 1988 Media Guide

BUCKS TRADE FOR "THE BIG O"

APRIL 21, 1970

The Milwaukee Bucks knew Oscar Robertson was a perfect fit for them. They could only hope that he'd feel the same way.

They were willing to part with their second-leading scorer and with the first player they'd ever drafted to acquire Robertson from the Cincinnati Royals, because they knew he would be the ideal outside complement to Lew Alcindor's inside dominance. But first they had to make sure the 10-time All-Star guard would go along with the deal.

Robertson had something rare for those times, a contract with a no-trade clause. What's more, he'd used it before when the Royals tried to deal him to Baltimore for forward Gus Johnson. But the Bucks had a couple of powerful persuaders on their side. One was Wayne Embry, their recently retired center and Robertson's former roommate at Cincinnati, who assured Robertson he'd be happy with the Bucks. The other was Alcindor, who'd made them an instant title contender when he was drafted a year earlier. Robertson badly wanted a championship.

It helped, too, that he didn't get along at all with coach Bob Cousy and that he wanted more money than the Royals were willing to pay him. The Bucks offered him a three-year contract with a $50,000 annual raise.

And that was good enough for Robertson, who waived the no-trade and came to Milwaukee for shooting guard Flynn Robinson and forward Charlie Paulk. The price was certainly right for Milwaukee. Robinson had averaged 21.8 points per game in the 1969-'70 season, but he had also played poorly in the playoffs and wound up sharing his starting job with Fred Crawford. And Paulk had contributed only three points a game as a rookie before going off to the Army for most of the next two seasons.

"I think they're going places," Robertson said of the Bucks, and he couldn't have been more correct. Where they were going was straight to their only NBA championship.

Although Robertson was 31, he was still one of the game's best all-around players. He averaged 18.3 points, 8.9 assists and five rebounds a game in the 1971 playoffs as his new team breezed to the title.

He promised to play out all three years of his contract and then see how it went after that. It went very well.

He played four years with the Bucks, and they never won fewer than 59 games in any of those seasons. They almost won another championship in his last one before losing to Boston in a seven-game final series.

Robertson retired in September 1974, and six weeks later the team retired his No. 1 jersey. Clearly, he'd made the right decision when he agreed to come to Milwaukee.

Milwaukee Bucks coach Larry Costello is surrounded by players Bob Dandridge (10), Lew Alcindor (33), Greg Smith, top right, Jon McClocklin (14) and Oscar Robertson (1).

TEENAGE BOXER DIES FOLLOWING MILWAUKEE BOUT

APRIL 22, 1948

Thirteen days from his 19th birthday, Kansas City middleweight Jackie Darthard was carried from the ring at the Milwaukee Auditorium on a stretcher. He was in a coma by the time he reached his dressing room just past 10:30 on a Wednesday evening and he never regained consciousness.

His death at the hands of fourth-ranked contender Bert Lytell ended a promising boxing career and a dream. As elusive as boxing's big purses were back then, Darthard still saw them as his only way to escape the wretched poverty that he had been born into.

Darthard died at 8:40 a.m. on April 22, 10 hours after collapsing in the ring. The cause of death was a severe subdural brain hemorrhage. Darthard had undergone surgery at 1 a.m., but never regained consciousness and died under an oxygen tent at Milwaukee County Emergency Hospital.

Darthard appeared to be a good match for Lytell. He was the sixth-ranked contender, and he'd lost only once in 36 fights. He had scored six previous victories in Milwaukee, all in the last 10 months.

But in his rematch with Lytell – they had fought to a draw two months earlier in Kansas City – Darthard was already in trouble in the third round when Lytell put him down for two nine counts. The second one seemed long to Lytell, who testified later that he thought the fight should have been stopped right there.

Darthard's manager, Jordan "Beau" Davis Jr., had his doubts as well. Between rounds, he asked his fighter where he was staying in Milwaukee, but Darthard had no trouble coming up with the address: 1624 N. 5th St., which, incidentally, was a rooming house. Davis held up two fingers, and Darthard counted them and told his manager to stop kidding around.

But then came the sixth. Darthard took two hard shots to the head, and when he went back to his corner, he couldn't tell Davis where he was staying or whether the manager even had his fingers up. He slumped in his chair, and Davis signaled referee Alfred "Dauber" Jaeger of Fond du Lac that the fight was over.

Darthard was rushed to the hospital by ambulance, and Lytell went there immediately from the Auditorium to check on his condition. By the next morning, Darthard's body was on a slab in the county morgue. His mother, unaware of his death, was en route from Kansas City, a grueling 13-hour drive. As she and five other passengers, including a younger son who was doing the driving, approached Milwaukee from the south on U.S. Highway 41, the green Buick they were in – recognizable by its Missouri plates – was stopped by a stranger, Dorothy Byrd.

Byrd had been at the fight and had waited for several hours along the highway so there'd be someone ready with a consoling hand when Darthard's mother first learned the terrible news. Richard S. Davis of *The Milwaukee Journal* described Byrd as "a round faced dolly who has plenty of mileage, as the boys say." The paper added, "They say she's the madam of a couple of bawdy houses." Byrd took the grieving mother home with her to try to mend her breaking heart.

The mother told everyone that her son, Jackie, had dropped out of school after the eighth grade and gotten married to Ernestine Alexander. Ernestine didn't make the trip because she was pregnant with the couple's fourth child. The first three had died at birth. Darthard's mother said her son didn't even have enough money to own a car, despite his success as a fighter.

Lytell, meanwhile, was taken into custody and charged with assault with intent to do great bodily harm, pending an inquest. The investigation never got that far. Lytell told the district attorney that he knew Darthard was hurt badly in the third round, and he believed that his young opponent would still be alive if the fight had been stopped. Sammy Aaronson, Lytell's manager, said the same thing, and the next day he announced his retirement from boxing, ending a 27-year career. Jaeger claimed that Darthard was in no great danger in the third round. In fact, the referee said he'd given him the fourth round.

Darthard's death was ruled accidental, and Lytell was released. He met Darthard's sobbing mother at the Safety Building and told her how sorry he was.

"It wasn't your fault," she told him. "Brace up, honey. Don't let it ruin your life."

APRIL 131

PACKERS DRAFT TONY MANDARICH

APRIL 23, 1989

His numbers were exceeded only by his hype. Tony Mandarich stood 6-foot-5 and weighed 315 pounds. His chest measured 54 inches, his biceps 22. He ran the 40-yard dash in 4.65 seconds, faster than some running backs. He had a 30-inch vertical leap, and he could bench press 225 pounds an amazing 39 times. Whole villages could survive on his 15,000-calorie daily diet.

He made the cover of *Sports Illustrated*, which called him "The Incredible Bulk" and described him as "the best offensive line prospect ever." George Perles, his coach at Michigan State, said he could have starred as a junior on any of the four Pittsburgh Steelers teams that he'd helped coach to Super Bowl victories in the 1970s. "The guy should have an 'S' on his chest," said Jerry Reichow, the Minnesota Vikings' director of football operations. "He's perfect," said Ernie Accorsi, the Cleveland Browns' top personnel man.

And so it came as no surprise when the Green Bay Packers made Mandarich the second choice in the 1989 NFL draft. Dallas had taken UCLA quarterback Troy Aikman with the first pick, gaining that right by splitting its last two games to finish 3-13 while the Packers were winning their last two and finishing 4-12.

Executive vice president Tom Braatz was on record saying Green Bay would take either Aikman or Mandarich depending on whom Dallas left. But Braatz acknowledged later that the Packers had strongly considered taking running back Barry Sanders right up until the last two days before the draft. Cornerback Deion Sanders and linebacker Derrick Thomas were never in his thoughts. Four of the top five draft choices that year went on to Hall of Fame caliber careers. The fifth was Mandarich.

He came to Green Bay with the highest rating of any player at any position, and he wasted no time announcing that he planned to be paid accordingly. He said he wanted to play at least 10 seasons with the Packers and be an all-pro for all ten. "Obviously everybody remembers Lombardi when they talk about Green Bay, and I want them to say 'Mandarich,' too," he declared.

While Mandarich invoked Lombardi, Packers fans would have settled for Forrest Gregg. They got neither. The rookie sat out the entire training camp insisting on a contract bigger than Aikman's. He finally settled for less, but his four-year, $4.4 million deal was still the best ever signed by an NFL offensive lineman. It included a $2 million signing bonus, and it may have been the worst money the Packers ever spent.

When Mandarich finally came to camp five days before the season opener, his weight was down 15 to 20 pounds, adding to long-standing speculation that he was a creature of steroids. He'd passed three tests in college, but the NFL did random testing, and the question on everyone's mind was whether he'd gotten off the juice to pass.

He said he was forced to get lighter to be an effective pass blocker. Besides, he hadn't worked out much, because he'd been frustrated by the contract negotiations. This was a major turnabout for a man who'd claimed that he could play at 340 when his "muscles matured."

Apparently, they never did. Mandarich was back on the cover of *Sports Illustrated* in September 1992, only this time the headline called him "The NFL's Incredible Bust." He'd had three embarrassing seasons in between as defensive linemen around the league treated him like a chew toy.

He weighed less than 300 pounds when he came to camp that year hoping to find a niche somewhere on the offensive line. He didn't make it.. The numbers were down. The hype was gone. And so was Tony Mandarich.

Five years later, Mandarich resurfaced and played three years with the Indianapolis Colts as a sometimes starter. Twenty years after he was drafted by the Packers, he confessed to being addicted to steroids and alcohol while he was still at Michigan State in his book, *My Dirty Little Secrets – Steroids, Alcohol & God: The Tony Mandarich Story*.

LOMBARDI JETTISONS BILLY HOWTON

APRIL 24, 1959

Billy Howton was fast, productive, capable of making big plays and self-confident. In short, he was the Green Bay Packers' best offensive player. But he wasn't indispensible.

Nobody was with Vince Lombardi. And the veteran receiver became one of the first to find that out when Lombardi traded him to Cleveland less than three months after taking over the team. Gone was Green Bay's second-leading career receiver, the man who had led the team in pass catching for six of the last seven years and a four-time Pro Bowl choice. In his place were defensive end Bill Quinlan and halfback Lew Carpenter.

It wasn't clear how much of Howton's departure could be explained by the pressing defensive needs of the 1-10-1 team that Lombardi inherited and how much of it was the result of a personality conflict between the 28-year-old player and the new coach. What was clear was who was in charge in Green Bay.

"We had to do something about the defense," Lombardi said. "We think we got help where we needed it most. You don't give away nothing in this league for something. We know Howton is a fine ballplayer, but we're trying like everything to build up the defense."

Acquiring the 6-foot-3, 250-pound Quinlan was certainly a step in that direction, because he gave the Packers a badly needed starter at defensive end who was both stout against the run and capable of providing some pass rush. At the same time, despite his gifts, Howton may have had a couple of serious deficiencies in Lombardi's mind. He wasn't overly eager to block or to catch passes over the middle, and he wasn't shy about speaking his mind. He also had been elected the first president of the fledgling NFL Players Association, which some owners were adamantly opposed to recognizing, particularly after Howton threatened to sue them for antitrust violations.

The Packers hired Lombardi in late January, and Howton arrived in Green Bay from his home in Texas to meet with Lombardi in early spring. The meeting, held at the Packers' downtown office building, was believed to have lasted maybe 15 minutes, tops. A few days later Howton was bound for Cleveland.

Quinlan and Carpenter should have been bound for Green Bay at the same time, but that wasn't a sure thing. A two-year starter with the Browns, Quinlan first learned about the trade in the newspaper, and he wasn't pleased. "Would you like to go from the Yankees to the Athletics?" he asked rhetorically. "It's the same thing as going from Cleveland to Green Bay."

Quinlan said he was considering an offer to help coach Hamilton of the Canadian Football League, but within a few days he dropped his objections and his baseball analogies and agreed to become a Packer.

He proved to be a pretty good one, too. He was a four-year starter for Green Bay and a major contributor to two championship teams before he wore out his welcome with Lombardi. Quinlan had a tendency to get into barroom fracases, and the boss apparently got tired enough of that to deal him to Philadelphia before the 1963 season. Some blamed Quinlan's absence for the Packers' failure to win a third straight championship.

Carpenter, meanwhile, turned into a useful handyman. He played some halfback, fullback, wide receiver and tight end, returned punts and kickoffs and even served as the team's third quarterback.

Howton's stay in Cleveland was short. He led the team with 39 catches in 1959, but he didn't appear to get along any better with autocratic coach Paul Brown than he would have with Lombardi. Brown shipped him to Dallas after one season, and Howton led the Cowboys in receiving in 1961 and '62. When he retired after the 1963 season, Howton held the NFL career records with 503 receptions and 6,459 yards, surpassing the marks of the legendary Don Hutson.

Still, the Packers got along quite well without him. Just as Lombardi knew they would.

HEARD'S RELAY TEAM BREAKS WORLD RECORD

APRIL 25, 1992

No one in Wisconsin ever ran faster than Floyd Heard. He set state records in both the 100- and 200-meter dashes while running for Milwaukee Marshall High School at the state meet in 1985, and he was just getting started.

He went on to Texas A&M where he wasted no time in beating the best collegiate sprinters by winning the NCAA championship in the 200 as a freshman. That same year, he outran Olympic gold medalist Carl Lewis to finish first in the 200 in the USA Championships. There was no doubt that he could travel safely in the world's fastest company. And that's exactly what he did six years later at the Penn Relays.

If the Olympics are track and field's Super Bowl, the Penn Relays are its Rose Bowl. Started in 1895, it's the longest uninterrupted collegiate track meet in the country, and the 98th edition was something special. It drew a crowd of 38,508 to Franklin Field in Philadelphia on a chilly, gloomy Saturday when four men combined to cover 800 meters faster than it had ever been covered before.

Running for the Santa Monica Track Club along with Heard were Lewis, Leroy Burrell and Mike Marsh. Lewis had already won two Olympic gold medals in the 100 meters and another in the 200. In all, he would eventually win nine gold medals in track & field. Burrell was a two-time world record holder at 100 meters, and Marsh would go on to win gold in the 200 meters that summer at the Barcelona Olympics. Lewis, Burrell and Marsh also would run on the U.S.'s 400-meter gold medal relay team at Barcelona. But back to the Penn Relays.

An hour-and-a-half before the 800 relay, the four had battled stiff winds and temperatures in the low 50s to win the 400-meter relay in 38.79 seconds. It was a meet record, but pokey by this team's standards. Nonetheless, it served as a good warm-up for the 800.

Marsh led off the race, and he was followed by Burrell and then Heard before Lewis ran the anchor leg. The clock read 1 minute 19.11 seconds when Lewis crossed the finish line, breaking the world record of 1:19.38 set by the Santa Monica Club three years earlier. Burrell, Heard and Lewis had combined with leadoff runner Danny Everett to set the previous record.

This time the mark would stand up for only two years before the same foursome broke it again by running 1:18.68 at the Mt. San Antonio College Relays, edging out the team of John Drummond, Dennis Mitchell, Tony Jarrett and John Regis, who also bettered the previous record with a 1:19.10.

Heard's individual 200 times tailed off over the next six years following the San Antonio Relays, and he sat out the 1999 season altogether. But he made a huge comeback in 2000 with a best of 19.88 in the Olympic Trials, which made him at age 34 the oldest American sprinter ever to qualify for the Games for the first time. Heard placed sixth in the semifinals, and the following year he retired from competition and went into coaching.

He joined the staff at the University of Houston as a volunteer before becoming a full-time assistant in 2003 to Burrell, his record-setting relay partner.

BOB KNIGHT CHANGES MIND, SPURNS BADGERS

APRIL 26, 1968

More than 70 coaches applied for John Erickson's job when he announced he was leaving the University of Wisconsin to become general manager of the Milwaukee Bucks. The UW athletic board narrowed that field to seven finalists and then to one man it considered ideal for the job.

He was young. He was disciplined. He was successful. He was Bob Knight. And in a little more than 53 hours, he was gone.

Exactly what happened from 2:26 p.m. on Wednesday, April 24, until 7:13 p.m. the following Friday will always be a matter of opinion, but one thing appears certain. If someone hadn't talked out of turn, Wisconsin basketball would have been changed forever.

Knight was coming off his third year as head coach at Army when the Associated Press reported on Wednesday afternoon that the Badgers had chosen him to succeed Erickson. Apparently the wire service had gotten the word from a member of the athletic board, and when the news leaked, the university confirmed the report.

Wisconsin Athletic Director Ivy Williamson called Knight in Columbus, Ohio, where he was visiting relatives, to tell him that the board had indeed picked him for the job. The plan was for him to return to Madison on Friday to tidy up a few details and sign a three-year contract. But these were not minor details. They included his salary, his assistants' salaries and his recruiting budget.

Williamson said he assured Knight that none of that would be a problem. But Knight didn't see it that way. He flew to New York from Columbus, and he said when he got off the plane his wife told him he had the position at Wisconsin. He wasn't pleased, and even at the tender age of 27, when Bob Knight wasn't pleased sparks flew.

He said there was no way he could negotiate the details of his contract when it had already been announced that he'd been hired. "I didn't want to go into a job like that," he said. "You decide if you want a job after you examine all the sides of it, and that premature news release – I wouldn't call it that; it was a news leak – precluded ever getting to the point of examining anything."

Williamson said it wasn't nearly that complicated. When Knight called to tell him he was staying at Army, the athletic director said it was just a case of the coach changing his mind. "That call came Friday morning. I think it was just a reconsideration, as simple as that," he said.

Whether Knight had developed a hot head or cold feet didn't really matter. Either way, with Big Ten tenders due to be sent to recruits in less than a week, the Badgers needed somebody to coach their basketball team. And in keeping with the week's chaotic theme, they picked a tennis coach.

John Powless had come to Wisconsin from the University of Cincinnati in 1963 to be the head coach of the tennis team and an assistant on the basketball staff. As Erickson's No. 1 aide, he had been one of the other six finalists. When Knight announced on Friday night that he had signed a new contract at Army, the athletic board went back into session.

Shortly before midnight, the board members announced that the 35-year-old Powless was their man. He gave up the tennis job.

Three years later, Knight left Army for Indiana where he would win 11 Big Ten championships and three national titles over 29 seasons. In those same 29 years, Wisconsin had 20 losing records and no conference titles. Powless compiled an 88-108 record in eight years at Wisconsin. Knight became the winningest college basketball coach ever while working at Texas Tech in 2007.

The difference? "It was just that damn news release," Knight said some 40 years ago. "That did it all."

BARKLEY, BUCKS FANS MIX IT UP

APRIL 27, 1991

Charles Barkley was having a busy night at the Bradley Center. He was on his way to a triple double against the Milwaukee Bucks and a date with the district attorney after an altercation broke out behind the Philadelphia 76ers' bench.

Fans were throwing water and debris at the visiting players, and the visiting players were throwing back. It was hard to tell who started what, but people definitely were getting wet when Barkley escalated the conflict by flinging a whole tray of Gatorade into the stands and significantly delaying the start of overtime.

When the smoke cleared and the floor was dry, the 76ers had a 116-112 victory and a 2-0 lead in their first-round playoff series. And Barkley had 22 points, 13 rebounds, 10 assists and a soon to be arriving disorderly conduct citation.

"The Round Mound of Rebound" might have contested the case, but the cops had him cold... or at least damp. Cable station TNT had caught the whole incident on videotape. It didn't help Barkley's case that a month before, he'd been fined $10,000 by the NBA for spitting on an eight-year-old girl during a game in New Jersey. He was actually aiming at a grown man at the time, but the penalty for bad aim came to five figures.

This time, the league declined to intervene and the 76ers took a pass, too, saying that it was a matter between Barkley and the police. In the end, Barkley mailed the city of Milwaukee a check for $109, and that was that. But only for eight months.

Milwaukee's famed *Gemutlichkeit* was plainly lost on Philadelphia's all-star forward when the 76ers came back to town the following December. Things didn't go nearly as well on the court this time for Barkley. He scored just 10 points and had only eight rebounds and three assists in a 110-97 loss, but that didn't stop him from going out afterward to sample the night life. What happened next wasn't totally clear.

According to one version of the events, Barkley and a female companion left a local entertainment venue called Rosie's Waterworks at about 2:15 a.m. on Sunday. Or was it two female companions or just some friends? In any case, Barkley encountered a 25-year-old former Army Airborne Ranger named James R. McCarthy along with two other men, ages 23 and 25, and McCarthy greeted him by saying, "So, Charles, you're the baddest dude in the NBA."

How loudly McCarthy said that or from how far away was in dispute. There was no consensus either on what was said next. But somewhere along the way, Barkley took off his shirt and shoes and McCarthy got his nose broken.

McCarthy was a physical therapy major at the University of Wisconsin-Milwaukee and a competitive weightlifter. He stood 5-foot-10½ and weighed 250 pounds. Barkley was listed in the Bucks' program at 6-6 and 252 pounds.

Two bouncers from an establishment across the street broke up the dispute and drove Barkley to his hotel. Police arrived at the hotel at 6:50 a.m. and arrested him for battery. He was taken to jail where he spent four hours. He later admitted to getting superstar treatment. "Everybody else got bologna and water," he said. "I got bologna and milk."

With his humor intact but his wallet $500 lighter, Barkley made bail but missed his flight out of town and had to take a later plane. He was back in Milwaukee on June 17, 1992, to stand trial on two charges, the battery and disorderly conduct. The jury took 1 hour 45 minutes to acquit him of both whereupon Barkley made it clear there were no hard feelings.

"This is not an indictment of Milwaukee," he said. "I've got a great attorney from Milwaukee. I've got a lot of friends in Milwaukee. We've probably got more knuckleheads in Philadelphia than you do in Milwaukee."

Some 17 years later, Barkley compared Milwaukee to Cleveland on national television and called them "the same dreary ass city."

MADISON MEETS CASSIUS CLAY

APRIL 28, 1959

The skinny high school kid from Louisville held his hands too low. He counted on his speed to duck punches instead of protecting his face, and he danced around the ring daring his opponent to catch him. But he was so fast, and his punches came so quickly that no one had ever beaten him.

Cassius Marcellus Clay Jr. would change his name to Muhammad Ali five years later, but he never changed the style that he took to the Pan American boxing trials at the University of Wisconsin Fieldhouse in Madison. America's best amateur boxers would be competing for three days – April 28-30 – in 10 divisions at the event, and the 17-year-old with the 34-0 record was attracting as much attention as anyone in the tournament.

"Heading the list of National AAU champions is rugged Cassius Clay, a 17-year-old high school champion from Louisville, Ky., who startled the amateur world this winter by winning Chicago Golden Gloves honors at 178 pounds... and following up by winning the National AAU title. He is listed as one of the United States' brightest hopes for an Olympic berth and title in 1960," *The Capital Times* of Madison wrote in its preview story. There would be much more to say about the 6-foot-3 teenager before the meet was over.

The man who would become the world's greatest heavyweight champion fought three bouts at the trials – in the 178-pound or light-heavyweight division – and it cost only $1 to watch him from a reserved seat, $1.50 from a ringside seat.

A sparse crowd of 3,139 took advantage of the opportunity on the first day, and they saw Clay deck LeRoy Bogar of Minneapolis with a thunderous right hand in the second round and win on a TKO moments later to run his record to 35-0. The next day, Clay was described by *The Capital Times* as "perhaps the most sensational battler in the tourney thus far." It added: "Doesn't look like there is much for him to learn about the manly art of self defense."

It didn't look that way in the semifinals either when Clay won by unanimous decision over James Jackson of the East Regional team, but his winning streak came to an end in the final when he lost a split decision to a U.S. Marine named Amos Johnson. Clay appeared to tire in the fight as the left-handed Johnson slowed him down with body punches. This time there were 5,368 people on hand to witness one of only five defeats Clay would suffer in a 108-fight amateur career.

Not everyone was sold on Clay's style at that point. Jim Doherty wrote in a guest column for the *Wisconsin State Journal* in 2005 that Clay approached John Walsh, Wisconsin's legendary boxing coach, shortly after his first bout. Clay took a seat next to Walsh, who was sitting ringside, and said, "Did you see me? I'm the greatest." Walsh, according to Doherty, said years later, "I couldn't stand it. I got up and left."

Walsh may have been old school, but he helped officiate at the Pan Am Games and was widely respected in the boxing world. He was legendary at UW, winning eight national championships from 1934-'57 and producing 38 individual NCAA champions. He was the John Wooden of college boxing coaches.

Doug Moe in his book, *Lords of the Ring: The Triumph and Tragedy of College Boxing's Greatest Team*, provided another interesting anecdote about Clay's time in Madison. Moe wrote that Clay stopped at Badger Sporting Goods on State Street to buy some equipment, charmed everyone in the store with his charisma and boasted on his way out the door, "I'm going to be the greatest."

Clay fulfilled his promise.

He went to the Olympics and won the light heavyweight gold medal, knocked out Sonny Liston in the seventh round in 1964 to win the world heavyweight championship and reigned as champion three different times in the sixties and seventies. Early in that chain of events, he converted to Islam and changed his name.

In 1999, he was named "Sportsman of the Century," by *Sports Illustrated*. But he never fought again in Wisconsin after the Pan-Am Games.

OSHKOSH'S HOEFT PITCHES THE MOST PERFECT GAME

APRIL 29, 1950

You could say Billy Hoeft faced 27 hitters on a Saturday afternoon at the Oshkosh High School baseball field, but that would be using the term too loosely. Actually, nobody hit anything.

There might have been 10 or 12 foul balls, but that was just an estimate. It hadn't occurred to anyone to count when the lanky senior struck out Hartford High School's first batter. Then he struck out the next one and the one after that to retire the side, establishing a pattern that would last for nine innings.

Baselines were optional for the visitors. They used them only once. That happened when Oshkosh catcher Don Biebel dropped the third strike on the last out and threw the runner out at first.

No one could remember seeing anything like it. Not only did Hoeft strike out all 27 men he faced in his memorable 4-0 non-conference victory, he extended his personal no-hit streak to 15 innings. Just a week before, he'd held Menasha High School hitless over six.

It was big news now anytime the 6-foot-3, 175-pound left-hander took the mound, and not just in the Fox Valley. Major league scouts from all over the country were paying attention, too. There were six of them, including Brooklyn's legendary Branch Rickey, on hand when Hoeft pitched his last high school game against Manitowoc. Oddly enough, Hoeft lost a no-hitter in that one when the leadoff man in the ninth inning got his only hit of the season.

Considering that the Oshkosh phenom was credited with a 49-8 record during his high school days, the question was never whether he'd pitch in the majors. It was just where and for how much. Those were the days of bonus babies, when high school prospects were getting thousands just for putting their names on big league contracts. The minor leagues were getting squeezed, and so a rule was passed that any prep player who received a bonus of $6,000 or more – in 1953, the amount was lowered to $4,000 – had to stay on the major league roster for two years before he could be farmed out.

The question then became whether a high school player was better off taking the money and languishing in a dugout for two seasons or developing his skills before making it to the big show. Hoeft's high school coach, E.J. "Snitz" Schneider, recommended the second option, and Hoeft took his advice.

Virtually every major league club had contacted him, but he liked what Detroit had to say the most. Hoeft signed a non-bonus contract with the Tigers and played in their organization for two years. His first stop upon his graduation from high school was Richmond, Ind., of the Ohio-Indiana League, where he went 10-1 with a 1.71 ERA in 12 games. Hoeft made the big time in 1952, but endured three relatively undistinguished seasons before he finally went 16-7 in 1955. The following year, he won 20 games and was named to the American League All-Star team.

After being traded by the Tigers in 1959, Hoeft went on to play for five more teams, including the Milwaukee Braves for whom he posted a 4-0 record and a 3.80 ERA in 42 relief appearances in 1964. Hoeft finished his major league career with a 97-101 record, but never threw a no-hitter.

BUCKS SWEEP BULLETS FOR NBA TITLE

APRIL 30, 1971

First they stopped the Baltimore Bullets, and then they stopped traffic. While the Milwaukee Bucks doused each other with champagne in a locker room in Baltimore, their fans were jamming up the main drag in Milwaukee. They figured it didn't get any better than this, and they were right. It still hasn't.

The Bucks were all of three years old when they claimed the only championship in their history by beating the Bullets, 118-106, to sweep the best-of-seven title series and trigger a spontaneous celebration back home. Horn-tooting motorists flocked to Wisconsin Avenue on Friday night, and more than 10,000 fans greeted the team at the Mitchell Field airport on Saturday afternoon.

It was a fitting conclusion to one of the most spectacular seasons the National Basketball Association had ever seen. The Bucks posted a 66-16 regular-season record that would have been much better if they hadn't let up and lost five of their last six starts before getting serious again in the playoffs. They warmed up for Baltimore by disposing of the San Francisco Warriors and Los Angeles Lakers in a pair of 4-1 series, and then they absolutely dominated the Bullets.

No other expansion team had ever won a championship that fast, and only one other NBA club had ever swept a four-game final series in the 25-year history of the league, and that was the Boston Celtics in 1959. All of this from a team that two years earlier had gone 27-55.

But everything changed when the Bucks drafted UCLA's Lew Alcindor, the 7-foot-2 center who later became Kareem Abdul-Jabbar, with the first pick of the 1969 draft. Alcindor led them to a 56-26 record in his first year and the Bucks' second, but he couldn't carry them any further than the second round of the playoffs. Then Alcindor got some high-powered help from Oscar Robertson.

After playing 10 years with the Cincinnati Royals without getting so much as a sniff of a title, pro basketball's best point guard asked to be traded. The Royals tried to deal him to Baltimore, but he vetoed the swap, and Cincinnati was forced to send him to Milwaukee instead for a gunner named Flynn Robinson and a draft bust named Charlie Paulk. It proved to be a fateful turn of events for both organizations.

Robertson averaged 19.4 points and 8.2 assists during the championship season, while Alcindor led the league in scoring with a 31.7 average per game. Their supporting cast featured second-year forward and future all-star Bobby Dandridge, and perimeter marksman Jon McGlocklin. The fifth starter was undersized forward Greg Smith. McGlocklin and Smith were two of only three players left from the original Bucks' roster.

Coach Larry Costello had an ideal blend of stars and role players, and Baltimore couldn't begin to match it. The Bullets had put together a lukewarm 42-40 regular season before hitting their stride in the playoffs and shocking the New York Knicks for the Eastern Conference title. The Bucks held the Bullets under 100 points in the first three games of the finals, while winning by 10, 19 and eight points.

The city of Baltimore seemed to sense the inevitable when a less-than-capacity crowd of 11,842 turned up at the Civic Center for the finale. If the fans were resigned, the players at least were feisty. Star guard Earl Monroe squared off with McGlocklin after being called for a foul in the first seven minutes of the game, and shortly thereafter, forward Jack Marin swapped punches with Dandridge.

None of it helped. The Bucks went up, 31-22, in the first quarter and expanded their lead to 13 at halftime, and Baltimore never got closer than seven points after that.

The Bucks shot 56.1% for the game while getting 30 points from Robertson and 27 from Alcindor, who was in a war all night with muscular Wes Unseld. The Bullets' center hauled in 23 rebounds, but Alcindor held him to 11 points while getting 12 rebounds of his own.

Robertson made 11 of 15 shots from the field and scored 21 of his points in the first half. "You know, this is the first champagne I've ever had, and it tastes mighty sweet," Robertson said as he held up a glass of it in the locker room.

The Bucks haven't tasted anything as sweet since.

BREWERS BEAT WHITE SOX IN 19 INNINGS

MAY 1, 1991

The longest home game the Milwaukee Brewers ever played produced 19 runs, 37 hits, two errors and two highly unlikely heroes, both of whom had their heads messed with.

Don August finished the 19-inning struggle with a bright red welt on his right ear, while Willie Randolph had his pride damaged when the Chicago White Sox intentionally walked Paul Molitor three times to get to him. But Randolph got his revenge, and August got credit for the victory when the Brewers outlasted their rivals, 10-9, in a game that took 6 hours 5 minutes to finish.

A crowd of 13,973 had no idea it would be getting a doubleheader's worth of action for the price of a single ticket when the teams met at County Stadium for the wrap-up of a two-day series. In fact, the game appeared to be all but over in the third inning when the White Sox led, 5-0, with the big hit being a two-run homer in the first by Frank Thomas.

The Brewers didn't score at all for the first four innings, but then Franklin Stubbs' three-run blast helped put them ahead, 6-5, in the fifth. Tim Raines' home run tied the game at 6-6 in the seventh, and then both teams put their bats away for the next seven innings.

Fresh out of relief pitchers, Brewers Manager Tom Trebelhorn pulled August out of his starting rotation to start the 15th inning. Four hitters later, Trebelhorn had significant reason to regret it. August had put runners on second and third before Ozzie Guillen came to the plate and lined a pitch off the side of the right-hander's head to score the lead run. Two doctors, two trainers and Trebelhorn rushed out to the mound where the pitcher was lying facedown.

But he got up, and he stayed up. "I checked my ear to see if it was bleeding, and when I didn't see any blood, I said, 'I must be half all right,'" August recalled after the game. "We didn't have anyone left."

After taking a few practice pitches August faced Scott Fletcher, who lofted a sacrifice fly. Raines followed that with a run-scoring single before the Brewers got out of the inning, although not before they had seemingly blown the game since Chicago now held a 9-6 lead.

But Milwaukee refused to end the madness. It came back with three runs in the bottom of the 15th with Randolph knocking in the one that tied things up again. This time White Sox Manager Jeff Torborg elected to pitch to Molitor, who immediately validated his earlier strategy by ripping a single. That left the game in Randolph's hands, and he responded with another single that made it 9-9.

When Guillen was asked later about the ball he bounced off of August's head, he said, "I think I woke him up. After that he pitched well." And so he did. The Brewers' right-hander shut out the White Sox for the next four innings, giving Torborg another chance to intentionally walk Molitor and giving Randolph another chance to make him wish he hadn't.

The bases were loaded with one out when Randolph, who was playing second base, lined a single up the middle, and the issue was finally settled.

While the game was the longest the Brewers had ever played at County Stadium, it wasn't even close to the longest in their history. That one lasted 25 innings and stretched over two days at Chicago's Comiskey Park before the White Sox finally won, 7-6.

It was played in 1984, and it took the Brewers seven years to avenge it with Randolph's hit in the 19th inning. Randolph was 2 for 9 officially. "With each at-bat, I felt more comfortable," he said. "I didn't want to be the one to make the last out."

For more than six hours, it looked like nobody would.

AUERBACH RIPS NELSON FOR RIPPING AINGE

MAY 2, 1983

Red Auerbach had been denied his trademark victory cigar, but he was smoking anyway when he encountered Milwaukee Bucks owner Jim Fitzgerald outside the Milwaukee Arena locker rooms.

Fitzgerald was expecting the traditional handshake from the Boston Celtics' president after his team completed a four-game sweep in the NBA Eastern Conference semifinal round. He got it, but it was perfunctory, and it came with a tirade.

"Don't touch me," Auerbach huffed at Fitzgerald. "That was the worst thing I've ever seen in basketball. The guy's a whore when he says something like that about a kid who can't do anything to fight back."

Boston's iconic godfather-like boss and former coach could have been talking about the 107-93 thumping the Celtics had just taken at the hands of Marques Johnson, Sidney Moncrief and friends, because that was pretty grim, but he had Don Nelson on his mind instead.

The Milwaukee Bucks' coach had helped Auerbach win one NBA championship as a coach and four more as an executive during his playing days in Boston, but all of that was forgotten because of something Nelson had said in *The Milwaukee Journal.* He had accused Danny Ainge of being "a cheap-shot artist" after the young Celtics guard was involved in three controversial incidents in Game 2 two nights earlier. Ainge had nailed Bucks swingman Junior Bridgeman on a breakaway layup, and followed that by undercutting Moncrief and Johnson on separate plays.

At least, that's how Nelson saw it. Ainge said he was just playing defense, and Auerbach agreed with his player. Strenuously.

"This is the first time I've ever lost a series that I won't go to the winners' dressing room," he told a flabbergasted Fitzgerald. "If it's the last thing I do, I'll get back at the Bucks."

It was hard to tell how much of Auerbach's complaint was legitimate outrage and how much was just frustration. The Celtics had never been swept in a four-game series before in their 37-year history, and they looked truly inept at times doing it. They lost the first game at home by 21 points and then fell behind in the series, 2-0, when they lost at home again. They fell by eight in the first game in Milwaukee before Johnson's 33 points and Moncrief's 25 tore them up in the clincher.

"Did it ever occur to you that our team is better than yours?" Fitzgerald said to Auerbach when he finally got a word in edgewise. "What's that got to do with it?" Auerbach shot back, and that pretty much ended the discussion.

Meanwhile, Nelson and Ainge had shaken hands on the floor after the game, which was almost as ironic as the rough and tumble Nelson calling someone a dirty player or Auerbach accusing an opponent of psychological warfare. As Fitzgerald pointed out, "Every trick Nellie knows he learned from Red Auerbach."

No question Nelson was an apt student. Ainge claimed much later that Nelson wouldn't have said a word about him if he hadn't scored 23 points in the first half of Game 2 in Boston. Ainge maintained that the Bucks' coach was just trying to get inside of his head, and maybe in the officials' heads, as well.

Nelson acknowledged later that it was wrong to go public with his feelings about Ainge – he also was fined $1,000 by the league – and he even wrote him a letter that sort of apologized while continuing to insist that the young man had had a lot to learn about taking charges. Ainge rejected the apology, and bad blood flowed between the Bucks and the Celtics for years.

Fitzgerald hadn't helped matters. In the closing moments of the game, he had lit up a victory cigar. And Fitzgerald didn't smoke.

BREWERS' WHITE MANAGER KILLS BLACK WAITER

MAY 3, 1917

Danny Shay managed the minor league Milwaukee Brewers for just 15 games, and the last one ended with a 3-1 loss and a fatal shooting. The shooting cost him his job, but not his freedom.

Shay, a white man, killed a black waiter named Clarence Euell in an Indianapolis hotel restaurant. That much is certain. Shay stood and fired a shot into the 30-year-old man's stomach from point-blank range after a dispute that never would have happened if the Brewers had left town following the game the way they normally did. But Shay had persuaded the team secretary to have the team stay the night.

He would spend the next six months in jail before a jury ruled that he had acted in self-defense and set him free.

No one will ever be certain what role race played in the verdict, but it was known that there were 38 reported lynchings of black citizens in the United States that year and that Indiana had the largest Ku Klux Klan of any northern state.

The defense's star witness in Shay's trial was a young woman named Gertrude Anderson, whom the manager had met in a beauty parlor where he'd gone for a manicure after having several drinks in a tavern following the Brewers' loss to the Indianapolis Indians. Anderson was 36 years old and had been divorced twice, both times following marriages that lasted four months. She had lived in at least seven other cities before moving to Indianapolis working as a milliner, hairdresser, manicurist and vendor.

Shay joined Anderson at the restaurant some time after Euell had seated her, and she claimed later that Euell had leered at her from across the room.

Anderson testified that Shay consumed two drinks after sitting down with her, and a dispute ensued with Euell over Shay's request for sugar. She said Euell was rude and argumentative and eventually he swore at Shay and lunged at him. At that point she said she ran toward the kitchen and heard gunfire, but she never saw the shooting.

Another witness had a much different version of the events. Cashier Elizabeth Braskett said she'd overheard the two men arguing over the sugar, and Shay said something that Euell took exception to before walking away. She said Shay called Euell back to the table, and then he shot him. She said that was when Euell lunged at Shay and knocked him down.

Herbert Miller, the restaurant manager, testified that he ordered Euell to stop beating Shay, and Euell turned to him and said, "Why shouldn't I kill him, Mr. Miller? He shot me, and I'm bleeding to death inside. I haven't got a chance to live." Euell died at a hospital an hour later.

Shay waited in custody for six months for the trial to begin. It took nine days. The jury got the case at 11 p.m. and returned its verdict at 9:20 the morning of Nov. 22, 1917. A near riot broke out in the packed court room, but it ended quickly when the judge threatened to jail anyone creating a disturbance. And then Shay walked out, a free man. A 40-year-old widower with two children who'd lost his wife three years earlier in a car accident, he was accompanied by his 13-year-old son.

He was not welcomed back by the Brewers. Shay had been hired before the 1917 season, having left Kansas City's minor league team in a disagreement with the club president. After Shay was charged in the shooting, Brewers President Al Timme promised to do whatever he could to help him, and American Association President Tom Hickey announced that the league would establish a fund to pay for his defense.

But a week later, Timme changed his mind and said he'd be getting a new manager. Shay never managed again, but he did find work as a scout for a number of major league teams.

And at the age of 52 he found another use for a pistol. He shot himself to death in a Kansas City hotel room where he was living alone.

BRAVES BEAT METS; BRAWL IS A DRAW

MAY 4, 1964

When Casey Stengel's fledgling New York Mets took the field, the result was usually a mismatch, but they did battle to the last out. Sometimes even longer than that.

And Stengel's perennial tail-enders had a little extra motivation when they came to County Stadium to face the Milwaukee Braves in a Monday night game. Six of them had played in the Braves' system at one time. The home team, on the other hand, was still smarting from a four-game sweep by the Mets the year before that dropped them out of first place permanently.

So it had been a hard-fought game when the Braves took a 2-1 lead into the ninth inning, and a 170-pound New York infielder decided to try to run through a 205-pound Milwaukee wall. The wall's name was Ed Bailey, and he was the Braves' catcher. The infielder's name was Ron Hunt, and he was the Mets' designated masochist.

Hunt would play 12 seasons in the major leagues and retire with the career, season and single-game records for getting hit by pitches. Collisions large and small came naturally to him, and maybe Bailey should have expected it when Hunt came careening toward the plate trying to score from second on a ground ball.

The problem was Hunt was only halfway down the third base line when Bailey stood waiting for him with the ball. And since there was no place to slide, Hunt figured he had no choice but to barrel into the catcher and hope he dropped it. The strategy failed spectacularly. Bailey went down, but he kept the ball. Hunt ricocheted into foul territory, and when he got up, Bailey was on his way over to discuss the matter.

"I could break the neck or knock out the teeth of a runner coming in like that if I wanted to," the catcher explained later. "Sure, I was mad."

Hunt's response was, "It looked like a double-play ball, and I had to try to score."

It turned out to be a double play after all, and it might have been the most expensive of Hunt's career if plate umpire Bill Williams and chief umpire Tom Gorman hadn't gotten hold of Bailey before he could do any lasting damage. Gorman was no flyweight himself, but he couldn't intercept the whole Braves team as it came pouring out of the dugout. Waiting for them at home plate was a substantial contingent of Mets, including Stengel himself.

Denis Menke

The "Old Perfessor" was 73 years old at the time, but it was a spunky 73, and he grabbed the first available Brave by the shoulders. That happened to be Denis Menke, the Braves' 23-year-old shortstop. Stengel was used to being an underdog with the Mets, but a half-century age differential was too much for him to overcome. Menke shrugged him off, and Stengel landed on the seat of his traveling gray flannels.

When order was eventually restored, Milwaukee's Gene Oliver had a bloody nose, but there were no other casualties. The Braves still had their 2-1 victory, and the Mets, a third-year expansion team, were heading toward their third straight season of more than 100 losses.

LOMBARDI TRADES ALL-PRO CENTER JIM RINGO

MAY 5, 1964

According to one of the more enduring Green Bay Packers legends, Pro Bowl center Jim Ringo was negotiating his contract in 1964, and he had the audacity to come to Vince Lombardi's office accompanied by, of all things, an agent. Lombardi promptly walked out of the room and came back a few minutes later and told Ringo he was talking to the wrong team. He had just been traded to Philadelphia.

It made a great story, one that Lombardi had no reason to dispute. But it wasn't true. In fact, Ringo wasn't even in Green Bay the day the deal was consummated and recorded in the NFL office.

Pat Peppler, the Packers' personnel director at the time, said the trade was actually made after he'd received Ringo's demands over the phone and relayed them to Lombardi. What's more, Peppler said he thought Lombardi had been working on the deal before he even talked to Ringo.

One thing was sure: Ringo was shipped to Philadelphia. He went there along with fullback Earl Gros in exchange for linebacker Lee Roy Caffey and a first-round draft choice. And Ringo announced the deal himself, revealing it on a radio show in Easton, Pa., the night of May 5, 1964.

It turned out to be a fine transaction for everyone involved, although it probably worked a little better for the Packers than it did for the Eagles. Lombardi had decided that he needed help on defense more than he needed Ringo on offense, even though the veteran had started on the last seven Western Conference Pro Bowl teams and he'd been named first team all-pro by the Associated Press six times. But Ringo had turned 32, and Lombardi thought his skills were slipping and that he was undersized – Ringo played at closer to 220 than his listed weight of 232 – for the offensive line.

Gros, meanwhile, had been taken in the first round of the draft two years earlier in the hope that he would become Jim Taylor's successor. But he'd lost favor with Lombardi and was deemed expendable because of a tendency to fumble.

Caffey was a stalwart for the Packers at right outside linebacker on three NFL championship teams from 1965 through '67, making the Pro Bowl in 1966. The Packers also received a No. 1 draft choice in the deal, and they used it to pick Donny Anderson, who doubled as a running back and punter for six years before Dan Devine took over as coach and traded him. Both Caffey and Anderson have been inducted into the Packer Hall of Fame.

On the other side of the fence, Gros was so happy to escape Lombardi's doghouse that he led Philadelphia in rushing in his first year there, although that turned out to be the best year of his nine-year career. And Ringo was glad to be going home. A resident of Easton, he'd grown tired of shuttling back and forth between his off-season home and Green Bay.

Lombardi also may have been a little hasty in writing him off. Ringo would make three more Pro Bowls in Philadelphia before retiring and being inducted into the Pro Football Hall of Fame.

Jim Ringo

BUCKS TAKE HETZEL, EMBRY IN EXPANSION DRAFT

MAY 6, 1968

Larry Costello didn't know a lot about some of the players he would be choosing to make up the Milwaukee Bucks' first roster, but he was extremely familiar with at least one of them. He knew he'd be taking a 36-year-old guard from Philadelphia named Larry Costello.

Picking himself may have been the easiest thing the new coach had to do as the Bucks and the Phoenix Suns took turns selecting talent in the NBA expansion draft. Each would be getting a total of 18 players left unprotected by the other 12 teams. Costello, who had been sidelined by an Achilles tendon injury for the final three months of the regular season, was one of those left exposed by the Philadelphia 76ers. If he wanted to keep open the possibility of being a player-coach in Milwaukee, he had to use up a choice on himself.

And so he did, but not until he was deep into the second round. Far more important was the list of earlier picks headed by Fred Hetzel and Wayne Embry.

Phoenix used the first choice in the process on New York's Dick Van Arsdale, and then the Bucks spent the next two on Hetzel, a 6-foot-8 forward from San Francisco, and Embry, a 6-8 center from Boston. One of them made a brief visit to Milwaukee and the other became a pillar of the franchise.

Other key Bucks acquisitions in the draft were Jon McGlocklin, Len Chappell, Guy Rodgers, Bob Love and Bob Weiss; although, three years later, when Milwaukee won its only NBA championship, its roster included just one player from the original 18 picks.

The Bucks were surprised that Hetzel was available. The first overall choice in the 1965 college draft, he'd averaged 19 points a game as a starter at San Francisco the year before. But the Warriors must have known something, because at the age of 25, Hetzel was nearing the end of his career. The Bucks traded him to Cincinnati 53 games into their first season, and he played only two years beyond that.

The 31-year-old Embry had an even shorter tenure as a player. A four-time All-Star with the Cincinnati Royals who'd last served as the backup to Celtics player-coach Bill Russell, Embry retired after just one year in Milwaukee. But he contributed 13.1 points and 8.6 rebounds a game to the Bucks' surprising 27-victory first season, and then he went on to become their general manager from 1972-'77, engineering some of the biggest deals of their formative years. He also served as a vice president and consultant from 1977-'85.

McGlocklin was the lone survivor from the expansion group to play on the title team. A deadly outside shooter left unprotected by San Diego, he played eight years with the Bucks and is still with them as a TV analyst.

Rodgers was another pleasant surprise. An All-Star in 1967, he was, as Costello put it, "dead in the water" in Cincinnati. But if he was out of favor with the Royals, he was just the veteran presence the Bucks needed at point guard in their maiden season. Like Rodgers, Chappell played two years with the Bucks and averaged 11.5 points per game.

Love, a slender 6-8 forward with a deft outside touch, may have been the most promising of the Bucks' choices, but he played only 14 games for them. Milwaukee packaged him with Weiss to acquire Chicago Bulls' guard Flynn Robinson, who became a major player in two ways. Robinson led the Bucks in scoring in their first season, and then he and forward Charlie Paulk were sent to Cincinnati for Oscar Robertson.

While the Bucks' 27-55 record was the second-best ever posted by an expansion franchise, Phoenix finished 16-66 despite the presence of three established starters in Van Arsdale, Gail Goodrich from Los Angeles and McCoy McLemore from Chicago.

The Suns could have created a minor annoyance for the Bucks by taking Costello in the expansion draft and forcing him to retire as a player, but they preferred not to waste a pick that way. Not that it would have mattered. Costello never played a game for the Bucks.

ANTIGO'S LUKAS GETS FIRST KENTUCKY DERBY VICTORY

MAY 7, 1988

In the seven years that D. Wayne Lukas coached the La Crosse Logan High School basketball team, he won 36 games and lost 81. But then Logan was the smallest team in its conference at the time. You might say that Lukas didn't have the horses in his first career.

That was definitely not the case in his second. The Antigo native was already one of horse racing's most successful trainers when he saddled a filly named Winning Colors in the 114th running of the Kentucky Derby. She led from wire to wire, holding off Forty Niner down the stretch to win by a neck.

It was the closest Derby finish in 19 years and only the third time a filly had won America's biggest race. It was also Lukas' first Derby victory. He'd had 12 other starters in seven previous Derbys, and no trainer had ever had that many before without winning. In addition to being very good at what he did, Lukas was very persistent.

He showed that when he was growing up on a 10-acre farm and racing his pony at fairgrounds around northern Wisconsin. Horse racing was always one of Lukas' great loves, but it wasn't his only one. He was also crazy about basketball.

Only an average player, he was a ferocious competitor and a student of the game. He graduated from the University of Wisconsin in 1957 as a physical education major and later coached the Badgers' freshman team while studying for his Master's degree. He also taught and coached at Blair High School, as well as at Logan.

He was still dabbling in racing while he was coaching, and after nine years of living on a teacher's salary, he decided there was more future in horseflesh. Starting with quarter horses and moving on to thoroughbreds in 1978, he became the first trainer ever to win $100 million in purses in 1990. Nine years after that, he became the first to win $200 million.

He was up to $252 million and 4,500 winners after the 2008 racing season, but no victory was more satisfying than the 1988 Kentucky Derby. Lukas had an affinity for fillies that wasn't shared by other experts who doubted that they had the strength to compete with stallions. But in this case, the oddsmakers didn't agree and neither did Eugene Klein, the former San Diego Chargers' owner who bought Winning Colors as a yearling for $575,000.

She went off as the second favorite at 3-1, and jockey Gary Stevens took her to the front immediately. She had a three-length lead at a mile, and she still held it at the top of the homestretch before Forty Niner made his move. Two more strides might have reversed the decision, but Winning Colors held on just long enough to give Stevens his first Derby victory and Klein his "biggest thrill in sports."

For Lukas it was the end of his personal Kentucky Derby jinx. He was excited enough about the victory to predict that Winning Colors would have a good shot at winning the Preakness and the Belmont Stakes, which would have made her the first filly ever to claim racing's Triple Crown. He was wrong about that, though. She finished third in the Preakness and ran out of the money at the Belmont.

But that's all trivia when you start looking at Lukas' accomplishments. In all, he has won the Kentucky Derby four times, the Preakness five times and the Belmont Stakes four times for a total of 13 Triple Crown winners. At one point, he had a virtual stranglehold on the three races starting with the Preakness in 1994 when his horses won seven out of eight. In 1995 he became the first trainer ever to win the three Triple Crown events with three different mounts.

He has won the Eclipse Award as the nation's top trainer four times, and he was elected to racing's Hall of Fame in 1999 when he acknowledged that he'd been criticized over the years by other people in the industry and by the media. But he was making no apologies for his methods. "If you want a coach who wants to walk the ball up the court, you better get another guy," he said.

The horsemen who hired Lukas were convinced he was the right guy. From the time he left La Crosse, his life has been one fast break after another.

BREWERS, WHITE SOX PLAY 25 INNINGS

MAY 8, 1984

The game lasted so long that...
White Sox pitcher Bob Fallon started it in Chicago and finished it with an option to report to the team's Class AAA farm team in Denver...

They had two seventh inning stretches and decided to skip the third one...

Hall of Fame pitcher Tom Seaver got two victories on the same day without pitching in a doubleheader...

Third base coach Jim Leyland got penalized for holding...

Hall of Fame pitcher Don Sutton quipped that he'd forgotten that he'd even participated.

It is not necessarily true that bad news travels fast. The Milwaukee Brewers learned that after they lost a game in Comiskey Park that raged on longer than the Chicago Fire.

On Tuesday evening, May 8, the Brewers and the White Sox squared off for a game that started at supper time, was interrupted at bar time and might have run into breakfast two days later if Harold Baines hadn't won it for Chicago with a 25th-inning home run. The Sox were playing it under protest at the time.

The scoreboard that flashed "Thanks Harold" when Baines' blast cleared the center-field fence may have been expressing the sentiments of both sides. After all, it was 9:12 at night – the next night, May 9 – and the two teams still had another game to play.

The final score of the suspended game was Chicago 7, Milwaukee 6 and it took a major league record 8 hours 6 minutes to complete. The total damage to both teams' bullpens was incalculable. Fourteen pitchers threw 753 pitches, gave up 43 hits and 18 walks, while striking out 33 and stranding 37 base-runners.

The winning pitcher was Seaver, the losing pitcher was Chuck Porter, and the biggest loser of all was Fallon, who was rewarded for pitching six innings of one-hit ball for the Sox by being optioned to the minor leagues for at least a 10-day stay. Manager Tony LaRussa didn't want to do it, but he needed the roster spot to call up another pitcher to get him through the week.

While Fallon started for the White Sox, Sutton opened on the mound for the Brewers and gave up only four hits and one unearned run over seven innings. It was a notable performance for the Milwaukee right-hander, or so he was told. When the affair finally ended the next night he joked, "It started so long ago it slipped my mind that I was in it."

Chicago had scored all three of its runs on errors when action was suspended Wednesday morning by a 1 a.m. curfew with the score tied, 3-3, after 17 innings.

The Brewers thought they'd won it the next night when Ben Oglivie's three-run homer put them up, 6-3, in the 21st inning, but they were undone once again by their own malfeasance. This time, third baseman Randy Ready's throw to first landed in the box seats and opened the gates for a three-run Chicago rally in the bottom of the inning.

Leyland and LaRussa got into the act in the 23rd inning by which time Chicago's public address announcer had led the crowd in seventh- and 14th-inning renditions of *Take Me out to the Ball Game* and then decided to give it a rest in the 21st. Chicago base-runner Dave Stegman was rounding third base and heading for extinction at home when Leyland appeared to reach out and stop him. That prompted Brewers Manager Rene Lachemann to come racing out of the dugout to cite the rule against a coach touching a base-runner. After a long discussion, Stegman was ruled out, and it was LaRussa's turn to come storming onto the field and eventually announce that he was playing the game under protest.

That proved to be unnecessary when Baines hit a hanging breaking ball from Porter 420 feet to dead center in the 25th. Seaver, who pitched the final inning of the game, his first relief appearance in 18 years, got the win. He also started the regularly scheduled game that followed, held the Brewers to three hits in $8\frac{1}{3}$ innings and got another win.

While 44 players were involved in the marathon, the one everyone wanted to talk to had nothing to say. Baines had a long-standing policy of not speaking to the press, and he answered three separate requests for interviews by saying, "Nope" three times. At least somebody was interested in making a long story short.

GRAZIANO SCORES TKO IN NEW MILWAUKEE ARENA

MAY 9, 1950

Rocky Graziano

More than 11,000 people flocked downtown in April to watch an assortment of bands, choruses and drill teams formally open the new $5 million Milwaukee Arena. Another 9,000 showed up there nine days later to see Gorgeous George pin Gypsy Joe in a pro wrestling show refereed by Jack Dempsey. But now it was time to get serious.

Milwaukee's state-of-the-art showplace for sports needed a major sporting event to really get it launched, and local boxing promoter Frank Balistrieri had just the thing. He had signed former world middleweight champion Rocky Graziano, a dead-end kid from New York City with a popular following, to a $10,000 deal to fight in Milwaukee. The only problem was finding an opponent.

Graziano said he'd take on anybody. Anybody, that is, whom he couldn't face for more money somewhere else. That eliminated all of the big names in the middleweight class, but Balistrieri wasn't discouraged. He came up with a Brooklyn brawler named Vinnie Cidone, and his long-shot wound up putting Graziano on the canvas.

Ticket prices ranged from $2 to $5 plus tax for the 12,813 fans who paid their way in to watch Balistrieri's six-bout card, the Arena's inaugural sporting event. The crowd was a Milwaukee record, and so was the $49,475 gross.

Nobody gave the unranked Cidone a chance as the two fighters waltzed through the first round, prompting the referee to tell them to step it up. Cidone got the message in the second round, and he caught Graziano with a left hook that dropped him to his knees. Graziano rose after a nine count and covered up while Cidone tried to end the bout with a flurry of punches.

Graziano fought back and landed a left hook of his own. It barely grazed Cidone's left eye, but it was enough to open a cut on his eyelid that immediately began streaming blood. Ring doctor John Heraty examined the eye after the round and allowed the bout to go on. But Graziano swarmed all over the Brooklyn fighter in the third, and Heraty stopped the contest before the bell for the fourth.

The bout was labeled "a savage brawl" by Ray Grody of the *Milwaukee Sentinel* and it attracted national attention. In fact, it was enough to get Graziano's manager, Irving Cohen, talking about staging a proposed title match with champion Jake La Motta in Milwaukee.

Graziano had held the middleweight title for 11 months in 1947 and '48, both winning it from and losing it to Tony Zale. La Motta had won the title in 1949 from Marcel Cerdan, who had won it from Zale.

As it turned out, Graziano didn't get his title match, at least not until two years later when he lost in Chicago to Sugar Ray Robinson, who had won the title from La Motta. Regardless, the Milwaukee Arena was off to a terrific start, and boxing would flourish there for about five years before starting a gradual decline in the mid-1950s.

The Graziano-Cidone fight was the first of 10 at the Arena in 1950 and the average crowd topped 9,000. By 1959, there were only three fights with an average attendance of a little more than 2,200.

KAREEM'S HOOK BEATS CELTICS IN DOUBLE OVERTIME

MAY 10, 1974

Arguably the most memorable basket in the history of the Milwaukee Bucks came on a busted play. The wrong man got the ball and took the shot from the wrong place. Only the results were right for the Bucks. Their 102-101 victory sent them home with a chance to win a championship.

Seven seconds remained in the second overtime of Game 6 of the 1974 NBA Finals at Boston Garden when Oscar Robertson stood near half-court ready to inbound the ball. Coach Larry Costello had instructed perimeter specialist Jon McGlocklin to break from under the basket and away from Boston's 6-foot-7, 230-pound Paul Silas to receive Robertson's pass. The play was designed to get McGlocklin a 20-foot jump shot, but if he was covered he was supposed to dump the ball into Kareem Abdul-Jabbar for a short hook.

As it turned out, the Celtics didn't put Silas on McGlocklin, so McGlocklin stayed put. That's when Robertson and Abdul-Jabbar decided to improvise.

Abdul-Jabbar took the inbounds pass from Robertson and dribbled toward the baseline where he was shadowed by Celtics backup center Henry Finkel, playing for starter Dave Cowens, who had fouled out. Finkel stood 7 feet tall, and his arms were as long as a New England winter. They just weren't long enough to reach Abdul-Jabbar's patented sky hook.

Official accounts say the shot traveled 15 feet, but Boston star John Havlicek said it was more like 18 feet, and it came from behind the basket. "Tell me that wasn't a tough shot," Havlicek said afterward.

Nobody did. It went through the basket with three seconds on the clock, leaving the Celtics just enough time to miss a 30-footer at the buzzer and send the series back to Milwaukee. The Bucks would go on to lose the seventh game, but that did little to diminish Abdul-Jabbar's dramatic shot or the memory of their sixth-game victory.

Had McGlocklin made the shot as planned, the story would have been almost as good. The veteran guard was playing with a torn calf muscle, an injury he'd

Milwaukee Bucks Kareem Abdul-Jabbar, right, lays up a winning basket over Boston Celtics Hank Finkel (29) to defeat the Boston Celtics.

aggravated when he missed a 15-foot jumper that would have won the game in the last second of regulation. He'd been sitting on the bench when Costello called his last timeout, but the coach put him back in the lineup because he wanted his best shooters on the floor for the final play.

The Bucks lost another chance to put the game away in the first overtime when they held the ball and a 90-88 lead with 13 seconds remaining. But Boston's Don Chaney stole a Bobby Dandridge pass, and got the ball to Havlicek. He missed a jumper, but he put back his own rebound to tie the game with five seconds to go, and the Bucks failed to get off a shot before the buzzer.

Havlicek finished the game with 36 points, and the last two came on a jump shot over Abdul-Jabbar with seven seconds remaining that put the Celtics ahead, 101-100, and set the stage for the Bucks' big finish. Abdul-Jabbar led Milwaukee with 34 points. Nobody remembers much about the other 32.

KENOSHA WELCOMES JOE LOUIS

MAY 11, 1937

Kenosha had known celebrities before. At one time, it had been the weekend home of colorful Chicago Mayor William Hale "Big Bill" Thompson, but when Joe Louis decided to train there for his title fight with James Braddock, the city was impressed.

More than 1,700 citizens and a host of photographers turned out to welcome the young heavyweight challenger upon his arrival at Kenosha's Lake Front Stadium on a Tuesday afternoon. The stadium had a quarter-mile cinder track and enough seats to accommodate the people willing to pay to watch him spar. It would do nicely for the six weeks that Louis would be in town.

The area had everything he needed to get ready for Braddock, including a 10-room lakefront mansion at Chiwaukee Beach, located five miles south of the city. With six bedrooms and two baths, the home was valued at a princely $96,000. "Big Bill" had slept there, and so would "The Brown Bomber" and his entourage, which included trainer Jack Blackburn, managers John Roxborough and Julian Black, bodyguard Carl Nelson and chef Bill Bottoms.

The rent wasn't cheap, either. Louis leased the place from Fred P. Fischer, a wealthy Chicago bed manufacturer, and it cost him $1,000. Louis also had to lease a nearby hotel for his sparring partners.

Louis scheduled 19 public appearances at Lake Front Stadium, where a ring was erected around 3,500 seats. His schedule called for public workouts at 2 p.m. every Sunday, Tuesday, Thursday and Saturday. The cost of admission on weekends was $1.10; the weekday rate was 55 cents. When bad weather hit, Louis moved the show inside to the local Moose Club.

Following Louis' last workout in Kenosha, just two days before the fight, the final tally showed that more than 20,000 people had passed through the gates at the stadium to watch him train. Not only did Louis draw a steady stream of sportswriters and photographers and boxing experts, but special trains also brought hundreds of fans from Chicago on some of the weekend dates. Among the visitors was legendary musician Cab Calloway, who was playing in Milwaukee at the time. In turn, Louis also traveled to Milwaukee to hear a Calloway concert.

"Fine, fine," Louis answered when asked on his final day there about his stay in Kenosha. "We've only had to work inside three times. The weather has been splendid... It's as good as any training place I know."

He had celebrated his 23rd birthday with a huge turkey dinner two days after arriving in Kenosha, and a month later Louis was celebrating much more than that. On June 22 in Chicago's Comiskey Park before 55,000 spectators, he became heavyweight champion of the world.

Braddock had shocked boxing two years earlier when he'd won the title with a unanimous decision over Max Baer, but he'd been resting on his laurels ever since. Louis entered the fight a 3-1 favorite to take him out, and he didn't disappoint anyone.

Braddock put Louis on the canvas with a right uppercut in the first round, but the punch merely got the challenger's attention. He was up immediately. The rest of the first round and the next six were a brawl with Louis hitting the champion with punishing blow after punishing blow. And then 1 minute 10 seconds into the eighth, it was over.

Louis caught Braddock in the face with a thundering right, and the champion went sprawling across the ring. He was down for the count – bleeding from the mouth, cut and battered – and he had to be helped to his feet to leave the ring.

While Louis had been favored to win the fight, many New York and Chicago writers had predicted doom for him after watching some of his uninspired workouts in Kenosha. In his dressing room after the knockout, Louis said his public appearances there were just for show. He added that he had done most of his preparation behind the scenes, much of it during early morning roadwork along the beach near his mansion and on rural Kenosha County roads.

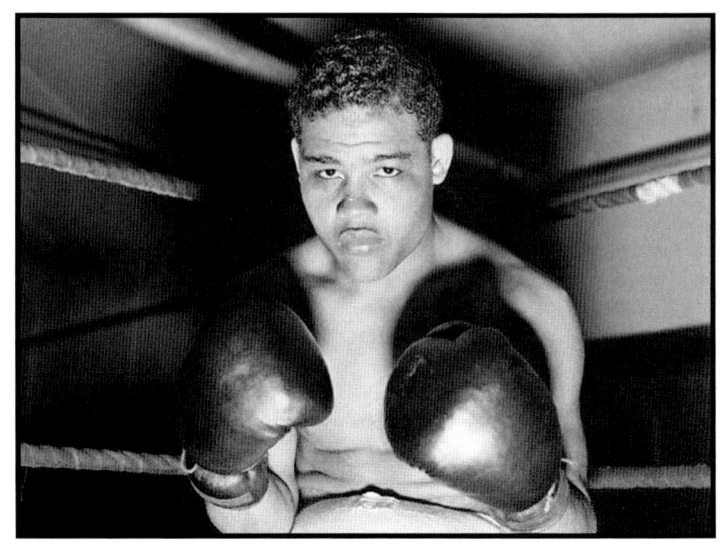

Joe Louis

BUCKS LOSE NBA TITLE GAME TO BOSTON

MAY 12, 1974

With a double-overtime victory at Boston fresh in their minds and a Sunday afternoon crowd of 10,938 bouncing off the walls of the Milwaukee Arena, the Milwaukee Bucks seemed poised for the second championship in their six-year history. But the visitors had different ideas.

They also had a different game plan.

The Celtics had spent the first six games of the series playing Kareem Abdul-Jabbar straight up instead of double-teaming him, the way everyone else in the league did. The strategy worked well enough to give them a split in the six games, but the Bucks' center had made them pay by scoring 34 points or more in five of them. And so Boston coach Tom Heinsohn decided it was time for a change.

He had forwards Don Nelson and Paul Silas take turns dropping off of their men and helping center Dave Cowens deny Abdul-Jabbar the ball. It took 12 minutes for the plan to work as the Bucks' star scored 14 points in the first period. But then the Celtics tightened up and Abdul-Jabbar went scoreless for 18 minutes. He got off only three shots in that span while a 20-20 tie was turning into a 65-50 Boston advantage.

The Bucks would never lead after that, although they mounted a dramatic comeback midway through the third quarter and early in the fourth to close the difference to 71-68. Cowens picked up his fifth foul during the run, but then the Celtics quieted the crowd with eight straight points and turned the game into a 102-87 rout.

Cowens finished with 28 points and 14 rebounds, while Abdul-Jabbar had 26 and 13 and got very little help. Oscar Robertson, possibly the greatest guard in NBA history up to that point, suffered through one of his most forgettable days, making only two of 13 shots and scoring six points. Cornell Warner and Curtis Perry, the power forwards whom the Celtics chose to ignore while concentrating on Abdul-Jabbar, totaled seven between them, and Jon McGlocklin, the Bucks' best perimeter shooter, was held to 13 while playing with a torn calf muscle.

Starting guard Lucius Allen, the team's third leading scorer that season, had suffered a knee injury March 15 and never returned.

The outcome was a shattering disappointment for the fans who had jammed the freeways and parking lots around the Arena more than an hour before tip-off. Hundreds came down from their seats to ring the floor during warm-ups. But the comforts of home never materialized for the Bucks.

Milwaukee won two of the three games played in Boston, but prevailed only once at the Arena, taking Game 2, 105-96.

The series was summed up in the post-game awards ceremony when the championship trophy fell to the floor and came apart in three pieces. Celtics President Red Auerbach put it together again, which was more than anyone could say for the Bucks. They have yet to return to the NBA Finals.

1974 NBA FINALS

DATE	SCORE	SITE
April 28	Celtics 98, Bucks 83	Milwaukee Arena
April 30	Bucks 105, Celtics 96 (ot)	Milwaukee Arena
May 3	Celtics 95, Bucks 83	Boston Garden
May 5	Bucks 97, Celtics 89	Boston Garden
May 7	Celtics 96, Bucks 87	Milwaukee Arena
May 10	Bucks 102, Celtics 101 (ot)	Boston Garden
May 12	Celtics 102, Bucks 87	Milwaukee Arena

Source: Bucks Media Guide

TERRY PORTER CUT FROM OLYMPIC SQUAD

MAY 13, 1984

Just in case Terry Porter wasn't feeling displaced enough when he got to the United States Olympic Trials, the coach was kind enough to tell him that nobody knew who he was.

Bobby Knight had 72 players on his hands when the tryouts began, and Porter was the only one of them who'd played at the lowly NCAA Division III level. But the University of Wisconsin-Stevens Point star was coming off a terrific run at the NAIA tournament where he'd averaged 25.6 points a game and been named the Most Valuable Player while leading his team into the championship game. So Porter figured that had to be worth something. But he figured wrong.

Recalling his first encounter with Knight much later, Porter, a 6-foot-2 guard, said, "He told me that no one on the selection committee knew anything about me. No one had seen any film on me, and because I was from Wisconsin, they just assumed I was a big white kid from a farm. It wasn't until the first day of practice that they learned I was black and a guard and that I could play."

And play he did. Three practices a day until the original 72 players had dwindled to 32. And then another ambush cropped up on what Porter had hoped would be his road to the Los Angeles Games. He came down with chicken pox. He went home to get well, and that probably should have been the end of his Olympic quest. But Knight had seen enough of him to want to get a longer look. So he called him back.

It was clear that Porter wasn't the most talented guard in camp, but he might have been the toughest. He could also pass extremely well, and he was refreshingly serious about defense. And so when the 32 were reduced to 20, he was still on the premises and gaining a reputation as the biggest surprise of the tryouts.

That, however, was as far as he would go. Halfway through a six-day mini-camp on the Indiana campus, Knight had a surprise of his own. He made an unscheduled cut and reduced the squad to 16. Porter was one of the four players sent home.

"My personal opinion is that he played outstanding here," said Iowa coach George Raveling, who was Knight's top Olympic assistant. "The thing I liked best about him was his basketball intelligence. It wasn't that he played poorly. Others just played better."

Porter couldn't be too disappointed about his dismissal because he was in such good company. Also let go that day was an undersized point guard from Gonzaga named John Stockton and an oversized power forward from Auburn named Charles Barkley, along with St. Joseph's swing man Maurice Martin.

Martin played 69 games in two pro seasons, while the other three lasted considerably longer than that. Stockton played in the NBA for 19 years, Porter for 17 and Barkley for 16. Porter's career was easily the least likely.

"When I first went to Stevens Point, I didn't even think about the NBA," he said. "The big start for me was making it to the final cut for the Olympic team. Then I figured I had a chance to be drafted."

Terry Porter looked for an opening while playing for UW-Stevens Point.

What's more, he figured he had a chance to be drafted by his hometown team. A Milwaukee native who didn't even make his South Division High School squad until his junior year, he was counting heavily on the Milwaukee Bucks to take him with the 22nd pick in the 1985 draft. In fact, he was in the building when the Bucks' Don Nelson passed on him in favor of Louisiana State guard Jerry "Ice" Reynolds. Reynolds proved to be a dismal bust. Porter went two picks later to Portland and went on to become the Trail Blazers' all-time leader in assists and three-point baskets.

While Nelson clearly made a mistake on Porter, Knight had no reason to regret his decision. The U.S. Olympic team cruised to the gold medal with an 8-0 record, beating Spain by 31 points in the final. The gold medal was only a little tarnished by the fact that the Soviet team boycotted the Games.

The guards Knight selected ahead of Porter included Steve Alford, Vern Fleming, Leon Wood, Alvin Robertson and Michael Jordan. Only one of them made a bigger name for himself than Terry Porter.

MILWAUKEE HOSTS FIRST MAJOR LEAGUE GAME

MAY 14, 1878

Big-time baseball fever came to Wisconsin on a Tuesday afternoon in May, but it was a fairly mild outbreak. A crowd of 1,500 gathered at the new Milwaukee Base-Ball Grounds to watch the Milwaukee Grays – also known as the Cream Citys – play the Cincinnati Red Stockings in the first major league game ever held in the city. The place held 4,000.

Prices were reasonable. A season-ticket could be had for $15, which seemed like a bargain when the local *Milwaukee Sentinel* practically promised a pennant for the home team.

The Grays justified the newspaper's optimism in their home opener by beating the Red Stockings, 8-5, but things went steadily downhill after that. The Grays would finish 15-45 and last in the six-team National League.

Local citizen W.P. Rogers acquired the franchise in the three-year-old National League at the previous winter meetings, thanks partly to a betting scandal. Four players had admitted to throwing games in 1877, getting themselves banned for life and costing Louisville its franchise. St. Louis and Hartford also lost their teams. Some thought the game would be ruined forever, but Milwaukee, Indianapolis and Providence leaped into the breach, with Milwaukee picking up the name and the manager of the Louisville club.

The manager was John Curtis Chapman, who'd led the Kentucky team through the two previous seasons. The name was totally in keeping with the colorful times. The league consisted of the Boston Red Caps, the Chicago White Stockings, the Indianapolis Blues, Cincinnati Red Stockings and two Grays, one in Milwaukee and one in Providence.

At least, the local Grays had a nice place to play. The stadium was bounded by 10th and 11th streets, and Michigan and Clybourn avenues, and it featured a double row of shade trees along the first baseline to shield the patrons from the sun. It was 395 feet to dead center, but the foul lines were a shallow 266, and any ball hit over the short fence in right was ruled a double.

That was not a problem since nobody hit home runs anyway. The home run title that year went to a Providence player who banged out four. Power was not a big item in those times, but pitching was. Rosters were limited to 11 players and pitching staffs to two. The Grays' pitchers were Sam Weaver, who finished with a 12-31 record, and Mike Golden, who was much worse. He went 3-13.

The highlight of the season occurred before the Grays even came home when on May 9, Weaver pitched a no-hitter in Indianapolis for Milwaukee's first victory. Another high spot was that Milwaukee outfielder Abner Dalrymple led the league in hitting with a .354 average.

But Milwaukee finished 26 games behind first-place Boston. Thus, it didn't come as a big surprise when the city's franchise was sold the following February to satisfy a bankruptcy judgment of $125.61. Milwaukee subsequently enjoyed a one-year, big league stint in the American League in 1901, as well as partial seasons in the Union Association in 1884 and the American Association in 1891. But it had to wait until 1953 to get back into the National League.

That's when the Braves came to town, and the fever ran much higher.

MILWAUKEE IN THE MAJOR LEAGUES

YEARS	TEAM	LEAGUE
1878	Grays (or Cream Citys)	National League
*1884	Grays	Union Association
**1891	Brewers	American Association
1901	Brewers	American League
1953-'65	Braves	National League
1970-'97	Brewers	American League
1998-present	Brewers	National League

*Inherited defunct Pittsburgh team on Sept. 19.   **Inherited defunct Cincinnati team on Aug. 17.

Source: Total Baseball: The Official Encyclopedia of Major League Baseball

MILWAUKEE WELCOMES THE WHITE SOX

MAY 15, 1968

They were clearly the Second City's second team. Chicago loved its Cubs and tolerated its White Sox, so when the American League club scheduled ten games in Milwaukee, it was hoping for a warm reception.

It got one, too, as 23,510 fans ignored a dire weather report to watch the reeling Sox play the California Angels. Milwaukee fans hadn't seen a regular-season major league game since the Braves skipped town in September 1965, and this was their way of stating the case for putting a franchise back in their city.

Bud Selig and his Milwaukee Brewers organization sponsored the White Sox visits, which included regular-season games against the nine other American League teams plus an exhibition with the Cubs. After the exhibition drew 20,759 people in near freezing weather, Selig and friends were hoping to draw 30,000 for California. But tornado warnings had been broadcast throughout the day, and there was also a 90% chance of rain. Still, the Wednesday night turnout more than doubled the best crowd the Sox had had all season at Comiskey Park.

The team wasn't doing any better on the field than it was at the box office. After surprising everyone by finishing three games out of first place in 1967, the Sox had dropped their first 10 games in '68 and limped into town with an 11-16 record. They limped out again in last place after dropping a 4-2 decision to the Angels.

A 29-minute rain delay dampened the fans' enthusiasm in the bottom of the sixth inning and a two-run California eighth sunk their adopted ball club. White Sox Manager Eddie Stanky's decision to move his outfield in resulted in a game-changing double by the Angels' Bobby Knoop, and that turned out to be the key hit of the game.

It also helped establish a season-long pattern for the White Sox, who were frankly terrible. They would finish 36 games out of first place with a 67-95 record and a different manager as Stanky got fired midway through the year. Milwaukee didn't do much to promote Stanky's job security as the Sox lost eight of their nine AL games there, but it did help the Chicagoans' bottom line.

While the Sox were averaging 7,493 fans at their own field, they were drawing 29,366 per game in Milwaukee, even though four of the games were played in bad weather. None of the White Sox County Stadium dates drew fewer than 20,000, while a July match with the Yankees attracted 40,575, and the series finale with the World Series-bound Detroit Tigers pulled in 42,808.

The disparity in crowds was so obvious that rumors began floating around that the White Sox might move to Milwaukee. Owner Arthur Allyn called that talk "silly," and he also downplayed a *Washington Post* report that Milwaukee and San Diego would almost certainly be getting National League franchises the following year.

Allyn proved to be right on both counts. The White Sox were back for 11 AL games in 1969, and this time their County Stadium crowds averaged 18,019, which was still almost triple the 6,633 they were pulling in at home.

The following year, Milwaukee didn't need the White Sox anymore as the Seattle Pilots moved into town permanently and became the Milwaukee Brewers. With a little help from Chicago, the city had proved its point.

MELGES STEERS U.S. TO AMERICA'S CUP

MAY 16, 1992

Multimillionaire Bill Koch had almost everything he needed to win sailing's biggest prize. He had a dedicated crew of 17, a stubborn "fools rush in" attitude and $64 million to spend on a lightning fast boat. What he lacked was experience.

The 52-year-old owner of America³ was a novice among yachting's jet set with only eight years of racing experience. But he solved that shortcoming by sharing the helm with two others: David Dellenbaugh, an experienced America's Cup tactician, and another even more experienced sailor, a two-time Olympic medal winner from Zenda, Wis.

Harry C. "Buddy" Melges Jr., brought more than 60 national and international championships to the Koch team, and it proved to be more than enough when the American defender swamped Italy's Il Moro di Venezia by 44 seconds in the fifth and final race in the best-of-seven series. As they crossed the finish line off the shores of San Diego, both Koch and Melges had their hands on the wheel.

Adding to the victory's Badger flavor were the contributions of former University of Wisconsin football players Larry Mialik, Art Price and Chad VandeZande, who signed on to crank the America³ sail winches.

In the end, it really was no contest. The Italians' only success came in the second race, which they won by three seconds in the closest finish in America's Cup finals history. And so a U.S. boat captured the Cup for the 27th time in 28 competitions since 1851, making it look easy, although certainly not cheap.

Koch, an MIT engineering graduate and heir to an oil fortune, spent $55 million of his own money on America3, much of it on computer-based research. The result was a technological marvel with a mathematical name. The boat was dubbed "America Cubed," and the "Cubed" stood for "talent, technology and teamwork."

Koch was expecting to invest about $20 million in the project, but the stakes were raised by the Italian syndicate, which spent $70 million. Asked if he would try to defend his title, Koch said, "Not if it costs $64 million."

To Melges, who grew up sailing the boats designed and built by his father on Lake Geneva, it was another solid gold experience. He won an Olympic gold medal in the Soling class in 1972, and he also earned a bronze in the Flying Dutchman class in 1964, three Yachtsman of the Year awards and seven world ice boat titles.

Nicknamed "The Wizard of Zenda" for the town of 200 where his boat works builds fiberglass sailboats and skiffs, Melges was inducted into the America's Cup Hall of Fame in 2001.

WISCONSIN WOMEN PIONEER PRO BASEBALL LEAGUE

MAY 17, 1943

1943 Racine Belles: Front Row (L to R): Irene Hickson, Edythe Perlick, Clara Schillace, Annabelle Thompson, Madeline English. Second Row: Eleanor Dapkus, Sophie Kurys, Dorothy Wind, Gloria Marks, Dorothy Maguire, Margaret Danhauser. Back Row: Charlotte Smith, Joanne Winter, Manager Johnny Gottselig, Mary Nesbit, Dorothy Hunter, Chaperone Marie Anderson.

Empty ballparks, not women's rights, were on P.K. Wrigley's mind. The Chicago Cubs' owner was concerned that with so many players overseas fighting a war that baseball parks across the country would be insufficiently used. He was looking for another attraction, and what could be more attractive than women?

That was the conclusion of a committee set up by Wrigley and headed by his assistant general manager, Ken Sells. With the blessing and the fiscal backing of his boss, as well as Brooklyn Dodgers President and General Manager Branch Rickey, Sells launched a recruiting drive for young athletes of the feminine persuasion. Hundreds of them were found, and the best of the prospects gathered in Chicago on May 17, 1943, for tryouts at Wrigley Field, although bad weather curtailed the first two workouts.

So began what is now popularly remembered as the All-American Girls Professional Baseball League, an ambitious effort that had a distinct Wisconsin flavor and would provide employment for more than 600 female ballplayers in the 12 years that it lasted.

The league wrestled with various names, not to mention rules, throughout its existence and, seemingly, for good reason. The players weren't all Americans, they weren't girls, and this wasn't baseball. The original four teams based in Racine, Kenosha, Rockford, Ill., and South Bend, Ind., included a number of Canadians; and the original rules were a hybrid of softball and baseball with bigger balls, underhand pitching, but with a longer pitching distance and base paths than in softball. And the rosters were made up of young women, not "girls." But this was a long way from the days of political correctness and Title IX.

Just how far was demonstrated by the players' contracts. All of them included clauses that required the players to observe high moral standards and rules of conduct. Femininity was crucial, and Helena Rubenstein's nightly charm school classes were compulsory. Boyish haircuts were banned, and each player was issued a beauty kit and told how to use it. There would be no shorts or slacks. The uniforms included short skirts and high socks, and each team traveled with 15 players, a manager, a business manager and a female chaperone.

Players were prohibited from working anywhere else during the season, but they didn't mind. They could make anywhere from $45 to $85 a week, and there were plenty of men who were not pulling down that kind of money.

The schedule called for 108 games beginning in mid-May before ending with playoffs in September. Wrigley's idea of using major league stadiums didn't fly with the other owners, but the sport was ideal for smaller cities such as Racine and Kenosha where it was the only game in town.

The schedule called for the first season to open May 30, 1943, a Sunday, with a doubleheader between the Racine Belles and the Kenosha Comets. Another doubleheader was scheduled for the next day. But the weather wasn't kind. A crowd of 600 paying 65 cents apiece for adults and 35 cents for children was held down by threatening skies as Kenosha beat Racine, 8-6, in the opener. The second game was rained out. The teams had the same problem on Monday with Racine winning, 6-3, before rain washed out the nightcap.

But, in the end, the first season was deemed a success, especially in Racine where the Belles won the playoffs by sweeping Kenosha in three games. Racine's Mary Nesbitt won two of the games and relieved in the third. In all, four Wisconsin women were on the playoff rosters of the two teams: Pitcher Merna Nearing of Milwaukee, and outfielders Darlene Mickelsen and Phyllis Kroehn of Madison, all played with Kenosha; while first baseman Margaret Danhauser of Racine played for the Belles.

The Milwaukee Chicks and a team from Minneapolis were added to the league in 1944, and Milwaukee won the title. But the new cities appeared to be too big for the sport, and their franchises were moved to Grand Rapids and Fort Wayne, Ind., after one season. The Racine Belles won the championship again in 1946, giving Wisconsin teams three of the first four titles.

Although Wrigley sold the league following its second season, it grew to 10 teams and attendance peaked at 910,000 in 1948. But then interest fell off. Racine dropped out following the 1950 season and Kenosha did the same after 1951. Three years later, the All-American Girls Professional Baseball League was no more.

THE ALL-AMERICAN GIRLS PROFESSIONAL BASEBALL LEAGUE (1943-'54)

TEAMS	YEARS
Battle Creek Belles	1951-'52
Chicago Colleens	1948
Fort Wayne Daisies	1945-'54
Grand Rapids Chicks	1945-'54
Kalamazoo Lassies	1950-'54
Kenosha Comets	1943-'51
Milwaukee Chicks	1944
Minneapolis Millerettes	1944
Muskegon Belles	1953
Muskegon Lassies	1946-'49
Peoria Redwings	1946-'51
Racine Belles	1943-'50
Rockford Peaches	1943-'54
South Bend Blue Sox	1943-'54
Springfield Sallies	1948

CHAMPIONS

YEAR	REGULAR-SEASON	PLAYOFF
1943	South Bend	Racine
1944	Milwaukee	Milwaukee
1945	Rockford	Rockford
1946	Racine	Racine
1947	Muskegon	Grand Rapids
1948	Grand Rapids	Rockford
1949	Rockford	Rockford
1950	Rockford	Rockford
1951	South Bend	South Bend
1952	Fort Wayne	South Bend
1953	Fort Wayne	Grand Rapids
1954	Fort Wayne	Kalamazoo

Source: aagpbl.org

BIRD-LED CELTICS SWEEP BUCKS OUT OF PLAYOFFS

MAY 18, 1986

Don Nelson never questioned the Boston Celtics' talent, but he did wonder about their origin. "I'm not so sure Boston isn't from a different planet from the rest of us mere mortal teams," said the Milwaukee Bucks' coach.

Wherever they were from, the Bucks would have been delighted to load them onto the next rocket and send them back. The two teams had met five times before the playoffs, and the Celtics had five victories to show for it. When they made it nine in a row with a four-game sweep in the NBA's Eastern Conference finals, Milwaukee's season was over.

And it had been such a promising season. The Bucks had put together the league's third best regular-season record at 57-25, and then they'd swept New Jersey and slugged their way past Philadelphia in the first two rounds of the playoffs. The four-games-to-three triumph over Philly was especially satisfying because the 76ers had demolished them in the conference semis the previous year.

If any other Boston team had been standing in their way, the Bucks might have had a legitimate shot at the franchise's second championship. But they were stuck with these Celtics, and Nelson was right. This group was a galaxy ahead of everyone else. They finished the regular season with a league-best 67-15 mark, and three of their victories over Milwaukee came by double-digit margins.

Steady Dennis Johnson and the irritating Danny Ainge gave them a competent backcourt, while Robert Parish, Kevin McHale and Larry Bird backed up by Bill Walton gave them one of the best front lines in the history of the game. It was all too much for the Bucks. Especially Bird.

When Bob Lanier walked away from the game two years earlier, he left a size 22 hole under the Milwaukee basket, and while Alton Lister did his best to plug it, the Bucks' baseline was undersized and overmatched. They might have been able to compensate for some of that with a healthy Sidney Moncrief, but their star guard played the series on a gimpy foot.

The Celtics disposed of their visitors with almost embarrassing ease in the first two games at Boston Garden, winning, 128-96 and 122-111. The Bucks regained some self-respect when they got back to the Milwaukee Arena, but still lost Game 3.

Forward Terry Cummings had a monstrous 27-point, 18-rebound game as the Bucks double-teamed Boston's big men and took their chances with Johnson and Ainge. The strategy worked until the fourth quarter when the Celtics got their perimeter game untracked, and Johnson hit a pair from long range and Bird buried a three to lock up a 111-107 victory.

Bird finished the night with a modest 19 points, but that final three-pointer served as fair warning. The following day, May 18, while another Arena sellout of 11,052 alternately crossed its fingers and held its breath, the Bucks gave the Celtics all they could eat until Bird took over the game.

These two teams never were fond of one another, and another example of that cropped up early in the second quarter when Ricky Pierce decked Ainge with an elbow. Pierce was ejected, and the already thin Bucks were without their sixth man.

Still, they were trailing by only two points with 6 minutes 47 seconds remaining when they went cold and Bird caught fire. While Milwaukee was missing eight shots in a row, Bird nailed four three-pointers in the last four minutes of play. The Celtics won going away, 111-98.

"We worked really hard and came out with our hands empty," said Cummings. "But we played well through all the playoffs and had nothing to be ashamed of. We lost to the team that will probably win it all."

The Celtics eliminated Houston in a six-game final series. They never did come back to Earth.

BREWERS DEMOTE "THE SUNDOWN KID"

MAY 19, 1977

Danny Thomas was seeking peace. The Milwaukee Brewers were seeking pitching. When the two searches couldn't be reconciled, Thomas was on his way to Spokane.

Religion, the Brewers insisted, had nothing to do with sending the slugging 26-year-old outfielder to their Class AAA farm club, even though he was hitting .271 – tied with Robin Yount for the fifth best average on the team – and batting in the clean-up spot. For an excuse, they had three injured pitchers, and they needed fresh arms. Besides, they still had plenty of options on Thomas.

Thomas expressed no hard feelings, but he had to know that his new found faith hadn't helped. He'd joined Garner Ted Armstrong's World Wide Church of God during the winter, and in keeping with the faith, he vowed not to play in games from sundown Friday to sunset Saturday. That meant he would be missing close to 40 starts.

The Brewers were scheduled to play a weekend series in Boston, and Thomas would be sitting out a Sunday doubleheader, as well, due to a holy day, when Jim Baumer, vice president of baseball operations, decided to farm him out. No one could have known at the time that Thomas' demotion would trigger a tragic three-year tailspin that would end in his death in a Mobile, Ala., jail cell.

Thomas' upside looked to be unlimited when the Brewers made him their No. 1 draft choice in 1972. He went on to win batting's Triple Crown in the Class AA Eastern League before making it to the big leagues at the tail-end of the 1976 season. He hit .276 with four home runs in 32 games for the Brewers that fall.

But he was a troubled young man. According to one report, he tried to kill himself while playing winter ball during the off-season in Venezuela. He was in and out of hospitals for several months suffering from depression. It was while he was in a St. Louis facility that he contacted the World Wide Church and decided to join. His wife joined, too, and they said their new religion gave them peace they'd never known before.

When Thomas came to spring training in 1977, he told Baumer of his conversion and of the limits it placed on when he could play. Baumer suggested he try to get a dispensation from the church. When that wasn't forthcoming, Baumer talked with a church official himself, but said that he wasn't at all understanding.

Meanwhile, Thomas proceeded to tear up spring training, and it was decided to keep him on the roster. "We've got to keep him," Manager Alex Grammas said. "He's swinging the hell out of the bat." When asked about the scheduling conflicts, the manager said, "We can't worry about it now. We hope somewhere along the line, something will be resolved."

Nothing ever was. Thomas was hitting better than .300 to start the season. Friendly and hard working, he was a popular figure in the clubhouse. His teammates joked about his selective schedule and took to calling him "The Sundown Kid." But then his production started to tail off, the Brewers started to lose, and Thomas' popularity started to wane.

"As a general rule, it's not healthy to treat one player differently than the other 24," said Baumer on the day he sent Thomas down.

The Brewers docked him two days pay per week to compensate for the weekends he didn't play, and still he wouldn't budge. He thought the Brewers were trying to make him hate the minor leagues enough to change his mind. Spokane clearly was not the answer for him. He was batting .237 when the Brewers tried to ship him back to the Eastern League. Rather than go, Thomas retired from baseball.

He got a job at a manufacturing plant in Spokane and lost it. Then he became a logger and moved his family to a cabin in the woods without electricity or running water. He returned to baseball in 1978 and starred for an independent league team in Boise, Idaho. The following year brought him to Miami and another independent team that folded in mid-season.

Thomas moved his pregnant wife and two children to Mobile in 1980 and began undergoing psychiatric care again. After a couple of months, he broke off treatment. And two months after that he was arrested for allegedly raping and sodomizing a 12-year-old babysitter.

He was found in his cell with a pair of blue denim jeans wrapped around his neck. He'd torn them up and tied them together and used them to hang himself.

BORCHERT FIELD OPENS IN MILWAUKEE

MAY 20, 1888

It would be home to rodeos, balloon races, mysterious blackouts, flying roofs and disappearing fences over the next 66 years, but on this historic Sunday afternoon in Milwaukee, the place that would later be renamed Borchert Field was all about baseball.

The fans – 6,000 of them or maybe 7,000 depending on who was counting – began gathering outside the entrances of the brand new $40,000 palace around 1 o'clock. By the time they opened the gates for the 3:30 game, there was hardly any place to stand. Second-floor porches across the street were packed with neighbors, and all of the best knotholes in the outfield fences were taken by the biggest kids.

Bounded by Burleigh and Chambers streets on the north and south and Ninth and Tenth streets on the east and west, this overgrown playground was shoehorned into its north side neighborhood, but it was the only place to be on opening day. The hometown Milwaukee Brewers – also referred to as the Cream Citys – were facing visiting St. Paul in a Western Association game, and who cared if the outfield was a little rough and the people seated in the right-field stands couldn't see left field, and vice versa?

The stadium was actually called Athletic Park when it opened, but that would change in 40 years. The quirky dimensions featuring foul lines only 266 feet long wouldn't. Home runs were cheap, but only if you didn't count the windows they broke across the street. The management paid for those.

The Brewers got off to a slow start, giving up three runs in the top of the first. But they got one back in the bottom of the inning, and then they rallied for four in the fifth and won, 9-5. And the fun was just beginning.

This was truly a park for all seasons. Boxing, wrestling, bicycle races, circuses, rodeos, hot air balloon races and donkey baseball were all staged there, as was a Green Bay Packers game in 1933. The Packers held the New York Giants without a first down that day and still lost, 10-7. Both the Milwaukee Badgers of the NFL and Marquette University's football team also played there in the 1920s.

It was the home field when Milwaukee spent a single year in the American League before the franchise moved on in 1902, but mostly it was known as the place where the American Association Milwaukee Brewers played more than 4,000 games and won eight pennants while an estimated 8.3 million people watched from 1902 through 1952.

Some of them watched standing up. The seating capacity was around 10,000, but standing room crowds of up to 17,000 were frequently accommodated by situating the customers behind ropes in the outfield. Hit a ball into the SRO section, and you had a ground-rule double.

In 1920, Otto Borchert, the descendant of an old Milwaukee brewing family, became the Brewers' sole owner, and he made some serious money developing young players and selling them to big league clubs. But his prosperity was short-lived. He collapsed and died of a cerebral hemorrhage at the age of 52 while making a speech at an Elks Club dinner given in his honor in 1927. His wife was listening to the speech on the radio when she heard what had happened.

The widow sold the team but kept the stadium, which was renamed Borchert Field on Jan. 3, 1928, in her husband's honor. She leased the field to a succession of Brewers owners, none of them more colorful than Bill Veeck, who revived a flagging franchise in the 1940s with dozens of zany promotions.

The most spectacular stunt of the Veeck era had nothing to do with the owner. Mother Nature staged it in the form of a fierce thunderstorm that blew a 100-foot section of roof off the grandstand during a game on June 15, 1944. Thirty fans were injured, and cars and houses all over the neighborhood were damaged.

Already showing its age, Borchert Field began to deteriorate more rapidly after that. The plumbing and electrical systems were wearing out, and the popularity of the automobile had overrun its limited parking. The lease with Mrs. Bochert was due to end in 1953, and the construction of the new Milwaukee County Stadium made the old place obsolete.

The Brewers played there for the last time on Sept. 21, 1952, when they lost to Kansas City in the final game of the American Association championship series. The park was torn down in 1954. A freeway runs over it now.

"TRADER" LANE LAYS INTO UMPIRE HANK SOAR

MAY 21, 1971

"Showboat" or "Shoe-brain?" It depended on whose side you took in a classic three-day duel of insults between General Manager Frank Lane of the Milwaukee Brewers and veteran umpire Hank Soar.

A cloudburst in Kansas City had left Lane storming mad. The Brewers were leading the Royals, 4-1, when Soar's crew called off a Friday night game in the fifth inning just two outs before it would have become official. The umpires cleared the field once for 42 minutes after the Royals' first batter in the fifth had struck out. And then when they removed the tarp, the skies opened again. This time they waited 35 minutes and sent everyone home, which meant the game had to be replayed from the start.

Technically, the decision was made by home plate umpire George Maloney. But Soar was the crew chief and the focus of Lane's wrath.

"Only a shoe-brain like Soar could have done it," raged the general manager. "He announced his retirement this year, but should have retired 20 years ago. The man is consistently inconsistent."

Even if Lane, who was 75 at the time, was right and the 57-year-old Soar was past his prime, Soar could still read a newspaper. And so he fired back in an interview of his own two days later. "Lane's just a showboat. He always has been and always will be," Soar fumed.

On Saturday, in between that volley, Lane also had blasted Larry Barnett, another member of Soar's crew, for his call on a close play at first base. And in an intriguing twist on an old theme, an umpire charged somebody else with being blind.

"I know that Lane can't see far enough to make any judgment on a play like he did about the one at first," Soar said, adding that he planned to call American League President Joe Cronin with a full report.

Soar was wrong about one thing. Lane was not just a "showboat." He also was a trading maniac.

He made his first big splash as a general manager when he took over the Chicago White Sox in 1948 and immediately put the entire team on waivers to gauge his players' market value. "Trader Lane," as he was popularly known, originated 241 transactions involving 353 players while turning the moribund Sox into pennant contenders. But when Chicago finally made it to the 1959 World Series, Lane had worn out his welcome and gone to St. Louis where he promptly traded future Hall of Famer Red Schoendienst and tried to deal Cardinals legend Stan Musial.

The most unpopular swap Lane ever made came at Cleveland where he sent local icon Rocky Colavito to Detroit for American League batting champion Harvey Kuenn. The most bizarre came when he fired Indians Manager Joe Gordon, then rehired him and traded him to the Tigers for Manager Jimmie Dykes.

Soar had an interesting past himself. Before becoming an umpire, he had played semi-pro baseball, coached in what became the National Basketball Association and played pro football. In fact, he caught the game-winning touchdown pass for the New York Giants when they beat the Green Bay Packers, 23-17, in the 1938 NFL title game.

But Lane wasn't interested in Soar's prowess as an athlete. He just thought he was a lousy umpire. Told of Soar's threat to contact Cronin, Lane one-upped him. He urged that umpires, even those with Soar's seniority, be shipped to the minors if their work was unsatisfactory.

Soar wondered aloud why Lane had never said any of these things to his face. He said he looked for him at the ballpark but couldn't find him. "I wanted to give him a piece of my mind," Soar said.

To which Lane replied, "Soar can't afford to give anybody a piece of his mind. If he does, he won't have that much left."

The verbal war between Lane and Soar ended in a draw, and the same might be said of their careers. The Brewers replaced Lane with Jim Wilson after the 1972 season, but kept him on the payroll for another year. Soar's last year was 1973.

JAMES LOFTON ACQUITTED

MAY 22, 1987

His former teammate was across the hall at the Brown County Courthouse being tried on three counts of second-degree sexual assault, but Mossy Cade's troubles were hardly the first thing on James Lofton's mind. He had troubles of his own.

A 30-year-old woman from Iron Mountain, Mich., had accused the Green Bay Packers' star receiver of forcing her to perform oral sex in the staircase of a Green Bay nightclub, The Top Shelf, early in the morning of Dec. 18, 1986. Like Cade, Lofton was accused of second-degree sexual assault. In Lofton's case, there was just one count, but if a jury of 10 men and two women believed his accuser could go to jail. Now he was waiting to see what the jurors had decided.

Forrest Gregg, the Packers' coach, had spent much of his time attending both trials. He said professional athletes could be targets because of their fame, that people didn't understand how hard it was to become a successful pro. No matter what happened at the trial, Gregg knew he wouldn't have the use of Lofton's services in the coming season. The Packers had already traded Lofton to the Los Angeles Raiders for a third-round draft choice and another conditional pick. Gregg said if there hadn't been a trial, there wouldn't have been a trade.

As Lofton waited, his wife Beverly waited with him. She was eight months pregnant with their second child. Her husband's lawyer didn't dispute that the incident in the stairwell had taken place, but he contended that the act was consensual. Lofton didn't testify in his own defense. The Loftons said they'd received dozens of cards and letters from people who said they were praying for them.

Their prayers were answered. The jurors, who were from Rock County, deliberated for two hours, and then they returned to the courtroom and announced their verdict. They said Lofton was not guilty. One juror said there were no witnesses and there wasn't enough physical evidence to convict him. He also said the verdict had nothing to do with the fact that Lofton was a football player.

Gregg said the verdict was what he expected. "After being in the trial for one day, I knew what the outcome would be," he said.

After it was read by Judge Alexander Grant, the Loftons cried, embraced and kissed. Reporters crowded around them outside the courtroom and Beverly said she forgave her husband. "I married James for life," she said. "I have to deal with this with him. I'm a Christian, No. 1, and I'm obedient as a Christian in my forgiveness."

James said he also forgave his accuser and regretted that he would no longer be playing for the Packers. "I've always been a Green Bay Packer," he said. "I would have liked to finish my career here a little bit differently."

Meanwhile, no one paid much attention to the woman's friends and relatives as they left the courtroom.

Several current and former Packers players attended at least one of the concurrent trials, either Lofton's or Cade's. So did former Packers coach Bart Starr and his wife Cherry, along with Gregg and his wife Barbara. It all created a media circus in Green Bay, and it caused a schism between the Packers and their fans like no other in franchise history.

As the trials began, *Sports Illustrated* came out with a story by Frank Deford, arguably its most respected and renowned writer, that was titled: "Troubled Times in Title Town." The subtitle was: "Court cases and losing seasons have strained the bond between the fans in Green Bay and their once-beloved football team."

Deford concluded at one point in the story that: "Actually, the answer to Green Bay's dilemma is simple. It should sell the franchise to Milwaukee..."

That didn't happen, of course, and Lofton's career wasn't over, either.

He was 30 at the time of his trial, but he played seven more years in the NFL with the Raiders, Buffalo, the Los Angeles Rams and Philadelphia. He was inducted into the Pro Football Hall of Fame in 2003, the 20th Packer to be so honored.

MOSSY CADE CONVICTED

MAY 23, 1987

Everyone was talking about the Green Bay Packers. *Sports Illustrated*, with its story "Troubled Times in Title Town," had hit the newsstands. People in town could have lived without the notoriety. Fans were fascinated. Many more seemed disgusted.

The team's former all-pro receiver, James Lofton, had been acquitted the day before of second-degree sexual assault. Now it was the starting safety's turn. Mossy Cade was facing three counts of the same charge.

A 44-year-old woman, a relative by marriage, alleged that Cade had assaulted her once in the den and twice in a bedroom of his house in De Pere on Nov. 4, 1985. Cade testified that he was at a restaurant in Ashwaubenon at the time the woman was assaulted. His lawyer, Donald Zuidmulder, said the charges had grown out of a divorce pending between the woman and a relative of Cade, and that the woman was trying to hurt her husband by hurting Cade. The case took 19 months to come to trial.

Barbara Gregg, wife of coach Forrest Gregg, testified briefly in Cade's behalf. Her husband said the team's troubles weren't as important as a man's life.

The jurors came back after four hours. Cade, 25, was visibly relieved when they found him innocent of the alleged assault in the den. But not for long. They found him guilty of the other two counts. They didn't believe his alibi. No one could say for sure that he was at the restaurant. There was a broken bathroom door at his home, gold chains that the woman said she'd ripped from Cade's neck, bruises on her body and seminal fluid.

The woman said she was relieved by the verdict. Gregg and his wife were brought to tears. "I can't believe that conviction," said the coach. "There was no basis for them to find Mossy guilty." Barbara declared, "This is sick."

The jurors declined to talk about their deliberations, but the foreman said they began them with five minutes of prayer.

Cade spent some time with his fiancé, his family and his lawyers before leaving the courtroom without comment. He was later sentenced to two years at the Fox Lake Correctional Institute. He was paroled in October 1988, after one year and three months. At Cade's sentencing hearing, a psychiatrist testified that Cade had finally admitted that he had assaulted the woman and was prepared to undergo intensive treatment during his incarceration. A year later, Cade did another about-face and denied that he ever made such a confession.

Unlike Lofton, who was suspended by the Packers for the final game of the 1986 season, Cade had not only been allowed to finish the 1985 season, but he played all of '86. His conviction contributed to some cruel jokes at Green Bay's expense. One of them was delivered by the Wisconsin attorney general, who was a former state senator from neighboring De Pere.

Donald J. Hanaway, the state's top justice official, told a convention of district attorneys a month following the season that Green Bay should be the site of a new state prison "so the Green Bay Packers can walk to work."

After Cade served his sentence, the Packers entertained thoughts of welcoming him back for the 1989 season, but drew so much criticism as soon as the public found out about their intentions that they promptly waived him. The Minnesota Vikings claimed him, but also quickly bowed to public pressure and released him.

Cade never played again. A once promising career – Cade had been drafted No. 1 by San Diego in 1984 and acquired by the Packers for another No. 1 pick a year later – was ruined after two seasons.

Gregg would coach the Packers one more season, following the trial, before taking a job at his alma mater, Southern Methodist. The Packers would eventually recover from the black-eye that resulted from the Lofton and Cade trials, but it would take awhile and almost a complete housecleaning of the organization.

BUCKS WIN THE LOTTERY

MAY 24, 2005

Close to three weeks removed from a disastrous, injury-scarred season, Milwaukee Bucks General Manager Larry Harris called a press conference to assure everyone that Terry Porter was still his coach. "We're basically in the same boat," he said. "I told Terry, 'We're going to sink or swim together on this.'"

Roughly six weeks later Harris was hollering, "Man overboard!" What happened in between was the NBA draft lottery.

Mathematically speaking, the Bucks had a 6.3% chance of moving from sixth to first when the lottery was held in New York in the third week of May. Practically speaking, Porter had a 0% chance of keeping his job when that's exactly what happened.

Harris was ecstatic and Milwaukee was curious when the ping-pong balls fell the Bucks' way. What were they going to do with the fourth No. 1 overall choice in their history? The obvious candidate for the pick was Andrew Bogut, a 7-foot-1 center from Australia by way of Utah. But there were other alternatives, the most likely being 6-9 Marvin Williams, a freshman phenom from North Carolina. Also entering the discussion were point guards Chris Paul of Wake Forest and Deron Williams of Illinois.

Any of the above would have made life much easier for Porter had he remained the coach. But in a startling about-face, Harris called another press conference just six days before the draft and heaved Porter out of the boat. The general manager said he wanted a "more experienced head coach to guide the Bucks to the playoffs." English translation: Now that the Bucks had the No. 1 choice, they thought they had a legitimate shot at the post-season and a big-name coach.

Skeptics sensed the fine hand of owner Herb Kohl in that logic, since it put Harris in the outrageously uncomfortable position of going totally back on his word. But Harris insisted that the decision had been his. "Everybody's allowed to change their mind," he said. "That's what I've done."

He did nothing of the sort, however, when it came to actually using the pick. The Bucks had kept their preference a secret right up until the night of the draft, but nobody believed they were seriously considering anyone but Bogut. They hadn't had a dominating big man since Bob Lanier retired more than two decades ago, and there was no telling when they'd have another chance at one as promising as the skillful Australian giant.

When draft day came, they were still without a head coach, however. Flip Saunders, who been jettisoned by the Minnesota Timberwolves, had been the name most prominently mentioned. Other potential candidates were Seattle's Nate McMillan, and current broadcaster and former longtime coach Doug Collins.

But none of them was particularly overwhelmed by the Bucks' opportunity. This despite the fact that not only was Bogut on his way, but the team also figured his presence would improve their chances of re-signing guard Michael Redd, who was an unrestricted free agent also being pursued by the Cleveland Cavaliers.

Finally on July 8, Harris named former Bucks assistant Terry Stotts as the team's new coach. This was a curious choice since Stotts had even less experience as a head coach than Porter, and his record was worse. He'd been in charge at Atlanta for a season-and-a-half and gone 52-85. Porter was 71-93 in two years with the Bucks.

But Harris insisted that he wasn't "settling" for Stotts, who ironically had been a candidate for the Bucks' job two years earlier when George Karl was fired and Porter hired. "We chose the right guy," Harris said.

Wrong again. Stotts was fired before the end of his second season. Then a year later, Harris lost his job. Meanwhile, Bogut's career got off to a slow start while Paul and Deron Williams became NBA stars. Then just as Bogut's career seemed to be taking off in 2009-'10, as the Bucks qualified for the playoffs for the first time in four years, he suffered horrifying and multiple injuries to his right arm.

All of which goes to show that even winning the lottery provides no guarantees.

BOB JOHNSON LEADS PENGUINS TO STANLEY CUP

MAY 25, 1991

Bob Johnson

One year after Bob Johnson came to the University of Wisconsin, the Pittsburgh Penguins came to the National Hockey League. While one was becoming "Badger Bob" the other became a typically struggling expansion team.

But no one was laughing at the Penguins now as they hoisted the Stanley Cup at center ice in a rink in Bloomington, Minn., not far from where Johnson had grown up and begun his coaching career. Down two games to one in the best-of-seven series, they'd won three in a row and capped their run by mauling the Minnesota North Stars, 8-0, in the most lopsided Cup finals game ever played.

It was a triumph not only for the Penguins but for American hockey in general and Johnson in particular.

The team had never played for the Cup before in its 24-year history. In fact, it had never played in May before, and it had made the playoffs only once in the past eight years.

Only seven years earlier, it was in danger of folding. But the Penguins began climbing out of the basement when they drafted a French Canadian named Mario Lemieux after finishing the 1983-'84 season with the NHL's worst record.

The climb was steep, and it culminated with the hiring of Johnson in June 1990. His stated goal was to make the playoffs that year, not to win them. He'd coached the Badgers to three NCAA championships between 1973 and '81, and now suddenly he found himself at the helm of the first U.S. based team to win the Stanley Cup since 1983. He was only the second American to coach an NHL champion and the first to win both an NCAA title and a Stanley Cup.

When Johnson was skating around the outdoor rinks of Minneapolis as a kid, American hockey was barely an afterthought. The NHL had only six teams, and the players were almost all Canadian. At the University of Minnesota, he skated with supremely talented American teammates who were never considered for the pros.

Things began to change in 1967 when the NHL expanded from six to 12 teams and American players began to get a look. American coaches, too. Johnson validated his NHL credentials by coaching the Calgary Flames for five years and reaching the Stanley Cup in 1986. But that was nothing like this. This in Johnson's words "was the top of the mountain."

Lemieux carried the Penguins through the playoffs, scoring a playoff-high 44 points and earning Most Valuable Player honors. In the final game, he scored a goal and had three assists.

When the Penguins returned to the Pittsburgh airport with the Cup in hand, they were joined at the top of the mountain by 40,000 cheering fans. The road had been long and bumpy. The celebration was tragically brief.

It was August, just three months later, and Johnson was coaching the U.S. team as it prepared for the Canadian Cup tournament when he was hospitalized with a brain aneurysm. While he was in the hospital, the doctors found two malignant tumors.

They removed one surgically, but all they could do was prescribe radiation for the other one. Vowing to coach the Penguins the next season, Johnson went home to Colorado Springs to recuperate. It was a promise he couldn't keep.

Though weakened by the radiation, he was still faxing suggestions to his team as the new season approached. Many of his players flew out to visit him, and the Penguins had a satellite dish installed at his home so that he could watch them play. Out of respect to Johnson, the Penguins delayed naming Scotty Bowman their interim coach until three days before the opener. They didn't hang their Stanley Cup banner until Oct. 19 when Johnson could watch the ceremony on TV.

He lapsed into a coma and died on Nov. 26, 1991, at the age of 60. It took four different cities to give him a proper good-bye. Memorial services were held in Colorado Springs, Minneapolis, Pittsburgh and Madison.

The Penguins wore a patch on the left sleeve of their jerseys during the 1991-'92 season when they defended their championship by sweeping the Chicago Black Hawks in the final series. It said "BADGER."

HADDIX LOSES HIS MASTERPIECE

MAY 26, 1959

Major league baseball's best-pitched game began on a Tuesday evening in Milwaukee and didn't really end until a Wednesday morning ruling in New York. You can't rush history.

But on this night at County Stadium the Milwaukee Braves couldn't hit the Pittsburgh Pirates' Harvey Haddix. At least not until the 13th inning when Joe Adcock ended an unforgettable pitcher's duel and sent Haddix home as the game's most celebrated loser. The final score was 1-0, but nobody knew that for sure until the next morning when National League President Warren Giles said it was.

Haddix faced 36 Braves' hitters in a row without letting any of them reach base. No hits, no walks, no errors, no hit batsmen. And no victory. That went to Lew Burdette, who shared the stage with Haddix all night long, although in a decidedly supporting role. Burdette gave up 12 hits, but he didn't walk anyone and he got out of trouble by inducing the Pirates to hit into three double plays.

Haddix was never in trouble through the first 12 innings. Mixing his fastball with an assortment of sliders and curves, he struck out eight and fell behind only four hitters. He was already in the record books when he recorded his first out in the tenth inning. Never before had anyone pitched a perfect game for more than nine innings or a no-hitter of any kind for more than 10. It had been 79 years since any National League pitcher had recorded a perfect game.

But perfection vanished for Haddix when Felix Mantilla, batting for the first time after taking over at second base in the 11th inning, opened the Milwaukee 13th with a routine ground ball to third. Pirates third baseman Don Hoak fielded the ball cleanly, but threw it past first baseman Rocky Nelson for an error. Haddix still had his no-hitter, though, after Eddie Mathews sacrificed Mantilla to second and he intentionally walked Henry Aaron to bring up Adcock.

Adcock had struggled even more than most of the Braves that night, striking out twice and grounding out twice. This time, he took a pitch for a ball, and then ended his struggles dramatically by ripping Haddix's next pitch 394 feet over the right-center field wall. Game over. Final score 3-0. Or maybe not.

Aaron hadn't seen the ball clear the fence, and he thought the drive had merely scored Mantilla. So he just touched second base and walked off toward the dugout. By the time Manager Fred Haney had yelled at Aaron to get back on the base paths, Adcock was standing on third. That made Adcock out

Harvey Haddix of the Pittsburgh Pirates walked back to the dugout at County Stadium the night he pitched 12 perfect innings, but lost in the 13th when he gave up a a ground-rule double to Joe Adcock. As a result, Haddix was credited with a one-hitter and also a 1-0 loss.

automatically, which meant he couldn't have scored. But first base umpire Frank Dascoli ruled that Aaron's run counted, because he'd gone out of the base path of his own volition and not to avoid a tag. So the score was 2-0. Or was it?

Giles took another look at the situation the next day and came up with a different take. Since Adcock was ruled out he couldn't have a home run. Instead he was credited with a double, and the only run that Giles counted was the one the Braves needed to win the game. The NL president offered a lengthy explanation for his ruling, but it didn't matter much to Haddix. All he cared about was that he'd lost the game.

As for Burdette, he thought it was a shame that Haddix's big night had been spoiled, but he pointed out that he wasn't there to lose. He had a point. This was one game neither pitcher should have lost. And Haddix would lose again 32 years later.

Three years before Haddix died, Major League Baseball issued another ruling on Haddix's masterpiece. It wiped it off the books as a perfect game because Haddix hadn't completed it perfectly.

DON NELSON RESIGNS FROM BUCKS

MAY 27, 1987

"I am the Milwaukee Bucks," declared Don Nelson, a dubious claim that he would later wish he could take back.

But lots of interesting things get said in a messy divorce, and if Nelson's break-up with the franchise he'd served for 11 seasons wasn't the most bitter in the history of Wisconsin pro sports, it was certainly the most inane.

Don Nelson looked on during a game against the Boston Celtics at the Boston Garden. Nelson took over as coach of the Milwaukee Bucks eighteen games into the 1976-'77 season and then coached 10 full years before resigning in May, 1987.

In the two-plus years that Herb Kohl had owned the Bucks franchise he'd made his general manager and two-time Coach of the Year the highest-paid person in his profession, raising his salary from $140,000 a year to $500,000. He'd praised him publicly and doubled his payroll, but something happened between the two strong-willed men that sparked a media feeding frenzy and ended with Kohl wishing Nelson success in his future career through gritted teeth.

The two were so far apart in fact that they couldn't even agree that they disagreed. Four days before Kohl accepted Nelson's resignation, the coach detailed a series of three heated meetings that he said he'd had with the owner late in the season, and he listed 37 criticisms that he recalled Kohl leveling at him.

Kohl responded by claiming there were no meetings, and he denied saying any of the above. He called the alleged criticisms "fictions" and said the feud was all in Nelson's mind.

Nelson's list of grievances was rambling and frequently redundant. He had long been known as an innovative coach, but it might have stretched even his imagination to make all 37 of them up. Included were charges that Kohl had blasted Nelson for botching his draft choices as well as the hiring of player personnel director Stu Inman and a trade for Seattle center Jack Sikma. Nelson also claimed that the boss had ripped him for not trying to trade longtime star Sidney Moncrief and for attempting to rule by intimidation while not respecting Kohl's opinions.

The longer the story played out in the media, the more muddled it became. Nelson produced a letter from Rick Majerus, the former Marquette coach who had resigned from the Bucks' staff to take the head coaching job at Ball State, saying that he'd left because he felt caught in the middle of a rift between two of his good friends. Nelson also said he'd actually resigned and then un-resigned during the late-season meetings. Kohl said it was all a "one-way feud."

Nelson was incensed. Kohl was unresponsive. And one thing was very clear. The Bucks would have a new coach for the 1987-'88 season. The only question was what would happen to Nelson.

It seemed everybody wanted him. The New York Knicks were interested in his services. The Dallas Mavericks courted him as their head coach. The Golden State Warriors, owned by Jim Fitzgerald who'd hired Nelson when he previously owned the Bucks, would take him in any capacity.

But as lucrative as Nelson's contract was, it contained a provision that put a major crimp in his career plans. A "no compete" clause stipulated that he couldn't serve as a coach or director of player personnel for any other team for two years unless that team compensated the Bucks. Nelson insisted that the clause didn't prevent him from becoming a general manager somewhere else, but that would be a hard sell with the NBA office.

Kohl was willing to grant Nelson permission to talk to anybody, but he insisted on compensation if he left for another franchise. And he wasn't talking about money. Kohl wanted players or draft choices or both. That did nothing to improve Nelson's marketability.

In the end, Fitzgerald came through for his good friend. He made Nelson a part-owner of the Warriors and said he'd sort out his duties later. Nelson wound up sitting out a season and eventually becoming Golden State's coach. Kohl got a second-round draft choice.

He'd made his point. Maybe Don Nelson was the Milwaukee Bucks. But Herb Kohl owned the Milwaukee Bucks.

PACKERS' NO. 1 PICK FLEES TO CANADA

MAY 28, 1980

In football as in real estate, location can mean everything. The Green Bay Packers found that out much to their regret in the case of Bruce Clark, their reluctant No. 1 choice in the 1980 NFL draft. When they learned it too late, Clark wound up in Canada, and they lost the services of one of college football's most promising defensive linemen.

Clark didn't want to be in Green Bay, and he didn't want to be in the middle of anybody's 3-4 defense. The Packers apparently didn't understand that when they made him the fourth overall pick in the draft. If they had, they would have been spared one of the most bitter and embarrassing negotiations in the history of the franchise.

Coach Bart Starr had decided to switch from a 4-3 defense to a 3-4 following the 1979 season, and he was in the market for a nose tackle. At 6-foot-3 and 270 pounds Clark seemed to have the ideal size and lateral speed to do the job, but he didn't see it that way. He'd played the position as a senior at Penn State and suffered a knee injury.

"I want to be playing five or 10 years down the road," he told the *Green Bay Press-Gazette* in a telephone interview on draft day, April 29, 1980. "But nose tackle has the life span like a back. I guess I'm not really sold on it."

Starr claimed that came as news to him. He said that when he'd visited Clark in late April the player had told him he'd love to play in Green Bay and at any position that would help the team. It was never clear whether Clark had changed his mind or Starr had gotten the wrong message, but either way it certainly didn't help the negotiations.

The Packers said Clark's agent, 28-year-old Richard Bennett, had opened the talks by demanding a $1 million signing bonus. Reports were that the Packers were offering a four-year, $650,000 deal with a $250,000 signing bonus. When Bennett got the numbers, he wasn't pleased. He said he called Packers Corporate General Manager Bob Harlan on a Thursday to say he was talking to the Toronto Argonauts of the Canadian Football League, but he never heard from the Packers again. He didn't think they were taking the Toronto threat seriously.

The Packers got very serious the following week, though, when Harlan learned second hand from a Pittsburgh reporter that Clark was on the verge of signing with the Argonauts, if he hadn't already. Reports were he'd accepted a two-year deal for $1 million, but subsequent reports suggested that figure was greatly exaggerated. Ironically, Clark's coach in Toronto would be Willie Wood, the former Packers' free safety and longtime teammate of Starr.

During a subsequent press conference in Toronto, Clark disclosed his reservations about Green Bay. "It's like State College," he blurted out. He then shifted direction and simply added that Toronto appealed to him more because it was a big city.

Meanwhile, Starr called a media session of his own and used it to blast Bennett. "I cannot for the life of me understand the selfish motives of an agent, sacrificing a person who could play in anonymity somewhere north of the border," he said.

Bennett shot right back, saying of Starr, "It's appalling that somebody could get so hysterical. I assume it was the act of someone frustrated after making a significant error, and that Mr. Starr felt that he had to lash out at someone."

There was no doubt that Starr was frustrated. The Packers' defense with Charlie Johnson at nose tackle would finish the 1980 season ranked 25th in the league.

Clark played out his option in Canada and returned to the NFL in 1982, but he still wanted no part of Green Bay. The Packers traded his rights to New Orleans for a No. 1 draft choice that turned out to be cornerback Tim Lewis. Clark played seven years with the Saints and made the Pro Bowl once. He played defensive end.

SHEBOYGAN REDSKINS COACH FINED FOR ASSAULT AND BATTERY

MAY 29, 1947

Labor relations were different in the early days of pro basketball. Take the case of John "Doxie" Moore.

The Sheboygan Redskins' coach was having a disagreement with his star player, Fred Lewis, on the afternoon of May 26, 1947. Lewis wanted a bonus. Moore didn't want to give it to him. When Lewis refused to drop his demands, Moore dropped Lewis. To the floor of his office. After Moore's second punch landed, Lewis was unable to call his union rep. He didn't have a union rep. He didn't even have a union. So he called the cops instead.

Moore was a former Navy lieutenant who had taught hand-to-hand combat. Lewis was a 6-foot-3 guard who had finished second in scoring in the National Basketball League. A warrant was issued for Moore's arrest. He appeared in Sheboygan Municipal Court on a charge of disorderly conduct.

The prosecution changed the charge to assault and battery. Moore's attorney, Frank Zummach, a former Redskins coach, pointed out that there was "plenty of provocation" for his client's action. In other words, Lewis had it coming. Zummach also said that Moore could have done what he'd done long ago, but he'd showed admirable restraint. Still, Moore pleaded guilty on May 29. He was fined $10 plus court costs.

You might say Sheboygan had a dysfunctional relationship with pro basketball. But it was a successful one for as long as it lasted. Sheboygan joined the NBL in 1938, won the league championship five years later and lost in the playoff finals four other times between 1941 and '46. The Redskins had a coach they liked named Dutch Dehnert from 1944-'46, but he was unable to work for them fulltime. One of the Original Celtics in his playing days, Dehnert had a summer job as a cashier at a New York racetrack that he couldn't afford to give up.

So at the beginning of the 1946-'47 season, the Redskins hired Moore, who had earned three letters apiece in football and basketball at Purdue. They made him coach and business manager. They also signed Lewis that year. The team finished the season with a 26-18 record, and Lewis was named Rookie of the Year. But the coach and the star never got along, and things got only worse after their two-punch fight.

The following October, Lewis jumped to Birmingham of the new Professional Basketball League of America. There were two leagues competing with the established NBL at the time. The other one was the Basketball Association of America, which would become the National Basketball Association. Lewis' new league folded only seven games into Birmingham's season.

Lewis had been permanently barred from the NBL for skipping out on his Sheboygan contract. But he went to a judge to get the ban removed, and after the judge ruled in his favor, the league let him back. In the meantime, the NBL held a dispersal draft of players on the Chicago Gears, a former NBL team that collapsed with the new league, and the Redskins were able to pick up a four-time league MVP named Bobby McDermott.

Moore didn't get along with McDermott any better than he did with Lewis. Moore wasn't what you'd describe as a players' coach. His charges called him a "slave driver" and when they staged a mutiny on an East Coast trip, the Redskins' board of directors installed McDermott as the temporary coach. *The Milwaukee Journal* sports editor R.G. Lynch thought the Redskins should fire the board of directors rather than Moore. "Most of them are busybodies, each jockeying around with a favorite player, so that in case of a change, he will be known as the man who picked the next manager," wrote Lynch.

Nobody got fired. McDermott, who was 33 at the time, was sold to the Tri-Cities franchise in late December. Moore returned as coach for the remainder of the season, but the Redskins finished last with a 23-37 record. Following the season, Moore was named commissioner of the NBL. Lewis finished out the season with Sheboygan, as well, but didn't return to his rookie form.

Before the 1949-'50 season, the BAA became the NBA and absorbed the Sheboygan franchise, but the Redskins lasted just one more year. Moore resurfaced as coach of the Milwaukee Hawks in 1951-'52 and then became the NBA's supervisor of officials.

WISCONSIN'S WEATHERLY DIES IN INDIANAPOLIS 500 CRASH

MAY 30, 1935

Safety was a big issue before the 1935 Indianapolis 500. It was the year that the race required crash helmets for the first time, and the year that the track installed its first green and yellow stop lights. It was also the year when four people died.

Clay Weatherly, a former Wisconsin high school football player, was one of them.

The 25-year-old Weatherly was a familiar figure around the dirt tracks of the Midwest, but he was a total newcomer to racing's biggest event, and he needed a car. The one he got became available in the worst possible way.

Nine days before the race, a Norristown, Pa., driver named Johnny Hannon had driven a jet black racer called the "Somber Bullet" to his death on a practice run. It was the same day that Los Angeles driver W.H. "Stubby" Stubblefield and his riding mechanic Leo Whittaker were killed on a qualifying lap. In those days, drivers had to carry a mechanic with them.

Owner Leon Duray had the car rebuilt after Hannon's death, and Weatherly begged him for a chance to drive it in the race. Duray gave him that chance and had great cause to regret it later.

It was Duray who was using a blackboard to signal Weatherly to slow down as he entered the northwest turn on the Indy oval just nine laps into the race. Weatherly either didn't get the message or he ignored it. He was traveling at least 110 miles per hour when he crashed into a retaining wall, caromed down the track and smashed through a wooden guardrail. The car went end over end into the infield, and Weatherly suffered a fractured skull and crushed chest. He was pronounced dead at the track.

That brought Indy's death toll to 31 since the race was started in 1911. Eleven drivers and mechanics had been killed in the last three races.

Ed Bradburn, Weatherly's 23-year-old mechanic, was thrown clear of the car, but he fractured two vertebrae in his back. He was taken to an Indianapolis hospital in "very serious" condition. Bradburn wasn't expected to live, but he pulled through.

Weatherly was the son of a potato farmer who moved with his family from Illinois to Rhinelander. He played halfback on the high school football team as a junior, and then moved the following year to Janesville where he played basketball and sang with the glee club in addition to being a fullback on the football team. He graduated with the class of 1928.

The tragedy at Indy was the second serious crash of Weatherly's young life, but the first one had nothing to do with racing. When he was 16, he was involved in a head-on collision on state Highway 47 outside Minocqua. One of the passengers in the other car lost an eye in the crash, but Weatherly wasn't seriously injured. Nine years later, he was dead.

UW'S GEHRMANN WINS FIRST CONFERENCE MILE

MAY 31, 1947

They called it the "elusive four-minute mile," and it was about the only thing that ever eluded Don Gehrmann on a cinder track. The University of Wisconsin's middle distance phenom dominated his event like no one before him ever had.

At 5-foot-9 and 130 pounds the bespectacled product of Milwaukee Pulaski High School didn't look like an athlete, but then it was hard for his rivals to tell because they never saw much but the backside of him. That was particularly true of his league rivals. Gehrmann suffered only 12 losses in 99 starts from 880 yards up to two miles, and none of those came in the conference championship mile. In the days before the Big Nine became the Big Ten, he won that four times in four tries, something no one else has ever done.

The first came in Evanston, Ill., at the expense of Illinois' heavily-favored Bob Rehberg. The Illini were about to run away with the team championship, and Rehberg was expected to begin the rout in the first event of the day. But after running third through most of the race and then falling back to fifth on the backstretch of the last lap, Gehrmann had a surprise for the Illinois star. He unleashed what would become his famous finishing kick, caught Rehberg with 30 yards to go and beat him by six feet.

Gehrmann's winning time of 4 minutes 19.6 seconds wasn't exceptional, but it would get much better over the next three years as he turned track's glamour event into his personal property. He won the NCAA 1,500 meter run as a sophomore in 1948 when the event was being run at the Olympic distance in an Olympic year, and then he repeated in the mile in 1949 and '50. He was also the first runner ever to do that.

What's more, he was just as good indoors as he was out. He had some memorable duels with FBI agent Fred Wilt in the famed Wanamaker Mile at New York's Madison Square Garden where he won four times in a row. But it took Gehrmann 10 months to do it the second time. Gehrmann and Wilt finished the fabled Jan. 28, 1950, race in a dead heat, and Gehrmann was awarded the victory on a vote of the judges. Thirteen days later, an Amateur Athletic Union committee overruled the judges and Wilt was named the winner. Then Gehrmann appealed, and by a 304-108 vote of AAU delegates at the national convention in early December, 314 days later, he was awarded the winner's cup and this time it was his to keep.

Gehrmann proved to be almost as good at winning races as he was at winning elections while putting together a string of 39 mile victories. By his junior year at Wisconsin, the media was billing him as the leading candidate to break the four-minute barrier in the mile. But these were the days of soft tracks and antiquated spikes, and Gehrmann never got closer than 4:05.3. He almost certainly would have done it with modern surfaces and up-to-date equipment, because he was clearly in the neighborhood.

If the four-minute failure was a disappointment to Gehrmann, his Olympic performance was a bigger one. He qualified for the 1948 Games as a 20-year-old college sophomore, but the race was held on a rainy day in London, and the undersized Gehrmann was no mudder. He slipped and went down to one knee on the final turn and finished out of the money.

"I was too young then to run in that kind of competition," Gehrmann recalled much later in a *Wisconsin State Journal* interview. "If I had had more experience, I would have been hard to beat."

He was always that. By the time he retired from the sport in 1953, he'd done enough to be named the Big Ten's greatest miler in the first 50 years of the conference's existence. He would be followed by a glittering array of Badger distance runners that included the likes of Ray Arrington, Mark Winzenreid, Steve Lacy, Tim Hacker and Chris Solinsky, but none of them owned an event the way Gehrmann did the mile.

SUZY FAVOR WINS RECORD EIGHTH NCAA TITLE

JUNE 1, 1990

Suzy Favor always made it look so much easier than it really was.

The pride of Stevens Point had established herself as the most accomplished runner in Wisconsin high school history by winning four state cross country championships and six individual track titles, and the victories just kept coming in college.

She had won her last 38 races when she traveled to Durham, N.C., for the NCAA Outdoor Track & Field Championships, the last meet of her collegiate career. She would be competing in the 800- and 1,500-meter events, and if she could win one of them she would become the first woman ever to claim eight individual NCAA titles.

The 800 came first for Favor. It wasn't her best race, but she was still clearly the runner to beat in the event. And nobody could. Jasmin Jones of Tennessee made a late run down the stretch, but Favor finished more than a full second ahead of the field with a time of 1 minute 59.11 seconds that not only broke the meet record but established her as the single biggest winner in the history of American college track.

Next up was the 1,500 the following day, June 2, and the results were the same. This time she broke her own record by finishing in 4:08.26 and becoming the first woman ever to claim an NCAA championship in the same event four times. Once again, Jones finished right behind her, but she didn't seem to mind. "How can you feel bad about finishing second to Suzy Favor?" Jones asked. "She's the future of our country in middle distance." Little did she know how much disappointment and heartbreak that future would hold for her rival.

Everyone in track knew Suzy Favor. Or so everyone thought. But what everyone didn't know was that the pressures of success had been building on the seemingly easy-going Wisconsin star since her prep days, and those pressures would take their toll 10 years later at the Olympics.

Although Favor had run world class times while dominating college track, she would never come close to winning an Olympic medal. She would finish 11th in her 1,500-meter heat at the 1992 Olympic Games in Barcelona, and she wouldn't even qualify in the 1,500 for the 1996 Games in Atlanta, where she would also fail to medal in the 800.

Her name was Suzy Favor Hamilton by then. She had married University of Wisconsin baseball player Mark Hamilton, and her new husband had encouraged her to deal with an eating disorder that she had struggled with before they met. She did and by 1998 she was ranked No. 1 in the United States in the 1,500.

So it was a stronger Favor Hamilton who stood at the start line for the 1,500 meters in the 2000 Olympic Games in Sydney. It was also a sadder one. A year earlier, her older brother Dan, who had been struggling with bipolar disorder, took his own life. At about that same time, her former college roommate and best friend was diagnosed with a fatal form of bone cancer.

All of this and more was going through Favor Hamilton's mind before the biggest race of her life. In a revealing interview with the *Wisconsin State Journal* eight years later, she disclosed that she'd been suffering from depression from the time she'd begun competing in the fifth grade. Running was her cure. And once again, running failed her on the international stage.

She was leading the field through the first 1,300 meters of the Olympic 1,500, but then she hit a wall and a runner passed her. And then two more passed her, and the thought of disappointing so many people once again was more than she could bear. She had a panic attack, and she literally took a dive.

As she told the *State Journal*, "I was thinking about everyone, and how happy they would be, and at that moment I had let them all down. So falling was the option, and I fell."

Then she got up and finished last. And then she fell again.

Favor Hamilton's career never recovered from that, but Favor Hamilton did. She became a mother, and a motivational speaker, and she found a therapist to help her with her depression.

BREWERS FIRE RODGERS, NAME KUENN MANAGER

JUNE 2, 1982

"Don't bury me yet," Buck Rodgers said after his Milwaukee Brewers beat the Seattle Mariners, 2-1, on a Tuesday night. Too late. The Brewers fired him close to 12 hours later.

Unfortunately for Rodgers, his last victory as a Brewers manager was only his seventh in his last 21 games. And that was only one of his problems. Another one was Rollie Fingers, the team's star closer. Fingers ripped Rodgers in the press, not once but twice during the last three days in May, objecting to the way he'd been used. "That's probably the final nail in the coffin," an angry Fingers shouted in the Brewers' clubhouse on May 31 after the Brewers had fallen to Seattle, 5-4, in the first of a three-game series.

General Manager Harry Dalton wielded the hammer. The next evening, he called Harvey Kuenn in from a scouting assignment to take over the club. The following morning, Dalton informed Rodgers and announced his decision. Rodgers reacted by blaming "a couple of cancers," players that he'd had a personality clash with. He didn't identify the two, but speculation was that Fingers wasn't even one of them. The suspects were catcher Ted Simmons and pitcher Mike Caldwell.

It was clear that something ailed the Brewers. They'd made the playoffs under Rodgers in the strike-shortened 1981 season by winning the American League East over the second half and finishing 62-47 overall, but they were a restless 23-24 and tied for fifth in the AL East when Dalton made his move.

Kuenn was a popular choice. A West Allis native and former University of Wisconsin star, he joined the organization in 1971 as a spring training and minor league instructor and was elevated to batting coach the next year. He knew a little about hitting, having won an American League batting title in 1959 and posting a career average of .303 in 15 seasons that included eight All-Star appearances.

He even had major league managing experience, although it was extremely limited. He managed the Brewers for the final game in 1975 when Del Crandall was fired. He won it, too, beating the Detroit Tigers.

Kuenn also had a compelling personal story, undergoing heart and stomach surgeries in the 1970s and losing his right leg in 1980 after suffering a blood clot. He was back at work six months after the amputation.

When Dalton hired Kuenn, he said "interim" could mean anything from two weeks to a full season. Kuenn wasn't worried about that. He said he didn't even know what the word meant.

It turned out to mean a full season and more. Kuenn's home-run happy "Harvey's Wallbangers" went 72-43 the rest of the way and won the only pennant in franchise history before losing the World Series to St. Louis in seven games. So it came as no surprise when Kuenn was named Manager of the Year by the Associated Press and United Press International.

Dalton lifted the interim tag after the season, but Kuenn didn't keep his seat in the manager's office for long. The Brewers fell to fifth place in 1983 with an 87-75 record, and he was fired at the end of the year.

After Harvey Kuenn led the Milwaukee Brewers to the American League championship in 1982, he was saluted on the scoreboard at County Stadium. Kuenn replaced Buck Rodgers on June 2 with the Brewers tied for fifth in the AL East.

BREWERS MAKE SURHOFF FIRST CHOICE IN DRAFT

JUNE 3, 1985

Harry Dalton, who was usually right, got a little carried away after he picked B.J. Surhoff first in major league baseball's free agent draft. "I know this is going to sound silly, because I'm comparing him with two outstanding players, but he reminds me of Robin Yount and Paul Molitor," said the general manager.

Dalton, who had personally scouted Surhoff three times, clearly missed the mark in his assessment. Surhoff had been an excellent catcher at the University of North Carolina, and he would become a solid major leaguer, but he was not a Hall of Fame talent. He wouldn't even turn out to be one of the top five players taken in a draft that included the likes of Will Clark, Barry Bonds, Barry Larkin, Rafael Palmeiro and John Smoltz.

Surhoff hit 188 home runs and finished with a lifetime .282 batting average over a 19-year career. It was just unfortunate for the Brewers that he played his best baseball somewhere else.

Dalton had a lot to think about as he prepared for the 1985 draft. The Brewers had built much of their success around Yount and Molitor, both of whom they'd landed while choosing third, and now they were coming off a 67-94 season and getting their first and only chance at the No. 1 pick.

The player some draft experts thought Dalton should take was Oklahoma State's Pete Incaviglia, who had just set an NCAA single-season home run record with 49. With the advantage of hindsight, the player many draft experts thought Dalton should have picked was Clark, a slugging first baseman from Mississippi State who was drafted second by the San Francisco Giants.

But Surhoff had hit .392 as a junior at North Carolina. He had struck out just 24 times in 676 collegiate at bats, and he could play the infield as well as catch. Dalton believed he had the best overall game of anyone available, and he was signable. The Brewers had already come to terms with him on a $150,000 bonus deal when they named him.

After just two minor league seasons, one at Class A Beloit where he was named prospect of the year in the Midwest League, Surhoff became the Brewers' catcher, and he started out by hitting a highly respectable .299.

Clark beat Surhoff to the big leagues by a season and in his second year, his career took off. He would hit 135 home runs over five seasons and top .300 in three of them. In a 1990 poll of fellow players, he was pegged baseball's best clutch player. By 1992, his numbers started to taper off and injuries began to hamper his career, but he played 15 seasons and batted .303 with 284 home runs.

If passing on Clark was a mistake, skipping Incaviglia was a gift. Montreal took him eighth, but he refused to sign with the Expos. He forced a trade to Texas where he hit 124 home runs but struck out 788 times in five years. The Rangers finally got tired of his whiffing ways and dealt him to Detroit. In seven more years with five different clubs he never hit more than 24 home runs in a season.

Surhoff played nine seasons with the Brewers and hit better than .300 just once before he signed with Baltimore as a free agent before the 1996 season and mysteriously discovered a power stroke. He hit a total of 57 home runs in nine seasons with Milwaukee, and he had 89 in his first four years with the Orioles.

If it had been home runs the Brewers were looking for, the real steal of the draft would of course have been Bonds, who hit 762 in 22 seasons. But Bonds wasn't even in the conversation when people talked about the top two or three picks. Pittsburgh took him sixth. Palmeiro, drafted 22nd by the Chicago Cubs, hit 569 home runs in 20 seasons. Larkin, who became an icon in 19 seasons with Cincinnati, also would have been a better choice than Surhoff.

But then hindsight is often painful when it comes to drafting in any sport. That was particularly true of the Brewers during the Sal Bando regime when they squandered top choices on such forgettable names as Ken Felder, Antoine Williamson, Chad Green, Kyle Peterson, and J.M. Gold. Bad personnel choices sent the franchise into a tailspin that ended only after Jack Zduriencik took over the scouting department and turned up such draft day gems as Prince Fielder and Ryan Braun.

MIDDLEWEIGHT KING KETCHEL WINS MILWAUKEE BRAWL

JUNE 4, 1908

A chartered boatload of fans arrived from Grand Rapids to back "The Michigan Assassin" while two special trainloads arrived from Chicago to cheer for "The Illinois Thunderbolt." Stanley Ketchell's middleweight title defense against Billy Papke was that big a deal, particularly in Milwaukee.

By mid-afternoon, police had to be called to control the crowd in front of the Alamo, a downtown saloon where the weigh-in was scheduled. Two hours before the preliminaries were slated to start, another crowd began lining up for tickets in front of the old Hippodrome at 620 W. Wells St., where the fight was scheduled to be held. Normally a brass band played at big events at the Hippo, but seats were at too much of a premium for that to happen this time.

"Milwaukee has been fight mad all day," *The Milwaukee Journal* wrote in an afternoon edition.

The attendance was never announced, but some accounts said the place overflowed with as many as 5,000 people, well above capacity. The receipts were $21,244 with the winner getting $7,640 and the loser $5,093. This at a time when Hart, Schaffner and Marx suits sold for $15.

The late Nat Fleischer, publisher of *The Ring* magazine for 50 years and known as America's foremost boxing authority, rated Ketchel the greatest middleweight of all time, a claim that took in a lot of territory.

Ketchel would post a 53-4-5 record with 50 knockouts and four no-decisions before he was shot to death two years after the Papke bout at the age of 24. According to some accounts, his killer was a jealous ranch hand. Papke would meet a similarly dramatic fate much later. He shot his estranged wife and then killed himself.

Ketchel was a slight favorite in Milwaukee, having won the middleweight title less than a month earlier with a 20-round knockout of Jack "Twin" Sullivan. However, some recognized Ketchel as champion as early as December 1907, after he had beaten Joe Thomas in 32 rounds. It was believed that Ketchel could outlast anyone, but the Papke bout was scheduled for just 10 rounds, and so he had to prove he could dispatch an opponent or earn a decision quickly.

As a result, Ketchel, a brawler who paid little attention to defense, was even wilder than usual in this fight. He decked Papke with a right hook in the opening seconds of the first round, but the challenger was up quickly. Still, Papke seemed stunned by Ketchel's power and the *Milwaukee Sentinel* said the knockdown caused him to back off for the first time in his career.

Stanley Ketchell

Billy Papke

Ketchel carried the fight most of the way, although Papke rallied with a flurry of punches in the eighth round and tried to do the same again in the 10th. When it was over, there was little doubt in anyone's mind that the champion had earned the decision. And then Ketchel was ready to celebrate. He called the proprietor of the roadhouse on Whitefish Bay road where he had trained and told him: "Fill that bathtub with champagne and make it snappy."

Ketchel and Papke would meet again in September. According to the *San Francisco Chronicle*, referee James J. Jeffries called the fighters to the center of the ring to start the fight, and when Ketchel extended his hand to shake, Papke ignored it and nailed his opponent with a left. Ketchel never appeared to recover, and Papke stopped him in the 12th round.

Ketchel would regain the title a little more than two months later with an 11th-round knockout of Papke and then he would beat Papke again in 20 rounds in a fourth fight in July 1909. While Papke held the middleweight title for only 80 days, he was rated seventh all-time by Fleischer. Three months after his last Papke fight, Ketchel took on Jack Johnson for the world heavyweight championship, but fell in 12 rounds.

Just one day short of a year later, on Oct. 15, 1910, Ketchel was shot in the back and killed by Walter Dipley, whose girlfriend was cooking breakfast for Ketchel at a ranch in Conway, Mo. Papke killed himself and his wife on Nov. 26, 1936.

The Hippodrome, a roller rink and dance hall as well as a boxing venue, survived until 1961 when it fell to a wrecking ball.

LARRY FRANKLIN SETS ENDURING BROAD JUMP RECORD

JUNE 5, 1965

They've replaced his school and renamed his specialty, but some things seem to go on forever. Larry Franklin's incredible leap is one of them.

The state high school broad jump record had stood for 21 years when the Madison Central senior arrived at the track at nearby Monona Grove High School intent on defending his title in the event at the Wisconsin Interscholastic Athletic Association state track and field meet. Ralph Welton of Shorewood had established the mark at 23 feet 7 inches during World War II, and it was literally the oldest record in the books. But now it was in more danger than anyone knew.

The broad jump field that Saturday afternoon included not just one but four athletes capable of bettering Welton's effort. In addition to Franklin, who had won the event with a leap of 23-6 the year before, there was Craig Ferris of Madison East, Cal Mallory of Milwaukee King and Peter Van Driest of Sheboygan North.

So it was only natural that the broad jump attracted plenty of attention when the competition began. Franklin fouled on four of his seven tries, but his first legal attempt fell just four inches short of Welton's record, and his second one broke it.

Franklin jumped 24-2¼, clearing the old mark by an amazing 7¼ inches, but he wasn't done yet. He soared 25-¾ on his final jump, missing the national high school record by four inches and beating the rest of the field by more than a foot.

Not that the rest of the field was bad. The next three finishers all broke Welton's record, as well.

Ferris finished second at 23-9¼, while Mallory was third at 23-7½. Van Driest's 23-7¼ leap topped the old mark by a quarter-inch and he placed fourth.

The state had never seen a broad jumping exhibition like that before, and it still hasn't. Madison Central was closed following the 1968-'69 school year, and the broad jump has been renamed the long jump, but Franklin's mark continues to stand after four decades. No other state track record has lasted that long. Even the incomparable Bob Beamon's world record in the long jump, set in the 1968 Olympic Games at Mexico City, fell after 23 years.

Franklin also anchored his school's winning half-mile relay team that day, but it wasn't quite enough to give Central the team title. It finished in a tie for second with 14 points. Kenosha Bradford won with 14¼.

Milwaukee Bradley Tech's Marcus Jenkins almost snatched the record from Franklin in 2008, but only for about 10 seconds. Jenkins was briefly credited with a jump of 25-5 at the state meet in La Crosse and the crowd erupted. But a second judge checked the measurement and found that it was really only 24-5. Jenkins soared 25-2¼ in a regular-season meet that year, but state records have to be set at the state championship meet. And so the granddaddy of Wisconsin high school track records was safe for another year…in what is the granddaddy of all state track meets.

The state meet in Wisconsin, first run in 1895, is the oldest in the country.

REX MAYS HITS A WALL, SAVES A LIFE

JUNE 6, 1948

Rex Mays had two choices, and the first one was to drive into a wall. The second would have killed a man.

Duke Dinsmore, a 35-year-old driver from Osborne, Ohio, who had started last, was on his seventh lap of a 100-mile Indy car race at State Fair Park when he hit a patch of loose gravel on the south turn. His right rear wheel nicked the concrete outer wall, tipping the car forward and throwing Dinsmore onto the track. He was lying there unconscious when Mays came around the turn.

A three-time winner in Milwaukee and a fan favorite everywhere, Mays saw Dinsmore and immediately spun into the wall while hitting his brakes to reduce the impact. With his car out of the race, Mays jumped out and started directing the other drivers around Dinsmore.

Dinsmore was still in the hospital recovering from his injuries more than a year later when he said, "If it wasn't for Mays I wouldn't be here. Nobody but Mays would have avoided running over me. And don't forget, he cracked up to do it. He's a great man. Everybody loves him."

They loved him in Milwaukee enough to name the race after him. In 1950 the State Fair Park event was rechristened the Rex Mays Classic. Tragically, the honor came posthumously for Mays. Seventeen months after saving another driver's life, he lost his own in an accident that bore an eerie resemblance to Dinsmore's.

Mays was running in Del Mar, Calif., on a track designed for horse racing. Newspaper accounts called the surface "ridiculously bumpy," and when Mays' car hit a chuckhole on the 13th lap, it flipped, throwing him onto the track and shearing off 13 posts on the inside rail. Mays had unfastened his seat belt, just as Dinsmore had in Milwaukee. Drivers often did in those times.

Now it was Mays lying unconscious on the track. Two drivers missed him, but a third couldn't avoid him. Hal Cole ran over him, crushing his head and chest, and Rex Mays was dead at 36.

The Rex Mays Classic lasted 35 years before it fell victim to the changing commercial times. Miller Brewing contributed $360,000 to sponsor the race in 1985 and renamed it the "Miller American 200 in Honor of Rex Mays." All mention of Mays' name disappeared shortly after that when it was changed one more time to the "Miller Genuine Draft 200."

When Mays died, he had won eight Indy car events and two national driving titles in addition to finishing second twice in the Indianapolis 500. He finished 17th in the 18-car Milwaukee field in 1948, earning $210 and the admiration of his entire sport.

Rex Mays was running in first place in a race in Milwaukee in 1939.

Rex Mays

JUNE 177

JESSE OWENS DOMINATES MARQUETTE TRACK MEET

JUNE 7, 1935

He was called "The Buckeye Bullet," and he had just accomplished more in 45 minutes than most track stars could manage in a lifetime. From 3:15 until 4 o'clock in the afternoon at the Big Ten championships in Ann Arbor, Mich., on May 25, Ohio State sophomore Jesse Owens was credited with tying the world record in the 100-yard dash, and breaking three others in the 220-yard dash, broad jump and 220-yard low hurdles.

The question now was what would he do for an encore?

Two weeks later, a crowd of more than 10,000 gathered on a Friday night in Milwaukee to find out. The occasion was the Central Intercollegiate Track and Field Meet, and the venue was Marquette Stadium.

The Central meet was first held in 1926 after the idea had been conceived in a Prohibition speakeasy by legendary Notre Dame football coach Knute Rockne; Ralph Young, then athletic director at Michigan State; and Conrad Jennings, longtime athletic director and track coach at Marquette. Jennings brought the meet to Milwaukee in 1928, and it was held there every year but two through 1961 when Marquette dropped track. And on this date, it would see the world's greatest sprinter dominating everyone he faced.

Owens easily won the 100, 220 and broad jump while leading Ohio State to the team championship by 1¾ points over Wisconsin. His 9.6 time in the 100 was a full two-tenths off the pace he'd set in Ann Arbor, but it was a damp evening, and he still beat second-place Bob Grieve of Illinois by three yards. The 220 was a little more entertaining as Owens trailed three runners by a yard coming out of the turn. But then he sprinted away from the field and finished in 21.8 seconds.

Finally, he won the broad jump by two feet with a leap of 26 feet 2½ inches. That was a quarter-of-an-inch better than the listed world record, but almost six inches short of his performance at the Big Ten meet, which was still to be registered. By now, the fans at Marquette knew they were watching someone special, but it would be another year before they found out just how special.

James Cleveland Owens was born in Oakville, Ala., the son of a sharecropper, and was given the name Jesse after his family moved to Cleveland, Ohio.

After setting national high school records in the 100, 220 and broad jump, Owens enrolled at Ohio State in the fall of 1933. There's probably nobody left who would remember anymore, but there's an interesting footnote to that story. As late as July of that year, Owens said he was still considering three schools and Marquette was one of them on his list. "I'd like to follow in the footsteps of Ralph Metcalfe at Marquette, but I'm afraid he's a little too fast for me right now," Owens told Ronald McIntyre of the *Milwaukee Sentinel.*

It wouldn't be long before there was nobody faster than Owens.

After dominating the NCAA and Big Ten meets again in 1936, Owens ran for the United States at the politically charged 1936 Olympic Games in Berlin where Adolph Hitler hoped to showcase his all-white team as the best of a "master race." But Owens enraged the dictator by winning gold medals in the 100 meters, 200 meters, broad jump and 400-meter relay. He set Olympic records in the 200 and broad jump, and his relay did as well.

Owens returned to New York and a ticker tape parade, but, sadly, he also encountered racism in his own country. He had to ride the freight elevator to a reception in his honor at the Waldorf-Astoria Hotel. With no endorsements coming his way, Owens made money by racing horses and dogs in exhibitions. It wasn't until years later, after a 1950 Associated Press poll named him the greatest track and field star of the first half-century, was that he was able to open a public relations firm and trade on his name by making speeches and corporate appearances.

On March 31, 1980, Owens died of lung cancer in Phoenix, Ariz. His death came two years after Marquette Stadium had been dismantled.

RECORD HOME RUN BARRAGE CAN'T SAVE BRAVES

JUNE 8, 1961

Talk about your seventh-inning stretches. Four batters, four home runs in a row.

Breaking records was the last thing on the Milwaukee Braves' minds when they entered the seventh at Crosley Field trailing the Cincinnati Reds, 10-2. In a matter of minutes they did something nobody else had done in 85 years of Major League Baseball, and still it wasn't enough to get them out of sixth place.

"I don't think anybody on the bench realized we were setting a record," said first baseman Joe Adcock. "All we were doing was trying to catch up."

That would be the case all season for the Braves. Charlie Dressen's team was a home run hitting machine, but it also was on its way to a middle-of-the-pack 83-71 finish. Eddie Mathews, Henry Aaron, Joe Adcock and Frank Thomas gave the Braves four sluggers, all of whom hit 286 or more home runs in their careers. Still, it wasn't enough to compensate for below average pitching.

That was the case again on a windy Thursday in Cincinnati when the great Warren Spahn struggled on three days' rest, and Moe Drabowsky was no improvement. The result was a 10-8 loss marked by a lot of futile fireworks.

The Reds had hit two home runs of their own while reaching Spahn for six runs and Drabowsky for four more when Frank Bolling singled to lead off the Braves' seventh. That's when the bombing began. Mathews drove a Jim Maloney pitch into the right-field bleachers, and Aaron followed with a drive over the left-field wall. Reds Manager Fred Hutchinson decided that was enough for Maloney and replaced him with left-hander Marshall Bridges. It didn't matter. Adcock greeted Bridges by sending one over the center-field wall, and Thomas wrapped things up with a drive to the same place.

The Braves had already hit three home runs in a row three times since coming to Milwaukee, but this was something brand new for baseball. And it wasn't the only record they set that day. Spahn had hit his 27th career home run in the third to extend his record for a pitcher, and Mathews struck again in the eighth. No other team had ever hit six dingers in a game and still found a way to lose.

That was just the kind of team the Braves were. The next day they traveled to Chicago, hit four out of Wrigley Field and still lost to the Cubs, 11-10. The Braves would lead the league with 188 home runs that year and finish in fourth place. But they were sure fun to watch.

Mathews would hit 32 home runs that year and finish his 17-year career with 512.

Aaron, who hit 34 homers that season, evidently had a fondness for Cincinnati. He tied Babe Ruth's career record of 714 home runs with his first swing of the 1974 season at the Reds' Riverfront Stadium, which was christened in 1970 with an Aaron homer. He hit his 715th home run in Atlanta and his 755th and final one in Milwaukee working for the Brewers.

Adcock had some ties to the Reds, too. He played his first three years with them but got stymied behind Ted Kluszewski at first base and demanded to be traded. The Reds sent him to the Braves where he flourished for ten seasons. He hit 35 homers in 1961 and finished his career with 336.

Thomas was just kind of passing through Milwaukee. He had been traded to the Braves from the Cubs a month earlier and would be traded again following the season to the New York Mets. But during his career he finished in double figures in home runs 12 seasons in a row and clouted 286 total. In 1961, he hit 27, 25 of them with the Braves.

It was Thomas' blow that broke the record in Cincinnati, but the Braves didn't take much joy in that. As Adcock put it after the game: "We would have been better off if we would have had some guys on base."

WIESNER SHARES NCAA HIGH JUMP TITLE IN MILWAUKEE

JUNE 9, 1945

High jumping wasn't exactly like riding a bicycle for Ken Wiesner, but it was close. Once he learned how, he never forgot.

So winning three NCAA championships in the event for Marquette University and then taking almost six years off before claiming an Olympic silver medal and setting a world indoor record came kind of naturally to the Milwaukee King High School graduate.

Wiesner, who also played center on the basketball team at Marquette, had a geographical advantage when he faced Utah's Fred Sheffield in the 24th annual NCAA meet. The meet was held at Marquette Stadium just as it had been in 1944, when Wiesner dethroned Sheffield. Now they were back at Wiesner's home track, only with Sheffield as the challenger.

There was a war going on, and many of America's best athletes were overseas, but Milwaukee fans still loved their college track. Marquette carried tremendous clout in the sport at the time thanks to its longtime coach Conrad Jennings. The NCAA meet has been held every year since 1921, but the 1944 and '45 championships were the only ones ever held in Wisconsin.

Illinois entered the 1945 meet as the defending team champion, having won the year before behind future NFL star Buddy Young, who had won the 100- and 220-yard dashes and finished second in the broad jump. The Illini were expected to get a stiff challenge from powerful Navy, while Wiesner and Sheffield commanded much of the individual spotlight. The competition couldn't have been much tighter in either case.

Navy edged out Illinois by 4¼ points, and Sheffield tied Wiesner for first place as both jumped 6 feet 6⅝ inches. Their efforts fell short of Wiesner's winning 6-7³⁄₁₆ leap in 1944. But, then, Wiesner made up for that the following year when he won his third title as a senior going 6-8⅜ as the University of Minnesota served as host.

Wiesner didn't know it at the time, but he would soar much higher later. He graduated from Marquette and opened a dental practice figuring his jumping days were over. When the Korean War broke out, he joined the Navy and continued to take in a few track

Ken Wiesner

meets when he got the chance. He was particularly interested in a sprinter and hurdler named Harrison Dillard, who had won the 100-meter dash in the 1948 Olympic Games at London and who would win the 110-meter hurdles in the 1952 Games at Helsinki.

Wiesner was stationed at the Great Lakes Naval base in suburban Chicago in 1952 when he decided to take a shot at jumping again in an Amateur Athletic Union meet in Milwaukee. "Dillard was about my age, 27, 28, and I thought if he's still competing, maybe I can do that," Wiesner recalled years later. It turned out that he could as he jumped 6-7 without so much as a single workout.

That was enough for the Navy to put him on its newly formed service squad and send him to California to train and participate in the Los Angeles Olympic Trials. Wiesner surprised everyone there by finishing second to Walter Davis and qualifying for the Games in Helsinki. He was an even bigger surprise in Finland when he finished second to Davis again and won the silver medal with a jump of 6-7.

With his career back on track, he went on to break the world indoor high jump record three times, the last of them in Chicago in 1953 when he went 6-10¾. He was discharged from the Navy the following year, and returned to Milwaukee and his dental practice. This time he really was through jumping.

BADGERS QUALIFY FOR THEIR ONLY COLLEGE WORLD SERIES

JUNE 10, 1950

Thornton Kipper

No one knew quite what to expect from the University of Wisconsin baseball team in 1950. The Badgers had finished last in the Big Ten the year before, but they were a senior-dominated squad with some outstanding all-around athletes.

Four of their starters also played football, and three of those four would be signing professional baseball contracts in late June. A fourth player who would turn pro was pitcher Thornton Kipper, a native of Bagley, Wis., a small town near Prairie du Chien, who became the most predictable part of this club. It was pretty simple: When Kipper pitched, the Badgers won.

And Kipper pitched a lot. Especially in the postseason when he carried his club into the College World Series by shutting down Ohio University, 4-1, in the championship of the NCAA District 4 tournament in East Lansing, Mich.

After losing his first game of the season, Kipper won his last 11 and, in the process, led the Badgers to a share of the Big Ten championship with Michigan and a 19-9 overall record. They would never win another conference title or play in another World Series. This was literally as good as it got for Wisconsin baseball until the sport was dropped following the 1991 season.

Without much doubt, this was the best team in the 116-year history of the program. It had five .300 hitters and a coach who was in his 11th season of a 31-year reign in Arthur "Dynie" Mansfield.

"Dynie" was short for "Dynamite," a nickname Mansfield acquired as an amateur boxer in his native Cleveland. The versatile Mansfield entered Wisconsin as a freshman in 1925 and basically never left. He served as a physical education teacher and as coach of the lightweight football team as well as the baseball coach.

But nobody was more important to the 1950 Badger baseball team than Kipper. He entered Wisconsin in 1945, pitched on the school's Big Ten championship team in 1946 and then went into service. He returned and had a lukewarm season in 1949 before finding his groove the following spring.

The Badgers swept Michigan in a late-season doubleheader to earn their piece of the Big Ten title and a trip to the District 4 meet, where they faced host Michigan State in the first round. They took a 7-4 lead into the fifth inning against the Spartans, but starting pitcher Ed Keating was struggling mightily. When Michigan State got two more runs in the top of the inning, Mansfield decided to play his ace and use Kipper in relief even though he was supposed to be starting the next game.

Kipper shut out the Spartans the rest of the way. Wisconsin won, 13-6, and the move didn't cost Mansfield a thing because Kipper was ready to go against Ohio the next day.

So ready in fact that he held the Bobcats scoreless until the seventh inning when they got an unearned run on a dropped fly ball by outfielder Bruce Elliott. But Elliott more than atoned for the mistake by driving in two runs with two doubles. Kipper finished with a nine-hitter, and the Badgers were headed to the national tournament in Omaha, Neb.

This was only the fourth College World Series, and Wisconsin might have won it if Kipper had been twins. He scattered nine hits again as Wisconsin beat Colorado State, 7-3, in its first game of the double-elimination tournament. But he wasn't available for the second one, and the Badgers lost to Rutgers, 5-3. Back for the third game, Kipper pitched a three-hitter to beat Alabama, 3-1. Then it was Rutgers again in the fourth game, and the Kipper-less Badgers were shelled, 16-3, leaving them in fourth place.

Within four days after they left Omaha, catcher Red Wilson of Milwaukee, second baseman Gene Evans of Green Bay and first baseman Bob Shea of Waukegan, Ill., signed contracts with the Chicago White Sox. Kipper signed with the Philadelphia Phillies with the understanding that he could finish his graduation requirements before reporting.

Wilson had by far the best major league career, spending ten seasons with Chicago, Detroit and Cleveland. Kipper had a 3-4 record over three seasons with the Phillies. He pitched only 55 innings, which would have been about two weeks' work in his magic season with Wisconsin.

MU'S METCALFE CREDITED WITH FOUR WORLD RECORDS

JUNE 11, 1932

He would become one of Marquette University's most accomplished alumni much later, but first Ralph Metcalfe staked a claim to being "the world's fastest human."

The sophomore sprinter from Chicago deserved to be part of that discussion after going home for the NCAA Track & Field Championships and running away from everybody. How fast was he? Well, he needed only two races to rewrite four records; or at least he was credited with breaking three world records and tying a fourth by the *Chicago Tribune*, as well as other newspapers of the day.

There were two sets of stopwatches operating at Metcalfe's races at Stagg Field on Chicago's South Side. One measured the times for the collegiate distances of 100 and 220 yards and the other the Olympic distances of 100 and 200 meters. And on a Saturday afternoon when the weather was warm and the cinders were firm, the timekeepers would get quite a workout.

The 220 was strictly no contest. Illinois Normal's J.A. Johnson stayed with Metcalfe for half of the race, but then the Marquette star hit his stride and won by four yards. He finished the first 200 meters in 20.3 seconds and the full race in 20.5, seemingly clipping three-tenths of a second off the first world record and one-tenth off the second, although neither time was ever officially recognized.

In the 100-yard dash, Metcalfe was timed at 9.5 and credited by the *Tribune* and others with equaling Eddie Tolan's world record, although official records later showed that Frank Wykoff of the United States and Daniel Joubert of South Africa had already broken the record by running 9.4s. Metcalfe's 100-meter time of 10.2 seconds was two-tenths of a second faster than anyone had ever run that distance before, but, again, his time was never officially recognized as a world record.

Metcalfe's victories in Chicago qualified him for the Olympic Trials the following month, and he advanced from there to the Summer Games in Los Angeles where he was edged out in a photo finish at 100 meters. Metcalfe and Eddie Tolan crossed the line in a dead heat, but Tolan was awarded the gold after officials reviewed films of the race. Metcalfe was also third at 200 meters.

He would get his gold medal four years later in Berlin, running on the victorious 400-meter relay team

Marquette's Ralph Metcalfe hit the tape.

after finishing second to the legendary Jesse Owens in the 100.

In time, Metcalfe also would get his world records. In 1933, he ran the 100 meters in 10.3 and the 200 meters in 20.6, and he was credited with tying the world marks in both events.

And his NCAA sweep of the 100- and 220-yard dashes as a sophomore was no fluke. He would win both races again in 1933 and '34.

Metcalfe's fame also went on long after his racing career was over. As president of his senior class he'd displayed a talent for politics at Marquette, and he took that talent back to his hometown. After serving in World War II, he became a successful businessman in Chicago and then a member of the Chicago City Council in 1955.

During his four terms as an alderman, he became one of the city's most powerful African-American politicians, a role that eventually took him to Washington, D.C. With the help of Mayor Richard Daley's Democratic machine, Metcalfe was elected to Congress in 1970. He would later break with Daley, but he was re-elected three times, and he was the co-founder of the Congressional Black Caucus.

BRAVES' RETREAD JIM WILSON PITCHES NO-HITTER

JUNE 12, 1954

It takes luck to pitch a no-hitter in the major leagues, but Jim Wilson was not what you'd call a lucky man.

His career almost ended in his rookie year with the Boston Red Sox when Detroit's Hank Greenberg hit a line drive back to the mound that fractured his skull. Many thought that would be the last pitch the 23-year-old right-hander would ever throw, but he came back the following season, just in time to get his leg broken by another batted ball.

That was enough for the Red Sox. They traded him to the St. Louis Browns, but Wilson persevered, shuttling back and forth between the minors and the big leagues before landing with the Boston Braves in 1951. When the Braves moved to Milwaukee, Wilson moved with them, but he'd become a largely forgotten man by 1954.

He hadn't started a game since the previous Labor Day, and the Braves exposed him to waivers in late May, offering his services to any club that wanted to pay $10,000 for him. Nobody did, and so Wilson remained on the Milwaukee roster.

Manager Charlie Grimm was running short of pitching when he decided to start Wilson in a June 6 Sunday doubleheader, and Wilson rewarded his confidence by shutting out Pittsburgh on four hits. That was enough to get him another start against Philadelphia the following Saturday and put him into the record books as the first pitcher ever to throw a no-hitter at County Stadium.

It took only one play that day to show that Wilson's luck was changing. Willie Jones, the Phillies' leadoff man, hit a hard smash to the left side, and Braves third baseman Eddie Mathews made a good stop to throw him out. Philadelphia never threatened again.

Phillies catcher Smokey Burgess reached Wilson for the only two walks he would surrender all day, and he never made it past first base. Wilson struck out six and had just one anxious moment, provided once again by Jones. With two out in the ninth, the Philadelphia third baseman lined a 3-2 pitch into the left-field corner, but it was foul by a foot. After fouling off another pitch, Jones grounded out to second baseman Danny O'Connell, and Wilson's teammates mobbed him on the mound.

That was almost more support than he'd gotten all day. The Braves managed only seven hits off Phillies ace Robin Roberts, who had beaten them nine times in a row and had one-hit them in April. But two of those hits were home runs by Johnny Logan and Del Crandall, and they were enough to provide a 2-0 victory.

Wilson said he had his slider working and good control, good enough that he almost knew he was heading for something special. "I sensed a no-hitter after the sixth inning," he said. "No one in the dugout said a word, but I knew. I knew."

Of course, he'd had that feeling before. Wilson had pitched a no-hitter for Buffalo in the International League in 1949 when he was fighting his way back to the big leagues. But that one, he said, didn't compare to this one.

Wilson would post an 8-2 record in 27 games including 19 starts for the Braves in 1954. He was 86-89 lifetime with a 4.01 earned run average when he ended his career with the Chicago White Sox in 1958 – 13 years after Hank Greenberg knocked him out with a line drive.

BRAVES TAKE NL LEAD AFTER BRAWLING WITH DODGERS

JUNE 13, 1957

Don Drysdale hit a modern National League record 154 batters over the course of his career, which in the opinion of Johnny Logan was one too many.

Logan was a 5-foot-11, 175-pound shortstop for the Milwaukee Braves. Drysdale was a 6-6, 215-pound pitcher for the Brooklyn Dodgers, and they were facing one another on a Thursday afternoon at Ebbets Field. It was only the second inning, and outfielder Billy Bruton had just hit his second home run of the game off Drysdale when Logan came to the plate. When the first pitch plunked Logan, he doubted that it was a coincidence.

So Logan said something to Drysdale as he reached first base, and Drysdale said something back, and suddenly just about every player on both teams was on the field punching, pulling or jawing at someone on the opposite side. It was fairly spectacular as baseball fights go as Logan wound up with about a half-inch cut over his eye and Drysdale, who appeared to have been flattened by Eddie Mathews, exhibited some redness in the throat area. But it had little to do with the outcome of the game, which was an 8-5 Milwaukee victory.

What it did do was obscure the Braves' move into first place and overshadow catcher Carl Sawatski's heroics. The first was an omen. The second was a crime.

There had been little love lost between the two teams since the Dodgers had edged out the Braves by one game for the National League pennant the previous September. Brooklyn's Jackie Robinson had since retired, but not without delivering a parting shot, claiming the Braves spent too much time in nightclubs. "You can't mix athletics and drinking and smoking," he said. "I don't mean you can't take an occasional drink if you're grown up, but these fellows didn't take care of themselves down the stretch."

The Braves weren't interested in hiring a chaperone, and they really weren't interested in losing another pennant race to the Dodgers. And they didn't. They never fell more than three games out after June 13, took over the National League lead for good on Aug. 6, and won the pennant while Brooklyn finished third, 11 games out.

Sawatski, who hit all of .238 in 58 games, made a minimum contribution to the pennant drive. Except for that one day.

At 219 pounds the squat Sawatski was a tight fit in any spotlight. He'd spent the last two seasons in the minor leagues, and he was getting his first start with the Braves only because Del Crandall, their No. 1 catcher, was hurt. Sawatski had been up just 13 times before and had only one hit to show for it. In other words, he was used to being slighted.

And perhaps he took it that way when Dodger Manager Walter Alston elected to pitch to him in the eighth inning with men on second and third, two out and the pitcher due up next. After all, Sawatski had already doubled twice that afternoon and driven in a run.

The Braves were up, 5-4, when Sawatski left the on-deck circle, and they were ahead, 8-4 when he trotted back into the dugout to accept congratulations. Ace reliever Clem Labine, who hadn't suffered a single loss in 38 appearances, tried to slip a fastball by Sawatski. But Sawatski drove it into the lower center-field seats. The Dodgers got a run back in the ninth, but it wasn't nearly enough.

The victory gave the Braves a half-game lead over Philadelphia and Cincinnati, and a full-game lead over the Dodgers in the tight NL race.

Meanwhile, Logan missed Sawatski's clout because he was in the clubhouse having been ejected after the tussle. Drysdale, who was just 20 years old at the time and who had allowed four runs in $1^{2}/_{3}$ innings, missed the moment as well. He, too, had been run, although it was a meaningless gesture. Alston had been on his way to the mound to take him out of the game when the fracas started.

Logan was in a good mood later as he talked about Drysdale. "They say he has a temper," Logan said. "I don't. It was a baseball fight. It's forgotten." Said Drysdale: "I'm sorry it happened."

Nobody believed that.

AARON SIGNS WITH EAU CLAIRE BEARS

JUNE 14, 1952

The salary was $350 a month. The rent was a dollar a day, and the signing bonus was a cardboard suitcase. It sounded like a good deal to Henry Aaron.

Eau Claire's Class C Bears couldn't have known what they were getting when the scrawny 18-year-old shortstop showed up at Carson Park and signed a minor league contract. The Boston Braves had bought Aaron's rights from the Indianapolis Clowns of the Negro American League and shipped him to the Bears, who promptly inserted him into their lineup in the No. 7 spot.

Boston parted with $10,000 to get Aaron, and the Clowns' owner tossed in the suitcase to seal the deal. The Braves outbid the New York Giants, who lowballed him at $250 a month and compounded the error by sending him a telegram with his named spelled 'Arron." If they'd been a little less thrifty and a little more attentive, they might have had the future home run champion in the same outfield with Willie Mays.

Then again, William Maughn, a Braves scout, practically begged his bosses to sign Mays two years earlier, but was overruled. So, conceivably, the Braves could have had both players, as well.

But back to Aaron and his one season in Eau Claire. A poor black kid from Mobile, Ala., Aaron had dropped out of high school to play ball and had never faced a white pitcher or an all-white crowd in his life. And now all of a sudden he found himself in a northern Wisconsin city of 35,000 people that included just seven African-Americans. There were two other black players on the Bears. One was future Braves outfielder Wes Covington and the other was veteran catcher Julie Bowers, and they both became anchors for the painfully shy newcomer.

"Wherever I went in Eau Claire, I had the feeling that people were watching me, looking at me as though I was some kind of strange creature," Aaron recalled in his biography *I Had a Hammer*. "I might not have said 50 words all summer if it hadn't been for Wes and Julie and a white family that sort of adopted me."

There was nothing silent about Aaron's bat, however. The game on June 13 was rained out, so Aaron didn't make his debut at Eau Claire's Carson Park baseball stadium until the following night. He drove in a pair of runs with two singles in four at bats against the St. Cloud Rox. And although he was thrown out trying to stretch that first single into a double and his error allowed the winning run to score in a 4-3 loss, he still made quite a first impression.

The impression just kept getting better as Aaron was named the Northern League's best rookie and wound up hitting .336 with nine home runs and 61 RBIs in 86 games.

In his book *A Summer up North*, detailing Aaron's season in Eau Claire, author Jerry Poling recounted how Aaron was met at the airport by local sports editor Clell "Buzz" Buzzell, who also served as the Bears' official scorer and the man in charge of finding housing for their players. Buzzell took the young man home to meet his wife Joyce, who remembered Aaron's reaction as he walked in the door. "He was shaking. He'd never been in a white person's home before," she said.

Buzzell's next stop was the downtown YMCA where Aaron was able to rent a room for $1 a day, along with his two black teammates. The white players were offered rooms in private homes or hotels.

It was a lonely existence, and Aaron later wrote that he was depressed enough at times to think about quitting. "I was ready to pack everything into that cardboard suitcase and go back to Mobile," he said. "I called home and told them I was on my way, but my brother, Hubert Jr., took the phone and told me I'd be crazy to leave. He said there was nothing to come home to."

Aaron took his brother's advice, changing the course of baseball history. Later that season, the suitcase dissolved in a rainstorm.

SCHOENDIENST TRADE BOOSTS BRAVES' PENNANT HOPES

JUNE 15, 1957

Bobby Thomson hit baseball's most celebrated home run to win a pennant in 1951, and his return to the New York Giants six years later helped win another one. Only this time, it wasn't for the Giants.

A four-player trade involving Thomson brought Red Schoendienst to Milwaukee, and while the deal was hardly "the shot heard around the world," it made enough noise to turn the Braves into clear National League favorites. In return for Thomson, second baseman Danny O'Connell and right-handed pitcher Ray Crone, the Braves got a 34-year-old switch-hitting second baseman who had played in nine All-Star Games.

Schoendienst had earned a reputation for clutch hitting and a great glove in 11-plus seasons with the St. Louis Cardinals, leading the league's second basemen in fielding for five of them before being traded to New York in 1956. He hit .302 that year, but the Giants were struggling and needed to shake things up.

Schoendienst was thought to be nearing the end of his playing career, but that didn't bother Braves General Manager Bob Quinn. He acknowledged that the swap might not be popular with everybody, but he called it "an all-out effort to get a pennant for the people of Milwaukee." He wasn't the only one who thought it would do that either.

There was Schoendienst himself, who all but offered a Joe Namath style guarantee, "I'm happy to be with the Milwaukee club. I feel sure they will win the pennant," he told *The Milwaukee Journal.*

And interestingly enough, there was O'Connell, who took a small parting shot at his teammates on the way out of town. In predicting that the Braves would make it to the World Series, O'Connell said, "If they don't it's the players' fault, because they get a little dead when things go wrong. A few of the boys get down when things don't go our way and don't put out that extra."

Schoendienst certainly offered that extra. In his 93 games with Milwaukee, he batted .310, had 122 hits and scored 56 runs. He finished the season with 200 hits, and the Braves won the pennant by eight games before beating the New York Yankees in seven in the World Series.

Of course, Schoendienst had plenty of help, but the argument could be made that he put the team over the top. The Braves were in first place by 1½ games at the time of the trade, but O'Connell, their starting second baseman, was hitting only .235, and Crone had a 4.50 earned run average. As for Thomson, he'd been a major disappointment ever since the Braves acquired him from the Giants for left-hander Johnny Antonelli as part of a six-player trade in 1954.

Antonelli had twice won 20 games for the Giants, while Thomson broke his ankle in spring training shortly after the trade and was never the same player again. He batted just .235 in 1956, and he was hitting .236 when he was shipped back to New York, much to his own surprise. "It was a shock to me," he said. "I wanted to stay in Milwaukee. I was happy there."

No happier than Schoendienst, who proved to have plenty of baseball life left in him even at 34. Playing with bruised ribs and a broken finger, he helped send the Braves to another World Series in 1958, although he played in only 106 games. The "all-out effort" to get Milwaukee a pennant went a long way toward getting two before he contracted tuberculosis in 1959 hastening the end of his career.

"All I know about the Braves is that they never won the pennant without Schoendienst or lost it with him," Leo Durocher, longtime National League manager, said a few years later. "Can you say that about any other Milwaukee player?"

BUCKS TRADE ABDUL-JABBAR TO LAKERS

JUNE 16, 1975

Everybody's dream player became the Milwaukee Bucks' nightmare when Kareem Abdul-Jabbar told the world that he wanted to get out of town. The Bucks had known for years that he was unhappy, but they'd done a decent job of keeping it to themselves until their three-time National Basketball Association Most Valuable Player confirmed the rumors that he was all but demanding to be traded.

He said it in March, and three months later he was gone to the Los Angeles Lakers. It was not only the biggest deal the Bucks ever made, it was a nice stroke of damage control. Today, half of the results are hanging in the rafters at the Bradley Center.

Abdul-Jabbar had led the Bucks to their only NBA championship in 1971, and he almost did it again in 1974 when they lost in the finals. He'd won two league scoring titles and he would play 14 more seasons on his way to the Hall of Fame. But it was clear that he was committed to getting out of Milwaukee.

At the time, some thought it was due to irreconcilable cultural differences. Two years later, former teammate Oscar Robertson said that was untrue. "Kareem didn't hate Milwaukee," Robertson told the *Milwaukee Sentinel* in 1977. "... He just didn't get along with Larry (coach Costello.)"

Jabbar's disenchantment left General Manager Wayne Embry with two choices. He could trade basketball's best player when the whole league knew he was holding a gun to the Bucks' heads, or he could make him play out his contract and possibly get nothing for him two years later. There was no compensation rule in the NBA for players who played out their option and signed elsewhere. What's more, Bucks President Bill Alverson claimed that the rival American Basketball Association had been trying to convince Abdul-Jabbar to sit out the 1976-'77 season, his option year, and jump leagues.

Embry talked to several teams, with New York, Atlanta and Buffalo heading the list. The Hawks had Lou Hudson, and the Braves had Bob McAdoo, but nothing could be worked out with either club. Abdul-Jabbar, a native New Yorker, had wanted to play for the Knicks all of his life, but they were an aging team without the goods to make a deal.

If New York was Abdul-Jabbar's preferred destination, Los Angeles was his second choice. It was a huge city with plenty of culture, and he'd played his college ball at UCLA. And that's where the Bucks solved their problem.

The swap was completed in mid-June, but the details may have been worked out before the college draft in late May when the Lakers made UCLA power forward Dave Meyers the second pick and Louisville swingman Junior Bridgeman the eighth. In any event, once the Lakers had them under contract, the deal was done.

Going to Milwaukee along with Bridgeman and Meyers were Brian Winters, a second-year shooting guard with a deadly touch, and Elmore Smith, a fifth-year veteran center who had led the league a season earlier in blocked shots. Gone to LA were Abdul-Jabbar and Walt Wesley, his barely used back-up in Milwaukee.

The deal was announced in simultaneous afternoon press conferences in the two cities, although it had been reported on an LA radio station late the night before. The Bucks' press conference featured Embry and Alverson, but curiously it did not include Costello, the team's coach for the past seven seasons. Costello's job status was a subject of great speculation following a 38-44 season; and if it was true that he and Jabbar weren't getting along, his security might have been tied to the trade.

As expected, the deal was a windfall for the Lakers. Abdul-Jabbar would lead them to five NBA championships. The Bucks might have missed out on several more NBA titles, too, but they fared about as well as could be expected.

They got a combined 50 points a game from their newcomers in the first season, with Winters averaging 18.2 points per game and making the NBA All-Star team. Milwaukee's record stayed the same at 38-44, but it was good enough to boost the team from last place to first in the weak Midwest Division.

Then 19 games into the 1976-'77 season, Don Nelson replaced Costello as coach, and the franchise won seven division titles over the next 10 years. Meyers was the best power forward they'd ever had before back problems cut short his career after four years. Smith was traded in 1977 for two No. 1 draft choices.

As for Winters and Bridgeman, both of them had their numbers retired and hoisted to the ceiling of the Bradley Center. Abdul-Jabbar's is up there, too.

UW MILER FENSKE SHOCKS PRINCETON CROWD

JUNE 17, 1939

The newspapers called it the "Mile of the Century," but then there were lots of those in the thirties. They needed fewer miles or more centuries for a race to truly live up to that billing.

But the field for the feature event at the sixth annual Princeton Invitational was better than most. It boasted five runners who had covered the distance in less than 4 minutes 10 seconds, which was considered lightning quick at the time.

The best of them were Glenn Cunningham, the biggest name in middle distance running, and world-record holder Sidney Wooderson, a British lawyer who was competing for the first time in the United States. Also entered but not attracting much attention was University of Wisconsin graduate Chuck Fenske, winner of the NCAA mile two years earlier and a three-time Big Ten indoor champion.

Wooderson had set the world mark at 4:06.4, and he was on record as saying that he planned to run 4:03 in this meet. A crowd estimated at 28,000 gathered at Palmer Stadium in Princeton, N.J., to find out whether he could back up his words and beat Cunningham to the finish line. As it turned out, the barrister couldn't win anything that day. Not even an argument.

As for Cunningham, the best he could manage was a distant second to the surprising Fenske.

Fenske recalled later that he felt "weak as a kitten" while he was warming up for the race, which he took as a good sign. He usually felt that way when he was about to run well. And Wooderson gave him plenty of time to regain his strength by taking the lead on the first lap and setting a leisurely pace throughout the race.

The crowd hoping for a world record was disappointed early when Wooderson ran a slow 64-second first lap. He didn't get any faster after that, running another 64 in the second and a 66 in the third. But things got interesting in the last 220 yards. As the runners made the turn for home, Wooderson collided with Blaine Rideout and hit the curb of the track. Fenske sailed past him and Cunningham followed.

The final dash wasn't even close, as Fenske pulled away from Cunningham and beat him to the tape by five yards.

Wooderson finished an angry fifth in the five-man field and lodged a protest saying that Rideout elbowed him aside. Perhaps, in part, because the other four runners were all Americans and because Wooderson stood 5-foot-6 and weighed 125 pounds soaking wet, the British press howled foul. But referee Asa Bushnell ruled that everything was perfectly legal.

Fenske ran a 56.8-second final quarter-mile to win the race, and while his time of 4:11 was mediocre, he still considered the victory to be the biggest of his career. That was saying something, too, because he won some impressive races and earned the nickname "Monarch of the Mile."

A Fond du Lac native and West Allis High School graduate, Fenske beat Cunningham again in 1940 in the famed Wanamaker Mile at the Millrose Games, finishing in 4:07.4, and he won the Amateur Athletic Union national indoor meet that same year. In addition, Fenske held world records at one time or another in the 1,000 yards and the three-quarter mile run before joining the Air Force.

He entered World War II as a private and left it as a major, but his racing days were over. If the Princeton showdown wasn't the "Mile of the Century," it was at least the biggest race in Fenske's life.

ANDY NORTH WINS HIS FIRST U.S. OPEN

JUNE 18, 1978

It was the final putt of the U.S. Open, and the man standing over it was Andy Who?

Hardly anyone recognized the lanky 28-year-old pro from Monona, Wis., but there he was just 43 inches from golf's biggest prize. This despite the fact that he'd blown four shots of the five-shot lead he'd held after 13 holes.

While a gallery estimated at 25,000 looked on quietly, he stood over his bogey putt for almost a minute, and then a gust of wind hit him, and he backed away. Then he stepped up and backed away again. He needed to be steady when he took the stroke. And, on his third look, he finally tapped the ball and it landed squarely in the center of the cup.

Now everyone would know who Andy North was.

"I'm not an egomaniac," North told the *Milwaukee Sentinel* after clinching his first major PGA Tour championship at Denver's Cherry Hills Country Club. "But it is nice for people to call you by your right name. My first couple of years I was called Jerry Heard by a lot of people, and the last few years they have taken me for Andy Bean."

North might have picked an easier way to make a name for himself. He played the last five holes on this Sunday afternoon in four-over par, allowing J.C. Snead and Dave Stockton to get back into the hunt. As North stood watching from the 18th tee, Snead missed a 20-foot birdie putt that would have tied him for the lead. Then Stockton missed a 15-footer for par that would have done the same.

Now all North needed was a bogey-five on the rugged 480-yard finishing hole. He had birdied the hole twice in the first three rounds, but he was in trouble immediately this time when he drove a 3-iron through the fairway into the right rough. Then his 8-iron second shot landed short of the green, and he pitched into the sand.

It was then that North saved the championship. His bunker shot stopped below the hole and inside of four feet, setting up the dramatic putt that gave him a final round 74 and a one-over-par 285 for the tournament.

He beat Stockton and Snead by a stroke. Hale Irwin and Tom Weiskopf finished three back. Lumped in a group of six four back were Jack Nicklaus, Gary Player and Tom Watson.

The victory was worth $45,000, and it came as one of the bigger surprises in Open history. North had won once before in his six years on the tour, and no one had taken him very seriously at Cherry Hills. He was just the other guy playing with Nicklaus on Saturday and Player on Sunday.

Seven years later, on June 16, 1985, North would prove his triumph was no fluke when he won a second U.S. Open at Oakland Hills in Birmingham, Mich. His final-round 74 gave him a one-shot margin, and he finished that one with a bogey, too.

Andy North

WHITWORTH CRUSHES FIELD FOR MILWAUKEE TITLE

JUNE 19, 1966

Kathy Whitworth was right when she said, "No one ever conquers golf." But sometimes a player can hold it hostage for awhile, which is exactly what the 26-year-old slugger did in the final round of the Milwaukee Jaycee Open.

Whitworth didn't think she'd been hitting the ball particularly well in the first three days at Tuckaway Country Club. She'd followed an opening round 68 with a 71 and a 69, leaving her two shots under men's par. But then along came Sunday and a five-under 65 that shattered one record and tied another.

"I could have kicked the ball, and it would have gone in," Whitworth said after she fired six birdies against a lone bogey and won the tournament by 12 strokes over Sandra Haynie. Her victory margin equaled the women's tour record and put her in select company. The record was first set by Babe Didrikson Zaharias in 1954, and matched by Betsy Rawls and Mickey Wright. Whitworth's 72-hole total of 273 broke new ground. The old record of 275 had been set by Wright in 1962.

An estimated 8,000 people lined the course in Franklin to watch the rangy Texan tear it apart. One of the tour's longest hitters, she got it on the green in regulation 13 times, and her putter did the rest. She needed only 27 putts over the 18 holes, scoring two birdies on the front nine and four on the back. When she was done, she said it was "the best she'd ever played."

Whitworth's comment echoed something she'd said three years earlier when she'd won the same tournament at North Shore Country Club, then located in the Milwaukee suburb of Bayside. That time she finished with a 286 to top the field by seven shots and said, "Far the best I've played on tour so far."

There was obviously something about the Jaycee meet that brought out the best in Whitworth. Milwaukee played host to the tournament six times from 1962 through '67, and she took home one-third of the titles. Curiously, the 1966 victory was worth $50 less than the one in 1963 as the winner's share dropped from $2,000 to $1,950.

But if Milwaukee wasn't making Whitworth rich, it was certainly helping to make her famous. She was on her way to passing Wright as women's golf's pre-eminent player when she turned in her record-breaking victory at Tuckaway. From 1965 through '73 she won seven scoring titles and eight money titles, and she was named LPGA player of the year seven times. She also won six majors during her career, but for 10 of her years on the LPGA tour there were only two women's major tournaments played per year.

Whitworth captured at least one tournament championship every year from 1962 through '78, and she was still in top form six years after that when she won three. Her last title came at the 1985 United Virginia Bank Classic 27 years after she turned pro. A three-time LPGA president, she became women's golf's first $1 million winner. She never conquered the game, but few women ever played it better.

MILWAUKEE LPGA TOURNAMENT CHAMPIONS

Year	Winner	Course
1962	Mickey Wright	Tuckaway Country Club
1963	Kathy Whitworth	North Shore Country Club
1964	Mickey Wright	North Shore Country Club
1965	Marlene Hagge	North Shore Country Club
1966	Kathy Whitworth	Tuckaway Country Club
1967	Susie Maxwell	North Shore Country Club

Source: Dan Blackman, U.S. Bank Championship media director

DWYANE WADE LEADS MIAMI HEAT TO NBA TITLE

JUNE 20, 2006

Hardly anyone wanted him when he left high school to go to Marquette University, and now no one could get enough of him. Dwyane Wade was clearly the flavor of the day in the National Basketball Association, an emerging superstar and the unquestioned leader of the league's new championship team.

Naturally, it happened for him the hard way. Only two other teams in NBA history had lost the first two games of the championship series and come back to win the title. This one had been left for dead in Game 3 when it fell behind 13 points with less than seven minutes to play.

But that was just basketball, and basketball was usually easy for Wade. It was life that had been hard. And so he took over that game and the next three as the Miami Heat beat the Dallas Mavericks, 4-2, in the best-of-seven series. He wrapped it all up with a 36-point, 10-rebound, five-assist effort in Game 6, which Miami won, 95-92, on the Mavericks' home court. It was a performance that Dallas coach Avery Johnson called Michael Jordan-like and it earned Wade the Most Valuable Player award for the series.

"To me, it's bad moments that make a person," Wade said in the *Sports Illustrated* story when he was named the magazine's Sportsman of the Year later that year. "You're going to fall. It's how you get up that defines you as a man. This is how I know what kind of player I am."

Wade was already a very good player in 2000, but nobody seemed to know it when Marquette's Tom Crean gambled on him and offered him a scholarship even though he didn't have the grades or the test scores to play right away. Only Illinois State and DePaul had been willing to take a similar chance.

Wade sat out a season, honed his skills in practice, and two years later led Marquette to the Final Four. "He just has an uncommon drive," Crean said once. "It's just amazing."

Wade amazed everyone during the NBA Finals, particularly in the last four games. He had gotten off to what for him was an average start, scoring 28 points in Game 1 and 23 in Game 2, and it was no coincidence that the Mavericks won them both. But then Wade put up totals of 42, 36, 43 and 36 and added 33 rebounds in the next four games.

He did his most important work in the third game when the Heat trailed, 89-76, with 6 minutes 34 seconds on the clock. If Miami had lost that game there would have been no hope. Instead, Wade contributed 12 points to a 22-7 finishing run that gave the Heat a 98-96 victory and turned everything around.

"Thirteen points down with six minutes to go? That's not life or death," he said. "I've been through more than anybody knows. To me this is joy."

What Wade had been through was a childhood in a drug-plagued family on some of Chicago's least forgiving streets. He'd moved in with his father at age six while his mother struggled with cocaine and spent time in and out of jail. He'd learned the game on the playgrounds before going to Richards High School in suburban Oak Lawn where bad grades and limited exposure limited his college options.

But Crean took the risk, and it paid off both for Marquette and for Wade and his family. One of his proudest moments came when the Golden Eagles beat Cincinnati to win their first Conference USA championship, and his mother was there to see her son play in a college game for the first time. She had fought off her addiction and was on her way to becoming a Baptist minister.

The Heat made Wade the fifth pick in the 2003 draft, and he was an NBA All-Star in 2005 and '06. But nobody predicted that he would become one of the four or five best players in the league. Not until he took the Heat to the championship.

SHOWMAN BILL VEECK BUYS BREWERS

JUNE 21, 1941

Milwaukee's minor league Brewers weren't making friends or money in the early forties while 27-year-old Bill Veeck was on his way to becoming a master at both. Veeck hadn't sent a midget to the plate yet or built his first exploding scoreboard, but he'd been around baseball his whole life, and he was about to change the game in some interesting ways.

When Brewers owner Henry Bendinger put the struggling American Association franchise up for sale for the eighth time in its 39-year history, young Veeck was the treasurer of the Chicago Cubs and Charlie Grimm was a Cubs coach. They didn't care that interest in the Brewers was at a dismal low or that the club had been running in the red for close to three years. They had big plans and $100,000 of other people's money to spend.

So they closed the deal to buy the franchise at 3 o'clock on a Saturday morning and the *Milwaukee Sentinel* broke the story that day, although the official announcement was delayed for two days. Four years and three American Association pennants later, Veeck sold the team to Chicago lawyer Oscar Salenger for a reported $175,000. In between, he took Milwaukee on quite a ride.

Veeck, known for his stubborn refusal to wear a tie, was 11 years old when he started working for the Cubs filling ticket requests. He got the job, as well as a pioneering mindset, from his father William Veeck Sr., who happened to be the team president. And when the younger Veeck installed the banjo-playing Grimm as his first manager of the Brewers, he let it be known that fans could expect anything when they showed up at Borchert Field.

Veeck gave away everything from live lobsters to guinea pigs, and he personally served coffee and donuts to the customers who came to the 8:30 a.m. games that he started for the benefit of graveyard shift workers during World War II.

He also was known to doctor the diamond, move the fences and rig the lights to enhance the home-field advantage. He pulled off his most original stunt in Milwaukee to commemorate Grimm's 45th birthday.

Veeck had asked his skipper what he wanted for a present and Grimm said what he really needed was another pitcher for the pennant race. So Veeck held a birthday party for him on Aug. 28, 1943, and presented his manager with a huge cardboard cake at home plate.

First a covey of dancing girls popped out of the cake. They were followed quickly by left-handed Cuban pitcher Julio "Showboat" Acosta, whom Veeck had acquired from the Richmond (Va.) Colts of the Class B Piedmont League. Grimm immediately sent Acosta to the bullpen to warm up for that night's game. In this case, Grimm should have looked his gift horse in the mouth. Acosta was rapped for 15 hits and the Brewers lost to Indianapolis, 6-5, in 10 innings.

Veeck's time in Milwaukee was interrupted by a three-year hitch with the Marines. While serving in the South Pacific, his lower right leg was crushed and needed to be amputated. But Veeck never lost his irreverent approach to baseball or his sense of humor. He sold the Brewers in October 1945, and the next year, he headed a syndicate along with comedian Bob Hope that bought the Cleveland Indians.

Over a 33-year span from 1946-'80, Veeck also owned the St. Louis Browns and the Chicago White Sox twice in addition to the Indians. In Cleveland, Veeck signed Larry Doby, the first African-American ever to play in the American League. In St. Louis, Veeck sent 3-foot-7 midget Eddie Gaedel to the plate as a pinch-hitter in a game against Detroit. And it was in Chicago that Veeck installed a 130-foot high scoreboard that set off fireworks whenever the White Sox hit a home run. In 1991, he was inducted into the Baseball Hall of Fame as an executive.

And it all started in Milwaukee.

NEENAH'S WHITLINGER RULES COLLEGE TENNIS

JUNE 22, 1974

He was aced six times before he figured out all the right moves. In this case, they were up and back and side to side, but if standing on his head would have worked, John Whitlinger might have tried that, too.

Anything to distract Stanford teammate Chico Hagey. Hagey had breezed through seven matches of the NCAA tennis championships without having his powerful serve broken even once. He appeared to be on his way to doing it again when he blew Whitlinger away, 6-1, in the first set of the final, and the Neenah native knew something had to change.

So the 5-foot-8 sophomore with the two-fisted backhand took a stroll. Lots of strolls. When Hagey got ready to serve, Whitlinger moved all the way back to the baseline, and then he moved up at the last second. Other times he'd go sideways. Hagey never knew whether to look north, south, east or west for his opponent, and that was just enough to disrupt his concentration.

Leading, 4-2, Whitlinger broke Hagey's serve in the second set and won it, 6-3. He did it again in the third with the score tied, 3-3, and won, 6-3, again. The final set was no contest. Whitlinger prevailed, 6-1, and claimed the intercollegiate singles crown as Hagey served only three aces in the last three sets. Barely more than a half-hour later, Whitlinger joined Jim Delaney to add the doubles championship, 6-4, 6-4, 4-6, 6-4 over the top-seeded pair, John Andrews and Sashi Menon, from Southern Cal.

Winning was certainly nothing new to Whitlinger. He had claimed four Wisconsin Interscholastic Athletic Association state championships from 1969-'72 while at Neenah and won a remarkable 109 consecutive matches. He'd also won a number of national junior tournaments and cracked the top 60 in the adult rankings in 1973. But after starting the season as the No. 6 player on Stanford's team, Whitlinger was hardly the favorite to win the national collegiate championship as a sophomore.

"What a job he did," Dick Gould, who produced 10 individual NCAA champions in his 38 years as Stanford's tennis coach, said in an interview with Bill Letwin of *The Milwaukee Journal* following the meet. "I don't know of a guy with a bigger heart."

Whitlinger never won the NCAA meet again, but he was a two-time All-American, and he finished at Stanford with a 40-9 dual meet record.

He spent six seasons on the pro tour after he left school, ranking among the world's top 50 players in singles and the top 40 teams in doubles, and he also played for Indiana in the World Team Tennis League. After serving from 1981-'86 as a club pro, Whitlinger returned to Stanford to become an assistant to Gould. He spent 18 years on Gould's staff, but his patience was rewarded when he got the head coaching job in 2005. Once again, he'd made a good move.

John Whitlinger

DeMERIT'S PERSEVERANCE PAYS AT WORLD CUP

JUNE 23, 2010

Now this was Jay DeMerit's kind of game. Four minutes from elimination from the World Cup, the United States soccer team desperately needed a goal to make history and avoid embarrassment at the hands of underdog Algeria. The Americans had seen two shots sail wide of an open net, one bounce off the post and one disallowed by a questionable offside call.

This was nothing new for the U.S. In its first two matches, both ties, it had done things the hard way, falling behind early and suffering a reversal or two along the way. Nobody understood how that worked better than DeMerit, the center back from Green Bay whose teammates had nicknamed him "Rags to Riches."

Eight years earlier after he'd finished a solid college career at Illinois-Chicago, no one could have imagined DeMerit starting for his country on soccer's biggest stage in Pretoria, South Africa. But now he and his teammates were on the verge of an ungainly exit as they battled to a scoreless tie with only four minutes of extra time remaining.

A draw would send the U.S. home. A victory would advance it to the Round of 16 for the first time in eight years and only the third time ever. But that seemed highly unlikely. At least it did until star midfielder Landon Donovan broke the deadlock with a breakaway goal a minute into injury time.

Donovan's heroics were described by US Soccer, the national governing body for the sport, as "the most dramatic moment in U.S. Men's national team history," and they gave the U.S. its first group championship since 1930. But while Donovan was clearly the headliner, DeMerit earned plenty of credit himself for his role as a defender in only the second U.S. shutout since 1950.

ESPN analyst Alexi Lalas identified DeMerit and forward Jozy Altidore as "two major reasons" for the victory. "Jay DeMerit had a phenomenal game in the back there," Lalas said. "The entire team did well in terms of creating those opportunities. But those are the two players who stood out for me."

It was high praise for a kid from Wisconsin who hadn't even been drafted by Major League Soccer when he left college. Judged technically challenged and only moderately athletic, DeMerit overcame any physical limitations with a constantly revving engine, freakish determination and a total disregard for his body. As he told *Sports Illustrated* after playing a key role in shutting down England's high powered and highly paid attack in America's 1-1 opening match tie, "If I'm not bleeding after the game, I'm not doing my job."

The hardest part for DeMerit was just getting a job. After participating in basketball and track, as well as soccer at Bay Port High School, he finally concentrated on soccer at Illinois-Chicago and earned all-conference honors three straight years. But he still couldn't get a nibble from the MLS, even after training with the Chicago Fire's developmental club.

In 2003, friend and fellow soccer player Kieron Keane talked DeMerit into moving to England to pursue his soccer dreams. DeMerit dabbled in Sunday pub leagues there, and he played for a ninth-tier semipro team called Southall FC until the following summer when he was invited to play in a pre-season game against Watford, a second-division British team.

DeMerit impressed Watford's manager enough to earn a spot on his squad, and two years later, he made a huge professional breakthrough by scoring the first goal in a match in Cardiff, Wales, that allowed Watford to advance to England's Premier League.

DeMerit made his debut with the U.S. national team in 2007 and established himself internationally two years later when he played every minute for the U.S. in a 2-0 upset over Spain in the semifinals of the Confederations Cup. By beating the world's No. 1 team, the U.S. advanced to its first FIFA men's final since starting play in 1916.

The U.S. lost to Brazil, just as it followed up on its dramatic victory over Algeria by getting knocked out of the World Cup by Ghana, 2-1, in overtime. Again, the Americans gave up an early goal and played from behind.

Sometimes the hard way isn't the best way, even though it's a career path that has served DeMerit well.

BUCKS TRADE RIGHTS TO NOWITZKE

JUNE 24, 1998

In all fairness, it doesn't qualify as the worst trade the Milwaukee Bucks ever made due to the circumstances involved. But the draft day deal that sent Dirk Nowitzke to Dallas and brought Robert Traylor to Milwaukee has been one undampened, enduring embarrassment for the franchise.

Dallas drafted Traylor with the sixth overall pick after reaching an agreement to move him to the Bucks for Milwaukee's two first-round choices. The Bucks then took Nowitzke ninth and Pat Garrity 19th for the Mavericks. As a result, Dallas wound up with a future Hall of Famer, Most Valuable Player and perennial All-Star, and the Bucks got a player who may have been, pound for pound, the biggest flop in their history.

It should be pointed out that Milwaukee probably never really had a shot at Nowitzke's rights. If they hadn't made the deal, Dallas coach and General Manager Don Nelson would have simply taken the German 7-footer at No. 6. But giving up two first-round picks to get Traylor was bad enough. And the maneuvering that the deal required suggests that the Bucks coveted Traylor more than Nowitzke, although Nowitzke's value was difficult to gauge because of a contract he had signed in Europe.

You might say former Bucks general manager Bob Weinhauer bears a heavy responsibility here. The 6-8 Traylor was nicknamed "Tractor" when he tipped the scales at 330 pounds before he even arrived at the University of Michigan. He was more of a lawn tractor when the Bucks got him at a svelte 288, thinking he would provide the inside presence they'd been lacking for years. Traylor thought so, too. He set his goals at making the NBA all-rookie first team, and averaging double figures in scoring and rebounding.

He fell a little short, averaging 5.3 points and 3.7 rebounds as a part-time starter as a rookie, and then he lost ground his second year. His averages dropped to 3.6 and 2.3 before the Bucks shipped him to Cleveland. Traylor would be traded twice more in his NBA career and never average double figures in anything. In fact, Milwaukee would have been better off with Garrity.

After the Mavericks packaged Garrity with a couple of veterans and a first-rounder to acquire point guard Steve Nash from Phoenix on draft night, the 6-9 product of Notre Dame spent 10 mostly solid years in the league, nine of them with Orlando.

As for Nowitzke, he's averaged more than 22 points and eight rebounds a game for Dallas while earning league MVP honors in 2007 and being named first-team all-NBA four times, more than any Bucks player in history other than Kareem Abdul-Jabbar. Nowitzke also turned what was a dreadful Dallas franchise into a perennial playoff participant. The year before he arrived, the Mavericks were 20-62. Three years later, they finished 53-29 and were on a roll.

Nobody knew that Nowitzke would be that good, although Nelson may have suspected it when he tentatively reached a trade agreement with Weinhauer 15 minutes before the draft began.

The Bucks' general manager had been trying all day to bundle his two picks to make a move in the draft, and this seemed to make sense. Traylor, a junior, was an all-Big Ten selection, the Most Valuable Player of the Big Ten tournament and a load in the paint. Milwaukee believed he could be the kind of offensive player who would demand a double-team if he could improve his 54.5% free throw shooting and control his calories.

Traylor showed all the signs of doing the latter when he dropped 40 pounds on a three-month crash diet before the draft, cutting his body fat from 19.5% to 12.4%. But in the end he was a shadow of himself in more ways than one.

BUCKS CON PISTONS, DRAFT MONCRIEF

JUNE 25, 1979

It took Dick Vitale a little more than a year to figure out that his future was not in the National Basketball Association, and Don Nelson helped him arrive at that conclusion.

Nelson was running the college draft for Milwaukee, and Vitale was in charge for Detroit in 1979 when the Bucks won a coin flip that gave them the fourth choice and the Pistons the fifth. It was pretty much a foregone conclusion at that time that Magic Johnson, Bill Cartwright and David Greenwood would be the first three players picked, but no one knew for sure whom the Bucks were interested in at No. 4. No one but Nelson, that is.

He was crazy about a slightly undersized off-guard from Arkansas named Sidney Moncrief. Vitale, on the other hand, liked Michigan State forward Greg Kelser. But somehow the Bucks had managed to leave the impression that they would take Kelser, a 6-foot-7 forward, at No. 4. That might have been because Milwaukee already had two outstanding shooting guards in Brian Winters and Junior Bridgeman, or it might just have been that Vitale was not only voluble, but gullible.

Either way, Nelson had Bucks owner Jim Fitzgerald call Vitale 40 minutes before the trade deadline on the Sunday night before the Monday draft. Fitzgerald offered to switch draft positions with the Pistons for cash considerations. Vitale hung up on him, but then he called back and made the deal after Fitzgerald got a 15-minute extension on the trade deadline.

And so Vitale wound up spending $50,000 of the Pistons' money for the right to choose a journeyman over a player who would become a five-time NBA All-Star. "We had Moncrief in mind the whole way," Nelson told *The Milwaukee Journal*. "Like a good poker player, you never let them know what you're thinking." Nelson added that Moncrief had "the chance to be a great basketball player. Not just a good basketball player, but a great basketball player."

Moncrief certainly took advantage of that chance. One of seven players whose number has been retired by the Bucks, he retired as their second-leading scorer. He was also first in career free throws made and attempted, second in assists per game and fourth in rebounding, and that didn't take into account his defensive prowess. Moncrief was the NBA's defensive player of the year the first two seasons that that distinction was awarded.

You might say Kelser's accomplishments were more modest. He averaged 14.2 points per game as a rookie, but he never reached that number again in his six seasons in the league. He averaged double figures only twice more before finishing with a 9.7 career mark.

Actually, the swap with the Pistons was Nelson's second coup prior to the draft. The Bucks owned the fourth pick because of a deal they made a year earlier with Cleveland. Prior to the 1978 draft, the Cavaliers shipped their first-round choice in 1979 to the Bucks for the 15th selection in '78 and used it to take forward Mike Mitchell.

That was at a time when it wasn't unusual for NBA teams to trade their top picks two, three years in advance. Actually, the Bucks had traded their own No. 1 pick in '79 – 10th overall – to the Buffalo Braves in 1977 for John Gianelli and cash. And the Braves, in turn, traded it to the Pistons in a deal involving Marvin Barnes.

As it turned out, the Pistons owned three first-round picks in 1979. They used the Bucks' original choice on UCLA guard Roy Hamilton, who lasted a year. And they chose Michigan forward Phil Hubbard with the 15th pick that they had acquired in a trade with Denver.

All of which comes back around to Vitale. He coached only 12 games for the Pistons in 1979 after going 30-52 the previous year. He lost eight of the 12 before he was fired and eventually moved on to ESPN.

WATERFORD'S ZISKE WINS WOMEN'S WESTERN OPEN

JUNE 26, 1960

The honor was as high as the budget was low when the pride of Milwaukee Pulaski High School staged a brilliant comeback to win one of women's golf's biggest events.

Joyce Ziske, playing out of Waterford, Wis., was five shots down with eight holes to play at Chicago's Beverly Country Club in the 31st Women's Western Open, which was considered a major tournament at the time. She'd never won a major before, and she was a bad bet to win this one, but then Ziske was used to doing things the hard way.

So was everybody else on the fledgling LPGA Tour. The circuit had begun in 1950, and Ziske had joined it five years later when there were still only about 25 regular players. The women would drive from one event to the next, make their own tee times and pairings, print their own programs, mark off the course, run the tournament and phone in the results to the local press.

And all for mad money.

Ziske had won two tournaments in her first five years on the tour, and those two victories had earned her about $2,300. If she could win this one at Beverly, she would collect $1,313. Which she did. Six months later, she quit the pro tour and never came back.

Ziske started the final Sunday of the Western four shots behind Betsy Rawls. Ten holes later, she was five shots behind Barbara Romack. Rawls had blown up by that time, but Ziske was just getting started. She carded a dazzling 33 for the back nine, catching Romack on the 16th hole and forcing a playoff when they each parred the final two holes.

Both players had fours on the first extra hole, and when Romack missed a four-footer for par on the second, the 26-year-old Ziske had her major. It boosted her earnings for the year to a lavish $6,710.

She would win three tournaments in all that season and finish second in the Women's U.S. Open, but when the tour resumed at Sea Island, Ga., in January to start another year, Ziske stayed home and married bowling proprietor Tom Malison. Five years later, Joyce Ziske Malison was raising three boys and helping out at the lanes.

"At that time, there were two things you could do," she told the *Milwaukee Journal Sentinel* some 37 years later. "Play golf the rest of your life or get married. I got sick of the traveling, and there wasn't much money out there at the time. I found the right man."

Ziske grew up on a farm on Milwaukee's south side, and she developed her interest in golf by retrieving balls at the driving range across the street. By the time she was 14, she was good enough to play an exhibition with the great Patty Berg, and three years after she graduated from Pulaski, she turned pro.

Her skills put her on a level with LPGA Hall of Fame players such as Rawls, Babe Didrikson Zaharias, Mickey Wright and Louise Suggs, but Ziske didn't play long enough to earn that honor, and she never regretted her decision to quit.

"It doesn't bother me one bit," she said. "I was happy with the choice I made."

Joyce Ziske

FUTURE GOLD MEDALIST WINS DECATHLON AT MARQUETTE

JUNE 27, 1936

When Glenn Morris came to Marquette Stadium he was a 6-foot, 182-pound car salesman. When he left two days later, he was a 6-foot, 174-pound Olympian. What happened in between was history.

Morris was 24 years old, and he had made a name for himself as a football player at Colorado State. He was good enough that he would play four games for the Detroit Lions in 1940 before an injury ended his career, but that was in the future. He was working at an auto dealership in Denver when he turned his attention to the Olympic Games, especially the decathlon. It just looked like something he could do.

And so he took a break from the showroom, entered the Kansas Relays in the spring of 1936 and won, becoming a bona fide Olympic contender. That was why he journeyed to Milwaukee to join track and field's top athletes for the final Olympic Trials in the decathlon and the Central Region semifinals for all other events. The finals of the Olympic Trials, for everything but the decathlon, would be held at Randall's Island, N.Y., two weeks later.

Morris' performance in Kansas made him a slight favorite in his event, but he knew the competition would be stiff. Waiting for him were the best decathletes in the country including two-time national champion Bobby Clark of San Francisco. Morris blew them all away.

It was a lively crowd at Marquette. Up to 3,500 people were on hand to watch the competition, including two young men in shorts who took a lap around the track between races with signs on their backs that said "Boycott the Nazis." Their political statement in advance of the Berlin Olympics didn't sit well with police who chased them into the stands but never caught them.

When they weren't watching the extracurricular activities, the fans were seeing some sterling performances. Marquette sprinter Ralph Metcalfe won both the 100- and 200-meter races. Marquette freshman Ed Burke won the high jump with a leap of 6 feet 6⁷/₁₆ inches. And distance star Glenn Cunningham, "The Kansas Flyer," won the 1,500.

But Morris was the star of the meet as he finished first in two of the ten decathlon events, tied for first in four others, and had a second and a third. Only the pole vault was not his friend. He finished eighth in that, but he still went into the final race well within range of a world record. All he needed was a time of 4 minutes 56 seconds in the 1,500-meter run. He ran 4:48.1.

Glenn Morris

When the grueling two days were done, Morris had compiled 7,880 points, shattering the old world mark of 7,824.5. He'd also dropped eight pounds, but it was a small price to pay for a trip to Berlin.

Clark and Jack Parker of Sacramento College finished second and third to Morris, which is also what they did at the Olympics as the Americans swept all three decathlon medals.

The world record that Morris set in Milwaukee didn't last very long, though. He broke it in Berlin.

He also apparently created a scene there that went virtually unnoticed at the time. Leni Riefenstahl, a famous German actress and film producer who directed the official film of the 1936 Olympics, wrote in her 1987 autobiography that after the lights dimmed for the medal ceremony, Morris came down the steps and headed directly toward her.

"I held out my hand and congratulated him," Riefenstahl wrote, "but he grabbed me in his arms, tore off my blouse and kissed my breasts, right in the middle of the stadium, in front of a hundred thousand spectators."

PANCHO GONZALES LOSES TEMPER, DOUBLES FINAL

JUNE 28, 1964

Pancho Gonzalez was famous for his blazing serve, and for his raging temper. Fans got to see a lot of both during the short-lived $10,000 Milwaukee Open tennis tournament sponsored by the Joseph Schlitz Brewing Co.

"Why don't you go home?" hollered a spectator at the temperamental Californian after he'd blown his cool at a baseline judge during the doubles final. "I would if I didn't have a lawsuit on my hands," Gonzalez fired back.

This was a frequent problem for Gonzalez, who was referring to the divorce action recently filed by wife Marilyn. He was married six times in his life, the last time to Rita Agassi, sister of Alex, another somewhat less volatile tennis great.

Gonzalez would spend a lot on lawyers during a Hall of Fame career that spanned four decades, but he'd win a lot of tennis tournaments, too. Just not this one. He'd lost the singles title the day before to Ken Rosewall; and he and partner Alex Olmedo were in the process of dropping the doubles final, 6-4, 6-3, to Rod Laver and Mike Davies when Gonzales decided to mix it up with a gallery of 450 at the Milwaukee Country Club.

At one point, he offered his racquet to one of the customers and told him to see if he could do any better. He hadn't gotten along very well with anyone during the singles final either, but then that was just Gonzalez being Gonzalez. He won the U.S. Open in 1948 and '49, and he was as big a drawing card as there was on the early pro tennis tours. But he was known as much for his antics as his game.

All of which made him one of the star attractions when he came to Milwaukee two months after a group of players had launched a series of sponsored tournaments. Schlitz put up the $10,000 purse for the five-day event, which began with two days of singles and doubles at the Milwaukee Arena and wound up at the all-weather courts at the Milwaukee Country Club.

Tournament organizers had a couple of causes to promote. Proceeds went to encourage youth tennis in Wisconsin, but the hope was that meets such as this would help the pros establish their own circuit, modeled after the pro golf tour.

Until that time, most of the top tennis competition was held during one-night stands. Players such as Gonzalez made a decent living that way, but everyone recognized that the long-term future of the sport demanded a more organized approach. The Milwaukee meet was the seventh on an eight-city tour.

It represented an early attempt, and there would be many more before the pros finally got what they were looking for. But it went well. An estimated 5,400 people paid their way into the five days of competition, and they weren't disappointed.

They saw some of the all-time greats of tennis. Laver and Rosewall would win a total of 19 Grand Slam singles titles; and Laver had already won all four of tennis' most prestigious events in the same year, 1962, and he would do so again in 1969.

Gonzales, who was 36 years old at the time, also made the finals in the singles, played on June 27. He dropped the first set, 6-4, before storming back to take the second, 6-3. Then the 29-year-old Rosewall wore him out to win the third, 6-2.

Still, Gonzalez made $1,200 for his efforts that week. It wasn't clear how much of that was claimed by his wife.

MARQUETTE SETTLES AGAIN ON GOLDEN EAGLES

JUNE 29, 2005

Eleven contentious years passed before Marquette University's board of trustees came up with a way to make its sports fans accept an unpopular team nickname. They threatened them with a worse one.

In an unannounced meeting at an undisclosed location, the rulers of one of America's leading Jesuit institutions came to a unanimous decision that was so completely nutty that they had to reverse themselves in seven days. They changed the name of Marquette's teams from the "Golden Eagles" to the "Gold."

The change to Gold was announced on May 4, 2005. The reversal came on May 11. The name Golden Eagles was restored 49 days later.

The reaction to the nickname "Gold" was immediate and overwhelmingly negative. Hundreds of calls and e-mails flooded in demanding to know why anyone would supplant a soaring bird with an inert metal. Students demonstrated. Alums threatened. Dwyane Wade, maybe the most talented Marquette athlete ever, promised to call somebody. SpongeBob SquarePants was suggested as the new mascot. And the local talk show hosts thought they'd died and gone to heaven.

At first the trustees were adamant. A day after announcing their decision, they insisted that it was non-negotiable. Six days after that they held an emergency session, and university President Robert A. Wild admitted there had been a terrible mistake.

"After we made the decision the board gathered together for dinner and people felt good about the job they'd done," he said. "But then you put it out there, and obviously the customers didn't buy it. The new name was being mocked. I think that was the issue that was most problematic."

That and the fact that everyone was feeling left out of the process. Wild made sure that didn't happen again. Instead he said more than 100,000 alumni, students, faculty, staff and donors would be invited to choose the next team name. And, lo and behold, when the votes were counted Wild was right back where he'd started from,

On a momentous Wednesday at the Al McGuire Center, he announced that "Golden Eagles" had gotten 54% of the vote, "Hilltoppers" had gotten 46%, and nothing else mattered. An obviously relieved Wild said the name fracas was the most difficult issue he'd faced in his nine years at Marquette.

Of course, none of it would have happened if he'd simply left well enough alone. His predecessor could have told him that.

Former university president Father Albert J. DiUlio had created a public relations shipwreck in 1993 when he decided that Marquette's 39-year-old nickname "Warriors" was offensive to Native Americans, and it had to go. The school had taken some steps in a more sensitive direction since it had replaced its old "Hilltoppers" moniker with "Warriors" in 1954, most notably dumping the blatantly stereotypical mascot "Willie Wampum." But DiUlio was determined to go much further than that.

He solicited alternative names, but cautioned that this would not be a contest. The school would make the decision. He got 500 suggestions and eliminated all but two of them. One of the first to go was "Jumping Jesuits."

And then he changed his mind and decided to hold a referendum after all. The final choices were "Lightning" and "Golden Eagles." The birds got the nod when write-in votes for "Warriors' weren't allowed. Hardly anyone was thrilled by the outcome, but people got used to it.

And then a millionaire named Wayne Sanders stirred things up all over again at Marquette's 2004 graduation ceremonies. Sanders, vice president of the board of trustees, used the occasion to make an offer. He would donate $1 million to the university, and he said another unnamed trustee would kick in another $1 million if the name got changed back to Warriors.

Wild declined politely to consider the Warriors proposal. He wasn't about to reopen that can of worms. But he popped the top on another one instead. He and the trustees announced that they'd revisit the naming issue.

The rest was theater with the last act playing out at the McGuire Center when the Golden Eagles were reinstated.

Speaking of the Gold, Wild had said, "We were not winning hearts and minds." Or using either.

BONTHRON EDGES CUNNINGHAM AT WIRE IN CLASSIC 1,500

JUNE 30, 1934

Glenn Cunningham was America's premier distance runner and one of the country's most inspirational stories when he came to Marquette Stadium for the 47th annual Amateur Athletic Union national track and field championships. But he met his match against Bill Bonthron, a more than worthy rival who ran 1,500 meters that day faster than anyone ever had.

Nicknamed "The Kansas Flyer," Cunningham had won the 800- and 1,500-meter runs in the 1933 AAU meet, and the mile in both the 1932 and '33 NCAA meets. He also had set the world record in the mile in 1934. And a year earlier, he had won the coveted Sullivan Award given annually to the top amateur athlete in the country. He did all of that on legs scarred by a childhood accident that doctors predicted would leave him unable to walk.

When Cunningham was seven years old, he and his brother Floyd had the job of lighting the schoolhouse stove in the winter time. That stove exploded one February morning in 1917 after someone had mistakenly put gasoline in the kerosene can. Floyd Cunningham, 13, died of severe burns two weeks later, while Glenn's legs also were horribly burned.

After several weeks in bed, Cunningham was able to walk on crutches. And when he got rid of the crutches, he found it was less painful to run than it was to walk. It would be years before he stopped running.

He might have owned every 1,500-meter and mile race in the world if it hadn't been for the emergence of Bonthron, Princeton University's star distance runner, at roughly the same time. Bonthron, who would go on to win the 1934 Sullivan Award, had faced Cunningham four times, including twice indoors, before they arrived in Milwaukee. Just a week earlier, Bonthron had outkicked Cunningham down the stretch to win a sensational mile in the 13th annual NCAA meet at Memorial Coliseum in Los Angeles. That gave each two victories, setting up a historic rubber match before 17,000 people.

At the time, the AAU meet was the most prestigious in the country. It had been first held in 1888 in Detroit and it had been held once before in Milwaukee in 1903. Milwaukee also would host the meet two more times, in 1937 and '48, before the AAU event lost its place as the premier track meet in the country in 1980 and eventually was replaced by the USA Track & Field Championships.

But it never got much better than the 1934 meet.

Four of America's best runners, jumpers and throwers were credited with world records, and another with a tie. Fourteen of 22 defending champions were beaten. Marquette's Ralph Metcalfe won both the 100- and 200-meter dashes for the third straight year, beating Ohio State sprinter Jesse Owens in the 100. Owens, in turn, won the broad jump. Cornelius Johnson, who would win the high jump in the 1936 Olympic Games, and Walter Marty, the world record holder at the time, tied for the high jump crown at 6 feet $8^{5}/_{8}$ inches. Jack Torrance of Louisiana State won the shot put for the second straight year and broke his own world record with a heave of 55-5.

But the biggest race of the day was the 1,500 meters. Five runners were lined up at the start, but only two were serious contenders. Two laps into the four-lap race, Cunningham had the lead and Bonthron was a close second. Then halfway through the third lap, Cunningham put on a spurt and looked as if he was ready to shake his rival.

With roughly 100 yards to run, Bonthron was roughly 15 yards behind. It was then that he mounted a historic finishing kick. He caught Cunningham with 30 yards to go, and the two ran together for another 10 before Bonthron's surge at the tape left him ahead by two feet.

Both men broke the world record of 3 minutes 49.2 seconds. Bonthron was timed in 3:48.8 and Cunningham in 3:48.9. When the race was over, Bonthron turned and shook Cunningham's hand. Then he retreated to the bleachers and collapsed. The victory ceremony was held without him, but the race is still remembered as one of the greatest 1,500-meter races in the annals of American track.

BUCKS GET SIKMA FROM SEATTLE

JULY 1, 1986

The Milwaukee Bucks needed a center, and they had a committee instead. Sharing the middle for them were Alton Lister, Randy Breuer and Paul Mokeski - 21 board feet of mediocrity.

Lister could rebound and block shots. Breuer could score from underneath. Mokeski was a good perimeter shooter. Taken together, they would have amounted to a competent NBA pivot man. After all, their combined scoring average was 21.4 points per game.

They had been good enough to help the Bucks to 57 victories in the 1985-'86 season, but coach Don Nelson knew he had a problem if he hoped to make a run at a championship against Eastern Conference powers Boston and Philadelphia. Fortunately for the Bucks, Lenny Wilkins faced a different problem.

The Seattle SuperSonics' general manager had one of the league's best big men in 6-foot-11 Jack Sikma, but Sikma had told him that he wanted to finish his career with a title contender. Since the seven-time NBA All-Star had four years left on his contract and the Sonics were coming off a 31-51 season, it seemed pretty clear that Sikma would not find happiness in Seattle.

But he found it in Milwaukee. Sikma, a native of Kankakee, Ill., who had played his college ball at Illinois Wesleyan, was delighted when Wilkins told him that he'd been dealt to the Bucks for Lister and two first-round draft choices. The Bucks were pretty pleased themselves. Not only had they acquired the inside presence they'd lacked since Bob Lanier had retired in 1984, but they got two second-round draft choices along with him, and they were able to keep Mokeski and Breuer as backups.

Nelson had no illusions that adding the 30-year-old Sikma would make the Bucks instant champions, but he figured it at least put them in the championship conversation. "I'm not saying that we're better than Philly or Boston or any of the others," he said, "but if anybody has an off-year or an injury, I think we can slip in the back door."

Sikma didn't care if they climbed in through the fire escape. He just wanted a second ring to go along with the one he'd won in Seattle in 1979. Asked for his goals with the Bucks, he said, "I don't think they're anything short of winning a championship."

There were some legitimate grounds for that kind of optimism. The Bucks had an acknowledged if fading star in Sidney Moncrief and three highly accomplished supporting actors in Terry Cummings, Paul Pressey and Ricky Pierce. Add Sikma's experience, along with his 16.8 career scoring and 10.8 career rebounding averages, and Milwaukee suddenly looked like a more dangerous challenger. Certainly, their playoff prospects looked better considering they had been swept by Boston in the Eastern Conference finals six weeks earlier.

In his first season, Sikma's scoring average slipped to 12.7 points, but he still got 10 rebounds a game during the regular season while the Bucks were going 50-32 and dropping to third place in the Central Division. But when the playoffs came, they were ready. They eliminated Philadelphia in five games in the first round and scared the Larry Bird-led Celtics half to death before losing to them, four games to three, in the Eastern Conference semifinals.

That, however, would be the last serious championship run the Bucks would make for 14 years. Nelson left the Bucks after a messy public dispute with owner Herb Kohl when the playoffs were over, while Moncrief's creaky knees forced him to retire in 1989. Cummings was traded the same year, and Pressey was traded in 1990.

Sikma played five seasons in Milwaukee and averaged double figures in all five, but his dreams of another title were never realized. The Bucks made the playoffs in every season that he spent with them, but they never won a division championship or advanced beyond the conference semifinals.

Nearly two decades after Sikma's retirement, the Bucks still hadn't found a dominant center.

MARICHAL BEATS SPAHN IN EPIC PITCHERS' DUEL

JULY 2, 1963

Both bullpens would have emptied if they'd played this game today. Pitch after pitch, inning after inning Warren Spahn and Juan Marichal set down enemy hitters until they were less than 20 minutes from curfew in San Francisco.

Marichal was 25 years old. Spahn was 42, but it didn't matter. The Milwaukee Braves' lefty scattered eight hits over 15 innings, while the San Francisco Giants' right-hander did the same. The game was just about 4 hours 10 minutes old when Willie Mays came to the plate for the seventh time at Candlestick Park. It was 2:31 a.m. in Milwaukee.

Mays had two fly outs, two ground outs, a strikeout and an intentional walk to show for his other six trips to the plate. Spahn had thrown 200 pitches at that point. The 201st did him in. There was one out in the bottom of the 16th inning when he aimed one more of his nasty screwballs at the plate. This one hung up in the strike zone, and Mays hammered it over the left-field wall.

Giants 1, Braves 0. The game was over. The praise had just begun.

Exactly 30 years to the day had passed since the immortal Carl Hubbell had pitched a record 18-inning shutout. He did it for the 1933 Giants, and watching this duel left him shaking his head over Spahn.

"He ought to will his body to medical science," Hubbell told the *San Francisco Chronicle*. "The world should be told what that man is made of and how it all got put together like it did. Here is a guy 42 years old, who still has a fastball... My arm was tired, and the fastball was gone, and I was through at 40. Spahnie's got me by two years, and he's still throwing 15-inning shutouts."

Spahn's only regret was that it wasn't 16 innings. The pitch that Mays hit didn't break at all. "What makes me mad is that I'd just gotten through throwing some real good screwballs to Harvey Kuenn," said Spahn, brushing off the notion that he'd just completed a masterpiece and had only a loss to show for it.

"I don't care about that," he said. "The thing I'm happy about is that I'm pitching good ball."

Much more than good actually. In his last start four days earlier, he'd shut out the Los Angeles Dodgers on three hits. Mays' home run broke his string of 27 1/3 scoreless innings.

All that proved was that it didn't pay for Spahn to work extended overtime. This was the second 16-inning game of his career, and he'd lost the other one as well. He'd also lost a 15-inning game in 1952 when he'd struck out 18 Chicago Cubs and gone down, 3-1. He'd also hit a home run that day.

He tried to provide his own offense in this game, too. Marichal gave up only one extra base hit, and it was a double to Spahn that almost cleared the fence in the seventh inning. Henry Aaron also had what could have been a home run blown back into the park in the fourth inning when the Braves' only serious rally ended after Mays cut down a runner at home plate.

Kuenn, with a double in the sixth, was the only batter other than Mays to get an extra base hit off Spahn. Just two Giants struck out, but then only one walked. Marichal, who threw 227 pitches, fanned 10 and walked four in what was becoming almost a typical performance for him. He finished the game with a 13-3 record, and he would finish the season 25-8. He was a 20-game winner five times over the next six years.

Spahn had an 11-4 record when the game was over. Some observers thought it took so much out of him that he was never the same, but that would be hard to prove. He went 12-3 the rest of the year for a 23-7 record, then fell to 6-13 the following season when he was 43 years old.

MATZDORF SETS WORLD HIGH JUMP RECORD

JULY 3, 1971

The bar was quivering and so was one of track and field's most enduring world records as Pat Matzdorf, a native of Sheboygan and a University of Wisconsin junior, lay motionless in the pit for close to 15 seconds after high jumping 7 feet 6¼ inches. The bar stayed up. The record fell.

Ironically it was a mark that had been set by a Russian in 1963 in the same meet, the United States-Russian dual track meet. Matzdorf was representing his country in an international meet for the first time and admitted later that he was both "excited" and "frightened" by the opportunity.

He had tried twice before that day at this historic height, and he had missed on both jumps. On his final try, he barely brushed the bar, but when it stopped vibrating, he leaped from the pit and a capacity crowd of 22,000 in Berkeley, Calif., let out a roar.

Wiped from the books was the oldest record in track and field, Valery Brumel's effort of 7-5¾. Matzdorf had to know what he'd accomplished, but he was new to this kind of attention and it didn't register at first. He said afterward that the only thing on his mind as he leaped up out of the pit was that he'd set a personal best. A math major with a 3.2 grade-point average, it took him just a little while to process the numbers.

It took him a while to catch up to the world's greatest jumpers, too. Matzdorf began jumping in grade school, but he didn't attract much attention until his senior year in high school at Sheboygan North. That's when he cleared 6-11 to shatter the Wisconsin prep record by four inches. He cleared the 7-foot barrier for the first time as a sophomore at Wisconsin and by the time he got to Berkeley, he'd topped it countless times.

Still, he was viewed as an obscure jumper on a national stage. He had won the NCAA outdoor championship the previous year with a leap of 7-1. But a month earlier he had finished fifth in the same meet. He qualified for the U.S.-Russian event by placing second the week before in the national Amateur Athletic Union meet. But in both the NCAA and AAU meets that year, he had finished behind Reynaldo Brown of Cal Poly at San Luis Obispo. Brown had won both with jumps of 7-3.

Brown did 7-3 one more time at Berkeley, but it was good for only second place as Matzdorf buried his previous personal best by three inches. With first place already his, he tried raising the bar to 7-7½, but he missed, and he was too tired to take another shot. He'd done enough for one day.

Certainly it was enough for Sheboygan. The day Matzdorf got back from California, his hometown was waiting for him with a parade. It happened to be July 5 and the city was having its Independence Day parade a day late. But the timing was perfect and when Matzdorf showed, he was placed near the head of the procession in a red convertible.

With his senior year still ahead of him, Matzdorf appeared poised to become the first high jumper ever to clear 7-7, but it didn't work out that way. He had to deal with tendinitis in his knee and other ailments in 1972, and finished a disappointing fifth in the U.S. Olympic Trials. He also used a bent-leg, straddle style that was becoming less and less popular.

The Fosbury Flop, a revolutionary back-first high jumping style came into vogue, and Dwight Stones used it in 1973 to top Matzdorf's record by one-quarter inch. Matzdorf switched to the "Flop" himself and cleared 7-4¼ in 1975, but he never came close to setting another world record. For Sheboygan, Wisconsin and America in 1971, once was enough.

NO WINNER IN FIVE-HOUR WRESTLING MARATHON

JULY 4, 1916

The combatants started at 4 o'clock in the afternoon, and after a few hours the spectators were tossing seat cushions at them. Dinner hour came and went. It was nearing bedtime, and still nobody had been thrown. When referee Ed Smith finally called off the much anticipated pro wrestling match, he had a lot of explaining to do.

People took their wrestling seriously in the early 20th century, and the crowd at the Douglas County Fairgrounds in Omaha, Neb., wasn't pleased when the man from Wisconsin who called himself "Strangler" Lewis had played five hours of defense against the world heavyweight champion from Nebraska. After Smith ruled the match a draw, Joe Stecher still had his title, and Stecher's manager branded the challenger a "four flusher."

It all came with the territory when wrestling was a real sport, and its champions enjoyed the same esteem as athletes like Babe Ruth, Jack Dempsey and Bill Tilden. The game made them rich and famous, and nobody took greater advantage of that than Robert Herman Friedrich, aka Ed "Strangler" Lewis.

Friedrich was born in a German settlement that would later become Nekoosa, Wis., and he wrestled more than 6,000 matches over 44 years and claimed to have lost only 33 of them. The one with Stecher was the longest.

"Disgusting in the extreme" was the way the *Omaha World-Herald* described Lewis' performance, and the sentiment was echoed by nearly 20,000 people who witnessed it. They'd come to see Stecher make short work of the pretender, but Lewis kept his distance from the Dodge, Neb., favorite's feared scissors hold all evening. Referee Smith consulted with several ringside doctors before he ended the marathon.

Smith's problem was that the contract specifically prohibited draws. The promoter went so far as to offer to resume the match the next day and let the customers in for free. But Smith doubted that that would change anything. As he explained in the newspaper, the wrestlers had simply been too exhausted to continue, and somebody could have been badly injured or even killed if he hadn't done what he did.

And so Lewis was allowed to leave town with his $8,950 share of the estimated $30,000 purse. It was a generous sum for those times, but just a fraction of the $1.5 million Lewis would earn before he left the sport. Over the course of his career he would attract an estimated $15 million from ticket-holders, and even Dempsey never did that.

Four years later, at the Seventy-first Regiment Armory in New York City, Lewis took the heavyweight title away from Stecher in a match that lasted a little over an hour. Lewis was much more aggressive this time, catching his opponent in several of his patented headlocks and finally forcing his shoulders to the mat. Lewis would hold the championship, or some form of it, five different times over the next 13 years, but by that time the sport was beginning to shade into theater. Nobody was sure which winners were determined by skill and which by script. Lewis didn't mind either way. As he put it, who was he to tell millions of fans what they should want?

There was no question that wrestling had been very good to Lewis, who began his career unofficially at the age of 16. The story goes that he was playing for Nekoosa's traveling baseball team at the time. The team was in Pittsville for a game, and when the gate proved to be much less than expected, the visitors had no money to get themselves home. Young Friedrich, as he was known then, was a giant for his day with a neck as big as some men's thighs. He offered to wrestle the local champion for travel expenses, and when he won he was on his way to a long and lucrative career.

Lewis was still in his prime when he contracted trachoma, which caused him to lose his sight temporarily and find religion permanently. He credited prayer when he was able to see again, and when he finally retired he spent most of his time working with young men in the service of his church.

He went blind again about five years before his death. He was 76 when he died in 1966 at a veterans' hospital in Muskogee, Okla.

EX-INFIELDER LOCKWOOD WINS HIS FIRST GAME

JULY 5, 1970

The Kansas City Royals had lodged a serious charge, and the Milwaukee Brewers' new starting pitcher met it with an unusual defense. After nine previous career starts and 67 frustrating innings, Skip Lockwood had finally posted a major league victory only to have his methods questioned.

He'd shut the Royals down on four hits and a single walk while striking out four and taking a big step toward a major career change. But he'd also sent pinch-hitter Bob "Hawk" Taylor to the hospital with a fastball to the head in the eighth inning and pitched much too far inside for his opponents' taste.

"He was doing a little headhunting," said Royals Manager Bob Lemon, "but two can play at that game."

Lockwood, a National Honor Society student in high school, was bright enough to know what that meant, and he had a special reason for pleading his innocence. "I don't throw at anybody," he said. "I've played long enough at third base to realize that. I didn't like guys throwing at me."

Lockwood's memories of life as an infielder were certainly fresh enough. He'd signed a $100,000 bonus contract as a third baseman with the Kansas City A's in 1964, but after watching him struggle to hit a slider for four years the A's decided to see if he could throw one, and so they switched him to the mound. It wasn't entirely new territory for the then-21-year-old right-hander, who had posted a 22-1 record as a high school pitcher in Boston. But that was high school, and this was the big leagues.

Lockwood acknowledged that he'd gotten some help from minor league pitching instructors, but he claimed to have made the transition pretty much on his own. "I learned primarily to pitch by myself," he said.

His homeschooling paid off as he went 6-3 at Peninsula of the Class A Carolina League in 1968, but that wasn't enough for the now Oakland Athletics to protect him from the new Seattle Pilots in the expansion draft that fall. When the Pilots moved to Milwaukee in 1970, Lockwood became a Brewer. He started the season with Portland of the Class AAA Pacific Coast League before being called up on May 6. The Brewers desperately needed starting pitching, but their offense didn't exactly go out of its way to make him feel welcome.

Lockwood entered the Kansas City game with a 4.57 earned run average and a misleading 0-5 record because his teammates just couldn't find a way to hit for him. They'd left a total of 32 runners on base in his last two starts, which helped explain why they were in last place in the American League West Division and on a five-game losing streak.

They weren't any more generous on this occasion as they managed just four hits and scored their only runs on a pair of Gus Gil sacrifice flies. On the other hand, they couldn't have been more accommodating in the field. Left-fielder Danny Walton, center-fielder Davey May and third baseman Tommy Harper all came up with defensive gems, and the Brewers turned two double plays as they prevailed, 2-1, before 10,323 fans at County Stadium.

Lockwood needed just 99 pitches to gain the victory, one of which he would have been very happy to have back – the one that hit Taylor. The former Milwaukee Braves bonus baby left the field under his own power and stayed overnight in the hospital only for observation. But Royals left fielder Lou Piniella wasn't happy. "All I've got to say is he better stay loose the next time he pitches against us," was Piniella's warning shot to Lockwood.

But control wasn't Lockwood's only problem. He lost his next five starts to fall to 1-10 as of August 19. Then he won four out of his last six decisions to finish the season with a 5-12 record and a 4.30 ERA. In four seasons with the Brewers, Lockwood compiled a 28-54 record before they traded him to California in a 10-player deal that brought them lefthander Clyde Wright.

SE RI PAK WINS U.S. WOMEN'S OPEN AT KOHLER

JULY 6, 1998

Blackwolf Run had thrown everything at the world's best women golfers, exhausting them, frustrating them, roasting them, blowing sand in their faces and hurling lightning bolts at them, and now it was trying to drown one of them.

One minute Se Ri Pak was standing in the deep grass along the 18th hole, and the next she was halfway up to her knees in a pond. Just surviving the 53rd U.S. Women's Open had been an accomplishment, and now the South Korean slugger was trying her soggy best to preserve her chances of winning it.

Naturally, that required removing her shoes and socks and wading into the temporary water hazard on the 18th hole in a Monday playoff. Pak had pulled her drive into the rough, and it had rolled down the bank to the edge of the water. She had two choices: Take a drop and a penalty or take a dip. She chose Plan B and blasted her ball out of the muck.

An 8-iron approach and a 15-foot putt later, she'd earned a bogey and new life against amateur upstart Jenny Chuasiriporn, who missed a 10-foot par putt and her best chance to win the longest U.S. Women's Open in history.

It took another two holes of sudden death to decide the issue between the two 20-year-olds. When Pak rolled in a 15-footer for birdie on the 20th extra hole, she became the youngest player ever to win the top prize of women's golf. A tour rookie, she'd already won the McDonald's LPGA two months earlier, and she would win three more majors over the next nine years on her way to the LPGA Hall of Fame.

But she was never in a tougher fight than she was in Kohler. With an opponent or with a course.

Chuasiriporn, an American-born daughter of Thai parents, had come from Timonium, Md., where she waited tables at the family restaurant when she wasn't playing golf or studying at Duke. She was a senior psychology major, which might help explain why she was driving Pak crazy.

Pak led the field at Blackwolf after both the second and third rounds, but Chuasiriporn put together a ferocious run on Sunday, coming from four strokes back and forcing the playoff by dropping a 40-foot birdie putt on the final hole. When the playoff began on Monday she picked right up where she'd left off in regulation, birdying three of the first five holes to take a four-shot lead.

But things started coming apart for her on the par 3 sixth hole when she lost three shots of her lead with a triple bogey. Pak finally pulled ahead by birdying the 14th hole of the playoff, but then she bogeyed No. 15, and the combatants were tied again. Both players were at one over par when Pak got wet on the 18th and Chuasiriporn missed her par putt. "My hands were shaking a lot," Chuasiriporn admitted afterward.

Pak, on the other hand, was as steady as a lady can be standing barefoot in the surf with a sand wedge in her hand and a $267,000 winner's prize at stake. It seemed only right that that would be the signature shot of this most cantankerous tournament.

Blackwolf Run had been a beast all week, serving up an evil mix of soaring humidity, howling winds, driving rain, rolling greens and thick rough. Two rounds had been suspended by darkness, and one had been delayed by rain and lightning.

Nothing about the week was easy, and it showed on the scorecards. Par was 71, and the average round was more than five shots over that. Only five eagles were shot through the whole tournament, and three of those were holes-in-one. There were only 703 birdies compared to 1,951 bogeys and 85 triples or worse.

When Pak and Chuasiriporn finished 72 holes, they were six over par, marking the first time since 1984 that a U.S. Women's Open winner had come in over par. The scoring was brutal, but the entertainment was superb. More than 21,000 fans survived Dan Ryan Expressway-style traffic to attend the first round, setting a record that was promptly broken the next day when 26,000 showed up.

Even the playoff, held on a Monday when most of Wisconsin went back to work, drew 8,000. Among the guests was former President George H.W. Bush, who made it a point to congratulate Chuasiriporn on her effort.

There could be no question that the customers got their money's worth. Anyone who disputed that was all wet.

BREWERS TRADE FOR SABATHIA

JULY 7, 2008

The future the Milwaukee Brewers had been waiting for for 26 years arrived from Cleveland, Ohio, and it weighed 290 pounds.

Ever since the World Series year of 1982, the Brewers had been promising their fans that they would be back in the playoffs, but it was all talk until Doug Melvin took a giant gamble on a huge man. The general manager sacrificed the top prospect in his farm system plus three other minor leaguers for what amounted to the temporary rights to reigning American League Cy Young Award winner CC Sabathia.

The Cleveland Indians had given up on re-signing Sabathia when their left-handed superstar turned down a four-year, $72 million contract in the spring, and the Brewers didn't figure to have a much better chance of keeping him after he became a free agent following the 2008 season. Melvin was effectively renting Sabathia for three months at the expense of slugging outfield prospect Matt LaPorta, along with pitchers Zach Jackson and Rob Bryson and a player to be named later that turned out to be outfielder Michael Brantley.

And the reason was simple. "We're going for it," Melvin said.

"It" was the playoff spot that had eluded the team for two-and-a-half decades because of bad decisions and short pockets. But a new stadium and a new owner were supposed to change all of that, and now it was time for the Brewers to prove that if they got close enough to the promised land, they'd do whatever it took to go the rest of the way. Playing the best ball in the National League over the past six weeks had put them 10 games over .500 and made them ready to make their move.

Sabathia, who stood 6-foot-7 and weighed a few good meals under 300 pounds, was a load both physically and financially. His 95 mile-per-hour fastball, sharp slider and mind-bending change-up had earned him the 2007 Cy Young Award with a 19-7 record, a 3.21 earned run average and 209 strikeouts compared to just 37 walks. His record was only 6-8 in the current season, but that was mainly because the Indians had scored two or fewer runs for him in nine of his 18 starts. A valuable bullpen saver, he almost always took his team deep into games, and on top of that he was a major asset in the clubhouse.

But he came with an $11 million salary, and when the Brewers picked up half of it, they pushed their payroll to nearly $90 million. That represented half of what Mark Attanasio paid for the entire team in 2004. If this didn't work, it would be one of the most expensive miscalculations the franchise had ever made, and it had made plenty of them.

But as Attanasio put it, "The fans put us in a position to do this... we're trying to give something back to them."

The customers rewarded the gesture by buying 27,000 single-game tickets on the day the deal was announced. They also gave Sabathia a standing ovation when he was introduced at a game on the night he came to town. He more than returned the favor over the next three months.

He compiled an 11-2 record and a 1.65 ERA in 17 starts with his new team, striking out 128, walking only 25 and eating up $130 2/3$ innings. A disputed single that could just as easily have been ruled his own error cost him a no-hitter against Pittsburgh, and best of all, he pitched a four-hitter against the Chicago Cubs on the last day of the season to put Milwaukee into the playoffs as the NL wild-card team.

The eventual World Series champion Philadelphia Phillies ended the Brewers' post-season run by taking their best-of-five playoff series, 3-1, but the fans weren't complaining about Melvin's gamble. They were just hoping he could follow it up by retaining the results.

The Brewers made a serious attempt, offering Sabathia $100 million over five years to stay, but they couldn't compete with the New York Yankees' record-setting seven-year, $161 million package. Just as quickly as their new hero had come, he was gone. It would be a while before anyone knew whether he was taking the future with him.

PACKERS' SHAREHOLDERS FLOCK TO LAMBEAU

JULY 8, 1998

It might be a stretch to say the Green Bay Packers' annual corporate meeting came to order at 10 o'clock on a Wednesday morning. When 18,707 co-owners gather at a football field, many of them fresh from tailgate parties and some of them wearing Cheeseheads, "order" is a relative term.

But there was nothing unruly about this gathering of capitalists as the franchise held its stockholders meeting at Lambeau Field for the first time out of pure necessity. It had nowhere else to put all those people.

Most of the participants were there because an unlikely stock sale had added more than 105,000 shareholders to the organization during a 17-week period that had ended in mid-March. One share was all it took to get invited to the meeting, and every shareholder was welcome to bring a guest. The combination of first-time curiosity and a second straight Super Bowl appearance told the Packers to expect a big crowd, and so they'd opened the stadium for the meeting.

Now under sunny skies with temperatures in the 70s, the people were listening to the treasurer give a financial report and the general manager battle a balky sound system to outline the state of the ballclub. Unlike most corporate meetings, this one was interrupted by frequent ovations, but no one seemed to mind. It was their team, after all.

It had been since 1923 when a group of Green Bay businessmen kicked off a stock sale hoping to sell 1,000 shares at $5 apiece to keep the team from going out of business. There were two other emergency stock sales after that, but this offering was something very different. Not only were the Packers doing fine at the bank, they had just been to the league's championship game for two years in a row.

But club President Bob Harlan saw a time not far away when the Packers would sink to the bottom of the league fiscally if not competitively if they didn't build a new stadium or at least rebuild the old one. And so he went to his executive committee with a plan to sell as many as a million shares of stock to raise money to revamp the facilities.

It should have been a hard sell, since the new stockholders wouldn't have any real say in running the team, and they couldn't sell their shares for a profit. What the Packers were really offering was an exclusive $200 souvenir, although it did come with bragging rights and a ticket to the annual meeting.

But this was Green Bay, and Harlan had no trouble convincing his committee to go for the sale. Some of the other NFL owners, on the other hand, had their doubts. Harlan got a cool reception from members of the NFL's finance committee at a meeting in Washington, D.C. They were suspicious that the Packers would use the money to pay players, and it was only after he'd stated his case to all of the owners that he got the green light.

The stock went on sale in November 1997, and the clearinghouse handling the transactions received 55,000 calls in the first 24 hours and sold $7.8 million worth of stock in the first 11 days. When the sale finally wound down in March, the Packers had raised $24 million. More than half of the buyers were from Wisconsin, but there were others from all 50 states plus Guam and the Virgin Islands.

People may not have come from quite that far to attend the annual meeting at Lambeau Field, but the ones who did come lent a game-like flavor to the occasion. They arrived at the parking lot hours before the meeting, and they were wearing green and gold. Once inside, they learned that the team had made a record profit of $6.7 million. Then Harlan and General Manager Ron Wolf held a question and answer session. The meeting lasted 1 hour 36 minutes. The memory lingered much longer than that.

Bob Harlan, president of the Packers, addressed stockholders at Lambeau Field.

MILWAUKEE BOOS, BLUSHES OVER ALL-STAR TIE

JULY 9, 2002

Henry Aaron, Robin Yount, Paul Molitor and Warren Spahn took turns throwing ceremonial first pitches for major league baseball's 73rd All-Star Game at Miller Park. Eleven innings and three-and-a-half hours later, Bud Selig had to be wishing he'd saved at least two of them for the game as a triumphant week of baseball in Milwaukee turned into a national embarrassment.

The stadium was only a year old and state-of-the-art, the biggest names were all on hand, the parties had been glittering, the five-day Fan Fest had drawn almost 90,000 people, and the Monday home run derby had been a soggy spectacular. But it was all forgotten when the commissioner was forced to call the game a 7-7 tie after the managers ran out of players.

Milwaukee's two other All-Star Games had been played at County Stadium in 1955 and 1975 without incident. But this one came with its own enduring image, and it was Selig standing in the company of two umpires, with both hands thrust in the air and a look of utter helplessness and disgust on his face.

"I had no alternative," he said later. He didn't, either, because no one saw this coming until it was too late.

Twenty-five hits, including a towering home run by the game's most prodigious power-hitter, a stirring seventh inning that brought two lead changes and a circus catch had provided a sellout crowd of 41,871 with plenty of entertainment. And National League Manager Bob Brenly and his American League counterpart Joe Torre were making sure the customers got to see everyone. All 60 players, including 19 pitchers, saw action. The problem was the 19 pitchers.

Selig was watching from his seat adjacent to the first-base dugout when he was approached by Sandy Alderson, the league's executive vice president of baseball operations, after the top of the 11th inning. Alderson told him that Vicente Padilla, the NL's last pitcher, had already thrown two innings and Brenly didn't think he could go a third. That prompted a conference among the managers and the commissioner at which both Brenly and Torre insisted that the game should end in a tie unless the National League scored in the bottom of the 11th.

The NL almost took Selig off the hook when it put the winning run on second base with two out. But San Francisco catcher Benito Santiago struck out to end the game, and the players walked off the field while the crowd booed, threw seat cushions and plastic cups on the field, and chanted, "Let them play!"

Selig would have liked nothing better than to accommodate the customers. The event had been staged against a backdrop of fiscal problems, labor strife and steroids, all of which had made him a stable target for his legion of critics. And now this.

He held a post-game press conference to apologize for the outcome and to explain his decision, but that didn't satisfy many fans. After all, they'd paid up to $175 a seat to see somebody win, and a number of them had parted with more than that. Scalpers had gotten as much as $700.

Only one other All-Star Game had ended with the score tied, and that had been because of rain more than 40 years ago.

Brenly suggested that the two teams hold an impromptu home run derby to decide the outcome, but Selig vetoed that as too gimmicky. The commissioner felt the same way about using position players to pitch or putting pitchers back into the game. He believed the risk of injury was too great, and the managers agreed.

And so the game was called with great regret, no decision and, incidentally, no Most Valuable Player either. Several candidates had emerged for that honor, with the early favorite being Barry Bonds. Bonds had hit a two-run home run in the third inning to help the Nationals to a 4-0 lead after being robbed of a homer in the first inning by Torii Hunter, who made a spectacular catch above the wall in center field. Damian Miller was a sentimental candidate. A native of La Crosse playing in his first All-Star Game and representing the defending World Series champion Arizona Diamondbacks, Miller doubled twice, and scored a run and drove in a run. But it was decided that since there was no winner there would be no MVP.

It may have been the only break Major League Baseball caught that night, because if it had been Bonds, he had left the game after the third inning and would not have been available to accept the award. The evening had been embarrassing enough without that.

BUCKS SIGN MOSES MALONE

JULY 10, 1991

Del Harris was always a big believer in communication. So it probably shouldn't have surprised anyone when the Milwaukee Bucks' coach accompanied a major player acquisition with a five-page memo to the press.

The player was Moses Malone. The memo outlined all of the reasons why an NBA team should never let its record slip just to get into the draft lottery. Coach Harris also happened to be General Manager Harris, and it had been suggested in the media that he was letting one job get in the way of the other. The charge was that he was making short-term personnel decisions at the expense of the team's long-term future in order to protect his coaching record.

"Some people say that Del keeps bringing in players to patch up the team so that they won't lose," Harris huffed at Malone's introductory press conference. "I'll tell you this: I'm not going to intentionally lose. When the time comes that this franchise doesn't want to win games, I don't want to coach anyway. Get the picture?"

You might say Harris was a little sensitive on the subject. You might also say that the Malone signing was a prime example of where the critics were coming from.

The Bucks had had some big men with big names play center for them since Kareem Abdul-Jabbar left town in 1975. People like Bob Lanier, Dave Cowens and Jack Sikma. But all of them were on the downside of their careers when they got to Milwaukee, and none of them had enough left to lead the team to a championship the way Abdul-Jabbar had.

Sikma, whom Milwaukee decided to cut loose in the off-season, was the latest case in point. Malone was about to become the next one.

The Bucks were badly in need of rebounding after getting swept out of the first round of the playoffs by Philadelphia in the spring of 1991. No question Malone was a rebounder. The 13-time All-Star had led the league in that category six times during his 16-year NBA career. He'd also won three Most Valuable Player awards, scored more than 25,000 points, made more free throws than anyone in the history of the sport and gone a record 1,047 games without fouling out.

But he was 36 years old, and his last rebounding title had come in 1985. And while he'd missed only five games in the past four seasons, he'd lost his starting job the previous year in Atlanta. The Hawks simply let him go in the spring.

But Harris went way back with Malone, having coached him for three years in Houston and seen him lead the Rockets into the NBA Finals in 1981. The coach believed there was enough left in this 6-foot-10, 255-pound tank to keep the Bucks in the championship picture.

"This is an opportunity to get one of the quality rebounders in the league, and the fact that he's 36 is not a big problem," said Harris. "We're getting him for two years, not five." Harris wouldn't guarantee that Malone's acquisition would make the Bucks a contender, but he said, "We will continue to seek to improve our team as we try for the championship."

It turned out to be a totally futile attempt. Malone's two-year deal called for a $1.6 million salary in the first season and $2.08 million in the second, and it was definitely not a bargain. He averaged 15.6 points and 9.1 rebounds in his first season in Milwaukee, but the rest of the Bucks kind of stood back and watched him work while the team skidded to a 31-51 record. It was the beginning of a very long and very dark period in the history of the franchise.

Harris relinquished his coaching duties in early December, less than five months after signing Malone, and then came to "a mutual agreement" with owner Herb Kohl to take a hike after the season. Meanwhile, Malone was gone after playing just 11 games the following year. It would be 1999, the lockout-shortened season, before the Bucks had another winning record.

They were in the lottery for eight straight years. Harris was right. It didn't do them much good.

RICHEYS SWEEP WESTERN OPEN

JULY 11, 1965

Nancy Richey and her younger brother Cliff were planning to go straight to the top, and they'd already made about half of the trip in a six-year-old Cadillac.

Twenty-two-year-old Nancy was the No. 1 ranked woman in the country while her 18-year-old brother Cliff was No. 11 among American men when they arrived at the 80th annual Western Open tennis tournament at the Town Club in Fox Point, a Milwaukee suburb. Joining them as usual were George and Betty, their parents, teachers, fans and chauffeurs. The first family of United States tennis traveled from tournament to tournament in its '59 Caddy, and this turned out to be one of their most rewarding stops.

Twelve of America's top 20 men's amateurs and five of the top 13 women were among 160 or so players from 11 different countries competing for one of the most important titles on the amateur circuit. The field included top-ranked defending champion Dennis Ralston, national collegiate titlist Arthur Ashe, and incidentally John Powless, who was on his way to becoming the head basketball coach at the University of Wisconsin. It also had Marty Riessen, who had finished second in the last four Western singles, and defending women's champion Julie Heldman.

Adding to the family flavor of the event were Clark and Carole Graebner, man and wife. But it was the Richeys who were shoving the singles trophies in the trunk after the competition was done.

Cliff had shocked Ralston in four sets to move into the final against Riessen, but he hadn't made many friends along the way. The intense teenager was just rude enough to ball boys and line judges to turn a crowd of 1,800 into Marty Riessen fans on the final day.

The former Northwestern star had upset Ashe, who was ranked No. 3 nationally, in the quarterfinals on Friday and looked as though he might be ready to renounce his bridesmaid role in the singles. He won the first set against Richey, 7-5, and took the first three games of the second. But Richey steadied himself after that and won going away, 5-7, 6-4, 6-3, 6-3, much to the disappointment of the customers.

Meanwhile, his sister was romping through the women's field. Nancy Richey had beaten 16-year-old Rosemary Casals, 6-1, 6-3, in the semis; and when she met Graebner in the singles final she barely broke a sweat. She won, 6-1, 6-0, making the Richeys the first brother-sister team ever to claim the Western singles.

A year later, they came back to the Town Club and duplicated their feat in the national Clay Court championships. The Town Club had played host to the Western Open in alternating years, starting in 1957, and would be the site of the U.S. Clay Court tournament for three years before canceling its option in 1969 following a dispute over gate receipts. Another pro tournament was held in its place that year, drawing a field of eight, but when the Town Club dropped its option on the Clay Court tournament it was essentially the beginning of the end of big-time tennis in Milwaukee.

The Richeys, on the other hand, kept riding and kept winning. Especially Nancy, who would become the world's third-ranked woman in 1968 with the arrival of open tennis when pros and amateurs began competing against each other. Over the course of her career, she captured 69 tournaments, including two Grand Slam singles championships.

Cliff never attained that kind of fame on the world stage, but his parents loved him anyway. Both were teaching pros and George had been the nation's eighth-ranked pro in 1952. The Richey family was all about tennis from the time the kids were little. In a 1965 *Sports Illustrated* story, Frank Deford wrote that Cliff dropped out of high school in Dallas to concentrate on the game, and neither sibling took time to date once their careers started to take off.

The parents hardly ever missed a match, which was no small trick since George was afraid of airplanes. So he packed up the kids and the gear, and they went everywhere in the car instead. That worked well for tournaments like the Western, but the folks had to make alternate travel plans when the kids started to play overseas. Cadillacs can't fly, and they don't float very well either.

MUSIAL'S BLAST WINS MILWAUKEE ALL-STAR GAME

JULY 12, 1955

To hear the losers tell it, it was "a lousy pitch" in a "lousy stadium," but when Stan Musial drove Frank Sullivan's fastball into the right-field bleachers, Milwaukee saw it as a perfect ending to its first Major League All-Star Game.

Sour grapes were hanging all over the American League clubhouse after Musial led off the bottom of the 12th inning with a first-pitch home run off Boston's 6-foot-7 right-hander. It was the fourth home run that Musial had hit in 12 All-Star games, and it capped a monumental comeback that saw the National Leaguers turn a 5-0 deficit in the seventh inning into a 6-5 victory.

"It was a lousy pitch," said Sullivan. "I gave him a fast ball right where he wanted it – over the plate and across the letters."

"What a lousy stadium," American League catcher Yogi Berra muttered to Musial as he stepped to the plate. "You can't even see the ball out there. Look at those shadows over the infield."

Too low. Too many shadows. Too bad, said the 45,314 fans who came to County Stadium to watch baseball's 22nd annual summer classic.

The Braves had been in town for just over two years, and the city was anxious to prove to everyone that they were in the right place. There was a parade, followed by a lakefront fireworks show that drew an estimated 250,000 people. And then there was this gripping baseball game.

It started at 2 p.m., a half-hour late to allow baseball officials and sportswriters to attend the funeral of *Chicago Tribune* sports editor Arch Ward, who had come up with the concept of an all-star game. And it started badly for the National League as the visitors jumped all over five-time All-Star starter Robin Roberts for four runs in the first inning. West Allis native Harvey Kuenn led off the rally with a single, and New York Yankees slugger Mickey Mantle finished it with a three-run homer.

When the Americans added a run in the sixth, they seemed to be on their way to a romp. At that point, Billy Pierce and Early Wynn had combined to pitch six shutout innings. But the NL team came back to tie it with two runs in the seventh and three in the eighth with the help of two errors and RBI singles by Milwaukee's Johnny Logan and Henry Aaron.

The score was still tied at 5-5 when Gene Conley took the mound for the NL in the top of the 12th. The Braves' lanky right-hander had some making up to do after taking the loss in the 1954 All-Star Game by giving up three runs in the eighth inning. He didn't give up anything this time. Instead, he struck out Al Kaline, Mickey Vernon and Al Rosen.

That left everything up to Musial, who just laughed at Berra's complaint. "I had only one thought in mind," he said. "That was to bust the ball out of the park." Which is exactly what he did, and as he circled the bases, Conley said he felt like leaving the dugout and running them with him.

Conley got credit for the victory, topping a big All-Star showing for the Braves. Aaron, who entered the game in the fifth inning, finished the afternoon with two hits, a walk, a run scored and a run batted in in three trips to the plate. Logan's single drove in the Nationals' first run, while Del Crandall caught the first five innings and Eddie Mathews played the first six at third base before leaving the game with a bruised wrist. No team had more All-Stars than the Braves, and nobody had more fun than Milwaukee's fans.

The crowd included 2,500 standing-room customers, and thousands more were turned away when they showed up at the park looking for last-minute tickets. The live gate was $179,545, and the event was just about the grandest thing that had ever happened in Milwaukee sports. From a local perspective, there was nothing lousy about that.

SOAP OPERA CONTINUES: UW NAMES MEANWELL

JULY 13, 1934

If daytime television had come to Madison in the thirties, this would have been a whole series. Turf wars, dueling doctors, secret shoe contracts, spiked coffee – it had it all.

The fracas between Walter "Doc" Meanwell and Clarence "Doc" Spears could have been scripted for *General Hospital*. It appeared to end when the university's board of regents named Meanwell as athletic director. He seemed like a logical choice. Meanwell had built Wisconsin's basketball team into a national power, winning three mythical national championships, and winning or sharing eight Big Ten titles.

But the war was just getting started. Two years later, both doctors would be fired.

The vote to name Meanwell AD was taken on Friday the 13th, and it couldn't have been any closer. University President Glenn Frank cast the deciding vote after an 8-8 deadlock on the first ballot.

Meanwell's election filled a vacancy that had been created more than two years earlier when George Little was forced to resign. Little was charged with being a Meanwell puppet when he oversaw the building of the new UW Fieldhouse. The facility was considered suitable only for basketball, which earned it the title of "Little's Folly."

Little's resignation was accepted on Dec. 28, 1931, and assistant football coach Irwin Uteritz was chosen to replace him. But Uteritz, 32, quit after four months because he said the strain of the position left him on the verge of a mental breakdown and business manager James Phillips emerged as acting AD.

Spears was named football coach at Wisconsin in 1932, following a controversial 13-week search. He replaced Glenn Thistlethwaite, who had posted a respectable 26-16-3 record, but was the target of critics, in part, for his work with the Woman's Christian Temperance Union.

Before naming Spears, the athletic council first tabbed UW assistant Guy Sundt, but the appointment fell through. Then it named Iowa State coach George Veenker, but that didn't fly either because of an outcry from both inside and outside the university. Finally, Spears, who was coaching at Oregon, accepted the job two weeks after he had first turned it down. There were reports that he had changed his mind because influential alumni had promised him the AD job within two years.

As the pro-Meanwell, faculty-dominated athletic council and the pro-Spears board of regents struggled for control of the athletic department, Meanwell and Spears battled each other. The two men had a lot in common. Both of them were strong-willed, both held medical degrees and both had designs on the athletic director's job.

Sure enough, two years after Spears was hired, the board of regents approved him as chairman of an advisory committee that was to serve under Phillips and that also included Meanwell and track coach Tom Jones. But within three months, the athletic council voted to give the AD post to George Downer, the athletic department's publicity director, instead. The board of regents favored Spears and rejected the recommendation. That opened the door for Meanwell to get the job.

Meanwhile, Spears hadn't posted a winning record since his first season and when his 1935 team went 1-7, team captain John Golemgeske circulated a petition demanding his firing. Golemgeske later told the press that Meanwell had put him up to it, touching off a pair of investigations: One by the council and one by the board.

The competing probes turned up all manner of juicy allegations. Spears was charged with ordering team trainer William Fallon to put whiskey in the players' coffee during halftime of a game. This would be before the age of Gatorade. Then Meanwell confessed to the regents that he'd given one of the football players a drink of whiskey on the way home from a different game.

Meanwell also admitted to having signed a secret contract with Bud Foster, his successor as basketball coach. The agreement forced Foster to use Meanwell's system for one season and made Foster promise to leave without a fuss if Meanwell decided to fire him.

Moreover, Meanwell was under fire for buying basketballs and shoes only from companies that paid him royalties.

When the smoke finally cleared over Bascom Hill on Feb. 15, 1936, the regents handed Spears, Meanwell and the unfortunate trainer Fallon their walking papers. The Big Ten, in turn, threatened to suspend Wisconsin for violating league rules on faculty control of athletics. A new faculty-controlled athletic board was named and within 90 days, the Badgers were readmitted to the Big Ten.

Unlike *General Hospital*, this soap opera had an ending.

STOCKTON WINS FIRST GREATER MILWAUKEE OPEN

JULY 14, 1968

Facing a field that included the reigning Masters, U.S. Open and PGA champions and shooting for the second-biggest purse in American golf history, Dave Stockton needed all the help he could get. But this couldn't have been what the gods of the game had in mind when they created hazards.

Stockton didn't just overcome them on his way to the first Greater Milwaukee Open championship, he was one.

The 26-year-old San Bernardino, Calif., pro shot a closing round 69 at North Shore Country Club to win the tournament by four strokes over the legendary Sam Snead, but only with the involuntary aid of the gallery. Stockton hit not one, not two, but three balls, into the spectators on the final Sunday, and all three of them helped pave his way to the $40,000 top prize.

He caught a woman on the arm with his drive on the third hole, drove over the green and into the gallery on the ninth where the ball rolled into somebody's foot, and nailed a man in the head with his tee shot on the 16th. Net result: One swollen arm, one knockout and three shots saved for the champion.

In all three cases, the ball bounced the right way off of the patrons and allowed Stockton to save par. In fact, he birdied the next four holes after he plunked the woman, effectively wrapping up the championship.

It was a bizarre way to win a golf tournament, but in Stockton's defense, the weather was hot and sticky and he'd had a long night. The plumbing system in his hotel had developed some strange knocks and rattles, keeping him up from 2 a.m. until almost 6. But if lack of sleep helped Stockton groove his swing, he was all for it. "The way I was hitting my shots and putting, only a coronary could have stopped me," he said.

Certainly, no one in the star-studded field could. Among the early favorites were Masters champion Bob Goalby, Open champion Lee Trevino, PGA champion Don January and Tom Weiskopf, the tour's second leading money-winner at that point. Weiskopf finished in a tie for third, but none of the others cracked the top 10.

Of course, the biggest name of all was Snead, who had won 84 tournaments in his 33-year career, but none in the last seven years. He showed all the signs of ending the drought by firing a course record 65 in the second round, but he followed that with a three-over 75, which meant he needed to shoot 67 on Sunday just to finish second. Still, runner-up money wasn't bad. His $24,000 share of the purse was the most he'd ever made from a single event.

Stockton grabbed the tournament lead in the second round and never gave it up, but he admitted he was keeping an eye on Snead throughout the final round. Snead pulled within three shots of the lead at one point, but his charge ended when he buried his approach shot in the bunker two inches from the 16th green "If the ball had cleared the trap, I had a chance for an eagle," he said. "... I had to blast the ball to get out of there. It went almost straight up... I went down so deep that I brought two Chinese up with it."

Stockton didn't feel really comfortable until he rammed home a 65-foot birdie putt on No. 15 to go ahead by four shots with three holes to play. The victory was the second of the summer for him – he'd won at Cleveland two weeks earlier – and it came on a course he really didn't like very much after he'd carded a 68 in the opening round.

"I didn't feel I could win, but as I went along, I improved," he said. "I appreciated that it was a 'heady' course."

He probably meant that North Shore made him think, although he could have been referring to the unfortunate customer on No. 16.

NL ALL-STAR STREAK STAYS ALIVE IN MILWAUKEE

JULY 15, 1975

Patience is a virtue, but it's possible to have too much of a good thing. That appeared to be the American League's problem at Milwaukee County Stadium as it dropped its 12th Major League All-Star Game in its last 13 tries. At least it appeared that way to Bill Madlock.

The Chicago Cubs' third baseman had just broken the American Leaguers' hearts again with a game-winning hit in the ninth inning when he said, "The American League was just sitting there looking like they were waiting to get beat."

Jon Matlack, the New York Mets' pitcher who threw two shutout innings to pick up the win, offered a different perspective. "I really think the National League has more talent," he said. "This is the cream of the crop from both leagues and it should be an even match, but it hasn't been."

Whether the American League's undoing had more to do with its talent or attitude, those comments by the game's co-Most Valuable Players had to sting. But no more so for the AL All-Stars than how they lost the game, 6-3.

After the National League took a 3-0 lead on back-to-back, solo homers by Steve Garvey and Jim Wynn in the second inning and an RBI single by Johnny Bench in the third, the AL tied the game, 3-3, in the bottom of the sixth. Pinch-hitter Carl Yastrzemski blasted a three-run homer off a Tom Seaver fastball with two outs.

But rather than seize on the momentum that had swung its way, the American League completely unraveled in the ninth. The National Leaguers' rally started when Reggie Smith's sinking line drive barely eluded Claudell Washington, continued when Al Oliver hooked a double over Washington's shoulder and culminated when Madlock slapped a two-run single under third baseman Graig Nettles' glove.

Washington had missed the Oakland A's last three games with dizzy spells, and the National Leaguers would soon have his head spinning again. After Smith's drive caromed off the thumb of Washington's glove, AL manager Alvin Dark motioned for his left fielder to retreat a few steps when Oliver came to bat. But while Washington seemed to know up from down, he was a little foggy on in from out, and he moved several feet in the wrong direction.

That allowed Oliver to hit the ball over his head and into the left-field corner. Then Madlock slapped a Goose Gossage change-up past Nettles to score the winning runs. Pete Rose's sacrifice fly wrapped up the scoring.

Just why a flame-thrower like Gossage would float a change-up to a future four-time batting champion like Madlock in a situation like that was something of a mystery. But then nobody could figure out why Nettles didn't flag down Madlock's grounder either. "It was almost a double play," groused the Yankees' third baseman.

As for Gossage, he was only 24 years old at the time and appearing in his first All-Star Game. "I made a big mistake," he said years later. "I should have gone with my fastball. We didn't even call for it. I changed up on my own. It was just inexperience."

"Could haves" were all the American Leaguers had to console themselves, although a crowd of 51,480 AL partisans didn't seem to mind. It was the largest gathering ever to see a baseball game in Milwaukee. The local fans had been pretty patient themselves, waiting 20 years since their last All-Star Game when Milwaukee was a National League city.

Having the mid-season classic back in town was particularly satisfying for Brewers President Bud Selig, who had pretty much devoted his life to returning a franchise to Milwaukee after the Braves bolted for Atlanta. Selig watched the game from a specially constructed box next to the American League dugout.

Sharing it with him were U.S. Secretary of State Henry Kissinger, Governor Pat Lucey, Mayor Henry Maier, Milwaukee County Executive John Doyne and baseball Commissioner Bowie Kuhn.

"It was a storybook evening," said Selig. "A lot went through my mind. I don't think necessarily that this was our finest hour, but I do think it was another tremendous chapter."

MILWAUKEE'S KRAENZLEIN WINS FOURTH GOLD MEDAL

JULY 16, 1900

Dapper Alvin Kraenzlein probably had one of those "Why didn't I think of that before?" moments when he decided to take a new approach to running hurdles. He tried gliding over them one foot at a time instead of using the traditional two-footed launch favored in those days, and the results were revolutionary.

The Milwaukee native literally had a leg up on the competition by the time he arrived at the Paris Olympic Games at the turn of the century. Five years earlier, he'd dominated the first state high school track meet held in Wisconsin, or the United States for that matter, when he won five individual titles and led his Milwaukee East Division team to the championship. At the University of Pennsylvania, he set world records in three different events and led his team to three straight Intercollegiate Association of Amateur Athletes of America championships or what were then the national collegiate championships.

Now, he was about to set an Olympic record that still stands today, although his accomplishments were diminished somewhat by a dispute over religious mores that, in turn, led to a fist-fight.

Over a three-day period, in the second Games of the modern Olympics, Kraenzlein won the 110-meter hurdles, the 60-meter dash, the broad jump and the 200-meter hurdles. His victory in the 200 hurdles came on Monday, July 16, when he easily outdistanced the field in a time of 25.4 seconds.

The 6-foot, 165-pound Kraenzlein was recognized almost as much for his curly-headed good looks and elegant wardrobe as he was for his skills in Paris where the Games weren't really a big deal. They were run mostly on a soft, lumpy grass track and overshadowed by the Universal Exposition being held there at the same time. Crowds of less than 1,000 were commonplace.

Kraenzlein won his first gold on Saturday, July 14, when he set a world record of 15.4 seconds in winning the 110-meter hurdles. Then came Sunday and the events that led to a bitter public feud among members of the U.S. team.

Long before the Games even started, the Americans had asked the French to reschedule the Sunday competition out of respect for their Christian members' religious convictions. When the French steadfastly refused, many on the U.S. team boycotted that day's events, including Meyer Prinstein, national collegiate champion in 1898 and 1900, and Kraenzlein's chief rival in the broad jump. Prinstein was Jewish, but his coach ordered him to sit out the Sunday competition, which meant that his jump of 23 feet 6½ inches in the preliminaries would have to stand as his best effort.

Prinstein expected Kraenzlein to sit out, too, but the Penn athletes were allowed to make their own choices and Kraenzlein changed his mind at the last minute and competed. His leap of 23-7 narrowly edged Prinstein for the gold medal. Incensed, Prinstein challenged Kraenzlein to a Monday jump-off, and when Kraenzlein said no, Prinstein punched him, and the two had to be separated by their teammates.

Kraenzlein also won the 60-meter dash on Sunday in a world record time of 7-flat.

On Monday, immediately after winning his fourth gold, Kraenzlein announced that he was retiring at the age of 23. "I am through with athletics, and shall devote myself to something more serious," he said.

When Kraenzlein announced his retirement, it was assumed that he'd make use of the dental degree he'd earned at Penn. But he wasn't quite as serious as that. The man who walked around Paris when he wasn't competing dressed to the hilt with a stylish cap and scarf became a vagabond track coach before dying of heart disease in 1928 at age 51.

Two of the four events in which Kraenzlein won gold medals have since been discontinued in Olympic competition – the 60-meter dash and 200-meter hurdles – but his record remains intact. Jesse Owens and Carl Lewis each won four gold medals in a single Olympics, but both ran on winning relay teams.

ADCOCK LOSES COOL, CHASES GOMEZ INTO DUGOUT

JULY 17, 1956

Joe Adcock had been known to chase a pitch in his time, but this was something new. Now he was chasing a pitcher.

Hotfooting it for the New York Giants' dugout was 6-foot, 170-pound right-hander Ruben Gomez in what might be called a fifties version of flight for life. On his heels and making up ground was the 6-4, 210-pound Adcock. Twice wounded and hopping mad, the slugging first baseman had had a brief conversation with Gomez on his way to first base, and now he was eager to resume it from closer quarters.

The discussion started in the second inning of a game the Milwaukee Braves were winning, 2-0, when Gomez hit Adcock on the right wrist with his first pitch. After an exchange of unkind words, Adcock charged the mound while Gomez was still holding the ball. So the Giants' pitcher decided to throw at him again. This time he cut loose from a distance of 20 feet and nailed Adcock on the left thigh, leaving a large bruise.

When that didn't stop the onrushing Louisianan, Gomez wisely decided to put safety first and flee to his dugout. All of Adcock's teammates flooded out of the opposite dugout and followed him across the field where they were met by the entire Giants roster. The result was gridlock on the third-base line at County Stadium and sheer delight from a crowd of 33,239 fight fans.

Umpires, ushers and local police rushed to the scene to restore order before anybody could really get hurt. And nobody did, although the cops decided later to escort Gomez to his hotel for his own safety.

This confrontation may have been inevitable given the two players' tendencies. Gomez tended to hit people with baseballs, and Adcock tended to get hit. The Giants' pitcher had plunked Brooklyn's Carl Furillo in 1953, and the National League batting champion broke his hand in the ensuing melee. A year after the incident with Adcock, Gomez would engage in a bean-ball war with St. Louis Cardinals pitcher Sam Jones, and he'd hit Frank Robinson in the head, putting the Cincinnati star in the hospital.

Adcock, meanwhile, had been nailed previously in the head, hand and forearm, and Gomez's pitch came uncomfortably close to the spot that had been hit the previous year resulting in a fracture. Adcock also entered the evening having whacked seven home runs in his last nine games, making him a prime target for any pitcher.

Gomez's teammates appeared to be generally disappointed with his hasty retreat from the mound. Two of them described his actions as "disgraceful." But Gomez didn't seem to care. "Why should I stay there and get killed?" he asked reasonably. "He is much bigger and stronger than I am. A lot of brave guys get killed. Why fight a guy who's bigger than you? It's better to run."

Adcock seemed to understand that he'd been spared a manslaughter charge. "He called me a name, and I chased him," he explained. "I was never so mad in my life. It's a good thing I didn't catch him."

Good for him and good for the Braves. As it was, Gomez and Adcock were both ejected from the game and the Giants wound up winning, 8-6, in 11 innings. But two nights later, Adcock hit a grand slam and a three-run shot in addition to a single and a double to beat the Giants, 13-3, and keep his hot streak very much alive. He would finish the season with 38 home runs.

He was fined $100, however, for his encounter with Gomez. Gomez was fined $250 and suspended for three games.

JIM CARTER DEFIES NFL PLAYERS' STRIKE

JULY 18, 1974

We're all taught to be careful crossing the street, and maybe the lesson just didn't take with Jim Carter. Never a fan favorite, the Pro Bowl linebacker risked a major rift with his teammates as well when he strolled into a practice session in the middle of a strike.

To get there Carter had to cross not only Oneida Street but a picket line of Green Bay Packers bent on changing the National Football League's labor rules. He could have made the trip easier by taking a bus, but that wasn't his style.

"What's the big deal?" he asked. "I've always walked to practice. I've walked to practice for four years. It wasn't for a stage play."

Maybe not, but Carter and reserve linebacker Larry Hefner created plenty of drama by breaking ranks with the other veterans in one of the first significant job actions in any pro sport. A week later, 14 of their fellow players would be arrested.

Organized under the banner "No freedom, no football," NFL players went on strike on July 1 demanding the repeal of the so-called "Rozelle Rule" that essentially bound a player to his team even after he'd played out his contract because of the compensation requirements. The players also wanted the waiver system and the college draft eliminated, but the owners weren't interested in changing anything.

And so when training camp opened for Packer veterans on July 12, they, as well as players from all over the league, walked picket lines instead of working out. In an effort to avoid ugly confrontations, the Green Bay management decided to transport the rookies and free agents who were practicing from the locker room to the playing field in buses. But when Carter and Hefner decided to break ranks with their fellow veterans and report to camp six days later, they declined to take the easy way out.

Carter said his philosophy was basically anti-union in general, while Hefner's explanation was simpler. "The longer I stayed out, the more chance somebody had of getting my job," he said.

Carter didn't have to worry about that. He'd been good enough to be named to the Pro Bowl the season before, although many Packer fans were still having trouble accepting him as Ray Nitschke's replacement at middle linebacker. Nitschke's popularity combined with Carter's outspoken manner and some off-field controversy got him booed more than once at home games.

Now his teammates were joining the chorus. "I don't see how Carter can be a captain and team leader when he dumps the whole bunch of us," said guard Gale Gillingham. Carter was the Packers' defensive captain, and Gillingham was the offensive captain at the time.

The differences would get more heated shortly after that. On the day that Carter and Hefner crossed the picket line, the Packers announced that they would hold a practice game at Lambeau Field against the Chicago Bears' rookies and free agents on July 25. A crowd of 36,210 showed up at the game, and so did the picket line.

This one was manned by 14 Packers and six other NFL players. All 20 of them were arrested for trespassing, creating a weird scene in the stadium parking lot. With Packer center Ken Bowman, a licensed attorney, quoting labor law from the back of a pickup truck, the players were politely taken away by local police and sheriff's deputies. Executive committee member and team attorney Fred Trowbridge had gotten a restraining order, and when the players wouldn't leave they were booked.

Packers President Dominic Olejniczak and coach Dan Devine both insisted that they didn't know anything about the order. Devine also said the conflict would have no effect on team unity. "I'm certain of that," he said. The Packers would finish the 1974 season in wild disarray with a 6-8 record; and Devine, on the verge of being fired, would announce that he was leaving to go to Notre Dame.

But it was the strikers' unity that dissolved first. Kicker Chester Marcol, quarterback Jerry Tagge and safety Al Matthews were among a handful of Packer veterans who later joined Carter on the practice field. The strike basically collapsed when the players union agreed to a two week "cooling off period" and the players went back to work on Aug. 14.

The union achieved many of its goals in court two years later in the John Mackey decision. Carter enjoyed a solid eight-year career in Green Bay.

WISCONSIN CANCELS LSU GAMES OVER RACE LAW

JULY 19, 1956

Politics and sports, never an ideal combination, got downright ugly when Louisiana passed a law banning interracial athletic contests. The University of Wisconsin responded by sending the Bayou State an important message while calling off a heck of a football game.

Both schools were excited when Wisconsin and Louisiana State signed a contract to play each other in football in 1957 and '58. The Badgers hadn't faced a Southeastern Conference team in 28 years, and the Tigers hadn't played a Big Ten opponent in 32. Now they had a home-and-home series scheduled to start in Madison in 1957.

But everything changed when the University of Pittsburgh came to New Orleans in January 1956 to face Georgia Tech in the Sugar Bowl. Georgia Tech won the game, 7-0, but state legislators were outraged when Pitt used a black fullback, Bobby Grier. A flurry of segregationist bills ensued, capped by a measure in early July outlawing "social events and athletic contests involving both Negroes and whites."

It passed both houses of the state legislature unanimously over the objections of Sugar Bowl officials, the LSU board of supervisors, the Tigers' coaches and most of the players. Governor Earl Long, younger brother of Huey Long, signed it, and the man who sponsored it predicted that future opponents would take the money and run. "They'll put first things first by accepting cash profits for playing LSU or competing in the Sugar Bowl," said Rep. H. Lawrence Gibbs, according to an article written by Richard Carlton Haney that appeared in a 2008 issue of Wisconsin Magazine of History. "This will be a strong inducement for leaving their colored players at home."

Wrong again.

When UW Athletic Director Ivy Williamson got the news, he said immediately that the 1958 game in Baton Rouge would definitely fall through, although he didn't know about the 1957 contest in Madison. He didn't have to wait long to find out. The UW faculty athletic board met quickly and issued a statement saying the contract for both games was canceled because the Louisiana law would deny Wisconsin "the privilege of selecting the members of its team without regard to race or color."

There were fewer than a dozen black players on the Badgers' roster at the time, but one would have been enough. The Badgers had a history in race relations dating back to 1900 when two blacks played on their baseball team. Four years later, UW hurdler George Poage became the first black runner to win an Olympic medal.

If Wisconsin wasn't interested in letting Louisiana's legislature dictate who could play on its teams, neither were several other northern schools. Marquette, Notre Dame, Dayton and St. Louis all canceled games with Louisiana opponents that year.

The Badgers had no trouble replacing LSU on their schedule with West Virginia in 1957 and Miami (Fla.) in '58, and they won both games easily. They were led appropriately enough by a black halfback named Danny Lewis against West Virginia and a black quarterback named Sidney Williams against Miami. But their success didn't stop anyone from speculating wistfully about what might have been.

Most people agreed that Wisconsin would have beaten the Tigers at Camp Randall without much trouble. They finished 6-3 in 1957, tying for 14th in the final AP poll, while LSU was 5-5 playing a much weaker schedule. But 1958 was a different story.

LSU went undefeated that year, beat Clemson in the Sugar Bowl and wound up the season ranked No. 1 in the country. Wisconsin had a 7-1-1 record and finished with a No. 7 Associated Press rating. No one will ever know if the Badgers would have spoiled LSU's season if they'd played in Baton Rouge, but Wisconsin coach Milt Bruhn insisted his team would have won that game.

In 1959 the United States Supreme Court ruled that the Louisiana law was unconstitutional, and the whole country won.

AARON HITS NO. 755

JULY 20, 1976

History was the last thing on Dick Drago's mind when he faced Henry Aaron in a meaningless mid-summer American League game at County Stadium. The California Angels' reliever had just given up a home run to George Scott, and he was already thinking too much.

Drago had replaced starter Gary Ross in the fourth inning, and he had struck out Aaron in the fifth on fastballs. Now it was the seventh, and Drago decided to try to cross him up and slip a slider past him on the first pitch. He hung it, and when the ball landed in the left-field bleachers just inside the foul pole, Drago knew he'd made a big mistake. It would be a couple of months before he learned how big.

Nobody could have known that Aaron's 755th career home run would be his last one. If anyone had, a lot more people would have been there to watch. As it was, a meager gathering of 10,134 came to witness one of baseball's truly monumental records being set very, very quietly.

The last-place Brewers of the AL East still had 77 games to play when they took on the last-place California Angels of the AL West. Drago rarely gave up home runs. In fact, he surrendered only seven that season in 79 innings, but the one he yielded to Aaron stayed on the books for 31 years before Barry Bonds displaced the Milwaukee slugger as baseball's all-time home run king in 2007.

Sore-kneed and 42 years old, Aaron had only 65 more at bats before retiring at the end of the 1976 season with a .229 batting average, 35 RBIs and 10 homers. He never hit another ball over the fence, but he still commanded plenty of respect when Drago faced him.

"The thing about hitters, the last thing to go is their bat speed," the pitcher recalled years later. "Their legs go, their arms go, but they can still swing the bat... I remember being upset because I had gotten him out with fastballs. I was a fastball pitcher, and I outthought myself."

Drago's loss was Jerry Augustine's gain. The Brewers' left-hander had been struggling all season, and he got credit for the 6-2 victory. But the biggest winner that night was a part-time groundskeeper named Richard Arndt. Arndt was the man who got the ball.

He got to it just ahead of a whole pack of people. What happened next is a matter of opinion.

In his 1991 autobiography *I Had a Hammer*, Aaron said Arndt simply refused to sell him the ball. "The Brewers fired him over it, but he still wouldn't give me the ball," Aaron wrote. "Every few years, I call him and try to buy it from him – I've offered him as much as $10,000 – but he won't part with it."

Arndt told a different story. He told the *Los Angeles Times* in 2007 that when he was summoned to the clubhouse after the game, all he hoped to do was hand the ball back to Aaron personally. But an equipment manager told him Aaron was busy packing for a road trip and didn't have time to meet with him. Arndt said he turned down an offer of a bat, an autographed ball and a picture of Aaron, and the next day he was fired, and his final paycheck was docked $5 to cover the cost of the ball.

Arndt moved to Albuquerque a few months later and put the ball in a safety deposit box where it stayed until he brought it to a card show in Phoenix in 1994 where Aaron signed it without knowing what it was. In the end, Arndt sold the ball to a Connecticut collector for $650,000 and donated $155,800 of the proceeds to Aaron's Chasing the Dream Foundation, an Atlanta charity for underprivileged kids.

Aaron played his final home game in Milwaukee on Oct. 3. He went one for three in a 5-2 loss to the Detroit Tigers. And, again, there weren't many people there. The attendance was 6,858. However, 16 days earlier, the Brewers had held "A Salute to Hank Aaron Night," and 40,383 fans had showed up at County Stadium to give him a more appropriate farewell party.

MAJOR LEAGUE BASEBALL CAREER HOME RUN LEADERS

Rank	Name	No.
1	Barry Bonds	762
2	Henry Aaron	755
3	Babe Ruth	714
4	Willie Mays	660
5	Ken Griffey	630

Source: mlb.com

BILL HALL IGNITES BREWERS' SWEEP

JULY 21, 2008

It couldn't get any better than this for Bill Hall. The Milwaukee Brewers' third baseman had gone on a tear in the middle of the summer, and he was taking his team with him.

On July 21, in the first game of a pivotal series in St. Louis, he drove a Ryan Franklin slider into the left center-field bleachers in the tenth inning, giving the Brewers a 4-3 lead in what would be a 6-3 victory and starting them on their way to a four-game sweep. It was Hall's 16th hit in 38 at bats since July 4, a .421 average that was a persuasive argument for keeping him in the lineup every day.

Manager Ned Yost had been platooning Hall at third base, but Hall would further strengthen his case for full-time employment the next night with another game-winning home run in the ninth inning. After completing its first sweep ever in St. Louis, Milwaukee was three games up on the Cardinals in the wild-card race and just a game behind first-place Chicago in the National League Central.

And by winning seven in a row away from home and eight straight overall, the Brewers completed the most successful road trip in the history of the franchise.

Hall's solo home run in the second game in St. Louis was his 14th of the year, and it wrapped up a 4-3 victory. Like the one the night before, it came off a right-handed pitcher. Manager Ned Yost had been alternating Hall with Russell Branyan at third because he'd been struggling against right-handers, but Hall was making Yost's strategy look bad. Not bad enough, though, for Yost to say Hall was his everyday third baseman.

Meanwhile, there were other heroes as the Brewers completed the sweep. In the third game, CC Sabathia threw his third straight complete game, carrying a no-hitter into the sixth inning, as the Brewers won, 3-0. Home runs by J.J. Hardy and Ryan Braun backed Sabathia, who improved his record to 4-0 since coming to Milwaukee in a trade with Cleveland. And then it was all Braun as Milwaukee won the finale, 4-3. His two-run home run in the ninth inning decided the outcome on a night when he also had three singles and a walk.

And so the Brewers headed home having won three of the four games with the Cardinals in their last at bat and boosting their road record to 28-26. That was a considerable improvement for a team that had gone 32-49 in other peoples' parks the year before.

Still, they were looking forward to getting home where the fans were making them feel welcome by buying every ticket in sight. Crowds of 40,000-plus were expected for all three games of a series with Houston, while a four-game set with the Cubs had been sold out for months.

The home stand proved to be a terrific commercial success and a competitive disaster. Milwaukee dropped two out of three to the Astros and then suffered a gruesome four-game sweep at the hands of the Cubs when they were outscored, 31-11. That effectively ended the pennant race in the NL Central, but not the wild-card chase. The Brewers righted themselves with an eight-game winning streak in August and wound up edging out the New York Mets by a game for the wild card.

The Cardinals, meanwhile, faded out of sight, but an argument could be made that they'd launched the Brewers into the playoffs for the first time since 1982. They did not, however, have the same effect on Hall.

Yost proved to be right about reserving judgment on his third baseman. Hall would hit only one home run the rest of the year, and he'd finish the season batting .225, including .174 against righties. Things really couldn't have gotten any better for the five-year veteran than they were at St. Louis that week. And they didn't. A year later, the Brewers designated Hall for assignment with $10.5 million remaining on his contract and he was traded to Seattle for a minor league pitcher.

MANAGERS GARNER, BEVINGTON MIX IT UP

JULY 22, 1995

Milwaukee Brewers Manager Phil Garner earned the nickname "Scrap Iron" in his playing days, and it wasn't because he was made from recycled parts. Chicago White Sox Manager Terry Bevington acquired a reputation for a quick temper in his days as a minor league manager in the Brewers' system. Thus, it was only natural that there was "a certain tension in the air" when the two clubs met on the same field.

That was Garner's description of the rivalry between the Brewers and White Sox, and he would offer many more comments on the subject over the years. But he was as much a man of action as he was of words, a fact that surfaced on a Saturday night at Chicago's Comiskey Park.

The White Sox were enjoying a 3-2 lead in the bottom of the seventh inning of a relatively tame game when their shortstop, Ozzie Guillen, stole third base. The play wasn't even close, but when third baseman Jeff Cirillo tried to tag Guillen, he fell back into him. Guillen took exception and shoved Cirillo twice. It wasn't much of a skirmish, and the fire had died down when Garner and Bevington arrived on the scene carrying kerosene.

"I did not want to fight Cirillo, and he did not want to fight me," Guillen said later. "We had no reason to fight. He was going back to his position and me to third base. Then I saw all these guys coming out."

Among those guys were Bevington and Garner. Both managers claimed later that they were there to protect their players, but as the dugouts emptied they wound up protecting themselves. Words were exchanged, and Bevington grabbed Garner in a headlock. Garner broke free, and a bad Worldwide Wrestling Federation bout ensued. The Brewers' manager gave away a little size, but he held his own. Bevington was 6-foot-2 and on the plus side of his 190-pound playing weight. Garner was 5-10, 175. He suffered a small cut on his right cheekbone that he explained away by saying, "I cut myself shaving."

When the umpiring crew finally succeeded in separating the "peacekeepers," they were banished from the game, which was not exactly a new experience for either of them. It was Bevington's third ejection of the season and the fourth for Garner.

Three weeks earlier, the players had swarmed the field at County Stadium when White Sox reliever Rob Dibble was subsequently suspended for throwing at the Brewers' Pat Listach. The Brewers lost that game, 17-13, and they lost this one, 4-2.

The traditional major league manager's role in a baseball fight is to restrain his players, and so the league took a dim view when it was the managers who had to be restrained. Predictably, Garner and Bevington were hit with four-game suspensions. Garner accepted his suspension, but Bevington appealed his. Then he changed his mind. About the appeal, not about Garner.

Speaking of the melee, the White Sox skipper said, "Phil Garner caused it. That's the facts... I know the man doesn't like me. I am aware of that. I am well aware of his feeling toward me. I don't care what he says in the paper. He can try and publicly make himself look good."

If Garner was trying to look good, it didn't work. He just looked like his normal combative self. Two years earlier, he'd been suspended for three games for participating in a brawl with the Oakland A's at County Stadium. But that was just Oakland. That same year, he'd challenged White Sox broadcasters Tom Paciorek and Ken "Hawk" Harrelson to a fight when they accused Milwaukee pitchers of throwing at Chicago batters and suggested it was time to retaliate. There was just something special about the White Sox.

Garner denied, however, that he harbored any bad feelings toward Bevington. He said he didn't have any feelings at all about the Chicago manager. "I don't even know Terry Bevington," he said. "He's just got the wrong uniform on."

After two more seasons, Bevington didn't have the uniform anymore. The White Sox fired him. At the same time, the Brewers moved to the National League and began playing Chicago's other team on a regular basis. But their feelings were never the same against the Cubs. Or maybe they just weren't as feisty without "Scrap Iron" in charge.

ASHE WINS U.S. CLAY COURT TITLE IN FOX POINT

JULY 23, 1967

Local tennis fans got some happy news when a busy Army lieutenant told the United States Clay Court tournament committee that he would be coming to Milwaukee. Suddenly a good week of tennis was shaping up to be the greatest week the sport had ever seen in Wisconsin.

For three years in the late sixties, Milwaukee was a mecca for amateur tennis. Next to the U.S. Open at Forest Hills, the 57-year old Clay Court tournament was the most prestigious in the nation at the time, and the Town Club in Fox Point hosted it from 1966 to '68.

What made the 1967 edition special was the addition of Arthur Ashe, the top-ranked amateur in the country and an African-American pioneer on his way to becoming one of sport's most influential figures. Army commitments had severely limited the 24-year-old Virginian's tournament schedule, and he didn't know until three days before the Clay Court was scheduled to start that he would be able to go. He figured to be rusty, but he was immediately seeded No. 1.

Second-seeded Cliff Richey was expected to give Ashe his toughest match as he and his older sister Nancy Richey came back to defend the men's and women's titles they'd won the year before. But that showdown never happened because Cliff Richey lost in the quarterfinals to Mike Belkin and went straight home.

Instead, Ashe disposed of two lesser known players, John Cooper and Ronald Barnes, en route to the championship match where he met former Northwestern star Marty Riessen.

The fourth-seeded Riessen started fast, breaking Ashe's service three times in the process of winning the first set, 6-4. But then Riessen wilted in the 90-degree heat and Ashe's ground strokes began taking their toll. Ashe won the second set, 6-3; romped through the third, 6-1; and then outlasted Riessen in the fourth, 7-5.

Meanwhile, Nancy Richey crushed 18-year-old Rosemary Casals, 6-2, 6-3, to claim a record fifth straight championship. Casals had upset top-seeded Billie Jean King, who had recently won the women's title at Wimbledon, in the semifinals.

A capacity crowd of 3,500 watched the final matches, bringing the attendance for the week to an estimated 20,000 people.

Ashe's victory was his first in the national Clay Court tournament, and it helped launch him on a career that would include 33 professional singles championships. Still playing as an amateur the following season in the first year of open tennis, where pros and amateurs competed against each other, Ashe won both the U.S. Amateur and the U.S. Open, something no one else has ever done in the same year.

He would later become the only black male to win a singles championship in a Grand Slam event. In fact, he won three of them, the U.S. Open, the Australian Open and finally Wimbledon in 1975 when he beat 10-1 favorite Jimmy Connors in four sets. Ashe's career ended in 1979 when he suffered a heart attack.

Ashe was every bit as active off the court as he was on. He was one of the founders of the ATP World Tour and a prominent spokesman on behalf of his sport. A longtime opponent of apartheid, he was the first black player to win a championship in the South African Open. And he was a leading figure in the Safe Passage Foundation devoted to helping needy kids, but he may have been best known for his work in the fight against AIDS.

Ashe contacted the disease through a blood transfusion in 1988, and five years later, he died at the age of 49.

OVERFLOW CROWD SEES BASEBALL RETURN TO MILWAUKEE

JULY 24, 1967

What should have been a routine out turned into something much more painful when Minnesota left-fielder Bob Allison went back to flag down a fly ball in a much ballyhooed exhibition game at Milwaukee County Stadium. The problem was there were 1,500 people and a rope standing between him and the warning track.

Allison tumbled over the rope and into the people, accidentally spiking a young fan in the leg. The boy was taken to the Twins' clubhouse where he was given an autographed ball and dispatched to a hospital for stitches. The play resulted in a ground-rule double and a bit of symbolism. If there was any doubt that Milwaukee was still head over heels in love with baseball, this should have been all the evidence anyone needed.

Allison was at County Stadium on a Monday night playing against the Chicago White Sox because the city was determined to prove that it was still big league. The people were standing on the warning track because there was nowhere else to put them.

When a group of businessmen calling themselves Milwaukee Brewers Inc., persuaded Major League Baseball to hold the first exhibition game ever between two teams from the same league smack in the middle of a pennant race, they were hoping to fill the place. They had no idea they'd overflow it. A total of 51,144 people, the biggest baseball crowd in Milwaukee history, paid their way in, and another 5,000 were turned away. The management made the stadium bigger and the field smaller by putting 1,500 fans behind ropes on the warning track, and letting others stand behind the last row of the lower grandstand.

This was much more than just a festive occasion. This was a city-wide rally held in perfect 80-degree weather. The first pitch had to be postponed for a half-hour because baseball Commissioner William Eckert and American League President Joe Cronin got caught in traffic. The game could have started without them, except that Eckert was throwing out the first pitch.

A fireworks display was scheduled for after the game, and a pig race broke out during it. At least the small animal that was thrown onto the field in the eighth inning and chased by a gleeful group of young boys looked like a pig. Other accounts said it was a dog. The way the beer was flowing that night, it was hard to tell.

The county let the teams use the stadium for free, and the Twins and the White Sox split the take with the Brewers organization. To say a good time was had by all would be a huge understatement, but that wasn't the point. Milwaukee was telling Major League Baseball what a terrible mistake the Braves had made leaving town, and a new team should be found to replace them as soon as possible. The message was received in several quarters.

"It leaves you kind of speechless," said White Sox owner Arthur Allyn as he surveyed the crowd.

"This is fantastic," said Twins owner Calvin Griffin. "They're crying for baseball here. If some clubs were smart, they'd consider moving here."

Unfortunately, the opinion that counted was Eckert's, and he was noncommittal. The only team going anywhere was Charlie Finley's Kansas City Athletics. There were rumors of Finley being interested in Milwaukee, but the smart money was on Oakland. There was also talk of expansion, but the Vietnam War was already diluting baseball's talent pool without adding franchises.

Speaking of expansion, the commissioner said, "To the best of my ability, I'm going to see that all these fine cities have fair and equitable treatment. There are several cities interested. Milwaukee certainly would be treated the same as other cities."

At least if Eckert wasn't impressed, Allyn was. While Milwaukee would have to wait three more years to get its own franchise, he took his White Sox to County Stadium to play a number of home games over the next two seasons.

Allyn didn't seem to mind that his team lost the exhibition, 2-1, and the fans barely noticed. They'd made their point.

MONTGOMERY TOPPLES BARRIER IN 100-FREE

JULY 25, 1976

It was hard to tell the American men from the East German women at the Olympic swimming competition in the 1976 Games at Montreal. Both teams were winning everything in sight. The difference was the Germans' muscles were bigger.

No one had ever seen a group of women athletes look quite so buff. The only thing more mysterious than the definition of their bodies was the consistency of their success. East Germany had never won an Olympic gold medal in women's swimming before, and now it was on its way to taking home all but two of the 13 available.

The American men, on the other hand, had been dominating the pool for years, and they were simply doing what they always did. They would win 12 of 13 events, but the East German women were attracting the most attention. At least, they were until Jim Montgomery shattered the sport's biggest barrier in the 100-meter freestyle.

Montgomery, a 21-year-old Madison native, started swimming when he was two years old, and he started racing in the Madison Country Club League when he was seven. He graduated from Madison East High School with six state championships and went on to Indiana University where he won seven NCAA titles. But it was overseas that Montgomery really made waves. At his first World Championships in Belgrade in 1973, he claimed a record five gold medals.

He held the world mark in the 100-meter freestyle when he arrived at Montreal, and so it came as no great surprise when he won the gold in swimming's glamour event. It's how he won it that grabbed everyone's attention.

Montgomery had already captured bronze in the 200 freestyle and gold in both the 800 freestyle relay and 400-meter medley relay when the 100 semifinals came around. After his anchor leg helped the 800 team shave a full seven seconds off the world mark, anything seemed possible for him. And when Montgomery broke his own world record by finishing the 100-meter semifinal in 50.39 seconds, one of the sport's most enduring milestones was within reach.

The 50-second mark in the 100 free was swimming's version of the four-minute mile. Because the race is so short, it's totally unforgiving. The start and the turn are crucial, and Montgomery was flawless in both in the final. He covered the first 50 meters in an unheard of 24.14 seconds, and then it was just a matter of holding off fellow American Jack Babashoff. He did that by 1.5 meters, finishing in 49.99 seconds.

When the race was over, Montgomery said he was more excited about the gold medal than the record. "When people ask me about the Olympics, I don't say I swam a 49.99. I say I won a gold medal," he said. "It's the gold that counts."

That point was driven home when Jonty Skinner, who wasn't allowed to compete in the Olympics because he was from South Africa, broke Montgomery's record three weeks later with a time of 49.44

Meanwhile, as Montgomery was celebrating his victory in Montreal, the American women were a frustrated lot. With the final competition scheduled for that same Sunday, the East Germans had won all but one gold, and the Soviets had taken that one. The Americans had one last chance in the 400 freestyle relay, and with the help of a Wisconsin swimmer named Wendy Boglioli they used it to end their drought.

Boglioli, the former Wendy Lansbach, had done most of her early training in a cramped hotel pool while growing up in Land O' Lakes in northern Wisconsin. Now she was in a full-sized Olympic venue, and she made the most of it by swimming the second leg on the victorious relay team. The gold medal salvaged a small measure of pride for the American women, and they would gain a much larger one when it was proved later that the East German authorities had given their swimmers performance enhancing drugs without even telling them. The mystery of the muscular German women was solved.

PACKERS TRADE QUARTERBACK TOBIN ROTE TO LIONS

JULY 26, 1957

The question was whether the Green Bay Packers had too many quarterbacks or just one quarterback making too much money. In either case, there seemed to be only one solution: Trade Tobin Rote.

Coach Lisle Blackbourn had four quarterbacks and a severe shortage of offensive linemen. Both Bob Skoronski and Forrest Gregg, two promising rookies the year before, had gone into military service; and John Sandusky, another tackle, had retired to go into coaching. On the other hand, Blackbourn had two veterans and two kids standing in line waiting for time at quarterback.

He made it sound like a simple choice in the press when he packaged Rote and defensive back Val Joe Walker and sent them to Detroit for tackles Ollie Spencer and Norm Masters, guard Jim Salsbury, and halfback Don McIlhenney in one of the all-time blockbuster trades in Packers' history.

But Rote wasn't buying the explanation. He learned about the trade when he walked into the Packers' offices after taking a three-day drive from his Texas home to Wisconsin for the start of training camp. He said he was shocked, and if the Packers had sent him anywhere but Detroit he said he would have turned around and driven home again. He learned something else, too.

He said years later that Blackbourn told him the Packers' board of directors had forced the trade because they couldn't live with the huge contract Rote had just signed. It called for him to make $25,000.

Those were hard times for the Packers, who were getting ready to play their first season in their new City Stadium after moving out of a creaky, 25,000-seat high school stadium. Otherwise, Rote certainly seemed to be worth the money.

He'd been the Packers' starter for seven years, and in that time he'd become the franchise's all-time leading passer. He'd also led the league with 18 touchdown passes the previous year. But the Packers hadn't had a single winning season under Rote, and they'd just traded with Cleveland to regain the rights to Vito "Babe" Parilli, the Packers' No 1 draft pick in 1952 who had shared duties with Rote in the '52 and '53 seasons. The Packers also had used the bonus pick or the No. 1 choice in the 1957 draft to select Notre Dame star Paul Hornung. Although Hornung had played quarterback for the Irish, the Packers were still debating whether they were going to play him there or at halfback.

But most importantly, Blackbourn had young Bart Starr, who seemed ready to take over the starting job. "He's the man," said Blackbourn, who may have recognized Starr's potential well before anyone else did.

In turn, while Spencer, Masters and Salsbury may have sounded like a law firm to some people, they sounded like the foundation of a new offensive line to Blackbourn.

At first, Spencer balked at the idea of playing for Green Bay. Considered to be the key to the deal for the Packers, the three-year veteran announced after the trade that he was retiring from football and staying in Detroit where he had an insurance business. That was ironic, because Walker was saying pretty much the same thing from the other side. The Packers' defensive back had already indicated before the deal that he would rather stay home than report to training camp. Home was Texas and an insurance business.

Had Spencer not changed his mind, the Lions would have had to supply a different player, but the rest of the deal would have stood. Had Walker made good on his threat, the Packers would have had to surrender a future draft choice to Detroit. But both players changed their minds, and the trade was valid. As it turned out, the Lions had better reason to be happy about that than the Packers did.

They already had future Hall of Fame quarterback Bobby Layne, but Rote shared time with him for most of the 1957 season. Then after Layne broke his leg late in the year, Rote took over fulltime and led the Lions to their last NFL championship. In the title game, Rote completed 12 of 19 passes for 280 yards and three touchdowns as the Lions routed the Cleveland Browns, 59-14.

McIlhenney led the Packers in rushing, but with only 384 yards and he was gone by 1960. Masters was a serviceable lineman for eight years, even alternating with Skoronski at left tackle early in the Lombardi Era, but Spencer and Salsbury each lasted for just two seasons. As for Starr, he turned out to be pretty good, but it took him four years to become the full-time starter.

And Blackbourn was fired following the 1957 season.

HARRISON WINS OLYMPIC TRIPLE JUMP

JULY 27, 1996

Reporters called them the "his and her" gold medals, and both athletes had gone through a lot of grief to earn them. The difference was she was willing to talk about hers.

Minutes after his girlfriend, Gail Devers, had won the 100-meter dash at the Atlantic Olympics, Milwaukee native Kenny Harrison was doing a back-flip to celebrate his own victory in the triple jump. He certainly seemed happy after becoming the first Wisconsin native to win an individual Olympic gold medal in men's track and field in 92 years. But then he declined to attend the mandatory press conference for medal winners.

Following the U.S. Olympic Trials six weeks earlier, Harrison had stormed out of the post-event press conference without saying a word. When a media member stopped him in a hallway, he barked, "I don't got nothing to say."

That left Devers to talk for both of them at the Olympics. "He's had a lot of struggles," she said. "If anyone deserves to win a gold medal in his first Olympics, it's Kenny Harrison."

Devers had done some struggling of her own while overcoming Graves' disease, a thyroid condition that had almost caused doctors to amputate both of her legs. Harrison's continuing problems with back and knee injuries seemed mild by comparison, but they had turned him from a world champion into an Olympic non-qualifier four years earlier.

A two-time state title winner at Brookfield Central High School, Harrison would hold the state triple jump record for 22 years. After leaving high school he won the NCAA outdoor title in the triple jump for Kansas State in 1986, and then he won a gold medal in the 1991 World Championships in Tokyo. But he had battled injuries from the time he was a teenager, missing all but one meet in his sophomore year in high school, and he was far from healthy when he entered the 1992 U.S. Olympic Trials in New Orleans. He finished sixth and off the team, but strangely, he'd taken defeat much better in 1992 than he did victory in Atlanta in 1996.

A story in *The Milwaukee Journal* said, "Harrison, a friendly outgoing person who is well liked by virtually everyone on the international track circuit, earned more respect by accepting his disappointment graciously." Shortly after that, Harrison was neither friendly nor outgoing to reporters. In fact, he barely talked to them at all, and he never explained why.

But media relations were the least of his problems when he came to Atlanta. He had Great Britain's Jonathan Edwards to contend with. The only 60-foot triple jumper in history, Edwards not only held the world record, but he hadn't lost since 1994.

Harrison gave his rival fair warning on the day before the Olympic final by qualifying with a single 57 feet 8½ inch effort, which was more than 15 inches better than anyone else in the field. And then he got serious on Saturday. He soared 59-¼ on his first attempt, eclipsing the Olympic record. Then he topped that on his fourth try by going 59-4¼. Edwards could do no better than 58-8 and the silver medal.

"I knew Kenny was going to jump a long way," Edwards said. "I wasn't surprised."

If Harrison was, he didn't tell anybody. But his performance came as quite a shock back home. Milwaukee's Arlie Schardt had been the last Wisconsin male to win an Olympic gold in track and that was in 1920, but he'd done it in a 3,000-meter team race. The last individual winner from the Badger State had been Dodgeville's Archie Hahn, who'd swept the 60-, 100- and 200-meter dashes in 1904. Milwaukeean Ken Wiesner won a silver in the high jump in 1952, and he was the last man to take a Summer Olympics medal of any color back to Wisconsin.

All of which made Harrison's accomplishment that much more impressive and his silence that much more puzzling. Much later, he said he just wanted "to go home and share the moment with Gail."

ALVAREZ STEPS DOWN AS COACH

JULY 28, 2005

Barry Alvarez always was pretty good at managing the clock. He'd set a goal of becoming a head coach by his 42nd birthday and missed by just three days, and now 15 years later, he figured he knew exactly when to walk away.

"This is my personal timeline," he said in announcing that he would coach one more season and then become the University of Wisconsin's full-time athletic director. "One of my close friends told me, 'You'll know when it's the right time.' I believe it's the right time."

Alvarez struggled with his emotions during the Thursday morning press conference at the Kohl Center, and it would have been all right if he'd let himself cry. Plenty of people laughed after he'd told his introductory media session on Jan. 2, 1990, "People need to be patient. They have to understand this is not going to turn overnight. (But) they better get their season tickets now because before too long they probably won't be able to."

More than five million tickets later, everyone understood what he meant. The Badgers had drawn at least 70,000 customers to every one of their last 75 home games. In Don Morton's final game as head coach before Alvarez replaced him, they'd gotten 29,776 for Michigan State.

Clearly, Athletic Director Pat Richter had hired the right man in 1990, and Alvarez was confident that he was doing the same in 2005 when he announced that defensive coordinator Bret Bielema would be the Badgers' next head coach and would take over at the end of that season. Alvarez and Bielema had some things in common. Both had grown up in small towns, both had been longtime assistants at Iowa, both were defensive coordinators, and neither had ever been a college head coach before.

Bielema would be 36 when he took over, but speaking from personal experience, Alvarez wasn't worried about that. "I don't think age has been a factor in any job I've received to this point," he said. "I feel truly fortunate to have a coach on my staff that will continue the level of success that we've enjoyed."

It was a nice compliment and a stiff challenge all at the same time. Barry Alvarez was one very tough act to follow.

There was a single telephone in the football offices and a $2.1 million debt on the athletic department books when Richter became AD and hired Alvarez three weeks later. Don Nehlen was widely believed to be the No. 1 candidate to replace Morton, but Richter never interviewed the West Virginia coach in person. When Nehlen told Richter over the phone that he had some doubts about making the move, Alvarez zoomed to the top of the candidates' list.

Barry Alvarez

Alvarez had a list of his own, and it had only one name on it. He was a highly sought assistant at Notre Dame at the time, and he told Irish coach Lou Holtz that Wisconsin was the only job he was interested in. If he didn't get it, he'd be back in South Bend.

He got it, and there had to be times when he wasn't sure it was such a good idea to have it. The Badgers were 6-27 and had won only three Big Ten games in Morton's three years, and they were even worse in Alvarez's first season when they finished 1-10. But they won their first three games in his second year and finished the season by beating conference rivals Minnesota and Northwestern. Things only got better after that.

When Alvarez completed his 16th and final season at UW, he was the winningest coach in school history with 118 victories, including three Big Ten championships and three Rose Bowl triumphs. He also had 10 straight seasons with a 1,000-yard rusher, eight bowl victories, two Big Ten Coach of the Year awards and a flavor in his name at the Babcock Hall ice cream shop.

A master of timing, Alvarez had wasted very little of it at Wisconsin.

BREWERS SWEEP WILD WEEKEND SET WITH YANKEES

JULY 29, 1979

It was a memorable series for the Milwaukee Brewers and a forgettable one for Thurman Munson. Two bench-clearing fights, a series of ugly incidents involving spectators and a one-for-eight performance at the plate by the New York Yankees' catcher were crammed into a weekend sweep by Milwaukee.

And then four days later, it all seemed so trivial. Four days later, Munson, the first captain of the Yankees since Lou Gehrig and the American League Most Valuable Player three years earlier, died in a fiery plane crash.

The defending world champion Yankees were happy to leave Milwaukee after dropping their third straight against the Brewers on July 29, but then the Yankees were usually happy to leave Milwaukee no matter what. With Sunday's 5-3 victory, the Brewers had won the season series for the second year in a row. But this visit was something special.

"I don't know what it is about Milwaukee," said Reggie Jackson. "I think it's because they drink so much beer here. I'm really afraid to play here."

The Yankees' superstar was being a little dramatic, but it wasn't hard to see his point. He'd been subjected to endless "Reggie sucks!" chants after getting involved in a brawl with pitcher Mike Caldwell in the fourth inning of the Brewers' 6-5 victory on Friday night, and fellow outfielder Lou Piniella had been showered with debris after a fight on Sunday with Jim Gantner.

Also over the course of the weekend, the wife of Milwaukee third baseman Sal Bando had been attacked in the parking lot, a woman spectator had run out onto the diamond and thrown her arms around Brewers third base coach Buck Rodgers, and a portly customer had jumped down onto the field and dropped his pants.

A brush-back war between Caldwell and the Yankees' Ed Figueroa culminated in Jackson flipping his bat toward the mound after popping out in the fourth inning of the Friday night game. When Caldwell picked up the bat and broke it by slamming the handle to the ground, Jackson charged him, and both dugouts emptied. Because Jackson was ejected and Caldwell wasn't, New York Manager Billy Martin played the game under protest. Cecil Cooper's third home run of the night with two out in the ninth decided the outcome.

The following night, the Brewers rapped out a team-tying record seven doubles in a 9-2 triumph that was spoiled by an ugly post-game scene. Sandy Bando was eight months pregnant when she was accosted by a man in the parking lot. He hit her in the face a couple times before she fought him off. Jackson, who had been Sandy Bando's friend since he'd played with her husband in Oakland, called that the worst incident of the weekend. But it wasn't the last.

In the seventh inning of the Sunday finale, Piniella had doubled in Jackson and then gotten caught in a base-running gaffe. He took off for third on a ground ball and with no chance to make it there safely he barreled into Gantner, who was playing third, hoping to knock the ball loose. It was a typical hard baseball play, but Gantner took exception and charged Piniella. Once again the field was filled with battling players. Gantner was ejected.

The Brewers had taken a 5-0 lead in the game, but they had to hold off a ninth-inning rally that was started by Munson's triple. It was his only hit of the series and the last at bat he'd ever have against the Brewers.

When Martin's team left Milwaukee it was 14 games out of first place with 59 to play, and winning pitcher Bill Travers proclaimed, "The Yankees are dead." Four days later, one of them was.

The Yankees played a three-game series with Chicago next, and when that was over Munson used an off-day to take a quick trip home to Canton, Ohio, in his own private jet. He'd bought the plane recently, and he was taking flying lessons. He was practicing landings with his flight instructor when the plane lost both wings and burst into flames on impact.

Ironically, Munson had invited Jackson along on the trip, but Jackson had declined because he'd had a previous engagement in New York. The flight instructor and another passenger tried to pull Munson out of the plane, but the flames forced them to flee. Munson's body was burned beyond recognition. He was 32 years old.

FAMOUS CINCINNATI RED STOCKINGS MAUL MILWAUKEE

JULY 30, 1869

Victory was out of the question for the home team, according to the *Milwaukee Daily Sentinel*, but then that wasn't the point. When the fabulous Cincinnati Red Stockings came to town, nobody expected to beat them. Watching them play was enough.

This was the Reconstruction Era, and baseball was still recruiting cricket players and just starting to gain a foothold in America. Making a living at the game was a radical new idea. And then along came the Wright brothers.

Not those Wright brothers. Harry and George Wright traveled by train, boat and stagecoach, but they were no less pioneers when they led their touring team of pros to Milwaukee to play the local Cream Citys. Other baseball teams had paid some of their players, but this was the first one that admitted to paying all of them. Harry was the manager, George was the shortstop, and both were the sons of an English cricket star, who was not pleased to see them desert his sport. Both were also on their way to the Baseball Hall of Fame, although it hadn't been built yet.

The visitors arrived on an afternoon train the day before the game, were escorted to the Plankinton House hotel and given a reception. They also arrived with a payroll of close to $9,300, a 36-game winning streak and an air of invincibility. "Our boys entered into the contest with their famous antagonists, not in the hope of victory, which was out of the question, but for the purpose of scoring a creditable number," wrote the *Daily Sentinel* the next day.

If the Cream Citys lacked confidence, they lacked pitching more. The Red Stockings won the game, 85-7. Still, an estimated 2,000 people, many of whom came by horse and carriage, had a fine time witnessing the rout.

They were in good company. The Red Stockings would go 57-0 that year, posting a 19-0 record against other pros. Then they'd win some more. They had amassed 81 straight victories – some sources claim it was as many as 130 – when they finally lost an 8-7 game to the Brooklyn Athletics before 10,000 people in New York in June 1870. The Red Stockings may just have been tired by then.

Their 1869 tour took them 11,877 miles, drew an estimated 200,000 people, and when all the salaries and expenses were paid, supposedly netted $1.39, leaving them $1,000 in the red. But then nobody said it would be easy.

The Cincinnati Base-Ball Club was formed in 1866 because the city fathers there thought a first-rate team would bring prestige to their town. The Red Stockings' name was adopted two years later and for the most obvious reason. The players wore high red stockings. The club was founded at a law office, and many of the first players were lawyers. But that changed when the organization made a deal with the local cricket club that allowed the cricket players to try out for the fledgling sport.

Harry Wright was recruited to run the team, and he recruited his brother George to play shortstop for $2,000. George was ostensibly an amateur with the Washington Nationals, but everybody knew better. He claimed his occupation was "clerk," and he listed a city park as his home address.

Harry would sign the best of the best over the next three years, and it all became legal when the national baseball sanctioning organization created a separate classification for pros. He would later be called the "Father of Professional Baseball," a name he earned by popularizing the game from coast to coast with his touring Red Stockings. He was the first to outfit a team in knickers, the first to introduce cooperative team play and the first to use hand signals. He also played in the first game where admission was charged.

The Red Stockings probably should have charged a little more for their games, because they went out of business after the 1870 season when their backers refused to take on any more red ink. That was not a problem for the Wrights. They moved their operation to Boston where Harry proceeded to manage his newly based Red Stockings to four straight pennants in the National Association, which was organized in 1871 and is recognized as the first major league.

The Boston Red Stockings would change their name and eventually evolve into the Milwaukee Braves. Today, they are the Atlanta Braves and the only franchise to have fielded a team in every season of professional baseball.

ADCOCK CRACKS FOUR HOME RUNS

JULY 31, 1954

The record book all but lay in shreds on the visiting clubhouse floor at Ebbets Field, and Joe Adcock had to be thinking maybe size does matter.

A few hours earlier, the Milwaukee Braves' first baseman had been looking for a bat, having broken his own the night before. For no particular reason, he decided to borrow one from reserve catcher Charlie White. When he took White's war club to the plate for the first time, he figured it was at least five ounces heavier than what he was used to. He joked that he could hardly pick it up.

Nine innings, four home runs, one double and seven RBIs later, he didn't want to put it down.

Four different Brooklyn Dodgers pitchers fell victim to Adcock's power surge as he broke two major league records and tied two more. His 18 total bases and 13 extra bases shattered the previous standards while his four home runs and five extra base hits equaled them. Only six big league batters had ever hit four home runs in the same game before, and no one would do it again until Cleveland's Rocky Colavito did it in 1959. The next National League player to hit four would be San Francisco's Willie Mays in a game at County Stadium on April 30, 1961.

Only 14 major leaguers have done it to this day.

Adcock had no idea what had brought this on. He'd never hit more than two home runs in a game before, and he'd never totaled more than 18 in his first four major league seasons. Now he had 19, as many as he had ever hit in the minors. He also had an abiding love for the Dodgers' ballpark. At the end of the night, his average in seven games that season at Ebbets Field was .467 with eight homers and 16 RBIs.

Adcock was particularly partial to the stadium's left center-field stands where he deposited all four of his home runs in his latest outing. The first came on a Don Newcombe fastball in the first inning, and the second on a slider by Erv Palica in the fifth. Palica also yielded his double in the third.

Adcock picked on a Pete Wojey curveball for his third home run in the seventh, and then he belted Johnny Podres' fastball into the stands in the ninth. Adcock was getting some grief from his teammates in the dugout before smacking that fourth one, but he said he wasn't particularly concerned about the record. The last thing coach John Cooney told him was to be sure to get under the ball, and when he complied the result landed in the customary place.

Adcock's display was not only impressive, it was contagious. Eddie Mathews contributed two more home runs to the Braves' 15-7 victory, and Andy Pafko chipped in with one. The Dodgers hit three themselves, accounting for a two-team total of 10 that tied the National League record. Mathews happened to be Adcock's roommate, so their total of six may have set an unofficial record for home runs from a single hotel unit.

When the fireworks were over, Manager Charlie Grimm was so pleased by the Braves' ninth straight victory that he offered to pay any price to retrieve Adcock's last home run ball from the fan who caught it. Adcock himself was probably more interested in keeping the bat.

For the record, White said his bat was really only two ounces heavier than Adcock's, but nobody was in the mood to argue. Adcock hit 23 home runs that season and would eventually hit as many as 38 in a season. Charlie White hit one in 1954, the only home run in his brief career. Maybe the bat wasn't the whole story.

MAJOR LEAGUE PLAYERS WITH FOUR HOMERS IN A GAME

PLAYER & TEAM	DATE
Bobby Lowe, Boston (NL)	May 30, 1894
Ed Delahanty, Philadelphia (NL)	July 13, 1896
Lou Gehrig, New York Yankees	June 3, 1932
Chuck Klein, Philadelphia (NL)	July 10, 1936
Pat Seerey, Chicago White Sox	July 18, 1948
Joe Adcock, Milwaukee (NL)	July 31, 1954
Rocky Colavito, Cleveland	June 10, 1959
Willie Mays, San Francisco	April 30, 1961
Mike Schmidt, Philadelphia	April 17, 1976
Bob Horner, Atlanta	July 6, 1986
Mark Whiten, St. Louis	Sept. 7, 1993
Mike Cameron, Seattle	May 2, 2002
Shawn Green, Los Angeles (NL)	May 23, 2002
Carlos Delgado, Toronto	Sept. 25, 2003

Source: mlb.com

HICKMAN DIES AFTER STATE FAIR CRASH

AUGUST 1, 1982

On a stock car speedway in Talladega, Ala., 28-year-old Gene Richards drove into the wall on the fourth turn and died of head injuries. On the water in Pasco, Wash., 44-year-old Dean Chenoweth, a four-time national hydroplane champion, failed to survive after he flipped his boat doing 175 miles per hour.

And on the one-mile oval at State Fair Park, 39-year-old Jim Hickman wasn't breathing when doctors got to the mangled wreckage of his March-Cosworth. Some 12 hours later, he was dead.

This grisly series of coincidences made its way across the country on a single Saturday. It took a few hours longer to finish its work in Milwaukee when Hickman died at Froedtert Lutheran Hospital at 4:50 Sunday morning, Aug. 1. Chenoweth had already survived three high-speed crashes in his career. Richards, normally a short-track driver, was racing at lightning quick Talledega for the first time. Hickman shouldn't have been racing at all.

He had failed to qualify for the 22-car field at the Tony Bettenhausen 200, but he had gotten a spot on a promoter's option because he had been named Rookie of the Year at the Indianapolis 500 two months earlier when he finished seventh. His car was under-steering badly, and his former crew chief said later that it had no business being on the track.

But Hickman was determined to get his machinery into racing shape. He was not easily discouraged. He'd survived the Vietnam War in the cockpit of a fighter plane, but he didn't survive the first turn at State Fair Park.

Less than five minutes were left in the practice session when his throttle stuck and he drove straight into the concrete wall. He hit the brakes, but it didn't matter. He was going full speed. If he had been on the straightaway, he might have been able to shut down the engine and coast to a stop.

It took track workers 15 minutes to pull Hickman out of the car. The track doctor got him breathing again and rushed him to the trauma ward at County General Hospital. He was transferred to the neurological intensive care unit at Froedtert, but his condition worsened steadily during the night, and he died of massive head injuries.

In one of the last interviews he'd given before his death, Hickman had praised the safety of modern championship racing cars. Even though they were going faster than they'd ever gone before, he'd said they had more "crashability." He added: "When they hit something, they collapse at a much better rate, so it absorbs the shock."

Hickman's death was the second on the Indy-car circuit that year. Gordon Smiley had died at a practice at Indianapolis in May. It was the first fatality at State Fair Park since 1968 when Ronnie Duman died driving in the Rex Mays 150, but it also was the 18th fatality in 79 years of racing at the track.

Tom Sneva won the Bettenhausen 200 that Sunday. It was an exciting race, but not only was Hickman missing, so was Al Unser. Unser had qualified sixth for the race, but he and his wife Karen went home to Albuquerque, N.M., on Sunday morning when they learned that their 21-year-old daughter had died in a dune buggy accident the night before.

LEGENDARY MICKEY WRIGHT WINS AT NORTH SHORE

AUGUST 2, 1964

In the cozy world of women's golf, Mickey Wright was Tiger Woods without the zeroes on the winner's pay check. She won 82 tournaments including 13 majors in a career cut short by the strain of carrying the pro tour on her shoulders, and two of those victories came in Milwaukee.

Wright made it look so easy when she won the first Milwaukee Jaycee Open in 1962 that it hardly seemed worth the effort of coming back. Shooting a seven-over-par 77 on the final day at Tuckaway, she still ran away from the field by seven shots. The next time around was a little more challenging.

The 29-year-old California native came to North Shore Country Club two years later with seven titles already under her belt that season and a remarkable 13 the season before that. She also came with a quarrelsome ulcer. The medication required to keep her touchy stomach under control along with the stifling August heat seemed to sap her strength. She said it was taking yards off her iron shots. Her rivals could only imagine how things might have gone if she'd been feeling good.

She got off to a slow start with a first-round 74, but made up for it with a three-under 69 the next day. Even with another 74 on Saturday she entered the final round with a three-shot lead on Californian Ruth Jessen. Fifteen holes later, Jessen had trimmed that to a single shot. But that's where the drama ended.

The runner-up went bogey-par-bogey the rest of the way, while Wright shot par to claim the $2,000 winner's check by three shots. And then with the cheers of a gallery of 8,000 still ringing in her ears, she hurried home to Texas to get that ulcer taken care of.

The health of the early LPGA was very much connected to Wright's well-being. The only woman ever to win all four major championships in the same year – she did it in 1962 – she was expected to be at every tournament if she could. At a time when it was hard to get 30 golfers in a field, she agreed to lower the winner's percentage of the purse just so the tail-enders could meet expenses.

To illustrate her commitment to the women's tour, from 1962-'64, she played in 90 tournaments, winning 34.

Wright's father gave her a $1,000 stake when she decided to leave Stanford to try her luck on the five-year-old pro women's tour in 1955. She had no trouble paying him back. She won her first tournament in 1956, and then she won at least one every year for the next 13. Along the way, she added to her fame with an appearance on the *Ed Sullivan Show*, and she was later named the greatest female golfer of the 20th century by the Associated Press, beating out Babe Didrikson Zaharias and Kathy Whitworth for the honor. Wright even had a tournament named after her while she was still playing, and the immortal Ben Hogan said she had the best golf swing he'd ever seen.

And then at the age of 34, five years after winning in Milwaukee, she decided to stop playing fulltime. She was having problems with her feet and her wrists, but mostly she was worn out. "It's just like my fishing," she told *Sports Illustrated* in a 2000 interview. "Caught all the bass I wanted to, and now I don't want to catch anymore. Been there, done that."

Playing a sharply curtailed schedule, she posted her final victory in 1973, six years after the final Milwaukee Jaycee Open.

METCALFE NIPPED BY OWENS IN BERLIN OLYMPICS

AUGUST 3, 1936

Racism trumped the races when the 11th modern Olympic Games were staged in Berlin under the aegis of the monster Adolph Hitler. Nazi propaganda had labeled African-Americans as inferior and criticized the United States for relying on what it called "black auxiliaries" to win medals. That made Jesse Owens and Ralph Metcalfe Hitler's nightmare.

Marquette University's Metcalfe and Ohio State's Owens had waged a spirited rivalry over the past several seasons, swapping championships and records back and forth. They were clearly the fastest runners in the world, and they also happened to be black.

Their dominance in the showcase 100-meter event at Berlin became apparent in the first preliminary heat when Owens finished in 10.3 seconds, tying the world record shared by Metcalfe. Owens broke that record in the quarterfinals, running a 10.2, but the time was disallowed because he'd had a wind of more than four miles per hour at his back. Then Owens won one semifinal while Metcalfe won the other.

When the world's top sprinters lined up for the final, Owens was the favorite, and the only question was whether he could hold off Metcalfe's celebrated finishing kick. True to form, Metcalfe started slowly while Owens roared out of the blocks and took the early lead. Owens was ahead by five feet at the 50-meter mark, but Metcalfe came on hard in the final 25. It wasn't enough. Owens broke the tape in 10.3 seconds, equaling the world mark once again and beating his longtime rival by a full yard.

Owens wasn't invited to Hitler's box following his triumph, but he wore a big grin anyway at the awards ceremony where he drew a loud cheer from the fans. Metcalfe wasn't smiling, though. This was his second major Olympic disappointment.

He had also taken silver in the 100 four years earlier in Los Angeles, losing a disputed race to another American, Eddie Tolan. Metcalfe had come from behind in that one too, drawing even with Tolan at 80 meters and running neck and neck with him to the finish line. Several hours later, the judges watched a film of the race and decided that Tolan had crossed the line first.

Under current rules, the runner who gets to the line first is the winner, and that would have given Metcalfe the decision. Metcalfe also earned a bronze in the 200 meters in 1932 in another disputed race when it was determined that he had been forced to dig his starting holes several feet behind the other runners. And so he was still looking for his first gold four years later. He finally got it in Berlin in the 400-meter relay on Aug. 9, but that too was an ugly chapter in Olympic history.

Just days before the event, coach Lawson Robertson said he planned to run an all-white team of Sam Stoller, Marty Glickman, Frank Wykoff and Foy Draper. Robertson said Owens already had won enough glory; but he didn't rule out inserting Metcalfe for one of the other runners. Then on the morning of the race, Robertson informed Glickman and Stoller that they were being replaced by Owens and Metcalfe.

There had been speculation that Robertson had been taking his orders from U.S. Olympic Committee President Avery Brundage when he replaced the only two Jewish members of the team with two black runners.

That subsequently led to accusations that the U.S. withdrew Glickman and Stoller rather than infuriate Hitler even more. Just days earlier, Stoller and Glickman had finished first and second, ahead of Wykoff and Draper, in a practice race called for by the two U.S. track coaches, Robertson and his assistant Dean Cromwell. The plot thickens here because Cromwell, Wykoff and Draper were all from the University of Southern California.

Whatever, Stoller and Glickman were the only two members of the U.S. track team who returned home without running in the Games. Were they victims of anti-Semitism even if they were replaced by two African-Americans?

"Of course I'm convinced it was the Jewish thing that was behind it," Metcalfe told William O. Johnson Jr., author of the 1972 book, *All that Glitters is not Gold*. "Glickman and Stoller should have run."

But it would be hard to argue that Metcalfe didn't deserve to run, too. And when the U.S. breezed to a 15-yard victory, Metcalfe finally had his gold medal.

GULDAHL SETS PACE IN MILWAUKEE GOLF TOURNAMENT

AUGUST 4, 1940

The first and last Milwaukee Open featured not only some of the greatest names in the history of golf, but also one of the most mysterious. And he was the man who won it.

Ben Hogan, Sam Snead, Walter Hagen, Tommy Armour – they were all there. And so was Ralph Guldahl, who had won 14 regular PGA Tour tournaments over a career that spanned nine years with one significant interruption. But he would never win another one – other than a four-ball tournament – after claiming the $1,200 top prize in Milwaukee.

Guldahl was short off the tee, but he had the shots required to capture three major championships – the U.S. Open in 1937 and '38; and the Masters in 1939 – and the temperament to drive his opponents crazy. As Snead put it once: "If Guldahl gave someone a blood transfusion, the patient would freeze to death."

But Guldahl demonstrated that something was bubbling under that calm exterior after he missed a short putt that cost him a chance to win the 1933 U.S. Open. The 21-year-old Texan had made up nine strokes in 11 holes to pull within a stroke of the lead, and he needed to make only a four-footer on the 72nd hole to take Johnny Goodman into a playoff. When he missed the putt, his whole game seemed to unravel. He returned to Dallas and a job selling used cars.

He resumed his career in 1936 and became one of the hottest players in golf. Over the next three years, he won three majors and three prestigious Western Opens. In addition to being supremely talented, Guldahl was unusually fashion-conscious. He was the last man to win a U.S. Open wearing a necktie.

And so Guldahl was both a natty and a welcome addition to what may have been one of the most potent fields ever assembled at a Wisconsin pro tournament when the $5,000 Milwaukee Open began on a Friday morning at North Hills Country Club. It was the only time the tournament was ever played and the last time Milwaukee would be host to a pro event until it staged the Blue Ribbon Open in 1951.

The competition was spread over three days, beginning on Friday and winding up with 36 holes on Sunday. A gallery estimated at 2,000 people gathered to watch the first round, and the crowds would grow to 5,000 for the final. With a field that strong, they were strewn all over the course, but as the tournament wore on, the man attracting the most attention was Johnny Bulla.

Unlike Guldahl, who was slim and patient, Bulla was built like a bull with a personality to match. He held a one-shot lead on the field and a four-shot lead on Guldahl after the second round on Saturday. After 18 holes on Sunday, Bulla had fired a tour-record 197 for 54 holes, and he was still four shots up on Guldahl.

The two towering figures – Guldahl was 6 feet 4 inches; Bulla, 6-3 – played together in the final threesome with Hinsdale, Ill., pro Jim Foulis, and that may have made all the difference in the tournament. Bulla still had a three-shot lead going into the last nine holes, but Guldahl's deliberate style was taking its toll.

The exasperated Bulla self-destructed down the stretch, soaring to a 39 while Guldahl shot a 32 on his way to 67 for his last 18 holes. That gave him a 16-under-par total of 268 and a two-shot victory over Ed Oliver. Snead was third at 271, while Bulla dropped into a fourth-place tie with Hogan at 272.

"I'll never be paired with Guldahl in another tournament again," vowed Bulla. "He's the slowest guy I ever saw." Guldahl shrugged and said, "I always play that way."

He didn't play that way much longer. He paired with Snead to win a four-ball event later that year, but his game deteriorated practically overnight. Some observers theorized that he'd made a fatal mistake by writing an instructional book and messing up his own swing by overanalyzing it. He retired from the game in 1942 at the age of 30.

MOREL WINS WBA FLYWEIGHT TITLE IN MADISON

AUGUST 5, 2000

Eric Morel couldn't have been much more confident when he weighed in for the title shot he'd been waiting for all his life. And why not? His opponent was totally out of his element.

World Boxing Association flyweight champion Sornpichai Pisnurachank had had only one fight outside of Thailand in his 19-bout career, but he traveled 32 hours to get to this one. And when he landed, he had to lose 12 pounds in 48 hours to make the 112-pound limit. Not only was he defending his title in Morel's adopted hometown, but no one but his translator could even pronounce his name, let alone understand him. In fact, Pisnurachank wasn't even his given name or his only name. It was his boxing name based on the gym where he trained, per a Thai custom.

Morel wasn't much help. "He won't be able to pronounce his name after the fight," boasted the Madison resident and Puerto Rican native, making the most of the home-ring advantage.

It is practically unheard of for a champion to travel to a challenger's city, especially when the city is on a different continent, but Pisnurachank had 100,000 reasons to make the trip or one for each dollar he had been guaranteed. Morel's manager wouldn't say what his fighter's take would be, but money wasn't the object anyway. Morel had won 26 bouts and knocked out 16 opponents since turning pro after the 1996 Olympics. A former national Golden Gloves champion, he had won the International Boxing Association super flyweight crown two years earlier and had been longing for a chance at a major title ever since.

His only concern was a chronic condition that tended to make his right hand swell during a fight, but a specialist assured him that there was no break. "My right hand is ready to knock some teeth down," Morel said. As it turned out, he was wrong about that.

A small but raucous crowd of 2,750 gathered at the Alliant Energy Center in Madison to watch the event, and it included Morel's father, who had taught eight sons to fight, but none of them as effectively as Eric. And the fans liked what they saw early in the bout as the local favorite decked the champion in the second round.

Morel was clearly ahead before the hand condition flared up again in the middle rounds, and by the seventh he was unable to punch at all with his right. That was a huge disadvantage against a left-handed opponent, but he was able to keep the onrushing Pisnurachank far enough away to earn a unanimous 12-round decision.

"We try. We try," said the frustrated Thai fighter through his translator. "But he keep running away." Morel hardly disputed him. In fact, he apologized to the fans for not being more aggressive, but he was taking no chances on one wild punch ending a lifelong dream.

"When the bell rang, I was happy because I knew all those years of hard work were worth it," he said. "The only thing that's going to change is I'm going to train even harder to retain this title, because this is not only mine, this is all my friends' and all my family's. So it's going to be hard for me to let it go easy."

Not only was Morel determined to keep the crown he had at 112 pounds, but he said he was aiming at every championship from 115 to 126 pounds. But he relinquished his flyweight title with his first professional loss in 2003 and then he lost much more.

In 2005 Morel pleaded no contest to second-degree sexual assault of a 15-year-old girl and was sentenced to two years in prison and two years of extended supervision. He was released in 2007 and resumed his career in February 2008, after almost three years off.

PACKERS TRADE FAVRE TO NEW YORK JETS

AUGUST 6, 2008

The picture in the *Milwaukee Journal Sentinel* sports section said it all. There was Brett Favre with a sickly grin on his face and a New York Jets jersey in his hands. "To a certain extent, I don't know what I'm getting into," he said.

Neither did anyone else when the greatest Green Bay Packer ever tearfully announced his retirement in March after 16 memorable seasons that included three Most Valuable Player awards. What followed were five bizarre months before the team and the quarterback parted ways in an ugly divorce.

In a complicated deal designed mostly to keep Favre out of the hands of division rivals Minnesota and Chicago, the Packers surrendered the face of their franchise for a conditional draft choice. The conditions were all about how much Favre played for New York and for how long.

If he played 50% of the Jets' snaps in 2008, it would be a third-round pick. If he played 70% and the Jets made the playoffs, it would be a No. 2; and if he played 80% and took them to the Super Bowl it would be a No. 1. Anything less and it would be a No. 4. But Favre's greatest value as an ex-Packer would come if the Jets traded him to either the Vikings or the Bears. Then they'd have to send three first-round choices to Green Bay.

Obviously, they weren't going to do that, but nothing else about Favre's messy parting with the Packers was obvious at all.

Favre's friends and family were quoted as saying the Packers in general and General Manager Ted Thompson in particular had done nothing to encourage him to play another year for them. The Packers claimed that just weeks after Favre announced his retirement he had contacted them and said he'd changed his mind, but when they offered to welcome him back, he changed it again and said he was going to stay retired.

If that was the case, he changed it one more time. Favre took the first step on his convoluted journey to New York by asking the Packers for his release so that he could play somewhere else. Thompson's answer was "absolutely not." Favre was a valuable commodity, and the team intended to get value for him.

The Packers were willing to trade his rights to another NFL team as long as that team wasn't in the NFC North Division. The closer it got to training camp, the clearer it became that the Packers also had decided the Favre era was over and their future was tied to Aaron Rodgers at quarterback.

Like every good drama, this one required a villain, and the Packers tried to cast the Vikings in the role. They filed tampering charges against their rivals, saying Favre had talked about a trade with Minnesota coach Brad Childress and offensive coordinator and former Green Bay quarterbacks coach Darrell Bevell. But the charges were dismissed by NFL Commissioner Roger Goodell.

With neither side budging, the Packers faced the unappetizing prospect of Favre coming to training camp as a backup, which was the last thing they or Favre wanted. Favre told ESPN's Chris Mortensen that he'd asked Thompson if he'd be welcome in the building, and Thompson told him, "Brett, you can't do that. You'll get me fired."

Enter Mark Murphy. The Packers' new president tried to head off a public relations catastrophe by visiting Favre in Hattiesburg, Miss. Instead he made it worse. When Murphy offered Favre a 10-year, $20 million "marketing agreement" to stay retired, he called it an opportunity, but the Favre camp and the public saw it as a bribe.

And so Favre came to training camp, but he never got on the practice field. Coach Mike McCarthy had a long talk with his ex-quarterback and came away saying that Favre's mindset was all wrong for a return to the Packers. He didn't want him.

Fortunately for everyone, the Jets did. Under pressure from Goodell, the Packers had contacted virtually every NFL team about a Favre trade, and the only serious candidates outside their division were the Jets and the Tampa Bay Buccaneers. The Jets were offering more than the Bucs, and when Favre finally agreed to a trade after talking to their coach and general manager, the deal was made and he joined them in Cleveland, where they were playing an exhibition game.

That left it up to the fans to decide who was at fault for the end of a rewarding relationship between Brett Favre and the Green Bay Packers.

MUCKS WINS FIRST NATIONAL SHOT AND DISCUS TITLES

AUGUST 7, 1915

At 6 feet 5 inches and 265 pounds, Arlie Mucks was a big man who had already made a big name for himself when he came to San Francisco for the 40th annual Amateur Athletic Union national track and field championships.

Three years earlier when he was just 20 years old and only days out of Oshkosh High School, Mucks had made the U.S. Olympic team and finished sixth in the discus at Stockholm, Sweden. He'd also been named an All-American in football in 1914 after playing guard for the University of Wisconsin.

A knee injury ended Mucks' football career, but he was just getting started as a national track star when he dominated both the shot and discus events in the AAU meet. He threw the discus 146 feet 9¼ inches and followed up with a 48-11¾ effort in the 16-pound shot to capture both medals and serve notice that he would be a force in track and field for a long time.

He won the national championship in both events the following year in Newark, N.J., and then he did it again in St. Louis the year after that, making him the only man ever to capture both titles three years in a row. No one has done it since, and that covers more than 130 years of national track meets.

The first national meet was held in 1876 and sponsored by the New York Athletic Club. The NYAC ran the meet for two more years before it was taken over by the National Association of Amateur Athletes of America from 1879-'88. The AAU also ran its first national meet in 1888 and continued doing so through 1979 when it was stripped of its role as the governing body for track and field by the Amateur Sports Act of 1978.

The Athletics Congress of the USA ran the meet from 1980-'92 before it was taken over by USA Track & Field in 1993.

Since Mucks swept the two events for the last time in 1917, only three men have won both events just once in the same year. John Godina captured both the shot put and discus in 1998; Parry O'Brien did it in 1955; and Bud Houser accomplished the feat in 1925.

Mucks was competing for the Chicago Athletic Association when he topped the shot and discus in St. Louis, but he was representing the University of Wisconsin in the first two national meets. Tutored by Tom Jones, who coached the Badger track team for 35 years, Mucks won the shot put and discus in the Big Ten outdoor meet in 1915 and '16, and he also won the shot put in the 1916 indoor meet.

He graduated from Wisconsin in 1917 with a degree in animal husbandry and started a career in agriculture that was as distinguished as his career in track. After working a hog farm in Mitchell, S.D., for eight years and serving as a county agriculture agent, he joined the UW faculty in 1925 and served on it for 31 years.

Still influential in the athletic department, he played a big part in the hiring of Doc Spears, the controversial Badger football coach. The university had negotiated with Spears for three days, but he turned down the job in March 1932. Mucks flew out to Oregon to meet with Spears and helped him to change his mind.

Mucks most cherished honor came in 1965 when he was inducted into the Wisconsin Sports Hall of Fame. He called it "the night of nights in my athletic life." The honor came 53 years after an Oshkosh High School publication first labeled him "A Phenomenal Athlete."

The title appeared in the school's 1912 June Index and was followed by these words of praise: "As it happens occasionally in the history of High School athletics, some school is fortunate enough to claim such a person among its numbers... Still less frequently one of these athletes is possessed of such extraordinary ability that his name and records cannot be forgotten. To this latter class belongs Arlie M. Mucks, the young man who has made himself and his school famous."

How prescient for a high school publication. Mucks may still be the greatest athlete ever to come out of Oshkosh.

ESTHER JONES RACES TO GOLD AT BARCELONA

AUGUST 8, 1992

This was Evelyn Ashford's last Olympic race, and she was taking no chances with the rookie from Milwaukee. She had to be sure the baton was in good hands.

So as the 35-year-old matriarch of American sprinters roared off the turn she used both of hers to pass it, steadying Esther Jones' left hand with her left and jamming the baton in with her right. It might have looked a little like Ashford was trying to tackle her 23-year-old teammate, but it worked.

Jones, the tallest member of the relay at 5 feet 9 inches, used her patented long stride to make up some ground and then passed the stick flawlessly to Carlette Guidry, who made up a little more before the final exchange with Gwen Torrence. The fleet, outspoken Torrence did the rest, making up the small lead that Russian star Irina Privalova had on her and winning the 400-meter relay for the United States by the slimmest of margins at the Barcelona Games.

Afterward, Jones called the race the most exciting thing that had ever happened to her, although she admitted it may have been a little too exciting when she was getting the baton from Ashford. "Evelyn was coming in very strong, running a tremendous corner, and she got there very fast," Jones said. "I didn't feel her grab my hand, because I was so keyed in on the race. We got a clean handoff. It wasn't that great, but we got the stick, and that's all that was necessary."

Ashford was an expert on necessary at the Olympics. She'd been in three of them, and this was her fourth gold medal and fifth medal overall. In addition to being on three winning 400-meter relay teams, she had twice medaled in the 100 meters, winning gold in 1984 and silver in 1988.

All that experience paid off when she had to pass the baton to Jones. It wasn't a clean handoff, but it was a safe one under the circumstances. "Maybe I stunned her that I was coming so fast," Ashford said. "I ran right up her butt. I really did, and I had to give her the stick with a two-handed pass."

It might have been considered typical if a failure to cooperate had doomed the American effort. Torrence had caused a fuss by alleging in public that some of the other sprinters were using drugs. She later apologized for the statement, but it was not exactly calculated to promote teamwork. Jones was Torrence's roommate at the time, but she said the team left the controversy behind when it got out onto the track.

The important thing to her was leaving the field behind. This was her first Olympics, and everything was happening so fast. Jones had only started running seven years earlier as a sophomore at Milwaukee Bay View High School, but she'd learned in a hurry, winning a total of four state championships in the 100 and 200 meters during her junior and senior years. Then it was on to Louisiana State where she became the most decorated female sprinter in the history of the school by capturing four individual NCAA championships.

But she was having a tough Olympic year. She'd failed to qualify in the 100 or 200, and she didn't know until she got to Europe whether she'd be picked for the relay. When she made it, the team had only the third-fastest qualifying time in the event.

Jones admitted she was all butterflies when she got to the track in Barcelona to run the biggest race of her life before 65,000 people and a whole world watching on TV. It would have helped if her family could be with her, but her mom and dad didn't even know if she'd make the team. They watched the race glued to their television set. Jones had called her mom in the morning, and then she'd used a homemade remedy for the jitters. She'd done a load of laundry back at the athlete's village.

And then she'd gone to the track where the Americans cleaned up.

Esther Jones

"HURRICANE" HAZLE DELIVERS BIG FOR BRAVES

AUGUST 9, 1957

The news looked bad when Billy Bruton blew out his knee on July 17 in the middle of a pennant race. Not only were the Milwaukee Braves losing a reliable bat for the rest of the season, but suddenly they had a big hole in the middle of their outfield.

They moved Henry Aaron to center field, put 36-year-old Andy Pafko in right and hoped somebody from their farm system could take up a little of the slack. That somebody turned out to be a 26-year-old stranger with six games of big league experience named Bob Hazle.

Hazle had come to the organization in April 1956 as a throw-in when the Braves traded first baseman George Crowe to Cincinnati for pitcher Corky Valentine. And while Valentine was never heard from again, Hazle would never be forgotten in Milwaukee.

He'd been on a hitting tear at Wichita when he got the call, and while that was against Class AAA pitching, he didn't appear to notice the difference after he arrived with the big club. As he put it later: "When they called me up, I said to myself, 'I'm up, and I'm not going back because I'm not swinging the bat.' I wasn't going to take called strikes."

It was a bold approach from a man with a bad leg and a good doctor. He'd been passed up in the draft by every major league team the year before after struggling with a chipped ankle and a wrenched knee on his right leg – his price tag at that time was a mere $10,000 – but none of that was apparent anymore.

"I'm playing baseball today because a chiropractor friend of mine in Columbia, S.C., made me stay off my leg all last winter," he said. "He put compresses on it, and I didn't run until spring training."

If Hazle's chiropractor was an unsung hero, Hazle was a whole chorus for the Braves. He was called up by them on July 28 and appeared in a game for the first time the next day. He started in right field for the first time on July 31, going 1 for 4, sat out two games and made his first big splash on Aug. 4, getting two doubles off Carl Erskine in a 9-7 victory over Brooklyn.

Over the next three weeks, Hazle crushed just about every pitcher that he faced. In the 17 games that he played, he went 29 for 53, a .547 average. Going into the game on Aug. 4, the Braves were in second place, one game behind the front-running St. Louis Cardinals and there were five teams bunched within seven games of each other in the NL race. At the end of the day, Aug. 25, the Braves were in command of the race, leading the Cardinals by seven games.

In the meantime, Hazle acquired an enduring nickname. What else would you call a young man who was taking the league by storm than "Hurricane?"

The game on Aug. 9 was Hazle's best of that stretch and it came against the second-place Cardinals.

Hazle whacked his first major league home run in the second inning and added three straight singles that night at what was then called Sportsman's Park before the Cardinals finally got him out on a foul pop in his last at-bat. When he was through, so were the Cardinals, both for the evening and for the season. They lost the game, 13-2, as Hazle drove in two runs and scored two, and fell three games out of first. They also dropped the next two games of the series – Hazle went 3 for 4 with three RBI the next night – to fall five behind and they never got that close to the Braves again.

Hazle didn't stop there. He went 3 for 3 and drove in six runs in a 7-3 victory over Philadelphia on Aug. 25; went 4 for 7 in a 23-12 bashing of the Chicago Cubs on Sept. 2; and 4 for 5 in another win over the Cubs on Sept. 22.

The "Hurricane" was reduced to a soft fall breeze in the World Series when he went 2 for 13 at the plate, but he'd done more than his share to get the Braves there. He finished the regular season with a .403 batting average, seven home runs and 27 RBIs.

Unfortunately, his fame outlasted his career by three decades. He was hitting .179 just 20 games into the 1958 season when the Braves sold him to Detroit. Hazle played 43 games for the Tigers that season and never appeared in another major league game.

But when he died of a heart attack at age 61 in 1992, he was still getting fan mail from Milwaukee.

RUTHERFORD WINS BETTENHAUSEN CLASSIC

AUGUST 10, 1980

The wheels were coming off in more ways than one as State Fair Park played host to its second Indy Car race of the summer. Johnny Rutherford finished the competition $20,150 richer, and the United States Auto Club finished it noticeably poorer as politics plagued motor sports as it often does.

Rutherford survived the Tony Bettenhausen 200-mile Classic as much as he won it, catching a break when front-running Al Unser lost the front right wheel of his Longhorn-Cosworth on the 165th lap. Unser had a three-car length lead at the time, and Rutherford acknowledged later that he probably would have lost if Unser's car had stayed together. Instead Rutherford won by 18.7 seconds over Rick Mears and took home the winner's share of the $137,000 total purse.

Unser's wheel shot about 50 feet up in the air and wound up in the parking lot, and it wasn't the first one to go. On lap 64, Mike Mosley's Starcruiser-Cosworth suffered a similar fate with greater consequences. Unser's car was merely obscured by a shower of sparks, while Mosley's was engulfed in flames when it hit the wall. The driver was lucky to walk away, as were several customers when debris flew over a restraining fence.

A crowd of 14,785 was relieved when Mosley was taken to the first-aid hospital and diagnosed with nothing but short-term memory loss. He couldn't remember a thing about the crash. "I guess I'm shook up," he said. "I can't really say."

Rutherford had been the pole-sitter, and his victory wasn't really much of a surprise. He'd already won four of the seven races of the season, while Unser had failed to finish six of them. Still, the winner understood that it took a mechanical quirk for him to earn the checkered flag. "I'd rather be lucky than good anytime," he said.

It was hardly Rutherford's best quote of the weekend. He got that one off on the Friday before the race when he said, "As far as I'm concerned USAC is dead."

The Bettenhausen 200 was the first race at State Fair Park to be sanctioned by Championship Auto Racing Teams, a new organization formed by drivers and owners who blamed the USAC for poor promotion and skimpy purses. When the teams went their own way, they touched off an alphabet soup war that has never really ended.

If it had, open-wheel cars, which are the kind that run at the Indianapolis 500, might not have been buried in the modern battle for auto racing dollars by stock cars, which are the kind that run NASCAR races like the Daytona 500.

Rutherford and friends couldn't have seen that coming that day at State Fair Park. USAC and CART had cooperated to put on the Rex Mays 150 earlier in the summer at the same oval. Curiously, both races were named after famous drivers who had died in crashes, a thought that may have occurred to some of the fans as they watched Mosley hit the wall.

CART began operating its own series in 1979, and before long it had enrolled all of the leading drivers and teams with the notable exception of A.J. Foyt. Twenty open-wheel races were held in 1979, and 13 of them were run by CART. Rutherford was right. USAC was dead.

But in another 12 years, CART wasn't looking so healthy either. Tony George, president of the Indianapolis Motor Speedway, tried to buy the organization in 1991, and when he was turned down he started his own sanctioning body called the Indy Racing League five years later. CART still had the best drivers, but George had the Indianapolis 500, which was the open-wheel sport's biggest event by 500 miles. When CART drivers began defecting to run at Indianapolis, CART went broke and eventually its remnants merged with the IRL.

None of which helped the State Fair Park oval. The venue that held two major open-wheel events in 1980 lost big time racing in 2010.

SPAHN JOINS ELITE COMPANY WITH 300TH WIN

AUGUST 11, 1961

Charlie Dressen had his own pet name for Warren Spahn. He called him his "Go to sleep pitcher" because the Milwaukee Braves' manager always got a good night's rest when he knew Spahn was on the mound the next day.

But Spahn himself was a bundle of nerves in the hours before he faced the Chicago Cubs looking for the 300th victory of his 17-year career. Well wishers had kept his phone ringing all day, and by the time he got to County Stadium, he just wanted the game to start.

So did a crowd of 40,775. It was the biggest gathering the Braves had had in two years. The Cubs had a junk-ball artist named Jack Curtis on the mound, which prompted Dressen to play a hunch and put journeyman Gino Cimoli in center field. Cimoli had started only one game in five weeks, and he would play only 37 in his one-half season in Milwaukee, but Dressen thought he might be able to pull Curtis. So he made Cimoli his leadoff man. If he'd known how that move would work out, he would have slept even better the night before.

Everyone was on edge through four scoreless innings as Curtis' soft stuff kept the Milwaukee batters off balance. But the Braves finally broke through in the fifth when Spahn took matters into his own hands and drove in a run with a sacrifice fly.

The Cubs came back to tie the game in the sixth on three singles, which represented half of their hit total for the night. And that's how things stood when Cimoli came up with one out in the eighth and vindicated his manager's faith.

As predicted he pulled Curtis' pitch halfway up the left-field bleachers for his third home run of the season and only the 30th of his six-year career. Spahn himself had 29 at that point.

The Cubs were down to three outs, and Spahn made the first one look easy by making Andre Rodgers his fifth and final strikeout victim. And then Cimoli came through again. This time he plucked Jerry Kindall's sinking line drive off his shoe top for the second out. The third should have come on pinch-hitter Ernie Banks' grounder to third, but Eddie Mathews threw the ball over first baseman Joe Adcock's head to keep the Cubs alive. They died one out later when Jim McAnany flew out to right.

After the ball settled into Henry Aaron's glove, Spahn raced halfway to the outfield to retrieve it. The final score was 2-1, and he had become the 13th pitcher in major league history to win 300 games. "I wanted that so bad I could taste it," he said later.

Spahn called the victory the biggest thrill of his career, adding that he "deserved it." There was no telling how much sooner the 40-year-old lefty would have gotten to No. 300 if he hadn't lost three years to military service. In those three years, he'd earned a battlefield commission, a Purple Heart and a Bronze Star.

Looking back on his career much later, he had no regrets about the time away from baseball. "I pitched until I was 44. Maybe I wouldn't have been able to do that otherwise," he said.

Or maybe he would have been a 400-game winner. Spahn was still at the top of his game at age 42 when he went 23-7 with a 2.60 earned run average in 1963, but then he hit the wall quickly. As it was, he compiled a lifetime record of 363-245, making him the winningest left-hander in major league history.

He had 13 years with 20 or more victories, including the 1961 season in which he reached the 300 milestone against the Cubs. An hour-and-a-half after the game was over, Spahn was throwing a party for his teammates at Ray Jackson's on Bluemound Road and buying champagne for the press room. The record was in the books. Now everyone could relax.

BREWERS FIRE GARNER; BANDO REASSIGNED

AUGUST 12, 1999

Wendy Selig-Prieb took over from her father Bud as the Milwaukee Brewers' president and chief executive officer in 1998, and people wondered whether she'd be able to make tough decisions. She'd been the team's general counsel since 1992, but her dad had done all the hiring and firing before he left to become the commissioner of baseball.

There hadn't been much of either after Sal Bando was put in charge of baseball operations in 1991. In fact, Bando was the only general manager Selig-Prieb had ever worked with, and Phil Garner was the only manager Bando had ever hired. But after the Brewers came within a weekend of making the playoffs in 1992 with a team built mainly by Bando's predecessor, Harry Dalton, they'd never risen above .500 again.

Things clearly had to change, and no one understood that better than Bando. So when the Brewers lost their sixth game in a row on Aug. 6, he went to Selig-Prieb and told her that two people had to go. One of them was Garner, and the other was Bando himself.

Selig-Prieb had to agree. She made the tough decision six days later when she discharged Garner and reassigned Bando as a special assistant.

"The bottom line for me personally is we didn't win," Bando said after essentially firing himself. "I didn't feel it was in my best interest to make a change in the manager and make a change in a number of areas and sit in my position and be the same person."

Garner, whose 563-617 record over seven-plus seasons gave him more victories and more losses than any other Brewers manager, didn't dispute the decision. "I've got to call it justified. We didn't play up to my expectations nor their expectations," he said, adding, "I'm leaving with a lot of managerial experience and hopefully a little more knowledge. I can't be bitter about that."

Garner could afford to be philosophical, since his name was already being mentioned for several possible managerial openings. Selig-Prieb, on the other hand, had to find someone to run her ballclub.

She gave no timetable for naming a full-time replacement, saying only that she'd pick a general manager, and he would hire the new manager. In the meantime, she plucked Jim Lefebvre off Garner's staff to be interim manager, but after the Brewers finished the season 13 games under .500, he was never a serious candidate to keep the job.

Framing the search project was Commissioner Selig's directive that minority candidates be given full consideration for any new managerial hirings. One name mentioned prominently in the early speculation was San Diego Padres coach Davey Lopes. One name that didn't get much mention in talk about the general manager opening was Dean Taylor. But Selig-Prieb hired Taylor from the Atlanta Braves' front office, and he promptly hired Lopes.

The combination proved to be no improvement on Garner and Bando. Lopes was fired 15 games into the 2002 season with a 144-195 record, and Taylor was gone at the end of that year. So was Selig-Prieb as the Brewers' president. She stepped aside as CEO at the same time, but remained head of the team's board of directors. Garner went on to manage the Detroit Tigers and Houston Astros, finally reaching the World Series with the Astros in 2005.

MILWAUKEE BREWERS' MANAGERS FIRED IN-SEASON

DATE	FIRED MANAGER	REPLACEMENT
May 29, 1972	Dave Bristol	Del Crandall
June 2, 1982	Buck Rodgers	Harvey Kuenn
Aug. 12, 1999	Phil Garner	Jim Lefebvre
April 18, 2002	Davey Lopes	Jerry Royster
Sept. 5, 2008	Ned Yost	Dale Sveum

Source: Milwaukee Brewers' media guides

SARAZEN RULES IN PGA TOURNEY AT BLUE MOUND

AUGUST 13, 1933

The competition on the course wasn't nearly as much fun as the conflict that preceded it when the 16th annual PGA Championship came to Blue Mound Country Club in Wauwatosa.

This was the first time that one of golf's four major tournaments was played in Wisconsin, and it almost didn't happen because many of the game's leading players had better things to do. Members of the United States Ryder Cup team had suffered a 6.5-5.5 loss in Southport, England, and most of them had lucrative exhibitions scheduled overseas at the same time as the PGA tournament. And so they threatened to skip the event unless it was moved back to September.

That didn't sit well with C. Ben Johnson, the tournament's executive director who had put up an extravagant $9,000 guarantee for the purse. Johnson informed the PGA that if he didn't get the top players, he was keeping his $9,000, and the prize money would have to come strictly from gate receipts. The PGA, in turn, threatened to move the meet elsewhere. Then the players got involved, and things got nasty.

Venerable pro Tommy Armour publicly ripped his reluctant colleagues, saying, "If it wasn't for golf and an organization like the PGA fellows like Hagen, Sarazen, Shute, Wood and myself would be lucky to have ordinary paying jobs today instead of strutting around like heroes with plenty of cash in our pockets...Hagen, Sarazen and myself are three outstanding golfers because we're just about all washed up and don't know it. We're living on our reputations and think we're more important than the game of golf itself. Well, we're mistaken."

Among those whom Armour was referring to were legends Walter Hagen and Gene Sarazen, and the 31-year-old Sarazen was not amused. He shot back, "I didn't know about the dates until I got to England. Armour is taking a lot for granted putting me in the class with himself and Hagen. They are 10 years older than I am. I'm not washed up yet, and I won't be for years to come."

With their players at war and the tournament just over three weeks away, PGA officials called an emergency meeting with Johnson, where it was decided that the tournament would be played in Milwaukee on the dates scheduled, but Ryder Cup players would be given automatic berths without having to qualify in sectional trials. But Hagen, British

Gene Sarazen followed his ball after a shot at the PGA Championship at Blue Mound Country Club in Wauwatosa. The tournament was held there in 1933.

Open champion Densmore Shute and Craig Wood still refused to come.

Once the competition began, Sarazen proved to be well worth waiting for. Over the next six days, the two-time PGA champion and two-time U.S. Open champion, demonstrated that he was anything but washed up.

At that time the PGA started with 36 holes of medal play followed by five days of match play. Sarazen finished tied for fourth in the medal competition and then simply trashed all of his match-play opponents. He played his final match on Aug. 13 against an obscure San Francisco municipal course pro named Willie Goggin.

Goggin was only one hole down after the first 18 holes of the final, but then his putter cooled down. Sarazen birdied the 31st hole to go four shots up and clinched the title on the 32nd when both players birdied and halved the hole. Sarazen's 5 and 4 victory gave him his third PGA title and the sixth of what would be seven major titles over the course of his career.

Organizers estimated the crowds at 15,000 for the six-day tournament, guaranteeing that the event was a financial success. Johnson got his money's worth, and so did Wisconsin golf fans.

LEE KEMP WINS THIRD WORLD WRESTLING TITLE

AUGUST 14, 1982

No iron cages or sleeper holds here. This was real wrestling, all hard work, quickness and technique. And Lee Kemp was doing what he always did, helping his opponent beat himself.

In this case, the opponent was a Czech named Dan Karabin, and he was on his way to a 3-0 defeat in the final 163-pound match of the World Freestyle Amateur Wrestling Championships in Edmonton, Alberta. By Kemp's standards the score was a landslide, but the result was familiar enough. It gave the former University of Wisconsin star and current UW assistant coach his third world championship.

Four years earlier, Kemp had been the youngest American wrestler ever to win a gold medal at the world meet, and now he was the first ever to win three of them. The Chardon, Ohio, native was consistency itself. He always won, and almost always by just a little bit.

He'd started this meet with a 2-1 victory over West Germany's Martin Knosp. It was his toughest match. Knosp had upset him in the world meet the year before, and Kemp was having trouble with a gash he'd suffered over his right eye in practice. The cut had opened, and the match had to be interrupted while he got medical attention.

But he overcame the injury and then went on to score one-point verdicts over Russia's Yuri Vorobiev and Iran's Mohamed Hossein Mohebbi. Beating Mohebbi was almost a matter of national pride because the Iranians had used the tournament to make a political statement. They'd even papered the walls of the American athletes' dorms with posters of the Ayatollah Khomeini. Their fans and the American fans took turns chanting at each other throughout the competition.

The only surprise in the title match was the three-point margin. Kemp truly believed that the best offense was a good defense. He bided his time and waited for his opponents to attack, and then he used the openings they created to score points. The usual result was low-scoring matches.

It was an unspectacular approach that had produced spectacular results. He'd begun using it in high school where he was drawn, at first, to more conventional sports like basketball and football. But he was a small kid who would never get very big, topping out at 5 feet 7 inches. He couldn't make the basketball team, and the football coach wouldn't let him play. So he gave wrestling a try and when he won 54 high school matches without a loss during his last two seasons, he decided he'd found his game.

Wisconsin applauded the decision when he collected three NCAA championships at 158 pounds. He won 30 matches and lost five as a freshman and then dropped only one and tied one out of the next 115 as a sophomore, junior and senior. He left Madison with the school's best career record ever, 143-6-1, and then entered the grown-up world of international competition. He was hoping to get some experience and maybe even pick up a bronze medal at his first world championships in Mexico City in 1978, but it was a long shot. Freestyle wrestling was so new to him, and he was so raw.

When he won the gold at the tender age of 21 years and eight months, he shocked the world and maybe himself a little bit. But he got over the surprise in plenty of time to win again in 1979. Knosp limited him to a bronze in 1981, but Kemp avenged that disappointment in Canada.

There were very few disappointments in Kemp's career. The biggest came in the Olympics. He'd made the American team for the 1980 Games in Moscow, but then the United States government decided to boycott the competition. So he went back to school and earned a master's degree in marketing. But he kept wrestling. He suffered another setback when he finished second in the U.S. Olympic Trials leading up to the 1984 Games in Los Angeles.

When he retired from the sport, he owned a 163-12-1 record in freestyle competition. In 2008 at the Olympic Games in China, he was inducted into the FILA International Wrestling Hall of Fame, one of only five Americans ever to be so honored.

SINGH PREVAILS IN PGA PLAYOFF AT WHISTLING STRAITS

AUGUST 15, 2004

The management of the Whistling Straits Golf Club disputed rumors that someone had broken a leg at the 86th PGA Championship, although it admitted to seven sprained ankles, a dislocated shoulder and countless knots and bruises. And that was just in the gallery.

The bumpy terrain, steep hills and slick grass on this breathtakingly gorgeous layout was wreaking havoc among the more than 40,000 spectators who came each day to witness the first major tournament in Wisconsin in 71 years. But it was being surprisingly kind to the participants.

No fewer than 43 players were under par halfway through the tournament, which was not at all what anybody expected when the famed Pete Dye designed his 7,514-yard monster along two miles of wind-swept Lake Michigan shoreline. But calm October-like weather, soft greens and thinned-out rough had taken much of the snarl out of Whistling Straits.

Then along came Sunday when the course claimed its revenge. Its tees moved back and its pins tucked into nooks and crannies all over the place, it allowed only 14 players to break par on the final day. The winner wasn't one of them.

If Vijay Singh wasn't the best golfer on the planet at this time, he was certainly the best on the leader board after 54 holes, with Tiger Woods having putted himself out of the debate with a first-round 75. Woods had needed a desperation 33 on the back nine on Friday just to keep his streak of 128 cut-free tournaments alive. Still, he finished in a tie for 24th.

The 41-year-old Singh, on the other hand, had already won four tournaments in 2004, and when he stepped to the first tee Sunday with a one-shot lead on playing partner Justin Leonard, he seemed a logical choice to claim his third major championship.

Until he double-bogeyed the fourth hole. And then he bogeyed the seventh. And then the 15th, clearing the way for Leonard to zoom right past him and take a two-stroke lead with three holes to play. But then Whistling Straits reached up and swatted Leonard, too. He bogeyed two of the last three holes, including the 18th when he missed a par putt, much to the relief of Singh and Chris DiMarco, who had rallied from five shots back to move into contention.

Singh was watching helplessly from the green while DiMarco was fidgeting in the scorer's trailer as Leonard putted for the championship. After his crucial 10-footer slid just right of the cup, the three formed a crowd on the first hole of a three-hole playoff.

It was there that Singh dropped in a six-foot putt for his only birdie of the day. When no one could do better than par over the last two playoff holes, Singh had his title and the $1.125 million winner's share of the purse. He called it the biggest accomplishment of his career, which was saying something since the 41-year-old Fijian had won 31 tournaments worldwide, including the 2000 Masters and 1998 PGA.

Singh couldn't have struggled much harder for any of his other victories. His 76 on Sunday was the worst final-round score ever posted by the champion in the PGA tournament. Leonard, meanwhile, carded a 75, while DiMarco was the only one in the playoff who'd had any luck at all that day. He had a one-under 71.

While the three finished the tournament at 8-under, 280, it would be fair to say that Whistling Straits had gotten at least a draw with the best golfers in the world. And that was the expectation when the course opened in 1998.

Herbert V. Kohler Jr. of Kohler Plumbing fame had spent a lot of money to hire Dye and move more than 13,000 truckloads of quarried sand onto an abandoned airfield in tiny Haven, just north of Sheboygan, to create one of the most formidable tests in pro golf. Designed to emulate the old seaside links of Great Britain, the course came with three stone bridges, eight holes directly on the water and a flock of black-faced Scottish sheep.

The sheep had a much easier time getting around the place than the customers at a major tournament, but that hasn't lessened the course's appeal. The U.S. Senior Open was held there in 2007 and the Ryder Cup is scheduled for there in 2020. The PGA Championship returned in 2010 and was decided again by a playoff. The finish came on the same date as the 2004 tournament. This time, Martin Kaymer of Germany won.

ZALE-PRYOR DRAWS 135,000 TO MILWAUKEE LAKEFRONT

AUGUST 16, 1941

Local authorities predicted that as many as 50,000 people would show up at Milwaukee's lakefront on a Saturday night to see Tony Zale fight. They may have been underestimating the power of a four-letter word. The word was "free."

Preliminaries were scheduled for 8:15 p.m., with the featured bout to go off sometime around 10. By 1:30 in the afternoon, the entertainment seekers were starting to gather around the makeshift ring at Juneau Park. By 6 p.m. the 13,000 bleacher seats were full. Another 1,000 would be escorted to ringside. The rest of the people were on their own.

The attraction was irresistible. Zale, a powerful puncher from Gary, Ind., was the world middleweight champion, and never mind that opponent Billy Pryor was what the fight game called "a survivor," a fighter whose main skill was going the distance. The Fraternal Order of Eagles was in town for its national convention, and the Pabst Brewing Co., had welcomed the 40,000 delegates by sponsoring the scheduled 10-round bout, along with five prelims.

Pabst not only let everyone in for nothing, it paid the fighters and the world famous referee. The immortal Jack Dempsey was there to officiate, and he had twice fought Gene Tunney in front of crowds of more than 100,000 for the world heavyweight championship. "This crowd reminds me of the night I fought Gene Tunney in Chicago," said Dempsey. That fight drew 104,000 to Soldier Field.

Milwaukee would do better than that. By 8 o'clock the people overflowed Juneau Park, west of Lincoln Memorial Drive. They swarmed the bluffs and filled streets. Many of them brought their radios because WTMJ was broadcasting the action.

The skies were starry, the weather was perfect, and there was a free fireworks show scheduled later. Father Flanagan of Boys Town was there, too, and he got a huge ovation.

How many people were there? With no turnstiles, it was impossible to tell exactly, but Milwaukee Police Captain Harry Erlach had been counting crowds for 20 years. He walked the grounds three times and came up with the amazing estimate of 135,000.

That was good enough for *Ring* magazine, which recognized it as the biggest boxing crowd in history. It was also the biggest gathering to see any sporting event in Wisconsin. Many of the tens of thousands who couldn't actually witness it with the naked eye improvised with field glasses and opera glasses. One enterprising fan brought a spy glass.

From a boxing standpoint, the distant viewers didn't miss much early as Zale seemed to be saving himself. Before the third round, Fred Saddy, chairman of the state boxing commission, ordered the fighters to pick up the pace. Before the sixth, Dempsey told them that they needed to punch more. They were making themselves look bad.

That was not good news for Pryor. He had gone down for a four-count in the third round and a nine-count in the fifth. Following Dempsey's warning, Pryor took two eight counts in the seventh, and he was decked twice in the eighth. Zale was dribbling him like a basketball before he finally put him down for good with a crushing left hook in the ninth round.

Most of the crowd stayed for the fireworks and then left in a most orderly fashion. A cadre of 132 police was on hand, and there wasn't a single arrest. A little boy got lost, but he was found quickly.

The Eagles held a parade the next day. More than 100,000 lined the Wisconsin Avenue parade route for that, too.

Tony Zale

SACHS WINS STOCK CAR RACE AT STATE FAIR PARK

AUGUST 17, 1961

Eight years before there was an Indianapolis 500, there was a Milwaukee Mile. The oval at State Fair Park began running races in 1903, and no track in the country had been operating longer without interruption as of 2009.

During the 28 years that the United States Auto Club sponsored or co-sponsored stock car races at The Mile, from 1955-'83, the list of winners had included the likes of A.J. Foyt, Parnelli Jones, Bobby Allison, Rusty Wallace, and Bobby and Al Unser. And it would have liked to have seen more of Eddie Sachs.

Called by some "The Clown Prince of Racing," Sachs was the kind of homespun, talkative driver who went over well in Milwaukee. It didn't hurt either that he owned a bar back home in Coopersburg, Pa.

And so when the top qualifiers went to the line for the USAC 200-mile stock car race at State Fair, Sachs was one of the crowd favorites. As many as four USAC stock car races were held in a single season in Milwaukee in the years between 1960 and '79, and this was the third of four in 1961. Sachs had already won one of those races on July 16, and he would need some help to repeat that success. That help came from a teammate.

The race got off to an ominous start when 11 cars were involved in a pile-up on the 22nd lap. Seven of them had to drop out, and there was a 29-minute delay, but fortunately nobody was hurt seriously. Sachs got through the mess without a problem, and so did pole-sitter Don White, the third driver on Sachs' Bill Trainor team.

White moved to the lead on the 161st lap and showed no signs of relinquishing it to Sachs, who had started in the sixth position and worked his way up to second. But then the Keokuk, Iowa, driver ran out of gas seven miles from the finish, and Sachs zoomed past him. Sachs averaged 87.58 miles per hour and took the checkered flag 10 seconds ahead of Dick Rathmann. Troy Ruttman finished third.

"Don sure had hard luck," Sachs said after the race. "I know I couldn't have caught him if he hadn't been forced out. But it would have been fun trying."

It was even more fun, though, to collect the $2,509 winner's share of the purse. It was Sachs' second victory in four stock car starts. It also was the last race he would ever win on the Milwaukee Mile.

Three years later, Sachs found himself in the cockpit of a new rear-engine racer at the Indianapolis 500. The controversial machine was made of fiberglass, which made it light but extremely flammable. What's more, it carried its fuel in large tanks mounted on either side of the car, which meant the driver was surrounded by danger. In those tanks was a gasoline blend that was far more volatile than the alcohol that powered the traditional front-engine cars.

On the second lap of the race, rookie driver Dave MacDonald lost control, spun into the inside wall and bounced across the track where he was hit by Sachs. Both cars burst into flames instantly. Track workers rushed to the scene, and they were able to free MacDonald from the wreckage and get him to a hospital. But it was too late. He died from his burns two-and-a-half hours later.

Sachs never even had that chance. He was dead before anyone could get to his car. Two days after celebrating his 37th birthday, he left a wife, a two-year-old son and a gaping hole in the field at his next scheduled race.

He was due in Milwaukee the following week for the Rex Mays 100 at State Fair Park.

Eddie Sachs (left) was a happy winner.

AUGUST 249

BURDETTE'S NO-HITTER STIFLES PHILLIES

AUGUST 18, 1960

This was Lew Burdette's day for yard work. He cut the grass during the day and mowed down the Philadelphia Phillies at night.

It had been kind of a hectic Thursday at home for the Milwaukee Braves' right-hander before he arrived at County Stadium. It didn't help that he hadn't made it to bed until 3 a.m. after returning from a road game in Cincinnati. When he got up he had lunch and went out and tended to the lawn. Things kind of deteriorated after that.

He was changing a light bulb in the kitchen when he dropped it, and it hit him on the head. That caused him to drop the fixture, which broke a valve off the stove on its way to the floor. So Burdette just took the next few hours off before heading out to the ballpark where he was planning to meet his wife after the game.

But Mary Burdette was having a busy day herself. Nine-year-old Kenny was late getting back from camp, and by the time she got him and the other kids ready for bed, it was too late to get to the game on time. So she spent the evening listening on the radio while her husband pitched the best game of his life.

Not only did Burdette hold the Phillies hitless over nine innings, but he came within inches of a perfect game. Mixing a sharp fastball with sliders, sinkers and the occasional screwball, he retired the first 13 batters he faced. But then a slider slid a little bit too far inside, and he nicked Tony Gonzalez on the right shoulder with a pitch in the top of the fifth inning. It didn't seem like a big deal at the time because Gonzalez was quickly erased in a double play.

When Burdette proceeded to set down the next 12 batters, it meant that he'd faced the minimum 27 on his way to only the second no-hitter pitched by a Brave in Milwaukee. All that was left was for him to score the winning run in a 1-0 victory. He did that by doubling in the eighth inning and coming home on Billy Bruton's double off old teammate Gene Conley.

It took Burdette just 91 pitches and 2 hours 10 minutes to dominate the Phillies, who managed only four fly balls and never came close to scoring. Their best chance for a hit came on Pancho Herrera's bunt in the second inning, and Burdette threw him out himself. Burdette struck out three and didn't walk anyone while pitching his second shutout in his last two starts.

The 33-year-old veteran had had two one-hitters in his 11-year career, but he'd pretty much given up hope of throwing a no-hitter. Known as "Fidgety Lew," he was famous for putting runners on and working out of jams. "I still can't believe it," he said. "For a guy who gives up more hits in one inning than anyone, I never thought I'd do it."

But he did, and Burdette called it one of the easiest games he'd ever pitched. He said his fastball was the best he'd had in a couple of years, and the balls the Phillies did hit went right to someone. The last three outs were a breeze. He got catcher Jim Coker on a tap back to the mound and then retired pinch-hitters Ken Walters on a ground ball to third and Bobby Gene Smith on a soft fly to right.

Naturally, no one in the dugout said anything about a no-hitter while it was in progress, although Burdette said he toyed with the idea of bringing it up himself just for fun. In the end, he was mobbed by his teammates and cheered by a sparse crowd of 16,338.

Mrs. Burdette was not among them. When it was over, she called her husband on the phone.

WEISSMULLER SWIMS TO VICTORY IN MILWAUKEE RIVER

AUGUST 19, 1922

When the man who would become Tarzan in a dozen movies journeyed to Milwaukee to claim another swimming championship, you might say the crowd went ape.

Johnny Weissmuller was a big man with a huge name in water sports when he and two competitors met at the banks of the Milwaukee River to vie for the Central Amateur Athletic Union 150-yard backstroke title. The 6-foot-3, 195-pound Pennsylvania native with the Hollywood looks was on his way to breaking at least 51 world records over a nine-year career, and he fully intended to knock off another one that day. He might have, too, if the guide boat hadn't gotten lost.

Thousands watched from the North Avenue Bridge, and hundreds more lined the banks or paddled boats alongside to see Weissmuller leave two local swimmers in his wake. It was clearly a different time as the waters were described by *The Milwaukee Journal* as "shimmering." Unfortunately, the guide boat headed off in the wrong direction and took a circuitous route that had the contestants swimming upstream for much of the race. And so Weissmuller's winning time of 2 minutes 14-plus seconds was 16 seconds short of his record, but no doubt respectable considering the circumstances. The *Milwaukee Sentinel* estimated that the guide added 35 yards to the race.

Weismuller didn't seem to mind, though. The important thing was that he won. He would go on to capture five gold medals in the 1924 and '28 Olympics, as well as a bronze for playing on the American water polo team, and he claimed never to have lost a race. Even more remarkable perhaps was that he held records in distances ranging from 50 to 800 yards.

While Weismuller was responsible for drawing the large crowd to the meet on the Milwaukee River, he wasn't the only future Olympian there. Eleanor Coleman, who grew up in Milwaukee and was representing the Milwaukee Athletic Club, won the 100-yard breaststroke. Coleman would qualify for the 200-meter breast in the 1924 Olympic Games, but she didn't place.

This wasn't Weismuller's only appearance in Milwaukee, either. In fact, seven months earlier in another Central AAU championship event at the MAC he was credited with a world record in the 100-yard backstroke. He also swam at the MAC in October and November of that year, getting credit for another world record in the 100 back on the second of those two visits. In all, Weismuller swam in Milwaukee roughly 10 times over a six-year period from 1922 to '28.

Weismuller was planning to compete in the 1932 Olympics in Los Angeles when the makers of BVD swimming suits offered him the staggering sum of $500 a week to promote their product. His travels for the swimwear company would take him to LA and one day, out of the blue, he was invited to audition for the role of Tarzan. Acting wasn't exactly Weissmuller's forte, but the role required a photogenic body and only a few lines, and he got to star with Maureen O'Sullivan, who also had a photogenic body.

Weismuller made a fortune in show biz, but he also went through a series of business partners and four wives and lost it all. The man who claimed 36 national swimming championships in his career before becoming a household name to movie-goers everywhere was reduced to taking a greeter's job at a Las Vegas hotel in 1973. Less than a year later he fell and broke his leg, and while he was in the hospital he suffered the first in a series of heart attacks and strokes.

He was an invalid, broke and living in Acapulco, Mexico, with his fifth wife when he died in January 1984 at the age of 79.

MILWAUKEE'S IKE RUEHL UPSETS DON BUDGE

AUGUST 20, 1933

Don Budge had a red face to go with his fiery red hair after making a little stop at the Wisconsin State Open tennis tournament.

The California teenager who would later become the best player in the world wasn't even the best amateur in Milwaukee on a Sunday at the Town Club, then located on Farwell Avenue, just south of Brady Street, when he ran into a local player named Milton "Ike" Ruehl. Budge had just captured the national junior championship eight days earlier in Culver, Ind., and he wasn't expected to have much trouble in a state tournament, even though this was no ordinary state tournament.

Between the twenties and the early fifties, the Wisconsin Open drew a whole passel of tennis heavyweights as they made their way east to the U.S. Open in Forest Hills, N.Y. Stars like Ellsworth Vines, Frank Shields, Herb Flam and Vic Seixas played in Milwaukee for expense money. This was in the days when everyone had to be an amateur to participate in the four Grand Slam tournaments – the U.S., the French Open, the Australian Open and Wimbledon – and, naturally, expenses varied according to how big a draw the player was.

Budge was just 18 when he came here, but everyone knew he was headed for stardom. Budge knew it, too, and according to press accounts of his match with Ruehl, it showed in his play.

Ruehl was no slouch. Holder of the state closed championship, he was Wisconsin's only nationally-ranked player and the best hope for a native son to win the Wisconsin Open for the first time in 11 years. Budge took a nonchalant approach to the local favorite, and before he knew it, he had nonchalanted himself into two service breaks as Ruehl took a 4-1 lead in the first set.

Budge rallied briefly, but he still lost the set, 6-3. By the time Ruehl had Budge's full attention, the Milwaukeean was in a groove, and he won the match easily, 6-3, 6-2, 6-4. As a result, Ruehl became the first Wisconsin player to win the tournament since Abbie Weller in 1922.

Looking back almost 50 years later in an interview with Bob Wolf of *The Milwaukee Journal*, Ruehl said, "I guess my shots were just dropping in. I always had a lot of stamina, and because this was before tennis was a game of the big serve and volley, I was the stronger player."

Not many men would be able to make that claim after matches with Budge, once the Oakland, Calif., ace refined his game. Never a big hitter, he was a maddening opponent, who simply hit everything back. As one rival put it, "Playing tennis against him was like playing against a concrete wall. There was nothing to attack."

Four years after losing to Ruehl, Budge turned Wimbledon into his private estate, winning the men's singles, the men's doubles and the mixed doubles. He also won the U.S. Open that year and was voted the Sullivan Award as the nation's best amateur athlete. And then he had an even better season in 1938.

That's when he swept all four Grand Slam tournaments, becoming the first player ever to do that in the same year. He turned pro in 1939, joining a fledgling tour, and won two U.S. pro championships before entering the Air Force in 1942.

The tour was suspended when World War II broke out, and Budge suffered a shoulder injury in the service that prevented him from ever regaining his past form. But he finished third behind Bill Tilden and Jack Kramer in a 1950 Associated Press poll to determine the greatest tennis player of the half-century, and he was inducted into the International Tennis Hall of Fame in 1964. By any standard, he compiled an outstanding record with one little smudge on it from his visit to Milwaukee, thanks to Ike Ruehl.

CONTROVERSY ERUPTS OVER HAMM'S GOLD MEDAL

AUGUST 21, 2004

He needed a miracle, and then he needed a lawyer. The first was to claim a gold medal. The second was to keep it.

On Aug. 18, Waukesha's Paul Hamm brought the crowd at the 2004 Olympic Games in Athens to its feet with a spectacular high bar routine that made him the first American gymnast ever to win the men's Olympic all-around competition. He had been lagging in 12th place with two events to go and hoping for a silver at best, maybe a bronze. But with an international television audience and everyone in the gym watching him, he posted a cold-blooded 9.837 score on his final rotation to win by .012 of a point over Kim Dae-eun of South Korea.

It was a record-low winning margin. It also led to a legal wrangle that started in Greece on Aug. 21 when the governing body for gymnastics announced that Hamm had won due to a scoring error and ended with a ruling in Switzerland on Oct. 21. Only when the painful two-month process was over could Hamm be sure he was still the Olympic champion.

Hamm's troubles began when the South Korean team belatedly noticed that the judges had given their star Yang Tae-young's parallel bar routine the wrong start value, erroneously deducting one-tenth of a point. If Yang had gotten that tenth, he would have edged Hamm by a .051-point margin for the gold. Instead, Yang was awarded the bronze medal.

Start values are crucial in gymnastics arithmetic. A routine begins with a specific number based on its difficulty, and then the judges make deductions for errors. In Yang's case, the start value should have been 10, but the three judges mistakenly recorded it as 9.9.

The mistake got the judges fired, but it didn't get the South Korean the gold. His team protested the scoring to the International Gymnastics Federation after the competition was completed. The federation acknowledged the error and immediately suspended the judges, but it disallowed the protest because it came too late. By FIG's rules, it had to be made before Yang went on to his next rotation, not after the meet was over. Doing it any other way would have been like flagging down an NFL instant replay official on the way to his car.

The Koreans appealed the ruling the next day and got turned down again. Then they appealed to the Court of Arbitration for Sports, or the court of last resort in international competition, in Lausanne, Switzerland. But CAS also ruled against the South Koreans, declaring that the protest had been filed too late and that it had no jurisdiction to change the ruling anyway.

And so finally Hamm was able to take his medal out of a drawer at home where he'd wrapped it in a sock. "I feel like I've won it three times," he said.

Hamm said the sock was to keep the medal from getting nicked up in case he had to give it to somebody else. It was very considerate of him, but his consideration also had its limits.

FIG learned that earlier when it sent him a letter in late August asking him to voluntarily turn the gold over to Yang in a gesture "that would be recognized as the ultimate demonstration of fair play by the whole world." FIG had asked the United States Olympic Committee to deliver the letter to Hamm, but it refused, calling the maneuver "deplorable." FIG was in effect asking Hamm to save it from its own mistake and he had no reason to do so.

As several experts pointed out, if Yang had gotten the right start value, he probably would have lost anyway. Hamm's own routine in the parallel bars had been clearly better than Yang's, and the judges would have had to up his score, too. Besides, a replay of Yang's routine showed that the judges had missed a crucial deduction that would have cost him any medal at all.

Hamm had already gotten a silver medal in the team competition before the all-around began. He went on to win a silver in the individual high bar on Aug. 23, giving him three medals for the Games, which equaled the American men's total from 1976 to 2004. He still has them all. Nobody knows what happened to the sock.

STATE ROWERS WIN OLYMPIC GOLD

AUGUST 22, 2004

Chris Ahrens began rowing at the age of seven, competed in his first race at 14 and led the powerful Princeton heavyweight eight to the top of the Ivy League. Beau Hoopman bumped into a guy with a clipboard at freshman registration and thought he'd check out crew.

Otherwise, they had a lot in common. Both were from Wisconsin and both brought home gold medals when the United States Olympic team ended a 40-year drought in the men's eight-oared shell with coxswain competition in Athens, Greece.

It takes a special kind of mindset to excel in crew. The sport is equal parts pain and anonymity, which may have been why America hadn't won a gold in the men's eights since 1964 in Tokyo or any kind of medal at all since taking a bronze in Seoul in 1988.

That wasn't supposed to change in the 2004 Games, but when Ahrens, Hoopman and friends overtook favored Canada in the final 500 meters of a first-round heat to win in a world-best time and advance directly to the final, the Yanks began to attract attention. A week later, they led the final race from start to finish and beat out the Dutch by 1.27 seconds. Australia won the bronze medal, and Canada fell to fifth.

"I had resigned myself to never winning gold," Ahrens later told the *The Daily Princetonian*. "So there was a certain amount of disbelief when we crossed the finish line."

Ahrens, a Whitefish Bay High School graduate, had been a long time arriving at that moment. He started his rowing career with his dad when he was in grade school and he stayed at it right through Princeton and beyond, helping the Americans to a fifth place finish at the Sydney Olympics in 2000. He walked away from the sport for three years and then decided to walk back. "I thought I might as well give it a shot now. If it doesn't happen, it doesn't happen," he said.

It happened.

It happened, too, for Hoopman, and a little more quickly. The Plymouth High School graduate and a former swimmer there was registering for his first classes at the University of Wisconsin when he noticed a stranger with a clipboard staring at him. "I thought, 'Uh oh, what's this guy want?'" he recalled in an interview with the *Milwaukee Journal Sentinel*.

"He said, 'You look like an athlete.' I said, 'Uh... yeah?' He said, 'Would you be interested in crew?' I'm like, 'What's crew?'"

Six years later, Hoopman had a pretty good idea as the American shell crossed the finish line in Athens. This didn't come as a total surprise given the Badgers' reputation in crew. They don't have Princeton's rich tradition, but there's been at least one UW rower at every Olympics since 1968. According to Hoopman, it's not because they love the sport either.

"We do it with tall, lanky kids from Wisconsin," he said. "I've never met a rower who loves rowing. They love winning and they love racing, and they love competition, but it's a brutal sport. It's a lot of hard work, a lot of hours, a lot of strokes taken for five-and-a-half minutes of utter pain."

Hoopman knows what he's talking about. He suffered two herniated discs in his back, but that didn't stop him from rowing with the national team for seven years and competing in five world championships. He won a gold medal in the world championships in 2005 and a bronze in 2006. Then in 2008 he was back at the Olympics along with another UW rower named Micah Boyd from St. Paul, Minn.

This time the U.S. men didn't finish first but they rallied from sixth place at the 500-meter mark to claim a bronze medal. The women's eight, meanwhile, won the gold. America's dry spell in the water was definitely over.

HIRSCH STARS FOR COLLEGE ALL-STARS

AUGUST 23, 1946

Elroy Hirsch had just finished his sophomore year at the University of Wisconsin the last time the collegians had beaten the NFL champions in the much ballyhooed College All-Star Game. That was in 1943, and there didn't seem to be much reason to think the pros' streak would end three years later, although 97,380 people paid their way into Chicago's Soldier Field looking for an upset.

The game had been played 12 times before, and the All-Stars had just three victories. But then the All-Stars had never had Elroy Hirsch before.

The pride of Wausau just wasn't used to losing. He'd played on back-to-back unbeaten teams as a junior and senior at Wausau High School, and then he'd led the Badgers to an 8-1-1 record in 1942. The following year, he was shipped to the University of Michigan as part of a special naval training program – because Wisconsin had no such program – and he helped the Wolverines to an 8-1 record. After one year at Ann Arbor, Hirsch was given the option of playing service football for the El Toro Marines in California rather than being shipped overseas.

Now he was getting ready to embark on a highly successful 12-year pro career, but first he had the NFL champion Los Angeles Rams to deal with in America's most celebrated exhibition game. Technically, that's what the College All-Star Game was, but it was much more important in the eyes of the fans in those days. From 1934, the first year of the All-Star Game, through 1954, it drew three crowds of more than 100,000 and seven others of more than 90,000. And it continued to draw well into the 1970s when interest began to diminish and the game was given its last rites.

The 1946 game was clearly one of the collegians' best showings. They not only beat the pro elite, they shut them out, 16-0, as Hirsch scored both of their touchdowns. He got plenty of help from another former Badger, fullback Pat Harder, who sprung him for one of the scores and kicked both extra points.

The game didn't start all that well for Hirsch as he fumbled the ball away twice in the first quarter. But with the All-Stars facing a second down with eight yards to go, he took a handoff from quarterback Otto Graham, skirted around left end as Harder blocked the first man in the secondary and sprinted 68 yards for a touchdown. Harder added the conversion, and the collegians had a 7-0 lead they'd never lose.

In the third quarter, Hirsch faked to the flat, turned up the field and caught a long pass from Graham in full stride. The play netted 62 yards and a touchdown. The All-Stars added a safety later, and the rout was complete.

"We just had more drive," said Harder in a joyous All-Star locker room, "and Elroy ran like a mad fool."

Hirsch was named the game's Most Valuable Player, joining his old teammate in earning that honor. Harder, a native of Milwaukee, was one of those rare players who participated in two College All-Star Games during the war years, and the collegians won both of them. He'd been named the MVP in 1943 and after playing again in '46, he went on to play eight years for the Chicago Cardinals, leading them in scoring in 1947 when they won the NFL title.

Hirsch played only one season at Wisconsin, but he didn't waste a minute of it. Some 27 years before he returned to Madison to become the Badgers' athletic director he'd taken them to the nation's No. 3 ranking. He also earned the nickname that stuck with him until his death in 2004. In a victory over the Great Lakes Naval Training Station in mid-October, Hirsch broke loose for a 61-yard run and Francis Powers of the *Chicago Daily News* wrote the next day, "His crazy legs were gyrating in six different directions all at the same time."

Hirsch liked it. "Anything was better than Elroy," he said.

After the College All-Star Game, Hirsch played three seasons with the Chicago Rockets of the All-America Football Conference before he jumped to the NFL and landed with the Rams. He played nine years in Los Angeles and earned a spot in the Pro Football Hall of Fame before coming back to Wisconsin and serving as athletic director from 1969 to '87.

Only six football numbers have ever been retired by the Badgers. Elroy "Crazylegs" Hirsch's No. 40 is one of them.

Elroy "Crazylegs" Hirsch

ARMOUR WINS WESTERN AT OZAUKEE COUNTRY CLUB

AUGUST 24, 1929

Dour Scotsman Tommy Armour was too stern to be a gallery favorite, but he was more than welcome when he came to rural Mequon for the 29th Western Open. The Western was one of golf's most prestigious tournaments at the time, and its presence at the seven-year-old Ozaukee Country Club marked the return of big time golf to the Milwaukee metropolitan area after a 13-year absence.

The Western was first played in 1899, and it had made two previous stops in the Milwaukee area. Alex Smith won the tournament at the Milwaukee Country Club in 1903, and the great Walter Hagen won at Blue Mound Golf & Country Club in 1916.

Armour, as a former U.S. Open champion, was one of the field's biggest names in 1929. He was also one of its more inspiring stories, although most of the people who watched him play may not have known it.

Armour was a promising amateur golfer in his native Edinburgh, Scotland, when he volunteered for World War I and saw his career very nearly end not once but twice on the battlefield. He was one of only two survivors when a tank he commanded was shelled in 1918, and then later in the war, a mustard gas explosion left him blind with a metal plate in his head and a badly wounded left arm.

He regained the sight in his right eye following a six-month recuperation, but when he came to the Western, he was operating with just one eye and a healed but still-weakened arm. Not that anyone would know it to watch him play.

Armour seized the lead in the opening round, tying the course record with a 65 on a rainy Thursday, and then ran away from everyone. He followed with a 71 and a 69 before his final 68 left him with a tournament record 273 and a whopping eight-shot victory over second-place Horton Smith of Joplin, Mo. Willard Hutchinson was third and Gene Sarazen fourth.

"There is really little to say in detail concerning Armour's golf, because it so utterly lacked sensational recovery shots or unusual strokes," Billy Sixty, golf writer for *The Milwaukee Journal*, wrote the next day. "To watch him was to look at a human golfing machine performing like a mechanical toy wound up and simply going over the hills and dales clicking off one perfect shot after another."

The crowds for Saturday's 36-hole final were estimated to be between 7,000 and 10,000, and tournament officials had already said after Friday's round that all expenses had been covered. The galleries saw Armour reel off 19 birdies over 72 holes and toy with most of the nation's best golfers. It was his biggest victory since he'd beaten Henry Cooper in a playoff for the 1927 U.S. Open title, but it was hardly his last. In all, he would win 25 PGA events, including the 1930 PGA Championship and the 1931 British Open.

And none of it might have happened if Armour hadn't gotten on a ship for the United States after winning the 1920 French Amateur and encountered Hagen on board. Hagen, who was returning from the British Open at the time, helped get Armour a job as secretary of the Westchester-Biltmore Club. That gave the young player a chance to become a U.S. citizen two years later and develop his game before he turned pro in 1924.

Armour's career took off with the 1927 Open triumph, and he won his last tournament in 1938. Thereafter, he became one of the great teachers of golf and was well known for his homespun golfing aphorisms.

Armour also has been credited with coining the term "yips" for the malady that affects terrified golfers standing over short putts. "Once you've had 'em, you've got 'em," he said. He clearly didn't have them when the Western Open came to Ozaukee Country Club.

MOLITOR EXTENDS HIT STREAK TO 39

AUGUST 25, 1987

On a night when his teammates got 10 hits, it was beginning to look as if Paul Molitor wouldn't get any.

Six weeks and 38 games had passed since the last time the Milwaukee Brewers' designated hitter had gone hitless, but the streak was in grave danger when he came to the plate in the sixth inning against Cleveland reliever Don Gordon. The Brewers had been beating up on the Indians' pitching all night, and Molitor had hit the ball pretty well himself, but all he had to show for it was a deep fly ball to right, a walk and a hard, one-hop groundout.

There had been only eight other times during the streak that he'd failed to get a hit in his first three at-bats, but with the weather threatening and the Brewers leading, 8-4, this was perhaps his last chance. Oddly, he took advantage of it by getting fooled on a pitch.

He was looking for a slider on Gordon's first offering, but he got a fastball instead and fought it off for a single to right field. When the ball landed, a County Stadium crowd of 15,580 could breathe again. The Brewers finished the night with a 10-9 victory, and the fifth-longest hitting streak in modern Major League Baseball history was alive and well at 39 games. But not for long.

Molitor's next target was the 40-game run put together by Ty Cobb in 1911, and then maybe he could think about Pete Rose's 44-game streak in 1978. The ultimate, of course, was Joe DiMaggio's 56 in 1941, but that was still considered one of baseball's least reachable records. Las Vegas was giving 75-1 odds that Molitor wouldn't get there, and Las Vegas was right. His streak ended the next night.

The main culprit on a cold and damp Wednesday, again at County Stadium, was 25-year-old right-hander John Farrell, who had been in the big leagues for little more than a week. Farrell would win only 36 games in an eight-year career, but he never let Molitor get close to a base hit. He struck him out in the first inning, got him to hit into a double play in the third, retired him on a ground ball to short in the sixth and would have gotten him a fourth time if Molitor hadn't reached base on an error in the eighth. Molitor gave Farrell all the credit afterward, saying that he hadn't hit a ball solidly all night, but the man most people remember for ending the streak was one of his own teammates.

Rick Manning was already popularity challenged with Brewer fans through no fault of his own because he'd come to Milwaukee four years earlier in the trade that sent Gorman Thomas to Cleveland. And then Manning did the unforgivable. He got a game-winning base hit.

His problem was the hit came in the tenth inning with Molitor on deck, denying him a final chance to extend the streak. Pinch-hitting for Juan Castillo, Manning rapped a one-out single to center off reliever Doug Jones that scored Mike Felder and gave the Brewers a 1-0 victory over the Indians. Molitor rushed to first base to congratulate Manning, who promptly apologized to him for getting the hit. Molitor wasn't sure he'd heard him right, but a sparse crowd of 11,246 understood the sentiment. Most of them booed Manning.

Molitor, on the other hand, was just happy to win the game, 1-0, preserving a three-hitter for Teddy Higuera. "In a lot of ways, it's a disappointment," he said. "But there is a sense of relief that maybe we can get back to a little sense of normality around here now and get the focus back on the ballclub."

Molitor hit .353 that year, and the Brewers finished 20 games over .500. In many ways it was the best year of his career.

Paul Molitor

LONG WAIT ENDS FOR EDGERTON'S STRICKER

AUGUST 26, 2007

Steve Stricker had been living on a steady diet of disappointment all season, and K.J. Choi was cooking up another batch. The South Korean star had sunk a 46-foot birdie putt on the 12th hole to tie the pride of Edgerton, Wis., for the lead on the last day of The Barclays tournament, and then he canned a 48-footer on No. 15 to go ahead by one stroke.

This was the fifth time that Stricker had either led or been within one shot of the lead in the final round of a tournament during the 2007 season. Two of them, the U.S. Open and the British Open, had been majors, and all of the previous four had ended with him as an also-ran.

Considering the fact that Stricker hadn't won a championship in his last 146 tries, this one looked like a killer. But he was nothing if not determined. In fact, he would go on to set some kind of arcane record for resilience before the year was over by earning the PGA Tour's Comeback Player of the Year award for the second year in a row.

Choi learned of his recuperative powers the hard way when Stricker reclaimed a share of the lead with a birdie on Westchester Country Club's 16th hole and followed that with two more birdies on 17 and 18 to claim his first tour title in six-and-a-half years by two shots. "I put myself in position enough times that I didn't want to screw it up again," said a tearful Stricker after his final two-under-par 69 left him 16 under for the tournament.

The winner's check was worth $1.26 million, but it was the trophy, not the money, that had the champion all choked up. Seven top ten finishes had earned him his first comeback award in 2006, but until he won a tournament there would always be doubt about his recovery from a slump that had made him consider abandoning the game a couple of years earlier.

This was the last thing anyone was expecting when the sixth-year pro won two tournaments and finished fourth on the money list in 1996. At age 29, Stricker was considered a "can't miss" star. But his only victory in the next 10 years came over a diluted field in the 2001 World Match Play tournament in Australia. By 2003 he'd fallen to 188th on the money list with $150,000.

Forced to go back to the PGA's qualifying school, he missed regaining his card by two shots in December 2005, and that was when he started to consider some other line of work. "The thought had crossed my mind during that year that maybe I should think about doing something else," Stricker said in a 2008 interview in *Golf Digest* magazine. "The guys I was playing with (at Q school) were hitting it 50 yards longer than me and straighter. I was thinking, 'What's going on here?'"

But there was really nothing else that Stricker wanted to do. So he went back to Madison and spent the winter hitting balls into the snow. After searching for the right equipment and fiddling with his swing for years, he found a combination that worked and used it to make an impressive $1.8 million in 2006 playing without a card.

But it was in 2007 that he served notice that he was all the way back. He moved back up to No. 4 on the earnings list that year in addition to winning the comeback award again. "It tells you how far I had to come back that I had the chance to win it two years in a row," he said.

Stricker didn't win a tournament in 2008, but he earned a highly coveted spot on the American Ryder Cup team. And then in 2009 he won the Crowne Plaza Invitational on May 31, the John Deere Classic on July 12 and the Deutsche Bank Championship on Sept. 7.

For a man who'd gone more than six years without a victory, Stricker was literally on top of the golf world. In fact, after he won the Northern Trust Open in Pacific Palisades, Calif., the fifth event on the 2010 tour, Stricker moved up to No. 2 in the world rankings, ahead of Phil Mickelson and behind only Tiger Woods.

The slump was clearly over.

TIGER WOODS TURNS PRO IN MILWAUKEE

AUGUST 27, 1996

Fifty people, give or take a few, decided to take a stroll around Brown Deer Golf Course on a Tuesday morning to see what the fuss was all about. The good-looking kid from Stanford was getting in a practice round for the Greater Milwaukee Open, and they wanted to watch.

With his swing coach and his mom keeping him company, the kid was giving the customers a good show. And then he blew them away by driving it 330 yards on the par-five 18th and hitting a three-iron 225 yards stiff to the pin. Tiger Woods' first gallery as a professional golfer had gotten its money's worth.

Veteran Dave Stockton played the practice round with him and proved to be a prophet when it was over and he said, "Everyone keeps saying how they're waiting for the next big star. Well, here he is."

The three-time U.S. Amateur champion walked off the course that day a pro for the first time, having announced his decision in a two-paragraph statement released by the PGA Tour earlier in the day. The next day, Aug. 28, following the pro-am, Woods entertained questions from the media.

No less an expert than Jack Nicklaus had declared Woods a can't-miss superstar, and the golf world had been waiting for months for him to make his move. He could have done it anywhere, but he did it in Milwaukee, thanks at least partly to a conversation between his dad and a newspaper reporter.

Earl Woods was being interviewed by golf writer Gary D'Amato of the *Milwaukee Journal Sentinel* while the two were in Augusta for the Masters. The elder Woods mentioned that he'd like to get his son into a couple of PGA Tour events on sponsor's exemptions, and D'Amato asked him if he'd be interested in bringing Tiger to Milwaukee. He said he would, and so D'Amato got Earl Woods' home phone number and called GMO tournament director Tom Strong. Strong took the number and made a call that brought what would become the tour's biggest name to one of its smallest stops.

Even as a 20-year-old, Woods was already a commercial success. Endorsement contracts worth more than $60 million over five years were waiting for him when he left the amateur scene. Nike wanted a piece of him, as did Titleist and Cobra Golf, and soon there would be so many more. Strong was just happy to have a week of his time.

The GMO had a better than usual walk-up crowd that week, thanks to its young star, and it wasn't because he was tearing up the course. Woods needed 277 shots to finish the 72-hole tournament, leaving him seven-under par and tied for 60th. The third round was his undoing. Tired and a little overwhelmed by all the attention, he shot a two-over 73 on Saturday and went back to his hotel to take a nap. But he was ready on Sunday.

A healthy crowd gathered to see him tee off at 8:28 in the morning, and it was rewarded when Woods took out his six-iron and aced the 202-yard 14th hole. It was the fourth hole-in-one of the tournament and the ninth of his career, and it topped off a good day and a good week for both Woods and Milwaukee.

He'd gotten a load of hats, shirts and bags from Nike as well as his first tournament check. And the GMO had gotten more attention from the golf world than it had ever known. The check was worth $2,544. The attention was priceless.

Asked if he'd be back, Woods said, "Sure. People supported me 110% here. I was very surprised that so many people got up so early to watch me play today, because I sure the hell wouldn't have."

The GMO, or U.S. Bank Championship as it was eventually renamed, never saw him again and then it lost its spot on the PGA Tour in 2010.

NEGRO LEAGUE LEGENDS APPEAR IN MILWAUKEE

AUGUST 28, 1935

They were names without faces, players denied their stage. Some of the best athletes the wide world had never known.

Josh Gibson, James "Cool Papa" Bell, Oscar Charleston and William "Judy" Johnson. All of them would be named to the Baseball Hall of Fame and none of them would ever wear a major league uniform. They were in the lineup of the now legendary Pittsburgh Crawfords that came to Milwaukee for a two-day series at Borchert Park.

This was 12 years after Milwaukee's own entry into the Negro National League had come and gone in less than a full season. That team was called the Milwaukee Bears, and it didn't play a home game after June 11. But Negro League teams continued to barnstorm in the state, even playing league games, particularly in the late 1930s and early '40s. The Crawfords weren't strangers in the state, either. A week earlier, they had played an exhibition in Madison and beaten the Madison Blues.

This time, the Crawfords were playing a league opponent, a team called the Chicago American Giants, who had been using Milwaukee almost as a second home, and they beat them soundly, although not quite as soundly on that Friday night as they had the night before. They'd won the series opener, 17-2, and then completed the sweep, 8-3, on Aug. 28.

It may have been the greatest display of baseball talent the city has ever seen, but probably no more than a few thousand people were on hand to witness it. And the results rated only a single paragraph with a box score in the *Milwaukee Sentinel* and even less space in the *Wisconsin News*, another Milwaukee daily. *The Milwaukee Journal* didn't even bother to mention it.

Gibson homered for the Crawfords, and lefty Sam Streeter, a longtime Negro League pitcher, earned the win, allowing only one hit until he was tagged for two home runs in the ninth inning.

The Crawfords began as an amateur team of Pittsburgh coal miners before night club owner Gus Greenlee took them over in 1930. He raided the rival Homestead Grays to acquire Gibson and Johnson, and his Crawfords won the league championship in 1935 and '36. He might have won it every year after that if the raider hadn't been raided himself. Dominican Republic dictator Rafael Trujillo convinced Gibson, his immortal battery mate Satchel Paige and several other teammates to join his Santo Domingo team in 1937, and the Crawfords never recovered.

Before there was Jackie Robinson, there was Gibson, a powerful catcher who some called the Babe Ruth of Negro league baseball. The 6-foot-2, 210-pound Gibson reportedly signed a contract with the Pittsburgh Pirates in 1943, four years before Robinson broke baseball's color line, but Commissioner Kenesaw Mountain Landis canceled the deal.

In a 17-year career, Gibson has been credited with a .391 batting average and as many as 962 home runs, although there were no exact statistics kept in the Negro leagues. He died at the age of 35 after spending time in a mental hospital in Washington, D.C.

Bell was a pitcher first and a center fielder later whose trademark was blazing speed. People liked to say that he was so fast that he once hit a ground ball up the middle and got hit by the ball as he slid into second base. Bell also has been credited with a .342 lifetime average. He was 48 years old and retired when he was invited to play for the St. Louis Browns of the American League. He politely declined.

Charleston was a big man who was always looking for a game or for a fight. He stood 5-11 and weighed as little as 175 pounds and as much as 240 during his career. He supposedly hit .350 or better for nine straight years and .400 twice. The fiery Charleston was famous for hitting five home runs in five games in a barnstorming series against the St. Louis Cardinals and for threatening to throw pro wrestling champion Jim Londos out of a train window.

Johnson was the captain of the Crawfords and one of the best defensive third basemen the game has ever known. He was credited with being a .350 lifetime hitter and went on to be a scout for the Milwaukee Braves, among other teams. He signed Billy Bruton for the Braves, and Bruton wound up marrying his daughter.

Gibson was elected to the Hall of Fame in 1972. Bell made it in 1974, Johnson in 1975 and Charleston in 1976. Much too late.

PACKERS BEAT COLLEGE ALL-STARS BEFORE 84,567

AUGUST 29, 1940

The College All-Star Game did lots of things in its early days. It was a moneymaker for Chicago charities, a showcase for college football and an advertising vehicle for the emerging National Football League. It was also a personal playground for Cecil Isbell.

When the Green Bay Packers traveled to Soldier Field for the seventh annual event, they needed to establish some credibility both for themselves and their league. The defending NFL champs and collegians had each won two games, and two others had ended in ties. The All-Stars had beaten Green Bay, 6-0, in 1937; and the following year, they'd whipped Washington, 28-16, behind a strong-armed back from Purdue.

The back was Isbell, and he'd been named the Most Valuable Player of the game. Now he was playing for the Packers.

Green Bay was favored to win in 1940, but not by much. College football was still king in those times, and the NFL needed the exposure of the All-Star Game while it struggled to gain a foothold among the nation's fans. Isbell and the Packers gave it plenty of that on their way to a 45-28 victory.

And they did it before a record crowd of 84,567. At that point, no NFL Championship Game had drawn more than 50,000 fans, and the Packers had played before only one other crowd of more than 50,000. That was in the 1937 College All-Star Game when they drew 84,560. Otherwise, their biggest regular-season crowd in their first 19 years was 48,279 for a game in New York against the Giants in 1938.

In those days before television, this was the biggest stage that the Packers could possibly play on and they started out with Isbell throwing an interception on their first possession that led to an All-Stars' touchdown. But then Isbell went to work. Before the first quarter was over, he had thrown an 81-yard touchdown pass to Don Hutson and a 26-yard touchdown pass to fellow end Carl Mullenaux for a 14-7 lead. Isbell's strike to Hutson traveled 60 yards in the air.

After the All-Stars tied the game, 14-14, the Packers struck for two more touchdown passes. Future Hall of Famer Arnie Herber came off the bench and teamed up with halfback Andy Uram for a 60-yard touchdown, and Isbell connected with Hutson again for a 35-yard touchdown. But former Iowa star Nile Kinnick threw a 56-yard touchdown pass to pull the All-Stars to within, 28-21, at halftime.

At this point, the two teams had already broken the record for most points in an All-Star Game, and they were far from finished. After Herber hit Hutson with a 29-yard touchdown pass in the third quarter, the All-Stars cut the difference again to 35-28 with nearly eight minutes remaining in the game. Then, the Packers clinched the outcome with a 25-yard field goal by Ernie Smith and a four-yard touchdown run by Isbell.

Twenty years later and just four years before his death, Lambeau called the victory his greatest coaching thrill, which was taking in a lot of territory since he'd led the Packers to six NFL championships. "That game established pro football," Lambeau told Lee Remmel of the *Green Bay Press-Gazette*.

The game had to rank pretty highly with Isbell, too. He finished with eight completions in 12 attempts for 210 yards with three touchdowns. It also would be his last appearance in the series. He retired following the 1942 season, seven months after throwing 24 touchdown passes to set a league record.

Isbell played only five years as a pro, leading the league in passing the last two. He was 28 years old when he left the Packers to join Purdue as an assistant coach, walking away from what might well have been a Hall of Fame career. When he retired, Isbell had received as much all-pro recognition as the great Sammy Baugh, who had entered the NFL a year earlier.

The Packers would play in six more All-Star Games and win five of them. But they dropped the 1963 game, 20-17, making them the first and the last NFL team to lose to the All-Stars. The series was terminated after Pittsburgh won, 24-0, in 1976 in a game called with 1 minute 22 seconds left in the third quarter due to a severe thunderstorm.

By then, the game was no longer competitive. The NFL champions won the last 12 games and the series, 31-9-2. But to this day, three of the eight largest crowds the Packers ever played before were in the College All-Star Game. In fact, the most people ever to watch the Packers play were the 92,753 fans who filled Soldier Field for the 1945 All-Star Game.

EZRA JOHNSON HOT DOGS IT

AUGUST 30, 1980

As if Bart Starr didn't have enough trouble... The Green Bay Packers' sixth-year coach had enjoyed exactly one winning season. He was coming off a 5-11 year, and the fans were losing patience even if the team president wasn't. The Packers were not only on the verge of going winless in the exhibition season for the first time in 34 years while scoring a total of 17 points in five games, but they were also in the process of getting mauled, 38-0, by Denver in the last of those games on Aug. 30. As they struggled, the Lambeau Field crowd not only booed them off the field, but they cheered the Broncos.

And now this.

Several observers said they'd seen players gesturing and talking to the fans during the second half of the game. And they'd spotted something else much goofier than that. Standing near the team bench was defensive end Ezra Johnson in full uniform munching on a hot dog!

It wasn't clear who had supplied the tube steak or whether it was slathered with mustard or secret stadium sauce, but there was no question that the scene led to a major uproar and a flurry of bad puns. Starr did not relish the controversy. "I assure you that you'll never see or hear that again," he promised.

But once was enough for Fred vonAppen. When Starr let Johnson off with a $1,000 fine and an apology to the squad that may or may not have been voluntary, the Packers' defensive line coach announced his resignation four days before the first regular-season game.

An unidentified Broncos player had already labeled the Packers "the worst excuse for a pro team" he'd ever seen, and the second-year assistant saw his club becoming a laughingstock. Declaring himself deeply disappointed and upset by the symbolism of Johnson's snack, vonAppen said his leaving was a matter of principle. He said he had other issues besides the hot dog, but he declined to elaborate.

If vonAppen was disappointed by Starr's reaction to the Johnson flap, his players were dismayed by vonAppen's leaving. In his first year as defensive line coach after spending the previous season as special teams coach, he seemed to be popular with most of them. And that included Johnson, who said he didn't feel responsible for vonAppen's departure but he regretted it anyway.

When asked why he was caught munching on a sausage while a game was in progress, Johnson spoke frankly. "I ate the thing because I was hungry," he said.

Johnson said he meant no disrespect, which may have come as a relief to Starr because he was getting plenty of that from the public. But he remained popular with the people who counted. Team President Dominic Olejniczak, responding to rumors that the executive committee had contacted prospective candidates to replace the coach, said Starr was in no immediate danger of losing his job and that his status was not on the agenda for the committee's next meeting on Sept. 4.

Starr, who had a 26-47-1 record at that point, said he wasn't worried about losing his job, and he appeared to be tired of talking about the possibility. He canceled his regular Monday and Wednesday meetings with the media.

And he kept his job. For four more years. The Packers put the great frankfurter controversy behind them by beating the Chicago Bears, 12-6, in the season opener, but they would finish 5-10-1. They had one winning record in the next three years under Starr, that in the strike-shortened 1982 season, and he was replaced by Forrest Gregg in 1984.

VonAppen spent the 1981 season as a defensive line coach at Arkansas, and he went on to hold seven different jobs in 15 years before taking over his own program at the University of Hawaii in 1996. Presumably, the training table there did not include hot dogs.

BEN PETERSON CAPTURES OLYMPIC GOLD

AUGUST 31, 1972

When Ben Peterson began wrestling he was easy to beat but hard to discourage. He was the fourth of four sons of a Comstock, Wis., dairy farmer, and they all wrestled and played football, so there wasn't much chance that he'd just come home after school and watch television.

Peterson wrestled seven matches as a Cumberland High School freshman and got pinned in all seven. And while he went on to a solid prep career he never won a state championship. When his high school coach took him to the 1968 United States Olympic Trials in Ames, Iowa, he was pinned and lost, 12-3, in his two matches. But Peterson had shown enough to earn a partial scholarship at national collegiate wrestling powerhouse Iowa State where he made a less than spectacular first impression.

He was so raw when he joined the Cyclones that some of his teammates told him later that they wondered what he was doing there. But after spending a rigorous off-season training with his older brother John Peterson, Ben came back as a sophomore starter at 190 pounds. Still, he had plenty to learn.

Ben got absolutely buried in an early-season match with another former Wisconsin high school wrestler named Russ Hellickson, and he was so embarrassed that he swore to his coach that that would never happen again. The coach would learn very soon and Hellickson a little later just how serious he was.

Peterson got much harder to beat after that, winning NCAA championships at 190 pounds his junior and senior years, as well as his last 52 matches. Still, he was nobody's favorite to win an Olympic medal at the 1972 Games in Munich, Germany. In fact, he wasn't even expected to make the Olympic team, but he had upset the favorite at 198½ pounds in the Trials.

The favorite was from the University of Wisconsin, and his name was Russ Hellickson.

Peterson was joined at Munich by his brother John, who had starred at what is now the University of Wisconsin-Stout for four years and qualified for the Games at 181 pounds. Both of them adapted quickly to the international style. John lost one match to Russia's Levan Tediashvili, a name that would crop up repeatedly throughout the careers of both Petersons. But John claimed the silver medal by outpointing East Germany's Horst Stottmeister just minutes before Ben faced reigning world champion Russi Petrov of Bulgaria.

Ben had gone undefeated in the earlier rounds, although he had a 2-2 draw with the Soviet Union's Gennady Strakhov. He'd had John in his corner for every match, but this time he'd have to do it without his big brother. No problem. Ben pinned Petrov in 2 minutes 41 seconds. That left him and Strakhov with identical records, but Peterson won the gold medal because he'd had one more pin than the Russian.

Four years later, the Peterson brothers were back at the Olympics. This time they were in Montreal, and their fortunes were reversed. John won the gold medal at 181 pounds, and Ben settled for silver. His only loss was to the family nemesis Tediashvili, who had gone up a weight class.

Ben lost four other matches to the Russian legend between the 1972 and '76 Games, but he beat just about everybody else afterward while qualifying for a third Olympics in 1980 in Moscow. Only three other American wrestlers had ever done that, but Peterson never got a chance to compete in Russia because the U.S. boycotted the Games.

After retiring from competition, Peterson coached wrestling for Maranatha Baptist Bible College for 28 years, and he now runs wrestling camps out of his home in Watertown. His campers learn never to be discouraged.

MILWAUKEE AC SHINES IN THE OLYMPICS

SEPTEMBER 1, 1904

It was considered part of the Olympic Games, but the track and field competition that was held over five days in St. Louis in 1904 was more of a triangular meet contested by the athletic clubs of New York, Chicago and Milwaukee, with only a few foreigners sprinkled in.

The proceedings were badly overshadowed by the World's Fair that was going on in town at the same time, and not even the prospect of Alice Roosevelt, daughter of President Theodore Roosevelt, handing out the medals was enough to attract the leading athletes from other countries.

The Russo-Japanese War was occupying the attention of some of them for one thing, and the entire program of events in St. Louis was spread out over four-and-a-half months, creating another deterrent. Still, the Milwaukee Athletic Club contingent distinguished itself in many ways while giving the big city clubs a run for their money in track and field.

The dearth of foreign competition was reflected by the United States athletes winning 21 of the 22 track and field events, and capturing 238 of the 284 available medals. Five MAC participants totaled 10 individual medals, and that didn't count the winning tug of war team.

The tuggers, who included Oscar Olson, Sidney Johnson, Henry Seiling, Conrad Magnussen and Pat Flanagan, highlighted a big Thursday for the Milwaukee participants when they dispatched the New Yorkers for the gold. The winning team was required to pull the losing team six feet from its starting point, and the MAC managed that in a mere 1 minute 14 seconds, despite being outweighed by several pounds a man. Chicago, which didn't make it to the finals, complained later that the winners were ringers recruited from the Windy City, but it didn't matter. It wasn't a violation of the rules.

Walter Liginger, chairman of the athletic committee of the MAC, explained after the athletes had returned home that the members of the tug of war team had been offered transportation costs to St. Louis and two nights lodging, the same as his other representatives.

There were also two individual medal winners from Wisconsin that day, and one of them was making important history. George Poage, who was born in Missouri but grew up in La Crosse, was one of the first two African-American athletes to win a medal in the Olympic Games. Poage had won a bronze in the 400-meter hurdles the day before – the same day that Joseph Stadler, another black athlete representing the U.S., finished second in the standing high jump – and he won another bronze in the 200-meter hurdles on Sept. 1.

The other local medalist on that day – the fourth of track competition – was Emil Breitkreutz of Wausau, the third-place finisher in a memorable 800-meter run. Breitkreutz, who had been sick in bed for two days, led much of the way but began to wobble down the stretch and had to lunge across the finish line in exhaustion to win his bronze. The first three runners all finished within four-tenths of a second of each other.

The most decorated Wisconsin athlete of the week was Dodgeville's Archie Hahn. Nicknamed "The Milwaukee Meteor," Hahn collected gold in the 60-, 100-, and 200-meter races. He won his events on Aug. 29 and 31, and Sept. 3, and drew complaints for his tactics in the 100, his final race. It was alleged that he flinched slightly but intentionally before the gun, causing his three leading rivals to false start. That entailed a one-yard penalty for the offenders, and Hahn won the race by about two yards.

Frank Waller of Menomonie won silver medals in the 400 meters and 400-meter hurdles, and Milwaukee's Oscar Osthoff rounded out the statewide contribution with gold and silver medals in weightlifting.

Among the U.S. athletic clubs, the MAC was a distant third in the team competition, which was won by the New York Athletic Club. New York finished with 63 points followed by the Chicago Athletic Club with 59 and Milwaukee with 46.

KNEE INJURY SHELVES PACKERS' IVERY

SEPTEMBER 2, 1979

Bart Starr was speaking for the moment, but his words would cover Eddie Lee Ivery's whole career. "I'm just sorry," he said, "that you people didn't get a chance to see what he could do."

Nobody ever did.

The Green Bay Packers' coach was talking to the media after the Packers had lost their season opener, 6-3, in Chicago. But they'd lost much more than that. Midway through the second quarter, the team's No. 1 draft choice had taken the ball on a draw play on his own 15-yard line, burst through the Bears' line and tried to make a cut 10 yards up-field. Then he'd fallen to the ground clutching his left knee.

Ivery was helped off the field, and he never came back. Not to that game and not to that season. He underwent surgery for torn cartilage and a torn ligament and embarked on a run of bad luck that derailed his life and hobbled the career of one of the most promising players the Packers ever had.

Starr had good reason to be excited when the Packers made Ivery the 15th choice in the 1979 NFL draft. Ivery had run for 3,517 yards and 22 touchdowns at Georgia Tech, getting 356 of them in one record-setting chunk against Air Force. The Yellow Jackets' Pepper Rodgers called him "the greatest football player I ever coached."

Soon after reporting to training camp, Ivery flashed the same kind of skills in Green Bay. Zeke Bratkowski, the team's backfield coach, said a year later that he had seen enough in just the pre-season to compare Ivery's cut-back ability to that of two of the greatest open-field runners in NFL history, former Chicago Bears Gale Sayers and Willie Galimore.

Ivery scored the winning touchdown on a 22-yard screen pass in the first exhibition game of his rookie year, ran for a game-high 49 yards on nine carries in the second one and caught a 42-yard pass in the last one. The Packers, it seemed, had a game-breaker at last. But they didn't have him for long.

When Ivery went down in the first regular-season game of his career, he said he didn't even feel the hit before he fumbled the ball away to the Bears' Alan Page. He blamed the turf at Soldier Field.

But Ivery bounced back from the injury better than expected and became the Packers' rushing leader with 831 yards in 202 carries in 1980. He wasn't a 1,000-yard back yet, but he appeared to have that potential until he was sidelined again. Same turf. Same knee. He tore it up again in the 1981 opener at Chicago and missed another season.

Ivery would play five more years for the Packers before suffering a back injury and getting cut in January 1988. He was a solid, versatile, football-smart player, but he never came close to being the runner he was when the Packers drafted him. The best he did was rush for 636 yards in 1985. Meanwhile, the frustration took a huge toll on his personal life.

In an interview with *The Macon Telegraph* in his home state of Georgia, Ivery talked of attending a party with several teammates during the 1983 season and trying cocaine for the first time. "I was caught up in the limelight," he said. "I was one of those young country boys wanting to fit in. The first time I tried it I liked it, because it took away the physical pain and emotional pain I was going through at the time."

Ivery acknowledged that cocaine and alcohol cost him his family and led him into bankruptcy. It also led him into treatment and then into a totally new lifestyle. He went back to serve as an assistant coach at Thomson High School in rural McDuffie County where he'd grown up in grinding poverty and gone on to become one of the nation's most highly-recruited players. And then he returned to school and got his degree in 1992.

In 2000 he was hired as an assistant strength and conditioning coach at Georgia Tech where people had seen him at his best. All the Packers ever saw was what might have been.

GREG NORMAN RALLIES TO WIN GMO

SEPTEMBER 3, 1989

Thousands of golf fans came from all over the state to root for Greg Norman at his first Greater Milwaukee Open, but he may have needed only one of them. Eighteen-year-old Jamie Hutton was the ultimate good luck charm for "The Shark," which may have seemed ironic because Hutton wasn't very lucky himself. He had leukemia.

The high school student from Monona, Wis., had watched his favorite pro play once before at the Heritage Classic in Hilton Head, S.C., and Norman not only won the tournament, he gave Hutton credit for the victory and handed him the trophy. Now Hutton was at Tuckaway Country Club following Norman again through the GMO's final 18 holes, and the result turned out to be just as good.

Norman rallied with three birdies in his last seven holes after blowing a four-shot lead to win the tournament and bring home the $144,000 top prize. This time he also brought home the trophy.

"The last time I won a tournament, Jamie, I gave you the trophy, but I've got to have this for my trophy case," Norman told his young friend at the awards presentation. Hutton didn't seem to mind.

He'd met the Australian star in April 1988 just days before he checked into a hospital for a bone marrow transplant. Thursday's Child, a foundation that grants wishes for seriously ill children, paid to fly Hutton and his mother to Hilton Head where Norman was competing at the Heritage. They were scheduled to fly back before the tournament was over, but Norman was so impressed by the Wisconsin teenager that he chartered a jet for him after the final round. In the meantime, Norman arranged for Hutton to accompany him inside the ropes during the tournament.

Norman made up four strokes in the final day to win the Heritage and said afterward that it was Hutton who inspired his victory. That's when he handed him the trophy.

Norman hadn't won a PGA event, other than one that used a Modified Stableford scoring system, since then, and the largest galleries in GMO history flocked to Franklin to see him rectify that situation. He gave them what they were looking for on the first day when he shot an eight-under par 64. He stayed on top of the leader board for the next two days with rounds of 69 and 66, putting him four strokes up on the field going into the final day.

Meanwhile, Andy Bean was gathering himself to make a charge. Once a major force on the tour, Bean had fallen on hard times and needed a sponsor's exemption to make the field. He went into Sunday seven shots off Norman's pace, but he looked like his old self while firing a final round 66. When Norman missed a 12-foot par putt on the 11th hole, Bean found himself in the clubhouse with a piece of the lead.

He didn't keep it for long. Norman birdied No. 12 to go back on top and then rammed in a 35-foot putt on the 13th. When Norman added a final birdie on No. 16, he ended all suspense. His 16-under-par total of 272 left him three shots ahead of Bean, who earned second-place money of $86,400. And so the gallery went home looking forward to seeing Norman the following year. Norman seemed to be looking forward to it, too.

"I thought I was in front of my home crowd," he said, praising the local fans and adding that he was "98% sure" that he'd be back to defend his title in 1990. He was as good as his word, although the payday was quite a bit lighter the next time around. Norman tied for 16th and earned $13,500. He also returned for the tournament in 1991 and '92, but he didn't finish in the top 50 either time.

As for Hutton, his experience with Norman at the Heritage was made into a book called, *A Victory for Jamie*. He achieved a much bigger victory years later when he was found to be free of cancer.

SCANDAL ASIDE, PARKER WINS U.S. OPEN TENNIS

SEPTEMBER 4, 1944

Milwaukee native Franciszek Andrzej Paikowski played in his first tournament on the city's East Side in 1926, and 40 years later he was inducted into the International Tennis Hall of Fame in Newport, R.I. Along the way he changed his name to Frank Parker, which fit better into headlines. And it may or may not have been a good idea because he made plenty of those with both his game and his personal life.

People said that playing Parker was like hitting against a wall. He wasn't a spectacular shot-maker, but he hit everything back. Nobody understood that better than Bill Talbert after Parker frustrated the Indianapolis pro to win the first of his two straight championships at Forest Hills, N.Y. in what is now called the U.S. Open.

Parker, a 5-foot-8½, 145-pound sergeant in the Army Air Force, was allowed to play in only one tournament in 1944, and he made the most of it in a war-time Open that included 16 active servicemen in its 32-man field. Parker had surprised second-seeded and former champion Donald McNeill in the semifinals, while Talbert pulled off an even bigger upset the next day against No. 1-seeded Pancho Segura.

Parker showed no signs of rust in taking out Talbert, 6-4, 3-6, 6-3, 6-3, in an hour-and-a-half. His play was described in one newspaper account as "impassive, cool and absolutely unsensational." In a sense, Parker's victory was as big a tribute to his former coach as it was to him. The coach's name was Mercer Beasley, and that was quite a story in itself.

It was Ted Bacon, a local tennis player and executive of the Cutler Hammer Foundation, who first noticed Parker when he was a skinny, 10-year-old kid shagging balls at the Milwaukee Town Club. Bacon, in turn, asked the Town Club to hire Beasley, a widely respected teaching pro in Pasadena, Calif., to tutor Parker, who didn't have the means to pay for private lessons.

Parker, the youngest of five children, was only two years old when his father died. His mother supported the family by doing laundry, and young Frank helped out by working at the club for $2 a week. While there he fell in love with tennis. Several years later, he also fell in love with Beasley's wife.

Beasley took Parker under his wing and eventually into his house. The second proved to be a major mistake. Beasley continued to hone Parker's skills as he moved from job to job. And Parker followed him, his wife Audrey and their two children, as he attended high schools in Los Angeles, New Orleans and Lawrenceville, N.J. While the 15-year-old Parker was living with them, the Beasleys tried to adopt him, but his mother objected and they dropped their efforts.

Imagine Beasley's surprise then when six years later Parker and his wife confessed to him during a trip to Bermuda that they had been in love for three years. The Beasleys were divorced on a Monday in March 1938, and Parker and Audrey were married with much newspaper fanfare the following Thursday. Parker was 22 and she was at least 40, although she admitted only to being "older than 21." In the end, Beasley gave the couple his blessings. What's more he continued to attend Parker's matches, at least for a period of time.

Parker ranked among America's top 10 players for 17 straight years from 1933 through '49, claiming the No. 1 spot in 1944 and '45. He played 14 Davis Cup matches and won 12 of them, helping the Americans to big victories over Great Britain in 1937 and Australia in 1948. Parker also won the French Open singles title in both 1948 and '49; and the doubles championship at the U.S. Open in 1943; and at both Wimbledon and the French Open in '49. But his biggest triumphs came at Forest Hills.

Parker had been nicknamed the "Boy Wonder" when he played there for the first time at age 16. When he beat Talbert in 1944, it was his 13th try at a U.S. Open title. Then Parker beat Talbert again in the finals the following year. Parker also finished second in 1942 and '47, and he was still trying 21 years later when he became the oldest man ever to enter the men's Open singles at age 52. He played one match and lost it, 6-3, 6-3, 6-2, to a young fellow named Arthur Ashe.

Franciszek Andrzej Paikowski, aka Frank Parker, died in 1997 at the age of 81. He had made quite a name for himself.

COCHEMS PIONEERS THE FORWARD PASS

SEPTEMBER 5, 1906

Coach Eddie Cochems thought a practice game with little Carroll College would help his mighty St. Louis University team prepare for a tough season. But instead of getting tuned up his team was getting shut down.

The score was 0-0 at some unknown point in a game played at Brown Field in Waukesha when a frustrated Cochems decided to try something different.

He called a timeout and, on the next play, Bradbury Robinson, a rangy transfer student from the University of Wisconsin, took the ball in one pie-sized hand and flung it downfield toward a teammate who had nobody around him from either squad. As Robinson's throw fell harmlessly to the ground, Carroll's dazed defenders had to be wondering, "What was that?"

By most historical accounts, it was the first time a forward pass was thrown in a football game in the United States, although the innovative Cochems had his own name for it. He called it a "projectile pass," and before the season was over it would spur a revolution.

Cochems was a 29-year-old Sturgeon Bay native who was in his first year as head coach at St. Louis after completing a spectacular playing career at Wisconsin. He had led the Badgers to a 35-4 record in his four years there, scoring four touchdowns in a 54-0 romp past Notre Dame in 1900 and running a record 100 yards with a kickoff return against Chicago in 1901. Cochems then served two years as head coach at North Dakota State, returned to Wisconsin as an assistant in 1904 and became head coach at Clemson the following year.

Robinson, who grew up in Baraboo and lettered at Wisconsin in 1903 before transferring, knew Cochems and convinced officials at St. Louis to hire him in 1906. Robinson liked Cochems' system and considered him to be a forward thinker.

And that was before Cochems turned college football on its ear in the game at Carroll. Cochems had taken the St. Louis team to Lake Beulah in Walworth County in July for weeks of pre-season training, and he was able to work on new strategies to take advantage of the sweeping new rule changes in college football.

The season of 1905 had been a dark one in the sport. The *Chicago Tribune* reported that there had been 18 deaths and 159 serious injuries. It was a game of flying wedges and hand-to-hand combat in tight quarters, and it was feared that President Theodore Roosevelt would ban the sport altogether. Instead he called a summit of leading university presidents, who decided to open the game up for the safety of the players. And so it was that the forward pass was legalized, but with several restrictions.

Under the new regulations, according to Philip L. Brooks' 2008 book, *Forward Pass: The Play That Saved Football*, if no one from either side touched the ball after it was thrown, possession reverted to the defense. What's more, if a team completed a pass into the end zone, it was ruled a touchback. Passes could only be caught between the goal lines.

As a result, many simple incompletions had the effect of becoming interceptions. Besides, throwing the bloated, turn-of-the-century football was roughly equivalent to heaving a watermelon. So it came as no surprise when coaches all over the country simply ignored the passing game.

But Cochems wasn't most coaches. He had spent the summer drilling Robinson, who had unusually large hands and a strong arm, on how to grip the ball across the laces and to put his shoulder into the throwing motion to create a spiral, according to Brooks. And then Cochems unleashed his "aerial game" on Carroll.

Because the first pass fell incomplete without anyone touching it, St. Louis lost possession in accordance with the rules of the day. But when it got the ball back, Robinson threw a 20-yard strike to Jack Schneider, who once again found himself all alone. This time he caught the ball and ran 20 yards for a touchdown and St. Louis was on its way to a 22-0 victory. Hardly anyone noticed at the time because the game wasn't even reported in the local media. But over the years, Cochems has received the recognition due him for leaving an indelible mark on the game.

FUTURE HALL OF FAME PITCHER NOT ENOUGH FOR JANESVILLE

SEPTEMBER 6, 1877

More than a century before multi-million dollar contracts and inane signing wars, baseball was already beginning to assemble the best teams money could buy. And then as now, it didn't always work out.

A case in point was the Janesville Mutuals, who were determined to claim the state championship at the expense of Milwaukee. The metropolis to their east was in the process of recruiting the pros from outside the state who were about to form a big league team. There was pitcher Sam "Buck" Weaver, outfielder Abner Dalrymple and catcher Charlie Bennett among others.

But the Mutuals had hired their own bonus baby to lead them through the best-of-five series that started in mid-August and ran into September. John Montgomery Ward brought them a big bat, speed on the base paths and a nasty curveball when they lured him from his home in Pennsylvania in early August for $20 a week and an upfront payment of $75. Never mind that Ward was only 17 years old. He had Hall of Fame talent before there was even a Hall of Fame.

Besides, Ward had already been branded as a baseball mercenary by his hometown newspaper, the *Bellefonte Democratic Watchman*, after being hired to pitch a trial game for the Philadelphia Athletics a month earlier.

"There is no reason why a baseball pitcher should not become eventually a great man," the paper wrote, "but the chances, for Monte's sake, we are sorry to say, are against it and trust he will pause and reconsider."

Ward ignored the advice, and the Mutuals had no reservations about throwing what was then big money at him. What they cared about was his live right arm, and they tried to take maximum advantage of it by pitching him in all five games of the so-called state championship series.

It worked at first when Janesville took a one-game lead with a 4-3 victory on Aug. 18, but after that, not so much. Milwaukee shelled him, 13-1 and 16-2, in the next two meetings, setting up an elimination game at West End Park near the city limits on Wells Street.

Ward was more effective this time, but not nearly as productive as Weaver, who threw a no-hitter in a 6-0 victory on Sept. 6 that wrapped up the title for Milwaukee. Some 28 years later, Frank L. Smith, who had played for the Mutuals, wrote a series about the history of baseball in Janesville for the local *Gazette* and claimed the score was 6-3 and that Ward pitched only the last five innings, shutting out the Milwaukee team over that stretch.

In any case, Milwaukee won and next year joined the National League, giving the city its first major league team. Dalrymple led the league in hitting that summer, and Bennett went on to enjoy a 15-year pro career before a railroad accident cost him both legs. But the new Milwaukee franchise lasted only one year.

Meanwhile, Ward spent the winter in Janesville working for the *Gazette* and then went big league, too, the next summer. He pitched a two-hitter in his debut for the Providence Grays, beating Indianapolis, 4-0, and went on to win a league-high 47 games in 1879 and 39 in 1880, including the second perfect game in National League history.

Providence traded him to the New York Giants in 1883, and the following year his arm went dead from overuse. So Ward became a full-time shortstop and led the Giants to world championships in 1888 and '89.

It was while he was with the Giants that Ward began taking law classes at Columbia University. He graduated in 1885 and literally became a clubhouse lawyer. He co-founded the Brotherhood of National League Players, a forerunner of baseball's potent Players Association. In all, Ward played 17 years in the major leagues, compiling a 164-102 record as a pitcher and batting .275, while twice leading the National League in stolen bases. He also served as a player-manager for seven years, winning 412 games and losing 320.

In 1964, he was inducted into the Baseball Hall of Fame.

MARCOL'S FLUKE TD BEATS BEARS IN OVERTIME

SEPTEMBER 7, 1980

Chester Marcol didn't have time to think, which was probably a good thing for the Green Bay Packers. Nothing was making sense anyway that Sunday at Lambeau Field.

Disaster appeared to be at hand for Bart Starr's free-falling team when it opened the 1980 season against archrival Chicago. The Packers had been outscored, 86-17, during a 0-4-1 pre-season and defensive line coach Fred vonAppen had resigned just four days earlier. He did so in the wake of the Ezra Johnson hot dog incident during the closing minutes of the final exhibition game, a 38-0 thrashing at the hands of Denver. Starr's approval rating also was at an all-time low. He'd posted four losing records in his first five seasons, while the Bears were coming off a 10-6 record and favored to rule the division.

But it was the Packers who won the game, 12-6, on a day the Bears couldn't get Walter Payton into the end zone or keep Marcol out of it.

Green Bay's defense surprised everyone by picking off three passes and limiting the fabled Payton to 65 yards on 31 carries. The Bears could do no better than two Bob Thomas field goals, and when Marcol matched those, the game went into overtime.

The suspense was hard on everyone, but it was killing Larry McCarren. Green Bay's veteran center was a surprise starter, having undergone hernia surgery just three weeks earlier. He was down about 30 pounds from his normal playing weight of 260, but he'd started 63 straight games dating back to 1975, and Starr told him the plan was to have him play a couple of downs to keep the streak alive. Four quarters later, McCarren was still on the field.

The Bears won the overtime coin flip, but it did them no good as the Packer defense continued to stymie them, forcing a punt after six plays. Quarterback Lynn Dickey immediately put Green Bay in field goal range with a 32-yard pass to wide receiver James Lofton, and after three running plays, Marcol found himself lining up at the left hash-mark just outside Chicago's 24-yard line. He'd already made field goals of 41 and 46 yards, so this one looked like a chip shot.

It just didn't look that way to Alan Page. The Bears' defensive lineman would block 28 kicks in his 15-year-career, and this one may have been the strangest of all of them. "He told his teammates, 'Don't worry. I am going to block this kick, so you guys better watch it,'" Marcol recalled. And Page certainly did.

Marcol remembered hearing two thuds after he kicked the ball – one when it left his foot and one when it collided with Page. "I don't think it was more than two, three yards away from me," he said.

McCarren heard it all, too, and it almost broke his heart. "It wasn't fun," he said. "I was really sore. When they blocked the field goal, it was at least partially, if not all, my fault. Then I heard that double thud, and I thought, 'Oh no, this is going to go on.'"

And it might have if Marcol had been a little less alert or the Packers hadn't been so overdue for a break. As the ball caromed off of Page, it bounded directly back to a bespectacled Marcol, who grabbed it and ran 24 yards for the game-winning touchdown.

"There was no time to get shocked until afterward," he said. "It was just a reaction to a play. Bang! There it was. The ball hit me right in my numbers. I didn't have to reach to either side. It was catch and run. Sometimes, that makes a huge difference when a tenth-of-a-second doesn't have to be wasted on reaching out for the ball."

No Bear even came close to Marcol as he lugged his way across the goal line. And no Packer was more relieved to see him score than McCarren. "People were all happy," he said. "I was just happy the damn game was over."

The Bears would get their revenge three months later when they smoked the Packers, 61-7, at Soldier Field. And the losing would go on for Green Bay as it finished the season 5-10-1. Marcol was cut shortly after the game at Lambeau Field. He finished his career with one touchdown.

But it capped one of the most bizarre plays and one of the most bizarre weeks in Packers history.

Kicker Chester Marcol took off running after a blocked field goal attempt and scored the winning touchdown against the Chicago Bears in the 1980 opener at Lambeau Field.

DAN PATCH SHOWCASED AT WISCONSIN STATE FAIR

SEPTEMBER 8, 1904

After Dan Patch ran against the clock at the Wisconsin State Fair in 1904, he returned in 1908 for display. This advertisement promoted another race in 1909, but Dan Patch pulled up lame at the Minnesota State Fair prior to the event.

One of the world's first sports millionaires wouldn't think of renegotiating his contract. He received 50,000 pieces of fan mail a year, according to an authoritative account of his life, and he never had a bad word to say about anybody. He was also considered quite handsome, even if he did have four legs and a long tail.

It was a very big deal when the legendary horse Dan Patch came to the Wisconsin State Fair, because harness racing was a very big attraction at the time. Next to boxing and baseball, nothing drew a crowd like a great pacer, and Dan Patch was the best pacer on the planet. A crowd estimated at between 40,000 and 50,000 people flocked through the gates where the eight-year-old, one-time cripple made his run against the clock.

The race had been rained out the previous day, creating a heavy track, but not dampening the customers' enthusiasm a bit. Even though conditions made a record time highly unlikely, the fans filled the grandstands, lined the slopes behind them, and climbed roofs and telegraph poles hours before the 5 p.m. post time. This was no ordinary hay burner they'd come to see.

Dan Patch was born in Oxford, Ind., in 1896, with a left hind leg bent so badly that he had to be helped to his feet to nurse, according to *Crazy Good: The True Story of Dan Patch, the Most Famous Horse in America*, written by Charles Leerhsen and released in 2008. Dan Patch started his adult life pulling a grocery wagon around Oxford, but the leg straightened out, and he ran his first race in 1900 as a four-year-old at a local county fair. He went on from there to dominate harness racing until his retirement in 1909, setting world records at one mile and earning more than $1 million. This at a time when Ty Cobb's $12,000 was baseball's biggest salary.

Dan Patch had an extra wide rump and big feet that required oversized horseshoes, but his mahogany brown coat and noble head made him the early 1900s version of a rock star. He also had an even temper, and he loved playing to his crowds.

Fairgoers in Milwaukee had been visiting his palatial stall all morning on the day of the race, and when he walked out onto the track the crowd erupted. The run itself was unspectacular.

While the spectators couldn't expect Dan Patch to lower his own record for a mile, they were hoping to see him break two minutes. But the track was extremely heavy near the rail and soft everywhere else. Closing fast after two lackluster splits, Dan Patch finished in 2 minutes 3¾ seconds, more than seven-and-a-half seconds off his world record pace. Still, he'd equaled the track record set in 1897 in a match race between his sire Joe Patchen and another legendary pacer named Star Pointer. And Dan Patch probably had a good payday. His purses in races against time usually ranged from $10,000 to $20,000.

Whatever the take, when the race was over, hundreds followed Dan Patch back to the barn.

Two years later on a much faster surface before some 90,000 people at the Minnesota State Fair, he ran a 1:55, setting a standard that would not be equaled by any other pacer for more than 30 years. Dan Patch still had four years of racing left at that point, but his owner, Marion W. Savage of Minneapolis, was widely accused of running him too much late in his career. It was alleged that Savage, who sold a patent medicine for farm animals, needed the purses because his business was failing.

Thoroughbred racing had eclipsed harness racing when Dan Patch died in 1916, and the story was barely mentioned in the newspapers. But he'd been loved for many years, and never more than he was in Milwaukee.

YOUNT GETS 3,000TH HIT AT COUNTY STADIUM

SEPTEMBER 9, 1992

Like 47,589 other fans, Bud Selig wouldn't miss this for anything, except that he almost did. The world's most relentless small-market battler had just gotten himself elected de facto commissioner of baseball. It was an enormous moment in the history of Milwaukee baseball. It was also the second-most important story of the day.

No one understood that better than the Brewers' president whose problem was that the most important story of the day figured to be happening in Milwaukee and he was in St. Louis. Robin Yount, better know as the "The Kid," was teetering on the brink of history after getting the 2,999th base hit of his career the night before. His next hit would make him only the 17th major league player ever to reach 3,000. There was no guarantee that he would get it that night, but it just seemed so likely.

The Brewers would be leaving on a seven-game road trip after facing the Cleveland Indians at County Stadium, and a whole city would be disappointed if he failed to reach the milestone at home. Yount had made a career out of not disappointing Milwaukee.

Selig, who'd always treated Yount like the son he never had, had to be there. Minutes after his colleagues elected him chairman of their executive council at a Major League Baseball meeting – he wasn't officially elected commissioner until six years later – Selig set out for the St. Louis airport where he'd chartered a plane to get himself and a few friends back to Milwaukee. He'd hired a private limousine to take him from Mitchell Field to County Stadium, and if everything worked out, he'd make it to the ballpark for the first pitch.

Of course, everything didn't work out. With almost a full house on hand, stadium traffic was nasty. The game had already started when Selig and his friends got to their box, but the good news was Yount hadn't come to bat yet. Selig's friends included American League President Bobby Brown, San Diego Padres managing partner Tom Werner and Texas Rangers owner George Bush.

Yount, batting second in the order, stepped to the plate for the first time against Jose Mesa in the bottom of the first inning, and he grounded out. He was up again in the third, and he struck out. When he came up for a third time in the fourth, Mesa fanned him again. The Indians' right-hander was clearly opposed to being part of history.

Disgusted and totally out of character, Yount threw his bat and his helmet to the ground after the second strikeout. Then he had a little talk with himself. He'd been saying for weeks that No. 3,000 would just be another base hit, but now he knew better. He'd been pressing, and he had to get hold of himself and get back to playing baseball.

Paul Molitor, Robin Yount and Jim Gantner were teammates for 15 years.

He faced Mesa again for possibly the last time in the seventh. Yount fouled off the first pitch. Then he lined the next one into right field, and when the ball hit the ground the stadium went nuts. As Yount rounded first, Jim Gantner and Paul Molitor were there to greet him. The three of them had been teammates for 15 years, and there was a gentleman's agreement in the clubhouse that they would be the first to celebrate with him.

Gantner and Molitor hugged Yount, and then all of their teammates were on the field, hoisting Yount to their shoulders. The game ground to a halt for nine minutes while clips of Yount's career highlights ran on the scoreboard. The show could have gone much longer for the two-time Most Valuable Player and the single most popular figure in Brewers history. He'd come to town in 1974 as an 18-year-old shortstop with just 64 games of minor league experience, and now Brewers fans couldn't imagine a lineup without him.

His first base hit had come against Baltimore's Dave McNally. It also landed in right field, but Yount had to admit he couldn't remember it. This hit, he'd never forget. "That was as exciting a moment as probably I ever had," he said. "It was a great feeling."

When order was restored to the stadium, Molitor grounded into a double play. And then the Indians rallied from a 4-3 deficit in the ninth inning to win the game, 5-4. The Brewers took the loss well. "When I'm 50 years old, I won't remember the defeat. I'll remember the base hit," said Gantner.

Selig was already older than 50, but he felt the same way. He broke into tears after the game. He'd have cried a lot harder if he'd missed the hit.

RACING OPENS AT ROAD AMERICA

SEPTEMBER 10, 1955

They were still nailing the press pagoda together hours before the first race began on the brand new course 15 miles northwest of Sheboygan. The asphalt was dry, the brats were cooking at the concession stands, and most important, there was plenty of hay.

Four thousand bales of the stuff had been placed around the turns and other dangerous spots on the four-mile route. The better part of two farms covering 523 acres had been converted into a state-of-the-art motor playground known as Road America, but not all of it. There was still enough left to grow the hay.

Now all anyone needed were cars and drivers. More than 200 of each showed up at little Elkhart Lake, a popular resort town, to kick off the first weekend at the circuit that all of the experts agreed was the best in the country. There would be seven races over two days culminating in a 148-mile feature on Sunday.

The man destined to win that finale had skill, experience and a very fast Ferrari. He also had hay fever. No one said it would be easy.

When Elkhart Lake held its first road race in 1950, it had two things going for it. It was popular, and it was cheap. All the organizers had to do was close off three-and-a-half miles of public highway, put up a few barriers and wait for the people to come. Some 5,000 watched Neenah's Jim Kimberly win in a Ferrari. But after a couple of years of that, the State Legislature got nervous about spectator safety and passed a law banning the closing of highways for racing.

That could have been the end of the sport in Wisconsin, but a civil engineer with a background in road building named Clif Tufte had a different plan. He spent months roaming the hills and valleys of Sheboygan County looking for a site that would work as a road course. When he found it, he put together a corporation that sold stock to raise money to build a course. The corporation was formed in 1954, construction started in April 1955, and five months later, workers were hammering the last nails into the pagoda.

History was made when 20 brightly colored sports cars roared across the start line on Sept. 10 for the opening event. It was the first time a road race had ever been run on a privately owned course anywhere in the world, and it was won by Salina, Kan., driver Roy Heath on a cold and windy day.

The second race was won by Paul O'Shea of Rye, N.Y. Frank Bott of Chicago won Saturday's feature, a 100-miler.

After an estimated 20,000 people braved the conditions on Saturday, there were 35,000 on hand for Sunday's races. The feature, a 36-lap race, turned into a two-man fight and the highlight of the weekend.

Filling the cockpit of a sleek D-type Jaguar was Sherwood Johnston, all 200 pounds of him, also from Rye. Piloting a Ferrari Monza was diminutive Phil Hill of Santa Monica, Calif., who weighed 150 pounds soaking wet.

Size didn't seem to matter as Johnston and Hill zoomed ahead of the rest of the field and swapped the lead back and forth for much of the race. Johnston had about a four-car length advantage when he made the mistake of looking over his shoulder to see what Hill was up to. Johnston swung a little wide in the process, and Hill ducked inside of him. The two cars were door to door down the stretch before Hill nosed ahead at the finish line.

He averaged just under 80 miles per hour while covering the course in 1 hour 51 minutes 4.2 seconds, coughing and wheezing most of the way. Hill said his hay fever had been a problem throughout the race, particularly as the fans walked around and kicked up the dust. "Going into the last lap, I was resigned to finishing second," he said.

Instead, he'd won the first big event in the history of what would become a storied track. That was nothing to sneeze at.

MILWAUKEE SITE OF AAU TRACK MEET FOR FIRST TIME

SEPTEMBER 11, 1903

There were the movers, and there were the shakers. On the one hand were 200 of the fastest, strongest and most agile athletes of their time. On the other were the driving forces behind the meet who would put their stamp on amateur athletics for decades. And they were all at State Fair Park.

It was a major coup for Walter Liginger to bring the National Amateur Athletic Union Track and Field Championships to Wisconsin, but then he was a major player. The Milwaukee native was president of the AAU, then the governing body for all amateur athletics in the United States, and he was also director of the Milwaukee Athletic Club, which was sending its first team to a national competition. There were 22 men on that team, and they didn't have to travel far because Liginger had moved the meet off the East Coast for only the fifth time in its 16-year history.

Next to Bud Selig, who became baseball commissioner almost a century later, Liginger may have wielded more power on a national level than any other sports official ever to come out of Wisconsin. In addition to serving as president of the AAU from 1902-'04, he was a founder and first president of the National Boxing Association, which was organized in 1921 and became the World Boxing Association in 1962. Liginger also served as chairman of the 1904 Olympics in St. Louis and was on the committee that organized the Games in Stockholm, Sweden, in 1912, and in Antwerp, Belgium, in 1920.

When he died at age 70 in 1931, he was lauded by Ronald McIntyre, a sports columnist for the *Milwaukee Sentinel*, as a man whose "name always was mentioned in tones of respect."

Joining Liginger at State Fair Park as referee was James E. Sullivan, one of the founders of the AAU and an early Olympic titan whose name is still synonymous with excellence in amateur sports. The Sullivan Award has been given every year since 1930 to America's top amateur athlete. The winners have included Wisconsin favorites Eric Heiden, Dan Jansen, Bonnie Blair and Paul Hamm.

And then there was the University of Chicago's immortal Amos Alonzo Stagg. At least he seemed immortal. Then a 41-year-old football and track coach, he still had 61 years to live. Before his death in 1965, Stagg would coach college football for 57 years, including 41 at Chicago, a Big Ten power for most of that period. When his last head coaching stint at the College of Pacific ended in 1946, Stagg had won 314 games, second all-time to Pop Warner.

On this occasion, Stagg brought 11 athletes to Milwaukee to compete in the junior portion of the two-day meet.

The New York Athletic Club was a heavy favorite to win the senior championship, held on Sept. 11. Track was serious business for this group. It had a $25,000 annual budget for training and staff, while Midwestern officials liked to point out that their athletes had to train pretty much on their own. The money certainly wasn't wasted. The New Yorkers had won this meet 10 times previously.

And they would win it again, this time with 50 points, 14 more than the runner-up MAC. Chicago's First Regiment was third with 29. Sometimes the NYAC ran up as many points as the rest of the field combined, but three MAC runners made sure that didn't happen on this occasion.

Dodgeville's Archie Hahn was the star of the meet. He edged out defending national champion P.J. Walsh at the tape in both the 100- and 220-yard dashes. Fred Schule won the 120-yard high hurdles, finished second in the high jump and third in the 220-yard low hurdles; and Michael Bochman was first in the 220-yard low hurdles and second in the 120-yard highs.

Others who added to the MAC point total were Emil Breitkreutz, who finished second in the 880-yard run; Charles Hennemann, who took a second and third in the weights; and Walter Knox, who took two thirds in the broad jump and pole vault.

When the competition was over, the MAC invited the New Yorkers to a reception. Sullivan used the occasion to praise Liginger's running of the event. He said it would be "a great boon for western athletics." As it turned out, it was certainly a boost for the MAC, and for Milwaukee and its place in track and field circles.

The city would serve as host to the national AAU meet again in 1934, '37 and '48.

BADGERS SHOCK TOP-RANKED MICHIGAN

SEPTEMBER 12, 1981

The Badgers' Tim Krumrie corralled Michigan quarterback Steve Smith after beating the block of tackle Ed Muransky (72) in a huge upset in 1981.

Losing four straight games to Michigan by a combined score of 176-0 was bad enough without the Wolverines being so happy about it.

The defending Big Ten champions were a maize and blue study in arrogance when they ran onto the Camp Randall field to face lightly regarded Wisconsin in the season opener. Instead of going straight to their side of the field, they circled the Wisconsin players, who were doing calisthenics, and shouted a few ill-chosen words at them.

This was beginning to look like typical Michigan behavior. Earlier in the week, some of the Badgers were stewing over quotes made by Green Bay Packers safety and Michigan alum Mike Jolly, who had said the Wolverines could always see fear in the Badgers' eyes and that they used to predict how many points they'd score.

They had good reason to gloat. It had been 19 years and 14 games since the last time Wisconsin had beaten Michigan. The Wolverines had lost only once before in Madison, and they held a ridiculous 32-7-1 advantage in the overall series. This was a Big Ten rivalry in the same sense that hawks and mice were rivals.

Michigan had won the Rose Bowl the previous January, and now it was everyone's choice to claim the 1981 national championship. Coach Bo Schembechler was 10-0 against the Badgers, and he was bringing in the top-ranked team in the country in the Associated Press pre-season poll. He would be leaving with something else entirely.

Naturally, Jolly's comments earned a conspicuous place on Wisconsin's locker room wall. And, of course, the Badgers were insulted. But they'd been insulted before. The difference this time was that they were good enough to do something about it. Some three hours after kickoff, they were mobbing each other at midfield and coach Dave McClain was proclaiming, "This is the greatest thing that's ever happened to me."

It was also one of the most surprising that had ever happened to the Wolverines. The final score was 21-14, but the game wasn't nearly that close. Wisconsin outgained Michigan, 439 yards to 229, and rolled up 23 first downs to the Wolverines' eight. Sophomore quarterback Jess Cole completed eight of 17 passes for 182 yards and two touchdowns for Wisconsin, while sophomore Steve Smith completed three in 18 tries for 39 yards for Michigan. Despite the presence of All-American receiver Anthony Carter, Smith's leading receiver in this game was Badger safety Matt Vanden Boom, who intercepted him three times.

Nothing made any sense. Wisconsin had finished the previous season with the league's worst offense both in scoring and total yards. The Wolverines had more than half of their starters back from the Big Ten's best defense. But it was Wisconsin that dominated on defense as Vanden Boom's thievery and nose guard Tim Krumrie's 13 tackles stymied Michigan all over the field.

The Wolverines took a 7-0 lead on a four-yard run by Smith, but only after the Badgers had fumbled a punt on their own 33-yard line. Wisconsin got those points back when Cole finished a 71-yard drive with a 17-yard scoring pass to wide receiver Marvin Neal, and it took a 14-7 lead on Chucky Davis' one-yard run with two seconds left in the half.

A less than capacity crowd of 68,733 turned quiet when Butch Woolfolk tied the score with an 89-yard touchdown run early in the third quarter, but that was the end of Michigan's scoring. Cole's screen pass to Muskegon, Mich., native John Williams covered 71 yards for the winning points, and Vanden Boom did the rest when his interceptions stopped three of the visitors' last six drives.

McClain, who had been Schembechler's assistant at Miami of Ohio, had never beaten Michigan or his old boss before, and that made him twice as proud. Schembechler would have preferred his understudy's happiness to come at someone else's expense, but he had no trouble understanding how he'd lost.

"Our problems were simple," he said. "Our offense wasn't any good. Our defense wasn't any good. Our kicking game wasn't any good, and our coaching game was poor."

The miracle was short-lived for the Badgers. They lost, 31-13, to UCLA the following week, but they did make it to the Garden State Bowl, where they lost to Tennessee and finished with a 7-5 record. Michigan fell off the top of the polls and never got back up. It was 9-3 and ranked No. 12 at the end of the season. Humility came hard for the Wolverines, and it started in Madison.

SEPTEMBER

JAY GETS REVENGE ON BRAVES

SEPTEMBER 13, 1961

He'd been the Milwaukee Braves' first bonus baby, and beating his old team was definitely a bonus for Joey Jay.

The 26-year-old right-hander had spent eight years in the Braves organization, long enough to win a modest 24 major league games and get himself called fat and lazy by his manager. He didn't look lazy at Crosley Field, though, as he turned in the best performance of his young career for the Cincinnati Reds while beating the Braves and Carlton Willey, 1-0.

The loss did more than drop the Braves 9½ games out of first place. It served as a symptom of their accelerating decline after they'd won back-to-back pennants in 1957 and '58. They were an aging team that got old when their young players either failed to pan out or reached their potential with other clubs.

Jay was a prime example of the second as he demonstrated at Willey's expense while throwing his fourth shutout and becoming the first National League 20-game winner of the 1961 season. Jay limited the Braves to four hits, struck out seven, walked only one and seemed pretty happy about the trade that had sent him to Cincinnati nine months earlier.

"I get satisfaction out of beating the Braves because they're one of the best clubs in the league and because they traded me," he said. "But that doesn't mean I'm bitter at them or anything like that. Tonight, for instance, I beat Carl Willey. He's my former roommate and my best friend."

The luckless Willey, who had lost three games by 2-1 scores that season, was also the pitcher the Braves thought they could plug effortlessly into Jay's spot in the rotation when they dealt him and left-hander Juan Pizarro to Cincinnati for shortstop Roy McMillan. They were wrong about that. Willey finished the season 6-12. Jay was 21-10 for the Reds, and he would go 21-14 the following year. Pizarro, who had moved on to Chicago in the three-cornered deal, was 14-7 with the White Sox.

McMillan's numbers didn't help either. He never hit better than .250 in three seasons with the Braves. But General Manager John McHale was convinced that he'd put together baseball's best infield when he acquired the slick-fielding shortstop. Besides, he wasn't sorry to see Jay go.

The first Little League product ever to make a major league club, Jay was also the first Milwaukee victim of baseball's arcane bonus-baby rule. In the days before the baseball draft, the rule required that players who received signing bonuses of more than $4,000 had to spend their first two professional seasons in the majors. The intent was to keep rich teams from signing all the best young talent. The result was to retard the players' development while they spent two years languishing on the bench.

Jay, who signed for $40,000 in 1953, was farmed out after appearing in only 18 games his first two years and spent most of the next three years pitching at the Class AAA level. He showed flashes in 1958, winning five games in July and being named the National League player of the month, but he broke a finger and finished just 7-5. The 1959 season was a definite downer when Manager Fred Haney banished Jay to the bullpen, accusing him of being fat and lazy. Jay said if that was true, it was all Haney's fault because he hadn't used him enough. Haney might have won the argument, but that also would be his last season as the Braves' manager.

Willey never did become the pitcher Milwaukee thought he would be. He had a fine rookie year, but then he lost 33 out of 52 games over the next four seasons before the Braves sold him to the New York Mets. There were many more examples of prospects who brought more frustration than production to Milwaukee.

Young arms like Bob Hendley, Cecil Butler and Kenosha native Bob Hartman never distinguished themselves at the major league level, and the problem wasn't limited to the pitcher's mound. Catcher Robert "Hawk" Taylor and Port Washington product, John DeMerit, two other bonus babies, proved they weren't worth the money. Mack Jones, who replaced Billy Bruton in center field, took three years to get untracked; and the career of Lee Maye, another outfielder, followed a similar path. Shortstop Amando Samuel had a three-year career batting average of .215, despite being touted as "potentially great" by venerable *Milwaukee Sentinel* baseball writer Lou Chapman.

Potential wasn't enough for the Braves. They finished fourth in 1961 while Cincinnati won the pennant with a big boost from Jay.

PACKERS ROMP IN THEIR FIRST GAME

SEPTEMBER 14, 1919

The jerseys were blue, and there were only 20 of them. The players lived in town all year long. The standing-room-only crowd was restrained by ropes ringing the field. There were no seats, but the estimated 1,500 who showed up didn't mind. They were watching for free.

Pro football was a very different sport when the Green Bay Packers played the first game in their colorful history on a sunny Sunday at Hagemeister Park where East High School now stands. How many of the changes represent improvements is a matter of taste. But one thing was certain. The first Packers were a whole lot better than any of the teams they played, with the possible exception of the last one.

History was a haphazard discipline in those days, and there was a lot about the founding of the Packers that's open to interpretation. The standard version of events had the franchise springing brand new from an Aug. 11, 1919, players' meeting in the cramped editorial offices of the old *Green Bay Press-Gazette* building. But others saw them as an extension of Green Bay's city team in 1918 or just the latest edition in a series of town teams that started in 1895.

Curly Lambeau, of course, was the first coach. Or was he? The *Press-Gazette* reported on Sept. 4, 1919, that "Big Bill" Ryan, the football coach at Green Bay West High School, would double as coach of the Packers, while Lambeau served as captain.

In any case, Lambeau had an enormous role in getting the organization off the ground. George Whitney Calhoun, who is credited with being the team's co-founder and who was working for the *Press-Gazette* in 1919, told the story that most people tend to believe. He said he bumped into Lambeau on a sidewalk in downtown Green Bay, and the two started talking about getting a football team going. The talk led to an organizational meeting at the newspaper offices, and when the Indian Packing Co. of Green Bay came up with $500 to cover expenses, the team had a name and a mission.

A month later, on Sept. 14, they were at Hagemeister Park beating the bejabbers out of a collection of former high school and college players called the North End Athletic Club of nearby Menominee, Mich. Quarterback Dutch Dwyer scored the first touchdown in the Packers' history by capping their first drive with a straight-ahead plunge through the center of the line. There would be many more as the visitors managed only one first down, and the Packers scored at almost a point-a-minute pace while winning, 57-0. All 20 players, one for each jersey purchased by the packing company, played, and according to the *Press-Gazette* account, "showed their mettle and worked like demons."

They were similarly demonic the following week when they rolled over the Marinette Northeners, 61-0, and the week after that when they clobbered New London, 54-0. Mercy was not one of Lambeau's qualities as was starkly demonstrated in the Packers' fourth game, an 87-0 stomping of Company C in Sheboygan.

But the Packers got their comeuppance in Beloit where they faced the Fairies for the so-called state championship in the final game of the season. Beloit scored only the second touchdown the Packers yielded all year, and then it used a colossal home-field advantage to hold off the Green Bay invaders for a 6-0 victory.

Twice in the third quarter, Lambeau crossed the goal line for apparent touchdowns. But referee Baldy Zabel, a name that will live in Green Bay infamy, claimed Lambeau's forward motion had been stopped on the first score and called the Packers for offside on the second. Then twice in the fourth quarter, two of the Packers' backs, Jennings Gallagher and Ray "Tudy" McLean, broke loose for what were potential touchdowns only to be swarmed or tripped up by Beloit fans who had come onto the field. Zabel, who was from Beloit, observed the proceedings without responding.

The favoritism was so outrageous that the Fairies agreed to a rematch two weeks later, but then backed out. And so the Packers finished their first year with a 10-1 record while scoring 565 points and giving up 12. Instant replay might have saved the loss, but that was also a long way away for pro football.

THORPE HOLDS OFF NICKLAUS TO WIN GMO

SEPTEMBER 15, 1985

Jack Nicklaus had won 17 of his eventual total of 18 majors and had collected 72 of his 73 PGA Tour victories when he made his only appearance at the Greater Milwaukee Open. Jim Thorpe had never won anything, but he'd come close.

The 36-year-old pro from the backwoods of North Carolina had enjoyed one day of fame four years earlier when he'd fired an opening 66 at the U.S. Open at Merion Golf Club to become the first black player ever to lead a round of a major. And a month earlier at the Western Open, he'd lost a playoff to amateur Scott Verplank, leaving him with the $90,000 winner's check, but not the trophy.

Now Thorpe was gunning for both. His tournament record 62 on Saturday had included an astonishing 29 on the front nine at Tuckaway Country Club and given him a one-shot lead over Jeff Sanders and a two-stroke edge on Nicklaus going into the final round. When Thorpe teed it up with golf's greatest player on Sunday, it wouldn't have surprised anyone if he'd just melted away. Nicklaus after all had been thriving on these situations for the better part of 25 years. Thorpe was 38th on the money list, a nice player with a swing that had about 100 moving parts.

But Thorpe knew something about pressure, too. He'd entered that first round at Merion without a dollar in his pocket. He said later that if the Open hadn't provided breakfast he would have teed off hungry. He'd joined the tour in 1976 and then lost his card immediately when he'd won only $2,000 in his first year. He didn't get it back again until 1979.

But by the time he was playing in his third GMO – he had missed the cut in 1976 and tied for 58th in 1979 – he was a better, more confident player. So when he hit the Tuckaway course with the five-time PGA player of the year, nerves weren't a problem. And when Nicklaus bogeyed the first hole, Thorpe never let him up for air.

He shot a steady, two-under-par 70, giving him a final 274, a three-shot margin over Nicklaus, and his first tour victory. It also gave Thorpe the $54,000 winner's check, but that didn't seem as important to him as the hardware that came with it.

"I needed that trophy, man," he said. "I would have traded checks with Jack just to get that trophy. It means the World Series of Golf and one or two endorsements out there, especially with me being one of the three black guys on the tour."

Nicklaus' take was $32,400 and it was the only purse he ever picked up in Wisconsin. He never returned, and his only previous tournament appearance had come in the 1961 Milwaukee Open when he'd tied for sixth as an amateur. Nicklaus may have come back if he'd won, because he always came back to defend his championships, but all he could offer as a runner-up was his thanks. "I enjoyed my week here," he said. "Everybody was so nice. I appreciate that. Obviously, I would have liked to eliminate Jim Thorpe from the tournament."

Nicklaus had agreed to play in the GMO when his son, 23-year-old Jack Nicklaus II, was given a sponsor's exemption. It marked the first time a father and son had played together in a PGA Tour event. And on the first morning of the tournament, Jack Sr. drew what was considered to be the largest ever first-day gallery at the GMO. In fact, one tournament official said that when Nicklaus finished his round and started to follow his son on the course, he might have drawn the second largest first-day gallery in the history of the GMO.

Nicklaus was 45 years old at the time and no longer the player he once was, although he had enough left in his tank to win the Masters the next year.

Meanwhile, Thorpe went on to win the Tucson Match Play Championship later in the year and then won it again in 1986. He also endured a long dry spell, illustrated by him playing in 10 more GMOs and missing the cut six times, before finding success on the Senior Tour.

In January 2010, he was sentenced to a year in prison for failing to pay federal income taxes.

SPAHN THROWS HIS FIRST NO-HITTER

SEPTEMBER 16, 1960

Fifteen big league seasons, 286 victories and 50 shutouts, and still Warren Spahn hadn't thrown a no-hitter. He had two one-hitters and a whole slew of other brilliant games, but never the kind of gem where they wanted a ball sent directly to the Hall of Fame. People had to be wondering what he was waiting for.

And then the Philadelphia Phillies found out. He was saving it for a rainy day.

With a drizzle filling the air at County Stadium, the visiting Phillies would have been happy to postpone the game and play it as part of a Sunday doubleheader. The fans might have liked that, too.

But General Manager John McHale wanted no part of it. The Braves still had a chance to win the pennant, although a slim one. Going into the evening, they were 6½ games behind Pittsburgh with 13 to go, and it's always harder to win two games in one day than one.

As Spahn drove to the ballpark, he was worried that he'd pitch four innings and the game would be called. He had a 19-9 record at the time, and he had his heart set on an 11th 20-game season.

When Spahn threw his first pitch, only 6,117 people were there to watch, the second smallest crowd in the eight years that the Braves had been playing in Milwaukee.

Only 29 Philadelphia batters came to the plate against Spahn, and just two of them got on base. They both walked. Another 15 struck out. Rule out foul balls, and just 12 hitters even got a bat on the ball. The Braves won, 4-0, and at the advanced age of 39, Spahn had his no-hitter.

The hardest ball the Phillies hit all night was also the last one. Bobby Malkmus, a .212 hitter who had played in 13 games for the Braves in 1957, rapped it right back at the mound, and when it caromed off Spahn's glove, it looked as if he'd be denied again. But shortstop Johnny Logan charged the ball, gobbled it up, dug it out of his glove and threw it to first baseman Joe Adcock all in one fluid motion. The throw was low, but Adcock dug it out of the dirt for the last out, and Spahn and catcher Del Crandall were all over him in seconds.

"I don't know what there's left for you to do in baseball," Adcock told Spahn later, "but I know damn well you'll do it."

Spahn actually had something in mind. He wanted to win 300 games, and he said he was disappointed that he wouldn't be able to do it that season. The no-hitter actually surprised him. He didn't think he was a no-hit kind of pitcher.

His teammates knew better. Five innings into the game, they were carefully avoiding the subject for fear of jinxing him. That was the last thing Spahn was worried about. So he decided to relieve the tension when he came back to the dugout. "All right, just nobody say I've got a no-hitter going," he said.

An 11-year-old boy sitting in the grandstand would have been appalled. His name was Greg, and he was sitting next to another boy named Lewis. In the seventh inning, Lewis told Greg, "Your dad's going to pitch a no-hitter just like my dad did," and Greg clamped his hand over the other boy's mouth.

Greg's dad was Warren Spahn. Lewis' dad was Lew Burdette, who had done just what his son had said. He'd no-hit these same Phillies on Aug. 18.

"After it was over, Greg rushed into the clubhouse and threw his arms around me," Spahn said. "He was close to tears. That was my biggest thrill about the whole thing."

Some seven months later, Spahn gave his son bragging rights over Burdette's boy by throwing a second no-hitter against the San Francisco Giants. It happened at County Stadium on April 28, 1961, and only 8,518 people watched. The weather, of course, was lousy.

BARABOO'S KOENECKE KILLED IN MID-AIR BRAWL

SEPTEMBER 17, 1935

Being confined in a tight space with a belligerent drunk is every air traveler's nightmare. When the traveler is the pilot, the situation can be deadly.

That's how it turned out for Len Koenecke, a 31-year-old major league outfielder from Baraboo, Wis., who chartered a private plane in Detroit and never made it to Buffalo alive.

Koenecke had shown a good deal of promise in his second year in the big leagues when he hit .320 with 14 home runs and 73 RBIs for the Brooklyn Dodgers in 1934. But his average was down to .283 and he had only four homers with 27 RBIs 100 games into the 1935 season. Not only had his play become erratic, but his behavior had, too, and Manager Casey Stengel had had enough. He sent him home after the Dodgers arrived in St. Louis following a four-game series in Chicago.

When Koenecke boarded an American Airlines plane en route to New York, he was carrying a bottle. During the flight he knocked a stewardess down and tried to start a fight with another passenger. He was thrown off the plane in Detroit, and so he chartered a private airplane to fly him to Buffalo, where he'd played minor league ball.

When the private plane took off, there were three people in it: Koenecke; pilot William Joseph Mulqueeney; and Irwin Davis, a friend of Mulqueeney's and a professional parachute jumper. According to Mulqueeney's account to police, Koenecke started the trip sitting alongside him in the cockpit, while Davis sat in back. But when Koenecke began poking the pilot in the shoulder and grabbed for the controls, Mulqueeney told him to switch places with Davis.

Koenecke did, but the move didn't calm his behavior. Koenecke, who stood 5 feet 11 inches and weighed 180 pounds, bit Davis, according to the pilot's story, and the two passengers fought for 10 or more minutes as the plane started rocking dangerously. At that point, as Mulqueeney struggled to keep the small plane under control, he decided he had to try to end the fracas before all three of them crashed. He grabbed a small fire extinguisher and hit Koenecke over the head with it several times until he lost consciousness.

At that point, the pilot knew the plane was somewhere over Toronto, but he couldn't tell exactly where. When he spotted Long Branch Race Track below, he made an emergency landing. The plane was damaged while touching down. The passenger was dead.

The coroner ruled that Koenecke had died from a cerebral hemorrhage brought on by the blows from the fire extinguisher. Koenecke's head and face were a bloody mess. Toronto police arrested Mulqueeney and Davis for manslaughter. Mulqueeney got a lawyer named E.J. Murphy, who signaled his intention to subpoena Stengel to testify at a hearing about Koenecke's state of mind. Murphy alleged that the player was trying to commit suicide.

Yet another sidelight was offered by Robert W. Creamer in his book, *Stengel: His Life and Times.* Creamer wrote that "veteran baseball men" claimed Koenecke made homosexual advances to the pilot and copilot.

The Dodger players were shocked when they heard of Koenecke's fate. He'd been a popular teammate, and they wore black armbands to honor him at their next game. Although Creamer wrote that it was someone else disguising himself as Stengel who actually made the call to the Associated Press, Stengel was quoted as saying: "I can't believe it. I won't believe it."

The hearing was held four days after Koenecke's death, and Mulqueeney and Davis were released following just a few minutes of deliberation by a coroner's jury. It was ruled that they had acted in self-defense.

Koenecke's funeral was held the following Saturday in Adams, located 24 miles north of Wisconsin Dells, and an overflow crowd packed the Norwegian Lutheran Church. Koenecke was survived by his wife and three-year-old daughter. The Dodgers sent flowers.

McGWIRE HITS 64TH HOME RUN AT COUNTY STADIUM

SEPTEMBER 18, 1998

The great home run chase between Mark McGwire and Sammy Sosa was entering its final days when the St. Louis Cardinals came to Milwaukee, and Brewers pitchers weren't doing a very good job of staying neutral.

The previous weekend, they'd surrendered four bombs to Sosa in a three-game series with Chicago, bringing the Cubs slugger's total to 10 on the year against Milwaukee pitching. "This is my lucky team," Sosa said of the Brewers.

McGwire, on the other hand, wasn't having much luck at all with Phil Garner's fifth-place club. He'd hit only two home runs against Garner's young pitching staff, none in County Stadium, and a crowd of 48,194 had come hoping to see that change.

There are many who say the McGwire-Sosa chase saved baseball from a wave of fan discontent following a canceled World Series. Whether that was true or not, it certainly didn't hurt Milwaukee. Although both McGwire and Sosa had surpassed Roger Maris' record of 61 home runs by the time the Cardinals arrived in Milwaukee for their final three-game series of the season at County Stadium, advanced sales had topped 154,000, breaking the Brewers' 20-year-old franchise record. Taking advantage of every opportunity, the management had even imported 100 beer vendors from St. Louis to make sure nobody went home thirsty.

Everyone wanted a piece of McGwire, and that included a certain NFL quarterback. Brett Favre had driven in from Green Bay to take batting practice and meet the Cardinals' strong man.

In turn, McGwire was obviously zeroed in for this game, and the Brewers seemed determined to make up for the favoritism they'd shown previously for Sosa. McGwire would send three balls into the outfield stands that night, but only one counted. Two other towering drives were ruled barely foul.

The one that stayed straight came at the expense of Rafael Roque in the fourth inning. The Brewers' rookie had made the fatal mistake of getting behind on the count when he aimed a 3-1 fastball for the outside corner. The ball caught too much of the plate, and 417 feet later, McGwire had his 64th home run, moving him one past Sosa.

He got a standing ovation as he rounded the bases, and it didn't stop when he reached the dugout. He finally had to pop back out and tip his hat to the fans. The Brewers lost the game, 5-2, but nobody seemed to notice.

McGwire was tipping his hat the next day, too, but it was to the Brewers' pitchers. He struck out four times in a 7-4 Cardinal victory. But McGwire was back in stride on Sunday when he hit No. 65 and might have been deprived of No. 66 by an umpire's ruling as the Cardinals pasted the Brewers, 11-6.

A struggling Scott Karl gave up the 65th in the first inning when McGwire mailed a 2-1 fastball 423 feet into the left-field bleachers. The blast was cheered by 52,831 fans, which may have been two too many. Four innings later, McGwire sent another drive to left field that looked like it might have made it over the fence, but second base umpire Bob Davidson said a couple of fans had reached over and touched the ball, making it a ground-rule double.

So McGwire left town with four homers for the season off the Brewers, and three days later the Cubs and Sosa appeared at County Stadium again along with the usual heavy complement of Chicago fans. A total of 45,338 people swelled the Brewers' coffers, and Sosa, who entered the game mired in an 0-for-21 slump, shook it off as soon as he recognized where he was.

Sosa hit his 64th home run against Roque in the fifth inning. In the sixth, he hit No. 65 off Rod Henderson, another Brewers rookie, and, once again, drew even with McGwire. Sosa's two homers gave him six in his last five games against Milwaukee and a total of 12 for the season. But Sosa's enthusiasm was dampened by two things. The Cubs blew a seven-run lead to lose the game, 8-7, and he wouldn't get to face Brewer pitching anymore.

That last obstacle proved to be too much for him to overcome. He would hit only one more home run for a total of 66, while McGwire would hit five over the final three days of the season against Montreal to finish with 70. The record was McGwire's. The fun was everyone's.

BREWERS' CALDWELL WINS 20TH GAME

SEPTEMBER 19, 1978

There had to be a reason why one pitcher could shut out the defending world champion New York Yankees three times in the same season. Lou Piniella thought he knew what it was.

"He's a cheater," said the Yankees' right fielder. "Yes he's a cheater."

Which just made Mike Caldwell smile. The allegation that he had something extra on his fastball that night was not going to spoil the enjoyment of becoming only the second Milwaukee Brewers pitcher ever to win 20 games.

"I didn't throw a single spitter all night," drawled the man they called "Mr. Warmth" for his cold-blooded approach on the mound. "I mess around with it in the bullpen, but I haven't thrown a spitball in the American League. I haven't found a way of throwing it to be comfortable with."

Mike Caldwell

The beauty of the spitball, of course, is that having batters worry about it is almost as effective as actually using it. Whether Caldwell was doing something illegal or not, he was certainly doing a lot of things right while he was handcuffing the Yankees, 2-0, and bettering his record to 20-9.

The fact that his sixth shutout of the year was also his third against New York only made the victory sweeter. He gave up just four hits and no walks while striking out 10. The previous year's World Series hero, Reggie Jackson, had gone down swinging three times, and he wasn't impressed with Piniella's argument.

"The man's good, that's all," said Jackson. "I don't know if he throws a spitter. If he does, so what? I'm swinging pretty good now and he made me look funny. So accept it like a man. He had a good sinker, and he won't give you a strike unless he has to. If not for Guidry, he'd be the Cy Young Award winner."

The Yankees' Ron Guidry was 22-2 at the time, and he denied Caldwell the Cy Young Award. But Caldwell achieved just about anything else he could have wanted in one dream season.

He finished the year 22-9 with a 2.36 earned run average while breaking club records for shutouts with six and complete games with 23. Jim Colborn had been the only other Brewers pitcher who'd had a season even close to that when he went 20-12 with four shutouts and 22 complete games in 1973.

That said, Caldwell didn't pitch the Brewers to a pennant. He would have had to be quadruplets to do that, but they did improve a staggering 26 games from 67-95 in 1977 to 93-69 in 1978. The Brewers finished third, 6½ games behind the Yankees, who edged out Boston by a single game for the American League East title and then repeated as World Series winners.

The tightness of the pennant race may have contributed to Piniella's skepticism, but it didn't explain Caldwell's dominance that night at Yankee Stadium. Getting all of the offense he needed from Robin Yount, who doubled and scored in the third inning and homered in the fifth, the 29-year-old left-hander became the first pitcher to shut out the Yankees three times in the same season since Dean Chance had done it for the Los Angeles Angels in 1964.

"All ballgame I kept my pitches on the corners," Caldwell said. "I don't think they knew what was coming. I outguessed them."

Caldwell did the same to many baseball experts who had written him off after he'd undergone elbow surgery four years earlier. When the Brewers acquired him from Cincinnati midway through the 1977 season for two long forgotten minor leaguers, Rick O'Keefe and Garry Pyka, Caldwell had a lifetime record of 35-50. He finished that year 5-8 and was in danger of being banished to the bullpen in spring training.

"Lots of people have given up on me, and maybe the people who have given up on me were responsible in an indirect way for my coming back," he said.

Caldwell was only a little bit more than halfway through his career at that point. He pitched six more years for the Brewers, the best of them coming in 1979 when he had a 16-6 record and in 1982 when he went 17-13 for the franchise's only pennant winner. The Brewers lost the World Series, four games to three, that year, but it wasn't Caldwell's fault. He won both of his starts and posted a 2.04 ERA.

No one could say for sure whether any of the pitches he threw at the St. Louis Cardinals in that Series were wet. But he probably wanted them to think so.

FAVRE IGNITES COMEBACK IN LAMBEAU DEBUT

SEPTEMBER 20, 1992

All legends have to start somewhere, and Brett Favre's began on a sunny, 70-degree Sunday when he was backed up on his eight-yard-line at Lambeau Field in the third game of the 1992 season.

Of course, nobody could have known that at the time. Not the Cincinnati Bengals, who had just taken a six-point lead on the Green Bay Packers, and certainly not the Packers themselves, who had been watching their 22-year-old quarterback being sacked five times and losing three fumbles. Favre had completed only 13 of 28 passes for 130 yards that day before leading his team on an 88-yard touchdown drive its previous series.

Now all coach Mike Holmgren could do as his team broke the huddle on its final possession with no timeouts was take the good with the bad and pray there was more of the one than the other. His prayers were answered with an unforgettable 54-second drive capped by a 35-yard touchdown pass that gave the Packers their first victory of the year.

The scoreboard read 24-23, and Brett Favre had arrived.

He had taken more than a slight detour to get there, though. Favre's misspent rookie season in Atlanta produced nothing but four incomplete passes in four tries, but General Manager Ron Wolf saw enough in the wild thing from Southern Mississippi to trade a first-round draft choice for him. Holmgren saw the potential, too, but started the season with six-year veteran Don Majkowski at quarterback.

Holmgren pulled Majkowski in the second half of a 31-3 flogging at Tampa Bay the next week, but Favre did nothing to get anyone excited. So Majkowski started again against the Bengals, only to tear up his left ankle on the Packers' sixth offensive play.

Enter Favre. Alternately erratic and brilliant, he kept the Packers in the game until Jim Breech's 41-yard field goal put Cincinnati ahead, 23-17. When rookie Robert Brooks stepped out of bounds on the eight-yard line on the ensuing kickoff, Favre faced a forbidding task that he turned into an adventure.

He started the winning march with a four-yard swing pass to running back Harry Sydney, and then he launched a 42-yard rocket to all-pro Sterling Sharpe, who landed awkwardly after making a spectacular catch. Favre hit running back Vince Workman for 11 yards to the 35 on the next play, and then he spiked the ball to stop the clock. It was at that point that the Packers' hopes looked a little dimmer. Sharpe had injured his ribs on the bomb, and he had to leave the game.

Replacing him was a fifth-year journeyman who had played for three other teams before the Packers picked him up as a Plan B free agent. His name was Kitrick Taylor, and he would be cut two months later. But at that moment, he was clearly in the right place at the right time.

The call was "Two jet, all go," a staple of the West Coast offense and a play that Favre said the Packers practiced at least five times a day for most of his career. It involved four vertical routes with Favre reading either or both safeties, then drilling the ball up-field. This one couldn't have come out any better. Favre pump-faked the Bengals' safety out of position and hit Taylor in full stride.

There were 13 seconds on the clock when Taylor caught the only touchdown pass of his career. Chris Jacke kicked the extra point, and 57,272 fans went nuts.

Thousands more would claim to have been there for the first of 40 game-winning drives engineered by Favre when the Packers trailed or were tied in the fourth quarter. With Majkowski sidelined indefinitely, Favre made the first of his NFL record 253 consecutive starts – 275 counting playoffs – for the Packers the next week. He became a welcome fixture at a position that had been in turmoil for most of the previous 21 seasons.

After all, the Packers had gone through 17 different starters looking for a quarterback since Bart Starr's retirement following the 1971 season. But they had one now.

Don Majkowski was helped off the field.

Brett Favre replaced him and seized the opportunity.

BRAVES REPEAT AS NATIONAL LEAGUE CHAMPS

SEPTEMBER 21, 1958

Twelve months earlier almost to the day, owner Lou Perini had stood in a champagne-soaked Milwaukee Braves clubhouse and declared, "It took us nine years to win this pennant. It won't take that long again."

The man knew what he was talking about.

Perini was celebrating the Braves' first championship in Milwaukee and the franchise's first since its days in Boston when he made his prediction. Henry Aaron's dramatic home run had just turned him into the happiest owner in the National League, and neither of them could have known that Aaron would do the same thing for him again the very next season.

The situation was much different, and so was the opponent this time around. The score had been tied, 2-2, in the bottom of the 11th inning when Aaron hit his pennant-clinching shot the year before at County Stadium. But now the Braves were in Cincinnati and cruising 4-0, with Warren Spahn working on a one-hitter going into the seventh inning.

Red Schoendienst was on first when Aaron stepped to the plate to face Cincinnati reliever Tom Acker. Aaron had smacked a two-run double and had scored on a throwing error in the Brewers' four-run fifth, and he immediately got Acker's attention by hitting a ball out of the park foul. Then Aaron straightened one out for his 30th home run of the year. When the ball landed in the left-field stands at Crosley Field the pennant race should have been over. But the Reds, now down 6-0, wouldn't leave quietly.

Spahn had looked untouchable. He hadn't given up a hit since the first batter singled in the first inning, but then Frank Robinson opened the bottom of the seventh with a home run to start a five-run rally that sent Spahn to the showers. Ace reliever Don McMahon restored order by surrendering just two hits over the last 2⅔ innings and wrapping up a 6-5 victory that clinched the pennant with four games to go and brought that champagne out once again.

"There's nothing quite like the first one," said Manager Fred Haney. "This time we did what people expected of us. Most people don't think of those things. But we won it, and that's what counts."

Haney had a point. Going into the season, the Las Vegas oddsmakers had made the Braves heavy favorites to repeat. "This one was tougher than last year, because they were all gunning for us," said Perini.

While the owner was relieved, the fans were jubilant. The celebration at home started a split-second after Billy Bruton caught the final fly ball in Cincinnati, and it stretched down Wisconsin Avenue from Lake Michigan all the way to N. 16th Street. An estimated 85,000 people swarmed Milwaukee's main drag shortly after 4:15 p.m., and they might have danced all night if they didn't have a plane to meet. The team charter was due in from Cincinnati, and almost everyone wanted to be there when it landed. It may have been the only time the Braves disappointed their fans all year.

The flight arrived on time, but it landed away from the main terminal, and only a few sharp-eyed observers actually saw the players get off before they disappeared into a mass of family, media and officials. People had lined the route from the airport to downtown expecting to cheer a busload of heroes. Instead, the players jumped into their cars, and they just kind of melted into the traffic.

That didn't cancel the party, but it dampened it. Especially for the 18 people arrested for drunkenness and disorderly conduct. The year before, excessive revelry brought only suspended sentences. This time, seven people were hauled in just for blowing their horns too close to Deaconess Hospital. Things were definitely different the second time around.

Especially later, when the Braves lost the World Series to the New York Yankees.

The Braves returned to Milwaukee by plane after winning the National League pennant in 1958, but they were greeted mostly by family, members of the media and officials when the flight landed away from the main terminal.

HUTSON'S FIRST CATCH BURNS BEARS

SEPTEMBER 22, 1935

Future Hall of Famer Johnny "Blood" McNally was lined up wide to the right and attracting most of the Chicago Bears' attention while the skinny rookie from Alabama was split left and getting single coverage. Bears safety Beattie Feathers had told his coach earlier in the week not to worry about the rookie, he'd "cover him like a blanket."

Don Hutson shrugged off the blanket with a wicked cut, and Arnie Herber's spiral hit him in full stride near midfield. Nobody came close to Hutson after that as he raced to the goal line with an 83-yard reception that gave the Green Bay Packers all the points they would need for a 7-0 upset of George Halas' Bears. It was Hutson's first start in the National Football League – he played sparingly the week before in the season opener against the Chicago Cardinals – and it was the beginning of one of the greatest careers any receiver would have in any era.

None of the 13,600 fans at old City Stadium that day could have known that Hutson would catch 487 more passes over his 11-year career or that the throw from Herber would amount to barely a fraction of the yards he would gain for the Packers. But it was pretty clear that pro football was about to undergo a fundamental change.

The Packers completed only six more passes against the Bears, and Hutson didn't catch another. But coach Curly Lambeau knew he had a special weapon in his rookie with 9.8 speed in the 100-yard dash, and there would be many more bombs in the future.

Lambeau wasn't the only one who knew it. After Hutson caught six passes including two for touchdowns against Stanford in his final college game at the Rose Bowl, the competition for his services was fierce. Halas was believed to be among the suitors, but it was Lambeau and the Brooklyn Dodgers' John "Shipwreck" Kelly who were there at the end.

This was a year before the college draft was instituted, partly to level the competitive playing field and partly to avoid expensive bidding wars for special talents like Hutson. When the Rose Bowl was over Hutson was confronted with two contracts, one from Lambeau and one from Kelly, and he eventually signed both.

The difference that brought him to Green Bay and not to Brooklyn wasn't dollars, it was minutes, or so the story goes. There's no longer any way to prove the veracity of it, but both signed contracts supposedly landed on NFL President Joe Carr's desk on the same day. Carr resolved the dilemma by looking at the postmarks on the envelopes. The Packers' had been mailed at 8:30 a.m., the Dodgers' at 8:47. Hutson became Green Bay property by a matter of 17 minutes.

The Packers announced his signing on Feb. 19, and it would prove to be a monumental triumph for the franchise. But not everyone in Green Bay celebrated it at the time. Hutson stood 6 feet 1 inch and never weighed any more than 178 pounds. His critics said he was too frail to play the pro game. They also said he was making too much money, although Lambeau took great pains not to reveal how much that was. He paid his star end each week with two equal checks drawn from two different banks so the other players on the team never knew how much Hutson was making.

In all, Hutson played 11 seasons, and he led the NFL in receptions and was an all-pro selection in eight of them. He also played defensive end and later safety where he topped the team in interceptions three times, and he kicked short field goals and extra points. Opponents designed special defenses for him. The Bears were especially obsessed with containing him, but nothing they did helped. He scored 105 touchdowns in 116 career games, and 15 of those scores came against Chicago.

It might be a toss-up whether the Packers' greatest player was Hutson or Brett Favre, and the two had something in common. They could never decide when to retire. Hutson actually announced his intention to retire before each of his final three seasons and considered it on at least one other occasion before he finally pulled the trigger following the 1945 season.

He had two Most Valuable Player Awards and 19 individual NFL records to his credit when he left the game. Included was the career mark of 488 receptions. Second-best was 190. A five-time league scoring leader, Hutson once ran up 29 points in a single quarter against Detroit with four touchdowns and five conversions.

Naturally, he was elected as a charter member of the Pro Football Hall of Fame. It was just one of many things that Don Hutson did first.

BRAVES WIN FIRST PENNANT ON AARON'S HOMER

SEPTEMBER 23, 1957

Two years after the fact, a panel of experts voted Henry Aaron's 715th career home run as baseball's most memorable moment. Aaron himself begged to differ.

He was willing to let the media members and the baseball officials who conducted the poll think what they wanted, but the blow he would always remember best disappeared over the center-field wall at County Stadium at 11:34 on a Monday night. It brought an end to a long, frustrating wait and sent a whole state into delirium. It was the home run that won the pennant for the Milwaukee Braves.

Johnny Logan was standing at first base when Aaron stepped to the plate to face the St. Louis Cardinals' Billy Muffett with two outs in the eleventh inning. Lew Burdette had pitched 10 solid innings before giving way to Gene Conley for the last one, but the Braves had left 13 runners on base. They'd come back from a 2-1 deficit in the seventh inning to tie the game at 2-2 and then blown two chances to win.

Red Schoendienst had hit a foul fly out to the first baseman with runners on first and second in the eighth, and Frank Torre had grounded into a bases-loaded double play in the tenth. It looked as if the game could go on forever. Instead, it lasted just one more pitch when Aaron strode to the plate in the 11th.

Muffett delivered it, and Aaron deposited it into the bleachers. While 40,926 people held their breath, Cardinals centerfielder Wally Moon leaped as high as he could. And then suddenly there was a scramble in the stands for the ball, followed by municipal hysteria. Final score: 4-2.

Aaron was heading to second base when the Braves' dugout emptied to greet him at home plate. While Aaron was getting carried off, Milwaukee was getting carried away.

One minute Wisconsin Avenue was a deserted strip of pavement, the next it was a scene from a Cecil B. DeMille movie. Horns blared, people screamed. A young woman turned handsprings in front of the Schroeder Hotel, and a young man climbed a light post. The citizens flooded out of the bars and restaurants, leaving their radios behind them but taking their drinks with them.

Sixty policemen took up positions around the avenue to keep things from getting out of hand, whatever that was. They closed the street for two blocks and kept it closed until 3:45 in the morning. Four hours of craziness was a minimum requirement for something as momentous as the Milwaukee Braves' first pennant.

Crowd estimates ran as high as 10,000 for just those two blocks, although some observers doubted that. Everyone agreed, though, that this was the city's wildest celebration since the Braves came to town.

Back at the stadium, the players were wasting champagne. More of the contents got sprayed or poured than got swallowed. A couple of visitors arrived from the visiting clubhouse. Fred Hutchinson, the St. Louis manager, and Alvin Dark, the team captain, wished the Braves luck in the World Series, which was due to start Oct. 2. The idle Yankees had clinched the American League pennant the same day when the second-place Chicago White Sox were losing in Kansas City; whereas, the Braves' victory over the second-place Cardinals gave them a six-game lead with five to play.

A year earlier, the Braves had been stung by blowing the pennant against St. Louis in the last series of the season. The Braves had a half-game lead with three to go when the Cardinals invaded County Stadium, but they lost the first two and finished a game behind Brooklyn.

Aaron wasn't thinking about that as he circled the bases. He said he was thinking about the home run that Bobby Thomson had hit to win a pennant for the New York Giants in 1951. If Aaron's 43rd home run of the season wasn't "the shot heard around the world," it was at least the one that got a whole state's attention.

"If I had to choose one great moment in my life, I'd have to say that one in Milwaukee was it," Aaron told the panelists in 1976.

Thousands of Milwaukeeans may have shared that opinion, although a few of them got a little too excited. Three were arrested for public drunkenness and four for disorderly conduct. They were among 20 cases that went before Judge Robert W. Hansen the next day. He suspended all of their sentences.

"Any Milwaukeean ought to be forgiven," said his honor, "because last night was a night to celebrate."

FREEDOM'S LOWNEY SCORES HUGE WRESTLING UPSET

SEPTEMBER 24, 2000

Garrett Lowney was so anonymous that he had to bring his own cheering section to the Olympics. His mother and father traveled all the way from Freedom, Wis., to Australia along with his two sisters and 25 or so other friends and relatives including his pastor. Nobody else thought he had a prayer against the world's best Greco-Roman wrestlers.

Lowney was a redshirt freshman from the University of Minnesota who had never been in a major international meet before, let alone the Olympics. He'd taken up the international form of the sport only two years earlier, and at 20 years old he was eight years younger than anyone else on the American team. But he'd learned a little secret while he trained for the Games in Russia. He could stay with these guys.

He proved it in his first match in the Sydney Games when he outlasted the Czech Republic's Marek Svec, 2-0, in overtime. Svec was a silver medalist in the European championships, which made this a heartwarming little story. But the story was sure to end later that day, Sept. 24, when Lowney faced Russian superstar Gogui Koguachvilli.

Koguachvilli, a five-time world champion, was the favorite to win the gold medal at 213¾ pounds, or the heavyweight division, but Lowney wasn't intimidated. He'd worked out with the Russian enough on his own turf to know that he had a chance.

Lowney's sturdy band of followers went wild when he took a shocking 3-0 lead early in the match. But he gave two points of that back when the referee penalized him for using his legs to defend. That was a violation of Greco-Roman rules, but Lowney was enraged because he thought it was a bogus call. When Koguachvilli picked up another point later, the match went into overtime.

"I knew that I wasn't getting no breaks," Lowney said afterward. "The only point that he earned was the point for the turn. The two points were a gift."

Lowney made good use of his anger in the overtime. He was looking for a one-point takedown when suddenly he spotted an opening and ducked behind the surprised Russian, throwing him into the air and onto the mat. It was a five-point throw, the biggest scoring move in the sport and more than enough to put the upstart two matches from the gold medal round.

Lowney truly believed Koguachvilli had no idea he could lose this match. "He was not real happy," he said. Later in the Games, Lowney expanded on his point. "A lot of people are looking at me and saying, 'Who is this guy?' No one in the world had heard of me except the coaches in the United States. They didn't think anything of me here," he said.

And who could blame them? No American had won an Olympic gold in Greco-Roman since the 1984 Games in Los Angeles, and those had been boycotted by the Soviet Union. As one writer for the Associated Press put it, Lowney's victory was like a Class A baseball team beating a major league opponent in the World Series.

But now he had everyone's attention when he faced Georgia's Genadi Chkhaidze. Once again Lowney was the underdog, and once again he won in overtime, 2-0, setting up a semifinal match with Sweden's Mikael Ljungberg. And that's where the dream took a detour.

Ljungberg, the 1996 Olympic bronze medalist, grabbed a 6-0 lead on an early lift and throw, and Lowney never recovered. Not only did he lose the match, 8-1, but he injured his neck in the process. He needed muscle relaxants and electric stimulation treatments overnight just to make it to the bronze medal match with Greece's Konstantinos Thanos on Sept. 26.

But once the wrestling started, Lowney forgot the pain and beat Thanos, 3-1, to claim a spot on the podium next to Ljungberg, who won the gold, and the Ukraine's Davyd Saldadze, who captured the silver. No one thought Lowney had a chance to medal. No one except Lowney.

"Maybe," he said, "I was just too young and stupid to know that I wasn't supposed to win."

Lowney would win U.S. national championships in Greco-Roman wrestling from 2001-'03, and he also qualified for the 2004 Olympics, but he didn't place.

BREWERS' SHAKE-UP STARTS AT THE TOP

SEPTEMBER 25, 2002

Ulice Payne was a former Marquette basketball player, a civic leader and a high-powered attorney. What he wasn't was a Selig.

And that made a big story even bigger when Payne was introduced as the new president of the Milwaukee Brewers at a hastily called press conference at Miller Park. Good or bad – and it was more good than bad – the Brewers were a Selig-run operation from the time future commissioner Bud led the group that brought them to town right through the day in 1998 when he turned the club over to his daughter Wendy and went off to run baseball.

Wendy Selig-Prieb had been a Brewer executive since 1990, and she would still be with the club as chairman of the board after the switch, but starting immediately she said Payne would be the boss.

With Payne came Doug Melvin, who turned out to be the only one involved in the entire shakeup who had any lasting impact on the franchise. Melvin was named as the club's new general manager, to replace Dean Taylor, whom Selig-Prieb had hired three years earlier in the last major Brewers restructuring. Taylor inherited a mess and left a catastrophe. The team was 74-87 when he arrived, and now it was closing in on a 56-106 finish. As bad as the Brewers had been over 10 straight losing seasons, they'd never lost 100 games before in a single year. Had Bud Selig seen enough?

The commissioner still had a 28% stake in the club that was voted by a blind trust, but he said his daughter's move had nothing to do with him. "It was her decision right from the start," he said. "I believe in people charting their own course."

Selig-Prieb, 42, had a daughter at home and a lot on her plate. What was causing her the most consternation at the moment was the Brewers' dreadful performance on the field. "This season has been tremendously disappointing and embarrassing," she said. "The season met no one's expectations."

Expectations, of course, were on everybody's mind, and Payne didn't do much to heighten them. "I don't have the answers," he said. "I'm going to find the answers."

The question was, how qualified was he to look for them? Payne was a highly visible figure around town. He had been a sub on Al McGuire's national championship basketball team in 1977 at Marquette, and then he'd gone on to serve on a number of corporate boards. He was the chairman of the Bradley Center board and the managing partner of the local office of Foley and Lardner, Milwaukee's leading law firm. But was he a baseball guy?

His firm had a long relationship with the Brewers, and he'd formed a good one with Bud Selig while serving on the Miller Park stadium board. But he had no experience and no credentials in personnel.

That's what Melvin was for. The Brewers signed their 50-year-old general manager to a four-year deal hoping he could do as much for them as he'd done for the Texas Rangers. Melvin had been the Rangers' GM from October 1994 through the end of the 2001 season, when they'd won three division titles. The Brewers hadn't been to the playoffs in 20 years.

Melvin also had been fired in Texas after the team had signed superstar Alex Rodriguez to a $252 million contract and then finished last in the American League West. So he was the lone newcomer to the organization who understood the peaks and valleys of baseball.

"My goal is to get the Brewers to a level where I can feel we're getting better," he said, but he was careful not to offer a timeline. "I don't believe in rebuilding plans," he said. "If there was a three-year plan, I'd wait and buy a ticket in 2005."

By early 2005 the Brewers had a new owner, Mark Attanasio. Melvin was still there and on the verge of turning the Brewers back into winners. But Selig-Prieb and Payne were gone.

GREEN BAY BOXER GOES 10 WITH JOE LOUIS

SEPTEMBER 26, 1934

Mixing concrete made Adolph Wiater's shoulders bigger, but it couldn't make his arms longer. That may have made all the difference.

Kids worked when young Wiater was growing up in Green Bay. Especially kids like Adolph who had 11 brothers and sisters. The family lived on his father's small construction business, and by the time Wiater turned nine, he was mixing concrete. By the time he was 18, he had the shoulders of a bull, and he was proud of them.

After attending East High School, he signed up with the National Guard to earn a little extra money. He'd done some big talking in his time with the Guard, and one day a boxer came to boot camp and offered to take on anyone brave enough to get in the ring with him. The corporal who was standing next to him lifted Wiater's arm and volunteered him. And so began his boxing career.

To everyone's surprise, Wiater won that first fight. When he returned to Green Bay, he started training with a group of fighters at the Columbus Community Center. Wiater was a full 6 feet tall, but his arms were short for his size, making it impossible for him to stand back and swap punches from long range. So he took a mauling, full-speed-ahead approach instead.

It served him well as a light heavyweight in the amateur ranks as he made a name for himself in Golden Gloves tournaments, and it was still working as he compiled a 17-1-1 record in his first two years as a pro. His record was good enough to get him mention as one of the leading heavyweight contenders, and that led to a match with another up-and-coming heavyweight contender named Joe Louis.

Louis was unbeaten when he met Wiater at Arcadia Gardens in Chicago, but he'd had only six fights. Some experts liked Wiater's chances because of his experience. Win it, and they figured he might be on the road to a title shot against Max Baer.

Wiater's aggressiveness put him in the path of a Louis right in the first round, and down he went before a packed house of 2,296. Wiater popped right up, refusing to take a count, and carried the fight to Louis for much of the night. He won the middle rounds, but the future champion rallied in the last two rounds to gain the decision.

Wiater had gone into those rounds thinking he was going to win the fight. Naturally, he was disappointed, but he still had something nobody could take away from him. He was the first opponent to go as many as 10 rounds with Louis. Moreover, some ringside observers thought the fight could have been called a draw.

"He was going to quit in the eighth round because he had taken too much of a beating," Wiater recalled some 50 years later. "Somehow his manager stuck a pin up his seat to make him fight." Jack Blackburn, Louis' trainer, would later say, "When Joe pulled through those 10 rounds, I knew that I was handling a great fighter."

Adolph Wiater

Wiater kept fighting, but by November 1935 he wasn't a contender anymore. What's more, his arms were killing him. Looking back, he thought his swarming style had put too much strain on his elbows. He had surgery to remove calcium deposits, but he was never the same fighter after the operation.

He split two more bouts and retired with a 19-6-3 record. He went to technical school, learned the printing trade and settled down in Chicago with a company called Roto Print. He stayed there for 41 years.

His career in the ring lasted less than a tenth as long as his career in printing, but it still left him in select company. Only three fighters ever beat Louis in his 70 pro bouts, and only 12 others in addition to Wiater lasted 10 rounds with Louis in his 67 career wins.

LOMBARDI WINS FIRST GAME WITH PACKERS

SEPTEMBER 27, 1959

Vince Lombardi introduced himself as the Green Bay Packers' fifth head coach by declaring that he'd never been on a losing team. It was an interesting way to start since most of his players had never been on a winning one. At least not in the pros.

Some new coaches have to reverse a losing culture. Lombardi had to revive a corpse. The Packers were coming off a 1-10-1 season when he got there, and they'd lost 93 games their last 11 years. The best they'd done in that time was go 6-6 twice.

And now just months from their opener against archrival Chicago, this obscure assistant coach from New York was telling them that they would achieve excellence by pursuing perfection. They didn't reach either one in Lombardi's first game, but they did beat the Bears, 9-6, before a sellout crowd of 32,150 at two-year old City Stadium or what is now Lambeau Field.

Lombardi didn't just change the Packers' mindset. He also shuffled their roster and radically revised their conditioning. In the eight months leading up to the opener, he got rid of five leading veterans including all-pro end Bill Howton, who had been the Packers' best offensive player for most of the 1950s. And he introduced a number of sadistic training devices, most notably the grass drill.

If Lombardi's first Green Bay team wasn't the most talented in the league, it may well have been the fittest. There was a reason why the Packers outscored their opponents, 67-37, in the fourth quarter over the course of the season.

Nobody suffered more from Lombardi's merciless methods than defensive stalwart Dave Hanner, who was said to have lost 18 pounds in the first two days of training camp. That would land Hanner in the hospital in July, but it would also pay a major dividend two months later in the opener against Chicago.

The Bears were heavy favorites in the game, but then everybody was favored against Green Bay in those days. They were able to build a 6-0 lead on two John Aveni field goals in a ragged affair, mainly because Lamar McHan couldn't get anything going offensively for the Packers. McHan was a highly skilled but totally erratic quarterback. He was also a little goofy, which was at least part of the reason why he would lose his starting job to Bart Starr eight games into the season.

With McHan completing only three of 12 passes for 81 yards that day, Green Bay needed to do something on defense or special teams to have a chance. That something turned out to be a Richie Petitbon fumble that Jim Ringo recovered on the Chicago 26-yard line following a Max McGee punt. Six plays later, Jim Taylor scored from five yards out, giving the Packers a tenuous 7-6 lead.

The lead became much more emphatic later in the fourth quarter thanks to the streamlined Hanner. Lombardi had made a curious decision at the beginning of the game when the Packers won the coin flip. He'd elected to kick off because of a 25 mile per hour wind that he wanted at his back in the final period.

The decision paid off when the Bears stopped the Packers on their second-to-last possession. With the gale blowing behind him, Max McGee got off a 61-yard punt that bounced out of bounds on the Chicago two-yard line. On the Bears' first play, quarterback Ed Brown dropped back into the end zone, and Hanner busted through the Chicago line and leveled him for a safety.

That made the score 9-7, and all the Bears could do was try an onside kick. Ray Nitschke recovered it, and Lombardi was carried off the field by his players with his first victory as the Packers' coach.

Curiously, Lombardi would coach eight more openers in Green Bay and win only four of them. But he'd also claim five NFL championships and two Super Bowls. And when he left, he still hadn't been on a losing team.

Vince Lombardi

BREWERS BACK IN PLAYOFFS AFTER 26 YEARS

SEPTEMBER 28, 2008

Even when it was over it wasn't over. Milwaukee Brewers fans had endured a 26-year wait since their team's last trip to the post-season, but they'd just seen CC Sabathia and Ryan Braun collaborate on a 3-1 victory that should have ended it.

Sabathia had brought new meaning to the term "tireless" by limiting the National League Central Division champion Chicago Cubs to four hits in his third straight start on short rest. If he'd had to, the 28-year-old left-hander would have been willing to go another nine innings, but Braun spared him the trouble by hitting a two-run homer in the Brewers' biggest game since 1982.

Braun's eighth inning blast left Milwaukee a half-game ahead of New York in the NL wild card race. But the sellout crowd couldn't celebrate until the other half was nailed down. If the Mets won, there would have to be a one-game playoff in New York to break the tie.

The Brewers' management arranged to show the last two innings of the Mets' finale on the Miller Park scoreboard. It was a bizarre scene as the fans stayed glued to their seats long after the Brewers' game was over and the players stood outside the dugout watching the New Yorkers battle the Florida Marlins. When the last out of the Mets' 4-2 loss was shown on the giant screen, the stadium went nuts.

The Brewers had retreated to their clubhouse area by then, leaving them free to pour adult beverages on each other in relative privacy. Sabathia got wetter than most, but then it takes a lot of bubbly to thoroughly soak a 300-pound man.

And it took a lot of pitcher to carry the Brewers into the playoffs. Since his acquisition from Cleveland on July 7, Sabathia had compiled an 11-2 record for the Brewers with a barely visible 1.65 earned run average. His four-hit victory over the Cubs was his seventh complete game for Milwaukee and his third start in eight days.

The Cubs had wrapped up the division eight days earlier, and Manager Lou Piniella could have made things easier on the Brewers by resting his starters. Instead, he chose to play most of them, and then he split the mound duties among seven pitchers.

The committee approach worked as the Cubs took a 1-0 lead on an unearned run in the second inning and held the Brewers scoreless until the seventh when Ray Durham doubled and eventually scored on a bases loaded walk. Braun did the rest after Mike Cameron singled in the eighth. When right-hander Bob Howry tried to slip a first-pitch fastball past him, Braun drove it into the left-field bleachers.

Sabathia closed out the Cubs with the help of a double play in the ninth, and 26 years of frustration vanished. It was impossible to tell who the happiest man was in the Brewers' clubhouse, but the most relieved had to be General Manager Doug Melvin. Melvin had taken two huge gambles to get the Brewers to where they were. The first was trading for Sabathia, and the second was replacing Manager Ned Yost with his bench coach, Dale Sveum, with 12 games left in the season.

After going 20-7 in August, the Brewers were clearly pressing in September. Sveum seemed to settle them down, and they won seven games with him in charge. But Melvin was quick to credit Yost for leading the Brewers through "93% of the season."

Meanwhile, many of the fans then took their celebration elsewhere. Wild times prevailed both inside and outside taverns from Bluemound Road to Water Street. The next evening, more than 14,000 Brewer backers gathered at the Summerfest grounds to cheer the team off to Philadelphia for the playoffs.

Those didn't go so well. The Brewers fell to the eventual world champion Philadelphia Phillies three games to one in the best-of-five NL Division Series, winning only Game 3 at Miller Park. But that didn't remove all the shine of a special season.

PACKERS DEDICATE STADIUM WITH VICTORY OVER BEARS

SEPTEMBER 29, 1957

A beauty queen, a TV cowboy and the vice president of the United States helped the Green Bay Packers dedicate their new home, but it took a backup quarterback to turn the occasion into a celebration.

Nobody had ever built a place quite like this just for pro football before the citizens of Green Bay passed a $960,000 referendum to put up their new City Stadium on the west edge of town. But then nobody had ever needed one more than the Packers.

They'd played in three different parks in Green Bay since Curly Lambeau established the franchise 38 years earlier, none of them much more luxurious than the previous one. Old City Stadium, their home for 32 of those years, was a wooden structure with a cinder track around it and a cubbyhole for a home locker room. It held only 25,000 people, and it wasn't even theirs. The school board owned it, and the Packers shared it with East High School.

When the players got a look at the new place, they were overwhelmed. "It was like you had died and gone to heaven," recalled end Gary Knafelc, who would catch the pass that left a capacity crowd of 32,132 feeling the same way after the Packers had upset the Chicago Bears, 21-17.

It took less than eight months to build the new facility and eight years to rename it Lambeau Field, so a weekend of ceremonies to dedicate it didn't seem out of place. There was a good-bye party at the old stadium, and of course there was a parade. An estimated 70,000 people watched the procession wind through two-and-a-half miles of city streets where Marshall Matt Dillon was on hand to maintain order.

James Arness, the actor who portrayed the lawman on the popular *Gunsmoke* TV series, drew some attention, but probably not as much as Marilyn Elaine Van Derbur, the reigning Miss America. The two were just part of the ceremonies that also included Vice President Richard Nixon and National Football League Commissioner Bert Bell.

If the spectators were excited about the stadium, Bell was positively euphoric. He called it "the greatest thing that has ever happened in professional football." That may have been a little excessive for a ballpark surrounded by a cyclone fence, but even George Halas agreed that it was a very big deal. Speaking at a rally before the referendum more than a year earlier, the Bears' owner had said, "I can say to you sincerely... that the best way for you to guarantee the current and future success of the Packers is to build the new stadium."

Halas may have been a little less enthusiastic about the Packers' current success after the game, because it came at the expense of his team.

The Bears were clear favorites over a Packer squad that had finished 4-8 the year before. But the defending Western Conference champions couldn't get out of their own way that day as they threw five interceptions and fumbled a punt.

As expected Chicago twice jumped out to leads in the first half, but quarterback Vito "Babe" Parilli threw a 38-yard touchdown pass to end Billy Howton and fullback Fred Cone scored on a one-yard run to tie the game at intermission. Parilli would throw just four touchdown passes all season, and he got two of them in this game. That was made even more remarkable by the fact that he was on the field only because coach Lisle Blackbourn had pulled a struggling Bart Starr in the second quarter.

George Blanda's 13-yard field goal put the Bears up again, 17-14, in the second half and set the stage for Parilli to send everybody home happy. Midway through the fourth quarter, he got flushed out of the pocket from the six-yard line, and he was running left and looking right when he spotted Knafelc in the end zone. He threw the ball a little behind the receiver, but Knafelc hauled it in for the winning touchdown.

It would be 13 months before the Packers won another game in their new home. But they have since won six NFL championships while playing there. The stadium has been expanded seven times, and was redeveloped in 2003, making it the longest continuously occupied stadium in the NFL.

It also is the most storied.

"THE BUD SONG" COMES TO CAMP RANDALL

SEPTEMBER 30, 1978

As the players danced around the field with the cheerleaders, there was no doubt that the University of Wisconsin had just pulled off one of the more astonishing comebacks in its history. But who deserved the credit? The third-string quarterback with the black eye or the 41-year-old band director?

Mike Kalasmiki, the quarterback, directed three touchdown drives in the fourth quarter, including two in the space of 42 seconds, to lead the Badgers to a 22-19 victory over winless and luckless Oregon. It was quite a performance from a young man with 11 stitches across the bridge of his nose and a left eye that he couldn't open in the morning without an icepack after falling on a fire escape earlier in the week.

Mike Leckrone, the band director, didn't throw any touchdown passes, but then neither did Kalasmiki before Leckrone dug deep into his repertoire and pulled out Wisconsin's special version of *The Bud Song*. Leckrone had used this rip-off of the beer company jingle at a hockey game three years earlier, and he figured he might as well try it out at Camp Randall Stadium where 63,988 people were just sitting on their hands anyway with the Badgers trailing, 13-0.

So the band struck it up, and about 20 seconds later Kalasmiki found split end David Charles in the end zone for Wisconsin's first touchdown with 10 minutes 29 seconds remaining.

The band continued playing the song over and over, and the Badgers continued rolling. By the time they scored their next touchdown, the visiting Ducks didn't know whether to rush the passer or tackle the tuba players.

The jingle clearly had the desired effect on a suddenly wide-awake crowd, and maybe it rallied Kalasmiki, too. The Addison, Ill., junior hadn't even expected to play that day, but then the first-string quarterback, freshman John Josten, went down with a knee injury in the first quarter and the second-string quarterback, senior Charles Green, couldn't get anything done. So Kalasmiki came on to complete 16 passes in 35 attempts for 232 yards and two scores.

Kalasmiki, who stood 6 feet 4 inches and weighed 210 pounds, had suffered a serious knee injury the previous fall and didn't appear to be a good fit in new coach Dave McClain's triple-option offense. But the fourth-quarter hole the Badgers faced against Oregon begged for a drop-back passer more than a runner. Kalasmiki's first touchdown pass covered 26 yards. After Oregon scored again to take a 19-7 lead, he completed his second to freshman receiver Tim Stracka for 12 yards with 2:14 remaining. Tailback Kevin Cohee scored the final touchdown on a five-yard run with 1:32 to go.

Oregon contributed mightily to its own demise in the last 3:04 left to play by having an ill-advised pass intercepted and failing to field an onside kick. As a result, the Badgers finished the afternoon with a 3-0 record and went on to a 5-4-2 season. And *The Bud Song* went on... well, forever.

It's still a Saturday staple at Camp Randall, along with the celebrated "Fifth Quarter" post-game music show and the playing of *Varsity*. One of Leckrone's predecessors, Ray Dvorak, gets credit for the arm-waving *Varsity* rendition, while Leckrone shares *The Bud Song* with the Anheuser-Busch Brewery and a fellow named Steve Karmen. When Karmen wrote the jingle in 1970, it had eight words: "When you say Bud—weiser, you've said it all." Leckrone substituted Wis—consin for Bud—weiser, and the rest is popular nonsense.

In the beginning, critics who weren't crazy about the beer connection were joined by customers in the upper deck who felt the stadium sway whenever the students danced to the music. In fact, Leckrone was asked to stop playing the song later in the 1978 season until the structural safety of Camp Randall could be checked out. The upper deck tested out just fine, and the band was given the OK to resume playing the song before the 1979 home opener.

McClain, who was coaching only his third game for the Badgers when they beat Oregon, made no mention of the band's contribution to his team's stunning victory, probably because he hadn't noticed it. He'd had a lot of other things on his mind, particularly after his starting quarterback, tailback and fullback all left the game with injuries before halftime.

"Gosh, darn. I still can't believe we won," he said.

Neither could his players, and just to be sure, many of them went back onto the field to check. A half-hour after the game, they were still out there dancing with the cheerleaders while the band played on. You know what they were playing.

BRADLEY CENTER OPENS WITH NHL EXHIBITION

OCTOBER 1, 1988

Not that they weren't grateful, but the city fathers just wanted to make a few minor adjustments when Lloyd and Jane Pettit offered to build them a $40 million hockey arena next to County Stadium over the next two years.

Three years and seven months later, a $90 million basketball facility opened downtown.

The mayor was there, and so were the county executive and the governor along with a sellout crowd when the doors officially opened and the Pettits bowed briefly and sighed deeply. The place was beautiful. The process was interesting.

Typically, the unassuming Jane Pettit wasn't even there on March 5, 1985, when her attorney, Joseph E. Tierney Jr., disclosed the family's intention to bestow its enormous gift on the Milwaukee sporting scene. The new building would be designed for hockey, but the Milwaukee Bucks and Marquette University would be welcome to use it. Construction would begin almost immediately at a cost of $30 to $40 million, and in two years the Milwaukee Brewers' baseball stadium would have a new neighbor.

The happiest man in town had to be Herb Kohl, who had bought the Bucks four days earlier without knowing that his team was about to get a brand new state of the art home. Asked about the proposed site, Kohl said, "If in fact it's built at County Stadium, I don't think there's anything to talk about."

But in Milwaukee there's always something to talk about. Mayor Henry Maier launched the discussion by praising the gift, which was the biggest the city had ever seen. That was no surprise coming from the Pettits. Before her death in 2001 Jane had given more than $250 million to her community.

And then Maier went on to issue "a forceful plea" that the place be built downtown. Brewers President Bud Selig liked Maier's idea or any idea that didn't involve putting it in his backyard, and months of wrangling ensued.

To the ordinary citizen, this seemed like getting a $40 million inheritance and bickering over whether to take it in tens or twenties. At times it seemed that way to the Pettits, too. After all the political smoke had cleared, Lloyd recalled that they'd been "perturbed" by the delay and had in fact considered calling the whole thing off.

On the other hand, he said, "As it turned out, Bud Selig was absolutely right. It would have been an absolute mess. The parking situation would have been unavailable to everybody."

The Pettits also revised their thinking on putting a National Hockey League team into the arena. One did become available to them later, but at such a high price that it didn't make sense to accept it. Instead they contented themselves with the minor league Milwaukee Admirals, who shared the facility with the Bucks, Marquette basketball, the Milwaukee Wave soccer team and as many concerts and special events as the building could attract.

At least hockey got first crack at the place. An NHL exhibition game between the Chicago Blackhawks and the immortal Wayne Gretzky's Edmonton Oilers was scheduled for the official opening. The Oilers took some of the shine off of that by trading Gretzky two months earlier, but it was still a grand occasion.

The Pettits were given a standing ovation as 17,915 people overflowed the seats and all 68 of the private suites. The mayor's office and the governor's mansion had changed hands since the Pettits' original announcement, and some less significant alterations had to be made as well. For instance, hot water was flowing through the cold water tap and the urinals in the Blackhawks' dressing room.

But there was no question that the actual playing area was top shelf. Oilers General Manager Glen Sather took one look and declared it "the best hockey facility in North America and maybe the world."

The opening ceremonies began at 7:30 p.m., and the game didn't get started until 8:23 because there was some problem installing the nets. The Blackhawks' Denis Savard scored the first goal 8 minutes 5 seconds into the first period, and everyone cheered whether they knew what was going on or not. It was pretty clear that the people in the seats weren't all hockey fans, since about a third of them were gone before the final period and could have cared less that the Blackhawks won, 6-4.

Most of the crowd had just come to extend a thank you to the Pettits. Lord knows they deserved it.

A capacity crowd filled the Bradley Center for its grand opening. The facility was a gift from Jane and Lloyd Pettit in honor of Mrs. Pettit's father, industrialist and philanthropist Harry Lynde Bradley.

WISCONSIN GETS PROBATION FOR "SHOEGATE"

OCTOBER 2, 2001

The shoe jokes started well over a year earlier, and now it was time for the University of Wisconsin to foot the bill. Fortunately for the Badgers, the penalties weren't as endless as the gags.

It took 15 months from the time the university began to investigate charges that scores of athletes at the school were taking illegal discounts and interest-free lines of credit from a nearby Black Earth, Wis., shoe store until the consequences came down. Considering the fact that this was the third time the Badgers had been nailed for violations over the past eight years, they seemingly were getting off lightly, although they didn't see it that way.

The NCAA hit Wisconsin with five years of probation, and a loss of 10 scholarships in football and one in basketball in addition to those that the university had already sacrificed. The penalty ran over a two-year period, but none of the school's teams was banned from post-season play, and none of its championships or records was tossed out. The last was a big item because the basketball team's 2000 Final Four appearance was at stake.

Football coach Barry Alvarez received a letter of reprimand, and the school had to disassociate itself for seven years from Steve Schmitt, the owner of the offending Shoe Box, who had donated $13,000 to the athletic department over the previous 13 years. There was also a $150,000 fine.

Alvarez would always believe that the whole ruckus had been blown hopelessly out of proportion, but he echoed the relief of people all over campus when he said, "It is over. It's final."

Kind of like the favored price on a pair of sneakers at The Shoe Box where a total of 157 UW athletes in 14 sports were found to have gotten too good a deal. UW officials pointed out that this was a discount shoe store, and so they asked, how could it be illegal to take a discount? The NCAA replied that the rake-offs the players were getting were heftier than anything the regular student population could expect. And, by the way, who else got interest-free loans to buy shoes?

This might have been a much smaller deal if the university wasn't already on probation for improper use of booster funds. It could be the NCAA was simply getting tired of dealing with the Badgers, and it decided to send them a message.

The message was officially received more than a year earlier. On Aug. 31, 2000, just hours before Wisconsin opened its football season in a nationally televised game, the NCAA suspended 26 players for their purchases at The Shoe Box. Eleven of them were determined to have received benefits of more than $500 and were given three-game suspensions. Five starters and six other players sat out the opener, which created some significant pre-game adjustments. But the Badgers were lucky enough to be facing Western Michigan that night.

The Broncos entered the game as 32-point underdogs against a Wisconsin team that was ranked fourth in the country. Still, with 11 players gone, the Badgers needed an 89-yard punt return from junior Josh Hunt, a walk-on from Mequon, to hold off the visitors, 19-7.

The game was played on a steaming evening when the on-field temperature reached 101 degrees, and nobody worked up a bigger sweat than Alvarez "This may be the longest day I've ever had to go through in coaching," he said.

There would be some other protracted ones before the year was over. The NCAA was kind enough to require Wisconsin to serve all of its suspensions in the first four weeks of the season, which meant they'd be over following the Big Ten opener against Northwestern. That should have been a huge break, but the Badgers took scant advantage of it. They won three non-conference games before losing their first three Big Ten games and finishing the year, 9-4, and a disappointing 4-4 in the conference.

A season later, after the penalties were announced, UW decided to drop the subject. "We're ready to close this and move on," said Chancellor John Wiley. Perhaps he had reached the conclusion that the shoe fit.

BREWERS RECOVER TO WIN AL EAST ON FINAL DAY

OCTOBER 3, 1982

"Harvey's Wallbangers" were becoming "Harvey's Headbangers." The Milwaukee Brewers were driving for a pennant, but they were driving their fans crazy first.

On Sept. 24, they held a four-game lead on second-place Baltimore in the American League East with nine games to play, only to drop the next two at home to the Orioles. But the Brewers got that lead back by winning two in Boston, and all they had to do was prevail in one of their last five starts to win their first full-season championship – they had won the second-half title in the strike-shortened 1981 season – since arriving from Seattle in 1970. Just to make things interesting, the Brewers lost four in a row.

Now it was down to a single Sunday game in Baltimore's Memorial Stadium. Win it and advance to the American League Championship Series. Or lose it and go home. Both teams were 94-67, so there was no chance of a playoff.

After losing the third game in Boston, the Brewers took two more on the chin as the Orioles trashed two of their star pitchers in a Friday doubleheader, beating Pete Vuckovich, 8-3, in the opener and Mike Caldwell, 7-1, in the nightcap. Then the Orioles destroyed Doc Medich, 11-3, on Saturday.

The home team had all of the momentum going into the crucial final game of the series. But the Brewers had something better. They had Robin Yount.

The pitching match-up couldn't have been much better. Earl Weaver started Jim Palmer, the Hall of Fame-bound right-hander who had registered a complete-game victory over the Brewers eight days earlier. Harvey Kuenn countered with spotlight-loving Don Sutton, also right-handed and also headed for Cooperstown. Sutton hadn't disappointed anyone since General Manager Harry Dalton acquired him from Houston on Aug. 30, winning three of his four decisions. And he didn't disappoint anyone this time.

He held the Orioles to two runs over eight innings before giving way to closer Bob McClure. Sutton gave up eight hits and five walks and said he relished the chance to pitch in such a crucial game. "It's a chance to be center stage, middle of the ring, with everything on the line," he said. "What more could you want?"

If Sutton was enjoying himself, Yount was having the time of his life. He hit two home runs and a triple and scored four times as the Brewers shelled Palmer and three other pitchers to win, 10-2.

Ted Simmons added a two-run homer to the Brewers' 11-hit attack, and Cecil Cooper chipped in with a solo shot and a two-run double. Ben Oglivie and Gorman Thomas contributed two spectacular catches in the outfield.

Back home, a raucous, horn-blowing, firecracker-popping celebration raged for five-and-a-half hours along Wisconsin Avenue, while the Brewers were packing up for the flight to Anaheim where they would open the ALCS against the California Angels.

While the Brewers were winning their only pennant, Yount was having the season of a lifetime. He was later named the American League's Most Valuable Player, and he might easily have won the batting championship as well. He lost that to Kansas City's Willie Wilson when Wilson's manager, Dick Howser, held him out of his last game to protect his average.

Wilson batted .332. Yount hit .331 after getting hit with a pitch in his last at bat, and he didn't care. "I'm very thankful I was able to help us win the game," he said.

The Brewers' clubhouse was jammed with thankful people. One of them was Dalton, who had signed on in 1977 and turned the Brewers into a contender in one season. Getting Sutton was vital, but that was only his second-best move of the year. The first was making Kuenn his manager on June 2.

The Brewers were 23-24 when Dalton replaced the tightly wound Buck Rodgers with his more laid-back batting coach. They were 72-43 under Kuenn, who never lost his cool or his faith. "I said I knew this ballclub could come back, and they came back," he said. "They were relaxed before the ballgame. I guarantee they're relaxed now."

And so at last were their fans.

YANKEES ARRIVE IN "BUSHVILLE"

OCTOBER 4, 1957

First in the American League and last in tact, Casey Stengel's New York Yankees managed to wear out three Wisconsin welcomes on a single train ride. If they could have scored runs as fast they made enemies, they might have won the World Series.

Instead they lost it and left Milwaukee with a self-imposed new nickname. "Bushville" said signs and banners all over town as the citizens turned an insult into a rallying cry.

World Series games were practically an annual event in New York, but they were brand new to Wisconsin. After splitting two games at Yankee Stadium, the two teams had a travel day before they'd meet in the first-ever World Series game in Milwaukee.

So when the Yankees rolled in on a special 17-car train, people were eager to display their hospitality. The Yankees' first scheduled stop was the Sturtevant station, outside Racine, where some members of the traveling party were scheduled to exit the train and board buses to the team's temporary headquarters at the Browns Lake Resort near Burlington.

When the train neared the depot, an estimated 2,000 well-wishers were waiting, and they literally had a cow. Along with the village president, a high school band and members of the local volunteer fire department was a local dairy farmer who'd brought his four-year-old Guernsey in the hopes that the sainted Mickey Mantle would milk it for the cameras.

Surprised by the crowd and amazed by the livestock, Stengel ordered his players to remain on the train while their wives and other club officials headed for the waiting buses. The players obeyed and refused to budge from their seats. A single exception was pitcher Whitey Ford, who slipped away long enough to pose for pictures with a dozen Little Leaguers, but he was hardly noticed.

The scene would have been a total public relations disaster if Edna Stengel, the crusty manager's wife, hadn't perched gamely on a stool and done the honors with the cow while wearing a fur coat. Then she and the rest of her fellow travelers moved on to Burlington where another crowd was about to be disappointed, although it had been warned beforehand that the players weren't arriving until later.

Meanwhile, the train chugged on to Milwaukee where it arrived at 11:25 a.m. to a crowd of more politicians and more autograph seekers, but no Guernsey. Among the 300 or so well wishers were District Attorney William McCauley, Sheriff Clem Michalski, Circuit Judge Robert Cannon and a representative from the mayor's office named Albert Davis. They all cheered and smiled as the train pulled in, and the Yankees returned the favor by striding right past them with their heads down and boarding three Greyhound buses bound for County Stadium and practice.

Once the train had emptied, Davis stuck his head in a bus and asked for Stengel. Two players told him that the skipper wasn't there and that he'd be coming later. Imagine the surprise among a group of reporters who'd seen Stengel board the bus. Either he'd vanished like a genie or the guests had been caught in a lie.

Banking on the latter, Cannon, who had met Stengel before, shouted for him through a bus window. Reluctantly, one of the players told his boss that Cannon was asking him to get off the bus to greet the crowd. Stengel sat tight and told Cannon to get on instead. When the judge complied, he was followed aboard by a band of reporters.

And that's when "Bushville" was born.

A particularly burly Yankee official began pushing the journalists out of the bus. "This," he told them, "is strictly bush league." The story spread quickly, and someone expanded it into the name.

The burly Yankee was widely reported to be a coach named Charlie "King Kong" Keller. Keller vehemently denied saying any such thing, while the Yankee brass expressed its regrets for the misunderstanding.

Burlington Mayor Ralph H. Larson said Yankee General Manager George Weiss told him he felt very bad about the whole thing, and it never would have happened if the Yankees had had some notice of all the welcoming ceremonies that their hosts had planned for them.

Bushville beat Mudville in the World Series, four games to three.

Fans reminded the New York Yankees of their "Bushville" faux pas during a celebration on Wisconsin Avenue after the Milwaukee Braves won the World Series.

OCTOBER 297

BRAGG WINS GRIM GRAND PRIX IN WAUWATOSA

OCTOBER 5, 1912

Death had claimed one driver, and it was gaining on another when Ralph DePalma drove into the rear wheel of Caleb Bragg's Fiat on the final lap of the international Grand Prix race held in what was then the rural township of Wauwatosa.

DePalma had made up most of the 2 minute 20 second lead that Bragg had taken into the final lap of the 7.88 mile course, and he was determined to pass him when the collision sent his Mercedes careening out of control and into a cornfield. Bragg drove on to the checkered flag, while DePalma and mechanic Tom Alley were rushed to Trinity Hospital. "Ralph DePalma Near Death After a Mad Ride for Prize," read a headline in the *Milwaukee Sentinel*.

A crowd estimated at 100,000 was on hand to watch the fourth Grand Prix, which when it was first run in Savannah, Ga., in 1908, was the first Grand Prix race ever held in the United States. This was the climax of three days of racing featuring the top names in the sport, including the legendary Barney Oldfield.

The week ranks as one of the biggest auto racing events in Wisconsin history. Some say it may still be the biggest. The Grand Prix and the Vanderbilt Cup race, which was run three days earlier, were the two biggest auto races in the country at the time.

By 8 a.m. Saturday, two hours before the Grand Prix's start time, the crowd began arriving in cars, buggies and streetcars, as well as on horseback and on foot. But they didn't all flock through the gates even though the price of a general admission ticket was $1. Instead, people overran nearby farms and watched the race from fences, barn roofs and even trees. Shrewd speculators who had purchased rights to all the water pumps for miles around made a small fortune selling water for five cents a glass.

The course started at the junction of Fond du Lac Road, and N. 35th and W. Burleigh streets. The course headed northwest on Fond du Lac, west on Capitol Drive, south on Appleton Avenue and east on Burleigh. The roads were narrow, unpaved and sprinkled with stones, some as big as baseballs. The road also had a high crown, so the edges of the course became dangerously soft.

Even before the races began, tragedy struck when Bragg's good friend, David Bruce-Brown, crashed during the Tuesday trials. Bruce-Brown was going more than 90 miles per hour when he lost a wheel and his Fiat cart-wheeled toward a ditch as he was thrown onto the road, suffering a crushed skull. He regained consciousness long enough to utter the word, "Mother," before being rushed into surgery. But he died three hours later. His mother was living in New York and was informed of the accident through a telegram sent from the course by DePalma.

Bruce-Brown had won the previous two Grand Prix races in Savannah, and if he had won this one, he would have retired the trophy. But the 12-car field went off without him.

DePalma had opened the program on the Wauwatosa course on Wednesday, Oct. 2, by winning the ninth Vanderbilt Cup race over 299 miles. The Vanderbilt Cup was the first international auto race ever held in the U.S., and DePalma had gotten lucky when the front-running Ted Tetzlaff went out with a broken crank on the 26th lap. DePalma went on from there to win by less than a minute over second-place Hughey Hughes.

Three days later, DePalma found himself in a furious battle with Bragg in the 410-mile Grand Prix. Going into the final five laps, Bragg was leading by a relatively comfortable margin. But DePalma hunted him down, only to miscalculate an opening and lose control of his car.

The crowd grew quiet when it was announced over the public address system that there had been an accident. People rushed the press box demanding details of the crash, and some angrily confronted Bragg at the finish line, accusing him of not giving DePalma enough room to pass. Bragg averaged 69 mph in collecting the winner's purse of $5,000, but he was visibly affected by the accident and declined to take a victory lap.

DePalma, who suffered a punctured abdomen and a broken leg, would spend more than two months in the hospital and would be forever grateful to the people of Milwaukee who sent him cards and gifts and even helped pay some of his medical bills. And he not only survived, he thrived. Two years later, he won the Vanderbilt Cup, and the year after that, he won the Indianapolis 500.

He also absolved Bragg of any blame for the accident. "He gave me all the road he could spare," DePalma told his doctors.

NIPPY JONES' SHOESHINE CALL KICK-STARTS BRAVES

OCTOBER 6, 1957

If it's true that baseball is a game of inches, the Milwaukee Braves may have won a World Series game by a foot. It wasn't the most dramatic victory in the team's history, but it was easily one of the stranger ones.

Nothing in the eight-season career of Vernal "Nippy" Jones indicated that he would play a brief but central role in the Braves' 1957 world championship. A journeyman first baseman, he had played in parts of seven seasons with the St. Louis Cardinals and Philadelphia Phillies from 1946-'52. But Jones hadn't appeared in a major league game in five years when the Braves purchased him from Sacramento of the Pacific Coast League on July 6, 1957.

After joining the Braves, he appeared in only 30 games and batted a modest .266. He had gone 0 for 2 in two pinch-hitting appearances in the World Series when Manager Fred Haney sent him up to bat for Warren Spahn leading off the bottom of the tenth inning in Game 4.

The Braves were in trouble. They were down two games to one in the Series, and they'd blown a 4-1 lead when Spahn gave up three runs in the ninth and another in the top of the 10th to the New York Yankees. Trailing, 5-4, they needed Jones to get something started for the top of the batting order. And so he did. But not with his bat.

Yankee left-hander Tommy Byrne started Jones out with a low fastball that landed at his feet and skipped all the way to the backstop. Umpire Augie Donatelli called the pitch a ball, but Jones told Donatelli that it was no such thing. "That pitch hit me," he said to the umpire, and just about that time, the ball came rolling back toward home plate.

Jones picked it up and pointed to a black mark that was clearly shoe polish. Jones argued that the polish could only have come from his shoe, which meant he'd been hit in the foot by the pitch. When Yankee catcher Yogi Berra, in perhaps an unparalleled moment of honesty, confirmed the smudge, Donatelli figured he had no choice. He directed Jones to first base.

Byrne wasn't happy. He claimed the spot had been on the ball when he pitched it. But not even Yankee manager Casey Stengel backed Byrne's argument, and so the Braves had a man on and nobody out to start their half of the tenth. They took full advantage of the opportunity.

Haney sent Felix Mantilla out to run for Jones as Stengel replaced Byrne with right-hander Bob Grim. Switch-hitter Red Schoendienst sacrificed Mantilla to second. Then Grim threw a 2-0 slider to Johnny Logan, who doubled in Mantilla to tie the score. That brought up slugging Eddie Mathews, who hadn't done much slugging at all lately. He'd gone hitless in the World Series until he'd finally broken through with a double in the fourth inning.

With first base open, it seemed likely that Stengel would walk Mathews intentionally. But all that would have done was bring Henry Aaron to the plate, and Aaron had already hit a three-run homer in the fourth. So Grim pitched to Mathews and immediately regretted it. He threw him a belt-high fastball and watched disconsolately as it sailed over the right-field wall.

The capacity crowd of 45,804 at County Stadium surged to its feet, and minutes later the celebration was on all over the city. The Braves had won, 7-5, and evened the Series at two games apiece.

Falling behind, three games to one, to the powerful Yankees would have been unthinkable. Instead, the Braves had new life and a home game to go. Who knows what might have happened if Nippy Jones hadn't started that winning rally with his freshly shined shoes?

"My only worry now," said Haney with a smile, "is whether Nippy Jones will be able to play tomorrow after getting hit on the foot with that pitch."

Jones was ready, but it didn't matter. That was the last at-bat of his major league career.

1957 WORLD SERIES

DATE	SCORE	SITE
Oct. 2	Yankees 3, Braves 1	Yankee Stadium
Oct. 3	Braves 4, Yankees 2	Yankee Stadium
Oct. 5	Yankees 12, Braves 3	County Stadium
Oct. 6	Braves 7, Yankees 5 (10 inn.)	County Stadium
Oct. 7	Braves 1, Yankees 0	County Stadium
Oct. 9	Yankees 3, Braves 2	Yankee Stadium
Oct. 10	Braves 5, Yankees 0	Yankee Stadium

Source: Total Baseball: The Official Encyclopedia of Major League Baseball

PACKERS WIN CLASSIC DEFENSIVE STRUGGLE

OCTOBER 7, 1962

Herb Adderley was a displaced person when the Green Bay Packers made him the 12th pick in the 1961 NFL draft. Vince Lombardi didn't know what to do with him. He tried him at running back where Adderley had starred at Michigan State, and he tried him at flanker in his rookie year, but it wasn't until the Thanksgiving game against the Detroit Lions that he tried him at cornerback.

Replacing an injured Hank Gremminger in the second quarter, Adderley responded by getting his first career interception and finding a new home in the Packers' secondary. In a way, the Lions helped launch him on a Hall of Fame career that day, and Adderley picked a strange way of paying them back the next time he faced them.

The Packers were the reigning NFL champions, and the Lions were the leading contenders when the two unbeaten teams met in a pivotal game in the fourth week of the 1962 season. This may have been Lombardi's best club, but the Packers weren't much better than Detroit.

The Lions had a fierce front four anchored by Alex Karras and Roger Brown, a future Hall of Famer at middle linebacker in Joe Schmidt, and a secondary that included three future Hall of Famers in Dick "Night Train" Lane, Dick LeBeau and Yale Lary. Their offense wasn't nearly as good, but they did have the returning NFL passing leader in Milt Plum.

The Packers had a much more potent attack, but it wasn't doing them much good against Karras and Co. on this sloppy Sunday at what is now Lambeau Field. The Lions would intercept two halfback option passes and recover a pair of fumbles before the afternoon was over while holding Green Bay without a touchdown for the first time in 36 games.

Karras caused the first fumble by leveling quarterback Bart Starr on the Green Bay 34-yard line, setting up a six-yard scoring run by former University of Wisconsin running back Danny Lewis. It was the only time either team reached the end zone.

The Packers were limited to two Paul Hornung field goals, while the Lions were held scoreless after Lewis' run. Their only other scoring opportunity was foiled by Adderley, who blocked Wayne Walker's 25-yard field goal attempt in the second quarter.

With just over six minutes to play in the fourth period, Hornung came up short on a 47-yard field goal attempt, and Pat Studstill returned it to the Detroit 22. Green Bay appeared to be doomed as the Lions ran almost five minutes off the clock. They were facing a third-and-eight situation at their 49-yard line with 1 minute 25 seconds to play when they made a curious decision.

Instead of eating up more time with a running play and then punting and turning the game over to their dominating defense, the Lions sent flanker Terry Barr on a square-out pattern. Plum had connected with Jim Gibbons twice before on the same play, but this time Barr slipped in the muck. Adderley stepped in front of him, picked off the pass and returned it to the Detroit 18. Two plays later, Hornung kicked a 21-yard field goal to seal a 9-7 victory.

The Lions got a measure of revenge seven weeks later when they sacked Starr nine times and crushed the Packers, 26-14, but that was Green Bay's only loss of the season. The Packers went on to a second championship, while Detroit was embarked on a five-decade drought.

Adderley, meanwhile, was headed for enshrinement at Canton. He recorded 39 interceptions for the Packers and ran seven of them back for touchdowns while being named first-team Associated Press all-pro five times. He also played in four of the first six Super Bowls, winning two with the Packers and splitting two with Dallas after he'd been traded to the Cowboys in 1970. What's more, he had the rare distinction of almost catching Lombardi in a mistake.

"I was too stubborn to switch him to defense until I had to," the coach admitted later. "It scares me to think how I almost mishandled him." The Lions would have benefited more than anyone if he had.

BREWERS STAY ALIVE IN ALCS

OCTOBER 8, 1982

No team had ever lost the first two games of the American League Championship Series and stayed alive in the playoffs, and no Milwaukee Brewers team had ever made it to the World Series. But thanks in large part to the efforts of a 37-year-old future Hall of Famer and a 26-year-old prison guard, that was all about to change.

The outlook was gloomy for the Brewers when they came home to County Stadium to face the California Angels in Game 3 of the ALCS. They'd lost four of their last five regular-season games and the first two playoff games in Anaheim, and they were facing a lineup featuring Rod Carew, Reggie Jackson, Fred Lynn and Don Baylor.

The Brewers had a couple of things going for them, though. There was a whole pennant-starved city cheering for them, and there was Don Sutton.

Since coming to the Brewers from Houston in late August, Sutton had won four of his five decisions, including the one that clinched the AL East in Baltimore on the last day of the season. Now facing an elimination game in the best-of-five series, he had a firm grasp of the situation. "I'm logical enough to know if we don't win today, we don't get to play tomorrow," he said.

Logic, along with $7^{2/3}$ innings of artistically placed fastballs, curveballs, sliders and change-ups, were more than enough for Sutton to shut down the Angels, 5-3, with the help of mid-season call-up Pete Ladd.

The red-headed Ladd didn't have anything approaching Sutton's credentials. He'd become Milwaukee's closer only because Rollie Fingers was out with a torn muscle in his right forearm, and he'd lost three crucial games during the stretch run. But he had an intimidating 6-foot-4, 230-pound body and a live fastball, and he used them to finish what Sutton had started and put the Brewers on the road to the American League pennant.

Sutton coasted into the eighth inning with a four-hitter and a 5-0 lead, compliments of a three-run Milwaukee outburst in the fourth and Paul Molitor's two-run home run in the seventh. Sutton had given up only two walks while striking out eight batters.

But the Angels weren't dead yet. They got a big boost from an unlikely source when Bob Boone led off the eighth inning with a fly ball to left that looked to be just another long out. Ben Oglivie ran back to the wall to make the catch, but the ball never got to his glove. A fan with a cheap seat and a taste for souvenirs reached over and grabbed the ball before it could get there. Umpire Larry Barnett ruled home run, and Oglivie went nuts. For good reason, too. Replays showed a clear case of fan interference, but Barnett was adamant, and the Angels were on the board.

They added two runs on Carew's bunt single and doubles by Lynn and Baylor before Manager Harvey Kuenn had a little talk with Sutton, who refused to use the fracas in left field as an excuse. "The thing that caused the next few pitches not to go where I wanted them was the fact that I'm 37 years old, I've pitched about 4,000 innings, and I was running out of gas," he said.

Kuenn appreciated the honesty and made the call to the bullpen. On came Ladd with two out, the tying run at the plate and the whole season hanging by a thread. It was a dicey situation, but Ladd had lived through worse during the off-season. There was the time for instance when he'd been punched out by a triple murderer in a game of one-on-one basketball. Ladd's winter job was working as a guard at the Cumberland County Jail in Maine.

He'd subdued the murderer, and he did the same to California's Doug DeCinces, getting him on a ground ball to third to end the rally. Then Ladd set the Angels down in order in the ninth, striking out the last two to preserve the victory.

The Brewers went on to win the fourth game, 9-5, behind Moose Haas, who pitched no-hit ball for $5^{2/3}$ innings, and then they wrapped up the series with a 4-3 victory when Cecil Cooper rapped a dramatic, two-out seventh-inning single to drive in the tying and winning runs. Sutton just watched that one from the dugout, but Ladd earned the save.

BRAVES BLOW GAME 7 OF WORLD SERIES

OCTOBER 9, 1958

In the end, Lew Burdette had to pitch too much. And maybe he talked too much, too.

After winning Game 2 of the World Series, the Milwaukee Braves' right-hander had created a stir when he said he wished the New York Yankees were in the National League. He didn't think they were any better than two or three clubs that the Braves played during the regular season.

It may have been true, but there was no reason to say it. The Yankees still hadn't gotten over losing the 1957 World Series to Milwaukee, and now their pride was being tested.

Besides, Burdette would have plenty to do without starting an argument. Just as he did the year before when he was the World Series hero, he would start three games.

There was no reason to think his words would come back to bite him after Milwaukee took what most people considered an insurmountable 3-1 lead in the Series. Only two teams had ever come back from that big a deficit, and one of those had needed eight games to do it. The 1903 Boston Red Sox – or Pilgrims as they were called then – had overhauled the Pittsburgh Pirates, 5-3, in a best-of-nine series, while the 1925 Pirates had come back on the Washington Senators in the conventional seven.

But that was 33 years ago, and with the last two games scheduled for County Stadium, the Braves couldn't imagine it happening again. At least not until the Yankees snatched the bats out of their hands.

It was probably just a coincidence, but Milwaukee's offense went missing right after Game 2 when Burdette had invited the Yankees to switch leagues. The Braves scored 17 runs in the first two games and a total of eight in the next five. Their biggest guns – Henry Aaron, Eddie Mathews, Joe Adcock and Wes Covington – didn't have a single home run in 91 at bats, while the Yankees hit 10 total, including four by Hank Bauer. What's more, Milwaukee totaled 56 strikeouts over the seven games and left 66 runners on base.

A huge part of the problem was Bob Turley, a 21-game winner who got off to a terrible start. The Braves shelled Turley for four runs in a seven-run first inning in their 13-5 victory in Game 2. But they barely touched him after that as he threw a five-hit shutout in Game 5, saved Game 6 by getting the last out in a 4-3 victory and then outlasted Burdette to win the finale.

Burdette was pitching on two days' rest in the seventh game, but it didn't appear to be bothering him as he breezed into the eighth inning with the score tied 2-2. The Braves had scored a run in the first on a hit, a walk, a sacrifice bunt, another walk and an infield out, but the Yankees had come back with two unearned runs in the second when Burdette had been unable to handle a couple of throws from Frank Torre on close plays at first base. One was on a sacrifice, the other on a ground out with a runner holding at third.

Torre was charged with both errors, but he said after the game that he thought they should have been chalked up to Burdette. "The throws were good and they beat the runners," said Torre. "Lew is a good fielder, but he just happened to drop them."

Turley got the Yankees out of a bases-loaded jam in the third when he took over for starter Don Larsen with two runners on, and then he limited the Braves to Del Crandall's sixth-inning home run after that. And the two right-handers looked like they could have squared off until Christmas when Burdette retired the first two batters in the eighth. But then he hit a wall.

Yogi Berra started the Yankees' winning rally with a double, and Elston Howard singled him home to break the tie. Another single by Andy Carey brought up Bill "Moose" Skowron, who had a powerful stroke and a long memory. He walloped a three-run homer into the left-center field bleachers at County Stadium to give New York a 6-2 victory, the world championship and the last word.

"They say the American League is a lousy league and they wish we were in their league," said the Yankee first baseman. "Well, we proved we could take them. We wish we were in their league."

Manager Casey Stengel was a little more gracious in victory. "It was an outstanding team we beat," he said. "The manager ran the series very wonderful. He had his men keyed up."

And maybe just a little too talkative.

302   365 BEST WISCONSIN SPORTS STORIES

BURDETTE PITCHES BRAVES TO WORLD SERIES VICTORY

OCTOBER 10, 1957

Lew Burdette may already have been Casey Stengel's biggest mistake when he took the mound in the seventh game of the World Series at Yankee Stadium. Seven years earlier, Burdette had made such a minimal impression playing for the New York Yankees that his manager hadn't even bothered to learn his name.

It would be a kindness to call Burdette's career in New York undistinguished. He'd given up three hits and compiled a 6.75 earned run average in $1^1/_3$ innings over two games in 1950, and he was back in the minors when he was traded to the Boston Braves the following year. No wonder he was John Doe to Stengel.

"Yes, sir, whenever Ol' Case wanted me, he'd yell over, 'Hey, you, get in there and warm up,'" Burdette recalled. "It was always 'Hey, you.' He never knew my name."

It was probably better not to know what Stengel was calling him now. Burdette had stymied the Yankees twice in this Series, and he was about to baffle them again by pitching the Braves to a 5-0 victory and the only world championship in their 13 seasons in Milwaukee.

He'd held them to seven hits while beating them, 4-2, in Game 2, and then he'd gotten serious. The Yankees reached him for seven hits in the fifth game, too, but that time they didn't get any runs. Joe Adcock's RBI single in the sixth was all Burdette needed to win the game, 1-0, and give the Braves a 3-2 lead in the Series.

Now he was back for a third time and pitching on two days of rest. His roommate, Warren Spahn, was supposed to start the seventh game, but Spahn had been bedridden for two days with the flu. Once again, Burdette gave up seven hits, as he became the first pitcher since Stan Covelski in 1920 to win three complete games in the same World Series and the first since Christy Mathewson in 1905 to throw two shutouts. For the record, Mathewson actually threw three.

Burdette struck out only three Yankees in the final game, but he walked just one and that was intentional.

As he raced through the Yankee batting order, Burdette began picking up support from the sellout crowd, which seemed peculiar since the game was being played in New York. But thousands of seats were filled by fans of the New York Giants and Brooklyn Dodgers stung by their teams' recent decision to move to the West Coast.

It wasn't until the ninth inning that the Yankees put together any kind of serious threat. They used three singles to load the bases with two out for Bill "Moose" Skowron, and the slugging first baseman threatened to clear them with a shot down the third-base line. But Eddie Mathews made a spectacular stop and stepped on third for the final out as the turncoat New Yorkers surged out of the stands and onto the field to celebrate with the Braves.

The losers contributed three errors to the Braves' nine-hit attack against five pitchers, none bigger than the one committed by Milwaukee-born, rookie third baseman Tony Kubek as the Braves scored four runs in the third inning. Bob Hazle, who had gone hitless up to that point in the Series, got things started with a one-out single, and he should have been erased in a double play when Johnny Logan, the next batter, sent a grounder to Kubek at third. But Kubek's throw pulled second baseman Jerry Coleman off the bag, and everyone was safe. Mathews followed with a two-run double, and then singles by Henry Aaron and Wes Covington and Frank Torre's infield out provided the rest of the runs.

That gave Burdette more than enough to work with, but Del Crandall added an eighth-inning home run just to make sure.

An overheated National League President Warren Giles called the Braves' success "the most popular victory in the history of baseball." It was pretty popular back in Milwaukee where an estimated 225,000 people took to the downtown streets to celebrate in what *The Milwaukee Journal* called "the craziest, wildest night Milwaukee has ever known."

Meanwhile, all the Yankees talked about was Burdette. "We never figured on that man," said catcher Yogi Berra. "The man we were worried about was Spahn."

Had they held Burdette in higher regard, they might have kept him.

BADGERS CELEBRATE AFTER SHOCKING IOWA

OCTOBER 11, 1969

Michael Leckrone was in his first year as the director of the University of Wisconsin marching band, and he brought plenty of optimism to the job. The Badgers hadn't won a football game in their last 23 tries, but Leckrone figured the slump had to end sometime, so he took out a parade permit for the first time Wisconsin won.

With Iowa in town four games into the season, it didn't appear that he'd need it anytime soon. Not only were the Badgers 0-3, but they'd been dismantled, 43-7, the Saturday before by a Syracuse team that would finish .500. And now the Hawkeyes had taken a 17-0 lead into the fourth quarter.

But Wisconsin sophomore fullback Alan Thompson piqued the crowd's curiosity with 12 minutes 26 seconds to play by capping a 16-play, 74-yard drive with a two-yard touchdown run. Then Iowa made things even more interesting by fumbling four plays later on the Badger 44. Thompson struck again, this time from six yards out, and it was 17-14 with 4:50 remaining.

Leckrone had to be reviewing the fine print on the permit when the Hawkeyes got off a lame punt five plays after that, giving Wisconsin the ball on the Iowa 36. The Badgers made it to the 17, but then the drive stalled. Or so it looked. But instead of going for a field goal and a tie, coach John Coatta called a pass play. Quarterback Neil Graff found Randy Marks in the end zone on a fourth-and-11 pass, and miraculously Wisconsin was ahead, 21-17, with 2:08 left.

The fans who had stuck around out of a Camp Randall Stadium crowd of 53,714 were stunned, and so were the Hawkeyes. In fact, the Hawkeyes were so stunned that they fumbled the kickoff back into their own end zone and got nailed for a safety. Final score: 23-17. Net result: General chaos.

Wisconsin hadn't won for so long that the fans literally didn't know how to act. With 1:10 still on the clock, an advance guard charged onto the field and had to be shooed off so the game could be finished. The Badgers hadn't won since former coach Milt Bruhn's last game at the end of the 1966 season. Under Coatta, they had lost their first four games in 1967, tied Iowa the fifth week, and had lost 18 straight since.

But that was all over now. This was the Vietnam era when unruly was the rule, but this celebration was different. It was uncontrollable joy. "We're No. 1," fans screamed. "Rose Bowl, Rose Bowl," they chanted.

Fans rushed the field again at the final gun, and were kissing cheerleaders and each other, and hoisting players and coaches to their shoulders and carrying them away. They were still there 45 minutes after the game trying to tear down the goal posts, but concrete and steel carried the day.

Coatta emerged from the locker room soaking wet to talk to reporters. This was before Gatorade showers, and the players had contented themselves with throwing their coach into the shower. He didn't mind. "It was one of the wildest scenes I've ever seen," he said.

It was certainly a novel sensation for Coatta, who had gone 0-9-1 his first year and 0-10 his second before losing the first three games of his third. He was a 36-year-old assistant to Bruhn when he'd gotten the job, and there were plenty of people who were wishing that hadn't happened.

One of the unsuccessful candidates for the position was a fellow named Bo Schembechler who went on to have some success at Michigan. Schembechler would create a stir in Madison several years later when he wrote in his book *Man in Motion* that his Wisconsin interview was so cursory that one of the athletic board members was asleep when he got there. Michigan officials had apologized to Wisconsin for that story, only to have Schembechler rescind the apology.

Nobody was sorry now. As Leckrone's band led a cast of thousands out of the stadium and through the streets of Madison toward the Capitol, the police more or less looked the other way. The parade was legal after all. Some of the things that happened weren't.

Those in the crowd blocked traffic, stopping cars just in case the drivers didn't know the score, all the while passing bottles of liquor and beer among themselves. State Street shops lost three plate glass windows and one glass door, and 13 parking meters were unaccounted for. Still considering the size of the demonstration, damage was light, and only seven arrests were made.

PACKERS COLLAPSE AGAINST DEFENDING CHAMPS

OCTOBER 12, 1952

What could have been Gene Ronzani's greatest coaching moment turned into one of the Green Bay Packers' biggest disappointments when they imploded in the fourth quarter against the defending NFL champion Los Angeles Rams.

In the three-plus seasons that Ronzani led the Packers, he had very few good coaching moments, let alone great ones, but this should have qualified. In the third game of what was Ronzani's third season at the helm, Green Bay had pushed the heavily favored Rams all over the field for three quarters while taking what looked like an insurmountable 22-point lead.

Ronzani had everything going for him. Not only had his defense limited the potent Los Angeles offense to two Bob Waterfield field goals, but he was coaching in front of 21,693 partisans at Marquette Stadium where he'd been a college hero.

The 43-year-old Iron Mountain, Mich., native had earned nine letters in football, basketball and track at Marquette before spending eight seasons with the Chicago Bears. And because of his Milwaukee ties, fans there perhaps were more willing to forgive him for his Bears background. But he was not a popular choice in Green Bay when he was named the second coach in franchise history. Moreover, he succeeded Curly Lambeau, a tough act to follow.

In Ronzani's first two seasons, the Packers finished with successive 3-9 records.

They started off the 1952 season by losing their opener to the Chicago Bears, but then rebounded the next Sunday to beat Lambeau's Washington Redskins, 35-20, in Milwaukee.

The Packers were back in Milwaukee again the following week, and the situation looked even rosier when they went into the final period against the Rams with a 28-6 lead. What Waterfield did in the final 12 minutes of the game lives in Green Bay infamy.

Waterfield was the Rams' 32-year-old, longtime quarterback and place-kicker and a lucky man if for no other reason than the fact that he was married to actress Jane Russell, America's reigning sex goddess. His only problem was he was losing his job to 26-year-old Norm Van Brocklin after two years of sharing it.

The Rams happened to be blessed with two future Hall of Fame quarterbacks, and the two had finished 1-2 in passing in the NFL when the Rams won the title the year before. Waterfield finished first after Van Brocklin had led the league in 1950, when the two alternated for the first time.

Van Brocklin started the game against the Packers, but he could manage no better than a couple of field-goal drives in the first half. Waterfield replaced him, and began whacking away at the Packers' lead as the fourth quarter began.

He started by leading the Rams on a 66-yard touchdown drive capped by "Deacon Dan" Towler's one-yard plunge. When Waterfield climaxed a 48-yard march with another field goal to cut the lead to 28-16, the fans started getting a little jittery.

Panic set in when Packers quarterback Tobin Rote fumbled on the Green Bay 33, and two plays later, Towler reciprocated with a fumble of his own, only to have teammate Bob Carey scoop up the ball and run 16 yards into the end zone. When Waterfield converted, the difference was 28-23 with 5 minutes 45 seconds remaining.

The clock had run down to 2:19 when following a Babe Parilli punt, the Rams took over on their eight-yard line. From there, Waterfield completed three passes covering a total of 76 yards to Carey, and backs Verda "Vitamin T" Smith and Volney "Skeets" Quinlan; and Towler punched the ball in from the two.

What had been unthinkable close to 12 minutes earlier had occurred. The Packers had blown their lead and trailed, 30-28.

That became the final score when Rote fumbled after being hit so hard he had to be helped off the field. Ronzani probably should been carried off on a stretcher, too, because his career was in critical condition.

The Packers finished the year 6-6, and they were 2-7-1 when Ronzani was forced out with two games left in the 1953 season. Thanks to the Rams' huge rally, he never had a winning record.

WITHOUT FINGERS, BREWERS' BULLPEN FALTERS

OCTOBER 13, 1982

The Rollie Fingers waiting game had been going on for so long that the Milwaukee Brewers were having trouble keeping their story straight. Yes, said Manager Harvey Kuenn, he could have used his star closer. No, said Fingers, he couldn't possibly have pitched.

As the St. Louis Cardinals loaded the bases in the eighth inning of Game 2 of the World Series, the only sure thing was that Pete Ladd was not Rollie Fingers. He wasn't even Pete Ladd.

It had all looked so good for the Brewers. They'd stolen the home-field advantage by smoking the Cardinals, 10-0, in Game 1. They had Don Sutton, their big-game specialist, on the mound, and they'd jumped out to a three-run lead. It was just a matter of finishing what they'd started.

What followed was a terminal case of the "What if's?" What if Cardinals catcher Darrell Porter had found peace in Milwaukee instead of waiting two years to locate it in St. Louis? What if veteran umpire Bill Haller's questionable call in the eighth inning hadn't gone against the Brewers? What if an inexperienced Ladd hadn't blown up as a result? And most important, what if Fingers had really been available to pitch?

The answer to any of the four might well have been that the Brewers would have won the World Series. Instead they lost it in seven games, and in retrospect, none of the other six seemed quite as important as Game 2.

Milwaukee had gone up, 3-0, in the top of the third inning, scoring one run in the second on Charlie Moore's double and two in the third on Paul Molitor's base-running and a solo home run by Ted Simmons. After the Cards came back with a pair of runs in the bottom of the third, Cecil Cooper's RBI single made it 4-2 in the fifth.

Enter Porter. The St. Louis catcher had been drafted No. 1 by the Brewers in 1970 and spent four full, but disappointing years with them before moving on to Kansas City where he blossomed as a player, but underwent drug and alcohol rehabilitation in 1980. Porter's struggles finally ended when he got hot in the 1982 National League Championship Series and was named its Most Valuable Player.

He was still hot when he belted Sutton's hanging slider into the left-field corner for a game-tying double in the sixth. "I would have to say the Good Lord has given me the power to relax right now," he said.

The Brewers could have used a little of that themselves in the eighth when the Cardinals put two runners on base with one out. Naturally one of them was Porter, who'd singled for his fourth hit of the Series.

At that point, Ladd was on the mound and Fingers was in the dugout where he'd been since Sept. 2 when he suffered what was first called a muscle spasm in his right arm in a game against Cleveland. The spasm was later described as a slight tear and then a bigger tear, and it might have morphed into a compound fracture at the rate the diagnoses were piling up. All the while the Brewers kept holding out hope that the American League's reigning Cy Young Award winner and Most Valuable Player would recover.

If they'd ever needed him, now seemed to be the time. Kuenn said after the game that Fingers was available, but he chose not to use him because Fingers only pitched when the Brewers were ahead. Besides, Ladd had been brilliant in the American League Championship Series, saving two of Milwaukee's three victories against California. Fingers had a different version. "I couldn't have pitched today," he said. "I'm a little stiff from not pitching for a month."

It would be spring training before he pitched again, leaving the heavy lifting to Ladd, who entered the game in the bottom of the eighth inning to face Lonnie Smith with runners on second and third. Smith worked the count to 3-2, and then took a letter-high fastball that seemed to catch the outside corner. It even seemed that way to Smith, whose first step was back toward the dugout. But Haller didn't agree. When he called it a ball, the Cardinals had the bases loaded and Kuenn had one badly shaken pitcher on his hands.

"It rattled me," Ladd admitted. "It shouldn't have."

Ladd stayed rattled for the next four pitches. He threw them all to pinch-hitter Steve Braun, and when none of them even came close to the plate, Braun walked to force in the winning run in the Cardinals' 5-4 victory.

It was the last game Ladd would pitch in the Series. He never recovered from the game-losing walk, and neither did the Brewers. In turn, Bruce Sutter, the Cardinals' bullpen ace and like Fingers a future Hall of Famer, won Game 2 and saved two others.

JACKE'S OVERTIME FIELD GOAL BEATS 49ERS

OCTOBER 14, 1996

In a game with giant implications, two of the smallest men on the field made all the difference. The Green Bay Packers might still have won Super Bowl XXXI if Chris Jacke and Don Beebe hadn't picked a Monday night match with San Francisco to turn in all-pro caliber performances, but it would have been much harder.

The 49ers carried a 4-1 record and a world of respect into Lambeau Field, whereas the Packers were still trying to establish themselves as an elite team. They had beaten San Francisco in an NFC divisional playoff 10 months earlier, but they still felt they had to prove that outcome wasn't a fluke. Most of all, they felt they had to prove it to the 49ers, who had won five Super Bowls and been to the playoffs in 13 of the previous 15 seasons.

Packer quarterback Brett Favre made sure a national television audience was entertained by throwing a club record 61 passes for 395 yards, but only one of those went for a touchdown, and that one created a terrible fuss. The 5-foot-11, 185-pound Beebe caught it, and Favre followed it with another completion for a two-point conversion. The rest of Green Bay's scoring was done by Jacke, all 200 pounds of him.

Jacke kicked four field goals in regulation, including a 31-yarder with eight seconds remaining that sent the game into overtime, and then he settled the issue with a 53-yard effort with just under four minutes gone in the extra period. When the ball flew through the uprights with room to spare, the Packers had a 23-20 victory, a 6-1 record and a major tailwind on the road to their first Super Bowl victory in 29 years.

They finished the season 13-3, giving them home-field advantage throughout the post-season while the 49ers ended up 12-4. If this game had gone the other way, the Packers might have had to travel to San Francisco in the playoffs, and who knows what would have happened then? What did happen was a 35-14 Green Bay romp in a divisional playoff at Lambeau Field almost three months later.

Neither Jacke nor Beebe seemed destined for stardom in the Monday night game. Jacke had one foot in coach Mike Holmgren's doghouse after starting the season by missing three of 10 field goal attempts, and he didn't improve his situation by blowing an extra point the week before in a game against Chicago. Holmgren was tempted to punt rather than take his chances with his kicker in overtime, but he went for the score and said later that it was the best decision he'd made all night.

The coach had no choice as far as Beebe was concerned. The eight-year veteran had been picked up as free agent insurance for $300,000 at the beginning of the season, and he proved to be a huge bargain when star receiver Robert Brooks suffered a season-ending knee injury on the Packers' first play from scrimmage against the 49ers. Holmgren plugged Beebe into Brooks' spot, and he responded with 11 catches for 220 yards and one greatly disputed touchdown.

It came in the third quarter when Beebe made a diving catch on a 29-yard pass, then got up off the turf and ran another 30 yards into the end zone. Cornerback Marquez Pope insisted that he'd touched Beebe down, and his position seemed to be supported by television replays. But there was no replay rule at that time, and the 49ers lost the argument and ultimately the game.

Beebe's performance was the most productive he'd ever had, while Jacke considered the game-winning field goal to be the best kick of his career. Not that it did much to improve his stock with his coach.

Jacke had a significant personality clash with Holmgren and with General Manager Ron Wolf, which resulted in his being let go in free agency after he'd kicked two field goals in the Super Bowl. At one point he and fellow free agents Andre Rison and Desmond Howard were excluded from the team's Super Bowl ring celebration, but fan backlash later caused the Packers to rescind that decision.

Without Jacke or the other two players, for that matter, there might not have been a Super Bowl victory.

Holder Craig Hentrich (left) and Chris Jacke celebrated.

DESERTING DEANS CAUSE NEAR RIOT

OCTOBER 15, 1934

Milwaukee baseball fans probably should have been suspicious when word went out that the fabulous Dean brothers were coming to town. The citizens had already been stung two years earlier when Babe Ruth, playing first base, tanked an exhibition game by letting a ground ball roll into right field in the 12th inning just to get things over with.

But the faithful were gullible, and 3,300 of them put up 75 cents apiece to watch the "Dean All-Stars" play the all-black Kansas City Monarchs in a game at Borchert Field that started at 3 p.m. on a Monday afternoon. These were the days when big league ballplayers made blue-collar salaries, and most of them supplemented their incomes by playing for barnstorming teams in the off-season. The Deans were particularly popular that fall because they'd been the pitching heroes of the world champion St. Louis Cardinals.

Jay Hanna Dean, who'd been dubbed "Dizzy" by his sergeant during his Army days, had won 30 games for the Cards in 1934 while leading the league in strikeouts and earning the Most Valuable Player award. His younger brother Paul, aka "Daffy," had won 19 games as a rookie. Promoter Eddie Stumpf promised to give the customers the best of both, with Dizzy pitching the first five innings against the Monarchs and Daffy the last four.

Little did Stumpf know that the brothers would be getting a phone call from Cardinals President Sam Breadon before the game. Breadon had heard that Paul was having arm troubles, and he told his young star he could play the exhibition but he couldn't pitch. He may have had similar concerns about Dizzy.

The elder Dean pitched in 50 of the Cardinals' games that season and then in three more in the World Series. He'd also started seven games over 19 days during the stretch run and the Series.

As Dizzy took the mound in the first inning, Paul trotted out to right field, and there he would stay for the next five innings. Dizzy, meanwhile, surrendered a run on two walks and a single over the first two innings and then retreated to left field. He proceeded to hit a home run in the third inning, but the patrons weren't pacified when he left the mound early and wasn't replaced by his brother.

And they were absolutely incensed when in the middle of the sixth inning, both Deans strolled off the field to the park office where they collected their pay. Hundreds stormed the box office demanding their money back, and police had to be called to prevent a riot. When the fans weren't shouting, they were circulating a petition insisting on the return of their six bits.

Promoter Stumpf definitely got the message. He threatened to withhold the purse, but when he took a better look at the contract, he discovered that it only required the Deans "to make a personal appearance." It didn't say anything about what they were supposed to do or for how long. While Stumpf pored over the fine print, the Dean brothers drove off with a $750 check safely tucked away. They had a flight to catch in Chicago, because they were about to embark on a vaudeville stage tour.

The Deans may have been halfway to the Windy City by the time the game was over. It ended in an 8-8 tie when the Monarchs came up with four runs in the ninth inning and the Dean-less All-Stars came back with three. Most of the people were in the parking lot by then looking for a refund.

"If they had only stayed around until the finish to satisfy autograph hunters, it wouldn't have been so bad," grumped Stumpf. But both he and the fans should have known better. The Deans had been drawing capacity crowds in other cities and were still hurrying to get out of town within an hour after arriving at the various ballparks.

Then again, that was in a day when news traveled a lot slower than a band of barnstorming ballplayers.

BREWERS' RALLY SQUARES WORLD SERIES

OCTOBER 16, 1982

The sound was clear enough, but this had to be a case of mistaken identity. Gorman Thomas was digging in at the plate, and boos were coming from the stands at County Stadium.

You don't shoot craps in church, you don't egg the ice cream truck, and in Milwaukee you don't boo Gorman Thomas. "I can't remember the last time I heard that," said Don Money. "I never heard that before," said Paul Molitor.

But the shaggy center fielder's teammates were hearing it now, and Thomas had to admit his critics had a point. He'd entered the fourth game of the World Series in an absolute grizzly bear of a slump, getting only six hits in his last 58 at bats and hitting only one home run in his last 15 games going back to the regular season. And then things got worse.

He flied out to center field in the second inning, fouled out to the catcher in the fourth and led off the seventh with another pop-up behind the plate for an easy out. In the field, he had played a warning-track fly ball to center into a two-run sacrifice fly in the second. All of which contributed to a 5-1 St. Louis lead that looked like it would be more than enough to put the Cardinals up, three games to one, in the Series.

But then with two outs and the bases loaded, Thomas got another chance in the seventh inning. The Brewers had tied the game, 5-5, with hits by Money, Jim Gantner, Robin Yount and Cecil Cooper, and with the involuntary aid of an old teammate. The rally began when Cardinals starter and former Brewer Dave LaPoint dropped a toss at first base that would have been the second out of the inning with nobody on. Instead, Ben Oglivie was standing at first.

Three batters later, Cardinals Manager Whitey Herzog replaced LaPoint and commenced to go on a shopping spree through his bullpen. When Thomas stepped in for his second at bat of the inning, he was facing Jeff Lahti, the fourth St. Louis pitcher of the inning, and elements of a record crowd of 56,560 were making it clear that they weren't especially happy to see their struggling slugger.

Lahti didn't help matters by getting ahead, 1-2, in the count. Thomas wasn't deterred by the situation or the reception. "It was an easy situation to hit in," he said later. "You can walk, you can get hit with a pitch, or you can drop a duck squirt out there. The game is tied, I'm just trying to keep it going. If I don't, it's still tied."

Thomas elected none of the options above when Lahti threw him an outside slider on the next pitch. Instead, Thomas lined a no-doubt single to left field, scoring Yount and Cooper. The hit capped a six-run rally and gave the Brewers a 7-5 victory and evened the Series at two games each. It also rewarded Thomas for working overtime.

With a day off on Thursday after the Brewers had split the first two games of the Series in St. Louis, Thomas made his way to the film room looking for answers. He watched four hours of video tape and whatever he found restored his standing with the Brewers' more fickle fans.

"I don't think it's a situation where they're upset at me," he said of the boo birds. "They're upset for me. They want to win. It's like they're in the batter's box, they made the out, and they're just as disgusted as I am."

It takes a keen ear to discern all of that from a booing crowd, but the patrons were in a much friendlier mood the next day when the Brewers played Game 5 before another record throng of 56,562. Yount got four hits as they won that one, 6-4, behind Mike Caldwell. But there would be no more good news as the Cardinals took the last two games in St. Louis to win the championship.

Thomas would wear out his welcome the next year. He was hitting .183 when the Brewers traded him to Cleveland on June 6, 1983, in one of the most unpopular deals in club history.

PACKERS WIN SHOOTOUT WITH REDSKINS

OCTOBER 17, 1983

The game started in controversy and ended with a miracle. Mark Moseley simply didn't miss chip shots.

Washington's defending Super Bowl champions had just gone 51 yards in 46 seconds to set up Moseley's 39-yard field goal attempt, and a Monday night crowd of 55,255 had to be thinking, "It was fun while it lasted." It was even more fun for those who had filled Lambeau Field when the league's reigning Most Valuable Player pushed the kick wide right on the last play of the highest scoring game in the Packers' history.

The final score was Green Bay 48, Washington 47. The final statistics were ridiculous.

The Redskins rang up five touchdowns and four field goals in 12 possessions. They gained 552 yards and 33 first downs, and they had the ball for 39 minutes 5 seconds to the Packers' 20:55. But the Redskins lost the game because they were helpless in their effort to stop Lynn Dickey.

The Packers' quarterback was feeling good enough before the kickoff to tell tight end Paul Coffman that he didn't think he could throw a wobbly ball that night if he tried. He didn't try. Instead he threw for three touchdowns while completing 22 of 31 passes for 387 yards. Coffman alone caught six for 124 yards.

Dickey got just enough help from a running game that produced 70 yards and a defense that came up with one crucial turnover. It happened on the Skins' third offensive play when quarterback Joe Theismann completed a swing pass to Joe Washington. Linebacker Mike Douglass hit Washington hard enough to separate him from the ball and then scooped it up and ran 22 yards for a touchdown.

Redskins coach Joe Gibbs swore that Washington never had possession and the play should have been ruled an incomplete pass, but those were the days before instant replay and so he lost the debate and ultimately the game. But not before the two teams put on the biggest offensive show in the history of *Monday Night Football*.

While the Packers could never stop anybody that season, they loved a shootout. They averaged 26.8 points a game and topped 30 six times with the league's second-ranked offense. Coffman and wideouts James Lofton and John Jefferson all caught more than 50 passes that year as did running back Gerry Ellis. Green Bay's problem was a 28th-ranked defense that yielded 27.4 points a game and gave up 47 to Atlanta and 38 to Houston and Detroit in addition to the 47 to Washington.

That defense must have been what one of the Redskins' players had in mind earlier in the week when he predicted in the Washington media that the game would be a rout. Packers coach Bart Starr seized on the quote and used it as bulletin board material all week, trotting it out one final time minutes before the teams were introduced.

A little psychological warfare never hurt, and the Packers needed all the help they could get. The Redskins were coming off a world championship. The Packers were coming off a strike-shortened 5-3 season that put them in the playoffs for the only time in Starr's nine-year tenure. Green Bay would finish 8-8 while the Redskins wouldn't lose another game en route to a 14-2 regular-season record and a return trip to the Super Bowl. But the teams couldn't have been more evenly matched on this night.

Theismann was even more productive than Dickey. He completed 27 of his 39 passes for 398 yards, and the Skins' running game helped him with another 184. But time after time, Dickey made the plays he needed to make, and with 54 seconds remaining, Jan Stenerud's 20-yard field goal put Green Bay on top, 48-47. What happened next could have been a nightmare.

The Redskins had no timeouts when they started their final drive, but they were still able to move the ball from their own 27 to the Green Bay 21 in less than a minute against a passive prevent defense. When Theismann completed an 18-yard pass to wide receiver Charlie Brown, Moseley was in business.

He'd already been perfect on attempts from 42, 28, 31 and 28 yards, which is what you'd expect from a 12-year veteran who had missed only one field goal in 22 attempts the previous year. He'd made 12 game-winners in his career, and he would make two more before the 1983 season was done.

But he didn't make this one. When it sailed outside the uprights, the Packers greatest fireworks show ever was over. It ended with a dazzling dud.

ABDUL-JABBAR DECKS KENT BENSON

OCTOBER 18, 1977

The Milwaukee Bucks had never sold out their home opener before, but then they'd never had a draw like this. Kent Benson, their new center and No. 1 overall pick in the draft, was facing Kareem Abdul-Jabbar, the man whose shoes he was being counted on to fill.

Abdul-Jabbar, who had led the Bucks to their only National Basketball Association championship before being traded two years earlier, was cheered warmly by 10,938 people when he was introduced before the game with the Los Angeles Lakers. Minutes later, he was being booed off the floor by those same people, and Benson was on his way to the hospital.

Nobody really saw the elbow that Benson delivered to Abdul-Jabbar's midsection as he flashed across the lane. Not the officials, not the spectators, not even Abdul-Jabbar. But Abdul-Jabbar said he felt it, and he reacted with a devastating right cross that left him with a broken hand, Benson with a concussion and the league with a headache.

It was the last thing the fans were expecting when the superstar faced the Bucks' 6-foot-10 rookie center who they hoped would soon lead them back to the NBA Finals. There was an electric atmosphere before tipoff that night in the Milwaukee Arena, and all because of the matchup.

It had little to do with Benson making it clear the week before the game that he would be as rough as he had to be to try and contain Abdul-Jabbar, who was four inches taller. And, later, it was a matter of opinion whether Benson took his own words too seriously. If he was trying to send a message, Abdul-Jabbar had one of his own to deliver, and it took him barely two minutes to do it.

Benson acknowledged later that he'd delivered the elbow, but he said it was a reaction to some rough handling on the last trip down the court. He didn't mean to hurt anyone. Abdul-Jabbar didn't seem to be too concerned about that when he swung at Benson.

The punch came with 9 minutes 51 seconds left on the first-quarter clock, and it was harder on Abdul-Jabbar's hand than it was on his opponent's head. Abdul-Jabbar walked out of the Arena with a fractured fourth metacarpal on his right hand. Benson was taken to Lutheran Hospital with a slight concussion and a cut over his eye that took two stitches to close. Neither would be in any shape to play their next game.

Two days later, Abdul-Jabbar was suffering some fiscal damage as well. Commissioner Larry O'Brien wasn't crazy about the prospect of sitting down the league's best player, but he had to do something to keep the NBA from turning into the NHL. He would have suspended Abdul-Jabbar, but he was spared the trouble when doctors said the injury might take four to six weeks to heal. So O'Brien fined the big man a league-record $5,000 instead.

Benson, meanwhile, was concerned about his reputation taking a hit. This was his first pro game, and he didn't want to become known as a dirty player. "I didn't do it maliciously or with intent to hurt him," he said. "I just let him know that I acknowledged the contact he was giving me going down the floor. I had bruised ribs, and I felt it."

He felt the punch more, and that was fine with Abdul-Jabbar. In an unrepentant conversation with Jim Cohen of *The Milwaukee Journal* as the two walked together to the Pfister Hotel while the game was still going on, Abdul-Jabbar said, "It's generally known around the league that they allow people to rough me up. That's the way it is, and I have to accept it. But I won't take cheap shots. They can throw elbows, but not at me. I have no second thoughts over what I did. The only thing I feel bad about is that I'm not playing, but I had to do it."

Ironically, this was the second time that Abdul-Jabbar had broken his hand as a pro. And it was the same bone in the same hand both times. The first time came in 1974 when he was playing for the Bucks and he took an elbow in the eye in an exhibition game from none other than Don Nelson, then playing for the Boston Celtics and now the coach of the Bucks. Frustrated, Abdul-Jabbar slammed his fist into the padded backboard support and was out of action for six weeks.

This time he would miss 20 games, not counting the Milwaukee opener. The Bucks won the game, 117-112, but hardly anyone remembers that.

WORLD CHAMPION WHITE SOX PLAY IN KENOSHA

OCTOBER 19, 1906

The 1906 Chicago White Sox were called, "The Hitless Wonders." Everybody wondered how they could win a World Series batting .198.

Five days after the Sox had dispatched the crosstown rival Chicago Cubs in the decisive sixth game of the Series, baseball fans in Kenosha got their chance to find out, and they were ecstatic about it. Most of the stars of the world champions came to town to play a local semi-pro team, and they were greeted with a 30-car parade and young women throwing flowers at them. A band paraded the streets, and hundreds of people gathered outside the old Eichelman Hotel to get a glimpse of the players.

Stores were shuttered and factories deserted, and the local superintendent was asked to close the schools so the kids would get a chance to see the game. The superintendent said no, but dozens of kids played hooky anyway and joined the throng that filled the grandstand and bleachers at Breen Park.

Five starters and two of the pitchers who had worked the Series were on the barnstorming club that came to Kenosha. They included catcher Billy Sullivan, a native of Oakland, Wis., located southeast of Madison in Jefferson County, and a player even more hitless and wonderful than most of his teammates.

Sullivan played in 16 major league seasons and held the rare distinction of having the second-worst lifetime batting average of any player with at least 3,000 trips to the plate. He was a .213 hitter, but he was such a terrific defensive catcher that the Sox wouldn't think of taking him out of the lineup. No less a luminary than Ty Cobb called him the best catcher "ever to wear shoe leather."

Sullivan led a whole band of banjo hitters. The White Sox batted only .230 as a team during the 1906 regular season, and that dropped off to .198 in the World Series. But the Cubs were worse. Their team batting average was .196 for the Series, and they lost two of the first three games by scores of 2-1 and 3-0.

Of course, the White Sox pitching had something to do with their struggles. Nick Altrock gave up only two runs in the two Series games he pitched, winning the opener, 2-1, and losing the fourth game, 1-0. And there he was on Oct. 19, sharing the mound against the Kenosha team with Frank Owen, who had pitched six innings of relief against the Cubs.

The Kenoshans had a pretty good pitcher themselves in left-hander Ed Killian, who had just finished his third season with the Detroit Tigers. A Racine native, Killian would become famous for a couple of things. He pitched both games of a doubleheader against Boston that clinched the 1907 American League pennant for Detroit, and he allowed only nine home runs in his eight-year career. Playing in the dead-ball era, Killian was the hardest pitcher to hit a home run against in major league history.

He didn't give up any to the White Sox that day, but he wasn't particularly sharp, either. The Sox got three runs in the fifth inning and four in the seventh to win the game, 7-1. Along with Sullivan, the other Sox starters from the Series who played in the game were first baseman Jiggs Donahue, third baseman George Rohe, center fielder Bill O'Neill and right fielder Eddie Hahn. Lee Tannehill, who split time at shortstop in the World Series, also played.

The three runs scored by the Sox in the fifth were aided by an error committed by Kenosha shortstop Jack Klopf, who had been knocked unconscious by a pitch earlier in the game. Klopf insisted on staying in the lineup, and the losers figured his injury had a lot to do with the error.

Altrock pitched four innings and Owen five for the White Sox, and while they limited the locals to seven hits, they couldn't shut them out. Kenosha got its run in the sixth on an infield hit, a walk and a solid single by Klopf, which was enough to keep the 2,500 spectators happy.

The Sox, meanwhile, had eight singles and three doubles. For one day at least, they weren't hitless at all.

HALL OF FAME PITCHERS BATTLE FOR LOCAL PRIDE

OCTOBER 20, 1901

Addie Joss

Bragging rights were a vital community resource at the turn of the century, especially where baseball was concerned. The citizens of Racine thought they had them. The people of Kenosha said, "Not so fast."

The much coveted if unofficial state championship was at stake when the two cities recruited a couple of young professional pitchers named Addie Joss and Rube Waddell for a showdown in Racine. Both would make the Baseball Hall of Fame. Neither would live to be 40.

Joss, a 21-year-old right-hander and native of little Woodland, Wis., in Dodge County, had just won 27 games for Toledo in the Western Association. He stopped in Racine and joined the local baseball team on the train ride back home. Waddell, 25, was raised in Pennsylvania farm country, and he had just finished his fourth season in the major leagues. He also had spent part of the 1900 season pitching for Milwaukee in the American League, then in its first year of existence and still a minor league. After winning 14 games for the Chicago Cubs in 1901, Waddell was recruited by Kenosha in early October.

When Joss pitched Racine past Appleton in the finale of a three-game series in mid-October, the winners laid claim to the state title, but a delegation from Kenosha challenged it.

After much wrangling, a game was scheduled to settle the argument. Twelve carloads of Kenoshans piled off the train when it reached the Racine station on game day, and they marched through the streets blowing horns, clanging cowbells and waving money. Thousands of dollars would be wagered that day, and attendance estimates ranged from 5,000 to 8,000.

Kenosha fans were feeling very good about their investment when Waddell struck out the first nine Racine batters. This was typical behavior from the colorful southpaw, who in an earlier game for Kenosha had waved his outfielders off the field with the bases loaded and then struck out the side on nine pitches.

A good hitter, Waddell appeared willing to go it alone again when he tripled in two runs in the second inning to put the visitors ahead, 2-0. But Waddell wound up walking five and hitting another batter, and his defense deserted him as Racine scored single runs in the fourth, fifth, sixth and eighth innings with the help of five errors, four by second baseman Bob Henderson.

Kenosha had two runners on and two out in the ninth when Waddell came to the plate with a final chance to save his own cause. Joss struck him out on three pitches, and Racine was the undisputed champion by a 4-2 score.

"Pandemonium reigned," wrote Scott Longert in his book *Addie Joss: King of the Pitchers*. "Delirious rooters dashed en masse out of the grandstand, hoisted Addie on their collective shoulders, and carried him around the park on a jubilant victory lap." Longert surmised that it probably was one of the greatest semipro baseball games ever played in the United States.

Waddell allowed five hits and struck out 19 batters. Joss gave up five or six hits and struck out six or seven, depending on which box score you believed.

Joss was signed by Cleveland before the 1902 season and pitched nine years in the major leagues. He compiled a lifetime earned run average of 1.89, completed 234 of his 260 starts and pitched two no-hitters, one a perfect game.

But Joss died in 1911 at age 31 of tubercular meningitis and because he hadn't played in the majors for 10 seasons, he was ineligible for the Hall of Fame. Finally in 1978, the Veteran's Committee loosened its rules, made an exception for Joss, and he was inducted into the Hall at Cooperstown, N.Y.

Waddell's career was just as impressive, despite his love for booze and a good time. Connie Mack called him the best pitcher he'd ever had in his 50 years as manager of the Philadelphia Athletics, and the great Walter Johnson said Waddell had "more sheer pitching ability" than anyone he ever saw. Waddell won 193 games with a 2.16 career ERA and led the American League in strikeouts six straight seasons.

In 1912 he was visiting in Hickman, Ky., when the Mississippi River flooded, and he joined the emergency crew and stood up to his armpits in icy water for hours stacking sandbags. He caught a bad cold, and a year later he contracted tuberculosis. He died in 1914 at the age of 37.

BRAVES ANNOUNCE MOVE TO ATLANTA

OCTOBER 21, 1964

This is what Milwaukee Braves Chairman William C. Bartholomay said on April 11, 1964: "We are positively not moving. We're playing in Milwaukee, whether you're talking of 1964, 1965 or 1975. I hope this is the last time anyone tries to link us with Atlanta or any other city."

This was the statement released by the team on Oct. 21: "The board of directors of the Milwaukee Braves, Inc., voted today to request permission of the National League to transfer their franchise to Atlanta, Ga., for 1965."

It's possible that Bartholomay had a lightning change of heart in six months. A more likely scenario was that published reports were true and the Braves had been dealing quietly with people in Atlanta for more than a year before they admitted they wanted to go anywhere.

When publicity director and former pitcher Ernie Johnson announced the team's intentions to move just before 2 p.m. following a board meeting at the posh Racquet Club of Chicago, he said he could offer no details until after the Braves formally requested permission at a National League meeting the next day. Two-and-a-half hours later, Milwaukee County proved it could sue as fast as Bartholomay could dissemble by getting an injunction from Milwaukee County Circuit Judge Ronald Drechsler banning the franchise from making its bid at the league meeting.

All of which kicked off a bitter two-year tug of war waged in local and state courts, that narrowly missed making it to the United States Supreme Court. When it was over, the Braves were in Atlanta.

Milwaukee's association with the Braves may already have been doomed shortly after the 1962 season when Bartholomay and a group of wealthy young Chicago investors bought controlling interest in the club from Lou Perini for a reported $6.2 million. Attendance had slipped from a 1957 high of 2.2 million to 767,000, but the group bought the team anyway.

It's not totally clear when Atlanta made its first overtures to the new owners, or vice versa, but it was reported as early as July 1963 that the Braves were looking south where Atlanta was building an $18 million stadium and there was a $1.5 million radio-TV package waiting for them. That was about three times what they could make from media rights in Milwaukee.

The vote in Chicago to seek a move carried, 12-6, with the six negative votes coming from the six Wisconsin board members who issued an angry statement saying they were "unalterably opposed" to the measure. But it didn't matter. The meeting took less than two hours, and the dissenting directors held only 14% of the stock.

Reaction was dramatic. Charles Finley, owner of the Kansas City Athletics, called the same day to inquire about moving his team to Milwaukee. County Executive John Doyne fired off a letter to Bartholomay warning him that the county would take every legal step to enforce its County Stadium lease with the Braves, which ran through the 1965 season. A local syndicate also offered to buy the team for more than $6 million.

The legal threat, at least, caused the Braves to postpone their request to move at a league meeting in New York the next day. But it was only a temporary respite. On Nov. 7, National League owners approved the move in a special meeting in Phoenix, but also decided that the Braves would have to honor their lease and spend one more season in Milwaukee.

The Braves played out the 1965 schedule at County Stadium and drew only 555,584 people while winning 86 games. And then they moved, but Milwaukee wasn't giving up. Milwaukee County Circuit Court Judge Elmer Roller ruled on April 13, 1966, that the Braves and the National League had violated Wisconsin's antitrust laws, and that, in turn, the Braves would have to move back to Milwaukee by May 18 unless the city was granted a new franchise for 1967.

Upon appeal the Wisconsin Supreme Court overruled Roller's decision, 4-3. The state and county tried to appeal that decision to the U.S. Supreme Court. When the justices declined by one vote on Dec. 12, 1966, to take the case, the battle was over.

And so was a 13-year love affair between the city and the team. The Braves had never had a losing season in those 13 years, and they'd led the major leagues in attendance in six of them. Four times they exceeded two million in attendance.

They would be in Atlanta for 18 years before they drew two million fans in a single season.

DESPERATE DEVINE TRADES FIVE PICKS FOR HADL

OCTOBER 22, 1974

Crime does pay. The Los Angeles Rams discovered that when they victimized the Green Bay Packers in one of the great robberies of any time in any sport.

The Rams made off with five premium draft choices and left nothing behind but John Hadl, their second-string quarterback. The deal would propel them to six straight division championships and cripple Green Bay's franchise for years.

A case could be made that the real perpetrator wasn't the Los Angeles management at all, but a desperate Dan Devine. The Packers' coach and general manager had a 3-3 team and the beginnings of a mutiny on his hands when he spent first-, second- and third-round picks in 1975, and first- and second-round picks in '76 on a 34-year-old quarterback who'd just been benched.

Hadl, of course, wasn't just any 34-year-old quarterback. He'd been named the Most Valuable Player in the National Football Conference the previous year. But he was sinking fast in 1974, completing just 46% of his passes in the first six games amid rumors that he was having arm trouble. Chuck Knox said Hadl's arm was just fine, but the Rams' coach sat him down anyway in favor of inexperienced James Harris.

That didn't discourage Devine, who badly needed a quarterback to rally his foundering team and rescue himself. Two years earlier, Devine had won a division championship and NFC Coach of the Year honors, but the Packers dropped off to 5-7-2 in 1973, and they'd lost two of their last three games. Strangely, their only victory in that stretch came against the Rams when Hadl had played poorly.

At the same time, it was being reported that Devine was barely speaking to Dave Hanner, his popular defensive coordinator, indicating a deep division within the coaching staff. The locker room was split as well, and when Devine made the Hadl trade without consulting the Packers' executive committee, the team's ruling body was incensed.

Hadl didn't seem too happy about the transaction himself at first. The deal was made on a Tuesday, and as late as Thursday morning it appeared that it might fall through because Hadl hadn't agreed to come to Green Bay. It was widely believed that he was demanding a cash settlement to switch teams. The Packers insisted they wouldn't pay that, and they didn't. The Rams did.

At least, it was reported that they gave their departing quarterback $200,000 so he'd report to Green Bay. Hadl never denied the report. "It's my business and I'm going to keep it that way," he said upon his arrival in Green Bay. He also dispelled rumors that he planned to retire after the season, leaving the Packers without a quarterback or their draft choices.

Devine said he hoped to have Hadl around for four or five more seasons. "There's no doubt in my mind that he can help us win a Super Bowl in the near future," said Devine. "... it will be proven that the price we paid for him is peanuts... Someone asked me if we were trading away our future. That's a ridiculous question because there's no way we're doing that. It's by far the best trade I've made."

In retrospect, it was one of the worst anyone had ever made. Hadl started the last six games of the 1974 season, and he was awful. He compiled a 54.0 passer rating with eight interceptions and only three touchdowns. He was worse the following year with a 52.8 rating and 21 interceptions compared to six touchdowns.

The Rams, meanwhile, turned the three draft choices in 1974 into defensive tackle Mike Fanning, a solid starter for most of his 10 years in the league; cornerback Monte Jackson, a two-time Pro Bowl choice; and center Geoff Reece, who was a bust. They traded the first pick in 1975 to Detroit for wide receiver Ron Jessie, who made one Pro Bowl with the Rams, and used the second on cornerback Pat Thomas, who made two.

Hadl outlasted Devine by a year at Green Bay before going to Houston in a trade for quarterback Lynn Dickey. Devine left the Packers one day after they finished the 1974 season with a three-game losing streak and a 6-8 record. The executive committee had decided to fire Devine and had agreed to pay him his next year's salary. And as soon as Devine received assurances that he would be paid for another year, he informed the executive committee that he was taking the head coaching job at Notre Dame. He had fleeced the Packers for a second time in two months.

OSHKOSH'S REVOLTA WINS PGA TOURNAMENT

OCTOBER 23, 1935

Johnny Revolta came into the 18th PGA Championship in Oklahoma City with a short swing, a peculiar putting stance and a ton of motivation. He had promised his wife the trophy for their wedding anniversary.

When a man puts that kind of pressure on himself, he'd better have the game to go with it. But then the 24-year-old pro from Tripoli Country Club in Milwaukee had already proved he had that. He was on his way to a five-victory season that also included seven seconds and a key role on the victorious United States Ryder Cup team.

All of which wasn't bad for a curly-haired kid who'd started playing the game in Oshkosh with homemade clubs fashioned from broomsticks. Revolta was born in St. Louis, but he grew up in Oshkosh where his father worked in a lumber mill and made the clubs. At age nine, Revolta became a caddy at a public course in Oshkosh. By the time he was 14, he had won his first state title. He was only 18 when he became a club pro and for the next several years he didn't stay long in one place. Before moving to Milwaukee, he had been the pro at courses in Portage, Chippewa Falls and Menominee, Mich.

"Back then, all you had to do was walk up, put up your dough and say, 'I'm a professional,'" Revolta said shortly before his death in 1991.

By 1935, the money was flowing the other way. Revolta joined the PGA Tour in 1933 and won the Miami Open, and then he won the St. Paul Open in 1934. When he became the pro at Tripoli, some members weren't thrilled when he neglected them to work eight hours a day on his game for the 1935 PGA tournament. But Revolta was intent on claiming his first major and the $1,000 check that went with it.

He finished five strokes behind the legendary Walter Hagen in the two medal rounds where another Wisconsin pro attracted some attention as well. Alvin "Butch" Krueger of Beloit tied for second at 142, and he went on to upset tournament favorite Gene Sarazen, 2 and 1, in the second round of match play before losing to Eddie Schultz one round shy of the quarterfinals.

Revolta's toughest opponent in match play was his first one. He drew Hagen, the five-time PGA champion and the winner of four British Opens and two U.S. Opens. Hagen was 42 at the time and his waistline was spreading a little, but he still had all the shots he needed to take his youthful opponent to the final hole. Revolta won the match, 1 up, mainly by hitting four chip shots from the sand that came up dead to the pin. There was no better bunker player than Revolta, who was accused sometimes of hitting onto the beach on purpose.

He had another close call in the second round when he beat Jimmy Hines, 1 up, and then he proceeded to eliminate Pat Circelli, Schultz and Al Zimmerman on his way to a 36-hole, final-round showdown with another legend, Tommy Armour.

Armour would win 25 tournaments including three majors in his career, but he was no match for Revolta on a Wednesday at Twin Hills Golf & Country Club. Revolta birdied the first hole and never surrendered the lead in a 5-and-4 victory built on a hot putter. He one-putted 13 greens in the final and had just one three-putt in the whole tournament.

When it was over, he wrote in a first person column for the *Milwaukee Sentinel* that he'd been confident all along. "The main reason I was so sure of bringing back to Milwaukee the PGA Championship was that I told my wife before I left home that I would give her the cup as our anniversary present, and here it is," he wrote. "The day that the PGA was to finish was yesterday, but owing to the delayed start on the second day, I was forced to miss my anniversary by a day. The fact still remains I was confident of winning."

Revolta would keep that confidence and make a fair amount of cash over a 19-year career. He led the pro money list in 1935 with the then handsome sum of $9,543, and he won 18 PGA Tour events, in all. His wife may not have gotten all 18 trophies, but one thing was sure. There was one anniversary Johnny Revolta would never forget.

MU FOOTBALL TEAM ROLLS TOWARD COTTON BOWL BID

OCTOBER 24, 1936

Marquette University football lived for 68 years before dying of an unbalanced budget. It was fun while it lasted.

The team called itself the Hilltopppers or Golden Avalanche for most of those years, and while it was never a perennial power it had some heady moments. None was headier than a 13-7 conquest of unbeaten Michigan State that led to a Cotton Bowl date with legendary Sammy Baugh and Texas Christian.

Michigan State hadn't joined the Big Ten Conference yet when it came to Marquette Stadium on Oct. 24, 1936, but it had shown that it could compete at that level by beating Michigan, 21-7, on the way to a 4-0 record. The Avalanche wasn't bad either. It had gone 7-1 the year before, and now it was 3-0 with a second straight victory over Wisconsin and a No. 20 national ranking to its credit. Four members of its backfield would be taken among the first 88 picks in the 1937 NFL draft.

This was largely a homegrown team led by Port Washington's Ray Buivid, a consensus All-American who finished third in the Heisman Trophy voting that year behind Yale end Larry Kelley and ahead of Baugh, who finished fourth. The quarterback was Art Guepe from Milwaukee North High School, and the wingback was Ray Sonnenberg from Milwaukee Marquette High School. Al Guepe, Art's twin brother, also went to North and was a versatile sub.

Buivid was the tailback and a triple threat. More than anything, he was a great passer, and his two touchdown strikes were the difference against Michigan State. The first was to Art Guepe in the first quarter, and it covered 40 yards. But when Guepe's extra point try was blocked, Marquette and an estimated 20,000 spectators were on their way to a nervous afternoon. Michigan State came back with a third-quarter touchdown and nailed the extra point to take a 7-6 lead that it maintained until the last seven minutes.

That's when Buivid struck again. This time, he teamed with end Herbert Anderson from 17 yards out for the winning touchdown. When fullback Ward Cuff, who hailed from Redwood Falls, Minn., kicked the extra point, Marquette had the victory and a great start on its most memorable season ever.

The following Friday the Avalanche beat 20th-ranked St. Mary's of California before 40,000 at Chicago's Soldier Field and jumped to fourth place in the national rankings. Conquests of Creighton and Mississippi in the next two games left the team as an unbeaten favorite to represent the eastern half of the country in the Rose Bowl, but that all disappeared when it lost its regular-season finale at Duquesne.

Still, coach Frank Murray's group had earned a trip to the first ever Cotton Bowl where Buivid more than held his own in his personal duel with Baugh.

Marquette took an early 6-3 lead when Art Guepe returned one of Baugh's punts 60 yards for the first touchdown in Cotton Bowl history. But the Marquette team had fallen out of shape in the weeks prior to the game due to the lack of an adequate practice facility and it lost, 16-6.

Buivid had been chosen third when the NFL held its draft in mid-December – again, ahead of Baugh, who was selected sixth – but his pro career lasted just two years. Art Guepe was a third-round choice who never played in the league, but spent 17 years as head coach at Virginia and Vanderbilt. Cuff was drafted in the fourth round by the New York Giants and had an 11-year pro career. Al Guepe was selected in the ninth round but never played, while Sonnenberg went undrafted and became a high school coach in the Milwaukee area.

The Golden Avalanche went more or less downhill after the Cotton Bowl, but the sport was still paying its own way until 1956 when it started losing fans and money. Four years of red ink and dwindling crowds did it in when Marquette began a $30 million fund drive in 1960. The Jesuit fathers didn't think they could very well ask friends and alums for funds when nonessentials like athletics were running a deficit. So they announced that football and track would be dropped.

It didn't help that the team had won only 10 games in the previous six seasons. There were no more Cotton Bowls in sight, and so Marquette football became a memory after 1960.

BUCKS BEAT SOVIETS IN FIRST-EVER EVENT

OCTOBER 25, 1987

The original "Dream Team" was still five years in the future, and the idea of NBA players competing in the Olympics seemed far-fetched. But the Milwaukee Bucks still had to make a point when they played host to the Soviet Union national team in a three-day tournament at the Milwaukee Arena.

Plenty of fans still remembered the 1972 Games in Munich when a group of college all-stars lost the gold medal to the Soviets in a highly controversial championship game. It was the first defeat ever suffered by an American Olympic basketball team, but then that was their pros playing American amateurs.

This was different. For the first time an NBA team was facing the Russians, and as Bucks coach Del Harris put it: "If somebody had to do it, it might as well have been us."

That was NBA Commissioner David Stern's thinking, too, when he scheduled the first McDonald's Basketball Open for two weeks into training camp. Joining the Soviets and the Bucks in what was the first of nine such tournaments was the Italian Tracer Milan club team.

The Italians had three-time NBA scoring champion Bob McAdoo and former journeyman pro Mike D'Antoni. And the Soviets had several players who'd been drafted by NBA teams, including forward Alexsandr Volkov and guard Sharunas Marchulenis. The Soviets didn't have their best weapon, though. Arvidas Sabonis, the 7-foot-3 center drafted first by Portland the year before, stayed home with an Achilles tendon injury.

The Bucks, who were on their way to a mediocre 42-40 season, were led by Jack Sikma, Paul Pressey and Terry Cummings, and they were taking this thing seriously. Losing to a team of traveling foreigners would have been a major embarrassment not only for them, but for the whole league. Even letting them come close would have looked bad.

And the Bucks did look bad in their first-round game against the Italians on Friday night. McAdoo, who had just completed his 14-year NBA career, torched them for 37 points as they'd let a 37-15 first-quarter lead diminish to nine points with 4 minutes 29 seconds to play. After the Bucks had squeezed out a 123-111 victory, a disappointed Harris said they'd have to play much better than they did in the second half to win the final game.

The Soviets, on the other hand, had no trouble handling Tracer Milan on Saturday, winning 135-108, which may have created some curiosity for the Sunday afternoon finale. A sellout crowd of 11,052 gathered to see how far the international players had come. The Russians may have been wondering that themselves. "For me personally, the entire team and the country, this is a big event," said Marchulenis through an interpreter.

It turned out to be a big loss. The Bucks took a 38-26 first-quarter lead and just kept building on it. They were ahead, 96-48, late in the third quarter and not one of their starters was still on the floor when the fourth quarter began. The Soviets were billed as a great perimeter team, but they made only three of their 25 three-point attempts. Coach Aleksandr Gomelsky summed up the situation when he said, "Many shoot, but nothing."

The final score was 127-100, and the final emotion for the Americans was relief. "It was a no-win situation," said Sikma. "I came in today all businesslike and ready to play, and everybody else did, too."

Harris was almost as pleased with his team's performance against the Soviets as he was unhappy with their showing against the Italians. "I wouldn't want to overstate an issue on the basis of one game," he said, "but I think the Bucks players answered the challenge and left no doubt that if you want to beat somebody from the NBA, you'd better pick on somebody other than the Bucks."

BRAVES' FRED HANEY CLEANS HOUSE

OCTOBER 26, 1957

The Milwaukee Braves had won the World Series, their first National League pennant and 95 games. It was a magical season, and Manager Fred Haney celebrated it by firing three quarters of his coaching staff.

Sixteen days after the Braves had disposed of the New York Yankees in seven games, Connie Ryan, Charlie Root and John Riddle were out of work in one of the more startling shakeups in the history of Milwaukee baseball.

It was no secret that Haney did not get along with Ryan, even though he'd just hired him the previous December. Haney had hired Riddle, too, but he had inherited Root from Charlie Grimm's staff when he took over as the Braves' manager following a loss in Brooklyn on June 16, 1956.

Now all of them were gone. Only bullpen coach Bob Keely survived the purge, and he would resign in March.

Without naming names, Haney explained, "I wanted loyalty to begin with, and it wasn't forthcoming." That was in reference to Ryan, the third base coach. He was accused of not only disagreeing with Haney in the clubhouse, but criticizing him in public.

Of one of the others, Haney said, "Some of the players disobeyed certain orders by one of my coaches in whom I had much confidence, and I couldn't stand for that." Most observers saw that being aimed at Root, the pitching coach. It was believed that Root had gotten along fine with the Braves' young arms, but not so much with the veterans. Haney apparently felt Root's authority had been compromised to the point where he couldn't even carry out orders to his pitchers.

As for Riddle, the first base coach, Haney said, "Johnny was 100% loyal and cooperative, but I wanted a complete staff of assistants who would go along with my thinking and do their job."

General Manager John Quinn certainly went along with Haney's thinking because he had signed off on the changes a week earlier. He may not have had much choice. Haney apparently insisted on the firings as a condition before signing a one-year contract extension.

The same day that Haney announced the firing of the three coaches, he named replacements for two of them. He plucked John Fitzpatrick from the Pacific Coast League team in Hollywood, Calif., to assume Riddle's job, and he named Whitlow Wyatt, who had been the pitching coach in Philadelphia for the previous three years, to take over for Root. Later, Haney picked up Billy Herman from the Brooklyn Dodgers to replace Ryan.

"I live or die possibly by my particular judgment," Haney said. "I don't think I will be adjudged as wrong."

And he wasn't. At least, not right away. The Braves won 92 games with their new brain trust the following season, and they won another pennant by eight games. But perhaps they would have won it by much more if the new third base coach had been a little more discreet. Herman had been asked about his old club in a spring training interview, and he'd said the Dodgers weren't a "hungry" team. He might have been right, but for some reason the Dodgers' mouths watered whenever they faced the Braves that year, beating them 14 times in 22 games. They said they'd been inspired by Herman's words, although the Dodgers were never a factor in the race, finishing seventh, 21 games behind the Braves.

That minor incident would have been forgotten, though, if the Braves had won the 1958 World Series. But they lost it in seven games to the Yankees, and once again Herman was in the spotlight. In the second inning of the sixth game of the Series, with the bases loaded and the score tied, 1-1, Herman sent Andy Pafko home on a short fly out to left field. Pafko was nailed at the plate by at least five feet, and a promising rally was extinguished. The Braves lost the game, 4-3, in 10 innings and then the Series the next day.

The following season they lost the pennant, too. The Dodgers swept them in a best of three-game playoff, and Haney got much of the blame. In fact in the *Bill James Guide to Baseball Managers*, published in 1997, the author rated Haney's performance in 1959 as the worst ever by a major league manager. The management seemed to agree and readily accepted his resignation a week after the season ended.

MU'S DUNN BEATS BOSTON COLLEGE WITH ONE ARM

OCTOBER 27, 1923

Joseph "Red" Dunn could run, pass, punt and place-kick. And as Boston College would learn in a long-awaited clash of Jesuit rivals, the Marquette University star could do it all with one arm virtually tied behind his back.

It had been 24 years since a college team from Wisconsin had traveled to the East Coast for a football game, but this meeting was well worth waiting for. Both teams were not only unbeaten over their first three games of the season, they were unscored upon. It was the ultimate defensive struggle and on one of the first plays of the game, Dunn went down under a pile of opponents and got up knowing that something wasn't right.

The Marquette quarterback's left arm was throbbing, but he wasn't about to mention that to his coach or his teammates and certainly not to his opponents. He hadn't come all this way just to watch. A Milwaukee native with a tough streak and a full head of red hair, Dunn didn't just play quarterback. He was also the Hilltoppers' starting safety, punter and place-kicker, and they needed him to do all of the above to win this game.

But finally after a scoreless first half, the pain had gotten to be too much, and coach Frank Murray told Dunn to take a seat. X-rays taken after the game would reveal a fracture in a small bone in his left elbow. In other words, he had played an entire half with a broken arm.

It had been quite a half, too. The Hilltoppers had pushed Boston College all over Braves Field, but they had nothing to show for it after Dunn missed three field goals. The final statistics would have Marquette outgaining its opponent, 235 yards to 55 on the ground and 63 yards to 40 through the air.

None of it mattered, though, when Boston College recovered a fumbled punt late in the third quarter and scored a touchdown. The Eagles missed the extra point, but they still had a 6-0 lead with less than five minutes to play. With darkness descending on the field, they were trying to run out the clock when they fumbled and Marquette center Earl Kennedy recovered at the Boston College two-yard line.

By now, Dunn was back in the game, and he would be immortalized for his courage by legendary sportswriter Grantland Rice, who wrote, "This, of course, is taking risks entirely too great." Whatever the risks, Marquette halfback Irv Leichtfuss dashed around right end to tie the score, and now it was all up to Dunn. He kicked the extra point with room to spare and Marquette held on to win, 7-6.

Two days later, an estimated crowd of 7,000 welcomed home the Marquette team at the train depot, and thousands more lined the streets as the players were escorted by the school's marching band to yet another celebration in the Marquette gym.

The victory was the first ever by a Wisconsin team on a trip to the East, the power base of college football at the time. In 1899, the University of Wisconsin had traveled to Yale and lost, 6-0.

More important, the game kept Marquette unbeaten. The Hilltoppers gave up only 12 points that season while scoring 161 and winning all eight of their games.

Dunn came back from the injury to lead them to a 20-0 victory over Vermont in the season finale at Athletic Park, which was later renamed Borchert Field, giving Marquette a 16-0-1 record in the two years that he started at quarterback. And for his efforts, Dunn was named to the prestigious Walter Camp All-American third team.

Dunn also played basketball at Marquette and was captain of the 1922-'23 team that compiled a 19-2 record. He later played professional basketball at a time when the game was loosely organized and most teams played independent schedules, but his greatest accomplishments came in pro football.

He led the Chicago Cardinals to an NFL championship in 1925 and then was the starting quarterback when the Green Bay Packers won three straight NFL titles from 1929-'31. One of the other stars on those Green Bay teams was Lavvie Dilweg, one of Dunn's teammates at Marquette and another player who performed a key role in the Hilltoppers' victory over Boston College.

Dunn retired from the pro game following the 1931 season and went back to Marquette where he coached the backs for nine years and taught his players a little something about toughness.

BABE RUTH WOWS MILWAUKEE CROWD

OCTOBER 28, 1928

Barnstorming was an American tradition that may have had its roots in vaudeville, but became distinct to baseball in the late 19th century. Fans from all over the country loved it, but major league officials and owners weren't always crazy about it.

Championship teams had been known to "replay" World Series in the fall, and the officials feared that those touring competitions would dilute the real thing. Owners, meanwhile, weren't making any money from them, and they worried that their players would get hurt.

And so soon after taking over as commissioner in early 1921, Kenesaw Mountain Landis invoked an old rule, largely ignored, that prohibited players on the World Series teams from barnstorming. The game's biggest star resented the ruling and challenged it.

The star was George Herman "Babe" Ruth, and 8,000 Milwaukee fans were glad he'd made his stand as they gathered to see him play on a Sunday afternoon at Borchert Field seven years later.

Ruth had been known to make five figures in an off-season of barnstorming, and he wasn't interested in giving that up when he clashed with Landis immediately after the New York Yankees had lost the World Series to the New York Giants in October 1921. Ruth and Yankees teammate Bob Meusel got a call from the autocratic commissioner as they were about to leave for a tour starting in Buffalo, and they were ordered to stay home. They ignored the order, and Landis banned them from baseball for the first 37 days of the 1922 season.

Soon thereafter, the barnstorming rule was relaxed and players on the World Series teams were allowed to play until Nov. 1 with a few restrictions.

"By 1928 Lou Gehrig and I were doing a lot of barnstorming together," Ruth wrote in his autobiography, *The Babe Ruth Story*. "That revolt by Bob Meusel and me in the fall of 1921 helped all ballplayers, especially those on championship teams."

It also gave fans in cities such as Milwaukee, which didn't have major league baseball at the time, an opportunity to see some of the greatest stars in the game. And there was none bigger than Ruth and Gehrig. Nineteen days earlier, the two had led the Yankees to their second straight World Series sweep.

They arrived in Milwaukee shortly before 11 a.m., three hours before the game was scheduled to begin, and immediately headed to Mass at St. Mary Parish on North Broadway on the city's east side.

The matchup at Borchert Field pitted Ruth's Bustin' Babes against Gehrig's Larrupin' Lous. Gehrig's team included Philadelphia Athletics outfielder Al Simmons, a Milwaukee native and one of four Wisconsin-born players in the Baseball Hall of Fame. Ruth had on his side Joe Hauser, another Milwaukee native who five years later would hit 69 home runs for Minneapolis in the Class AAA American Association.

It probably shouldn't have come as any surprise that the Bustin' Babes won the game on a Ruth home run in the eighth inning. He whacked it high up onto the scoreboard, and it might have left the park altogether if it hadn't been for a stiff north wind.

Just to round out his afternoon, Ruth took the mound in the top of the ninth and whiffed Gehrig for the last out. Then all of the leftover balls from the game were tossed into the stands.

The score was 5-4, but the spectators really didn't care about that, especially not the young ones. Kids under 12 got bleacher seats for 50 cents apiece, and they followed Ruth just about everywhere asking for his autograph. He signed alongside the stands; he signed at first base; and he even signed from the pitcher's mound. Gehrig attracted some attention, too, when he put on a show during batting practice and, again, when he hit a home run during a five-minute stint at the plate in the ninth inning, but he was totally upstaged by his teammate.

Gehrig was used to that of course. When Ruth retired following the 1935 season with 714 career home runs, he had 336 more than the guy in second place. That just happened to be Gehrig, who played four more years and finished with 493.

Ruth led the league in home runs 12 times and changed the game forever from its plodding dead ball days. To this day, he remains one of the most recognizable names in the history of sports.

ANCIENT M&M RIVALRY DRAWS NATIONAL ATTENTION

OCTOBER 29, 1949

The whole country couldn't come to Walton Blesch Field. There wasn't room. So *Life* magazine did the next best thing. It brought Walton Blesch Field to the whole country.

The five million-plus circulation publication did it in a six-page spread featuring everything from weeping fans to bleeding players. The citizens of Marinette, Wis., and Menominee, Mich., had never seen anything like it, and they'd seen a lot since their high school teams first met on a football field on Thanksgiving Day 1894. Actually they met on a horse racing track, but that wasn't unusual for the time.

This was the 53rd edition of the nation's oldest interstate prep rivalry, and it was sold out as usual when the two squads clashed in the concrete marvel that was Walton Blesch.

Local businessman Gustavus A. Blesch had collaborated with the taxpayers of Menominee in 1920 to build the stadium in memory of his son, who had died the summer before he was to start his freshman year of high school. The elder Blesch split the $100,000 price tag evenly with the public. Eighteen houses had to be moved to make room for the place, which was tucked into a residential neighborhood and contained almost 3,000 seats bounded on three sides by an eight-foot high concrete wall. On this particular Saturday afternoon it held 8,268 fans and one VIP – the Very Important Photographer from *Life*.

The magazine had come looking for a slice of Midwestern life, and this was a thick one. "They are brotherly enough during most of the year," *Life* said of the two towns, "but every fall they are exploded by a football rivalry if anything keener than that which convulses high school communities all over the U.S."

It was an even match. The two cities separated by the Menominee River both had populations of roughly 11,000 to 14,000 people, and neither team had really gained the upper hand. Marinette had won 25 of the games, Menominee 21, and six had been tied going into this showdown.

Over the life of the series, both programs would claim illustrious alums. For Marinette: Earl "Jug" Girard, who starred at the University of Wisconsin and played for the Green Bay Packers and Detroit Lions; and later Mike Messenger, also a standout for the Badgers. For Menominee: Billy Wells, the Most Valuable Player for Michigan State in the 1954 Rose Bowl and a former NFL running back; and Bill Rademacher, who played on the New York Jets' 1969 Super Bowl champions.

This time, Marinette was the favorite. The Marines were unbeaten in seven games. Menominee's Maroons were 5-2. Marinette may have had a microscopic edge in fan enthusiasm as well. Both schools held Friday night parades ending in pep rallies. But the Marinette students continued with a snake dance across the Interstate Bridge into Menominee. The Menominee police chief was concerned about possible rowdiness. He said the situation was like "having a lion by the tail."

There were no extracurricular injuries, and the game kicked off on time under sunny skies. Marinette's all-state back Jim Strem took it over almost immediately. He threw a 20-yard scoring pass to end Don Miller and fell on a fumble in the Maroons' end zone following a wayward snap to give his team a 14-0 halftime lead. In the second half, Strem threw two more touchdown passes to Allan Blohm and sophomore fullback Allen Felch, who later led the University of Kentucky to a berth in the Cotton Bowl. Strem also kicked three extra points. The Maroons made just one serious offensive threat, and the final score was 27-0.

It was a big day for Marinette coach Howie Stiehm, who was quoted in *Life* as saying, "No coach stays at either school after three M&M defeats." He compiled a 35-9-1 record in six years with the Marines, including a 3-2 mark vs. Menominee, and then went on to launch a potent program at D.C. Everest High School. Menominee coach Ken Radick had his fair share of success, too. He had played on two of the Packers' NFL championship teams in 1930 and '31, and he would win 70% of his games as coach of the Maroons. However, he also lost six of seven to Marinette.

Life ran its spread two weeks after the game. The magazine has disappeared, but the rivalry goes on. There were interruptions because of scheduling complications, but the teams were still playing each other into a third century.

STARR, REPORTERS CLASH OVER DUANE THOMAS

OCTOBER 30, 1978

A normally quiet Monday press session turned into a major media event after four reporters spotted a celebrated running back strolling through the Green Bay Packers' locker room.

The running back was 31-year-old Duane Thomas, who had made quite a name for himself while leading the Dallas Cowboys to victory in Super Bowl VI, six years earlier. But the recalcitrant Thomas had a short-lived career and hadn't played in a pro game since the World Football League folded in 1975. Now, his presence on the Packers' premises threatened to cost the team a draft choice while creating a noisy explosion in coach Bart Starr's press relations.

Thomas had come to Green Bay for a perfectly legal workout, but the reporters' curiosity was aroused when they saw him in the locker room a week later. The league's "stashing" rules said a player could only be brought into town for a one-day trial. He couldn't be worked out more than once, and he couldn't use the team's equipment or facilities beyond that time. The rules also banned the team from covering his expenses beyond that one workout.

Considering that Thomas had been seen running around the practice field under the watchful eye of pro scout Burt Gustafson two days after his official tryout and now had been observed wearing Packer sweats in the Packers' locker room five days after that, the Packers seemed to have two strikes against them. A third zoomed across the plate when a desk clerk at the nearby Midway Motor Lodge said the Packers were paying for Thomas' room.

Starr wasn't pleased when the reporters, Dave Begel of *The Milwaukee Journal*, Mike O'Brien of the Associated Press, Cliff Christl of the *Green Bay Press-Gazette* and Dale Hofmann of the *Milwaukee Sentinel* questioned him about Thomas later that morning.

He said the team was doing nothing wrong. After all, he couldn't make Thomas leave town if he wanted to stay. He also suggested that the reporters could make better use of their time. "I'm not going to get my fanny in the wringer about some guy who is here who isn't supposed to be," said Starr. "I don't know why you guys want to make so much of something that might not even come to pass."

Starr was understandably sensitive on the issue because the Packers had just lost a fourth-round draft choice for illegally working out several college players before the 1978 draft. If they were caught again, the maximum penalty might be an even higher draft choice.

Not satisfied with the answers they were getting, the reporters contacted NFL public relations director Jim Heffernan for clarification of the rules. Then they asked to talk to Starr again to tell him what the league had said. That meeting was held in the afternoon, and it got hostile.

Starr admitted that the Packers had "bent the rules," but he insisted that they hadn't violated them. He also denied that they'd paid for Thomas' room. And then he told the reporters if they broke the story, they'd be banned from the Packers' facilities.

They broke it anyway, and Starr closed the locker room to the press during the week, eliminated one of his three weekly news conferences and barred the print media from the other two without acknowledging that the changes had anything to do with the Thomas fracas. The three newspapers involved were flooded with mail from loyal Packer rooters, not many of whom were writing to praise the reporters' work or defend the freedom of the press.

League officials reminded Starr, however, that he couldn't exclude the four reporters while letting everyone else in, and it also proceeded to conduct an investigation of the whole Thomas affair. A week later, it cleared the Packers of any wrongdoing.

Heffernan said the reporters had correctly interpreted the rules, but he couldn't explain the decision to exonerate the team. "I don't have those answers," he said. "This is something strictly between the commissioner and the Green Bay Packers."

The Packers, who were 7-2 when the Thomas story broke, won only one of their last seven games and finished 8-7-1. Thomas went home, signed with the Packers in the off-season and was cut in training camp the next summer.

BADGERS UPSET NO. 1 OHIO STATE

OCTOBER 31, 1942

The University of Wisconsin had never beaten a top-ranked team when Paul Brown brought undefeated Ohio State to Madison seven games into the 1942 season. But then Wisconsin hadn't been this loaded since the Associated Press poll was introduced in 1936.

UW coach Harry Stuhldreher had nine seniors who would be picked in the NFL draft the following spring, including end Dave Schreiner. Sharing the spotlight with Schreiner were two underclassmen, sophomore halfback Elroy Hirsch and junior fullback Pat Harder. All three would eventually be inducted into the College Football Hall of Fame. Hirsch also would be elected to the Pro Football Hall of Fame.

Schreiner was considered to be the best two-way end Wisconsin had ever had. A two-time Associated Press, first-team All-American, he was named the Most Valuable Player in the Big Ten Conference following the season.

Harder, who had led the Big Ten in rushing and scoring as a sophomore in 1941, was good enough to be taken second overall by the Chicago Cardinals in the 1944 NFL draft. As a sophomore, in his only season at Wisconsin, Hirsch would lead the Badgers in rushing with 767 yards and finish fifth in the country.

Two starting linemen, sophomore center Fred Negus and junior guard Evan "Red" Vogds, also would play in the NFL.

The Buckeyes weren't so bad themselves. Fullback Gene Fekete would finish eighth in the Heisman Trophy voting, and halfback Les Horvath would win the Heisman two years later. End Bob Shaw, tackle Charles Csuri and guard Lindell Houston were all chosen to at least one All-American team.

This was Wisconsin's homecoming game, and it served as a welcome wartime diversion for fans everywhere. With Bill Stern at the microphone, NBC broadcast the game to 184 domestic radio stations and several more overseas.

In Madison, an estimated 9,000 people gathered for a raucous pep rally on Friday night before the kickoff, and plenty of them stayed on the streets well into the morning. As it happened, the Ohio State team was staying at the Park Hotel on the capitol square, so there may have been some sleepy Buckeyes arriving at Camp Randall the next day.

The stands were filled with an estimated 45,000 spectators, and thousands of seats were occupied by local servicemen hoping to see the sixth-ranked Badgers beat No. 1 Ohio State for the first time since 1918. The Buckeyes were 5-0, while Wisconsin's record was blemished by a 7-7 tie with Notre Dame.

The marquee matchup was Harder vs. Fekete, but it didn't take Hirsch long to steal the show. Early in the second quarter, he skirted the right side of the line and ran 59 yards to set up the game's first touchdown. It was Harder who threw the key block on the play, and it was Harder who scored from a yard out and kicked the extra point to give Wisconsin a 7-0 lead. When Harder added a 27-yard field goal later in the period, Wisconsin went into the locker room with a 10-0 halftime lead.

After a scoreless third quarter, the Buckeyes' offense finally came to life early in the fourth. Halfback Paul Sarringhaus scored from the three to cap a 96-yard drive and close the difference to 10-7. But Wisconsin responded with a 66-yard scoring march of its own. Schreiner's 14-yard touchdown catch sealed the victory, and it came on a halfback pass from Hirsch. Harder's extra point made the final score 17-7.

Before Hirsch ran off the field, he received a big hug from Harder. He'd earned it, finishing the game with 118 yards on 13 carries, a touchdown pass and even an interception on defense. Harder carried 21 times and contributed 97 yards rushing to what may have been the biggest victory in Wisconsin football history.

It gave the Badgers a 2-0 conference record, while Ohio State fell to 3-1. With just three games remaining they seemed to have a lock on the Big Ten title. Then they suffered a huge letdown the following week and lost, 6-0, at Iowa. Ohio State won the rest of its games and climbed back to the top of the national polls with a 9-1 record, while Wisconsin finished 8-1-1 and ranked No. 3 with what may have been its most gifted team ever.

Sadly, it was broken up after the season, not so much by graduation, but by players going off to war or at least officer training school. It also was star-crossed. Schreiner and senior tackle Bob Baumann were killed in action on Okinawa in the last major campaign of World War II.

FAVRE GETS REVENGE IN LAMBEAU RETURN

NOVEMBER 1, 2009

He spent 16 seasons collecting superlatives at Lambeau Field, and 40-year-old Brett Favre wasn't done yet. The most anticipated, the most crowded and possibly the loudest game in Lambeau Field history was about to begin, and there stood the visiting quarterback grinning through his face mask while boos rang down all around him.

The grin was brief, the boos were prolonged, and it all made great TV. While 29.8 million people tuned in, Favre demonstrated that he was delighted to be back at Lambeau in a Minnesota Vikings uniform, even if the fans who had loved him so long and so well were anything but thrilled to see him there. Some three hours later, a regular-season record crowd of 71,213 was unhappier still.

"I didn't expect a standing ovation," Favre deadpanned after leading the Vikings to a 38-26 victory that not only provided him with the ultimate vindication against his former team, but left the Green Bay Packers in a deep hole in NFC North race.

Given the events preceding this spectacle, that couldn't have been too hard to figure out. Weary Green Bay fans seemed more relieved than disappointed when Favre bounced from a messy divorce with the Packers and General Manager Ted Thompson into the arms of the New York Jets entering the 2008 season. But when in the summer of 2009 he ended a second retirement to join the hated Vikings, there was general outrage.

Favre's relations with his former admirers further deteriorated when he threw three touchdown passes for the Vikings in a 30-23 victory over the Packers in Minneapolis on Oct. 5. And when he was quoted later saying, "Physically, from a talent level this is the best team I've ever been on," even his old teammates from the 1996 Super Bowl champions joined the chorus shouting "treason!"

In the week leading up to the rematch, Favre tried to back off from any comparisons, just as he sought to play down earlier remarks that he wanted to "stick it to" Thompson and the Packers for sending him away after a Hall of Fame career in Green Bay. But it was too late for that. By the time he arrived at Lambeau Field at noon on Sunday, the fans were spoiling for a fight.

He emerged from the visiting team's tunnel 48 minutes from game time to the cheers of many, but those were drowned out by the boos of the majority. And there was much more of the same when he took the field for the Vikings' first possession.

A couple of days before the game, Packers wide receiver Donald Driver had said he was eager to see how his old friend responded to the reception of the crowd. "He hasn't even gotten booed before," Driver said. "I want to see the expression on his face." The TV viewers wanted that, too, and what they got was a cross between a rueful smile and a smirk. Favre was clearly not intimidated.

It was the home team that seemed overwhelmed by the occasion as Green Bay managed just three first downs and 47 yards of offense in the first half. The Packers' only score was set up by a miscommunication between Favre and his center that resulted in a fumble and a field goal as the Vikings strolled to a 17-3 halftime lead. Aaron Rodgers tried vainly to direct the Packers' offense from the seat of his pants as he was sacked four times. It was familiar territory for the man Thompson had hired to replace Favre. He'd gone down eight times a month earlier at the Metrodome.

The question was what Favre would do for an encore after throwing three touchdown passes in that game. He answered it by throwing four in this one. The second of them was a 51-yard rocket to rookie Percy Harvin early in the third quarter that made the score 24-3 and left the Packers for dead. Rodgers finally got some protection after that, suffering just two more sacks as he pulled Green Bay within four points, but Favre still had two touchdown passes to go.

The final numbers for the two games showed him with 59 passes, 41 completions, 515 yards and seven touchdowns. No interceptions, no sacks. No "I told you sos" either.

"Am I pleased with the way these two games have turned out?" Favre said. "Absolutely. But it had nothing to do with trying to prove myself to anyone. I know it makes for a good story, but I'm glad it's over. I'm not going to sit here and throw any daggers."

AARON COMES BACK TO MILWAUKEE

NOVEMBER 2, 1974

Henry Aaron had just finished reestablishing his credentials as the world's premier home run hitter when he got a long-distance call from Bud Selig. Make that a really long-distance call.

Selig was in Milwaukee, and Aaron was in Japan when the Milwaukee Brewers' president reached him in the wee hours of the morning with an important message. Aaron was being traded to the Brewers for outfielder Dave May and a minor league player to be named later, who turned out to be a never-to-be-heard-from-again pitcher named Roger Alexander.

That might not have been welcome news coming from any other place. Aaron was 40 years old, and he'd played for only one team in his 21-year career, although he'd done it in two cities. He had hit 398 home runs for the Milwaukee Braves and 335 more for the Atlanta Braves, breaking Babe Ruth's career record of 714, and he didn't have much left to prove on the field. Off the field was another story.

Aaron had let it be known that he would like to be the first black executive in baseball history, and Braves Board Chairman William Bartholomay hadn't shown much interest in his career ambitions when he'd changed managers the previous July.

"To get to be a millionaire, you've got to step on people's toes," Aaron said. "Disappointment I should have expected a long time ago. I had a good career with the Braves. Now I'm only happy that someone would see fit to use me in more ways. We haven't talked about my becoming a general manager or anything other than playing baseball next season. But Bud Selig has been talking with my attorneys, and I hope things will work out a lot better than in Atlanta."

Aaron had tied Ruth's record in the 1974 season opener and broken it four days later. After the season ended, just to put an exclamation mark on the accomplishment, he went head-to-head with Sadaharu Oh, the Babe Ruth of Japan, in a home run contest in Tokyo. That's where Selig found him after Aaron had won the battle, 10-9, before 50,000 people.

The Brewers' boss was ecstatic for a couple of reasons. In the first place, he may have been Aaron's biggest fan, and in the second place he happened to be in the market for a designated hitter. The DH spot had been a glaring weakness for the Brewers, and while Aaron's skills were fading he still had enough pop to have hit 20 homers and driven in 69 runs in the past season. He couldn't hurt at the gate either. When the Braves came to Milwaukee for an exhibition game in May, Aaron got three standing ovations from a crowd of 21,153.

The Brewers' interest in him was no secret, and the least surprised person in the world may have been May. He said he and outfielder Johnny Briggs had been wondering which of them was headed for Atlanta ever since they'd noticed a Braves scout in the stands in late September.

May, who had been chosen for the All-Star Game a year earlier, was coming off a disappointing .226 season in which he'd hit only 10 home runs. He'd also had a confrontation with Brewers Manager Del Crandall late in the year, so he was a logical candidate to go somewhere else. Aaron figured to be able to top May's production without too much trouble, and if he couldn't, he'd know it. "If I find I can't play baseball, I'm man enough to walk away from it," he said.

It would be two more years before he walked away as a player. Aaron hit 22 home runs and drove in 95 runs while batting .232 for the Brewers in those two years. And then he went back to Atlanta, where there was a new owner, Ted Turner, and where Aaron got something close to his wish and was named vice president and director of player development.

CAMP RANDALL STADIUM DEDICATED

NOVEMBER 3, 1917

Alexander Randall would have been proud of the Badgers on the day the University of Wisconsin officially opened its new football field on the grounds that bore his name. Wisconsin's sixth governor had been instrumental in raising state troops for the Civil War, and the Union rewarded him by building an Army camp in Madison and naming it after him.

Later in the war, the camp also served as a military prison, and now it was the site of the university's new 10,000-seat concrete stadium. The Badgers were taking no prisoners on this Saturday afternoon, however, as they muscled past archrival Minnesota, 10-7, in their annual homecoming game. A drop-kick field goal in the first quarter by Eber Simpson, a touchdown pass in the third from Simpson to end Frank Weston and a whole day of stout defense were all the Badgers needed to get the $30,000 facility off on the right foot.

Halftime dedication ceremonies featured the raising of two American flags atop the flagpoles at each end of the field, while the band played the *Star Spangled Banner* and two squads of student officers looked on in one of the last truly sober moments the place would see.

It was somehow appropriate that the Badgers' new house got its start partly because the fans almost tore the old one down. A section of temporary wooden stands collapsed during a 1915 game, also against Minnesota, and an estimated 20 spectators were hurt.

No one was seriously injured, but the State Legislature knew it had dodged a bullet, and it appropriated $20,000 to build the new Camp Randall Stadium adjacent to where the old one stood. When voluntary contributions to finish the job tapped out at just over $2,000, the Legislature kicked in $10,000 more to complete the job.

The lawmakers had no idea what they were getting into. Both before and after the Civil War, the site was used as a state fairground. But when the state fair was moved to West Allis in 1892, the land was nearly sold and divided into lots. Outraged Civil War veterans put a stop to the plan, and the Legislature donated the land to the university as a memorial athletic field.

The old stadium at the site was first used in 1895. The new stadium actually opened for the first game of the 1917 season against Beloit, almost a month before it was officially dedicated. Today, Camp Randall is one of the most storied college football stadiums in the country. Entering the 2009 season, it was the fourth oldest Football Bowl Subdivision stadium in the country and the 19th largest.

Camp Randall Stadium in 1940

It also is being sold out on a regular basis, a vivid contrast to the Don Morton era in the late eighties when a gate of 50,000 was becoming a rarity and a capacity crowd was a pipedream. But then Barry Alvarez came along in 1990 and warned fans to get their seats early because they'd be going fast. It seemed like an idle boast at the time, but three Rose Bowls later, a ticket at Camp Randall was harder than ever to get.

Meanwhile, the place kept getting bigger. By 1951 a series of expansions had boosted seating to 51,000. The track was removed and the playing field lowered 10 feet in 1958 as capacity climbed to 63,435. An upper deck on the west side bumped it to 77,745 in 1966. Most recently, a massive $109.5 million renovation that started in December 2001 and took four years to complete increasing its size to 80,321.

The place owes much of its popularity in recent years to winning teams, but not all of it. Over time, a football game at Camp Randall has become almost as much a party as it is an athletic event. Nearby bars are packed, and the surrounding neighborhoods become a sea of red and white tailgate parties in the festive pre- and post-game hours. Between the third and fourth quarters, fans shake Camp Randall to its foundation by jumping up and down to the strains of a hit song by House of Pain. And when the game ends, fans stick around the stadium for 20 minutes or more to listen to the band's fun-loving "Fifth Quarter" routine. The singing of *Varsity* and *The Bud Song*, also contribute to one of the most colorful and spirited game-day atmospheres in college football.

MARQUETTE JOINS BIG EAST CONFERENCE

NOVEMBER 4, 2003

Marquette had gone through three coaches, three conferences and a nickname since leaving the vanishing ranks of independents in 1989.

So its administrators, coaches and other supporters couldn't have been more excited when they gathered in Alumni Memorial Union on the day it was announced in New York that the Golden Eagles were joining the Big East Conference, one of the nation's most prestigious leagues.

Rumors had been circulating for months that the school would bolt Conference USA, a move that most observers believed had to be made to establish the program in college basketball's big time. No less a force than Al McGuire had been advocating MU's affiliation with the Big East for years, and Athletic Director Bill Cords had put it at the top of his agenda as he neared retirement.

Marquette was just one of the major players in a game of high-stakes collegiate dominos at the time. It was joined in its move to the Big East by Conference USA schools Cincinnati, DePaul, Louisville and South Florida.

The Big East sought them as new members to compensate for the loss of Virginia Tech, Miami (Fla.), and Boston College, which had migrated to the Atlantic Coast Conference mostly for football reasons. Conference USA, in turn, plucked Central Florida and Marshall from the Mid-American Conference; and Rice, Southern Methodist and Tulsa from the Western Athletic Conference.

But with no major basketball powers left besides Memphis, Marquette's old league clearly paled in comparison to its new one. The Big East was formed in 1979 with seven schools. They were Boston College, Connecticut, Georgetown, Providence, St. John's, Seton Hall and Syracuse.

In its new format, to take effect two years down the road, it would have 16 members. The 11 holdovers had won four national championships in men's basketball, and its five new members had won five.

The only question was whether the Golden Eagles were getting in over their heads after spending the better part of 14 years in more lightly regarded company. But Tom Crean's club resolved that issue by going 10-6 in 2005-'06, its first season in the Big East.

Bob Dukiet was the coach when Marquette decided it could no longer go it alone in basketball and played its last independent schedule in 1988-'89. It started play in the Midwestern Collegiate Conference the next year against Butler, Dayton, Detroit, Evansville, Loyola, St. Louis and Xavier. And it finished 9-5 in what was coach Kevin O'Neill's first season. After two seasons in the MCC, it was on to the Great Midwest Conference, and four years after that it was Conference USA.

The team began its wanderings as the Warriors before becoming the Golden Eagles in 1994 while replacing Dukiet with O'Neill, O'Neill with Mike Deane and Deane with Crean. Marquette won two regular-season championships in that time, topping the Great Midwest in 1993-'94 when O'Neill took it to the Sweet 16, and Conference USA in 2002-'03 when Crean led it to the Final Four.

The Final Four run combined with the McGuire tradition and attractive rivalries made Marquette a good fit for the new Big East. At the same time, Marquette alone couldn't do for the conference what the Big East could do for Marquette.

It has provided the kind of television and press exposure that the Jesuit university never could have commanded if it hadn't joined with schools located in most of the country's largest media markets, including New York, Chicago, Washington D.C., and Philadelphia.

The conference also preserved two of Marquette's oldest and fiercest rivalries with DePaul and Notre Dame, maintained two budding ones against Cincinnati and Louisville, and created a whole slew of new ones against some of the most prestigious basketball powers in the country.

As a result, the Eagles aren't likely to be moving again any time soon.

PACKERS BEAT BEARS IN INSTANT REPLAY GAME

NOVEMBER 5, 1989

The score, the rules, the rivalry and maybe even the career of the NFL's top official were all changed by one play in a Green Bay Packers game with the Chicago Bears. If Don Majkowski did nothing else in his six years with the team, he'd still be remembered for that.

Of course, "The Majik Man" accomplished a bit more before losing his job to Brett Favre. He led the Packers to a 10-6 record in 1989, their first winning season since 1982, and he was selected to the Pro Bowl for his efforts. Just as important, he helped end a four-year, eight-game losing streak to the Bears.

None of that might have happened, though, if he hadn't gotten the benefit of the doubt in one of the most famous rulings in the checkered history of instant replay.

Majkowski was not having a Pro Bowl kind of day when the Packers lined up for their final drive against the Bears on a cloudy Sunday at Lambeau Field, although he'd certainly been busy. Coach Lindy Infante had more or less forgotten about the ground game, calling 17 passes and just three runs up to that point in the second half as a 7-3 lead melted into a 13-7 deficit. Majkowski had stalled two drives inside the 25-yard line with a fumble and an interception. But after the pick, Infante had told his quarterback to stay positive, that he would be a hero before the game was over.

Majkowski must have taken his coach's words to heart as the Packers took over on their own 27 with 4 minutes 44 seconds to play following a Bears punt. He marched them 66 yards in 10 plays, giving the Packers a first-and-goal on the Chicago seven-yard line. But then a sack and two incomplete passes left them with one final shot from the 14 with 41 seconds on the clock.

The Packers called for a slant route, but the Bears might as well have been in the huddle. Their zone defense was tailor-made for the play, and the Packers had to improvise. Majkowski scrambled while wide receiver Sterling Sharpe cut across the field to give him a target. Majkowski found him, and Sharpe caught just his second pass of the day, maybe two yards deep in the end zone.

Meanwhile, line judge Jim Quirk was throwing his yellow flag. He ruled that Majkowski had crossed the line of scrimmage before he threw the ball.

That's when replay official Bill Parkinson got into the act. He reviewed the play not once, not twice, but as many times as it took to fill up 4 minutes and 54 seconds. The whole drive required less time than that.

The players stood around on the field talking to one another while Parkinson ran the tape again and again. Finally he relayed his ruling to referee Tom Dooley, and Dooley made 56,556 spectators very happy by announcing that Quirk had been overturned and the play was a touchdown. When Chris Jacke added the extra point, the Packers had a 14-13 victory, and their Chicago drought was over. The controversy, on the other hand, would linger for years.

In explaining the reversal, Dooley made a point of saying that the ball was behind the line of scrimmage when Majkowski let it go, even if Majkowski wasn't. The rule at the time stated that it didn't really matter where the passer's feet were. It was just a question of the release point.

Bears President Mike McCaskey wasn't impressed by that subtle difference. He was so unimpressed in fact that he led a relentless campaign to get instant replay abolished. He finally got his way after three years, and replay wasn't reintroduced until 1999. For nine years, the Bears also marked the game with an asterisk in their annual media guide, conveying the message that it was a tainted victory for the Packers.

In the meantime, the rule on passes beyond the line of scrimmage was changed. Now a passer's feet had to be behind the line. While McCaskey groused, NFL Supervisor of Officials Art McNally agonized. *Sports Illustrated* magazine reported that McNally spent so much time going over the play that he knew it was time to get out of the business. So he retired.

Quarterback Don Majkowski rolled right looking for a receiver on the play that led to an instant replay delay of more than four minutes and a long-awaited victory over the Chicago Bears.

BREWERS MOVE TO NATIONAL LEAGUE

NOVEMBER 6, 1997

It was all good for the Milwaukee Brewers, and that was Bud Selig's problem. Baseball's acting commissioner was still the Brewers' president when the game's realignment committee decided it needed to move one team from the American League to the National to accommodate expansion franchises in Phoenix and the Tampa Bay area.

It was either that or have 15 teams in each league, an odd number that would have created a scheduling head-scratcher every year. The Brewers were more than happy to make the switch to prevent such a conundrum. Maybe too happy, or at least that's how Selig was afraid it would look.

Clearly, he was leaving himself open to his many critics, who could make the argument that what Selig was doing was much better for the Brewers than it was for Major League Baseball. And the last thing Selig wanted was a conflict of interest debate.

A poll of Brewers fans showed they were in favor of the move by almost a 4-1 margin, numbers that impressed both club and league officials. Milwaukee had been a National League city during the Braves' 13-year stay, and fans liked the idea of renewing acquaintances with old rivals such as the Chicago Cubs and St. Louis Cardinals. The team figured those sentiments could produce a big plus at the box office, and other owners figured it would solve their math problem without making anyone mad. But Selig was still concerned about appearances.

In fact, when the owners voted on Oct. 15, 1997, to move a team from one league to another for the first time in modern major league history, they also announced that the Kansas City Royals would have the first option to make the switch. But the Royals made it clear almost immediately that they weren't interested if only one team was going to be involved and it made no sense to involve more than one. The plan was to create a 16-team National League and leave the American League with 14 teams.

Unlike the Royals, the Brewers had no such reservations about moving. They had been members of the American League since 1970 when the one-year old Seattle Pilots moved to Milwaukee. In the years since, they had developed a strong rivalry with the Chicago White Sox, and they also could count on almost any game against the New York Yankees to be a strong draw. But the Brewers had never really found a home in the American League. They had switched divisions three times from the AL West to the AL East in 1972 and then to the AL Central in 1994 when a third division was added.

"We are in a unique position," Wendy Selig-Prieb, Bud's daughter and vice president of the Brewers, said after the October vote. "We have a 28-year history as an American League club, and preceding that we have the National League history of the Braves."

The Minnesota Twins were the only other team considered for the switch, but there was too much uncertainty about the franchise's future in the Twin Cities at that point. So a week before the final vote, the owners on baseball's realignment and expansion committees wrote a letter to Selig urging him to move the Brewers. And that took the pressure off him.

It also allowed Selig to do what he wanted to do all along. And so the Brewers became part of the National League Central Division, along with Pittsburgh, Houston, Cincinnati, St. Louis, and best of all, the Cubs. "It's a great day for Milwaukee," is how home run king Henry Aaron put it.

Not a bad day for the Brewers' treasury either. With $50 million in debts and a new stadium, which at that time was scheduled to open in 2000, their accountants couldn't have been happier.

Meanwhile, in Selig's mind, this was only the beginning of a much more radical realignment. He'd tried earlier to push through a plan that would have shuffled as many as 15 teams based almost entirely on geography, but that died when many of the affected clubs said no. Still, he wasn't giving up. He said the Brewers' move was only Phase I. He hoped at least six clubs would agree to switch leagues the following season. Realignment, he said, was the wave of the future.

But his colleagues stemmed the tide, and in the end only the Brewers changed leagues.

BADGERS BEAT IOWA IN A BLIZZARD

NOVEMBER 7, 1925

The rain started early in the morning, turned into sleet and then into snow. By kickoff, a three-inch blanket of white covered the field at the University of Iowa's old football stadium. Still, the crops appeared to be in greater danger than the Hawkeyes.

A stormy October had already left their acreage soggy, and the farmers were concerned that they wouldn't have time to get the corn husked. On the other hand, there was no reason to worry about the football team. The unbeaten Hawkeyes had won five games, shutting out three opponents in addition to beating Red Grange's potent Illinois outfit, 12-10.

Next up was a better than average Wisconsin squad. The Badgers carried a respectable 3-1-1 record into the game, but they were known to favor the forward pass far more than Iowa did, and the conditions couldn't have been worse for that. Wisconsin football teams had experienced more than their share of ridiculous weather over the years, and there would be much more of it in store, but most historians agree that this was as atrocious as it ever got.

There was no tarpaulin on the field, and so the yard-markers were already obliterated before kickoff. In fact, Doyle Harmon, the Wisconsin kicker, needed the assistance of the umpire to find the 40-yard line to start the game. Thereafter, the grounds crew fought a losing battle all afternoon trying to clear the lines with brooms and shovels. By the fourth quarter, six inches of the stuff was being blown around by winds gusting up to 50 miles per hour through the open north end of the stadium. The temperature dropped steadily all day and settled under the freezing mark.

The players' numbers became invisible almost immediately, and a thin coat of ice formed and re-formed on the ball despite the unstinting efforts of the towel-wielding officiating crew. Just holding onto the ball was an accomplishment. Throwing it was out of the question. The Badgers didn't try a single forward pass. The Hawkeyes tried one, and it fell incomplete.

According to the final statistics in *The Des Moines Register*, there were 32 fumbles in the game, 19 by Iowa. Another account claimed there were 40 fumbles in all. The *Register* also put the number of punts at 28, 14 for each team. With snow pouring into the open press box and soaking all of the papers, nothing was official. Telegraph operators stuck their hands and machinery into cardboard boxes while they tried to file newspaper copy. Fortunately, they didn't have much scoring to worry about.

Most of the action was limited pretty much to somebody dropping the ball onto the ground and somebody else picking it up, although the Badgers shut down two Iowa drives inside the five-yard line in the first half. Gloves were issued to both teams by the third quarter. It didn't help. Iowa would still lose more yards on fumbles than its offense gained. The *Register* had the Hawkeyes losing 95 yards on fumbles, while gaining only 65. Wisconsin was credited with 66 yards from scrimmage. The home team had three first downs; the visitors had two.

The Badgers caught a break at the start of the fourth quarter when they blocked an Iowa punt and fell on the ball in the end zone for a touchdown. They were delighted until they realized an offside penalty would cancel the score.

The Badgers were chilled, soaked and exhausted, but they weren't discouraged. Iowa had to punt again, and this time the kick was shanked out of bounds. Again, the various newspaper accounts differed on what transpired next. According to the *Register's* play-by-play, Wisconsin took over at the Iowa 11 and after right halfback Leo Harmon was stopped for no gain, left half Doyle Harmon ran for five yards. An offside penalty against Iowa put the ball on the one-yard line and Badgers fullback Robert "Red" Kreuz plowed over for the touchdown.

The Badgers fumbled the snap on the conversion attempt, but they held on for a 6-0 victory that disappointed what was left of a crowd estimated at 10,000. There would have been more if there weren't so many cars in the ditch in the roads leading to the stadium.

In the Badgers' locker room, coach George Little proclaimed, "It's the greatest victory I have ever had anything to do with," and then he dropkicked a ball through a window.

Iowa played two more games that year and didn't score another point, finishing 5-3. The Badgers won their last two to go 6-1-1. No update was available on the corn crop.

"FOUR HORSEMEN" TRAMPLE BADGERS

NOVEMBER 8, 1924

The name was new, but the results were familiar when football's most famous backfield visited the University of Wisconsin. "The Four Horsemen" turned Camp Randall Stadium into a bridle path.

Three weeks earlier, Jim Crowley had been a very good halfback playing on an exceptional Notre Dame team. But then the incomparable and poetic Grantland Rice of the *New York Herald Tribune* wrote his stirring description of the Irish's 13-7 victory over Army, and suddenly the Green Bay native was one-fourth of what would become the most storied backfield in the history of college football.

"Outlined against a blue, gray October sky, the Four Horsemen road again," wrote Rice. "In dramatic lore they are known as famine, pestilence, destruction and death. These are only aliases. Their real names are Stuhldreher, Miller, Crowley and Layden."

Rice never did say which back was which, but they were all too much for the Badgers as Notre Dame rolled to a 38-3 victory. The game was close for a quarter, but only because "The Four Horsemen" had spent most of the first 15 minutes on the sidelines.

Coach Knute Rockne liked to keep them under wraps for a quarter while his second-stringers, or "shock troops" as they were called, probed the opponent. In this case, the probing got painful, even though the *Wisconsin State Journal* had written that morning that it was "not reasonable" to expect victory. When the Badgers ventured inside the 50-yard line for the only time all afternoon, Rockne sent in his stars.

They couldn't prevent the Badgers from getting a field goal, but they exacted a terrible revenge. Playing only two quarters, "The Four Horsemen" scored 28 unanswered points. Overall, the Irish outgained the Badgers, 350 yards to 76, and nobody was more productive than the home-grown Crowley. He was credited with a team-high 118 yards from scrimmage, including a spectacular 60-yard run in the third quarter to set up a touchdown. He also scored a touchdown on a three-yard run and kicked three extra points. Rockne went back to his bench in the final period, or the score would have been much more lopsided.

But then there was no great shame in getting routed by the Irish that season. Rockne had put together the combination of Crowley at left halfback, Don Miller at right half, Elmer Layden at fullback and Harry Stuhldreher at quarterback two years earlier when all four were sophomores. They weren't giants by any means but they made Notre Dame all but unbeatable. Layden was the biggest at 6 feet and 162 pounds, and Stuhldreher the smallest at 5-7 and 151.

While Rice gave them their nickname, the man who made it stick was student publicity director George Strickler, who would later become sports editor of the *Chicago Tribune*. When the Irish returned from New York following their victory over Army, Strickler posed the four on horseback, in uniform, and saw to it that the wire services picked up the photo and transmitted it across the country.

The Irish were 5-0 when they came to Camp Randall, and they finished their season 10-0 with a Rose Bowl victory over Stanford. "The Four Horsemen" played 30 games together and compiled a 27-2-1 record. As seniors, they not only went unbeaten, but Stuhldreher, Crowley and Miller joined Red Grange of Illinois in that year's consensus All-American backfield.

All four of "The Four Horsemen" were inducted into the College Football Hall of Fame, and all four coached.

Stuhldreher, a Massillon, Ohio, product, must have liked what he saw of Madison that day because he came back to serve as head coach at Wisconsin from 1936-'48. Layden became head coach at Notre Dame for seven years, while Miller served as an assistant at Georgia Tech and then became a lawyer.

Crowley, who was nicknamed "Sleepy Jim," was Wisconsin through and through. He starred for Curly Lambeau at Green Bay East High School when Lambeau was leading the Green Bay Packers at the same time. After finishing his Notre Dame career, Crowley's brief career in the pros included two games with the Packers. He later spent 13 seasons coaching at Michigan State and Fordham where another famous nickname was born. He coached the fabled "Seven Blocks of Granite," which included a stocky lineman named Vince Lombardi.

KENSETH WINS NASCAR TITLE

NOVEMBER 9, 2003

The adage has it that "slow and steady wins the race," and while Matt Kenseth was never the first he was clearly the second.

The former short-track star from Cambridge, Wis., just needed to stay out of trouble on a sunny Sunday at Rockingham's North Carolina Speedway to wrap up NASCAR's Winston Cup championship. But that proved to be a major accomplishment in a race that featured 10 caution flags. It was called the Pop Secret Microwave Popcorn 400, which was totally appropriate because something was always shaking on the track.

Kenseth wound his way through a single-car spin, two cars banging into one another, an exploding engine that dumped oil all over the track and finally another car hitting the wall before coming home fourth in the race behind Bill Elliott. That left Kenseth 226 points ahead of the field, with just 185 points available in the final weekend of the season, and the $4.25 million first prize was his.

"I feel like the world has been lifted off my shoulders today," he said.

There was some grumbling about the fact that Kenseth had won only one race all year, but it didn't bother him. The 31-year-old racer had come a long way in the 15 years since he launched his career as a teenager at the Columbus 151 and Jefferson speedways. Nothing was going to spoil that.

After dominating the tracks around home in 1994 and '95, Kenseth decided to go south to NASCAR in 1996. He did well in the Busch series, and two years later, he finished sixth in his first Winston Cup race at Dover, Del. In 2000, he won his first race, the Coca Cola 600, and he also captured the Raybestos Rookie of the Year title over Dale Earnhardt Jr. In 2002, Kenseth would win a series-high five races, but he finished eighth in points.

He would win fewer races in 2003, but achieve a much higher level of consistency. Kenseth's only win was in the UAW-Daimler Chrysler 400 in Las Vegas in March. But he seized the points lead the next week at the Atlanta Motor Speedway and stayed there for 33 consecutive races.

He would place in the top ten in 25 of the 36 races and finish worse than 20th only four times. Ryan Newman, on the other hand, won eight times but he was 38th or worse in six races, which would leave him sixth in the final standings.

Only three drivers had ever won a Winston Cup championship before with just one victory – Bill Rexford in 1950, Ned Jarrett in 1961 and Benny Parsons in 1973 – and Kenseth was delighted to be in their company. He'd never finished higher than eighth in the point standings, so he found his accomplishment to be "a little overwhelming."

Matt Kenseth

The same could have been said of the championship-clinching race. Things got interesting for Kenseth when Newman spun out in front of him on the 84th lap, and Tony Stewart bumped him from behind when he hit the brakes. Kenseth was running 19th at the time, and he had to pit for repairs. But the damage wasn't significant, and he kept working his way up through the pack.

Kenseth admitted after the race that all the extracurricular activity was frustrating, because he was getting passed by seven or eight drivers on every restart. His car was slow on the short runs, but it was good enough to keep him around when he caught a break on the 242nd lap. That's when teammate Mark Martin's car exploded. Most of the leaders had pitted under the green flag, but Kenseth saw the waving yellow and was able to stay among six cars on the lead lap.

Earnhardt, who had come into the race second in the standings, was running ahead of him at the time, but he was one of the drivers who got caught in the shuffle. Earnhardt wound up 13th, two laps down, while Kenseth drove steadily toward the finish line and his seven-figure reward for consistency.

WISCONSIN ROUTS NO. 1 NORTHWESTERN

NOVEMBER 10, 1962

The biggest crowd in Camp Randall Stadium history up to that point gathered to watch the University of Wisconsin challenge top-ranked Northwestern on homecoming Saturday. Among the 65,501 in attendance were members of UW's last unbeaten, untied football team. As it turned out, the 1912 outfit might have given the Badgers a better game.

The Rose Bowl and a national championship were on the 6-0 Wildcats' minds when Ara Parseghian's flying circus arrived in Madison to face eighth-ranked Wisconsin. The Badgers had lost only one game, but it was to Ohio State, a team Northwestern had beaten, 18-14, en route to taking over the top spot in the Associated Press rankings.

Northwestern had a spectacular passing attack led by sophomore quarterback Tom Myers and senior flanker Paul Flatley. Wisconsin had a former walk-on quarterback from the Green Bay area named Ron VanderKelen, who had played only 90 seconds in his first two years on the varsity, throwing to All-American receiver Pat Richter. VanderKelen and Richter both had big days against the Wildcats, but it was Wisconsin's recently healed defense that made the difference.

Myers completed 16 of 26 passes for 181 yards and a touchdown, but he threw most of them on the run. The Badgers sacked him three times, intercepted him once and did their best to make Flatley invisible. Myers' favorite target caught just two balls for 17 yards all afternoon, thanks to the pass rush and the efforts of defensive backs Jim Nettles and Bill Smith.

With their passing game contained and their rushing game almost non-existent, the Wildcats took a 37-6 thrashing that left America wondering what the pollsters could possibly have been thinking.

Smith and Nettles were both recovering from injuries suffered early in the season, and Wisconsin coach Milt Bruhn started with them in explaining the victory. "The biggest thing was that Jim Nettles was ready and Billy Smith was ready," he said. "With them in there we could cover Flatley with one man."

If the recovery of Smith and Nettles was the big thing, there were plenty of smaller things going for the Badgers as well. There was VanderKelen, who completed 12 of 22 passes for 181 yards and three touchdowns, and there was Richter, who caught five of those passes for 77 yards. Richter didn't catch any touchdown passes, but halfbacks Gary Kroner and Lou Holland more than made up for that.

Kroner scored on an 11-yard pass from VanderKelen on Wisconsin's first possession and kicked a 38-yard field goal in the second quarter. That gave the Badgers a 10-0 lead at halftime, and then things got worse for Northwestern.

Kroner returned the second-half kickoff 45 yards to set up the first of three Wisconsin touchdowns in a space of 7 minutes 42 seconds. Kroner scored on a 23-yard pass three plays after his kickoff return, and Holland followed with touchdown runs of nine and four yards. The Wildcats contributed an interception and a fumble to the Badgers' binge, and the game was over before the final period began.

The score didn't quite match the 56-0 pasting that the 1912 team had put on Northwestern, but it was enough to humble Parseghian, who was in his eighth season at the school. "We were just overpowered," he said.

The victory wasn't enough to put the Badgers at the top of the AP poll. They jumped to fourth the next week, but never got any higher than second.

They won the Big Ten championship and earned a trip to Pasadena where they came to the Rose Bowl ranked No. 2. Southern Cal was ranked No. 1, and the Trojans showed why by holding off Wisconsin, 42-37, in one of the most thrilling Rose Bowls ever.

The Rose Bowl had been on everyone's mind after the Badgers thumped the Wildcats despite Bruhn's best efforts to the contrary. "When you start thinking about roses, you get into trouble," he'd warned.

That would have been good advice for Northwestern.

UW'S SHAFER FATALLY INJURED IN GAME

NOVEMBER 11, 1944

Allan Shafer, Jr.

The score was 7-7 early in the fourth quarter, and the University of Wisconsin had the ball on the Iowa one-yard line. One of the Hawkeyes jumped offside, and when the play was over, one of the Badgers didn't get up.

His name was Allan Shafer Jr., and he was 17 years old.

Wisconsin's freshman quarterback was still conscious when teammate T.A. Cox helped him off the field while a sparse, wartime crowd of 15,000 looked on. Coming off a 1-9 season and mired in a four-game losing streak, the Badgers were attracting only the truly faithful fans. Among them that afternoon were Mr. and Mrs. A.J. Shafer, who didn't just attend all of the home games, they went to most of the practices as well.

It was Dad's Day, and the elder Shafer had been introduced along with the fathers of other players at halftime. Wisconsin was dominating the Hawkeyes, despite the tie score at that point, and the Shafers, no doubt, were looking forward to celebrating the end of the skid. Then suddenly their festive afternoon turned into a nightmare as they watched their only child collapse on the sideline before being carried from the stadium on a stretcher.

Shafer was rushed by ambulance to old Wisconsin General Hospital, not far from Camp Randall. The Badgers scored on the next play and scored two more touchdowns in the final 11 minutes 42 seconds for a 27-6 victory. But as Badger fans cheered the late surge, they were ignorant of the gravity of Shafer's condition.

He never regained consciousness after reaching the hospital and was pronounced dead at 5:30 p.m. Coach Harry Stuhldreher and his parents were at the hospital with him.

The autopsy showed a lung hemorrhage apparently caused by a blow to the chest, but no one could say exactly when the young man had been fatally injured. After viewing the game films with the coroner, the university's medical and coaching staffs, and members of the Shafer family, Stuhldreher said, "The officials were on top of every play in order to protect the boys. They and we failed to see any play or plays that might have contributed to this unfortunate circumstance."

It was Wisconsin's first football fatality, and it would be its last until 1979 when freshman Jay Seiler died during spring practice. Speaking of Shafer's death, Stuhldreher said, "I have never had anything hit me harder."

There was no question that Shafer was a special kid. A center on Madison West's unbeaten high school football team of 1943, he also was senior class president and a top student. He was pursuing an engineering major at Wisconsin, and he'd just taken an examination for appointment to the Naval Academy.

The Badger coaching staff had moved him to quarterback in pre-season drills, and he'd immediately won the starting job. He suffered a back injury in the opener and missed two games, but he had returned to the starting lineup a week before the Iowa game.

Funeral services for Shafer were held the Tuesday after his death at the First Congregational Church in Madison. He was buried under a bright sun at Forest Hill Cemetery.

The Badger players were all there as were many of Shafer's teammates from Madison West. A mix of both carried his body to the gravesite. Also among the 1,500 mourners were Big Ten Commissioner John Griffith and Iowa coach Ed Madigan. Hundreds of floral arrangements were placed along the chancel of the church, and so was a large cardinal "W" against a background of white.

"He is part of the immortal community that make up the prime influence of Alma Mater," the Rev. Alfred W. Swan said in his tribute to Shafer. "Every time *Varsity* is sung, it will have a deeper truth because of this bright and shining lad."

Shafer's parents "bore their grief with subdued dignity," sports editor Henry J. McCormick of the *Wisconsin State Journal* wrote the next day.

There was talk of canceling Wisconsin's last two games of the season against Michigan and Minnesota, but Shafer's parents wouldn't hear of it. "That's the last thing Allan would have wanted," his father said the day before the funeral. "Allan loved football."

The university later retired Shafer's number 83. Only five other Badger players have ever been accorded that honor.

TRAVIS WILLIAMS' RETURNS CRUSH CLEVELAND

NOVEMBER 12, 1967

Ten players from the Vince Lombardi era are in the Pro Football Hall of Fame and 14 others were selected to play in at least one Pro Bowl. But no player in the nine years that Lombardi coached the Green Bay Packers ever made a bigger and more immediate splash than Travis Williams.

Williams, a rookie speedster out of Arizona State who had played little in the first eight games of the season, electrified a Milwaukee County Stadium crowd as the Packers smothered the Cleveland Browns, 55-7. The Browns, who had won four league championships in their first 15 years in the NFL, had never been so badly embarrassed. And pro football had never seen the likes of Williams' first-quarter performance.

He returned two kickoffs for a total of 172 yards and two touchdowns as the Packers grabbed a 35-7 lead. Entering the 2010 season, the 35 points still stood as the NFL record for most points by a team in the first quarter.

Williams took the opening kickoff and ran 87 yards for his first TD. The game was only 13 seconds old at that point, and things got steadily worse for Cleveland after that.

Quarterback Frank Ryan's first pass was picked off by cornerback Bob Jeter, leading to another Green Bay score. Then defensive end Lionel Aldridge knocked the ball out of Ryan's hands and, following a short drive, halfback Donny Anderson scored the first of his four touchdowns on a two-yard run. After the Browns fumbled the ensuing kickoff and Jim Flanigan recovered for the Packers, Anderson scored again on the first play, racing 27 yards for a touchdown. Incredibly, the Browns found themselves trailing, 28-0, and they'd run only five offensive plays.

They finally caught their breath enough to score a touchdown of their own, but that was a mistake, because it meant they had to kick off to Williams again. This time he ran 85 yards tying an NFL single-game record with his second kickoff return for a touchdown and a season record with his third. The entire process was lightning quick and remarkably simple. There were still 2 minutes 59 seconds remaining in the first quarter.

The Packers finished the game with a 28-11 edge in first downs and a 456-228 edge in total yards. It was clearly one of the most dominating performances of the Lombardi era, and bear in mind that it didn't happen against a bad team. The Browns would finish 9-5 and win their division that year.

The victory also came just one week after the Packers had lost more than a game in Baltimore. They also had lost their two starting running backs, Elijah Pitts and Jim Grabowski, with season-ending injuries. But Lombardi plugged in journeyman Ben Wilson for Grabowski, and he responded with 100 yards on 16 carries against the Browns. Anderson, playing for Pitts, accumulated 159 total yards.

And then there was Williams, who had carried the ball only twice from scrimmage going into the game. Now the backup halfback, he also rushed four times for 43 yards.

After Williams' second touchdown, the Browns never kicked off again. But when the game was over, Williams had returned a total of six kickoffs on the season, and he'd scored on three of them. Two weeks earlier, he'd returned three kickoffs for 151 yards, including a 93-yard touchdown against the St. Louis Cardinals. He'd get another touchdown later in the season to give him four for the year, another NFL record that still stands, although it was tied by Chicago's Cecil Turner in 1970.

Williams, who had been a fourth-round draft pick, finished his rookie year with 18 returns for a 41.1 average, which is still a league record, and he got to carry the ball 35 times from scrimmage for 188 yards, a stunning 5.4 average.

Then things tailed off for him quickly. He led the Packers in rushing in his third season with 536 yards, but that represented more than half of his total in his four years with the team. After an injury-plagued 1970 season, he was shipped to Los Angeles where he played a year, sat out a year with a knee injury, and then got cut by the Rams and eventually two other NFL teams. When the 1973 season kicked off, Williams was 27 years old and about to move back into a housing project in Richmond, Calif., with his wife and seven children.

His inability even to hold an odd job left him broke, depressed and alcohol dependent. Williams' fall was every bit as meteoric as his rise. He died of liver and kidney failure in a California hospital at the age of 45.

DAYNE BREAKS NCAA RUSHING RECORD

NOVEMBER 13, 1999

It was the biggest play of Ron Dayne's life, and he didn't know what to call it. "We ran a 23-something," he said haltingly. "We've got a couple of names for it."

If that sounded like Mozart claiming he couldn't read music or A.J. Foyt forgetting which pedal was the clutch, it didn't matter to Dayne. The University of Wisconsin's most decorated football player maintained that he never did care much about numbers.

The play Dayne couldn't remember was a "23-zone," and he ran it 31 yards from the Badgers' 17-yard line late in the first half to claim college football's most coveted individual record. His burst through the middle gave him 6,287 yards for his career, eight more than any college player had ever rushed for before.

Not content to better the mark set a year earlier by Texas' Ricky Williams, Dayne proceeded to obliterate it by rushing 27 times for 216 yards in a 41-3 rout of Iowa that put Wisconsin on its way to a second-straight Rose Bowl appearance. Dayne finished the afternoon with 6,397 yards in regular-season games, and those were the only ones that counted toward the record.

When he was asked which was sweeter, setting the record or going to Pasadena, Dayne had a much easier time than he did recalling the play. "Going back to the Rose Bowl," he said. "We get a ring for that."

Not that Dayne would ever lack for trinkets. Before the year was out, he would collect plaques for the Maxwell Award, the Doak Walker Award, the Walter Camp Award, and player of the year awards from the Associated Press, *The Sporting News* and *Football News*. There was also a Heisman Trophy in there, one of only two ever won by a Wisconsin player.

That's called history, and a Camp Randall sellout crowd of 79,404 went to a lot of trouble to witness it. The highways leading into Madison and most of the city's arterials began to back up hours before the kickoff against Iowa. Parking spots on people's lawns were selling at $20 a pop a half-mile from the stadium. Desperate ticket seekers went from corner to corner waving money and signs, and scalpers were getting $150 and up. The lucky ones who did get seats were handed red and white towels with Dayne's name and number on them when they entered the stadium, and they had plenty of reason to wave them.

This was a huge game in a lot of ways. Not only was Dayne chasing Williams' record, but this was the local fans' last chance to see him at Camp Randall. Over Dayne's four-year career, the Badgers would win 37 of 50 games and capture two Big Ten titles, while he surpassed 200 yards rushing in 11 games to tie another NCAA record and become the first player in history to win three Big Ten rushing titles.

But none of that was uppermost in his or the patrons' minds as ninth-ranked Wisconsin took the field against the unranked Hawkeyes. A victory over Iowa along with a Penn State loss to Michigan would send the Badgers to the top of the standings and back to Pasadena, an outcome that didn't seem likely when they stumbled early in the season. They followed a non-conference loss to Cincinnati with a five-point setback at home to Michigan, dropping them out of the Associated Press top 10. Then they bounced back by winning six games in a row, including four over top 25 teams.

Much of the Rose Bowl suspense evaporated in the first quarter when it was announced that the Wolverines had knocked off Penn State. That left the Badgers with fewer worries as they concentrated on helping Dayne get the record. He did it with 4 minutes 32 seconds left to play in the first half, and he was mobbed by his teammates and saluted by a streaker, who popped onto the field from the north stands and ran 100 yards into the waiting arms of the police.

On his record-breaking 31-yard run, Dayne started left, cut back right and broke through a hole in the middle of the line, eluded the free safety and veered toward the sideline before powering his way past a cornerback and finally being knocked out of bounds. Center Casey Rabach, guard Dave Costa and tackle Mark Tauscher threw key blocks at the point of attack.

"The whole week leading up to the Iowa game, everyone knew we were going to get Ron the record," said Tauscher. "But it took a little longer to get than we thought it would."

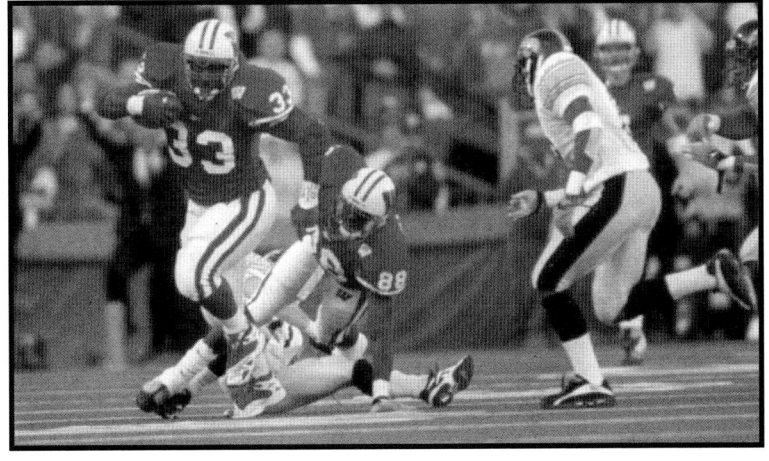

Ron Dayne broke through a hole on his record-setting day against Iowa.

PACKERS FIRST NFL TEAM TO FLY

NOVEMBER 14, 1940

Hoping to make history, the Green Bay Packers only made Cleveland.

The modern American airline industry was barely 14 years old when Curly Lambeau announced plans to put his players on a flight to New York for a crucial game with the Giants. No pro football team had ever flown to a game, and Lambeau created quite a fuss when he said the Packers would be the first.

When Lambeau announced his decision to fly to New York, he said it would be less disruptive to the Packers' practice schedule. This way, he said, his team would miss only one day of workouts. As it turned out, unusually cold November weather played havoc with the Packers' practice schedule anyway, but Lambeau was still hoping to get in two good workouts in Central Park upon his team's arrival in New York.

With much fanfare, the Packers boarded a Milwaukee Road train bound for Chicago at 7 o'clock on a Thursday morning, took limousines to the Chicago airport and, by shortly after noon, were winging their way east on two United Airlines Mainliners that took off 25 minutes apart. The first plane was filled to capacity with 21 passengers, including assistant coach Red Smith, publicity man George Whitney Calhoun, equipment man Tim O'Brien and 18 players. Lambeau, trainer Bud Jorgensen, a writer and photographer from the *Green Bay Press-Gazette*, and 16 players were on the second flight.

But 15 tons of equipment and the oversized personnel forced the two planes to make a fuel stop in Cleveland at 4 p.m. local time.

While the Packers sat on the ground, weather conditions deteriorated on the eastern seaboard. Airline officials consulted with Lambeau almost close to an hour before deciding that there was too much fog and traffic over New York's LaGuardia Airport to proceed. The planes were grounded, and the Packers took a train the rest of the way after spending more than three hours sitting around a hotel lobby in downtown Cleveland.

But they did fly back the following Monday, completing three-quarters of their scheduled round trip and cementing their place as the pro game's aeronautical pioneers. They had an interesting time doing it, too.

As the Packers were preparing to depart from Chicago, photographers were everywhere and the team's players were in an accommodating mood despite chilly, wind-swept weather in the outdoor boarding area. One of the photographers asked for a shot of quarterback Cecil Isbell throwing a pass to star receiver Don Hutson, but nobody could find a football. So Isbell tossed a stewardess, Roberta Schilbach, in Hutson's direction instead.

United Airlines also made the players feel welcome by painting "Green Bay Packers Special" on the planes. On the return trip, the airline handed out travel kits and allowed the players, two-by-two, to visit the cockpit.

There was some grumbling in Cleveland until the hotel management treated the team to a performance by a string ensemble, and there was more when the train pulled into New York at 8:30 Friday morning, a day late, and Lambeau informed his players that they would still be practicing in Central Park, despite a raw drizzle.

Not that it did much good. The 5-3 Packers badly needed to win the game against the Giants, who were 4-3-1. The Packers trailed Chicago by only one game in the Western Division with three to go, and the Bears were playing the dangerous Washington Redskins and Sammy Baugh. A Packer victory and a Bears defeat would pull them into a tie for first. No wonder Lambeau was nervous about practice time.

The Redskins did their part for Green Bay's title hopes by knocking off Chicago, but the Packers played themselves out of the race by fumbling the opening kickoff at the Polo Grounds and losing to the Giants, 7-3. They would win one of their last two games, settle for a tie in the other and finish second, a game-and-a-half behind the Bears.

The return trip went off like a 100-yard punt return. The Packers left New York at 8:30 a.m., Eastern time, Monday and stopped again in Cleveland to take on fuel, a process that required only 15 minutes. Then it was on to Chicago and a quick train ride home. The team had breakfast in New York, lunch over Indiana and dinner on the train somewhere in Wisconsin.

Modern travelers have had much worse trips than that, but the loss to the Giants had to sting. Not only were the Packers the first team to fly for a road game, but they also experienced the first long plane ride home.

STAR-CROSSED KULWICKI WINS WINSTON CUP

NOVEMBER 15, 1992

He arrived on stock car racing's biggest stage in a borrowed pickup truck, and he earned thousands of fans and millions of dollars before he left it seven years later in a private plane. Less than six months after Alan Kulwicki reached the top of his game, he was gone.

The highest point of the Greenfield, Wis., native's highly unlikely NASCAR career came on a Sunday afternoon at the Atlanta Motor Speedway when he won the Winston Cup championship by finishing second. He trailed Bill Elliott across the finish line in the Hooters 500, but he edged his Ford teammate for the drivers' title by 10 points.

It was the slimmest margin in the history of the circuit, and it came only because Kulwicki led 103 laps of the race to Elliott's 102. The rules awarded five bonus points for every lap led, which meant that if Elliott had nosed ahead on just one more lap the two drivers would have tied for the points lead. That would have given Elliott the title because he'd won five races that year to Kulwicki's two.

Actually, Kulwicki's biggest break of the day came on lap 253 when Davey Allison was knocked out of the race. Allison had won the Pyroil 500 two weeks earlier at Phoenix International Raceway to take the points lead going into the final race. Allison led Kulwicki by 30 points and Elliott by 40. In all, six drivers were still in contention, including Harry Gant, who was 97 points behind Allison; Kyle Petty, who was 98 back; and Mark Martin, who was 113 behind.

All Allison had to do in the Hooters 500 was finish sixth or better to win the Cup. And he was running sixth when Ernie Irvan lost control of his Kodak Chevrolet just in front of him and Rusty Wallace. Wallace avoided Irvan's car, but Allison T-boned it and was knocked from the race.

That gave Kulwicki the inside track on the Cup, and he celebrated his victory by turning his car around and circling the track the wrong way. He'd done that only once before when he'd won his first race at Phoenix in 1988, and he would never do it again.

Kulwicki was on his way to Bristol Motor Speedway for a race on April 4, 1993, when he and three other men approached Tri-Cities Regional Airport in a twin-engine plane after making a promotional appearance at a Hooters restaurant in Knoxville. A light rain was falling, and there was some fog in the area, but the approach seemed normal enough until suddenly the plane nosedived to the ground. All four men died instantly. Kulwicki was 38, and one of racing's more inspirational stories was over.

Almost three weeks after winning the Winston Cup, Kulwicki was feted in New York City, and he said the experience still hadn't sunk in yet. "It's an enormous accomplishment and the dream of a lifetime," he said. Kulwicki began pursuing that dream long before he started competing on the NASCAR circuit.

He started as a 13-year old kart racer, moved on to dirt and short-track racing, and then late-model stock cars, mostly at tracks within a short drive of Milwaukee. Late in 1985, he sold most of his earthly possessions and piled the rest onto a trailer for the trip south. He pulled the trailer with a pickup truck he had borrowed after his own truck had been totaled in an electrical fire two days earlier.

There he was, a Yankee from Wisconsin with a mechanical engineering degree from the University of Wisconsin-Milwaukee walking through garage areas wearing his driving uniform and carrying a briefcase. Kulwicki had raced five times in 1985 for Bill Terry's Ford team, finishing no better than 13th. The following year, Kulwicki started his own one-man team so to speak, functioning as owner, driver and chief mechanic. The engineering background helped, and so did his stubborn independent attitude, as he finished in the top 10 four times and won 1986 Rookie of the Year honors.

Kulwicki won his first Winston Cup race in the second-to-last race of the 1988 season. He captured the Checker 500 at Phoenix and invented his patented "Polish Victory Lap" that he reprised in Atlanta four years later when he became the first driver-owner to win the overall standings since Richard Petty in 1979.

Bristol would have been Kulwicki's 208th Winston Cup start, but he never got a chance at another victory lap. Wallace won the race, and when it was over, he circled the track the wrong way.

BADGERS, McCLAIN SHOCK BUCKEYES AGAIN

NOVEMBER 16, 1985

Something about Ohio State brought out the best in Dave McClain's football teams. The University of Wisconsin had beaten the Buckeyes only six times in 66 seasons before McClain came to Madison. He did it four times in five years.

The fourth came in Columbus, and it was the last game he would ever win. Less than six months after his Badgers stunned the nation's third-ranked team, 12-7, McClain died of a heart attack at the age of 48.

The football program was in a rut when the new coach arrived from Ball State. The Badgers had posted just one winning record in the previous 14 years, and they were coming off their third straight six-loss season under John Jardine. McClain had learned from the best while serving as an assistant under Bo Schembechler and Woody Hayes, and he put that knowledge to work immediately with a 5-4 record.

But it would take a couple more years before McClain really got the operation untracked. He lost his first three games to Ohio State, and after finishing above .500 in his first season, he had back-to-back 4-7 records. Then, from 1981 to '84, the Badgers had four winning seasons and went to three bowl games. They beat Ohio State three times in that span by a total of 11 points.

When the Badgers won at Camp Randall in 1981, it snapped a 21-game losing streak in the series. When they won at Columbus in 1982, it was their first victory there since 1918.

That was the game the Badgers had on their mind when they returned to Ohio State's horseshoe stadium three years later to face the team most people figured was headed for the Rose Bowl. The Buckeyes were 5-1 in the Big Ten and 8-1 overall, and Wisconsin's best chance seemed to rest on the hope that they would be looking ahead to their season finale with Michigan. The Badgers were 1-5 in the league, 4-5 overall, and a 21-point underdog.

Ohio State had five starters in Pepper Johnson, Chris Spielman, Cris Carter, Keith Byars and Tom Tupa who would become longtime pros, but even the best teams struggle when they don't take care of the ball. The Buckeyes were leading the Big Ten in turnover ratio with just seven lost before Wisconsin linebacker Michael Reid changed all of that by recovering three fumbles in the second half. The first one led to the winning touchdown, and the second came at the Wisconsin three-yard line with 9 minutes 45 seconds remaining and helped preserve the victory.

The Badgers got Ohio State's attention when Todd Gregoire kicked two field goals on their first two possessions, but a 37-yard touchdown pass from quarterback Jim Karsatos to Carter late in the second quarter gave the Buckeyes a 7-6 lead at halftime.

Reid recovered his first fumble when Karsatos and freshman running back Vince Workman, who was filling in for an injured Byars, mishandled a handoff at the Ohio State 22 with 4:38 remaining in the third period. Four plays later, freshman fullback Marvin Artley scored from the one to put Wisconsin back on top. A two-point try for the conversion failed, but the Badgers had all the points they needed for one of the biggest upsets in their history.

They were elated. The Buckeyes were grumpy. Asked after the game why McClain seemed to have his number, Ohio State coach Earl Bruce said, "You'll have to ask Dave McClain about that."

Bruce's demeanor wasn't improved the following week when the Buckeyes lost to Michigan and were relegated to the Citrus Bowl. The Badgers, meanwhile, got smoked, 41-7, by Michigan State in their finale at Camp Randall. But McClain wasn't discouraged. He told Hayes after the season that he thought the 1986 team would be his best ever. He never got a chance to find that out.

McClain had lost his mother, his father and a brother to heart attacks, and he was zealous about staying in shape. He liked to follow a strenuous workout on a stationary bike with some downtime in the sauna. That's where he was when he collapsed on April 28, 1986, at Camp Randall Stadium.

Dr. Stephen Zimmerman, an associate professor in the UW Medical School, found him. Five minutes later, the ambulance arrived, but McClain was unconscious when he was wheeled from the stadium on a stretcher. He was pronounced dead at 3:12 p.m. at St Mary's Hospital, and a whole campus went into mourning.

"Why someone so good?" asked senior linebacker Craig Raddatz. "He cared. I loved him because he was a real person, not just a coach behind a door."

JESS WILLARD DISAPPOINTS MILWAUKEE FIGHT FANS

NOVEMBER 17, 1913

He had the size and the skills to give the fans the bout they were expecting, but he was the first to admit he didn't have the heart. Jess Willard looked much more like a gentle giant than he did a future heavyweight champion of the world when he fought South African George Rodel at the Elite Roller Rink in Milwaukee.

The fight went the full scheduled 10 rounds as the much smaller Rodel took the action to the 6-foot-6, 220-pound Willard but could do no real damage. Willard jolted Rodel with a right uppercut to the jaw in the seventh round, but quickly backed off and allowed the bell to ring. The verdict was officially listed as a no-decision in accordance with state boxing laws at the time, although the local newspapers of the day gave the decision to Rodel.

"Awkward, clumsy, unable to move his feet, he was about as agile as a kangaroo with its tail cut off," Manning Vaughan wrote of Willard in the *Milwaukee Sentinel*. "Nerveless Willard Fights Rodel Lightly," blared the headline in the next day's *Milwaukee Daily News*. Willard himself might not have disputed the description. He had too much on his mind to put up a good fight.

In a bout three months earlier in Vernon, Cal., Willard had landed a hard uppercut to the jaw of William "Bull" Young, and Young had died from a brain hemorrhage. Willard had been charged with second-degree murder, according to the book *White Hopes and Other Tigers*, and although the charges were dropped he couldn't get that fight off of his mind.

"I could not fight. Poor Bull Young's face was always before me," he said after the Milwaukee bout. "I did not have the heart to strike Rodel."

That wasn't much consolation to a crowd of 2,000 that had come to see the man who was billed as the next "white hope" to dethrone heavyweight champion Jack Johnson. But the customers might not have been so disappointed if they'd known the real story.

Willard went into the fight game reluctantly and didn't have his first bout until he was 29 years old. Three years later, when he took a 17-2-1 record with two no decisions into his fight with Rodel, there also might have been some pre-fight shenanigans going on.

In John Lardner's 1947 book about "white hopes," he wrote that James J. Johnston, Rodel's manager, paid a visit to Willard in his dressing room before the fight and told him, "Jess, there's something I think you ought to know, for your own good. My Boer has got a very weak heart. A doctor told him a really good punch might kill him. You do what you like about it, but remember, there's a lot of tall trees around here for lynching a fellow that's killed two men in a row."

Willard later learned that it was a hoax, according to Lardner, and knocked out Rodel in two subsequent fights. Johnston, in turn, boasted that he delayed Willard's shot at Johnson for a year.

But Willard finally met the champion on April 15, 1915. The title bout was held in Havana, and it went 26 rounds before Willard won on a knockout. Johnson would claim later that he'd taken a dive, but Willard's supporters pointed out that if he were going to do that he wouldn't have waited 26 rounds.

Once Willard had won the championship, he wasn't particularly eager to defend it. He had only two fights in 1916, and one of those was a two-round exhibition. Then he took all of 1917 off and fought just two 10-round exhibitions in 1918.

Willard spent most of his time instead touring in Buffalo Bill's Wild West show, making up to $2,500 per appearance. But his gate appeal depended on his holding the title, and when a promoter offered him $100,000 to fight a young comer named Jack Dempsey, Willard couldn't pass up the bout.

Dempsey was also much smaller than Willard, but size didn't seem to matter when the two squared off on the Fourth of July, 1919, in Toledo, Ohio. Dempsey decked the "Pottawatomie Giant" seven times in the first round, and when the match ended after three rounds, the game Willard had broken ribs and a broken jaw.

He retired from boxing, but he was persuaded to make a comeback four years later. That ended badly when he was knocked out in eight rounds by Luis Firpo. Willard got into real estate after that and eventually opened a supermarket in Hollywood. He died Dec. 15, 1968, two weeks shy of his 87th birthday.

CLAY'S RECORD DAY RALLIES RACINE PARK

NOVEMBER 18, 2005

As Brent Moss was leading his school and its city to the 1988 state football championship, the people of Racine had to be thinking they'd never see a running back that good again. They were wrong. His successor was living across the street and getting his diaper changed.

It's strictly coincidence, of course, that John Clay was born the same year that Moss carried Park High School to the first Wisconsin Interscholastic Athletic Association football title in Racine's history. Or that he grew up at 2002 12th Street, directly across the street from the school. But it's a happy coincidence.

Seventeen years after Moss ran for three touchdowns and 202 yards in a 34-14 championship game romp past Superior, Clay topped him. He ran for three touchdowns and 259 yards at the expense of Wisconsin Rapids. When Clay was done, Park had the second WIAA football title in Racine's history.

If anything, Clay's performance was a little more dramatic than Moss'. The Panthers were trailing, 9-7, in the third quarter before Clay did most of his damage.

Wisconsin Rapids had contained him fairly well in the first half when he'd run for 83 yards and a three-yard touchdown. But Park had turned the ball over three times, and the Red Raiders weren't kidding themselves. "We did everything we could in the first half just to keep him where we did keep him," said Rapids coach Tony Biolo. "We knew he was going to break a few long ones, but we just had to respond to it."

Clay, who stood 6 feet 2 inches and weighed 220 pounds, broke the first long one on Park's first play of the second half. It went for 70 yards and a touchdown, and Rapids didn't respond to it well enough. Clay broke another one for 65 yards with 6 minutes 33 seconds left in the game. That put Park ahead, 21-9, and pretty much sealed its 28-9 victory. The Panthers' defense did the rest, and Clay played a major role in that, too. He finished with six tackles as a defensive end, two of them for losses.

Clay's 259 yards rushing set a Division 1 record and capped a junior season in which he scored 30 touchdowns and totaled 2,032 on 166 attempts for a ridiculous 12.2 yards per carry. Clay's numbers were made even more spectacular by the fact that he'd missed two games and most of a third early in the year with ankle problems.

So it didn't surprise anyone when he became the first junior ever to be named the Associated Press player of the year. Clay had already become only the third sophomore to make the AP's all-state first-team the year before.

"He's the best there is," said coach Joe Koch of conference rival Oak Creek. "This Clay is a man. I don't care what you draw up schematically. I don't care how many people you put in the box. He hits the hole like a freight train, and he makes those nice little cuts that almost go unnoticed, but he doesn't slow down."

Surprisingly, Clay did slow down his senior year. He'd hurt his hamstring during spring track season, and the injury lingered, retarding his summer conditioning and causing him to gain weight. And then he sprained his ankle in the second game of the year, and he didn't fully recover until the season finale.

Meanwhile, four of the five starting offensive linemen and the quarterback from the state title team had graduated, allowing opponents to concentrate almost exclusively on him. Park finished the season 4-5, and Clay's production dwindled to 1,485 yards.

Many college recruiters lost interest in him, but he was still a first team all-state choice, and he still received a Division I scholarship. He got it from the University of Wisconsin, the school that Moss had led to the 1994 Rose Bowl. It seems the comparisons were destined to go on.

Park coach Dennis Thompson had been a Panther assistant in 1988, so he knew Moss well. "I think Johnny's a step better," Thompson said.

In Racine football, there's no higher compliment than that.

BREWERS CARRY OUT "SATURDAY NIGHT MASSACRE"

NOVEMBER 19, 1977

News of the biggest front office shakeup in the Milwaukee Brewers' brief history broke at 10 o'clock on a Saturday night. What happened next was enough to make people wish the team made all of its major moves after normal business hours.

Gone were Vice President and Director of Baseball Operations Jim Baumer, Manager Alex Grammas and Director of Player Development Al Widmar. On its way were a new management team and the closest thing the Brewers would have to a golden age.

There had been rumblings as early as the World Series that Brewers President Bud Selig wanted to make changes, but when nothing happened for several weeks, it looked like nothing would. At least, it looked that way to Grammas.

"I wasn't shocked, but a little surprised they waited that long," he said. "You do it quickly or don't do it at all."

Or you do it like Richard Nixon. This was the Brewers' own "Saturday Night Massacre," a send-up of the president's 1973 late-night firing of special prosecutor Archibald Cox. Nixon left office within the year, but Selig wasn't going anywhere.

Within 48 hours after Hank Stoddard, sports director of WTMJ-TV, broke the news of the Brewers' purge, Selig introduced Harry Dalton as his new general manager. Under Dalton's reign as vice president of player personnel from 1966-'71, the Baltimore Orioles had won four American League pennants and two World Series.

Dalton left the Orioles following the 1971 season to become general manager of the California Angels, where he was much less successful. But his reputation in baseball circles was still intact. Dalton also was being squeezed out in California by Buzzie Bavasi, who had recently been hired by owner Gene Autry, and so Dalton was looking for a new opportunity.

He would take maximum advantage of this one, leading the Brewers on a six-year run of winning records highlighted by the team's only pennant in 1982. Before Dalton's arrival, the Brewers had endured eight losing seasons and had never finished any better than 10 games under .500.

Baumer was supposed to reverse the trend when he replaced Jim Wilson as director of baseball operations before the 1975 season, but he wasn't up to it. The Brewers went 201-284 in his three years in charge. Baumer hired Grammas, who had been a coach with the Cincinnati Reds, in his second year, and that didn't help. Grammas made some powerful enemies while winning 133 games and losing 190.

He was charged with failing to relate to young players, and he drew particularly heavy fire for a couple of incidents during the 1977 season. Grammas kept promising left-hander Billy Travers in for $7^2/_3$ innings during a brutal 18-hit, 14-run shelling in Cleveland in August. And he'd actually walked out of the dugout and up to his office in County Stadium during the last inning of a doubleheader on July 10 when the Brewers were swept by the Boston Red Sox.

"He lost the players' respect after that. And he could have ruined Travers' arm keeping him in that long," one club official told Lou Chapman of the *Milwaukee Sentinel.*

Grammas also had gotten into hot water by trying to protect two of his coaches, Jimmy Bragan and Hal Smith, and for trying to bounce another one. Word was that he considered first base coach Frank Howard to be a threat to his job. When Grammas was fired, Bragan and Smith were axed as well. Howard was retained.

Typically, the manager thought the team that had fired him was close to turning a corner, particularly after the Brewers had signed slugging free agent Larry Hisle to a six-year, $3 million contract 10 days earlier. "Now, with the addition of Hisle, and Paul Molitor looks like he will develop, the Brewers should be respectable," Grammas said.

Widmar, who had come with the franchise, also felt wronged. "They'd always mentioned that the kids were coming along well in the minors," he said. "I'm satisfied that I did a damn good job."

But Selig wasn't satisfied. "We are grieved by the whole situation," he said, "but we concluded after months of long and agonizing thought, that it simply was time for a change."

Brilliant conclusion. Dalton returned to his Baltimore roots and named Orioles pitching coach George Bamberger as his manager. The Brewers responded to Bamberger immediately and finished the 1978 season with a 93-69 record, a reversal of 26 games.

YOUNT WINS SECOND MVP AWARD

NOVEMBER 20, 1989

Robin Yount

Most baseball franchises have a face. When you think about them over time, you think of one man first. The New York Yankees have Babe Ruth, the Boston Red Sox have Ted Williams, the St. Louis Cardinals have Stan Musial, and the Milwaukee Brewers have Robin Yount.

Only two Brewers have ever been voted baseball's Most Valuable Player: Pitcher Rollie Fingers, the winner in 1981; and Yount, who won twice, although the balloting was much closer the second time around.

Yount had left no doubt when he missed being elected unanimously by one vote in 1982. This time, Yount, who was now 34 years old but still called "The Kid," edged out Texas outfielder Ruben Sierra by 28 points in one of the closest MVP races ever.

In a year when no one player dominated in the American League, six of them received first-place votes. And only 51 points separated the top four vote-getters. Baltimore shortstop Cal Ripken and Toronto outfielder George Bell finished third and fourth, respectively. In 1982, Yount won by 157 points over runner-up Eddie Murray of the Orioles.

When he won again seven years later, Yount became the first player to win the AL MVP award while performing for a team that didn't compile a winning record. The Brewers finished 81-81 and in fourth place in a tight AL East race. But four teams finished within eight games of division champ Toronto, and the Brewers were only a half-game out as late as Aug. 20.

Sierra had better power numbers with a .306 batting average, 29 home runs and 119 RBIs compared to Yount's .318, 21 and 103. But Sierra was shaky in the field, and the Rangers faded fast after a 17-5 start in April. They won two more games than the Brewers, but they, too, finished fourth, 16 games behind eventual World Series winner Oakland in the AL West.

While Yount finished in the league's top 10 in 12 offensive categories, he beat Sierra in only three: Batting average, hits and doubles.

Yount received the news with typical modesty and said the award also belonged to "my teammates, the organization and the great fans of Wisconsin."

Sierra was no gracious loser. "He had only the three statistics better than me," he said of Yount. "I don't think it's a good decision to call him the MVP. I feel sad, but there's nothing I can do about it."

Yount was the first multiple winner since Mickey Mantle captured his third MVP award 27 years earlier. And he joined Detroit's Hank Greenberg and Musial as the only players to win the award at two different positions. Yount had been a shortstop until 1985 when a shoulder injury sent him to the outfield.

He played four more years after winning his second MVP award, and then, with his skills fading, he turned down a $3.2 million offer and called it a career after 20 years with the same team.

What a career it was. Yount retired as the Brewers' all-time leader in at bats, total bases, walks, runs, hits, doubles, triples, home runs and RBIs. He also is a member of baseball's exclusive 3,000-hit club. But curiously, he made the All-Star team only three times, and one of those times wasn't 1989 when he won the MVP.

If that mattered to Yount, he never said so. He said the best time he ever had in baseball came in 1982, but that wasn't because he'd won his first MVP. It was because the Brewers won their only pennant that year.

Although Yount never led the league in hitting, home runs or RBIs, it was a foregone conclusion that he would be voted into the Baseball Hall of Fame the first time he became eligible in 1999.

"Robin Yount is close to a fictional player, something out of Kevin Costner's dreams," Tom Trebelhorn, who managed Yount from 1987 through '91, once said. "He is the pure baseball player."

HACKBART DRIVES BADGERS TO BIG TEN TITLE

NOVEMBER 21, 1959

Coach Milt Bruhn hadn't even been born yet when the University of Wisconsin won its last outright Big Ten football championship. Star back Dale Hackbart was in ninth grade when UW had shared its only other title in the 47 years since. That's how rare the opportunity was when the two of them led the Badgers into Memorial Stadium in Minneapolis for their last regular-season game of the 1959 season.

At stake was not only the league championship, but a bid to the Rose Bowl in Pasadena. And Wisconsin had played there only once since the Big Ten lifted its ban on post-season play and entered into an agreement to play a Pacific Coast Conference team, starting with the 1947 Rose Bowl.

Clearly, a victory over the University of Minnesota in this latest installment of the oldest rivalry in major college football would set some kind of record for perseverance for the Badgers. While they had shared the Big Ten title in 1952 with Purdue and gone to their only Rose Bowl, they hadn't won the championship outright since 1912, the year before Bruhn was born.

Moreover, after being ranked No. 6 in the Associated Press pre-season poll, the Badgers' whole season had been a struggle. They started with a 16-14 non-conference squeaker over Stanford, a team that would finish 3-7. Including the opener, five of UW's six victories had come by nine points or fewer, while the two losses were a 21-0 whipping at the hands of Purdue and a last-second, 9-6 homecoming heartbreak against Illinois the week before.

But if Wisconsin could beat the last-place Gophers and get some help from Illinois, it would become the first team to finish all alone on top of the Big Ten standings with two losses.

In Hackbart, Bruhn's senior quarterback, the Badgers had a strong leader. The Madison native was on his way to leading the Big Ten in total offense with 319 yards rushing and 367 passing while becoming a first-team all-conference pick. He also played some ferocious defense.

The line featured tackle Dan Lanphear, another Madison native, and a consensus All-American, along with guard Jerry Stalcup, an all-Big Ten choice. Bob Zeman, one of the starting halfbacks, would play six years in the old American Football League.

The Badgers' afternoon started well as Illinois jumped in front of Northwestern and rolled to a 28-0 victory, while Bruhn kept his players abreast of the score. Northwestern entered the day tied with Wisconsin at 4-2 and was the only team that could tie the Badgers for the title. Meanwhile, with "Paul Bunyan's Axe," at stake, the Gophers were eager spoilers.

They waited exactly four plays before sophomore quarterback Sandy Stephens threw a 57-yard touchdown pass that gave them a 7-0 lead that they kept through halftime. The Gophers were still leading late in the third quarter when defensive back Bob Altmann, who had replaced an injured Zeman, intercepted his second pass of the game and returned it 27 yards to the Minnesota eight-yard line. Bruhn called the play the turning point of the day. While Wisconsin came away with only a field goal by Karl Holzwarth, it at least put the Badgers on the scoreboard.

Hackbart took charge after that. He directed the Badgers on an 80-yard drive on their next possession and capped it himself with a quarterback sneak for a touchdown. On the extra point, Hackbart pulled off a fake out of kick formation and hit end Hank Derleth in the end zone for a two-point conversion that put Wisconsin up, 11-7, with eight minutes to play.

There would be no more scoring, but there would be a lot more suspense. The Badgers stopped one Minnesota drive on their 10-yard line, and they needed an interception by Hackbart as time expired to assure the victory. He finished his day with 74 yards rushing and 149 yards passing, as well as the game clinching theft and a 56-yard quick kick.

When the gun sounded, elements of an estimated 6,000 Badger fans stormed the field, while Hackbart's teammates carried him off on their shoulders. On the streets of Madison, meanwhile, pandemonium broke loose. "I've been through wringers before," said Bruhn, "but never any like this."

He would have one more wringer to go, and it proved to be much more painful. The Badgers went to Pasadena in a party mood and got drilled, 44-8, by Washington.

LOMBARDI TAKES WORST LICKING IN DETROIT

NOVEMBER 22, 1962

A great linebacker, Ray Nitschke was also a better than average prognosticator after he watched the Detroit Lions kick the stuffing out of the Green Bay Packers on Thanksgiving Day. It would prove to be the most humiliating defeat of the Vince Lombardi dynasty, but Nitshcke was determined to take it in stride.

"We were due to lose one," he said, "but one is all we'll lose."

Nitschke was correct. The Packers went on to win their next three games to finish the regular season, 13-1, and they defended their NFL championship with a victory over the New York Giants. But they were mauled so badly at Tiger Stadium that day that to label it merely a loss was a euphemism of the highest order.

Nitschke's defensive unit actually had a decent afternoon, intercepting two passes and recovering three fumbles. But Green Bay's offense was a study in confusion, and quarterback Bart Starr was a major insurance risk by the time Detroit got through with him. The 26-14 final score didn't begin to do justice to the Lions.

The Lions had a great linebacker in Joe Schmidt and an extremely talented secondary led by Dick "Night Train" Lane and Yale Lary, but the best part of their defense was their front four, featuring Alex Karras and Roger Brown. A quick and powerful unit, it was virtually unstoppable when it chose to be tricky as well.

Stunting and/or blitzing on almost every play of the first half, Detroit's pass rushers spent more time in the Packers' backfield than the Packers. "We couldn't find them," said tackle Forrest Gregg, although that shouldn't have been a problem. They just had to locate Starr and see who was lying on top of him.

Usually it was Brown, who claimed to have six sacks that day, although sacks weren't an official statistic at the time. The terminology didn't matter to Starr. He just knew that he'd been tackled on the wrong side of the line of scrimmage 11 times for 109 yards in losses.

This could only be the work of an angry group, and the Lions clearly qualified. They'd finished second to the Packers in 1960 and '61, and then they'd lost to them, 9-7, on a slick field in the fourth week of the season in Green Bay. They really thought they should have won that game, and they were almost maniacally dedicated to winning this one.

Their fans were pretty pumped, too. Hundreds of them stood in line outside the stadium the night before hoping to buy the few remaining tickets. When the gates were opened on a cold, dark and blustery Michigan morning, 58,431 people swarmed in to see the proud Packers brought to their knees.

This was by all accounts Vince Lombardi's best team. It had won 11 straight regular-season games going back to the 1961 finale, and it was a logical choice to retain the championship it had captured the previous year by thumping the New York Giants, 37-0, in the NFL title game. But logic fled the premises in a matter of 18 minutes 16 seconds while Detroit was racing to a 23-0 lead.

Milt Plum threw a 33-yard touchdown pass to end Gail Cogdill to put the Lions up, 7-0, and then he threw another one of 27 yards to Cogdill to make it 14-0 with just 58 seconds gone in the second quarter. Meanwhile, Starr was running for his life, and Brown, at the time a rare 300-pounder with exceptional speed, kept catching him.

Just 21 seconds after Plum threw his second touchdown pass, the Detroit giant nailed Starr hard enough to force a fumble that defensive end Sam Williams returned six yards for a touchdown. Four plays later, Brown ran Starr down in the end zone for a safety. The score was 23-0 at halftime, and it became 26-0 when Plum kicked a 47-yard field goal after Lane had intercepted a Starr pass on the second play of the second half.

The Packers managed two fourth-quarter touchdowns, thanks largely to an interception and a fumble recovery, but the players had no illusions. Their offense ended the day with a net gain of 13 yards, and their line had been thoroughly whipped.

When it was over, Lombardi seemed almost relieved by the spanking. He thought his players were showing the strain of the 11-game winning streak, and now the pressure was off. "We'll be a lot better ballclub for it," he said.

For one day at least, it was hard to imagine them being much worse.

CHARLES MARTIN BODY-SLAMS BEARS' McMAHON

NOVEMBER 23, 1986

This is how bad it had gotten between the Green Bay Packers and the Chicago Bears when they met for the second time of the season at Soldier Field. Several of the Packers' defensive players came onto the field with white towels hanging from their waists. Scrawled on the towels were the numbers of different Bears offensive players.

The Bears thought the towels represented hit lists – players the Packers would be trying to take out of the game. The Packers insisted they were just players they wanted to slow down. Only the Green Bay defenders knew which version was correct, but one thing was certain. There was a No. 9 on Charles Martin's towel, the number of Bears quarterback Jim McMahon.

Pro football's oldest series was edging past rivalry and bordering on assault when the two teams collided for the 132nd time in the regular season. Bears coach Mike Ditka had gone on TV and said the Packers had become a band of thugs since Bart Starr had been replaced by Forrest Gregg as head coach. Two months earlier before their first meeting of the season, safety Ken Stills had promised that the Packers would pick McMahon up and dump him on his separated right shoulder.

As it turned out, McMahon didn't play in that game, and it was relatively free of extracurricular activity. Still, the bad blood between the two teams was boiling. In the second of the two games in 1985, Stills had been whistled for a hit on fullback Matt Suhey that was so late the Bears were practically back in their huddle.

Now these bitter enemies were at it again with Chicago owning a 9-2 record and aiming for a second straight Super Bowl, whereas the Packers were 2-9 with nothing to lose.

McMahon's shoulder had kept him out of the last three games, but he was ready for this one, and that gave the Packers a chance to make good on Stills' threat, albeit a game later. Martin, a 6-foot-3, 275-pound nose tackle who had been signed by the Packers in 1984 as a free agent after being cut by Birmingham of the United States Football League, was the man who carried it out.

With 7 minutes 55 seconds to play in the second quarter, McMahon threw a pass that was intercepted by cornerback Mark Lee. As McMahon turned and walked away from the play, Martin roared in from behind, picked the quarterback up and body-slammed him onto the hard artificial turf. McMahon landed on his injured shoulder.

Referee Jerry Markbreit immediately threw a flag, penalizing the Packers 15 yards and ejecting Martin from the game. When Martin got to the sidelines, several teammates high-fived him. He was showered by beer as he was escorted off the field.

The play fired up the Bears. About a minute later, they blocked a Don Bracken punt and recovered it in the end zone for their only touchdown in a 12-10 victory. McMahon stayed in the game until the fourth quarter and stunk up the place, completing only 12 of 32 passes with three interceptions before Ditka replaced him.

The Bears were livid after the game. "That wasn't just bad, it was cheap, the cheapest play I've ever seen," said cornerback Dave Duerson. "I think he was trying to end Jim's career... Rozelle is going to have to step in."

NFL Commissioner Pete Rozelle did exactly that. Two days later, he suspended Martin without pay for two games. It was the stiffest penalty Rozelle had handed out for an on-field incident in 26 years as commissioner, and it cost Martin $15,000.

But the play cost the Bears much more. On the same day, they announced that McMahon would undergo shoulder surgery and miss the rest of the season. Many believed all hopes of a Chicago dynasty ended that day. The Bears had one of the most formidable defenses in NFL history, and they had Walter Payton, probably one of the two or three greatest running backs the league had ever seen. But McMahon was never the same again, and without their quarterback, the Bears fell short.

Martin apologized later that week, calling the incident the worst moment of his life. "It's like committing a terrible crime," he told the *Green Bay Press-Gazette*.

There would be many worse moments in Martin's life. He was released by the Packers in September 1987 following a number of off-field fracases. He also spent time in an alcohol treatment facility before the Packers cut him. Kidney failure claimed him in 2005 when he died at the age of 46.

SAPP'S BLOCK ENRAGES MIKE SHERMAN

NOVEMBER 24, 2002

Looking at the statistics of the Green Bay Packers' disappointing late-season loss at Tampa Bay, it was hard to tell that Warren Sapp was even there. No tackles, no sacks, no fumbles caused or recovered.

There was just this one crushing block, and it sent tackle Chad Clifton to the hospital and Mike Sherman over the edge.

The Packers were clinging to a 7-6 lead with 7 minutes 27 seconds to play in the third quarter when Brett Favre threw an interception. The ball was intended for wide receiver Terry Glenn, but it went to Bucs cornerback Brian Kelly instead, and Kelly took off up the sideline for 31 yards. Clifton was on the other side of the field jogging behind the play. There was no chance that he could ever catch Kelly when suddenly he was leveled by 305 pounds of Sapp.

As Clifton lay on the turf, Tampa Bay's star defensive tackle did a little dance celebrating the hit. At least, that's the way Sherman saw it, and his view led directly to an ugly post-game confrontation between the 29-year-old all-pro and the 47-year-old head coach.

Sherman was feeling pretty grumpy anyhow after the Packers faded badly in the second half and lost the game, 21-7. Favre had gone on to throw three more interceptions as 12 of his team's 13 possessions had ended either in a punt or a pick. That gave him seven interceptions in Green Bay's last two games, both road losses. The Packers were 8-3 and definitely in a funk, and now they were facing life without their starting left tackle.

Clifton had to be placed on a stretcher and taken away on a cart before being driven to a local hospital. His symptoms included numbness in his legs and fingers, and all because of a hit that Sherman considered totally unnecessary even if it was legal. But it wasn't the block that infuriated the coach so much as the fact that Sapp seemed to enjoy it so completely.

The assistant coaches in the press box told him that Sapp was laughing on the sidelines while Clifton lay motionless on the field, and Sherman was determined to let the Bucs' big man know he didn't see anything funny about the play. So determined in fact that after shaking hands with opposing coach Jon Gruden following the game, Sherman actually asked directions from a Tampa player as he hunted down Sapp. Then he waited for him to finish a TV interview.

What followed was a shouting match that would be replayed on network TV for days. Sherman told Sapp it was a "chicken-shit hit." Sapp told Sherman that if he was so tough he should "put a jersey on." Sapp liked that line so much that he repeated it three times. Other less delicate words were exchanged before Sapp had to be restrained and Sherman pulled away by Packers security personnel.

The argument didn't end there. "He's lucky I'm not 25 without kids and a conscience," Sapp said of Sherman in a post-game interview. He also instructed reporters to tell Sherman "to carry his tail home with that loss."

Clifton's recovery took time. He was transferred to a Green Bay hospital where he stayed until the following Saturday, then he left in a wheelchair. Meanwhile, recriminations flew from both sides.

"I don't think you approach a player after a game," said Gruden. "There were some unethical plays on their side of the ball, too... I'm not going up to those players after the game and asking them to please not do that."

If Sherman said please, nobody heard it. As for ethics, Larry Beightol, Clifton's position coach, made it clear that they would be out the window the next time the Packers saw Sapp. "Everyone is fair game," he said. "When we see him again, we'll see how that dog fares. We'll cut him every single time. I want him to know that."

The NFL office, meanwhile, chose not to take any action against Sapp, Sherman or anyone else involved. The Packers lost Clifton for the rest of the year, and while he didn't need surgery, he was unable to walk on his own for nearly six weeks. Then he required extensive rehabilitation to recover from what was diagnosed as a badly sprained pelvis. But Clifton was able to play all 16 games the following year, and he said later that he bore no ill will toward Sapp.

Six years later, Sherman was coaching a college team and Sapp was on *Dancing with the Stars.* Clifton was still playing for the Packers.

PACKERS SIGN BOB MANN, THEIR FIRST BLACK PLAYER

NOVEMBER 25, 1950

The Green Bay Packers were NFL pioneers in many ways, but race relations weren't among them. Curly Lambeau never had a black man play for him, and it wasn't until Gene Ronzani took over as head coach that the team's color line disappeared.

This wasn't unusual for NFL franchises. As early as 1922 the old Milwaukee Badgers had three African-American players in back Fritz Pollard, end Paul Robeson and tackle Duke Slater. Pollard was inducted into the Pro Football Hall of Fame in 2005 and Slater was a two-time finalist in the voting, but from 1934 through '45 black players mysteriously vanished from the league.

Finally, one year before Jackie Robinson made Major League Baseball history in 1947, Kenny Washington and Woody Strode signed with the Los Angeles Rams. It took the Packers four more years to catch up, and still they were the first Wisconsin major professional sports team of the so-called modern era to crack the racial barrier.

Strangely, while it took the Packers almost 32 years to hire a black player, they couldn't wait to get him into a game once they did. End Bob Mann signed on a Saturday and caught his first pass on Sunday as the Packers beat the San Francisco 49ers, 25-21, at Green Bay's City Stadium. Mann would catch 108 more passes and score 17 touchdowns before a knee injury ended his career two games into the 1954 season, raising the question of what the Packers were waiting for.

Mann was wondering the same thing after he led the league in receiving yardage for Detroit in 1949. He caught 66 passes for 1,014 yards for the Lions, and they rewarded him by cutting his salary $1,500. When Mann refused to take the cut, the Lions traded him to the New York Yanks for quarterback Bobby Layne. Layne would go to the Hall of Fame, but Mann would never play a down for New York. The claim was that the 5-foot-11, 175-pound Mann was too small to handle his blocking assignments, and the Yanks waived him before the season.

The former Michigan standout thought there might be some other reason why he had been let go. He doubted that the Yanks ever planned to use him, and when nobody picked him up, he charged that he'd been "railroaded" out of the league. It wasn't until the 10th game of the 12-game 1950 season that the Packers signed him as a free agent.

Ronzani, in his first year as coach, had signed two other black players the day before training camp started. They were guard James "Shag" Thomas and halfback James Clark, both World War II veterans who had played at Ohio State. But neither of them made the team. Mann not only made it, he led the Packers with 50 receptions in 1951, and he was a starter for the next two seasons as well.

Athletically, Mann and Green Bay were a good fit. Socially, it could have been worse. "I really didn't have much of a problem," Mann said in a 1996 interview with the *Milwaukee Journal Sentinel*. "When I needed to socialize, I just went to Milwaukee or Chicago."

Mann still had to stay in a different hotel from his white teammates when the team was on the road, but he said that was never an issue in Green Bay. The only issue Mann had with the Packers came when they let him go and he sued them for $25,000, claiming they had cut him illegally while he was injured. But in the end there were no hard feelings. Mann was inducted into the Packer Hall of Fame in 1988.

Once he broke the color barrier in Wisconsin pro sports, other players weren't far behind. Robert Wilson, a 6-4 forward from West Virginia State, was believed to be the first African-American to play for a Wisconsin pro basketball team when he signed with the Milwaukee Hawks, less than a week after they moved from the Tri-Cities in September 1951. The minor league Milwaukee Brewers signed their first black player, first baseman Leonard Pearson, in July 1950, but Major League Baseball didn't come to the city until three years later. Baseball's Braves had already signed their first black player, outfielder Sam Jethroe, in 1950 when they were still in Boston.

Mann became an attorney in Detroit after leaving football. When he died in 2006, he was eulogized as a trailblazer for all the black athletes who followed him on Wisconsin's pro sports teams.

BLACK PLAYERS BOYCOTT UW FOOTBALL BANQUET

NOVEMBER 26, 1968

Director Stanley Kramer won two Oscars with his 1967 movie *Guess Who's Coming to Dinner?*, a commentary on modern American race relations. A year later, the University of Wisconsin was doing a takeoff. Call it "Guess Who's Not?"

Hours before the school's annual football banquet, the players gathered to vote for the team's Most Valuable Player and to elect a captain for the following season. Everyone was there. But when the dinner began at the UW Fieldhouse with a crowd of more than 800 on hand, 18 varsity players were missing. All of them were African-American.

In fact, the only black players who showed up for the banquet were four members of the freshman team. UW officials claimed to be flummoxed by the absence of the others. University President Fred Harrington called it "sort of a protest," while Athletic Director Ivy Williamson said he had no idea what led to it. Public relations director Harvey Breucher theorized it might be an extension of general demonstrations going on around campus.

Only John Coatta acknowledged having a clue. "Some of this protest cropped up last week, and tonight is a part of it," said the head coach. None of the boycotting players was available for comment.

But they would have plenty to say later as would their white teammates, their coaches and university administrators. Charges ranging from racism to treason flew all over Madison in the next two weeks, and while this drama lacked the likes of Sidney Poitier and Katharine Hepburn, it had a thicker plot.

It probably wouldn't have been staged at all if the football team hadn't been so abysmal. Coatta had taken over for Milt Bruhn two years earlier and turned a 3-6-1 squad into a 0-9-1 outfit, and then the Badgers got worse. They were coming off a 0-10 year when the flak began to fly.

The day after the boycott, two black players speaking anonymously made it clear that it was about football and only football.

The next week after the 18 black players met with the UW athletic board, receiver Mel Reddick served as their spokesman at a press conference where he offered few details about their grievances. But it seemed clear that part of the problem was Coatta's staff. It was all white except for assistant Les Ritcherson, who happened to be the father of backup quarterback Lew Ritcherson.

By then, rumors had been floating around that the black players had threatened to boycott something much more than a banquet – namely the Badgers' final game against Minnesota. There were denials, but no one disputed that the locker room had been highly explosive before the game. White quarterback John Ryan said, "There are some white players on the team who don't like black people," but he doubted that that had affected the Badgers' performance.

Following a series of meetings, including one involving the black players, the grievances were eventually brought out into the open.

The black players alleged that they were being switched from positions that they'd been recruited for and stacked up in spots where they'd be competing with each other. They also said they'd been largely excluded from recruiting new players and not been allowed to move out of dormitories in their first two years the way white players were. They also wanted a fifth year of scholarship help for all players after their eligibility elapsed.

And, as many had speculated, there was one more thing. They wanted the coaching staff "re-evaluated." English translation: They wanted up to four coaches fired.

Only one left, and he didn't do it quietly. Gene Felker, a former Badger star and Coatta's line coach, resigned nine days after the boycott saying the whole mess left him "sick to his stomach." He ripped the administration for being "frightened," "soft," and "prejudiced," and he charged the black players with treason for their actions before the Minnesota game. He went on to say that Ritcherson had been given a five-year personal contract with the university president when all of the other assistants got only one because the school had leaned on Bruhn to hire a minority coach.

Coatta said he was shocked by Felker's resignation. No matter, the UW board of regents pledged their support of Coatta. That support lasted one more dismal season.

PACKERS NAME WOLF GENERAL MANAGER

NOVEMBER 27, 1991

Four years is a long time not to take no for an answer, but Bob Harlan was Iowa stubborn. When the Green Bay Packers were in the market for someone to run their football operation Harlan knew just the man for the job, even though that man had already taken a pass on the position in 1987.

Harlan was on his way to becoming the Packers' president then, but he didn't know it at the time. His title was corporate assistant to the president, and his duties included such sacred missions as picking people up from airports. In this case, he'd been dispatched to welcome a personnel administrator from the Los Angeles Raiders named Ron Wolf.

Wolf had flown to Green Bay to interview with then president Robert Parins for the position of vice president of football operations, and he was famished when he got off the plane. Harlan had given him the typical Wisconsin red-carpet reception. He'd taken him to the local Denny's restaurant and bought him a hamburger.

Over the next three hours the two talked about everything from the Packers' corporate structure to Wolf's brief unsatisfying tenure as a vice president in Tampa Bay. When they finally broke up after midnight, Wolf felt he'd found a friend, and Harlan hoped the Packers had found a general manager.

He vowed that night that if Wolf wasn't hired he'd go back to him if the job ever came open again and he had anything to say about it. Wolf took himself out of the running soon after the interview, and Atlanta's Tom Braatz got the job.

Four years later, Harlan was the team's chief executive officer, and he was shooing Braatz out the door. The organizational inertia that had started long before Braatz got there was becoming more and more strangulating. It had contributed to the Packers' 25-37-1 record in Braatz's first four years, and they were headed toward a 4-12 season in 1991. They were 2-9 when Harlan fired Braatz and went after Wolf.

Harlan had heard from his friend, New York Giants General Manager George Young, that other teams were interested in Wolf, and so he wasted no time in going to the Packers' executive committee on Nov. 20 and telling the members he wanted to make a change even though the season still had five games to run. They told him to go ahead.

Braatz was out of town at the time, and Harlan was forced to give him the bad news over the phone. Then he called the New York Jets to get permission to talk to Wolf, who had joined them almost a year-and-a-half earlier as director of player personnel. Once that was obtained, Harlan finally had his chance to make his own pitch.

It was the first time the two had talked since the burgers at Denny's, but it didn't take them long to get reacquainted. Harlan had a contract, a salary and a description of duties all in hand, and he faxed them to Wolf, who was on a scouting trip at the time. That was on a Friday afternoon. On Saturday morning, Wolf called back and said they had a deal.

Wolf had spent 25 years working for Al Davis and the Raiders, but he'd interrupted that run with two years at Tampa Bay where he'd gotten badly stung in a turf war. Harlan promised him absolute control over all football decisions at Green Bay along with a reported $400,000 a year salary. But it was the control issue that got Wolf's attention.

Harlan also wanted to get the fans' attention, because there had been talk that he and the executive committee were micromanaging the football operation. When Wolf was introduced on Nov. 27, as the Packers' new executive vice president and general manager, Harlan kept emphasizing the words "total authority."

Wolf clearly made the most of his power. The Packers had advanced to the playoffs just twice in 24 years from 1968 through '91. They made them six times and went to two Super Bowls over the next seven years. A franchise that many thought would be left for dead if free agency ever hit the league compiled the best regular-season record in the NFL from 1993, when free agency came into being, through the end of Wolf's tenure.

Wolf fired coach Lindy Infante within a month after taking the job. He replaced him with Mike Holmgren three weeks later, and he made the greatest trade in franchise history, a month after that when he gambled on an unproven, young quarterback named Brett Favre. And when Wolf finally retired after the 2000 season, Harlan could still taste that Denny's hamburger.

CLASS OF 14 INAUGURATES WISCONSIN HALL OF FAME

NOVEMBER 28, 1951

Connie Mack's dinner was getting cold. Even legends have to eat, but with hundreds of people asking for his autograph, baseball's grandest old man couldn't put his pen down long enough to pick up his fork.

He wasn't the only one having that trouble. Some of the greatest names in sport were sharing the attention of 800 fellow diners and another 1,000 or so assorted students and musicians sitting in the bleachers at the Milwaukee Arena. The occasion was the installation of 14 charter members into the brand new Wisconsin Athletic Hall of Fame.

Among the inductees were baseball's Charles "Kid" Nichols, Al Simmons and Addie Joss. All three were Wisconsin natives. Nichols was born in Madison, Simmons in Milwaukee and Joss in Woodland. All three are enshrined at Cooperstown today.

Former Green Bay Packer stars Don Hutson and Clarke Hinkle were inducted as was Ernie Nevers, who grew up in Superior, and played for both the Duluth Eskimos and Chicago Cardinals. Hutson and Nevers were inducted as charter members of the Pro Football Hall of Fame when it opened in 1963; and Hinkle was voted in a year later. Nevers still holds the NFL record for most points scored in a single game. He scored 40 for the Cardinals against the Chicago Bears in 1929.

Track was represented by Ralph Metcalfe, a star sprinter at Marquette; and bowling by Charles Daw and boxing by Richie Mitchell, both of whom were from Milwaukee. Mitchell, who won nearly 50 fights in a pro career that spanned 11 years, was best known for his game showing against the legendary Benny Leonard in a world lightweight championship bout in 1921. Even pro wrestling was represented by Ed "Strangler" Lewis, who was from Nekoosa.

The college football contingent included Bob Zuppke, a native of Germany who graduated from Milwaukee West Division High School before becoming the winningest coach in the history of the University of Illinois; and former Wisconsin stars Pat O'Dea and Dave Schreiner. A native of Lancaster, Schreiner was killed on Okinawa near the end of World War II and was honored by a poignant rendition of "Taps." The UW band also sang *Varsity* in his honor.

One other inductee also was a former major league star, Clarence "Ginger" Beaumont, a native of Rochester, Wis., in Racine County, and the first player to bat in a World Series game. He was in poor health, but he was determined not to miss the event. He arrived by ambulance from his home in Burlington, and he rallied gamely when he was greeted by the immortal Cy Young and Deacon Phillippe, the starting pitchers in that 1903 milestone game.

The 88-year-old Mack was there to unveil Simmons' plaque. He called the local slugger his all-time greatest player, which took in a lot of territory. After his 11-year major league playing career came to an end, Mack took over as manager of Milwaukee's franchise in the Western League from 1897-'99. In 1900, he was manager of the Milwaukee Brewers in the American League – then a minor league – and then he served as manager of the Philadelphia Athletics for the next 50. He won five World Series and four other American League pennants, and managed several other Hall of Fame players, including Jimmie Foxx and Mickey Cochrane. Mack even managed "Shoeless Joe" Jackson at the start of his career and Ty Cobb at the end of his.

Young was there to present Joss' plaque, and Olympic great Jesse Owens had come to do the same for Metcalfe. It was an eclectic mix, and the athletes were as awed as the audience. They were taking programs around to be signed by each other.

The driving force behind the creation of the Hall of Fame and the selection of the one-year-old Arena as its home was Milwaukee City Treasurer Joe Krueger.

The organizers had been hoping to sell 1,400 dinner tickets and fill the Arena stands with onlookers. But the sales fell 600 short, and the stands weren't close to sold out. That was fine with the hundreds of youngsters, and high school and college band members who were sitting in the crowd. They were there to watch, perform and eventually to collect autographs from the stars.

Four people were honored posthumously. Three were represented by their widows and the other by his mother. The other ten were all there.

Dinner was $10 a plate and worth it. Connie Mack ate for free. If he ate at all.

PACKERS CAPTURE THIRD STRAIGHT NFL TITLE

NOVEMBER 29, 1931

According to one newspaper account the field was "knee deep in goo" when the Green Bay Packers faced the Brooklyn Dodgers in New York, and the same might be said of the economy.

The Packers needed a victory to clinch the National Football League championship, and if they could pull it off, it would provide a big dose of civic pride for a city mired in the Great Depression.

This was the last of three games in eight days on an eastern road trip for Curly Lambeau's crew, which had knocked off the New York Giants and Providence Steam Roller in the first two to boost its record to 11-1. Championships were decided by the final standings at the time – the first NFL championship game between division winners wasn't played until 1933 – and a 12-1 mark would leave Green Bay all alone at the top of the standings where nobody could reach them.

A modest crowd of 10,000 people ventured to Ebbets Field to cheer the Dodgers, who were 2-10 going in, and they later went home damp and dissatisfied. Left halfback Verne Lewellen scored the game's only touchdown on a two-yard run in the first quarter, and the rest of the game was mud wrestling. The ball spurted out of Lewellen's hands after he crossed the goal line, but the official ruled he had scored, and the Packers by virtue of their 7-0 victory became the first team ever to win three NFL titles in a row. Only the 1965-'67 Packers have done it since.

"We've never had a bunch of men so eager to win, so willing to train and stay in physical condition as this 1931 squad," said Lambeau. "During the entire eastern trip... the players displayed a willingness to keep every single training rule, even to getting to bed early at night."

The coach's praise was topped by no less a personage than famous American sportswriter Grantland Rice, who called the Packers "the best team ever to play football," adding that they could defeat any team in the country by several touchdowns.

But the plaudits that mattered most to the Packers came from the people at home, and there were thousands of them waiting to meet their train at the Milwaukee Road depot when they arrived on Tuesday night, two days after the game. The local American Legion band and the Boy Scouts led the welcoming party, and the station was festooned in blue and gold, the team's original colors. When the players finally made their way through the crowd and onto the bus that would take them to the nearby Astor Hotel where some of their families were waiting, they moved at a snail's pace. Crowds lined Washington Street and kids jumped onto the bumpers of the bus.

A city starved for good news couldn't get enough of its football team, and that didn't go unnoticed by the national media. A full page editorial in *Editor and Publisher* magazine praised Green Bay for its efforts to pull out of the Depression.

"The other day the national professional football championship was won by the Green Bay Packers for the third consecutive playing season," the editorial read. "The Packers are one of the elements of justified local pride. Half-hearted people of other communities might have greeted this triumph with the usual hip-hooray, with a couple of tigers and a goal-post parade, their real spirits, however, neatly concealed in depression's boots. But Green Bay isn't built that way. She thinks she can, and by golly she can!" It wasn't clear where the tigers were coming from, but the message came through.

For all the hoopla, the city didn't schedule an official celebration because the Packers still had a game to play. And as it happened, they lost it, 7-6, to the Bears in Chicago, leaving them with a 12-2 record.

The second-place Portsmouth Spartans, who finished 11-3, claimed that they had tentatively scheduled a game with the Packers for Dec. 13 – the two teams never met during the 1931 season – but it wasn't listed on the official schedule. NFL President Joe Carr ruled that the Packers didn't have to play, and they didn't. Green Bay had its championship, and it wasn't taking any chances on giving it back.

AMECHE NAMED HEISMAN WINNER

NOVEMBER 30, 1954

Alan Ameche

With deep ties to the auto industry and as the home of an American Motors Corporation plant, Kenosha knew a little something about horsepower in the fifties. The city produced Nash and Hudson cars for the nation's motorists, and it produced Alan Ameche for college football.

The former Kenosha High School star earned the nickname "The Horse" while starring at fullback for four years at the University of Wisconsin. And when his collegiate career was over, he earned something much bigger. More than 1,000 sportswriters and sportscasters throughout the country voted him the 20th winner of the Heisman Trophy.

There was no higher individual honor in college football, and so when its native son won it, Kenosha knew just how to mark the occasion. Six weeks after the Heisman announcement, civic leaders held a dinner in Ameche's honor at the Eagles Club and showered him with gifts. It was one heavy shower.

Among the presentations was a 1,500-pound horse. Ameche was also given a bushelbasket full of $1 bills that added up to $3,212 or a buck for every yard he'd gained for the Badgers. And he received a new wardrobe, a ride in a fire engine and, of course, a new car. In this case, it was a 1955 Hudson Hornet made right there in Kenosha.

The palomino that was presented to Ameche was brought up by elevator to the third floor and he dutifully climbed into the saddle to pose for newspaper pictures, but it wasn't for him to keep. Besides, his wife, Yvonne, was terrified of horses.

The Heisman Trophy, on the other hand, was something that Ameche got to take home, although the fanfare surrounding it wasn't anything like it is today. First and foremost, the announcement about the award, which was made on Nov. 30, preceded the dinner by nine days.

Ameche won the voting in a landslide. He received 1,068 points compared to 838 for runner-up Kurt Burris, Oklahoma's All-American center. Ohio State halfback Howard "Hopalong" Cassady finished third; Notre Dame quarterback Paul Guglielmi, fourth; and California quarterback Paul Larson, fifth.

As it was, Ameche won the award more for his career accomplishments than what he did during the 1954 season. In fact, his injury-marred senior season was his least productive from a rushing standpoint. He gained only 641 yards with a 4.4 average. He had rushed for 824 yards as a freshman, 1,079 as a sophomore and 801 as a junior. But Ameche also had set the NCAA all-time rushing record in a game against Northwestern, doubled as a linebacker in those days of one-platoon football, and led the Badgers to a 7-2 record and a No. 9 ranking in the final Associated Press poll.

Ameche was awarded the trophy on Dec. 9 at a dinner at the Downtown Athletic Club in New York. Five hundred people gathered there in the gymnasium and then the people of Kenosha upstaged the event. Their dinner drew 1,000 guests and maybe more publicity. *Life* magazine sent a full crew of reporters and photographers.

At 6 feet and 212 pounds, Ameche was an unusually big back in his day and he was fast enough to have been a sprinter in high school. With his broad shoulders that required special shoulder pads and his high-stepping style of running, he personified his nickname.

He was the Big Ten's Most Valuable Player in 1954 and a first-team all-conference choice in each of his last three seasons. When his college days ended, Ameche was selected by the Baltimore Colts as the third overall selection in the 1955 NFL draft.

Ameche ran 79 yards for a touchdown against the Chicago Bears on his first pro carry and led the NFL in rushing as a rookie with 961 yards. He also was named the league's Rookie of the Year. He would be named to the Pro Bowl four times and would finish second in the NFL to Jim Brown in rushing when the Baltimore Colts won their first championship in 1958.

Ameche's biggest day as a pro came in the '58 championship game, which is often referred to as "The Greatest Game Ever Played." He scored the game-winning touchdown as the Colts beat the New York Giants, 23-17, in overtime.

After two more seasons, Ameche was out of football, his career prematurely ended by an Achilles tendon injury. He died of a heart attack in 1988 at age 55.

PACKERS BURY BUCS IN A BLIZZARD

DECEMBER 1, 1985

Fortunately, Forrest Gregg had put his team up in a hotel the night before the Tampa Bay Buccaneers learned all about winter in Green Bay. It would have been embarrassing for the Packers players not to show up for their own home game.

As it was, more than 36,000 fans failed to get there when 10 inches of snow turned the roads around Lambeau Field into toboggan slides during the biggest blizzard in National Football League history. Most of the players couldn't even move their cars out of the hotel parking lot on the morning of the game, but enough of them had Jeeps and trucks to get everyone where they were going. If they'd all had to leave from home, they might have needed an airlift.

The Buccaneers arrived at the stadium by bus and had every reason to wish they hadn't after suffering a 21-0 loss that ranked as one of the least attended and most humiliating in their brief history.

Only 19,856 ticketholders, the smallest crowd in Lambeau Field history, made it to the park to watch quarterback Lynn Dickey put on one of the more impressive offensive shows of his career, while the Bucs set or tied two team records for futility. Dickey barely noticed the precipitation as he completed 22 of 36 passes for 299 yards. Tampa Bay, on the other hand, gained only 65 yards and managed just five first downs compared to the Packers' 31.

The visitors had two significant problems, one emotional and one physical. They left balmy weather in Florida for sub-freezing temperatures with wind gusts between 20 and 30 miles per hour. In turn, they had a 2-10 record at the time, and there wasn't much point to going through all that discomfort. "Those guys just didn't want to be there," recalled Packers linebacker Mike Douglass. "It was so bad that day. It was wet snow and very thick. You got wet and stayed cold the whole game."

But at least the Packers stayed upright as well. That was the Buccaneers' other problem. They'd taken the field wearing half-inch cleats designed for grass and dry days, and that's all they'd brought. When tackle Greg Koch saw what the opponents had on their feet before the game, he told Bucs linebacker Scot Brantley, "It's not going to be pretty for you guys today."

But it was a thing of beauty for Dickey, who is kind of the Packers' forgotten quarterback. According to the team's passing records, he's No. 1, No. 2 or No. 3 in the most important categories, although it's usually No. 3 thanks to Brett Favre and Bart Starr. But the 4,458 yards he gained passing in 1983 is more than either of those fellows ever got in a season, and the 418 he rolled up against the Buccaneers in 1980 also still stands as the club record for a game. Dickey arrived from Houston in 1976 to rescue the Packers from the gruesome John Hadl trade, and when he was healthy he was as dangerous a passer as the team ever had.

His problem was he couldn't stay healthy. He'd been in the league seven years and missed two others completely before he played a full season as a starter. He had two screws in his hip socket, another one in his shoulder and an 18-inch plate in his leg, all from devastating injuries that would have ended the careers of more faint-hearted players. But he was in good health and better spirits against the Bucs when he saw all of that white stuff coming out of the sky.

"Lynn was a mudder," Koch said. "He played best in mud games and snow games."

The same could not be said of Steve Young. Tampa Bay's rookie quarterback completed only eight passes in 17 tries while getting sacked five times. Dickey completed six to James Lofton alone as the Packers rolled up 512 yards in the muck. They got all three of their touchdowns on the ground: One by Dickey on a one-yard scramble up the middle, and one each by running backs Gerry Ellis and Jessie Clark. Ellis and Eddie Lee Ivery each surpassed 100 yards rushing. Ivery gained 109 yards on 13 carries; Ellis, 101 on nine carries, including his 35-yard touchdown run.

But it was Dickey's passing that was most remarkable considering the playing conditions.

"You can't say enough about him," said Ellis of Dickey. "He was a guy who could throw a football through the eye of a needle, and he had five guys who could catch a B.B. at night... I think in those conditions it would have been hard for anybody to beat us."

PACKERS LAND TAYLOR, NITSCHKE IN WINDFALL DRAFT

DECEMBER 2, 1957

Scouting was not a big budget item for the Green Bay Packers in the 1950s. The Packers had no big budget items in the 1950s, but they did have a scouting department. His name was Jack Vainisi.

Hired in 1950 as a 23-year-old straight out of college, Vainisi had been on the freshman team at Notre Dame before entering the military and coming down with rheumatic fever. The disease ended Vainisi's playing days, but it didn't end his football career.

When Gene Ronzani became the Packers' head coach he made Vainisi his lone talent scout, which was the best thing Ronzani ever did for the franchise. Operating with minimum funds and virtually no help, Vainisi unearthed such Packer stalwarts as safety Bobby Dillon, defensive tackle Dave Hanner, linebacker Bill Forester, center Jim Ringo and receiver Max McGee, all in the third round or lower over just three drafts from 1952-'54. And Vainisi was just learning his trade.

In the 1956 draft, the Packers picked tackle Forrest Gregg in the second round, tackle Bob Skoronski in the fifth and quarterback Bart Starr in the 17th of 30 rounds. The following year, the Packers chose back Paul Hornung with the bonus, or No. 1, pick of the draft; and tight end Ron Kramer with the fourth overall selection. There were three future Hall of Famers in that group, but it was all a prelude to the greatest draft in Green Bay Packer history and one of the best ever in pro football.

The NFL brass met on a Monday in Philadelphia to complete the first and most important phase of what was officially the 1958 draft. The first four rounds were held in December to combat the Canadian Football League, which was sometimes paying better money and drawing players away from the NFL. The other 26 rounds were scheduled for late January. With Vainisi doing the pointing and coach Lisle Blackbourn doing the picking, the Packers used those first four rounds to lay the cornerstone for the Vince Lombardi dynasty.

The Packers selected linebacker Dan Currie of Michigan State with the third overall selection. They followed up by taking fullback Jim Taylor of Louisiana State in the second round, both halfback Dick Christy of North Carolina State and linebacker Ray Nitschke of Illinois in the third round, and guard Jerry Kramer of Idaho in the fourth round.

Christy didn't make it with the Packers, but he spent a year with the Pittsburgh Steelers and four in the newly formed American Football League, twice leading the league in punt returns.

Two of the other four made the Pro Football Hall of Fame, and the other two were all-pro selections.

Currie was the consensus All-American center during the 1957 season, but he played outside linebacker for the Packers. He started there on Lombardi's first two NFL championship teams in 1961 and '62. Currie made at least one all-pro team each season from 1961-'63, and he was named to the Pro Bowl in 1960.

Taylor became the Packers' all-time leading rusher on his way to the Pro Football Hall of Fame. Nitschke played 15 years with the Packers and is in the Pro Football Hall of Fame, as well.

Kramer turned out to be the only guard chosen on the NFL's 50th anniversary team in 1969, and he has been a finalist in the Hall of Fame voting 10 times. He was selected to three Pro Bowls and was chosen first-team all-pro four times.

While Blackbourn felt good about his draft class, he never got a chance to take advantage of it. The Packers finished the 1957 season with a 3-9 record, leaving him with a 17-31 overall mark and without a job. He was replaced by Scooter McLean before the second draft phase on Jan. 28.

With Vainisi at his elbow, McLean took lineman Ken Gray in the sixth round and then made the mistake of cutting him. Gray went on to play in six Pro Bowls as a guard for the St. Louis Cardinals.

McLean himself lasted just one season before he was replaced by Lombardi, who elevated Vainisi to business manager as well as chief scout. Nine games into Lombardi's second season as coach, Vainisi was found dead in his Green Bay home, the victim at age 33 of a chronic heart condition.

Like Blackbourn, he never got to enjoy the fruits of his labor. But no one ever did more with less for the Green Bay Packers.

BADGERS JOLT NO. 4 KANSAS

DECEMBER 3, 1968

As a second choice coaching his second sport, John Powless was definitely enjoying the ride after his first home game. He was taking it on the shoulders of his players and as many fans as could get their hands on him following one of the biggest upsets ever by a University of Wisconsin basketball team.

Powless' toughest job that week had been to convince his players that they belonged on the same floor with fourth-ranked Kansas, and now he was being carried off of it. The Badgers had showed the poise of a veteran team under their first-year coach while knocking off senior guard Jo Jo White and the more talented Jayhawks, 67-62.

It wasn't the most thrilling finish ever witnessed at the UW Fieldhouse. The Badgers wrapped up the victory by sinking six of nine free throws and scoring only one basket in the final three minutes as Kansas committed foul after foul. But a crowd of 9,113 was excited enough by it to come flooding onto the court. They weren't expecting this, and the truth was neither were some of the Badgers.

"There was sort of a lackadaisical air with two or three of them," said Powless. "I told them if I don't have all the guys who believe we can win, they should dress out and go sit in the stands."

Powless didn't have to motivate 6-foot-5 forward James Johnson. The UW co-captain took special satisfaction in scoring a game-high 29 points against the school that first showed interest in him as a high school recruit and then changed its mind. "I guess they didn't like me," said Johnson, who was from Memphis, Tenn. "They didn't write any more after my junior year. I would have come to Wisconsin anyway."

Chuck Nagle, also a 6-5 forward, added 17 points. But it was the ball-handling of homegrown guards Tom Mitchell and Clarence Sherrod against Kansas' pressure defense that allowed Wisconsin to hold off the Jayhawks. Mitchell, who hailed from Monroe, also made three free throws in the final 19 seconds. And Sherrod, a sophomore from Milwaukee Lincoln, drew two fouls on White in the last five minutes with his nifty dribbling.

White, who had starred for the gold medal-winning U.S. Olympic basketball team six weeks earlier, finished with 19 points to lead the Jayhawks. But he wasn't able to offset the Badgers' big edge at the free throw line. They made 17 of 23 free throws in the second half and 23 of 35 overall, while Kansas made just 10 of 17.

The victory would prove to be a career highlight for Powless. That year's Kansas team wasn't one of the school's better ones. No more than three or four other schools can match Kansas' rich basketball tradition. As of the end of the 2009-'10 season, Kentucky and North Carolina were the only Division I schools in the country that had won more overall games. And only Kentucky, North Carolina, UCLA and Duke had won more NCAA tournament games. Kansas' first coach was Dr. James Naismith, who invented basketball, and its great tradition has been carried on by legendary coach F.C. "Phog" Allen and more recently by Roy Williams, among others.

So by Kansas' standards, a 20-7 finish and an appearance in the National Invitation Tournament at the end of the season made for a rather ho-hum year. But White, a 6-3 senior guard, would have his number retired by both Kansas and his future NBA team, the Boston Celtics. And 6-10 sophomore forward Dave Robisch also would have his number retired at Kansas and play in the old American Basketball Association and NBA for a total of 13 years. So it was a formidable lineup that the Badgers faced.

Powless had gotten the Wisconsin job only after Bob Knight had turned it down, and that first team would finish 11-13. But at times that first season, it appeared that Powless might not be a bad fallback choice. Along with knocking off Kansas, the Badgers also upended third-ranked Kentucky, No. 12 Ohio State and No. 16 Marquette. But Powless would have only two winning seasons in his eight years in charge. His final record was 88-108, and his best Big Ten finish was a fourth-place tie.

Powless' second sport was tennis and he had a more distinguished career there. He coached the UW tennis team in the sixties and later became one of the world's leading senior players. In 2009 he was ranked No. 1 in the 75-and-over class after having both knees replaced in the previous three years.

BADGERS BEAT MICHIGAN STATE IN JAPAN

DECEMBER 4, 1993

When sponsors approached the University of Wisconsin in 1991 about moving a home football game against Michigan State to Japan it seemed like a good idea at the time.

The Badgers were coming off a 1-10 season in Barry Alvarez's first year as head coach, and Camp Randall crowds of 40,000 or so were not uncommon. The game in Japan would provide a bowl game atmosphere for a school that hadn't been to one since 1984 and there was a $400,000 guarantee on the table, plus expenses for the team, the band and the cheerleaders. And so Alvarez and Athletic Director Pat Richter agreed to the game. Little did they know what a far-reaching decision it would turn out to be.

The Badgers had back-to-back 5-6 seasons over the next two years, and then suddenly Alvarez's young program took off. In 1993 Wisconsin beat Michigan and tied Ohio State in the same year while losing only once to Minnesota. Incredibly, the Badgers found themselves 8-1-1 going into their final game against the Spartans with their first trip to the Rose Bowl since 1963 at stake. And the game was scheduled half-a-world away, or about 6,000 miles.

Because Ohio State had been to Pasadena more recently, a victory assured Wisconsin of the bid. A loss or a tie meant a low-profile trip to the Holiday Bowl in San Diego. The Badgers hadn't been to the granddaddy of bowls in 31 years, and while their fans were excited about their 10th-ranked team, there was plenty of grumbling about the surrender of the home-field advantage. Pressed by State Senator Michael Ellis, Richter acknowledged that he would have kept the team home if he had it to do all over again, but it was too late for that now. The Badgers would have to make the best of it.

On the plus side, they hadn't played since beating Illinois on Nov. 11, while Michigan State had no time to rest after dropping a 38-37 heartbreaker to Penn State a week earlier. That gave Alvarez extra time to get his league-leading offense ready for the Spartans' trademark 4-3 stunt defense. It also gave Alvarez a chance to consult with the university's sleep disorder clinic, which came up with a scientific program involving sunglasses, bizarre hours and fluid intake, among other things, to battle jet lag for the 16-hour trip to the Orient.

The two teams boarded the same flight from Chicago, and in the interest of keeping the peace, the Badgers occupied the top floor of the jumbo jet while the Spartans were seated on the main floor.

On game day, a crowd of 50,000-plus filled the Tokyo Dome, the home of baseball's Yomiuri Giants, intent on having a good time whether they knew what was going on or not. Red and white pompons were placed on every seat on one-half of the stadium. Green and white ones were distributed to the other half, and they all got waved regardless of which team scored. Music played throughout the game, and sometimes, people would cheer during the huddles and sit on their hands during the action.

The Badgers scored on a 35-yard field goal by Rick Schnetzky on their first possession, but Michigan State came back to take a 7-3 lead on a 33-yard pass. And then Wisconsin's rushing attack took control of the game and never gave it back.

Safety Scott Nelson intercepted a pass to set up a one-yard touchdown run by Terrell Fletcher early in the second period, and then Fletcher struck again from 40 yards out. Brent Moss followed with a three-yard scoring run to cap a 99-yard drive. It was 24-7 at halftime, and Wisconsin was never in serious danger after that against a Spartan team that finished the regular season 6-5 and was headed to the Liberty Bowl.

Moss, the nation's No. 3 rusher, finished the game with 146 yards on the ground, while Fletcher had 112 as the Badgers outgained Michigan State, 525 yards to 378, and never punted on the way to a 41-20 victory. Next up: UCLA at Pasadena.

The players celebrated on the field for 40 minutes after the game, even dancing a few polkas while the band played on. It was even more raucous back home. The game started at 10 p.m. Wisconsin time and didn't end until early Sunday morning. And when it was over, the bars and dorms in Madison emptied and an estimated 30,000 people flooded the streets and stormed the field at Camp Randall Stadium.

The faithful would have even more reason to celebrate a month later when the Badgers beat UCLA, 21-16, at the Rose Bowl some 1,600 miles from Madison. After Japan, it must have felt like a commuter flight.

BRAVES GET RUSH IN FIVE-PLAYER TRADE

DECEMBER 5, 1957

The Milwaukee Braves were suspected of wielding a deadly weapon in completing a five-player trade with the Chicago Cubs. According to at least one rival general manager, it had to be a heist.

The world champions had an all-star pitching staff headed by Warren Spahn, Lew Burdette and Bob Buhl even before they added Bob Rush, a good arm toiling for a last-place team. The Braves gave up lefty Taylor Phillips and catcher Sammy Taylor for Rush, and they also received two prospects, outfielder Eddie Haas and pitcher Don Kaiser, who were thrown into the deal.

"What did they use on those poor Cubs, a shotgun?" asked Philadelphia Phillies General Manager Roy Hamey. "Why, that's awful. I couldn't believe it when they told me."

Hamey wasn't the only one dazed by the swap. San Francisco Giants Manager Bill Rigney claimed his team had offered five players for Rush including regulars Bobby Thomson and Whitey Lockman. "They were looking for a center fielder and a third baseman," Rigney said. "Instead they settled for a pitcher who won three games and a catcher who hit .257 at Atlanta. How do you figure a thing like that?"

It certainly took a lot of figuring to get it done. Braves General Manager John Quinn said he began negotiations in October, following the World Series. Then at the winter meetings in Colorado Springs, Colo., Quinn, scout Wid Matthews and Manager Fred Haney began negotiations with Cubs Vice President John Holland at around midnight, took a recess about 7:30 a.m. and completed the deal at 9:30 p.m. (Milwaukee time). "We threw around almost every name on both rosters before we finally reached an agreement," said Quinn. "Offhand, though, I'd say it was a night's sleep well spent."

The Braves actually had shown interest in Rush off and on over the previous five years, and for good reason. He'd won 13 games for the woeful Cubs three of his last four seasons, and he'd led his team in starts and innings pitched five times between 1949 and '56. In 1952, the one year when Chicago was actually decent, he'd posted a 17-13 record with a 2.70 earned run average. But Rush was almost 32 years old and coming off a 6-16 season, and the Cubs were looking for youth.

The 24-year-old Phillips, a stocky southpaw, offered that. He'd been the Braves' Rookie of the Year in 1956 when he'd gone 5-3 with a 2.25 ERA after being called up from the minor leagues in mid-June. But then he'd dropped off severely with a 3-2 record and a 5.50 ERA in 1957. Phillips wouldn't be much better with the Cubs, where he was 7-10 the next year. Thereafter, he would win just one more game in his six-year career. Taylor, also 24, had no major league experience at the time of the trade. A left-handed batter, he had hit .257 for the Class AA Atlanta Crackers during the 1957 season. He became Chicago's semi-regular catcher for two years, but he never played in more than 110 games in six major league seasons.

The throw-ins didn't amount to anything for the Braves, either. Haas played nine games for them in 1958 and then broke his ankle in spring training and appeared in just 32 games after that. Kaiser never pitched for them. Actually, there were some who thought Kaiser could turn out to be the steal of the trade. He was 22 years old at the time, had been the Cubs' first bonus baby, and had pitched a two-hitter against the Brooklyn Dodgers in his first major league start in 1956. But he won only 26 games in the minor leagues in the four years following the trade and was out of baseball by 1962.

Rush proved to be a lifesaver for the Braves in 1958 when Buhl injured his shoulder in May and pitched in only one game the rest of the year. Rush had a 10-6 record with a 3.42 ERA as Milwaukee won a second straight National League pennant. He lost a World Series game to the New York Yankees and lasted just one more complete season with the Braves, but they might not have won the pennant without him. The trade also kept Rush out of the hands of their major competitors.

San Francisco and Cincinnati, in particular, had been pursuing him at the winter meetings, but Quinn beat them to the punch. The Giants finished third, 12 games out of first place, and the Reds were fourth, 16 games back, in 1958. As for the Cubs ... well they were still the Cubs. They finished 10 games under .500 and 20 behind Milwaukee.

BREWERS GET COOPER FOR SCOTT ON BUSY DAY

DECEMBER 6, 1976

Cecil Cooper

George Scott was unhappy, Darrell Porter was unhappy, and the fans were pretty discouraged themselves. With his team foundering on the field and sagging badly at the gate, Milwaukee Brewers Director of Baseball Operations Jim Baumer had to do something at the winter meetings in Los Angeles.

He did a lot. He traded away the best hitter and the only 20-game winner in the six-year history of the franchise in two separate deals. It may not have been the most momentous Monday the Brewers ever experienced, but it was certainly one of the busiest, and it netted one of the team's all-time best players.

Baumer began his day by sending right-hander Jim Colborn and catcher Darrell Porter to Kansas City for a player who would be named later and two who would be quickly forgotten. Coming from the Royals were a young utility man named Jamie Quirk and a nondescript outfielder named Jim Wohlford.

It didn't seem like much for a starting battery, but Colborn's victories had fallen while his earned run average had risen since he'd gone 20-12 in 1973. And Porter, who had been the Brewers' first first-round draft pick in 1970, had taken some shots at management, never a great idea for a young player who had batted .208 over the previous season. But Porter was hardly the leading malcontent on the team.

That honor went to George Scott, the boisterous 32-year old first baseman who held all of the franchise records for home runs, RBIs and batting average. Scott had come to the Brewers in a trade with Boston five years earlier, and he was about to leave them the same way. Baumer packaged him with outfielder Bernie Carbo and swung a deal with the Red Sox for 26-year-old first baseman-designated hitter Cecil Cooper.

In a minor transaction, Baumer also picked up off waivers Larry Haney, a veteran influence who flat out couldn't hit, to provide some protection at catcher.

When he'd finished his day's work, Baumer had gotten six years younger at first base without any appreciable loss of offense. In the previous season, Scott had hit .274 with 18 home runs and 77 RBIs, while Cooper had batted .282 with 15 homers and 78 RBIs. Carbo had been acquired from the Red Sox the previous June and was pretty much an afterthought.

But Scott wasn't through making waves. As a 10-year veteran with five years with the same team, he could veto any trade and he threatened to do so unless Boston signed him to a multi-year contract. It took the Red Sox three days to do that and two years to regret it. "The Boomer" had a huge year for them in 1977, batting .269 with 33 home runs and 95 RBIs, but the following season he tailed off to .233 with 12 homers, and his career was all but over.

Cooper, meanwhile, became the first Brewer in four years to hit .300 in 1977, and he went on to do it six more times. He also became a fan favorite, twice led the American League in RBIs and played 11 years with the Brewers.

Baumer's other trade didn't pan out as well.

Colborn played just two more years, but was 18-14 with a 3.62 earned run average for Kansas City the next season. Porter bumped his batting average to .275 while hitting 16 home runs and driving in 60 runs. He played four years with the Royals and then signed as a free agent with the St. Louis Cardinals. In 1982, he came back to haunt the Brewers when they lost the World Series to the Cardinals and Porter was named the Most Valuable Player.

Quirk and Wohlford contributed next to nothing during their brief stays in Milwaukee. Quirk hit .217 the next year and was traded back to the Royals. Wohlford played three seasons for the Brewers and hit a grand total of four home runs. All that saved the trade from being a disaster was pitcher Bob McClure, the player to be named later. He pitched nine full seasons for the Brewers, mostly as a reliever, and he went 12-7 and started 26 games when they won the American League in 1982.

The two trades had no immediate impact on the Brewers. They finished 66-95 the year before and 67-95 the next year. But Cooper, alone, was worth the wheeling and dealing, and he paid off big down the road. As of the end of the 2009 baseball season, he was third on the Brewers in all-time batting average, second in RBIs and fourth in home runs.

BREWERS LOSE MOLITOR TO FREE AGENCY

DECEMBER 7, 1992

The Dark Ages of the Milwaukee Brewers began after the 1992 season when they went from a 92-70 contender to a 69-93 afterthought. That was also when they let Paul Molitor leave for Toronto.

If the second didn't cause the first, it was at least a major symptom of a disease that sent the franchise into a 14-year funk. It would be 2007 before the Brewers had another winning record, thanks to baseball's skewed economic system and a grim list of their own personnel errors. For many of their fans, allowing the Blue Jays to claim Molitor in free agency topped that list.

After 15 years with the Brewers, Molitor was still their best offensive player in 1992 when he led them with a .320 batting average and 89 RBIs. A five-time All-Star with a .303 career average during his time with the Brewers, Molitor was also their second-most popular player, right behind the recently re-signed Robin Yount. But when Molitor's contract expired, General Manager Sal Bando's best offer was close to a $500,000 cut in base salary to about $2.6 million a year.

Asked if he could have saved money somewhere else to give Molitor a more competitive offer, Bando said, "If Paul could pitch left-handed, if he could be a utility player, if Paul could be a fourth outfielder, sure you could do that," he said. "But all he can do is be a designated hitter and part-time first baseman."

His "just a DH" stance would plague Bando long after he left the club, and it would help Molitor decide to accept the Blue Jays' bid of $13 million, or roughly $4.3 million per year, for three years, which was about $900,000 more than he'd made in his last season with the Brewers. It seemed like a no-brainer, but Molitor insisted that he could have been persuaded to stay in Milwaukee where he'd spent his whole career if the Brewers had negotiated seriously with him early in the process.

"It's been a surprise the lack of success we had negotiating with the Brewers," he said.

The team had one more surprise for Molitor when at the last second it offered him arbitration. But the move came about an hour after he'd agreed to the Toronto contract. The arbitration bid gave the Brewers a first-round draft choice as compensation. More important, they hoped it would convince their customers that they'd made a good faith effort to keep Molitor.

But that was a hard sell. Three weeks earlier, the Brewers had traded with Colorado for former Texas outfielder Kevin Reimer, a long-ball hitter with an iron glove who had just been acquired by the Rockies in the expansion draft. It was assumed by many that the Brewers had Reimer in mind as Molitor's replacement as their DH. Reimer would be paid less than a quarter of what Molitor made in 1992, and the Brewers were determined to trim their player costs by $8 million to $22 million.

Their payroll was in the upper third of Major League Baseball while their revenue was in the lower third, and Bando pointed out that they couldn't stay in business doing that. "I don't understand why people don't understand why we can't spend what we don't have," said Bando.

Paul Molitor

Bando's point was if the fans wanted to keep better players, they had to buy more tickets, and he needed to look no further than Toronto to make his argument. The Blue Jays drew four million fans while winning the 1992 World Series with a $46 million payroll.

The critics' answer was that the Brewers would have had enough money to compete if they hadn't spent so much on the wrong players. They cited several examples. In Molitor's last season in Milwaukee, Teddy Higuera made $3.5 million and didn't pitch because of an injury, Ron Robinson made $1.1 million to go 1-4 in eight appearances, and Franklin Stubbs pulled down $2.17 million to hit .229 with nine home runs. Worse yet, they were all going to be on the payroll again in 1993.

The Brewers also had recently jettisoned Chris Bosio, a 16-6 starter; Dan Plesac, their onetime closer; and the enormously popular Jim Gantner in free agency, although Gantner didn't sign with anyone. And still Bando insisted, "I think we're every bit as good as last year's team."

They turned out to be 23 games worse, while the Blue Jays won the World Series again and Molitor was named Most Valuable Player. He hit .332 during the regular season with 22 home runs and 111 RBIs, and then he played two more years in Toronto and three with Minnesota before being elected to the Baseball Hall of Fame in 2004.

PACKERS CAPTURE THEIR FIRST CHAMPIONSHIP

DECEMBER 8, 1929

Only a scoreless tie with the Frankford Yellow Jackets separated the Green Bay Packers from perfection as they ran onto Wrigley Field on a Sunday afternoon for the last game of the season. One more victory would make them champions of the 10-year old National Football League.

Could the hated Chicago Bears deprive them of the first title in the history of the franchise? They couldn't even come close.

When the final seconds ticked away, the Packers hadn't just beaten their archrivals, they'd blanked them for the third time that season. The Bears crossed Green Bay's 35-yard line just once while suffering a 25-0 rout to go with a 23-0 loss in September and a 14-0 disappointment in November.

Fullback Cal Lidberg was the star of the game as he led the Packers' rushing attack, scored a touchdown on a 12-yard run and chipped in on defense with two interceptions. Eddie Kotal, a halfback from Lawrence College, added two touchdowns, and fellow halfback Verne Lewellen scored the other. Tackle Cal Hubbard and guard Mike Michalske showed the way for a line that dominated both sides of the ball. The Bears picked up just one first down, that on a run by the fabled Red Grange.

And so the Packers became the first undefeated team in the history of the league, finishing with a 12-0-1 record and edging out the New York Giants, who would finish 13-1-1. At the time, the NFL title was decided by winning percentage during the regular season. The Packers were a perfect 1.000; the Giants' .929.

It was a far different NFL than it is today. There were 12 teams in all, and the league was moving from its original base of mostly small Midwestern cities to larger ones in the East. But it still included such teams as the Staten Island Stapletons, Providence Steam Roller and, of course, the Yellow Jackets, who represented a neighborhood in Philadelphia.

The Packers have now won a league-record 12 NFL championships and the 1929 team is still the only one that went unbeaten. It also may have dominated its opponents more than any other. The Packers outscored them, 198-22, over the course of the season, pitching shutouts in eight of their games.

Hubbard and Michalske had been signed in the summer, as had halfback Johnny "Blood" McNally. Hubbard was purchased from the Giants, while Michalske and McNally came from the New York Yankees and Pottsville Maroons, two teams that had gone out of business. All three would make the Pro Football Hall of Fame.

This was a great football team. And it was on its way to a great party.

The *Green Bay Press-Gazette* had been soliciting public contributions to show the community's support for its favorites. A total of 1,123 individuals and 103 companies responded to the tune of $5,073.60. They definitely got their money's worth.

An eerie orange glow lit the sky as the train carrying the team home from Chicago pulled into the Chicago & North Western station at 8:30 on Monday night. Some of the Packers feared there had been an accident on the tracks. But it wasn't that. It was thousands of fans lining the way and waving red flares welcoming the players. An estimated 20,000 people showed up, more than half of Green Bay's population at the time.

While other small Midwestern cities such as Canton, Rock Island, Racine and Kenosha had lost their franchises; Green Bay had endured, and its citizens were proud of that fact.

Four hundred people filled the dining room at the Beaumont Hotel on Tuesday evening to celebrate again. There would have been more, but that was all the room there was. Everyone else had to settle for a live broadcast of the event on radio station WHBY.

Dignitaries ranging from the mayor to the state attorney general paraded to the podium to congratulate the players. Team President Dr. W.W. Kelly spoke and called the Packers "the cleanest, most wholesome group of men" he had ever known.

Each player was awarded a wristwatch and $220 in cash, back before the league passed out championship game checks. When the speeches were done, the band began to play and a dance began. While this was during the height of Prohibition, the mayor had declared earlier that the Packers would have "freedom of the city," and everyone knew what that meant in a city that never really went dry.

Green Bay had a champion, and everyone partied all night.

NFL DRAFT HELD IN MILWAUKEE HOTEL

DECEMBER 9, 1939

Choosing new talent wasn't an art, and it wasn't a science in the early days of the National Football League draft. It was more of a pre-game party.

When roughly 30 officials from 10 teams congregated at the gleaming Schroeder Hotel in the heart of downtown Milwaukee, they were in a hurry to divvy up the top college players in time for dinner. They started the NFL's fifth annual draft – it's the 1940 draft in the record books – at 2 p.m. and seven hours later, they were all gathered at the Schlitz Brown Bottle for drinks. By then, they already had feasted on tenderloin steaks at a dinner hosted by the Green Bay Packers. Somehow those movers and shakers also found time to pick 200 players over 20 rounds.

Today, it takes personnel experts along with an army of scouts wielding computers back at their teams' headquarters at least half that time just to finish the first round. In the 1930s the participants relied on magazines and picked names off of a big board posted in front of the room. The process in this case was conducted in the Schroeder's posh Empire Ballroom.

The Packers were playing the New York Giants for the NFL championship the next day at Milwaukee's State Fair Park, and, back then, the draft was always conducted at the site of the title game.

The Packers used their first-round pick – the ninth choice overall – on a triple-threat tailback from Minnesota named Hal Van Every, who also tied for the top spot in the nation with eight interceptions.

Van Every played with the Packers as a backup in 1940 and '41, left for World War II and never returned. In May 1944, his plane was shot down over Germany and he spent a year in a prison camp in Poland. He wanted to rejoin the Packers in 1946, but he had injured his back when he ejected from his plane and he wasn't physically able to play again. So he went back to Minnesota and sold insurance. He died in 2007 at age 89.

The Packers took Lou Brock, a back from Purdue, in the second round, and he played six years, and was inducted into the Packer Hall of Fame in 1982. But he was about all they got out of their 20 selections.

The Chicago Cardinals, who had the first overall pick, didn't do any better. They wasted the choice on All-American tailback George Cafego of Tennessee. Cafego had suffered a late-season knee injury, which the Cardinals might not even have known about, and he never played a down for them, although he spent four lackluster seasons in the NFL.

The Chicago Bears' George Halas, on the other hand, must have known something that his colleagues didn't, because he wound up with two future Hall of Famers that day. He tabbed center-linebacker Clyde "Bulldog" Turner of Hardin-Simmons with his own first-round pick and walked away with Philadelphia's first-round selection, halfback George McAfee, through a trade.

In those days, there also was such a thing as "sleeper" picks, players that most teams knew nothing about. And in the 19th round, Halas took a flyer on halfback Ray "Scooter" McLean of tiny St. Anselm College, located in Manchester, N.H. McLean would play eight years for the Bears. He also would coach the Packers for one year, although not very well.

Halas was one of a dozen future Hall of Famers attending the draft, joining the likes of Art Rooney, Bert Bell, Wellington Mara, Charles Bidwill and, of course, Curly Lambeau. They were pro football's royalty, and the Schroeder was clearly up to the task of entertaining them. Built 11 years earlier by insurance and hotel magnate Walter Schroeder, it towered 265 feet above Wisconsin Avenue, and it featured 811 state of the art guest rooms and all of the luxury anyone could want. It's now the Hilton City Center.

Sportswriter Stoney McGlynn covered the draft for the *Milwaukee Sentinel*, but it was far from a major event in those days. McGlynn said the writers spent the day in an adjoining room taking in refreshments.

PACKERS PACIFY FANS BY WINNING FIFTH TITLE

DECEMBER 10, 1939

Winning the game would be the easy part. The Green Bay Packers had earned four National Football League titles in the previous 10 years, and they were a good bet to make it five when they took on the New York Giants at Milwaukee's State Fair Park.

The rugged Giants were the defending NFL champions, but it wasn't the opponent that had caused Curly Lambeau's team a world of grief in the days leading up to the game. It was the site.

At a special meeting held in Pittsburgh on Nov. 28, the league decided that if the Packers beat Detroit in the final regular-season game to win the Western Division and advance to the championship game, it would be held in Milwaukee, rather than Green Bay. The Packers beat the Lions, but before the game was even played, a howl went up in Green Bay that could be heard all the way to New York.

While Lambeau probably had little choice in the matter, fans in Green Bay felt betrayed. This was their first chance to play host to a championship and they wouldn't get another opportunity until 1961. But Green Bay's City Stadium held only 22,370 people at the time, whereas State Fair Park's capacity could be expanded to more than 30,000, and the league reasoned that the extra sales would go a long way to boosting the players' share of the gate. And that was that.

Tickets priced from $1.10 to $4.40 went on sale at *The Milwaukee Journal* lobby the day after the Detroit game, and they were all snapped up in 24 hours. Green Bay got an allotment of 11,000, and despite the local outrage, those sold immediately, too. The Packers, however, declined to make tickets available in New York, which really incensed the Giants.

Denied the chance to bring any of their fans along, they were also told they wouldn't be allowed to practice at State Fair Park before the game. Captain Mel Hein spoke for his teammates when he said, "One thing is certain. They'll have to let us use the same size football, and they can't soften up our blocking and tackling as those inhospitable mugs will soon find out."

But it didn't work out that way. The Packers were even less hospitable once the game started. As a record 32,279 badly chilled spectators looked on, Green Bay proceeded to drag the Giants all over the field on the way to a 27-0 victory. It was the first shutout in the seven-year history of the NFL championship game, and it was every bit as lopsided as the score made it look.

The Packers intercepted six passes and limited the vaunted New York ground game to 56 yards. Green Bay native Arnie Herber threw a seven-yard touchdown pass to end Milt Gantenbein, who grew up in La Crosse, in the first quarter. Tailback Cecil Isbell completed a 31-yard touchdown pass to right halfback Joe Laws in the third quarter. And fullback and Milwaukee native Eddie Jankowski scored on a one-yard plunge in the fourth quarter.

Steve Owen, the Giants' coach, was spared a close-up view of the carnage because he was in Oklahoma attending his mother's funeral, but his players offered no excuses. "We just haven't got enough for those guys," said Giants back Tuffy Leemans, a native of Superior and future Hall of Famer.

Naturally, the New York writers had nothing good to say about the Giants, but they reserved their greatest scorn for the venue, dubbed the "Dairy Bowl."

"The National Football League can't stand many more events of this kind and expect to be taken seriously by the football public," wrote the *New York Herald Tribune's* Stanley Woodward. He added, "The setting struck a new low for league competition. The press box, hung out on a projecting lip of the grandstand roof, waved and wobbled in a 35-mile gale."

Nobody could do anything about the gale. Forecasters called for variable winds from the west and southwest, but Mother Nature delivered something much fiercer straight out of the north. It was true, though, that the State Fair crew had done some scrambling to get ready for the event, adding 2,000 temporary steel bleachers and jerry-rigging a wooden press box in less than a week.

Fortunately, there were no major injuries except to the Giants' pride, and the winning players collected $703 apiece, thanks to the beefed-up gate. They were also met by several thousand fans when their train pulled into Green Bay the next afternoon.

The Packers were forgiven.

DAYNE WALKS AWAY WITH HEISMAN TROPHY

DECEMBER 11, 1999

Before Ron Dayne was presented with the highest honor in college football, he promised to give "the shortest speech in history." He may have come close, covering the subject in roughly 300 words.

He thanked God, the other finalists, his coaches, his teammates and family. He mentioned eight people by name or nickname, starting with his coach at Wisconsin, Barry Alvarez. "And finally," he said, "I'd like to thank the real Heisman winner to me, my uncle Rob."

Rob Reid, the uncle who raised Dayne like a son, didn't break the collegiate rushing record. He wasn't a starter for the University of Wisconsin football team for four years, and he wouldn't be taken in the first round of the NFL draft. Dayne did all of that, but he understood that he might have done none of it if it hadn't been for Reid. And so in his typical terse fashion he put the credit where he thought it belonged.

Calling Ron Dayne self-effacing is like saying he's big. He was already packing 240 pounds on his 5-foot-10 frame in seventh grade, and before long he'd have to wear braces on both knees to help them handle the weight. He was 270 when he left Overbrook High School in Pine Hill, N.J., and headed to Wisconsin where Alvarez promised to let him play tailback when everyone else wanted to make him a fullback.

Dayne might have turned out to be neither. He might have been just another street kid if Reid had not taken him in when Dayne's parents split and his mother got into drugs. Brenda Dayne lost her marriage and then her job after she found cocaine, but she kept her head long enough to know she wouldn't be able to raise her daughter and son. So she sent daughter Onya to live with relatives who had a daughter about the same age, and she sent Ron to Berlin, N.J., to live with her brother Rob, his wife Debbie and their three kids.

Reid, a social worker at a detention center who'd played some college football himself, made it clear from the day that Dayne moved in that he would be treated exactly the way the other kids in his family were being treated. Whatever that meant, it worked.

When Badger assistant Bernie Wyatt went to recruit Dayne for the first time, he found him cleaning up the house, and he figured he had a keeper. He certainly got that right.

Dayne would become one of only five players to rush for more than 1,000 yards in all four of his collegiate seasons and the first to top 7,000 for his career when bowl games were taken into account. Again counting bowl games, Dayne carried the ball 1,220 times for the Badgers, gained 7,125 yards and averaged 5.8 yards per carry. In his senior year, he finished with 2,034 yards and a gaudy 6.0 average per carry, while breaking Ricky Williams' national career rushing record. And Dayne did it all while barely opening his mouth.

Ron Dayne

Always polite but forever private with the press, he simply didn't like to talk about himself.

After struggling through an injury-plagued sophomore season that he considered a disappointment, a major event in his young life broadened his conversational reach. At age 19 Ron Dayne became a dad. He named his daughter Jada and had the name tattooed on his arm. He called her "the most important thing in my life," and he could talk about her forever.

Yes, there were far more important things in Dayne's life than joining Alan Ameche as the only Badger to win the Heisman Trophy. But it also was obvious that he was deeply touched when he was announced as the winner on a Saturday night at the Downtown Athletic Club in New York in what had become by then a much more gala and hyped affair than when Ameche won in 1954. When Dayne's name was announced, he embraced Alvarez before walking to the podium to accept the award.

The balloting wasn't even close. Dayne received 586 first-place votes from a panel of 921 voters and finished with 2,042 points. Georgia Tech quarterback Joe Hamilton, the runner-up, received 96 first-place votes and 994 points. Finishing a distant third and fourth were two quarterbacks, redshirt freshman Michael Vick of Virginia Tech and junior Drew Brees of Purdue.

Both of them were on their way to glory in the pro game, but Vick was also on his way to trouble. Dayne didn't need either. He'd already had one of the greatest college careers ever, and he could sum it all up in about 300 words.

BREWERS GET FINGERS, SIMMONS, VUCKOVICH

DECEMBER 12, 1980

Rollie Fingers

The St. Louis Cardinals were looking for youth, and the Milwaukee Brewers could have been looking for trouble when the two clubs completed a seven-player trade at baseball's winter meetings.

The Cardinals received Milwaukee's best minor league prospect, plus two young pitchers and a 27-year outfielder who had hit well over .300 two seasons before.

The Brewers got two pitchers who were in position to become free agents a year later and a catcher who could have vetoed the deal as a 10-year veteran with five years on the same team. Two years later, the Brewers also got the only pennant in the history of the franchise.

Closer Rollie Fingers, right-handed starter Pete Vuckovich and catcher Ted Simmons may not have been the best players on the team that went to the 1982 World Series, but the Brewers never would have made it there without them.

General Manager Harry Dalton knew he was taking a big chance when he sent minor league outfielder David Green, outfielder Sixto Lezcano, and pitchers Lary Sorensen and David LaPoint to St. Louis for a couple of guys he might not be able to sign the next year and another one he'd have to pay not to veto the trade.

Green had been compared to a young Roberto Clemente by Pittsburgh Manager Chuck Tanner. Sorenson, 25, had gone 18-12 in his first full major league season in 1978 and had won 27 more games in the two seasons since. LaPoint was a promising 6-foot-3, 21-year old southpaw pitcher. And while Lezcano had slumped badly in 1980, batting only .229, he'd had a monster year in '79 when he hit .321 with 28 home runs and 101 RBIs.

But the Brewers had never been to the playoffs, and they had the kind of offense that could get them there if they could land some pitching help. That's really all Dalton was looking for when he went to the winter meetings in Dallas.

He had been involved in talks with the Cardinals about Vuckovich since September. And now Fingers, who had just finished his fourth season with San Diego, was put at the top of his shopping list. But the Cardinals' Whitey Herzog beat Dalton to the punch by landing Fingers in an 11-player swap on Dec. 8.

Herzog, however, was just getting warmed up. He acquired another star closer in Bruce Sutter the next day, putting Fingers back on the market. Herzog, who doubled as manager and general manager for the Cards, doubted that he'd be able to sign Fingers after his option ran out. He had the same worry with Vuckovich and a different one with Simmons.

When the Cardinals signed free agent catcher Darrell Porter a week earlier, Herzog planned to move Simmons to first base. That was not in Simmons' plans, however, and he told his agent to look for a trade that would send him somewhere where he could catch.

The agent could find only one team interested in using him that way despite Simmons' 13 years of experience behind the plate, his .298 career batting average to that point, his selection to six All-Star games and his standing as one of the game's premier switch-hitters. That team was the Brewers.

But there was one final hurdle to clear. Simmons had to agree to surrender his no-trade option before the deal could go through; and so Dalton had to hand over a $750,000 bonus to him.

It was well worth it. Fingers won both the American League Cy Young and Most Valuable Player awards in his first year with the Brewers when he saved 28 games with a 1.04 earned run average. Then he saved 29 more in 1982. Vuckovich claimed the Cy Young Award that year and Simmons was a .269 hitter with 23 home runs and 97 RBIs for the pennant-winning team.

Things didn't work out nearly as well for the other side. Lezcano played only 72 games in St. Louis and hit .266, while Sorensen pitched just one season there and went 7-7. LaPoint won 34 games in four years as a sometimes starter. Green was the biggest disappointment of all. He lasted six seasons and ended his career with a .268 batting average and just 31 home runs.

Still, it was the Cardinals who beat the Brewers in the 1982 World Series. Of course, it helped that the Cards had packaged Lezcano in a deal at the winter meetings in 1981 for future Hall of Fame shortstop Ozzie Smith.

366   365 BEST WISCONSIN SPORTS STORIES

PACKERS WIN NFL TITLE WITH AERIAL BARRAGE

DECEMBER 13, 1936

George Preston Marshall had this dilemma. His Boston Redskins were playing the Green Bay Packers in the National Football League title game, and they were doing it in New York. If they won, the Redskins owner would have a team of homeless champions on his hands.

Under NFL rules at the time, the top finishers in the Eastern and Western divisions took turns hosting the title game. This was the Eastern team's turn, and Marshall knew one thing for sure: He wasn't going to play in Boston.

"Beantown" had treated pro football to an enormous collective yawn. Marshall had lost $95,000 over the past five years, and the Redskins had drawn only 3,715 people to their last game. So he borrowed the Polo Grounds, the home of the New York football Giants, for the title match and announced his decision just six days before the game.

"We have to be fair to the kids who won the divisional championship," Marshall said of his players who had won the East with a 7-5 record. "If we meet Green Bay in Boston they wouldn't get enough out of it to buy Christmas presents."

This was just one glaring example of how the NFL has changed over the past seven decades. Another was the game itself.

The Packers won it, 21-6, to claim their fourth NFL championship, but their first under the four-year-old playoff format. And they did it with what newspaper accounts described as their "great aerial barrage." To get an idea of how great, you needed only to read the report from the *New York Herald Tribune*.

"Green Bay is a strange football team in that it makes no pretense of having a consistent running attack," wrote Stanley Woodward. "Hank Bruder apparently calls running plays only to distract the attention of the defense from the passes on which he relies to score."

Bruder, the quarterback but really a blocking back, was the Packer who called the plays in the huddle, not the one who threw the passes. That was halfback Arnie Herber, who started the day with a 48-yard touchdown connection to end Don Hutson in the first three minutes. After making the extra point, Green Bay had a 7-0 lead it would never lose. Boston came back with a touchdown in the second quarter, but missed the conversion. Herber threw an eight-yard touchdown pass to end Milt Gantenbein in the third quarter and Bobby Monnett scored on a two-yard run in the fourth quarter.

It was a beautiful sunny day, and the crowd of 29,545 also was treated to some extracurricular activity. Marshall ran up and down the sideline full of glee and maybe something even more intoxicating when the Redskins scored their only touchdown; and a fight between the two centers, Frank Butler of the Packers and Frank Bausch of the Redskins, led to their ejections in the second half.

About that aerial barrage. Herber threw 14 passes in the game and completed six for 129 yards. What would later be a bad first quarter for Brett Favre was actually an average day for these air-minded Packers. They had led the league in passing by a wide margin that year, gaining 1,629 yards on 108 completions in 255 attempts. Doing the math over 12 starts – the Packers had won the Western Division with a 10-1-1 record – they put it up 21 times a game and completed nine for an average of 136 yards. The league as a whole averaged 83 yards a game passing.

As it was, the Packers' top-ranked passing offense was more than enough to overwhelm Boston's top-ranked passing defense and earn the praise of the Gotham press. "The Green Bay Packers, a burly band of bone busters from the tall timber of northern Wisconsin, are the finest pro footballers in these United States if not in the whole of God's green footstool," wrote the *New York Daily News*' Jack Miley.

It was an opinion widely shared by the estimated 10,000 people who welcomed the team when it arrived at the Milwaukee Road depot in Green Bay the next evening. Curly Lambeau's players had grown used to being greeted as conquering heroes over the years, but Hutson for one thought this team was special. He called it "the greatest offensive machine in the history of the game."

The Redskins' Marshall would have been pleased to attract as many people to his games as the Packers drew to their train station. Three days after the championship game, Marshall announced he was taking his team to Washington, and the move became official two months later, solving the dilemma.

Meanwhile, the winning share for each Packer was $224. Each Redskin got $160, or more than enough for Christmas presents back then.

PORTSMOUTH TIE GOOD ENOUGH FOR PACKERS

DECEMBER 14, 1930

Getting a National Football League franchise was easy during the Great Depression. Keeping one was hard.

Green Bay with its population of 37,327 was the smallest city in the league when the Packers traveled to Portsmouth, Ohio, needing at least a tie in their final game to clinch their second straight championship. The second-smallest city was Portsmouth, which was enjoying its first season in the league. All it took to get in was a $500 fee and a $1,500 deposit.

Built on the production of steel, bricks and shoes, the Ohio River town of 42,560 was growing and eager to become big time. It had been a semi-pro football hotbed for at least 20 years before the Portsmouth National League Football Corporation gained entry to the NFL in June 1930 after offering 250 shares of stock to local citizens and businesses at $100 a share. Construction also had begun on a 20,000-seat concrete stadium that would open in September.

In some ways, the Portsmouth Spartans were a mirror image of the Packers, but they lacked Green Bay's staying power.

One of the Spartans' best players was Roy "Father" Lumpkin, a talented back with a reputation for toughness earned by his refusal to wear a helmet. The coach was Harold Griffen. Another prospective star was a back named Keith Molesworth, who was cut before the season and later played seven years with the Chicago Bears. The speculation around Portsmouth was that Molesworth had lost his roster spot because he'd stolen Griffen's girlfriend, a woman Molesworth would later marry.

The Spartans started their maiden season well, winning four of their first six games, but then things came apart, and they took a 5-6-2 record into their battle with the 10-3 Packers. Championships were determined by final standings then, and the Packers needed a tie to finish ahead of the New York Giants.

The other nine teams in the league had already finished play, including the Giants, who had gone 13-4 for a .765 winning percentage. A loss to Portsmouth would drop the Packers to 10-4 and a .714 winning percentage. A tie with the Spartans would leave the Packers with a final record of 10-3-1 and give them the title by a mere .004 margin. At the time, ties were simply thrown out and not factored into the math.

While Portsmouth was playing for nothing but pride, it salvaged plenty of that by battling Green Bay to a 6-6 standstill before 4,500 fans at Universal Stadium. Nevertheless, the Packers had their title by virtue of their .769 winning percentage.

They scored in the first quarter on a 16-yard pass from quarterback Red Dunn to right halfback Wuert Engelmann, but Dunn's extra point kick sailed wide. The Spartans came back and scored in the second quarter on a short touchdown run by Chuck Bennett and missed the conversion as well. There was no more scoring, which was fine for the Packer players who headed home for a lavish victory celebration and bonus checks from a $5,000 championship fund raised by the people of Green Bay.

The Spartans came back stronger in 1931, compiling an 11-3 record and finishing one game behind the champion Packers, who went 12-2. The two teams didn't face each other, but the Spartans argued that they had a game scheduled with the Packers at the end of the season that would have given them a shot at a share of the title. The Packers countered that the game was only "tentative" and refused to play. NFL President Joe Carr backed the Packers, and the Spartans were out of luck.

They were also out of cash, blaming their financial woes partly on the Packers for refusing to play them, and they needed to sell more stock to survive. After raising enough money to field a team again in 1932, the Spartans gained a measure of revenge when they used only 11 men to beat the Packers, 19-0, on Dec. 4, and essentially deprive them of their fourth straight league title.

But the bad economy was taking an ever-mounting toll, and Portsmouth's players were forced to take shares of stock in the team in lieu of salary during the 1933 season. The Spartans finished 6-5 and badly in debt.

Despite the team's four-year record of 23-10-4, the directors in Portsmouth gave up in the summer of 1934 and sold the franchise to a Michigan businessman named George Richards. The Portsmouth Spartans were no more, and so ended their bitter rivalry with the Packers. But they became the Detroit Lions, and another bitter rivalry was born.

UW-WHITEWATER DETHRONES MOUNT UNION

DECEMBER 15, 2007

The NCAA Division III football championship was becoming a private argument between the University of Wisconsin-Whitewater and Mount Union College, which would have been fine with Whitewater, except that Mount Union kept winning the debate.

The Warhawks had made it to the title game in the last two years and lost both times to the top-ranked Purple Raiders. Now they were back for a third try that looked even less likely to succeed than the first two.

Whitewater had 23 seniors and 11 starters back from its 2006 runner-up team, but the coach had retired and the quarterback had graduated. When Justin Jacobs left, he took the school's career passing record with him. When coach Bob Berezowitz retired after 22 years, he left a legend behind him.

On the other hand, Mount Union, located in Alliance, Ohio, about 15 miles northeast of Canton, never seemed to lose anything. The Raiders came into this Amos Alonzo Stagg Bowl with a 37-game winning streak that stretched back to the seventh game of the 2005 season. Coach Larry Kehres had compiled a 260-20-3 record since becoming the head coach in 1986, which was better than any other college football coach on any level. And the Raiders had won nine of the last 14 Division III titles and had suffered only three losses since 2000.

Mount Union was winning its games by an average margin of 54-5, and no one had come within three touchdowns of the Raiders all season. But that changed in a big way on a cold and rainy Saturday in Salem, Va., when Whitewater upended the 20-point favorites, 31-21, under new coach Lance Leipold.

Leipold was a former Whitewater quarterback and a surprise choice to take over for Berezowitz. Most people thought the job would go to longtime offensive coordinator Stan Zweifel. Nobody knew who the quarterback job would go to until Danny Jones, a senior transfer from California Lutheran University, reached out to the Warhawks.

Jones had become acquainted with Whitewater when he watched the title game the previous year. When his coach left Cal Lutheran, also a Division III school, he sent Leipold an e-mail, and he followed that up with tapes. Leipold was impressed, and he became more impressed throughout the season as Jones threw 22 touchdown passes.

But Leipold's biggest weapon was there all along. Returning senior tailback Justin Beaver of Palmyra, Wis., was awarded the Gagliardi Trophy as the nation's top Division III player for just the kind of performance that he turned in against Mount Union. Still recovering from a fractured rib suffered more than a month earlier, Beaver carried the ball 31 times for 249 yards, an eight-yard average, against a defense that had been giving up an average of 24 yards rushing a game.

Beaver, who stood just 5 feet 7 inches and weighed 191 pounds, surpassed that number on his first carry when his 26-yard run set up a one-yard sneak by Jones that put the Warhawks ahead for good. Then he went for a 45-yard gallop that led to a 32-yard field goal by Jeff Schebler and a 10-0 halftime lead. That in itself was a monumental accomplishment, considering Mount Union had outscored its previous opponents that season, 548-22, in the first half alone.

It became 17-0 when tackle Michael Sherman recovered a Beaver fumble in the end zone in the third quarter, and that finally seemed to get Mount Union's attention.

The Raiders scored back-to-back rushing touchdowns to close the difference to 17-14, but then Beaver scored from 13 yards out. Mount Union's final touchdown with 3 minutes 36 seconds to play narrowed the gap to 24-21, but Jones scored again on a one-yard sneak two minutes later, and the Warhawks had their title.

"Change is sometimes difficult, but once everybody realized we were all Warhawks and that I was someone who was more or less coming home, we've worked together for a common goal," Leipold said. "And while many didn't think we had a chance to be here at this point in the day, here we are."

Not only that, but they were back the next year playing for the championship again. Same opponent, but a different result. Then in 2009, it was Whitewater's turn again. The two schools played in the title game for the fifth straight year and Whitewater won its second title. The argument rages on.

The UW-Whitewater football team celebrated its victory over Mount Union in the NCAA Division III football championship.

MARAVICH, COWENS JUST PART OF "CLASSIC" SHOW

DECEMBER 16, 1967

Sophomore sensations Pete Maravich and Dave Cowens dominated the statistics in the sixth annual Milwaukee Classic at the Milwaukee Arena, but it was a couple of guys in stripes who claimed much of the attention.

Maravich, the 6-foot-5 gunner from Louisiana State University, scored 84 points in two games and lost both of them; while Cowens, Florida State's 6-8 red-headed center, pulled down 42 in addition to his 36 points and got a split for his efforts.

And then there were Fred Huiet and Don Wedge. Both officials were from Ohio, and both would have been welcome anytime in Madison after calling one technical foul in the tournament's first round on Friday night that boosted Wisconsin into the finals and then calling another that helped the Badgers upset Marquette, 70-62, for the championship 24 hours later.

Cowens, who had had been held to 12 points and 11 rebounds before fouling out with eight minutes to play against Marquette in the semifinals, set the stage for the Saturday night final with a monster performance in the consolation game. He ripped down 31 rebounds and scored 24 points as Florida State turned a 54-52 halftime deficit into a 130-100 rout of LSU. Maravich, who would go on to become the nation's top scorer for three years in a row, scored 42 points for the losing Tigers.

And then the co-hosts faced off for the title, with Wedge and Huiet calling the game. Wisconsin took a 3-1 record into the contest, whereas Marquette had won its first four games by an average margin of 28 points. The heavily-favored Warriors grabbed a 10-point lead early in the second half, but Wisconsin squared matters at 58 after Marquette lost the ball on a five-second violation, called by Wedge, with just over two minutes to play.

Marquette coach Al McGuire was enraged by the call, but he was about to get much angrier. With 32 seconds to play and the score tied at 62, Huiet charged Marquette forward Joe Thomas with a flagrant foul against Wisconsin's Jim Johnson. McGuire erupted and drew a technical.

Johnson converted both free throws on the flagrant foul, and guard Mike Carlin sank another on the technical. And then after the Warriors fouled Mel Riddick as he took the ensuing inbounds pass, he made one more free throw for a 66-62 lead.

That decided the game and prompted a small group of unruly fans to jostle Wedge and Huiet as they tried to leave the floor. The officials needed a police escort to their locker room while McGuire was uncharacteristically stonewalling the press. He was so incensed that he declined all comment and referred reporters instead to LSU coach Press Maravich.

Press, the father of Pete, knew just how McGuire felt. He had been the victim of the first controversial technical the night before when LSU played Wisconsin.

The Badgers had held a five-point lead early in the second half of that game when Wedge's whistle took center stage. As Tigers' guard Jeff Tribbett broke away for an uncontested layup, the official stopped play and called a T on stunned LSU assistant coach Jay McCreary. It seems they had a communications problem.

According to an unnamed witness at the scorer's table who was quoted in the next day's edition of the *The Milwaukee Journal*, McCreary was shouting at his player to "shoot the (expletive deleted) ball!" But Wedge thought he heard "Make the (expletive deleted) call," and he T'd up the LSU bench.

The Tigers lost both the ball and the chance at an easy basket. And when Wisconsin's Chuck Nagle made the free throw on the technical and then scored on the subsequent possession, it was essentially a five-point play. A 65-60 UW lead was now a 68-60 lead whereas it could have been a 65-62 game.

LSU almost recovered, but not quite as the Badgers won, 96-94, to advance to the final against Marquette despite 42 points by the conscience-less Maravich. Pistol Pete jacked up 42 shots and made 16 of them in the days before the three-point shot.

The Warriors beat Florida State, 78-58, in the other semifinal when George Thompson scored 28 points, but all that did was put Wedge and Huiet back in the spotlight the following night.

PACKERS OUTLAST GIANTS, HERBER FOR NFL TITLE

DECEMBER 17, 1944

Ted Fritsch's heroics were almost spoiled by Arnie Herber's revenge when the Green Bay Packers beat the New York Giants, 14-7, to win their sixth National Football League championship. It was a case of one Wisconsin native outshining another, but not by much.

Herber was born in Green Bay, attended the University of Wisconsin as a freshman and played one year at Regis College in Denver before he began his pro career with the Packers in 1930. Herber and Don Hutson virtually redefined the passing game in the NFL, but then Cecil Isbell came along to take over much of the Packers' passing duties. So before the 1941 season started, Curly Lambeau cut his 31-year-old homegrown tailback.

Normally, that might have been the end of a Hall of Fame career, but there was a war going on, and players were in short supply. So when the Giants called three years later, Herber came out of retirement.

He wasn't a major factor when the Giants and Packers met in a regular-season game on Nov. 19. Herber completed just one pass, although it went for a 36-yard touchdown. But, in truth, the Giants didn't need to mount an aerial game of their own as long as they contained the Packers' passing attack, and they did that well. With Isbell now retired and tailback Irv Comp suffering an injury early in the third quarter, the Packers completed just 14 of 34 passes and Hutson had only four catches for 31 yards in a lopsided 24-0 loss.

It was a typical performance for the Giants' league-leading defense. They would post five shutouts that year while allowing only 7.5 points a game in winning the Eastern Division with an 8-1-1 record. And they were hoping to stymie the Western Division champion Packers, who went 8-2, again in their rematch for the NFL title.

The Packers had one big advantage going into the showdown at the Polo Grounds. They'd had three weeks to rest up after their last game, while the Giants had ended the regular season just the week before against Washington, and their star halfback Bill Paschal had suffered an ankle injury that limited him to two carries in the championship game.

If the Packers were rusty at all because of the layoff it didn't show. They never allowed the Giants to get past their own 35-yard line while holding them without a first down in the first half. Meanwhile, Fritsch, a 5-foot-10, 210-pound fullback, scored both of Green Bay's touchdowns in the second quarter.

The Spencer, Wis., native ran in from the one for the first one after setting the score up with a 27-yard run, and he caught a 24-yard pass for what proved to be the game-winner when Hutson drew double coverage as a decoy. No one was near Fritsch when he caught the ball.

The league put on a show featuring jugglers, skaters and acrobats at halftime, but it did little to pacify the New York fans. One of them shouted at Giants President Jack Mara, "Hey, Mara! So you're giving us a circus, huh? How about giving us a first down?"

Mara couldn't supply that, so Herber put on an aerial circus instead. While Green Bay stayed mainly on the ground, Herber threw for 114 yards in the second half after being blanked in the first half. Four of his attempts were picked off by the Packers, three in the second half, all by 34-year-old utility back Joe Laws.

Still, Herber managed to kick-start the New York offense. The Giants registered all nine of their first downs in the second half, and they scored their only touchdown after Herber completed a 41-yard pass to the one-yard line on the last play of the third quarter. Herber had the Giants on the march again in the closing minutes before a final interception by Paul Duhart put the game away for Green Bay.

Fritsch rushed for 59 yards on 18 carries and Laws for 72 on 13 attempts. Hutson caught only two passes that day, and when the game was over, he said his career was, too. "If I play another game here, you can push me off the top of the Empire State Building," he said.

This was at least the third or maybe even the fourth or fifth time that Hutson announced his retirement, and when Lambeau heard about it, he just laughed. But Hutson did hang it up after the 1945 season. So did Herber. This time for good.

PACKERS WIN THEIR LAST GAME IN MILWAUKEE

DECEMBER 18, 1994

The Green Bay Packers' president was approaching Port Washington at the same time as the Green Packers' quarterback was diving into the end zone. Each had to say goodbye to Milwaukee in his own way.

In Bob Harlan's case it was a precautionary measure when three policemen met him in the press box with seven minutes left in a tense game with the Atlanta Falcons and escorted his wife and him out of County Stadium. The last thing the Packers' CEO wanted was to miss the climax of his team's final game in Milwaukee, but the cops had convinced him of the danger of some fanatic in the crowd looking for him or his family on the way out.

In Brett Favre's case, there were hardly ever any precautionary measures. The Packers were down to 21 seconds and trailing by three points in a game they had to win when they lined up on the Atlanta Falcons' nine-yard line. Favre had three wide receivers deployed, along with his tight end and running back, and when he saw all five of them covered and started to feel pressure, he pulled the ball down and headed diagonally toward the right corner of the end zone.

Favre had to make a choice. He could try to get out of bounds with enough time left for a game-tying field goal attempt, or he could go for broke and try to reach the end zone. Falcons defensive end Chuck Smith had a third option in mind. He could chase Favre down, and maybe time would run out before the Packers could accomplish either of the first two.

Favre made his decision, and the race was on. The normally speedy Smith was slowed by a sprained knee suffered in the second quarter, but he still got his hand on Favre's ankle, causing him to stumble at the six. Then the quarterback righted himself at the three and dived into the end zone, barely evading fast-closing Falcons cornerback Anthony Phillips.

Favre reached the goal line with 14 seconds on the clock at the same time as Harlan reached the northern suburbs, his ear glued to his car radio. The Harlans' cheers might have been heard all the way back in Milwaukee if 54,885 people hadn't gone completely crazy back at the stadium.

As the Packers ran off the field, coach Mike Holmgren stopped at a snowbank along the first-base line and pumped his fists in the air in front of the crowd. "I'll never forget this," said the Packers' coach. "It was a very special moment." The final score read 21-17, and the franchise's 62-year stay in Milwaukee had ended in a rising wave of emotion.

Favre said afterward that he had "no idea" what made him decide to run with the ball, but his teammates weren't surprised. "It's vintage Brett Favre," said kicker Chris Jacke. "Dumb and brilliant at the same time."

Jacke had missed two field goals, and the Packers had blown a 14-3 lead when they huddled on their own 33 with 1 minute 58 seconds to play. Favre said then that they were going for the touchdown, not the field goal, and 10 plays later they had it.

They left the game with an 8-7 record needing to win at Tampa Bay the following weekend to make the playoffs. When the Packers beat the Buccaneers, 34-19, they were in, and the fans were feeling very good about their football team. Even their Milwaukee fans.

Harlan was extremely pleased by that. In his autobiography *Green and Golden Moments*, the Packers' former president said that moving the team out of the state's largest city was the hardest thing he'd ever had to do. The Packers played in Milwaukee for the first time in 1933 when they lost to the New York Giants at the old Borchert Field baseball stadium, and they would go on to play a portion of their schedule each year at State Fair Park, Marquette Stadium and County Stadium. But that was before millions of dollars in renovations turned Green Bay's Lambeau Field into a cash cow and made staying in Milwaukee fiscally unfeasible.

Harlan, recognizing that Milwaukee fans had kept the club afloat during the Depression and had remained loyal ever since, insisted that they still have the option to buy tickets for two regular-season games and one exhibition each year. Only now they'd be watching those games in Green Bay. When 96% of the Milwaukee season ticketholders picked up their option for the "Gold Package" in 1995, he was more than relieved to see there were no hard feelings.

PACKERS FIRE BART STARR

DECEMBER 19, 1983

He left with his head held high and his pocket full of timeouts. Bart Starr had coached the Green Bay Packers for 131 regular-season games when Judge Robert Parins announced at a Monday morning press conference that he was firing him and his entire staff. Who knows how many more he would have coached if he had won the last one?

The Packers' president said the team's last-second loss at Chicago in its regular-season finale wasn't the determining factor in ending Starr's 26-year association with the franchise, but he acknowledged that if they'd won, he wouldn't have made the decision he did that day.

A victory at Soldier Field would have given the Packers a 9-7 record and put them in the playoffs for only the second time in Starr's nine seasons in charge. Instead, they lost, 23-21, on Bob Thomas' wobbly 22-yard field goal with 10 seconds to play. The Bears had eaten up almost three minutes on their final drive while Starr declined to use his three remaining timeouts to stop the clock and give his explosive offense a chance to bail out his collapsible defense. Asked later why he hadn't called a timeout during the march, he snapped, "That's our business."

The testy response was symptomatic of the bunker mentality Starr adopted toward the media to the very end. At his final press conference he told photographers to stop taking pictures and warned television reporters to turn off their live broadcasts or he would refuse to answer questions.

Then he thanked his family and his staff for their support while making a long statement that quoted Teddy Roosevelt extensively. Starr went on to say he would be the Packers' No. 1 fan, and he declared that the organization was far better off than when he took over.

That might have been true because he inherited a shipwreck from Dan Devine, but Starr never lifted it out of an orbit of mediocrity. He finished with a 52-76-3 regular-season record and only two winning seasons and two .500 years. His teams had never won as many as four games in a row, and their only playoff appearance came after the strike-shortened 1982 season. Just 13 of his victories came against teams that finished with winning records, and 20 of his losses came by 20 points or more.

Instability plagued the process. Starr went through three player personnel directors, creating a fair amount of confusion in the draft room. In 1979, despite the pleadings of Midwest scout Red Cochran, Starr bypassed a Notre Dame quarterback to take running back Steve Atkins in the second round and nose tackle Charlie Johnson in the third. The quarterback's name was Joe Montana. Two years later, Starr opted for quarterback Rich Campbell, who had a long, slow delivery, although his personnel director at the time, Dick Corrick, tried everything to persuade him to take defensive back Ronnie Lott instead.

Montana and Lott are in the Pro Football Hall of Fame. Atkins, Johnson and Campbell were spectacular busts.

In 1980, Starr was stripped of his general manager's title, although he kept control of the football operation. That was also the year that he fired defensive coordinator Dave Hanner. At the same time, his offense was without a coordinator and being run by committee. Starr would have 24 assistant coaches in his nine years. Dallas' Tom Landry had 27 in 29 seasons.

Some circumstances were beyond Starr's control. Devine's disastrous trade for John Hadl had left him in terrible shape for his first two drafts. Some of his best draft picks had to deal with serious injuries, including running back Eddie Lee Ivery, tackle Mark Koncar and linebacker John Anderson.

Nevertheless, Starr appeared to be totally ambushed when Parins walked into his office shortly before 8 a.m. the morning after the Bears' game and informed him of his decision. Three days earlier, when Starr was asked about his job status before the game, he said, "I'm just getting started."

Almost 20 years after his firing, Starr told *Packer Plus* that accepting the job to coach the Packers was "the biggest mistake I ever made in my life," adding that he took full responsibility for his record. "I just didn't get it done," he said.

WISCONSIN EDGES MARQUETTE IN LOCAL STARFEST

DECEMBER 20, 2003

This wasn't a basketball game, it was a commercial. The product was Wisconsin high school basketball, and the message was that it had come a long way.

Wisconsin and Marquette had clashed 109 times before, but this was only the second time that both were nationally ranked when they met. Wisconsin was 18th in the ESPN/USA Today coaches' poll and 22nd in the Associated Press poll, while Marquette was 23rd in both.

The two had done it with homegrown talent. Four of the starters on each side had played as preps in the Badger State. Three of the five players on the 2001 *Milwaukee Journal Sentinel*/Wisconsin Basketball Coaches Association all-state first-team were there.

Marquette coach Tom Crean had said all week that this was a very big deal, while Wisconsin's Bo Ryan had insisted that it was just another game. When a record 176 media credentials were issued, Crean won the argument. But Ryan won the game as his Wisconsin thumpers outlasted Marquette's marksmen, 63-59, in the closest contest in the series since 1985.

The Badgers scored 36 points in the paint, while Marquette made nine of 18 three-point attempts. In a nutshell that was the difference. But a lot of delicious issues were raised first.

For instance, how advantageous was the home-court advantage? Wisconsin made 22 of 32 free throws to Marquette's six of nine before a sellout crowd of 17,142 at the Kohl Center. The Badgers were called for 12 fouls, the Golden Eagles for 23.

And which team had recruited the better point guard? Wisconsin's Devin Harris had been voted Mr. Basketball in the state for 2001 after a stellar senior year at Wauwatosa East. Marquette's Travis Diener had finished a close second in the balloting after starring at Fond du Lac. In a way, the results were duplicated on the court in what was now their junior year in college.

The 6-foot-1 Diener finished the day with 19 points, five rebounds and three assists in a team-high 33 minutes. The 6-3 Harris had 15 points, four rebounds and four assists in a team-high 36 minutes. But the important thing to both was that Wisconsin won and Marquette didn't, and it took them all game to sort that out.

Marquette made six of its first nine shots, and Wisconsin missed its first seven and fell behind, 9-0. Diener scored 11 of his points in the first half as the Golden Eagles raced to a 32-20 lead. But the Badgers went on a 12-0 run just before intermission, and the game was tied at 32 at halftime. Then it was Harris' turn as he scored 11 of his points in the final 20 minutes.

The play of the game came with 45 seconds remaining when sophomore forward Alando Tucker spun around Steve Novak, another sophomore forward, for a basket that gave the Badgers a 61-58 lead. Tucker, who was starting his first game of the season after recovering from a broken foot, scored 17 points and claimed six rebounds. An Illinois native, he showed no respect for the game's local flavor, while Brown Deer's Novak showed no great inclination to get in his way. Novak had four fouls, and he knew the Eagles might need him at the end.

They did, too. They got him the ball with 13 seconds remaining for a three-point attempt that would have the tied the game. It was the kind of shot that Novak usually made in his sleep. This time it didn't happen to fall, and Wisconsin wrapped up the fifth victory in its last six games against Marquette.

Novak finished with 12 points, while his fellow members of the Eagles' frontline, Scott Merritt of Wauwatosa East and Terry Sanders of Milwaukee Vincent, combined for 12 rebounds and nine points. UW guard Freddie Owens of Milwaukee Washington made a key free throw with 21 seconds left. And Mike Wilkinson, who had played at Wisconsin Heights High School, grabbed 10 rebounds and scored nine points. Boo Wade, who also played at Vincent, scored six for the Badgers.

Harris would enter the NBA draft following the season and be selected fifth. Diener would be chosen 38th the following year and Novak 32nd two years later.

The Golden Eagles finished the 2003-'04 season with a 19-12 record that left them in the NIT. The Badgers went 25-7 and lost in the second round of the NCAA tournament. None of their victories that season were better appreciated than the one over Marquette. It came on Ryan's 56th birthday in a game that was a gift to the entire state.

PRINCETON'S BRADLEY BEDEVILS BADGERS

DECEMBER 21, 1963

You didn't have to be a Rhodes scholar to tell that the University of Wisconsin basketball team was in for a long night against Princeton. The Tigers were bound for a second straight Ivy League championship and NCAA tournament bid, and they were led by one of the most prolific scorers in collegiate history.

Bill Bradley, a 6-foot-5 junior, had been recruited by upward of 60 major colleges as a high school All-American at Crystal City, Mo., but he had chosen Princeton, in part, because of its Woodrow Wilson School of International Affairs. Wilson, the 28th president of the United States, was a Princeton alumnus and Bradley was considering a career in Foreign Service. In addition to being an incredible athletic talent, Bradley was an exceptional character. He would become an Olympian, a United States senator, a presidential hopeful and ... a Rhodes Scholar.

The Badgers encountered him in the consolation game of the Kentucky Invitational Tournament, and they took some consolation from the fact that they were able to extend his team into overtime before losing, 90-87.

Coach John Erickson had led a less than average group into Lexington, Ky., where it was demolished, 108-85, by the University of Kentucky in the windup of the Friday night semifinals. That outcome led to Wisconsin's matchup against the Tigers, who had lost, 86-67, to Wake Forest in the other semifinal. Bradley had scored 30 points against Wake, or just under the 32.3 points that he would average that season, but he would have a much better night against the Badgers, who were on their way to an 8-16 season.

Bradley broke the tournament record by scoring 47 points, including seven of the Tigers' 11 in overtime. His hook shot with 41 seconds left in regulation tied the score at 79 and sent the game into the extra period, and his two free throws in the final five seconds clinched the victory. It also was his three-point play with 1 minute 17 seconds remaining that put the Tigers ahead for good, 88-87.

UW senior guard Don Hearden scored 23 points, including 16 in the second half and overtime, but his two traveling violations in a 38-second span late in overtime paved the way for Bradley's heroics. Senior guard Mike O'Melia added 21 to the Badgers' scoring output.

Bradley's 47 points were a personal best at that point and they easily broke the Kentucky Invitational record of 37 that Jerry West of West Virginia had set in 1959. Bradley would score 49 in an Ivy League game against Cornell less than a month later and top out with a 58-point performance against Wichita State in the third-place game of the 1965 Final Four.

In three years of college basketball – freshmen weren't eligible to play on the varsity then – Bradley scored 2,503 points and averaged 30.1 points per game. Forty-six years later, he was still one of only 10 players in NCAA Division I history to have scored 2,500 points or more in only three seasons.

These weren't the kind of numbers normally associated with a player at a non-scholarship Ivy League school, but then Bradley wasn't much for normality. He was touted in the Midwest, at least, as perhaps the best high school senior in the country during the 1961-'62 season and he had decided two years earlier that he was going to Duke, but he changed his mind at the last minute after doing some more research on Princeton.

It was an expensive decision, but Bradley's father was a bank president, and he really didn't need the scholarship. Three varsity seasons, three Ivy League titles, one Olympic gold medal and one Sullivan Award later, Bradley was back to turning down money. This time the New York Knicks picked him first in the 1965 NBA draft, and he rejected their offer and went overseas on a Rhodes scholarship instead.

Two years later, Bradley signed with the Knicks and wound up playing 10 years in the NBA, before retiring from basketball and going into politics. He was elected to the U.S. Senate in 1978 and served the State of New Jersey for three terms. In 2000, he challenged Al Gore for the presidential nomination of the Democratic Party and lost.

To this day, he's one of the best players Wisconsin has ever faced in more than 110 years of varsity basketball and certainly one of the most famous.

FAVRE STARS DESPITE FATHER'S DEATH

DECEMBER 22, 2003

Considering the source, this stood as one of the great compliments of Brett Favre's career. He ran onto the field at Network Associates Coliseum, and he was met with cheers. Not an ovation by any means, just polite applause, but that never happened in Oakland.

The Oakland Coliseum – as it's once again known – is the home of the dreaded "Black Hole," where the fans are famous for treating all of their visitors like kidnappers. True to form, they had booed the Green Bay Packers' starters enthusiastically one by one during the pre-game introductions. Until Favre's name was called last. Then the crowd of 62,298 clapped.

The quarterback had spent 12 years earning these people's respect, and he would spend the next three hours destroying their football team.

There was a serious question of whether Favre would be there at all after word spread that his father had died a day earlier, the victim of a heart attack at age 58. Irvin Favre had always been his son's hero, coach and confidante. Brett said his dad hadn't missed a game since he was in fifth grade. And he was convinced that he didn't miss this one either.

"I didn't expect this kind of performance, but I know he was watching tonight," Favre said afterward.

No one could have expected that kind of performance. In the first half Favre was, by National Football League standards, merely perfect. He achieved the maximum quarterback rating of 158.3 by completing 15 of 18 passes for 311 yards and four touchdowns, with eight of the 15 completions going for 20 yards or more. When Raiders coach Bill Callahan was asked at halftime what could be done to slow Favre down, he said, "I have absolutely no idea."

The final numbers showed Favre with 22 completions in 30 attempts for 399 yards. He hit on his first nine passes, gaining 184 yards. Setting the tone on the Packers' first possession, an 80-yard drive, Favre connected with wide receiver Robert Ferguson on a 47-yard bomb and threw a 22-yard dart to tight end Wesley Walls for a touchdown.

Walls, a 14-year veteran who had signed with the Packers as a free agent in August, went high into the air to snare the ball in the corner of the end zone. Asked later what he said to Favre, Walls replied, "I just said, 'I love you.' He played an amazing game for us, and we all felt we had to do the same for him."

And so they did. Favre completed passes to 12 different players, and they dropped just one ball. It didn't seem to matter how many Raiders were around the Green Bay receivers. If Favre could get the ball into the same area code, they'd come down with it. Wide receiver Javon Walker caught touchdown passes of 43 and 23 yards, and tight end David Martin caught the other touchdown on a six-yard pass following a 46-yard reception by Walker.

Running back Ahman Green complemented the passing game with 127 yards on the ground, and the offensive line allowed only one sack. The Packers' defense limited the Raiders to a single first-quarter touchdown. Defensive end Kabeer Gbaja-Biamila contributed three sacks, and cornerback Michael Hawthorne, filling in for an injured Mike McKenzie, had two interceptions.

The final score was 41-7, and Favre was as amazed by the result as anyone. "I'd like to take credit for a lot of it, but when you make catches like those guys did and block the way our guys did, I don't know if I've ever seen an effort quite like that before," he said.

Favre's appearance boosted his record consecutive game streak to 205 starts, but that was hardly the main consideration in his decision to play. Shortly after getting the news of his father's death in a cell phone call from his agent, Favre stood in front of his teammates and told them he had no intention of leaving his football family at a time like this. The Packers were 8-6 at that point, and they needed the game badly to stay in playoff contention.

"I knew that my dad would have wanted me to play," he said. "I love him so much, and I love this game. It's meant a great deal to me, to my dad, to my family..."

And on a Monday night in one of the world's toughest places to play, it loved him back.

LOMBARDI PACKERS SCORE RARE UPSET ON HOME TURF

DECEMBER 23, 1967

With 40 tons of hay spread over the field to keep it from freezing, County Stadium resembled a 50,000-seat pasture. The Green Bay Packers would be playing a post-season game there for the first and last time, and the grounds crew in Milwaukee wanted to be sure it was ready for the raw 20-degree weather.

There could have been some symbolism involved, too. The Packers were being portrayed as the old gray mares that weren't what they used to be as they prepared to face the Los Angeles Rams in the Western Conference championship game. The oddsmakers were reflecting that sentiment by making the Rams one-point favorites, marking the first time the Packers had ever been underdogs in a playoff game in their own state.

In what was the NFL's first year of a four-division format, Vince Lombardi's defending titlists had topped the lukewarm Central Division with a 9-4-1 record. Los Angeles had gone 11-1-2 in the much tougher Coastal Division, tying the Baltimore Colts for first place and earning the playoff berth based on point differential in head-to-head competition.

Two weeks earlier, Green Bay, with a playoff berth already secured, had blown a last-minute lead in a 27-24 loss at the Los Angeles Memorial Coliseum, and now the Rams were back with their indomitable 6-foot-4, 225-pound quarterback and their ferocious pass rush. Lombardi, on the other hand, was down to playing his third-string backfield at times.

The Rams had their "Fearsome Foursome" of Deacon Jones, Merlin Olsen, Roger Brown and Lamar Lundy, who had chased quarterback Bart Starr all over the field two weeks earlier, and they had Roman Gabriel, who had thrown three touchdown passes, including a decisive five-yard toss to wide receiver Bernie Casey with 26 seconds to play.

While a sellout crowd of 49,861, much of it bundled in blaze orange, watched nervously, the Rams jumped out to a 7-0 lead with the same combination that won the game in Los Angeles. Gabriel hit Casey with a 29-yard touchdown pass after a Green Bay fumble. And then another Packer turnover, an interception thrown by Bart Starr, helped put the Rams on the Green Bay five early in the second quarter. But the visitors came away with nothing when linebacker Dave Robinson blocked a chip-shot field goal attempt.

"If we score at all down there, we win," said George Allen. There was no way to tell whether the Rams' coach was right about that, but the momentum had definitely switched to the Packers, and they never let go of it.

Rookie halfback Travis Williams, who was spelling Donny Anderson who had replaced the injured Elijah Pitts, broke loose for a 46-yard run to tie the game, and then Starr connected with wide receiver Carroll Dale on a 17-yard touchdown pass that was set up when Willie Wood returned a short field goal attempt 44 yards.

The Rams couldn't figure out what to do with Williams. Lombardi took advantage of their fervent dedication to the pass rush by gouging them for 163 yards on the ground. Williams got 88 of those yards on 19 carries and earned Allen's praise as "the best third-string halfback in America."

The Packers opened the second half with an 80-yard drive capped by a six-yard touchdown run by Chuck Mercein, who was their third fullback, and then Williams scored again on a short run in the fourth quarter to seal a highly satisfying 28-7 victory.

Starr led the offense by completing 17 of 23 passes for 222 yards, but this day belonged to the grunts. The Packers' graying offensive line limited Jones, Olsen and friends to a single sack, while their own front four got to Gabriel five times for 44 yards in losses. Four of the sacks came from 32-year-old defensive tackle Henry Jordan.

Lombardi took great pride in the fact that his team had held the league's most productive offense to 217 yards and a single touchdown, even though his offense had turned the ball over four times. "There's a special sort of satisfaction in winning this one," he said. "Everybody has been saying we were dead, that we won in a patsy division in the league, that we weren't the Packers we once were. We had something to prove, and we proved it."

And they weren't done proving things. They beat Dallas the next week for their third straight NFL title and then won Super Bowl II.

PACKERS BOW TO DEMAND, NAME STARR COACH

DECEMBER 24, 1974

If football coaches were elected, Bart Starr would have run unopposed in Green Bay. The public and members of the media had nominated him well before the job became vacant, and when the unpopular Dan Devine left the Packers on Dec. 15 to coach Notre Dame, there were few regrets in Titletown.

Starr had quarterbacked the franchise to five NFL championships. Devine had gotten his dog shot, although it should be noted that the shooting occurred after Devine had been warned by a neighboring farmer whose animals were being chased by the wandering dog. And while Devine had been named NFC Coach of the Year by United Press International in 1972 for leading the Packers to their first division championship in five seasons, Starr's legion of backers said Devine never could have done it without their man as quarterback coach.

They cited as evidence the Packers' failure to reach .500 in the two years after Starr left the coaching staff. And so after Devine skipped town for South Bend, Ind., before the franchise's seven-man executive committee even had time to announce that it had fired him, it was almost a foregone conclusion that Starr would get the job.

The executive committee interviewed only one other candidate and that was defensive coordinator Dave Hanner, who never really had a chance. After signing Starr to a three-year contract as coach and general manager, the Packers introduced him at a packed press conference on the morning of Christmas Eve.

Starr asked Packers' patrons for two things: "Prayers and patience." He said he would earn everything else.

It was a stirring inaugural, replete with self-effacement, gratitude and optimism. The new head man said he'd had other offers, but none that excited him like this one. He said he was "humbled," but "not awed," adding, "I'm not as qualified as I'd like to be, but I'm willing."

Starr was 40 years old at the time and had played quarterback for the Packers for 16 years, nine of them under legendary coach Vince Lombardi, but he had spent only one year as an assistant coach. After a week of training camp in 1972, Starr had determined that he could no longer play because of arm problems and agreed to join Devine's staff.

Starr handled most of the play-calling that year as the Packers compiled a 10-4 record and won the NFC Central Division. But, then, in the playoffs against Washington, Devine overrode him and stuck with his vaunted running game, although the Redskins lined up with five defensive linemen. The Packers couldn't move the ball; lost, 16-3; and Starr left coaching. He tended to his business interests for two years and did some work as a game analyst for CBS.

At his opening press conference, Starr declined to predict when the Packers would make it back to the playoffs, saying that he didn't feel qualified to evaluate the talent on the roster. Devine was happy to help in that regard. "There's no way they can't make it to the Super Bowl," he said, dropping a 100-pound sandbag on his successor.

The truth was Starr had inherited an aging and badly divided team that was in a near state of mutiny. Things were in such turmoil that at least some players had openly talked about boycotting the final game of the 1974 season just to assure that Devine wouldn't be back.

Starr also said at his press conference that he'd have to take a crash course before the Jan. 28 college draft. "I couldn't name five college players," he said. Not that it mattered. Devine had spent the Packers' first three choices in that draft, as well as the first two in the next one, on over-the-hill quarterback John Hadl, adding years to the rebuilding process.

The Packers also still owed one of the two second-round draft picks that Devine had shipped to Miami for an unproven quarterback named Jim Del Gaizo and a fifth-round choice that Devine had given to Dallas for yet another quarterback, journeyman Jack Concannon. What's more, the Packers owed Kansas City a third-round selection in 1976 for quarterback Dean Carlson. Never heard of Carlson? That's because five weeks after Devine traded for him in Sept. 1974, he cut him and Carlson never played again.

On the day Starr was hired, linebacker Jim Carter echoed the sentiments of most of the players on the team when he praised the decision and referred to Devine's last year as "a nightmare." But Starr's reign as coach was never the Camelot that many expected it to be.

TYPHOID FEVER CLAIMS "KECKIE" MOLL

DECEMBER 25, 1912

The letter from Ohio State arrived at Madison General Hospital on Christmas morning. Along with it were hundreds of Christmas cards and get-well wishes. John "Keckie" Moll was a popular young man who was engaged to be married in less than a month. He had a very bright future. Or so it seemed.

One of the best football players ever to wear the University of Wisconsin uniform, Moll was only 25 years old and already in great demand as a coach. He'd taken over the Purdue program the previous fall and led the Boilermakers to three victories and a tie in their last four games. Purdue wanted him back, but Ohio State wanted him, too.

That was what the letter was about, but Moll never got to answer it. At 9 a.m., shortly after doctors thought they had seen some improvement in his condition, Moll died, a victim of typhoid fever.

The funeral was enormous. The church was filled, and people lined up outside for more than a block. Moll had made thousands of friends, first as a standout drop-kicker at Madison High School and then as a gifted quarterback with the Badgers. He starred as a sophomore in 1908, missed his junior year with what was described as "an attack of rheumatism" and returned for the 1910 and '11 seasons. The Badgers' record over the three years that Moll played was 11-4-3.

Wisconsin was 5-1-1 his senior year when he scored the only touchdown on a 60-yard punt return in a 6-6 tie with archrival Minnesota. Moll almost won that game in the waning seconds when he intercepted a pass at midfield and took it to the end zone, but the officials ruled that he'd stepped out of bounds at the one-yard line.

He was also the captain of a Badger baseball team that had won its first league championship in 20 years, and by all accounts a fine person off the field. According to one newspaper, Moll had ended severe hazing at Wisconsin when he got into a fight with an upperclassman who was abusing a freshman. He was expelled and then reinstated when the full story came out.

No one could say just how Moll had contacted the disease that claimed his life, but it probably happened in East Lafayette, Ind., where he worked long hours rescuing the football team. He'd taken a job as an assistant and then become head coach on Oct. 30, 1912 when M.H. "Bill" Horr was dismissed for improper conduct, according to the book *Purdue University Football Vault: The History of the Boilermakers.*

When Moll took over, the Boilermakers were 1-2, a record that included a 41-0 loss at the hands of Wisconsin. But then he seemed to get the most out of his material over the remaining games. Purdue beat conference opponents Northwestern and Indiana, and tied Illinois; and it shellacked Rose Poly, 91-0, in a non-conference game. The Boilermakers were expecting Moll to return the next season.

But he came down with the fever a few days after the season ended. Typhoid fever was a major health threat in those days. It spread by drinking water or eating food contaminated by bacteria. Over the years it has claimed Wilbur Wright and composer Franz Schubert, as well as Teddy Roosevelt's wife and Abraham Lincoln's son. And soon it would claim "Keckie" Moll.

He didn't take the fever seriously at first, but it kept getting worse. Finally he returned home to Madison where he was hospitalized. He was in the hospital for only three days before he died.

"... had he lived and never done another thing, he would nevertheless have accomplished much more than most men do, and to that extent, life was worthwhile," the *Milwaukee Sentinel* wrote in an editorial.

Moll's parents had been summoned to his bedside the night before he died. Shortly after New Year's Eve, Moll was to be married to a woman from Fox Lake, Wis.

John "Keckie" Moll

DISPUTED KICK DOOMS MATTE-LED COLTS

DECEMBER 26, 1965

It would come to be known as the "Tom Matte Game" in most of the country, but in Baltimore it would always be remembered as a gross miscarriage of justice. To the Green Bay Packers, it was just another step to yet another NFL championship.

When Don Chandler's 25-yard field goal sailed home 13 minutes 39 seconds into sudden death at Lambeau Field, the Packers had a 13-10 Western Conference playoff victory on the books and an enduring argument on their hands. Chandler's second field goal of the game split the uprights with room to spare, but it was the first one that caused all of the fuss. In the Colts' considered opinion, that one didn't split them at all.

It came from 22 yards out with 1:58 to play in the fourth quarter, and it capped a comeback that saw Green Bay wipe out a 10-point deficit to send the game into overtime tied at 10 all. The Baltimore players closest to the scene swore the kick was at least three feet wide, a claim Chandler himself appeared to support when he dropped his head as the ball cleared the goal line.

Quarterback Bart Starr, who was holding on the play after watching most of the action from the sideline, insisted that the attempt was good. Chandler offered no opinion on the subject. Coach Vince Lombardi told Chandler never to drop his head again.

One thing was certain: The ruckus distracted much of the attention from a sterling performance by Zeke Bratkowski and an interesting one by Matte. Bratkowski, the Packers' veteran backup quarterback, entered the game when Starr bruised his ribs on Green Bay's first offensive play and completed 22 of 39 passes for 248 yards.

Matte was a running back who hadn't taken a snap from center since his days at Ohio State. But he played the whole game at quarterback for the Colts because they had nobody else to do the job. Johnny Unitas had undergone knee surgery three weeks earlier, backup Gary Cuozzo had separated his shoulder the week after that in a 42-27 loss to the Packers at Baltimore's Memorial Stadium, and two late-season replacements had been ruled ineligible for the playoffs.

What necessitated the playoff game was that the Packers and Colts had finished the regular season at 10-3-1 and atop the Western Conference. At that time, there were only two conferences in the 14-team NFL and the winners met in the championship game. So the victor in the Colts-Packers game had a date set for the next weekend against the Eastern champion Cleveland Browns.

The Colts' predicament at quarterback left Matte to read the plays from a wristband and hope for the best. He didn't get that, but he could have been worse. He threw just 12 passes all day and connected on five of them for 40 yards, which was good enough to put the Colts ahead, 10-0, at halftime.

Linebacker Don Shinnick scored Baltimore's touchdown on the Packers' first play of the game when he picked up a fumble by journeyman tight end Billy Anderson and returned it 25 yards.

Matte drove the Colts 68 yards to the Packers' seven-yard line in the second quarter to set up a 15-yard field goal by Lou Michaels.

The Packers needed a bad snap on a Baltimore punt to set up their only touchdown in the third quarter. Paul Hornung scored it on a one-yard run after Bratkowski had completed a 33-yard pass to wide receiver Carroll Dale. Then the disputed call on Chandler's kick forced the second playoff overtime in NFL history.

Eleven months later, ABC-TV aired a film that the network claimed proved that Chandler's kick was wide. It didn't change the outcome, but it may have helped change the rules of the game. The following year the league extended the uprights to 20 feet above the crossbar and painted them bright yellow, which didn't help the Colts a bit. They were still seeing red over Chandler's kick.

Don Chandler, with Bart Starr holding, kicked the game-winning field goal in overtime as the Packers beat the Baltimore Colts in a Western Conference playoff.

FAVRE WINS THIRD MVP AWARD

DECEMBER 27, 1997

It was one of those King Kong vs. Godzilla arguments that adult males had when they were young boys. Who was tougher, Superman or the Incredible Hulk? When a nationwide media panel couldn't make up its mind, Brett Favre was forced to share the NFL's Most Valuable Player award with Barry Sanders.

The Green Bay Packers' quarterback had given some thought at the beginning of the year to winning a third straight MVP all by himself, and he'd clearly posted the numbers to get it done. He'd led his team to a 13-3 regular-season record with 3,867 yards and 35 touchdowns through the air.

But Detroit's Sanders had been just as impressive while running for 2,053 yards, missing the NFL record by just 53. And while the Lions were only 9-7, he had surpassed 100 yards an unprecedented 14 games in a row. So how to measure value? Without Favre, the Packers would not be serious contenders for the Super Bowl. Without Sanders, the Lions might have struggled in the Big Ten.

There also was a change in the makeup of the voters. The Associated Press had trimmed the number of electors from 93 reporters and broadcasters to 48. The idea was to give more weight to journalists who covered the whole league rather than just one team. There's no telling what effect that had, but the outcome was a tie, something that had happened only once before in the 41-year history of the balloting.

Favre got 18 votes, Sanders got 18 votes, and the AP announced that it had co-MVPs for the first time since Philadelphia quarterback Norm Van Brocklin and Detroit linebacker Joe Schmidt deadlocked in 1960. No one else other than Favre and Sanders received more than four votes, but five other players were named on at least one ballot.

Running back Terrell Davis of Denver received four votes, and San Francisco quarterback Steve Young drew three. Defensive tackle Dana Stubblefield of San Francisco and running back Jerome Bettis of Pittsburgh were each given two votes, and safety Carnell Lake of Pittsburgh received one.

Neither winner appeared to mind the outcome.

"Sure, I'd like to win it outright, but I can't complain," said Favre. "I'm sharing it with probably the best running back ever to play the game."

"I guess it puts me in elite company," Sanders said. "I'm glad he let me share it with him this year, because the last couple, he's taken it for himself."

Favre was still officially credited with three MVPs in a row. No one had ever won three before, and only one other player, San Francisco quarterback Joe Montana, had ever claimed the honor in back-to-back seasons.

Statistically, Favre and Sanders had been standing toe to toe since 1994. Favre had become the first NFL quarterback to throw for 30 or more touchdowns for four seasons in a row, while Sanders was becoming the only running back to rush for 1,500 yards or more for four straight. The difference was the Packers enjoyed more success as a team in that time.

They had won the Super Bowl the year before and been to the playoffs four straight years. The Lions had been to the playoffs three times, but hadn't won a game and had finished 5-11 in the other year.

There were those who believed that Sanders might have received some votes simply because he'd never won it before. Because he was only the third NFL back ever to run for 2,000 yards in a season, it just seemed like it was his time. It might even have seemed like that to Favre.

"I remember sitting here at the beginning of the season and I said, 'It would be nice to do it again, but the chances of doing it again are very slim,'" he said. "You know, I've won it twice, I can't be selfish. I'm very honored. I just can't believe a little country kid like me has won it three times."

Favre was a little greedy, though. He wanted more out of the season than the league's highest individual honor.

"It was a wonderful year, but if we don't win the Super Bowl, I would feel as though something's missing, and I don't want to end up that way," he said.

The Packers went on to lose to Denver in the Super Bowl. But Favre is still the only player to have won three straight MVPs.

UW RALLIES PAST COLORADO IN ALAMO BOWL

DECEMBER 28, 2002

Brooks Bollinger

Brooks Bollinger was always doing things at the last minute. The winningest quarterback in University of Wisconsin history had won 29 games in his four-year career, and the Badgers had trailed in the fourth quarter in eight of them.

But this time he may have gone too far. Unranked Wisconsin had come into the 10th annual Alamo Bowl as a 7½-point underdog to No. 14 Colorado and proceeded to push the Buffaloes all over San Antonio's Alamodome. But the Badgers had turned the ball over four times, and now they found themselves on their own 20-yard line behind, 28-21, with 2 minutes 5 seconds and one timeout left.

The dilemma was grim, and it would get worse, but Bollinger resolved it by directing a 10-play drive that tied the game with 51 seconds left in regulation. Along the way he had to overcome two fourth-and-long situations. The first came with 18 yards to go on the Wisconsin 44-yard line, and he'd responded by throwing a 27-yard strike to wide receiver Brandon Williams. The second came on the Colorado 29 four plays later, and Bollinger completed a 28-yard pass to wide receiver Darrin Charles. Bollinger scored from the one after that, and when Mike Allen kicked the extra point, the game was headed for overtime.

This was the last thing anyone was expecting from the Badgers based on their regular-season results. They'd won their first five games and then gone into an enduring funk, dropping six of eight on their way to a 2-6 Big Ten record. If they hadn't drilled Minnesota, 49-31, in their final game they would have been done in November for the second season in a row.

But there was something about coach Barry Alvarez and bowl games. He'd been in seven of them and won six, and the Badgers were obviously prepared for this one as they outgained Colorado, 356 yards to 200. In addition to passing for 163 yards, Bollinger ran for 82 more, but that wasn't a surprise. He'd been the Badgers' second-leading rusher in his first three seasons as a starter.

"He can hurt you carrying the football, and obviously he is efficient on his passes," said Colorado defensive coordinator Vince Okruch.

The Buffaloes, on the other hand, were so inefficient on their passes that they changed quarterbacks at halftime after Wisconsin used three interceptions to take a 21-14 lead. But then a muffed punt and a fumble by the Badgers put Colorado on top until the game-tying fourth-quarter drive.

The Buffaloes got the ball first in overtime and did less than nothing with it, losing three yards before kicker Patrick Brougham missed a 45-yard field goal attempt. Wisconsin promptly went into a shell, gaining all of five yards on three plays and leaving the issue up to Allen, who had not exactly distinguished himself during the season by making only 11 of 18 field goal attempts.

But there was no question that the former Prescott High School star had plenty of leg. The attempt was from 37 yards out, and Allen had already kicked four of 40 yards or more during the season, including a 48-yarder against Penn State. He'd even nailed one from 57 yards out at Prescott. And when he hit this one with room to spare, the Badgers had a totally unexpected 31-28 victory.

"I like playing the underdog role," said safety Jim Leonhard, who had one of the Badgers' three picks, giving him 11 for the season. "We played a lot of games this year as the underdogs. A lot of the guys on this team like to play like that."

Apparently, Bollinger was one of them. Why else would he give so many opponents a head start?

NFL GIVES MILWAUKEE BADGERS THE BOOT

DECEMBER 29, 1925

Schedules were fluid in the National Football League's earliest days. So were rosters. Franchises, too, for that matter.

But there were limits. And if a Chicago operator named Ambrose McGurk hadn't tested those limits to the breaking point, Milwaukee might have a pro football team today.

It had one in 1922 when McGurk and Joe Plunkett, another Chicago promoter, were granted a franchise to operate in Milwaukee. They called the team the Badgers, and they said it would be headed by the legendary Jim Thorpe, but that never happened. Instead Fritz Pollard, one of the league's first black athletes, became the co-head coach as well as the star player. Duke Slater and Paul Robeson, two other African-American standouts, were on the roster, too. They'd made the Milwaukee organization a racial pioneer.

What they couldn't do was make the Badgers a great football team. Even in future years when they signed such stars as future Hall of Famers Jim Conzelman and Johnny "Blood" McNally, and former Marquette University standouts Red Dunn and Lavvie Dilweg, the Badgers were able to muster only one winning season.

The fans responded by staying home as McGurk tried to run the operation on a shoestring. He'd even canceled a game when the crowd was too small, blaming it on a rainstorm.

But he was always looking to make a few extra bucks, and so when Chicago Cardinals owner Chris O'Brien came along with an offer to play an extra game in 1925, McGurk took him up on it.

The Badgers' season was over, and the Cardinals' should have been. Chicago had lost a Dec. 6 contest to the Pottsville Maroons in what was billed as a showdown for the NFL title. Championships in those days were determined by final records, and Pottsville finished that game at 10-2 while the Cardinals were 9-2-1. Doing some simple math, O'Brien figured he could still claim a championship by winning two more games. And so he scheduled the first one with Milwaukee for four days after the Pottsville loss and another one with Hammond, Ind., two days after that.

The Badgers had a problem, though. They'd played their last game on Nov. 22, and they didn't have enough players left around town to play again. O'Brien had a solution. Art Folz, one of the Cardinals' backs, recruited four players from Chicago's Englewood High School on behalf of the Badgers, and the game was on.

It was a travesty. The Cardinals didn't even bother to charge admission as they thumped their patched-together opponent, 59-0. Two days later, the Cardinals beat Hammond, 13-0, and now had an 11-2-1 record, half-a-game better than Pottsville, and O'Brien had his championship.

The four high school players never got a dime, but the Chicago school board wasn't overly sympathetic. It permanently banned the four from any further competition.

NFL President Joe Carr began his investigation of the Cardinals-Badgers game on Dec. 16 and handed down his decision to expel the Badgers on Dec. 29 from his home in Columbus, Ohio. Carr slapped O'Brien with a year of probation and a $1,000 fine. It was worse for McGurk. Carr fined him $500 and ordered the Badgers to dispose of their assets within the first 90 days of the next year and leave the league.

The Badgers were back under new ownership the following July, but they weren't any better or any more popular. After they stumbled through a poorly attended 2-7 season, new owner Johnny Bryan shut them down.

Three years later, in 1929, McGurk applied for another NFL franchise in Milwaukee, but he backed out at the last minute. He couldn't come up with the fee.

Meanwhile, the controversy over the league championship continues to this day. Supporters of the Pottsville Maroons have continued to appeal to the NFL, asking it to belatedly grant the 1925 championship to their team and take it away from the Cardinals.

PACKERS SURVIVE ELEMENTS, GIANTS TO WIN NFL TITLE

DECEMBER 30, 1962

Everybody recognized what Green Bay Packer weather was. It was gray, it was blustery, and it was savagely cold. But until Vince Lombardi's football team came to New York in search of a second straight NFL championship, nobody knew it was portable.

Still stung by a 37-0 whipping in the 1961 title game in Wisconsin, New Yorkers had spent all week trying to maximize their Giants' home-field advantage. They were even chanting "Beat Green Bay!" at a college basketball tournament at Madison Square Garden on Friday night, and they were still chanting it in the third quarter on Sunday afternoon at Yankee Stadium. But it didn't matter. The Packers had brought their weather with them, and they could barely hear the crowd over the howling of the gale.

The mercury read 20 degrees at kickoff, and it was headed in the wrong direction. It would read 17 at halftime and 14 at the end of the game, which might have been bearable if the wind wasn't gusting up to 45 miles per hour out of the northwest, burning hands and cheeks and turning the field into asphalt.

There were gas heaters behind the benches, smudge pots in front of them, and shoes all over the locker rooms. The Packers were provided with three different kinds to cope with the elements. The shoes helped some, the heaters not much. "They would have to double my salary to get me to play one more quarter," said Green Bay's Paul Hornung. Some Packer players who had participated in this game and in the celebrated Ice Bowl five years later in Green Bay said New York was every bit as cold.

Thanks to a defense that held the vaunted Giants' attack without a touchdown for the second championship game in a row and to the frozen toe of Jerry Kramer, Hornung didn't have to put in any extra time. The Packers scored in all four quarters on the way to a 16-7 victory that may have capped their greatest season ever.

Green Bay's offense amounted to Kramer field goals of 26 yards in the first quarter, 29 yards in the third and 30 in the fourth, plus Jim Taylor's seven-yard touchdown run less than three minutes before halftime. Kramer also missed two attempts, but that was understandable given the swirling winds and the fact that he'd assumed the place-kicking duties only two months earlier when Hornung had hurt his knee.

Green Bay's defense involved a fair amount of run stuffing, a good deal of pass rushing and a whole lot of Ray Nitschke. The Packers' ferocious middle linebacker won a Corvette from *Sport* magazine as the game's Most Valuable Player for recovering two fumbles, one that set up Taylor's touchdown and another that set up a field goal, and for deflecting a Y.A. Tittle pass that turned into an interception by linebacker Dan Currie. But it was a different Packer defender who attracted the most attention.

That was Willie Wood, who was ejected in the third quarter for knocking back judge Tom Kelleher onto his frozen stripes. Kelleher had whistled the Packers' safety for pass interference, and Wood sprung to his feet in protest, colliding with the official. Wood said the collision was inadvertent. Kelleher said it was intentional. The difference of opinion cost Wood at least $50, the mandatory minimum fine for being thrown out of a game. It also cost the Packers the services of an all-pro safety for much of the second half, but that didn't seem to matter.

The Giants outgained the Packers, 291 yards to 244, but 61 of their yards came on a final meaningless drive that ended on the Green Bay seven as time ran out. The Giants scored only by falling on a blocked Max McGee punt in the third period.

Frustrated on offense, they contented themselves with abusing Taylor on defense. According to outraged Packers fans, Green Bay's fullback was the victim of constant unnecessary roughness. Middle linebacker Sam Huff was cast as the leading villain. "I never took a worse beating on a football field," said Taylor.

But it was the Giants and the 64,892 people watching in person who suffered the most as they witnessed the Packers wrapping up their eighth championship, the most of any team in the league. "I think we saw football as it should be played," said Lombardi, and he got no argument from the folks at home.

Some fans partying downtown celebrated by hanging Huff in effigy in front of Prange's Department Store. There were an estimated 10,000 more waiting to greet the team at the Green Bay airport.

It was nine degrees below zero in Green Bay. Just right.

PACKERS CHILL COWBOYS IN ICE BOWL

DECEMBER 31, 1967

The vital statistics: 16 frostbite victims, 11 frozen musicians, a wind chill of minus-46 degrees and a final score of 21-17.

The last number was clearly the most significant, and possibly the least memorable. The Green Packers have played dozens of huge games in dreadful weather, but never one that was more defined by the conditions. When Bart Starr's quarterback sneak downed Dallas with 13 seconds on the clock, it not only sent the Packers to Super Bowl II, it put a signature on the franchise.

When Starr surged over the goal line behind the double-team block of right guard Jerry Kramer and center Ken Bowman, it provided the Packers with their third straight National Football League championship and allowed 50,861 spectators to go find a sanctuary where they could get warm.

After the game, 16 fans were treated for frostbite at St. Mary's Hospital after 11 members of the University of Wisconsin–La Crosse marching band had been treated earlier. The band was there for the halftime show, which was mercifully canceled when its instruments froze.

How cold was it? Well, the temperature was minus-13 at kickoff and expected to plunge another seven or eight degrees when the sun went down. Up in the CBS booth, where broadcaster Ray Scott had insisted that the windows stay open, analyst Frank Gifford set a cup of coffee down and picked it up a few minutes later to find it frozen. Bob Hayes, Dallas' star wideout, was so miserable that he stuck his hands in his pants on every play except for the ones when he was the Cowboys' primary receiver.

There are certain advantages to playing a December home game in Wisconsin against a team from Texas, and the Packers used them all early in the game to take a 14-0 lead on a pair of Starr-to-Boyd Dowler touchdown passes. The Cowboys were getting nothing at all done on offense at that point, but you might say their defense warmed to the occasion when defensive end Willie Townes sacked Starr and jarred the ball loose in the second quarter. George Andrie, the other defensive end, scooped it up and ran seven yards for a touchdown to cut the difference to 14-7, and it was shaved further to 14-10 just before halftime when the Packers' Willie Wood fumbled a punt to set up a Dallas field goal.

Starr suffered eight sacks in the game, resulting in 76 yards in losses, which was kind of demoralizing, but not nearly as much as the 50-yard halfback pass that the Cowboys pulled off to take their only lead of the game eight seconds into the final period. Dan Reeves threw the pass to wide receiver Lance Rentzel, making the score 17-14, which is what it was when the Packers started their final drive on their own 32-yard line with 5 minutes 4 seconds remaining.

It took them nine plays to get to the Dallas one, and an emergency fullback named Chuck Mercein figured prominently in three of them. The anonymous Mercein had been cut by the New York Giants and had spent time earlier in the year in the semi-pro Atlantic Coast Football League before the Packers picked him up to replace the injured Jim Grabowski. Mercein, a Milwaukee native, contributed 34 yards to the final march, seven on a run over right end on the second play of the drive, 19 more on a pass from Starr to give the Packers a first down at the Dallas 11 and eight on another run on the next play.

And Mercein fully expected to be carrying the ball on the final play.

But Starr had something else in mind. He had just watched halfback Donny Anderson stumble on the frozen field on the Packers' last snap, and he didn't want to chance another handoff. So he spent Green Bay's final timeout on the sidelines suggesting the quarterback sneak to coach Vince Lombardi.

Starr came back to the huddle and called "Brown right, 31 wedge," a play that normally called for the fullback to get the ball. But Starr kept it instead, much to the surprise of Mercein and everybody else in the huddle. The Packers never ran quarterback sneaks.

They ran this one to perfection, though, as Kramer with help from Bowman buried Dallas tackle Jethro Pugh, while Starr plunged into the south end zone. The Packers had won, and the quarterback's judgment was vindicated.

Asked later how Lombardi had reacted to the idea of a sneak, Starr replied, "He said, 'Run it, and let's get the hell out of here.'"

It was a sentiment that everyone shared.

BIBLIOGRAPHY

NEWSPAPERS

Appleton Post-Crescent: 4/26/1964.

Chicago Tribune: 10/20/1906, 12/26/1912, 11/18/1913, 11/9/1924, 12/30/1925, 6/12/1932, 9/26-27/1934, 8/30/1940, 3/9-12/1942, 5/17/1943, 8/24-25/1946, 6/1/1947, 12/6/1957, 3/1/1959, 4/29-30/1959, 5/1/1959, 6/27/1960, 11/11/1962, 6/2-3/1965, 2/4/1968, 5/10/1984, 11/24, 26/1986, 7/23/1995, 4/16-17/1996, 1/30/2003.

Des Moines Register: 11/8/1925.

Eau Claire Leader: 12/16-17/1949, 6/14-15/1952.

Fond du Lac Reporter: 1/2/1900, 2/11/1913, 3/15, 17/1913, 2/23, 25/1914, 1/6-7/1915, 2/25/1986.

Green Bay Press-Gazette: 8/13-14/1919, 9/6, 15/1919, 9/24/1920, 12/9-11/1929, 12/15-17/1930, 11/30/1931, 12/1-2, 4, 12/1931, 9/26/1934, 2/22/1935, 9/23/1935, 12/14-15, 17/1936, 11/29/1939, 12/11/1939, 8/30/1940, 11/13-15, 18-19/1940, 12/18-20/1944, 11/23/1946, 9/30/1949, 10/31/1949, 12/1-2/1949, 1/10, 13, 24-25/1950, 2/1, 3/1950, 7/21/1950, 11/25/1950, 10/13/1952, 9/14/1954, 7/26/1957, 9/30/1957, 10/14, 25/1958, 1/29-30/1959, 2/3/1959, 4/25, 27-28/1959, 9/23, 28/1959, 10/13/1959, 12/2/1959, 1/4, 16, 18/1960, 2/2, 15-16, 19-20, 22-23, 25-26, 29/1960, 10/8/1962, 11/23/1962, 12/31/1962, 5/6/1964, 5/12/1965, 12/27/1965, 1/3/1966, 1/10, 16, 17/1967, 11/13/1967, 12/6, 24/1967, 1/2, 15/1968, 2/4-7, 27/1969, 3/6/1969, 9/21/1969, 1/22-23, 25, 27-28/1970, 2/25/1970, 7/6/1970, 4/19/1971, 10/12/1971, 1/18, 22/1972, 2/7-10, 12, 14-15, 28/1972, 6/14/1972, 3/24/1974, 6/30/1974, 7/11, 13, 18-19, 26/1974, 8/2/1974, 10/23-25/1974, 12/24/1974, 7/26, 29/1976, 8/1/1976, 9/3/1978, 10/31/1978, 7/30/1979, 8/3, 5-6, 29/1979, 9/2, 4-5/1979, 1/20/1980, 3/8/1980, 4/29/1980, 5/29-31/1980, 7/16/1980, 8/31/1980, 9/2, 5, 8/1980, 6/11/1982, 10/18/1983, 12/19/1983, 1/8/1984, 12/2/1985, 3/29-31/1985, 9/13/1985, 11/7/1985, 6/13/1986, 11/24, 26/1986, 5/8/1988, 4/24/1989, 11/6/1989, 2/15/1990, 5/2/1991, 3/18-19/1994, 3/28/1995, 1/28/1997, 11/14/1998, 8/16/2004, 12/25/2004, 1/2/2005, 2/15/2005, 10/24/2006, 6/26/2009.

Janesville Gazette: 9/1, 6-7/1877, 3/13/1905, 4/7, 11, 17/1905, 12/12-13, 15-16/2001.

Kenosha Evening News: 10/19, 21/1901, 10/19-20/1906, 2/27/1911, 5/12-15, 17-22, 24, 26-29/1937, 6/1, 7-9, 11-12, 14, 18, 21, 23, 25/1937, 2/18/1943, 4/6, 8/1943, 5/18, 26, 29/1943, 6/1/1943, 9/2, 7/1943, 8/21-22/1952, 1/13/1955.

Louisville Courier-Journal: 12/20, 22/1963.

Manitowoc Herald-Times: 5/16-18/1971.

Marinette Eagle-Star: 10/28, 29, 31/1949.

Milwaukee Journal Sentinel: 1/2/1994, 3/20/1994, 3/19/1995, 4/2/1995, 7/23-24, 27-28/1995, 8/2/1995, 12/31/1995, 1/7/1996, 4/16-17/1996, 5/13/1996, 6/16/1996, 7/14, 27-28, 31/1996, 8/28/1996, 9/2/1996, 10/15, 24/1996, 1/13, 27-28/1997, 6/29/1997, 7/27/1997, 10/16/1997, 11/6-7/1997, 12/28/1997, 1/14, 18, 26/1998, 4/26/1998, 6/25-26/1998, 7/3-7, 9/1998, 9/19-21, 24/1998, 1/9, 11/1999, 2/17/1999, 6/26/1999, 8/10, 13, 28/1999, 9/26/1999, 10/11, 12, 16, 23, 29-30/1999, 11/6, 13-14/1999, 12/12/1999, 3/19, 24, 26/2000, 4/2/2000, 5/5/2000, 6/4/2000, 8/6/2000, 9/1, 24-27/2000, 12/16/2000, 1/26/2001, 3/18, 29-30/2001, 4/7/2001, 7/19/2001, 8/15/2001, 9/11/2001, 10/3/2001, 11/22/2001, 1/30/2002, 2/13, 18, 28/2002, 4/16/2002, 7/2-3, 9-11, 26/2002, 9/8/2002, 11/25-26/2002, 12/29/2002, 1/31/2003, 2/21/2003, 3/6, 9, 28, 30/2003, 4/23/2003, 9/17/2003, 11/5, 9/2003, 12/21-23/2003, 1/5, 12, 29/2004, 2/22/2004, 3/13/2004, 8/13-15, 19, 22, 28/2004, 3/14, 17-18, 20, 23, 25, 28-29/2005, 5/5-6, 12, 25/2005, 6/21, 23, 26-27, 29-30/2005, 7/9, 28/2005, 11/19-20/2005, 1/1, 4/2006,

Milwaukee Journal Sentinel (cont.): 6/21-22/2006, 8/26/2007, 12/15-16/2007, 1/21/2008, 3/26-27/2008, 5/31/2008, 6/3, 25/2008, 7/7-8, 22-25, 31/2008, 8/18/2008, 9/2, 29-30/2008, 2/16, 23/2009, 5/24/2009, 8/20/2009, 10/28, 31/2009, 11/1-2/2009, 6/24-25/2010.

Milwaukee Sentinel: 7/30-31/1869, 8/20/1877, 9/3, 7/1877, 1/18/1878, 4/2/1878, 5/14-15/1878, 5/20/1888, 7/15-17/1900, 8/30/1903, 9/6-7, 9, 11-12/1903, 8/30/1904, 9/1-2, 4-5, 6-9/1904, 6/4-5, 7/1908, 2/23/1910, 10/16/1910, 9/29/1912, 10/1-3, 5-6/1912, 11/17-18/1913, 3/13, 15/1914, 4/2-3/1916, 5/4/1917, 11/4, 23/1917, 1/26/1918, 2/23-24, 26/ 1918, 8/20/1922, 10/27-28/1923, 2/1/1924, 6/16/1924, 12/20/1924, 11/8/1925, 12/11, 16-17, 30/1925, 4/28/1927, 2/21/1928, 10/28-29/1928, 8/22-25/1929, 4/14/1931, 12/29/1931, 1/14, 17, 21-24/1932, 2/29/1932, 3/13, 15, 22, 24, 30/1932, 4/28/1932, 6/12/1932, 7/21-22, 24/1933, 8/2, 8-14, 21/1933, 3/15/1934, 6/17/1934, 7/1, 14/1934, 10/15-17/1934, 5/31/1935, 6/8-9/1935, 8/29/1935, 9/17-18/1935, 10/18-24/1935, 1/16, 29-31/1936, 2/6-7, 16/1936, 6/28/1936, 8/4/1936, 10/24-25/1936, 4/6/1937, 8/5/1940, 3/23, 30/1941, 6/22, 24/1941, 8/16/1941, 3/7, 12/1942, 6/11, 16/1944, 12/18/1944, 6/10/1945, 10/28/1945, 3/17/1946, 3/11/1947, 5/27, 30/1947, 4/22-23/1948, 2/3/1950, 4/9-10, 18/1950, 5/17/1950, 11/27/1951, 6/17/1952, 10/13/1952, 3/14, 17-20/1953, 4/14/1953, 8/1/1954, 2/10/1955, 7/13/1955, 1/22/1956, 12/7/1956, 6/14/1957, 10/5-6, 7-8, 27/1957, 12/3, 6/1957, 4/25/1959, 9/17/1959, 8/19/1960, 9/18/1960, 12/16/1960, 6/9/1961, 7/16/1961, 8/12, 17-18/1961, 9/14, 16/1961, 9/5-6/1962, 11/23/1962, 12/31/1962, 4/18/1963, 8/3/1964, 10/22-23/1964, 7/12/1965, 6/20/1966, 7/18/1966, 1/16/1967, 7/11, 15, 17, 19-22, 24-25/1967, 11/13/1967, 12/11, 25/1967, 2/5/1968, 3/6, 18/1968, 5/7/1968, 7/15/1968, 2/3, 7/1969, 3/24/1969, 2/24-26/1970, 4/1-3, 7/1970, 7/6/1970, 4/19/1971, 5/1, 22, 24/1971, 7/5/1971, 5/7/1972, 2/6, 15/1974, 3/25/1974, 6/25/1974, 11/4/1974, 12/25/1974, 1/20/1975, 7/16/1975, 8/12/1975, 7/14, 21/1976, 12/7/1976, 2/14/1977, 3/8, 29/1977, 4/1, 5, 13/1977, 5/20/1977, 8/11/1977, 10/19-20/1977, 11/21/1977, 2/9/1978, 6/19/1978, 9/20/1978, 10/31/1978, 11/2, 7/1978, 7/30/1979, 8/3/1979, 9/3/1979, 2/7, 19, 27/1980, 4/10/1980, 5/29/1980, 8/9, 11/1980, 9/1-3, 5, 9/1980, 12/13/1980, 4/10, 20/1982, 8/2/1982, 9/17-18, 25/1982, 10/1-2, 4-5, 9, 14/1982, 12/20/1983, 5/9-10, 14/1984, 11/3/1984, 3/2, 6/1985, 5/7/1985, 6/4/1985, 9/16/1985, 10/7/1985, 5/10, 19/1986, 7/2/1986, 5/2, 23-24, 28/1987, 8/25-26/1987, 2/15, 19/1988, 10/22/1988, 4/21/1989, 9/4/1989, 11/21/1989, 3/6/1991, 5/2/1991, 7/11/1991, 12/23/1991, 1/9/1992, 2/12/1992, 4/20/1992, 6/18/1992, 11/16, 19/1992, 12/8-9/1992, 10/9, 12/1993, 2/24/1994, 4/28/1994, 5/3/1994, 12/13/1994.

Omaha World-Herald: 7/2, 5-7/1916.

Oshkosh Daily Northwestern: 6/11/1912, 3/7, 11-13/1942, 5/1/1950, 6/3, 5/1950, 7/10/1967.

Packer Plus: 5/2002, 4/3/2003, 2/10/2005.

River Falls Journal: 12/22/1949, 1/22/1950.

Stevens Point Journal: 5/14/1984.

Superior Evening Telegram: 4/5-9, 12-14, 16/1937.

The Beloit Daily News: 1/31/1924, 2/1/1924, 1/31/1949, 3/24/1969.

The Capital Times of Madison: 6/10, 13/1950, 7/19/1956, 4/27, 29/1959, 11/27-28/1968, 10/2/1978, 11/18/1985, 11/20/1987, 6/4/1990, 10/8-10/1993, 10/18-19/1997, 1/14/1998, 3/24/2000.

The Indianapolis News: 11/22/1917, 5/30/1935.

The Indianapolis Star: 5/4, 11/1917.

The Milwaukee Daily News: 7/31/1869, 9/7/1877, 2/27/1911, 10/7/1912, 11/17-18/1913.

The Milwaukee Journal: 5/21/1888, 7/16/1900, 10/7-8/1912, 12/26/1912, 8/8/1915, 4/2, 4/1916, 7/5/1916, 11/4/1917, 2/26/1918, 8/20/1922, 10/28-30/1923, 11/9/1924, 9/7/1927, 10/27-29/1928, 8/25/1929, 1/17, 22-25/1932, 6/12/1932, 8/6, 13-14, 20-21/1933, 4/5/1934, 7/14/1934, 10/14, 16/1934, 6/8/1935, 6/26, 28/1936, 8/3/1936, 10/25/1936, 11/28/1939, 12/1, 8, 10-11/1939, 7/28/1940, 8/2-5/1940, 6/23-24/1941, 8/17-18/1941, 11/1/1942, 8/29/1943, 6/11, 16/1944, 9/3, 5-6/1944, 11/12-13, 15/1944, 6/10/1945, 6/12/1946, 6/1/1947, 12/11-12, 16, 19, 30/1947, 2/25/1948, 4/21-23/1948, 5/30/1948, 6/6-7/1948, 10/21/1948, 5/22/1949, 11/22/1949, 2/10/1950, 4/9-10/1950, 5/7, 10, 28/1950, 6/11, 18, 22/1950, 10/31/1950, 2/4, 7/1951, 3/11/1951, 5/6/1951,

The Milwaukee Journal (cont'd): 9/25/1951, 11/28-29/1951, 1/25/1952, 6/17, 30/1952, 8/24/1952, 10/13/1952, 3/12, 14-15, 18-19/1953, 4/10, 15/1953, 10/29/1953, 3/9/1954, 5/21, 30/1954, 6/13/1954, 8/1/1954, 2/13/1955, 7/10, 13/1955, 9/9, 11-12/1955, 11/24/1955, 3/31/1956, 4/12/1956, 7/18-20/1956, 8/17/1956, 12/6/1956, 1/20/1957, 3/7/1957, 6/14, 16/1957, 7/26-28, 30/1957, 8/1, 10, 26/1957, 9/24/1957, 10/4-5, 7-8, 11, 27-28/1957, 12/6, 8/1957, 3/2/1958, 9/22, 28/1958, 9/15/1958, 10/1, 9/1958, 2/21/1959, 3/3, 7, 14, 20-22/1959, 4/1, 2, 10, 25/1959, 5/1, 27/1959, 9/16/1959, 11/22-23/1959, 2/26, 28-29/1960, 4/18/1960, 5/11/1960, 6/27/1960, 7/8/1960, 8/19/1960, 9/17-18/1960, 12/9, 16/1960, 5/9, 21, 30/1961, 6/9/1961, 8/12, 18/1961, 9/14/1961, 2/25/1962, 3/11/1962, 4/8/1962, 9/5/1962, 10/8/1962, 11/11-12, 23/1962, 12/31/1962, 4/18-19/1963, 7/3/1963, 8/5-6/1963, 10/6/1963, 12/21-22/1963, 4/12/1964, 5/5-6, 31/1964, 6/1-2, 21,23, 28-29/1964, 8/3/1964, 10/21-22/1964, 4/20/1965, 6/6/1965, 7/4, 6, 10-12/1965, 9/28/1965, 10/21/1965, 1/3/1966, 4/14/1966, 6/20/1966, 7/27/1966, 12/12/1966, 2/16/1967, 7/10, 24-25/1967, 11/13/1967, 12/16-17, 24/1967, 1/15, 22-24/1968, 2/4-6/1968, 3/5-6/1968, 4/4, 6, 24-25, 27/1968, 5/5-7, 12, 16/1968, 7/13-15/1968, 8/25/1968, 11/27-28/1968, 12/4, 6-7, 10/1968, 2/3-7/1969, 3/11-14, 16, 18-21, 23/1969, 4/2-4, 8/1969, 10/12/1969, 1/22-23/1970, 4/1-3, 8, 21-22/1970, 5/7/1970, 7/6/1970, 4/19/1971, 5/1-2, 22, 24/1971, 7/4, 11/1971, 1/10/1972, 2/7, 9-10/1972, 8/31/1972, 2/4/1973, 3/18/1973, 2/6-7/1974, 3/22, 24, 25-27/1974, 5/7, 11, 13/1974, 6/23, 25/1974, 11/3-4/1974, 1/17, 19-20/1975, 3/10/1975, 6/16-17/1975, 7/16-17/1975, 1/6/1976, 7/21/1976, 9/18/1976, 12/7, 9/1976, 2/14/1977, 3/27-29/1977, 4/13/1977, 5/20, 22, 24/1977, 8/11/1977, 10/19-20/1977, 11/20/1977, 2/9/1978, 6/19/1978, 9/20/1978, 10/1/1978, 3/29/1979, 6/26/1979, 7/28-30/1979, 12/20/1979, 1/26, 29/1980, 2/5-7, 23-25, 27/1980, 3/4, 7-10/1980, 4/11/1980, 5/29/1980, 8/10-11/1980, 9/3/1980, 10/19/1980, 12/13-14/1980, 1/8, 11/1981, 6/25/1981, 9/13/1981, 1/31/1982, 3/25, 27-28/1982, 4/14, 19/1982, 6/1-3/1982, 8/1-2, 12/1982, 9/3-4/1982, 10/4, 9, 14, 17/1982, 11/10/1982, 12/19/1982, 3/3/1983, 5/1, 3/1983, 1/6-8, 24/1984, 5/9-10/1984, 3/2, 11, 31/1985, 6/2- 4, 17/1985, 9/11, 15-16/1985, 11/17/1985, 4/25, 29/1986, 5/16, 19/1986, 6/8/1986, 7/2-3/1986, 1/29/1987, 4/16, 20-22/1987, 5/10, 23-25, 27-28/1987, 7/28/1987, 8/26-27/1987, 10/23-26/1987, 11/28/1987, 8/18/1988, 9/30/1988, 10/2, 20/1988, 11/12/1988, 12/19, 30/1988, 4/24/1989, 9/5-6/1989, 11/21/1989, 1/18/1990, 2/15/1990, 3/4/1990, 6/2/1990, 2/18/1991, 4/28-29/1991, 5/2, 9, 26-27/1991, 7/11-12/1991, 11/16, 21, 27-28/1991, 12/1, 22-23/1991, 1/19/1992, 2/12/1992, 4/26/1992, 5/17/1992, 6/17, 19, 21-22/1992, 7/21/1992, 8/9/1992, 9/10, 21/1992, 11/19-20/1992, 12/6, 8/1992, 1/10, 17/1993, 3/7, 21/1993, 4/2, 4, 6-7/1993, 6/7, 20/1993, 10/9, 12/1993, 11/2/1993, 12/5, 26/1993, 2/18, 20, 22-23/1994, 3/5/1994, 5/2/1994, 7/29/1994, 12/16, 19/1994.

The New York Times: 7/17/1900, 9/12/1903, 9/3-4/1904, 2/27/1911, 7/1/1934, 9/17-18,20/1935, 12/8/1936, 6/17-19/1939, 12/10-11/1939, 8/30/1944, 9/5/1944, 11/20/1944, 12/18-19/1944, 4/22-23/1948, 11/7/1949, 3/10-11/1951, 8/1/1954, 12/1, 10/1954, 7/18/1956, 10/7/1957, 1/30/1963, 7/24/1967, 11/3/1974, 5/8/1988, 4/26/1992, 5/17/1992, 1/21/2008, 6/25, 29/2009, 11/2/2009.

The Oconomowoc Enterprise: 1/15, 22, 29/1932.

The Racine Daily Journal: 10/21/1901.

The Racine Journal-Times: 5/18-19, 26/1943, 11/18-19, 22/2005.

The Rhinelander Daily News: 5/31/1935.

The San Francisco Chronicle: 7/3-4/1963, 6/4/1985.

The Seattle Times: 5/18/2008.

The Sheboygan Press: 6/12/1946, 5/26-27, 29/1947, 10/13/1947, 11/13, 17, 19, 22, 25/1947, 12/1, 8, 12, 31/1947, 2/10/1950, 9/10, 12/1955, 8/23/2004.

Waukesha Freeman: 2/26/1988.

Wisconsin News: 10/28/1928, 8/27-29/1935.

Wisconsin State Journal: 11/2/1908, 12/26/1912, 11/4/1917, 4/6, 8/1924, 11/7, 9/1924, 11/8/1925, 6/18/1939, 11/1/1942, 11/12-13, 15/1944, 3/17/1946, 6/11, 14, 25/1950, 4/10/1953, 12/1/1954, 7/20/1956, 3/3, 8-9/1959, 4/28/1959, 5/1/1959, 11/21/1959, 4/10-12, 18/1960, 11/11/1962, 12/22/1963, 3/21/1964, 6/6/1965, 11/27/1968,

Wisconsin State Journal (cont.): 12/4-6/1968, 10/12/1969, 1/1, 3/1971, 12/10, 12/1971, 3/17-19/1973, 2/6-7/1974, 1/6/1976, 7/26/1976, 10/1/1978, 9/12-13/1981, 12/6/1981, 4/10, 14-15/1982, 8/15/1982, 1/6, 8-9/1984, 11/17-18/1985, 4/29/1986, 1/3/1990, 2/7, 11, 15/1990, 6/2-3/1990, 1/30-31/1995, 4/1/1995, 1/14-15/1998, 3/23-24/2000, 8/4-6/2000, 9/25/2000, 12/21/2003, 2/17/2004, 3/19/2006.

BOOKS

Addie Joss: King of the Pitchers, by Scott Longert, The Society for American Baseball Research, 1998.

All that Glitters is not Gold, by William O. Johnson Jr., G.P. Putnam's Sons, 1972.

Al McGuire, the Colorful Warrior, by Roger Jaynes, Sports Publishing L.L.C., 2004.

A Summer Up North: Henry Aaron and the Legend of Eau Claire Baseball, by Jerry Poling, The University of Wisconsin Press, 2002.

Baseball Barnstorming and Exhibition Games: 1901-1962, by Thomas Barthel, McFarland & Company, Inc., 2007.

Baseball's Bonus Babies, by Brent Kelley, McFarland & Company, Inc., 2006.

Baseball: The Biographical Encyclopedia, edited by David Pietrusza, Matthew Silverman, Michael Gershman; Total/SPORTS ILLUSTRATED, 2000.

Basketball Hall of Fame, Class of 1994, Yearbook.

Bucking the Odds, by Marv Fishman and Tracy Dodds, Raintree Publishers Ltd., 1978.

Cages to Jump Shots, by Robert W. Peterson, Oxford University Press, 1990.

Complete Pro Football Draft Encyclopedia, compiled by Dave Sloan, Sporting News, 2004.

Cooperstown: Baseball's Hall of Fame Where the Legends Live Forever, The Sporting News Publishing Co., 1983.

Crazy Good: The True Story of Dan Patch, the Most Famous Horse in America, by Charles Leerhsen, Simon & Schuster, 2008.

ESPN College Football Encyclopedia: The Complete History of the Game, edited by Michael MacCambridge, ESPN Books, 2005.

Forward Pass: The Play That Saved Football, by Philip L. Brooks, Westholme Publishing, LLC, 2008.

Frank Parker: Champion in the Golden Age of Tennis, by Cynthia Beardsley, Havilah Press, 2002.

Green and Golden Moments: Bob Harlan and the Green Bay Packers, by Bob Harlan with Dale Hofmann, KCI Sports, 2007.

Green Bay Packers: A Measure of Greatness, by Eric Goska, Krause Publications, 2003.

Green Bay Packers Official 2008 Yearbook.

Green Bay Packers 2009 Media Guide.

Green Cathedrals: The Ultimate Celebration of All 271 Major League and Negro League Ballparks Past and Present, by Philip J. Lowry, Addison-Wesley Publishing Co., Inc., 1992.

Hawkeye Legends, Lists & Lore: The Athletic History of the Iowa Hawkeyes, by Mike Finn and Chad Leistikow, Sports Publishing LLC., 1998.

I Had a Hammer: The Hank Aaron Story, by Hank Aaron with Lonnie Wheeler, HarperCollins Publishers, 1991.

Indianapolis 500 Chronicle, by Rick Popely with L. Spencer Riggs, Publications International, Ltd., 1998.

Lords of the Ring, by Doug Moe, The University of Wisconsin Press, 2004.

Marquette Basketball 2007-'08 media guide.

Milwaukee Braves 1957 Yearbook.

Milwaukee Braves 1958 Yearbook.

Milwaukee Brewers 1971 Media Guide.

Milwaukee Brewers 2009 Media Guide.

Milwaukee Bucks Media Guide 2008-'09.

MPS High School Sports: Celebrating 100 Years of Interscholastic Athletics, by Cliff Christl.

Mudbaths & Bloodbaths: The Inside Story of the Bears-Packers Rivalry, by Gary D'Amato and Cliff Christl, Prairie Oak Press, 1997.

My Dirty Little Secrets – Steroids, Alcohol & God: The Tony Mandarich Story, by Tony Mandarich as told to Sharon Shaw Elrod, Modern History Press, 2009.

NCAA Final Four: The Official 1996 Final Four Records Book.

NCAA Football: The Official 1996 College Football Records Book.

Notre Dame 1998 Football media guide.

Official Handbook, 1940, Amateur Skating Union of the United States.

Official 2009 NCAA Men's Basketball Records Book.

Oh, How They Played the Game: The Early Days of Football and the Heroes Who Made it Great, by Allison Danzig, The Macmillan Company, 1971.

100 Greatest Moments in Olympic History, by Bud Greenspan, General Publishing Group, Inc., 1995.

Only The Ball Was White: by Robert Peterson, Prentice-Hall, Inc., 1970.

On Wisconsin: Badger Football, by Oliver Kuechle with Jim Mott, The Strode Publishers, Inc., 1977.

On Wisconsin: The History of Badger Athletics, by Don Kopriva & Jim Mott, Sports Publishing, Inc., 1998.

On Wisconsin: The Road to the Roses, by Dennis Chaptman, Taylor Publishing Co., 1994.

Pilots (Milwaukee Brewers) 1970 Log Book.

Purdue University Football Vault: The History of the Boilermakers, by Tom Schott, Whitman Publishing, 2008.

Road America: Five Decades of Racing at Elkhart Lake, by Tom Schultz, Beeman Jorgensen Inc., 1999.

Rome 1960: The Olympics That Changed the World, by David Maraniss, Simon & Schuster, 2008.

Shooting Star: The Bevo Francis Story, The Incredible Tale of College Basketball's Greatest Scorer, by Kyle Keiderling, Sport Classic Books, 2005.

Sleepers, Busts & Franchise-Makers: The Behind-the-Scenes Story of the Pro Football Draft, by Cliff Christl and Don Langenkamp, Preview Publishing Inc., 1983.

Stengel: His Life and Times, by Robert W. Creamer, University of Nebraska Press, 1996.

The American Association: A Baseball History, 1902-1991, by Bill O'Neal, Eakin Press, 1991.

The Babe Ruth Story, by Babe Ruth as told to Bob Considine, Pocket Books, Inc., 1948.

The Ballplayers: Baseball's Ultimate Biographical Reference, edited by Mike Shatzkin, Arbor House William Morrow, 1990.

The Baseball Draft: The First 25 Years, 1965-1989, edited by Allan Simpson, A Baseball America Production, 1990.

The Baseball Encyclopedia: The Complete and Official Record of Major League Baseball, Seventh Edition, edited by Joseph L. Reichler, 1988.

The Baseball Hall of Fame: 50th Anniversary Book, Prentice Hall Press, 1988.

The Baseball Timeline, by Burt Solomon, DK, 2001.

The Big Ten, by Kenneth L. "Tug" Wilson and Jerry Brondfield, Prentice-Hall, Inc., 1967.

The Boxing Register: International Boxing Hall of Fame Official Record Book, 4th Edition, by James B. Roberts & Alexander G. Skutt, McBooks Press, Inc., 2006.